Computer Networks and Open Systems

An Application Development Perspective

Lillian (Boots) Cassel

Richard H. Austing

JONES AND BARTLETT PUBLISHERS

Sudbury, Massachusetts

BOSTON   TORONTO   LONDON   SINGAPORE

World Headquarters
Jones and Bartlett Publishers
40 Tall Pine Drive
Sudbury, MA 01776
978-443-5000
info@jbpub.com
www.jbpub.com

Jones and Bartlett Publishers Canada
2406 Nikanna Road
Mississauga, Ontario
Canada L5C 2WG

Jones and Bartlett Publishers International
Barb House, Barb Mews
London W6 7PA
UK

Cataloging-in-Publication Data

Cassel, Lillian N.
    Computer networks and open systems : an application development perspective / L. N.
  Cassel, R. H. Austing
      p.   cm.
    Includes bibliographical references and index.
    ISBN 0-7637-1122-5
    1. Computer networks.   2. OSI (Computer network standard).   I. Austing, Richard H.   II.
Title.
TK5105.5.C38   2000
004.6—dc21   99-058677

Production Credits
Chief Executive Officer: Clayton Jones
Chief Operating Officer: Don W. Jones, Jr.
V.P., Sales and Marketing: Tom Manning
V.P., College Editorial Director: Brian L. McKean
V.P., Managing Editor: Judith H. Hauck
V.P., Director of Design and Production: Anne Spencer
National Sales Manager: Paul Shepardson
Director of Manufacturing and Inventory Control: Therese Bräuer
Senior Acquisitions Editor: J. Michael Stranz
Senior Marketing Manager: Jennifer M. Jacobson
Production Editor: Rebecca S. Marks
Editorial and Production Assistant: Christine Tridente
Cover Design: AnnMarie LeMoine
Packaging: PageMasters & Company
Printing and Binding: Courier
Cover Printing: Courier

Printed in the United States of America
04 03 02 01 00   10 9 8 7 6 5 4 3 2 1

Contents

List of Figures

Preface

This text delivers principles, theory, and techniques from a practical perspective. It is grounded in real systems and real network applications, while emphasizing a strong foundation in the framework for network development. We have selected a set of topics that form a core of material in computer networking. Our emphasis is on methods and the environment for application development. By using the OSI model as an abstract structure, we expose students in an orderly way to the tools and techniques necessary for application development in a TCP/IP environment. Our goal is to make readers immediately comfortable in today's networking environment while equipping them to keep pace in one of the fastest moving and most exciting areas of computer system development.

Our approach to the study of computer networks is from an application development perspective. Looking at networks from this point of view reverses the traditional order of networking topics; instead of proceeding from the Physical layer upward, we move from the Application layer downward. Immediate benefits to this approach are:

- Students enter the study of networking through their own experiences as a network user.
- More attention is given to material in the upper layers, specifically the Application layer.
- Students encounter upper-layer material while there is still sufficient time in the course for comprehensive treatment and implementation.
- Students have the opportunity to practice in the course the kind of networking tasks they are expected to do in the workplace.

In a course using this applications development perspective, students first encounter the World Wide Web, a familiar network application. This leads them naturally to question what facilities and requirements must a network provide for the user. As a logical next step, they investigate the services and protocols of the topmost layer, the Application layer and, subsequently, the lower layers. At appropriate stages, relevant topics are addressed, such as data compression, encryption, ASN.1, routers, and LANs.

Our approach is a practical way to motivate the study of techniques and concepts; it parallels the approach commonly taken by an applications developer when confronted with a problem: enter through a user's perspective and find out what is required to solve the problem. For example, assume a new service is required in an electronic mail system. The

Our approach is a practical way to motivate the study of techniques and concepts; it parallels the approach commonly taken by an applications developer when confronted with a problem: enter through a user's perspective and find out what is required to solve the problem.

applications developer is more likely to review first what services already exist and how the new service relates to them rather than be concerned about the bit representation of messages that would be sent using the new service. The developer would determine what the specifications are and what set of functions is required to accomplish the task before deciding what functions to use or create.

In deciding what topics should be treated in this book, the authors grappled with the role of the OSI reference model in the study of networking given the widespread use of the Internet. In particular, what are the roles of the Open Systems Interconnection (OSI) and Internet (TCP/IP) environments in network-based applications development? Each offers something significant. Because the OSI reference model provides a widely accepted framework for describing networks and the interactions required in distributed applications, we use the reference model to divide the subject of computer networks into manageable pieces arranged in a logical order. These pieces consist of network protocols and services. Protocols and services designed to fit the OSI reference model offer a detailed definition of all aspects of network operation. Knowledge of them enables the developer to determine what needs to be implemented in a network application. In particular, a number of OSI services define common components of, and useful supporting modules for, applications. Applications developed in a TCP/IP or other network environment will require these services, and the developer can rely on knowledge of the OSI services to create the needed ones. Thus we use the OSI services to heighten awareness of what modules are needed and to suggest how they can be developed. Both OSI and TCP/IP protocols are included where appropriate, with OSI more prominent in chapters dealing with the upper layers.

The book is divided into three parts to help guide students: Fundamentals, the Application layer, and the supporting layers. Other pedagogical features are included; they are identified later in the Preface.

Part I, "Fundamentals," consists of four chapters, beginning with a short overview of computer networks. We differentiate among the various types of networks, describe the types of network-related problems that the students of computing disciplines must expect to encounter, and provide a rationale for studying networks. We distinguish the areas of data communications, networking, and distributed systems and identify our concentration on networking. We discuss the need for standards, and indicate how some came about. Major types of networks, including LANs are introduced in preparation for a more thorough treatment later in the book. Some highlights in the history of network evolution are included.

The World Wide Web provides an appropriate starting point for network application development. Tools such as the hypertext transport protocol (HTTP) and hypertext markup language (HTML) provide a quick entry into applications that span systems. HTML forms expand the environment to include general-purpose processing that may involve any number of heterogeneous systems. Metadata allows more efficient search based on descriptions rather than words or phrases. Java allows "documents" to include application invocation as well as more conventional text, images, video, and audio components. This early introduction of the Web as an application development environment allows students to begin work on significant projects before they are immersed in details of network operation.

With interest engaged and meaningful projects underway, we introduce vocabulary of the networked environment and examine the necessary layers of support to network-based applications. Fundamentals of open systems networking are identified, including an overview of the seven layers in the OSI model to give us a frame of reference with which to examine the operations of networked computers.

Part I concludes with a chapter on ASN.1, a language for describing information to be shared across a distributed environment, independent of any computer architecture or programming language. Liberal use of examples clarifies elements and features of the language. This placement allows us to use abstract syntax notation in examples within appropriate layers.

Part II, "The Application Layer," includes five chapters. The first provides a sample of the services that are common to many network applications and that provide a basis for discussion of common characteristics of distributed applications and the kinds of services that are frequently needed. The remaining four chapters of this section address specific network service areas in detail. These specific services—message handling (including electronic mail); terminal emulation; file transfer, access, and maintenance; and the distributed directory—are recognizable applications in their own right and can also be incorporated into other applications.

Our treatment of message-handling systems includes the user interface to the message-handling system, the requirements for local processing to serve the user's needs, and the requirements for communication between message-handling systems on separated computing systems. This must include facility for transporting messages and an agreement about communication between the processes in the end systems and the transport facilities that move the messages. We describe a number of mail systems and discuss both the SMTP and X.400 services.

Our discussion of virtual terminals looks at the types of terminals that an application may encounter, and considers terminal emulation with Kermit and with Telnet. We provide a balanced perspective between the user's workstation environment and the larger host environment.

In introducing file access and transfer, we look at file system features to see the similarities and differences existing on a network, and the special challenges these provide in application development on a network. We explain data transfer modes, such as XMODEM and YMODEM, and look at commonly available file transfer programs such as Kermit and FTP. The OSI FTAM protocol and services go well beyond file transfer to provide transparent remote access across a heterogeneous platform. The concept of a virtual filestore that incorporates all types of file systems is an important abstraction for general distributed file access. The need for a single general-purpose file access paradigm to and from which all other file system access is translated is key to successful application development in a networked environment.

The chapter on the Directory deals with the need to find resources in a widespread distributed environment. Like the general model of an electronic messaging system, the problem of a global directory involves communication among a collection of local user agents through network service agents (message transfer agents for messaging systems, directory service agents for directory systems). There must be flexibility in local systems to use many different types of database facilities, but with continuing common access. Naming, location, data integrity, and privacy are among the issues addressed in this chapter.

Part III, "The Supporting Layers," begins with a chapter on encryption and compression, primary aspects of data encoding during communications. Though encryption and compression may occur in several layers, we present the material in one place at the beginning of this part, so that it is available as appropriate in other layers. Other chapters in Part

III describe the services and protocols of the Presentation, Session, Transport, and Network layers. In addition, features of the Data-Link and Physical layers are included. Presentation and Session layers are terms from the OSI suite and not found in the TCP/IP protocols. Whether accomplished in distinct layers or integrated into applications directly, the services associated with these layers describe important functions in cooperative processes distributed over separate computer systems.

Communication between application entities imposes a number of requirements on the network services. First, there must be an agreed syntax for information exchange. The OSI Basic Encoding Rules (BER) and the External Data Representation (XDR) used in some UNIX systems deal with the issue of a common representation of data in transit.

The Session layer deals with establishing, maintaining, and managing a connection between two communicating processes. Quality of service options, dealing with disruptions of service during long operations, and synchronization are among the issues that are addressed. We include special cases among sessions: the client/server relationship and remote procedure calls.

At the Transport layer, we cross an important boundary. Our orientation shifts from services to the network user to dealing with the network itself. The Transport layer is responsible for end-to-end communications, across a possibly complex network topology, at a level that satisfies the quality of service required by the higher layers. The Transport layer masks network irregularities from the higher layers and provides the illusion of smooth functioning. The Transport layer is also important as it is often the lowest layer that the local system has under its control. Attaching to the Network layer is much like subscribing to a particular long-distance phone carrier. We can request the level of service that we require, but we cannot control how the carrier provides that service. The Transport layer is the local system's opportunity to improve on the service provided by the network carrier. We consider the requirements for joining networks that use different Transport layer protocols.

The Network layer is responsible for safe delivery of communications through the network. Its tasks include routing, congestion control, and the fragmentation and reassembly of messages too long to pass through some intermediate networks. Because the services of the network and lower layers will often come from a network utility, the interface between Transport and Network services is especially important. Implementation of standards affects the ability of a particular system to connect to the network service. Of practical concern when considering the safe delivery of communications is the vulnerability of an organization's network to access from the outside. Firewalls, as a protective mechanism, are introduced at this point in the book.

Selected features of the Data Link and Physical layers serve as an introduction to, or a review of, data communications. The goal here is to provide sufficient understanding of the underlying technology of computer networks to enable the application developer to feel comfortable with the environment. We give particular attention to the evolution and the properties of the most common local area network technologies: the Ethernet/IEEE 802.3 and the Token Ring. We give some attention to the interconnection of local networks. We introduce the characteristics of the evolving very high-speed networks and how they differ from the common LANs.

A course in networking is a key element in computer science, computer engineering, or information systems degree programs. Graduates of these programs have experienced campus networks throughout their undergraduate or graduate work. The network industry provides important and still developing career paths for qualified graduates and returning adults who take networking courses for career enhancement. Computing professionals in software development, systems, and many other specialties within computing must be knowledgeable in networking. At least, they must be able to develop and implement new software in a network environment, manage a network, convert a database to be accessible through a network or a myriad of other applications requiring networks. The network is the platform for development now, as the mainframe was in the past.

Because of the variety of curricula implementations among the computer science, computer engineering, and information systems fields, it is reasonable to question whether the traditional approach to the topic of networking satisfies the large diversity in student populations and needs. We believe there is a different approach to presenting and studying the topics generally contained in a networking course. In fact, we believe the answer to the query "Is there a better way?" is yes. As in any paradigm change, however, a shift in viewpoint is required to accept that a different approach is viable.

INTENDED AUDIENCE AND SUPPLEMENTARY MATERIALS

The approach and material of this book have been successfully class-tested in an upper-level undergraduate computer science course, and a graduate computer science course that included a mix of traditional and returning adult students.

The approach fits the needs of another significant audience, the working adult student. This type of student has some background and practical experience in computing with an interest in, and need for, applying knowledge in the workplace. Adult learners want exposure to the big picture first so they have a context to integrate topics as they are presented, rather than the more traditional details-first, bottom-up presentation that only later makes the context evident. Our approach to networking, through an applications development perspective, conforms with the adult learner's perception of education. Because the number of adult learners is increasing, and because many traditional colleges and universities are adapting courses to provide a more applications-oriented approach to concepts and theory, our book serves a population of considerable size.

An emphasis on clear, meaningful explanations of the many new terms and concepts required in studying this material characterizes the text. An extensive bibliography is included, including http addresses, for additional study.

The topics included in the text provide flexibility for the instructor to plan a course suitable for the environment in which it is used. An instructor who chooses to use all the material on applications and application development may have time for only light treatment of local area network protocols and the types of devices for joining networks. An instructor who wishes to give full coverage to the latter topics may choose to cover only one of the applications in great detail and review the others lightly. The decision will depend on the backgrounds and interests of the instructor and students, and on the number and types of related courses available.

An instructor's manual, including solutions to exercises in the book, will be available. Updates to the text, additional references, and discussion sessions with the authors should also be available online through the World Wide Web. The availability of materials online and the capability for conferencing through the Internet will make the book suitable for courses offered in a distance format.

As networking is a subject that is based on communications and cooperation, we invite the users of this text to join an online support group maintained and moderated by the authors of the text. Two discussion groups are offered: one limited to faculty, the other open to faculty and students. In the faculty group, we encourage suggestions for course examples, laboratory exercises, assignments, and exam questions. We will offer our own experiences and also hope to benefit from others' thoughts. We will answer questions when we can and invite others to contribute their ideas about the questions. In the student group, we invite the exchange of questions, answers, and open-ended exploration of ideas. Experience with assignments, discoveries of tools and methods that overcame difficulties, pointers to useful articles, and so forth are all welcome. We look forward to getting to know our colleagues and students in this exciting subject.

Computer Networks and
Open Systems

Fundamentals

The emergence of networked computers as the computing platform for many applications afffects every aspect of the study and use of computing.

Networks form a major part of the computing environment today. They are the backbone of the information superhighway, support automatic teller machines (bank machines), connect branch and main offices, allow international corporations to communicate efficiently, support fund transfers and news services, make reservation systems possible, and generally extend the potential of computing power for practical use. The emergence of networked computers as the computing platform for many applications affects every aspect of the study and use of computing. Architecture and operating systems, programming languages and tools, algorithm development and analysis all reflect the fundamental change in the nature of the system in use. The implications affect every type of application development, whether artificial intelligence, computer–human interface, databases, file systems, symbolic computation, visualization, and every other area where the presence of economical incremental increases in processing power affects the potential accomplishments.

Part I collects in one place the fundamental terminology, concepts, and notation required for a serious study of computer networks from the perspective of an application developer. The set of three chapters also includes a familiar application—the World Wide Web—so that you can experience the work of a developer early in the study.

Chapter 1 establishes the environment in which the study of open networking and network-based application development take place. Computer networks are a major platform for application development, just as individual systems had previously been. Basic issues of open networking and proprietary networks are introduced. Communication requirements are identified. The role of standards and protocols is explored, and the two significant models that are discussed in more detail in later chapters are introduced, the OSI reference model and the TCP/IP suite. The seven layers of the OSI reference model and the TCP/IP suite are viewed from a functional point of view. This provides the basic framework for examining network applications. The terminology, notation, and basic concepts essential to an understanding of layering, interactions between successive layers, service specifications, and protocol specifications are included. Typical components, such as repeaters, bridges, and routers, are associated with appropriate layers. Networks are characterized as local area, wide area, and metropolitan area, with a number of topologies possible for each type.

In Chapter 2, we discuss an application, the World Wide Web, that you have already experienced. It is included this early to demonstrate that meaningful developmental work can be done with only a fundamental knowledge of networking. This is analogous to learning application program development before obtaining a detailed understanding of computer system organization and architecture. Moreover, this gives you the opportunity to try your hand at application development while probing more deeply into the study of networks in later chapters. Familiar topics such as browsers, document preparation, Web forms processing, and Java are included.

Chapter 3 provides the last of the fundamental tools of Part I, the abstract syntax notation ASN.1. A selection of syntax rules and numerous examples are included. The notation will help you understand illustrations that use it in later chapters. This chapter can serve as a reference as you work through more detailed discussions of the network application environment that begin in Part II.

Networked Computers

Networks and network services are evolving rapidly. Most applications that run on a computer interact with a network, but the nature of that interaction varies greatly. At a minimum, the application accesses files stored on a file server. At the other extreme, the application may be distributed over a number of computer systems and require carefully coordinated cooperative work. The integrity of the program and its files depends upon the security of the network to which the computer is attached. The program may have to display its output on a remote system whose characteristics are unknown to the program developer. It may have to access data stored in a number of locations, on file systems with very different features and access modes, some of which are unknown to the program developer. Moreover, as time passes, the characteristics of resources and devices accessed by the program will change; the program must continue to work correctly.

The application development effort often includes not only writing programs that work correctly and efficiently on a particular type of computer—and perhaps port easily to other systems—but also cooperate with programs running on different systems. Simple file access may require interaction with a file server. Printing may include specifying which of many printers to use. Performance of a program using network resources can vary substantially, depending on the load on the network. Some of the resources that the program requires may be inaccessible because some part of the network has failed or one program may be competing for the same resources as programs running on other computers. Although a general user of the Internet and the World Wide Web need not be concerned with the underlying software, a networking applications developer needs to know more about the concepts, tools, and techniques that provide the basis for the software. To work in this type of environment, computer programmers and systems developers must understand the special nature of the computer network as an application development environment. Therefore, more than half of this book is devoted to applications and application services.

In this chapter, we enter an application from a user's perspective and move into the fundamentals that make the application work in a network environment. We begin by giving an example of an office supply company with three stores to illustrate issues and provide insights into networking.

With this application and some issues in mind, we step back and briefly describe networks and give some rationale for their design and use. We give a brief introduction to network software and distinguish among types of networks.

We introduce the seven-layer model of network components, the **Open Systems Interconnection (OSI) Reference Model**, which provides an established and recognized common framework for describing network software elements. We compare its layered structure with the most common implementation of network protocols, the **Transport Control Program** and **Internet Program (TCP/IP)** of the Internet.

We examine the concept of each layer having distinct functions, yet operating in conjunction with adjoining layers. We identify the service and protocol specifications that are common to a number of the layers. Finally, we briefly cite characteristics of various network topologies and three common types of networks, local area networks (LANs), wide area networks (WANs), and metropolitan area networks (MANs).

1.1 A NETWORKING APPLICATIONS EXAMPLE

The following scaled-down example typifies the kind of work to be done in network-based applications.

Office Supplies Unlimited, an office supply company, has three stores. Each store maintains its own stock, but can sell an item from another location if the item is not available in the store's stock. Each store has a computer system that keeps track of its inventory. There is no centralized system, and currently each local inventory system runs independently of the others.

The computers and inventory software of the various stores were acquired independently, and are not alike. However, all the systems include standard **protocols**. These are standard agreements about what messages will be sent and expected, under what conditions, in what format, and with what meaning. Adequate communication links exist such that each system can exchange messages with each of the others.

The project: We need programs, to run on all the systems, that will allow a salesperson at one store to check on stock availability at the other stores. The solution must not depend on a centralized system, nor on sending copies of one store's inventory to the others. Program input will consist of a stock identifier and the quantity needed. The program will first check store stock; then, if necessary, it will check the stock at the other stores. Output will include the stock identifier, a description of the item, quantity on hand, and the quantities in other stores if needed. The salesperson will then claim the stock needed, and the program will notify the other stores(s) to hold the claimed stock for pickup.

1.1.1 Proprietary vs. Open Systems

An application developer presented with the preceding problem, would consider the possible communications options required among the participating systems. If the application is built on communications components that run on only a particular type of equipment, then future expansion or modification of the application would require that same type of equipment. Furthermore, if it is later decided to integrate this application into another so that information can be shared and the two can interoperate to achieve a new result, the choice of equipment would again be constrained by the communication requirements of the current application.

These considerations point to the choice of network software designed and constructed to use particular equipment and address the needs of a particular environment. This kind of software system is called **proprietary** and is exemplified by IBM's System Network Architecture (SNA), among others. These systems offer distinct advantages in communication among like computer systems. When software on these systems must interact with software on systems from a different vendor, the proprietary network approach hinders communication and application development.

Open systems allow software developed on different manufacturers' equipment to interact with a common understanding of network operation.

Open systems alleviate these problems. Open systems allow software developed on different manufacturers' equipment to interact with a common understanding of network operation. Often individual systems will run both a proprietary solution for efficient interaction with like systems and an open system that allows them to participate in network applications independent of individual host machines. Figure 1.1 illustrates the differences in communication between open systems and between systems that use proprietary protocols.

1.1.2 Communications Requirements

We look at the requirements for communication in this example system, then determine which requirements the application programmer must meet and which are provided in a standard network system. The requirements are divided into seven categories to correspond, roughly, with the seven layers of the OSI model presented in more detail later in this chapter.

The Office Supplies Unlimited project illustrates many of the major issues of applications development that spans systems connected over a network, including considerations that do not enter into ordinary programming. Some of the elements required in a solution to this problem are unrelated to the communications requirements: there must be a convenient method to enter the request and a response that is easily understood; the program must check the local files to determine if the item is in stock; the program must update the local files when an item is sold. All these are ordinary aspects of an online inventory system.

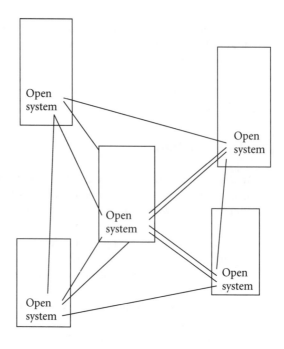

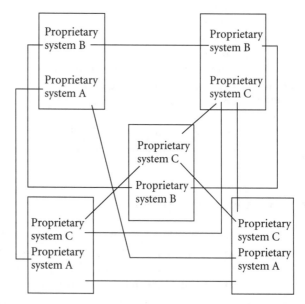

Figure 1.1. Open systems vs. proprietary systems in communications

The system must also have the ability to communicate with its counterpart on another computer. It must be able to exchange messages with the other inventory program to make and answer inquiries. Although this remote processing is similar to any other input/output operation, some differences make this type of programming more complex than accessing a new peripheral device:

1. The program must establish contact with the correct partner. This is much more involved than choosing the correct printer from several available. It includes contacting the computers in the other stores and specifically establishing contact with the inventory program running on each computer.

2. The program cannot know all the characteristics of the other system. The situation is not the same as installing a new printer to use with a word processor. In that case, an elaborate description of the printer is given to the word processor so that the software can use all the special features of the printer. When we develop our application to interact with the inventory system on the computers at other branches of the business, we will not restrict ourselves to the specific characteristics of the hardware used at the present time. Since the stores are independently managed, updates in equipment and the programs may occur without notice or coordination with the other stores. Thus, when the program communicates with a partner on another computer, any number of configurations are possible at the other end of the connection. Our program development should concentrate on what information (part numbers and description, requests for information and orders to hold stock) has to be exchanged, not how that information is made accessible to all other systems.

3. Since the two or more cooperating systems are partners, information must flow both ways between them. Inquiries and responses about stock availability flow both ways. Either partner may send a message to the other at any time. Once the connection between the two is established, either side may terminate it. Thus the dialogue must be managed.

4. Message delivery between separated systems must overcome obstacles. Some messages, perhaps the product descriptions, may be very long and must be broken down into units small enough to travel over the available connections. The message units may travel by different routes and arrive out of order. The units may arrive faster than the target system can accept them. Some units may be lost and need retransmission.

5. Each of the cooperating inventory programs runs on one specific machine. That machine must be addressed, with no chance of ambiguity. The address may be as simple as a phone number if the connection is by phone line. Given a unique address, the network must provide a path to that machine. If more than one path exists, the network must make a good choice.

6. Just as a journey of a thousand miles begins with a single step, the trip through a complex network begins with a message passing along a physical connection to an adjacent machine. The messages between our inventory programs will follow strict rules to access a communication channel and will be checked for transmission errors.

7. The bits of the message must be represented in voltages on the communication line so that both ends of the connection have the same understanding of what is 0 and what is 1.

How many items in this list of tasks must the application programmer accomplish? Not many because most of the tasks listed belong to the communication protocol set. Nearly all require that the programmer understand the communication requirements inherent in the problem and make choices from an array of options.

This, of course, is a familiar way to work. Every programmer is accustomed to using the services of the operating system to simplify the task at hand. The operating system provides input/output processes, paging, memory management, and a library of common procedures. The application programmer selects existing modules that are useful and writes code for those components of the application that are unique to the application. The programmer takes for granted many services of the operating system and of the computer hardware. You will learn to develop network applications in the same way, taking some services for granted, specifying parameters for others.

1.2   WHAT IS A NETWORK?

Now that we have seen a network application example and identified several issues, we consider some basic notions beginning with the following simple, but complete, definition of computer networks: a **computer network** is a set of computers that are connected and able to exchange messages.

Note that this definition excludes a large time-sharing system with a collection of terminals attached, a type of system sometimes called a network. In our descriptions and discussions of networks, we assume that each station on the network is a computer that can be used independently of the network; the network is an extension of the computing environment offered by that computer. Our networks may also include devices, such as printers, used only through the network. Because these devices cannot operate in a stand-alone mode, we do not consider such devices to be stations or nodes on the network, but as a separate category of peripheral devices, accessed through the network.

The connection between computers in a network can be point to point, shared medium, wireless, or a combination of these forms. The simplest form is point to point, a cable connecting two computers directly. Messages are passed by writing to the connecting cable and reading from it. More commonly, connections among networked computers require that a communication medium be shared by all the computers in the network. The medium could be a cable (copper or fiber optic) or a radio/microwave/satellite transmission channel. Figure 1.2 illustrates these two connection options for networked computers. To make communication possible, it is necessary to provide a scheme for coordinating sharing of the facility.

Individual stations on the network may be of the same or different types. There are, for instance, networks composed exclusively of large host computers, all made by one manu-

We assume that each station on the network is a computer that can be used independently of the network; the network is an extension of the computing environment offered by that computer.

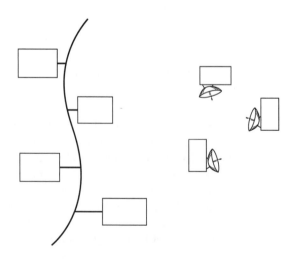

Figure 1.2. Connecting computers for network communications

facturer and all running the same operating system. There are also networks composed of stations from nearly every maker of computing equipment, running all the major operating systems and some that are very specialized. Participation in the network requires only the ability to send a message in a form other stations can use and to receive a message from another station.

1.3 REASONS FOR INSTALLING NETWORKS

Though electronic mail (e-mail) and the World Wide Web have evolved as critical uses of computer networks, there are other reasons to install and use a network. Often the first planned use of a network, and frequently the reason for the decision to network, is resource sharing. The increased use of personal computers and workstations emphasizes the importance of this facility. The advantages offered by networked small computers over a single, large, time-shared system include a superior price–performance ratio, better reliability through resource sharing, greater access to resources outside an organization, and easier growth of computing power through incremental addition of computer stations.

Not every characteristic of a networked system is an advantage, however. Distribution of disk space illustrates this point. In a single large system, all the disk space is available and can be divided among the users as needed. In a collection of workstations, the storage is distributed with the processing power. The decision about how much disk space each user will need is essentially static and made when the machine is purchased. If one user encounters a need for a very large block of storage, which is not available on the local machine, the fact that more than that amount of space is available on another machine may not help.

Thus, there are reasons to compromise on the complete separation and independence of the users. A solution used in many networks is to make disk storage a common shared resource like printers and other devices. This requires a facility to allocate space on the shared file system and to protect the files of one user from unauthorized access by another. This is accomplished by having a computer act as a **file server,** a computer with a large volume of disk space and the software needed to control its use. Other computers in the network use the storage space on the file server as if it were locally attached. A network may have one or several file servers. Individual workstations may have private disk storage as well, or may be diskless, relying entirely on the network to provide the storage required. Clearly such a configuration affects the operating system on the user's machine. The operating system must communicate with the servers to gain access to storage in response to the file access commands from its user. Dependence on file servers also increases the amount of traffic on a network, affecting access to other shared resources, such as printers. A network whose stations use a file server will support fewer stations than a network whose stations depend primarily on local file systems.

1.4 NETWORK SYSTEM SOFTWARE

A computer network requires three major components:

- A transmission medium
- An interface between the network station and the medium
- Software to drive the network connection

In addition to controlling the connection, software provides support for the network user or application developer similar to the support the operating system provides in a single computer system.

In a single computer system, the role of the operating system is twofold. The operating system *serves the user* by providing access to systems resources while masking the complexity of many operations. Thus many users have little or no understanding of the tasks required to read and write to a disk, or to manage memory, for example. The operating system also *protects the system* from a careless or malicious user. Critical functions in the system operation can be executed only by the operating system—users *must* issue requests through the operating system. This prevents users from accessing the areas in memory where system functions are stored, and the storage areas that belong to other users.

Computers connected to a network require systems software not only to function as independent, separate devices, but also to make explicit use of the network through operations such as e-mail, file transfer, and remote login, among others. A user invokes these operations by running specific programs. The network software that allows processes running on a computer to interact with the network and to send and receive messages supplements the other operating system functions. Sending a message requires making a system call on the operating system module that forms the message into packets suitable for network transmission. The packets include the message, but also information about what process is sending the message and what process is to receive it, as seen in Figure 1.3. The degree of difficulty involved in delivering the message to the intended destination depends on the nature of the network in use. Some networks require little effort to deliver the message since every station on the network receives every transmission. All that is needed is that the destination node accept the message and pass it to the proper process (the electronic mail or file transfer process, for instance) and that other nodes disregard it.

Receiving a message is actually more difficult. A node that can receive messages has no way of knowing when a message will arrive. Thus its network software must always be listening to the network connection in case a message arrives. A process that expects to receive a message must coordinate itself with the **daemon**, or background process, that is always listening for incoming messages. The daemon must know which process to deliver the message to, if one should arrive. The destination process must execute statements of the form "check for incoming messages; if any exist, proceed to process."

In some networks, however, the separate systems are more closely tied together through software. Resources located on the network are accessed nearly as easily as the resources attached directly to the individual user station. Software provides a sense in such networks that the whole collection of networked computers is a type of system. All the resources of this extended system are accessible to any process running on any station.

Figure 1.3. A packet includes a header and a message part

Destination	Source	Text, images, etc.
Header		Message

This degree of connectivity requires an extension of the operating system. The **network operating system** consists of a layer of software between the operating system and the application software on each computer in the network. The network operating system software captures calls for system resources, interprets them, and passes them to the usual operating system routines or to a network resource provider as needed.

Network operating systems most often connect personal computers or workstations and provide a file server and print server. To use network resources, the user must login to the network, as he or she would login to a multiuser computer system. The login identifies the user and determines what resources the user may access. The network operating system includes code that runs in the personal computer or workstation and other code that runs in the server. The user interacts with the code in the station, which in turn interacts with the code in the server. The net effect is increased resources for the user of each station.

The network operating system thus corresponds to a single system operating system. It assists the user in gaining access to resources, masking much of the complexity actually involved in such access. It also protects network resources from inappropriate use by authenticating users and restricting access.

1.5 NETWORK PROTOCOLS AND STANDARDS

Interoperability means that distinct processes, each running on its own processor, cooperate in accomplishing some goal.

Network operating systems provide access to network resources for user processes, but much more is needed to realize the goal of **interoperability** between processes running on separate systems. Interoperability means that distinct processes, each running on its own processor, cooperate in accomplishing some goal. They cooperate by exchanging information; by notifying each other as various tasks are completed; and by requesting services from, and granting services to, each other. The processes run in separate and perhaps very different operating environments; they are related only in the cooperation. Their cooperative operation depends on a common understanding of the protocols that determine how their interaction will proceed.

1.5.1 Protocol Example

Suppose we want to have the ability to send a message from one station in a network to another, have the receiving station confirm that the message arrived and then display the message on the screen. Sending the message is not sufficient, even if we are sure the message will be received by the destination machine. What is needed is an agreement, a protocol, that says

- I will send you a message with a header containing my identification and yours and message body containing the letters C and D.
- I understand that when you receive the message, you will know that C means Confirm and D means Display.
- I expect that when you receive the message, you will send me a message with a header containing your identification and mine and message body containing the letters OK. You will also display my message on your screen.

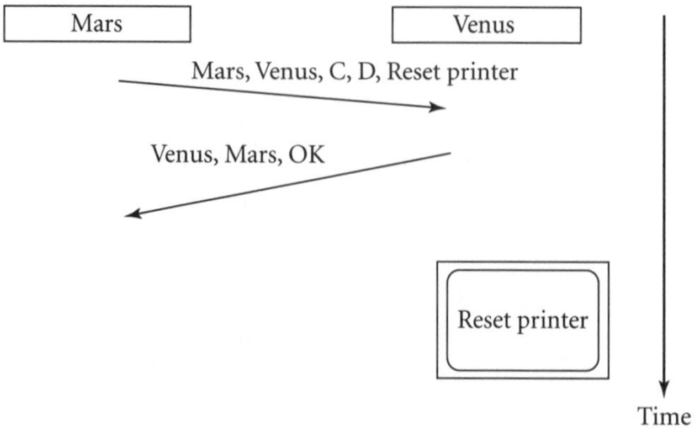

Figure 1.4. A simple protocol operating between two stations on a network and allowing each to display a message on the other's screen

- Furthermore, I agree to respond to a message from you, containing my identification and yours and the letters C and D, in the same way that you respond to my message. (This is the reciprocal agreement in a protocol specification; it allows each side to be the initiator or the responder in this interaction.)

Figure 1.4 shows this simple protocol in operation.

Let's call this protocol *ConfirmAndDisplay*. Now suppose two other stations in the network, or in a different network, use a protocol called *AcknowledgeAndShow*. AcknowledgeAndShow works exactly the same as ConfirmAndDisplay, except that in the message transmission, the letter S is used instead of C and D. (The S indicates that the message is to be Shown on the screen. An acknowledgment of receipt of the message is always expected and not explicitly requested in the message.) If stations named Mars and Venus use the protocol ConfirmAndDisplay only, and stations Neptune and Uranus, in the same network, use the protocol AcknowledgeAndShow only, then Mars and Neptune cannot display messages on each other's screens.

Why would such a situation arise, and what can be done about it? Perhaps the idea of the mutual screen write by separate computers occurred to more than one person and each implemented it on the computers on which he or she wanted it. Neither was aware of, or even interested in, the other's existence. Only later did someone recognize a reason to have the same facility on all the systems. What can be done about it? There are four potential solutions to the problem:

1. Drop one protocol entirely and use the other on all the systems.
2. Drop both protocols and develop a new one that all stations use.
3. Have each station run both protocols, using the correct one for each communication.
4. Keep the original protocol in each set of stations and also adapt the new global protocol to extend the range of stations each can work with.

At first glance, solution 1 seems reasonable. Unfortunately, it turns out that each protocol has spread beyond its initial use and is deeply embedded in a number of applications. If the protocol is discontinued, all the applications that use it will have to be identified and modified to use the replacement. Neither side is willing to go to that trouble. Further, each side is convinced that its own approach is better.

In solution 2, the new protocol would be carefully designed after thorough study and would address all the situations in which such a protocol might be useful. Since the new protocol would be installed in a very large collection of systems, not just the original Mars, Venus, Neptune, and Uranus, each of these systems would gain access to many other partners in using the protocol. The problem of applications with the old protocols embedded would remain.

Solution 3 is very practical for a simple case of two competing, similar protocols. However, if there are many other versions of this protocol, the burden on each system to keep all of them is substantial.

In solution 4, Mars and Venus will still use ConfirmAndDisplay when they work together because each knows the other will work correctly with that protocol and each has a number of application programs that include ConfirmAndDisplay. To display a message on Neptune's screen, Mars will use the new global protocol.

1.5.2   An Argument for Standards

This example illustrates the problem of developing network protocols. There are many reasons why a number of different protocols exist for accomplishing similar goals. Some of the differences result from requirements that demanded specific features that are not consistent with other requirements. Others grew out of historic events and have become deeply ingrained in the products and practices of the industry. The various stations on a network come from different manufacturers, each with a long history of its own way of working. Allowing processes to interoperate, machines to communicate with each other, and to cooperate to share a common transmission medium requires another kind of cooperation— the development of standards. The standards define protocols independent of individual manufacturers and applications. Appropriate standards can reduce development effort otherwise expended in preparing programs to run in different environments, such as the incompatible personal computer systems initially built by IBM and Apple.

Joining incompatible independent systems by agreeing to some common principles is not a new activity. In the 19th century, a railroad built for one region had a different width of track from a railroad in another region. As long as the regions remained separate, and the equipment was manufactured specifically for use in one region, the differences were immaterial. When use of the railroads expanded, however, and the ability to travel and ship goods over long distances was recognized, the problem illustrated in Figure 1.5 had to be solved. The solution was an agreement to build railroad equipment according to a common, or *standard* specification. Agreement on a standard gauge track did not, of course, allow trains to travel between narrow and wide gauge tracks. The original tracks and trains could still be used for transportation within the region but when travel between regions occurred, only standard gauge track and trains built to run on it would work.

The situation is similar to the developing network standards. Older proprietary protocols can still be used between the systems that implement them. However, to interoperate with other systems, the global standards must be observed. As a result, more than one set of protocols may exist in many systems. As more and more systems adopt the global standards,

> Allowing processes to interoperate, machines to communicate with each other, and to cooperate to share a common transmission medium requires another kind of cooperation—the development of standards.

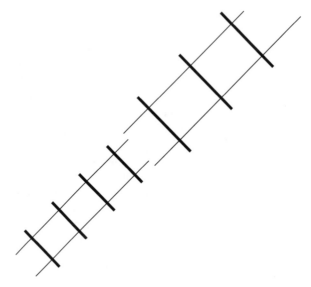

Figure 1.5. The importance of standards was recognized before computer networks were developed

there will be less reason to use the older, more restricted, protocols. However, because of the investment in the current systems and the number of applications that depend on them, these older protocols will continue to be important for some time.

1.5.3 Communication Modes

Communication between components of interconnected systems occurs in one of two modes: connection-oriented or connectionless. These distinctions affect many of the layers, so they must be understood before each of the layers is discussed.

Connection-oriented mode resembles communication by telephone: one party makes the call, waiting for the other to answer; then people at the two ends converse; finally, the call is terminated when the phones are hung up. Connection-oriented mode of communication between processes also involves three phases: connection establishment, data transfer, and connection release. Besides having a distinguishable beginning, duration, and end, a connection-oriented communication has other significant characteristics:

- Two forms of agreement are required: between the peer participants concerning the transmission of data between them and also between the users of the connection and the providers of the service.
- During the connection-establishment phase, it is possible to negotiate parameters and options regarding data exchange.
- Once established, the connection provides all the identification necessary about the participants so that data can move without the overhead required for addressing and direction finding.
- All the data carried over the connection can be related in a common context; data units can be kept in sequence and their flow rates controlled.

In contrast to connection-oriented mode, connectionless mode communication resembles communication using the postal system. Someone prepares an item to send, places it in an envelope or package that must contain the full address of the intended recipient, and drops it in the mail. For effective use of the system, the sender must know that the recipient is at the address placed on the envelope and is able and willing to receive the item sent. Connectionless communication between parts of an interconnected system consists of transmission of a single unit of data from a source to a destination without previously establishing a connection. No agreements about the context of the communication are possible, and no negotiation of services expected or required can occur. Each item sent must contain all the information about the destination and the quality of service expected from the service providers. Each unit sent may travel by a different route; no sequencing or flow control is available. On the other hand, there is no need for a connection establishment phase or a connection termination phase, and copies of a single unit of data may be sent to multiple destinations. The implications and impact of these two communication modes appear repeatedly in the the various choices available throughout the suites of protocols.

1.6 LAYERING AND NETWORK REFERENCE MODELS

1.6.1 The Concept of Layering

The interaction of application processes running on separate systems and communicating over a network is a complex task requiring a large number of operations. Since many of the operations are common to most processes, they can be grouped and provided as a library of functions called when needed. There are many ways to combine these operations, depending upon the needs of the application processes calling them. Since the number of operations that may be required is large, and the number of possible combinations is much larger, some structure is needed to organize the options and the practical combinations. In networked applications, a layered structure best serves the requirement of grouping operations and finding combinations that work well together to meet a particular need.

> In networked applications, a layered structure best serves the requirement of grouping operations and finding combinations that work well together to meet a particular need.

The layers defined in a suite of network protocols isolate particular services and define the relationship among the services. For example, communication between processes on separate computers requires that messages sent from one computer arrive at the other. It is useless to consider message exchange between processes unless that capability exists. An application, therefore, invokes a service to facilitate communication with its peer application and that service, in turn, invokes a service to locate and establish contact with the machine where the peer application is running.

Layering does more than assist the application in selecting from a variety of services. By isolating the details of each service from the others, layering allows each service to be developed and revised as needed with minimal impact on the other components of the network software. Some services, such as sharing the communication medium, change as new technology becomes available. Others change with the needs of new applications, perhaps for time requirements or security.

The layers in a protocol suite identify the required components of each network communication between application processes. Within each layer, a number of choices allow the processes to select the type of service most appropriate for their needs. Each service is defined in terms of its interaction with the layer above it, the layer below it, and the net effect of its use. Within those constraints, its internal operation can be implemented in any way and can be revised when better techniques are found. Additional services can be added at each layer as needed, without affecting the services that are currently available.

A suite of network protocols consists of a collection of layers of services to support communication between application processes. Each of the layers consists of one or more options for the type of service provided at that layer. The layers are often referred to as a **protocol stack**.

The sections that follow show several different approaches to layering network services and to the choices offered at each layer. There are others. We briefly identify the TCP/IP protocol suite and the SNA layered architecture. The OSI Reference Model, an attempt to define a set of standards for network interaction that all network applications can use, is then considered in more detail. These models are conceptual—convenient packagings of the many operations needed for process interoperation.

1.6.2 The TCP/IP Suite of Protocols

The TCP/IP protocols were developed for the ARPAnet, beginning in the 1960s under funding from the Advanced Projects Research Agency (ARPA). Figure 1.6 shows the layering of the TCP/IP protocols. The TCP/IP suite includes an Application layer, which provides networking-related services to the user; a Transport layer, which addresses the need for moving messages from a process on one system to the corresponding process on another system; and a Network layer, which concerns addressing and routing of messages. TCP/IP does not define how messages are put onto the communication medium or how bits are represented. Instead, TCP/IP runs on top of other protocols that provide these services. Systems that implement the TCP/IP protocols can interoperate with each other.

At the core of the TCP/IP protocols are a network protocol, called the Internet Protocol (IP), and a transport protocol, Transmission Control Protocol (TCP). IP is responsible for routing packets through interconnected networks, and TCP is charged with breaking messages into network-size packets, handing them off to IP, putting the packets back to form the original message at the destination, and recovering from errors that may have occurred

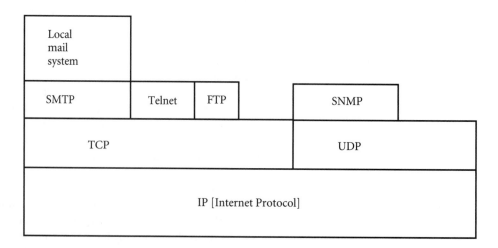

Figure 1.6. Layering in the TCP/IP protocols

in the network operation. TCP provides the appearance of a reliable connection between processes running on separate systems. TCP in turn relies on IP to deliver the packets of data from the sending machine to the destination machine. Combined, the two allow processes on separate systems to interact as if they were in direct contact with one another. Because the services provided in the ARPAnet and its descendants rely heavily on the combined services of TCP and IP, the entire suite of protocols and services is often referred to as TCP/IP.

In section 1.6.1, we noted that several versions of a service might be offered at one layer of a protocol suite. In the TCP/IP protocols, this is illustrated by the presence of the User Datagram Protocol (UDP) as an alternative to TCP at the Transport layer. Though TCP attempts to provide a very high-quality service, compensating for lost or reordered packets, this service comes at a relatively high cost in terms of processing required. UDP provides a much lighter best effort service, sometimes characterized as "Send it and pray," and involves a much lighter processing price. The appropriate choice depends on the type of service the application requires. If speed is more important than perfect accuracy, then UDP delivers the needed service. If the processing overhead of TCP is not an undue burden and a very reliable service is required, TCP meets the need. Both TCP and UDP can support a network communication using IP, as shown in Figure 1.6.

IP runs in many network environments, connecting systems over local area networks, wide area networks, and combinations of interconnections. The principal application services are File Transfer Protocol (FTP), e-mail support (SMTP, the Simple Mail Transfer Protocol), and telnet (a form of virtual terminal facility for remote login). Local mail systems use SMTP for moving mail from sender to receiver. SNMP (Simple Network Management Protocol) is an example of a service that uses UDP because it is faster.

TCP/IP has been widely available and used for more than 25 years. Consequently, a large base of applications depend on it, and many application developers are comfortable with it. In particular, the collection of networks that are interconnected by common use of the TCP/IP suite of protocols is called the **Internet**.

1.6.3 SNA

Work on IBM's System Network Architecture (SNA) began in the 1960s, and SNA was announced in 1974. SNA is a layered architecture that allows terminals to be shared by multiple programs in a single-host, tree-structured network. In 1976, enhancements allowed programs in two or more separate hosts, each using SNA, to communicate with one another and with the terminals.

An SNA network consists of nodes, each one of a particular type depending upon its function. Type 1 nodes are terminals. Type 2 nodes are terminal controllers. Type 2.1 nodes, introduced in 1983, can establish and support direct, peer-to-peer sessions. There are no type 3 nodes. Type 4 nodes are communications processors, attached to hosts to relieve the host of the processing requirements associated with communications. Type 5 nodes are the hosts. SNA network architecture consists of the physical entities that comprise the network plus logical entities (software) related to them. Three types of logical entities make up the *network addressable units (NAUs)*: *logical units (LUs)*, *physical units (PUs)*, and *system services control points (SSCPs)*. End users, either human users at terminals or application processes, access the SNA network through the logical units. LUs establish a session, the logical connection through which the communication occurs. The physical units provide administrative and network operation services at a node in the network. A system services control point resides in a host computer and includes complete knowledge of the other nodes associated with the host. The SSCP is the focus of configuration management, problem determination and directory services. SSCP runs in either a host or a communications front-end processor (type 5 or type 4 node). A *domain* comprises all the nodes known to an instance of SSCP. Each host or communications controller, along with its directly attached peripheral devices, makes a subarea. A domain includes a single instance of SSCP and is made up of one or more subareas [Pic89]. Figure 1.7 shows an SNA network consisting of two domains, each made up of several subareas.

The hierarchical approach to networking is the dominant architecture for SNA backbone networks. Establishment of sessions between LUs requires that a session first be established with the local SSCP. SSCP maintains the directory services tables required to convert the name of the requested LU to an address that allows connection establishment. After resolving the LU, the SSCP determines whether the destination LU is able to participate in the requested session and issues instructions to attempt the session establishment [Pic90].

The hierarchical nature of networking in subarea SNA uses manually established, static tables for name-to-address resolution and routing among subareas. Routing changes require major system adjustments, usually requiring that the affected hosts and communications front-ends be taken out of service. Problems associated with static definition of network nodes, resources, and routes are burdensome in today's networks, which involve hundreds of hosts and communications front-ends; the prospect of adding large numbers of personal computers and workstations to the SNA networks makes the problem unreasonable [Pic89]. This system also does not lend itself to dynamic response to changing network conditions.

General-purpose networking, involving session establishment between any machines without the need to predefine network membership, is a basic tenet of Open System Interconnection and a growing demand of the user community. This peer-to-peer networking is a significant departure from the master–slave relationship central to the networking strategies of IBM's SNA and the proprietary systems of other companies as well. IBM's

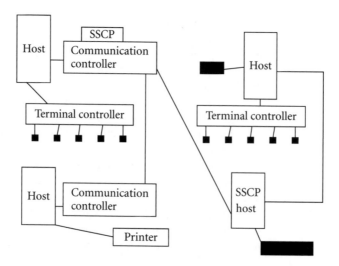

Figure 1.7. An SNA network with two domains each with several subareas

move toward meeting this demand is implemented in the Advanced Peer-to-Peer Network (APPN) protocols [Sac90]. Independent logical units using the APPN protocols reside in type 2.1 nodes. They can be the master or slave in a session, use a dynamic, distributed directory to find destination LUs, and use dynamic topology update and route-determination protocols.

Users of IBM's SNA have stated a requirement for communication and interoperability between their SNA network nodes and non-SNA devices. IBM selected OSI as the vehicle to enable communication between SNA and non-SNA nodes [Sac90]. Further, most IBM systems currently support TCP/IP. IBM, like other computer manufacturers, continues to develop its proprietary network systems to meet its customers' needs, while participating in the development and deployment of services required in heterogeneous networks. Like TCP/IP, SNA has a large installed base and a large group of satisfied and expert users.

1.6.4   The OSI Reference Model

To facilitate standardization of all aspects of communication and cooperation among systems, the Open Systems Interconnection (OSI) model of the International Organization for Standardization (ISO), referred to as the OSI reference model, identifies seven layers of interaction. The seven layers defined in the OSI reference model, and their positions relative to each other, are shown in Figure 1.8.

Each layer represents a group of tasks required in applications that communicate over network connections. The seven layers are always shown as a stack. The top of the stack is the set of functions most closely related to the application itself. The bottom of the stack is the farthest removed from the application, and closest to the physical requirements of the system.

The seven layers of the OSI model provide a framework for developing standards that permit open systems interconnection. A number of principles affected the particular sub-

7	Application	Those aspects of the application process that are concerned with communication
6	Presentation	Common representation of information exchanged between applications
5	Session	Establish and maintain a communication between application processes, synchronization
4	Transport	Reliable communication between machines, end-to-end through possible inter-network connections
3	Network	Routing, addressing
2	Data link	Reliable communications between machines that share a common communication channel
1	Physical	Electrical and mechanical interface to the transmission medium

Figure 1.8. The seven-layer OSI model

division of open system interconnection into the OSI model. These include use of past experience to determine where boundaries are most successful, putting layer boundaries where the description of services can be kept small and the number of interactions across the boundary minimized, separating functions that are manifestly different, keeping for each layer boundaries only with its immediate neighbors, and allowing a layer to be completely redesigned and its protocols changed as appropriate to take advantage of advances in technology, while not changing the services expected from or provided to the adjacent layers [OSI].

Both the TCP/IP and SNA models predate the OSI reference model. There is no direct correspondence of layers between the OSI model and either of the other two models. However, functions of the Application, Presentation, and Session layers of the OSI model are generally found in the Application layer of the TCP/IP model. The remaining layers of the two models approximately correspond on a one-to-one basis. The approximate correspondence between layers of the SNA and OSI models is shown in Figure 1.9. Although the OSI stack was modeled in part on SNA, the specific separation of duties varies somewhat in the two models. There are a number of similarities, but the layers in the two stacks do not match exactly [Ste91].

Functions of the Application, Presentation, and Session layers of the OSI model are generally found in the Application layer of the TCP/IP model. The remaining layers of the two models approximately correspond on a one-to-one basis.

Application Layer

The Application layer provides to an application process the ability to communicate with another application process, to exchange information and interoperate in the accomplishment of a particular goal. Of all the seven layers of the structure of network resources, only the Application layer interacts directly with the other components of an application process. It is the only way available for an application to gain access to the resources needed for communication, and the only way for an application to determine the characteristics of that communication.

Two concepts are key to the Application layer and its relationship with an information processing task: **application entity** and **abstract syntax**:

Application entity Application entities are those components of an application process that correspond to capabilities concerned with Open Systems Interconnection. That is, application entities are particular parts of an application process concerned with enabling communication and interaction with a corresponding application process in another open system.

SNA and OSI Protocol Layers		
	SNA	Approximate OSI Association
1	Transaction services	Application
2	Presentation services	Presentation
3	Data flow controls	Session
4	Transmission control	Transport
5	Path control	Network
6	Data link	Data link
7	Physical	Physical

Figure 1.9. SNA and OSI Protocol Layering

Abstract syntax Abstract syntax is specification of data or control information independent of the encoding technique used to represent them.

An application entity is the conceptual embodiment of all aspects of an application process that have to do with communication with another system. In the application example of section 1.1.2, an application entity must establish contact between the inventory programs running on separate systems, must access the remote inventory files to determine stock availability, and must provide that information to the application process for use in answering the salesperson's query. These several functions that make up an application entity for this example may be further grouped into application objects for efficiency or convenience in developing the application.

Abstract syntax corresponds to type declarations in programming languages such as Java or C. For example, declaration of a variable as an integer implies properties of values the variable may hold and operations allowed on it, but does not determine how the value will be represented (2's complement, perhaps, or a specific number of bits). In the Office Supplies Unlimited inventory example, consider the problem of exchanging inventory information. The application may call for the transfer of an inventory record consisting of an item number, an item description, and the count of the item in stock at that site. In Chapter 3, we will identify a representation, ASN.1 (Abstract Syntax Notation One), which could specify inventory information in the following way:

```
inventory_record::=

{item: character string, length 5;

description: character string, length 30;

item_count: integer;

}
```

An application entity belongs to only one application process, though another identical application entity may exist for another process simultaneously. A number of application entities may belong to one application process. These application entities may be of the same or different types. For example, a given application may consist of a number of complementary activities requiring communications activity of very different descriptions. Activities requiring interactive exchange of information could occur concurrently with activities requiring bulk transfer of large volumes of data. These might be designed and implemented as separate, but co-existing, application entities.

Application entities communicate by using application protocols between themselves and by using the services of the Presentation layer to transmit the messages required by the application protocols. Communication between application entities occurs in either connection-oriented or connectionless mode.

In both modes of operation, in addition to the transfer of information, the application entities may support the identification of intended partners in the communication, determination of acceptable quality of service (including acceptable probability of error occurrence, cost, time requirements, and so on) and identification of abstract syntaxes. In connectionless mode, the data unit transferred may include an indication of authority to send the data and to enter communication with the destination. In connection-oriented mode, the services provided by application entities may also include synchronization of the cooperating application, negotiation of responsibility for error control and for various security aspects of the communication. Because the Application layer is the only contact between the application process and the requirements for communication with another system, all choices must be made, all specifications of service requirements must be completed, in the invocation of application entities.

1.6.5 Presentation and Session Layer

The Presentation and Session layers are defined in the OSI protocol stack, but not in others, at least not explicitly. The functions provided by these layers are not unique in that stack, but are not usually defined in terms of separate, distinct elements. We will look at these tasks as defined in the OSI model because it allows us to examine some important characteristics of communications between cooperating entities. In many cases, these functions are built into individual application programs.

The function of the Presentation layer is to relieve the application process of any concern about representation of data transferred between interconnected systems. The application process is concerned with the exchange of information; the Presentation layer is responsible for conveying the information from one partner in the communication to the other. After the application entities have selected the abstract syntaxes to be used, the Presentation layer must select a mutually acceptable representation for the exchange.

Key concepts of the Presentation layer include **concrete syntax**, **transfer syntax**, and **presentation context**:

Concrete syntax refers to the realization of an abstract syntax in terms of a specific representation of the data. The concrete syntax relates an abstract syntax notation such as INTEGER to a specific storage model such as 32-bit 2's complement notation.

Transfer syntax is a concrete syntax used during transmission of data. This may be different from the concrete syntax used for local storage. The transfer syntax must be negotiated between the sender and the receiver.

Presentation context is the association of an abstract syntax with a transfer syntax. For example, {Inventory, Compressed} pairs the Inventory abstract syntax definition with a set of rules for compressing the information during transmission.

Concrete syntax refers to the representation of that data in some environment. Perhaps it is stored locally, as shown in Figure 1.10(a). We see that the characters are represented as ASCII codes stored in adjacent 8-bit bytes (octets) and that the integer is represented in 2's complement in a 32-bit word. In Figure 1.10(b), we see a different concrete syntax, perhaps what is used at the destination of this transfer. The characters are represented as EBCDIC codes, and the integer is stored in packed decimal format in which each individual digit of the number is given 4 bits and the low-order half-byte contains the sign of the number.

Transfer syntax is the representation of the data while in transit between the systems. Figure 1.10(c) shows the inventory record in a form that does not match either local representation, but which both ends of the connection have agreed to use. The characters are coded in ASCII, and the integer is transmitted as four ASCII characters for the digits. Since

```
Record to transfer: XJ32ELECTRIC THREE HOLE PUNCH     3
```

a)

```
584A646362454C4543545249435452494320544852454520484F4C45//
2050554E434820202020202000000003
```

b)

```
E7D1F4F3F2C5D3C5C3E3D9C9C3E3D9C9C340E3C8D9C5C540C8D6D3C5//
40D7E4D5C3C84040404040003F
```

c)

```
584A646362454C4543545249435452494320544852454520484F4C45//
2050554E434820202020202030303034
```

Figure 1.10. Concrete and transfer syntaxes

the integer represents a count of items in stock, no sign is needed. The presentation service on each end of the connection transforms the representation of the data between the local concrete syntax and that used in transit. Though the figure shows three different concrete syntaxes involved in this communication, that is by no means necessary. One, two, or three syntaxes are possible. Transfer syntax may also represent encryption or data compression between the ends of the communication. Clearly, the Presentation layers must both be able to transform between the local concrete syntax and the transfer syntax that is used. Negotiation of transfer syntax allows the two to settle on one that both can use. In Chapter 10, we will identify a specific representation BER (Basic Encoding Rules) for transferring data.

The Presentation layer offers to the application entities the ability to select a transfer syntax. In connection-oriented communication, the transfer syntax is negotiated between the Presentation layer peer processes. In connectionless communication, the transfer syntax is selected and specified with each data unit transferred, but no negotiation occurs.

More than one transfer syntax may be available for a given abstract syntax, for example, a common representation that most end systems are expected to understand, a compressed mode, and an encrypted mode. The combination of abstract syntax and transfer syntax is called a **presentation context**. The Presentation layer also offers to the application entities access to the services of the Session layer.

The Session layer allows cooperating presentation entities to organize and synchronize their dialog and to coordinate the exchange of data between them. For connectionless communication, the Session layer is effectively null; it merely maps the transport address to the session address and provides exception reporting in error conditions.

In connection-oriented mode, session services allow connection establishment, orderly exchange of data, and a graceful release of the connection. More specifically, the Session layer provides the following types of services:

Session establishment and release allows the connection of two presentation entities and the eventual termination of the connection.

Data transfer is provided in four forms: normal, expedited, capability, and typed. Normal data transfer is the ordinary data delivery method. Expedited data has some priority and is able to bypass some restrictions that might impede the transfer of normal data. Expedited data is restricted to small packets, whereas normal data has no such restriction. Typed and capability data types are specific to the Session layer. They are used principally to permit overrides of dialog control mechanisms that may be in effect.

Dialog control provides tools to control which side of a connection is able to send data at any given time and also to partition the dialog using synchronization points. Permission to send data is limited to the presentation entity that possesses a token. Synchronization facilities allow the presentation entities to define and use synchronization points and to reset the connection to a defined state and resume the session at that point. The significance of the synchronization points is determined by the presentation entity (on behalf of the application entity) and is transparent to the session service provider.

Activity management allows the session service user to distinguish logical divisions in the connection.

Exception reporting allows the session service provider to notify the presentation entity of exceptional conditions.

The collection of services available on a particular connection is subject to selection by the presentation entity that establishes the connection. Specific Session-layer services are grouped into functional units. Functional units define a number of frequently chosen operational styles, and their selection is a matter of negotiation at the time of connection establishment.

1.6.6   Transport Layer

Services provided by the Application through Session layers are oriented toward providing support for communication directly between application entities, with little or no notice of the characteristics of the network over which the services will be realized. The next layer, the Transport layer, is the first to concern itself with the actual transport of the data, rather than services presented to the application. In many cases, the Transport layer is also the last one to reside in the user's system.

The Transport layer provides the desired quality of service in the delivery of data units between session entities, while masking the complexities and the deficiencies of the underlying network connections. It operates between the interconnected systems where the application entities reside. The Transport layer also provides the service quality required by the session entity without the burden of routing and relaying that might be required for transit through the networks between the end systems.

The transport entity selects the appropriate network facilities to provide the service needed on behalf of the session entity. For connection-mode communication, this may include multiplexing more than one session entity onto a single network connection sharing the cost of the connection. Alternatively, a single session connection could be split over multiple network connections to provide more service to the session entity than is available from a single network connection. Also in connection mode, the Transport layer may provide a large number of services, including sequencing of data units, end-to-end error detection and error recovery, end-to-end flow control and monitoring of the quality of service as well as the establishment and orderly release of the connection and the transfer of

The Transport layer provides the desired quality of service in the delivery of data units between session entities, while masking the complexities and the deficiencies of the underlying network connections. It operates between the interconnected systems where the application entities reside.

normal and expedited data. In connectionless mode, the Transport layer provides address mapping between the transport address and the network address, the mapping of end-to-end transport connectionless mode transmissions onto network connectionless mode transmissions, and end-to-end error detection and monitoring of the quality of service.

A connection-oriented transport connection can be established over a connectionless network connection. This allows the session entity to benefit from the advantages of a connection-oriented communication, unaware of the nature of the network connection in use.

1.6.7   Network, Data Link, and Physical Layers

The Application through Transport layers are under user control. The remaining layers—Network, Data Link, and Physical—are essentially transparent to the user. Only brief indications of their services are included here. More detail is provided in later chapters, but a thorough discussion of these three layers is more appropriate to a course in data communications.

The Network layer provides the means for transmission among transport entities, independently of routing and relay considerations involved in such communication, including situations of transit through multiple intervening networks. In fact, the network service hides from the Transport layer all characteristics and operations of the underlying communication media except the quality of service. Quality of service is negotiated between the transport entities and network service at the time a network connection is established.

Functions performed by the Network layer include the following [OSI]:

Routing and relaying	Network connection and connection multiplexing	Segmentation and blocking of data units
Error detection and recovery	Expedited data transfer	Reset
Mapping between network addresses and data link addresses	Mapping network connectionless mode transmissions to data link connectionless mode transmissions	Converting from data link connection mode service to network connectionless mode service
Enhancing a data link connectionless mode service to provide a network connection mode service	Service selection	Network layer management

For the most part, these services are transparent to the application process. The application process specifies parameters that determine the quality of service needed for delivery of data across a network connection. That quality of service will be provided or the application entity will be notified by the Presentation layer of a failure to meet the requirement.

Increasingly, the network service will be provided by a communication utility, such as the telephone company. The communication user will have limited control over the operation of the Network layer, except to specify expected levels of service and react to failures to deliver that service.

The Data Link layer provides for data transmission between adjacent machines, where adjacent should be understood to mean either directly attached by a point-to-point link or sharing a common communication channel possibly with other machines. Services provided by the Data Link layer are similar to services provided by the Transport layer, except that the Transport layer applies its functions end system to end system, whereas the Data Link layer is confined to the communication defined between two adjacent systems. The Data Link layer provides connection establishment and release, framing of message units, error detection and recovery, reset, restricted routing and relaying, and Data Link layer management. The Data Link layer does not handle forwarding; it assumes a direct link between two systems.

In addition to the services listed here, the Data Link layer must provide the functioning that allows an attached station to participate in the sharing of a communication medium in a local area network. In these situations, the Data Link layer is subdivided into two sublayers, one providing **logical link control** and the other **media access control**.

"The Physical layer provides mechanical, electrical, functional and procedural means to activate, maintain, and de-activate physical connections for bit transmission between data link entities" [OSI]. The data units exchanged between physical entities are bits and streams of bits delivered in the same order they were sent. The Physical layer allows the transmission of bitstreams across a physical medium such as a cable or radio signal.

1.7 THE OSI MODEL AND THE WORLD WIDE WEB

Though the World Wide Web is built on Internet (TCP/IP) protocols that do not conform precisely to the OSI reference model, we can identify the roles of the OSI layers in the Web. The World Wide Web does include an example of an application entity: **http**, the protocol that allows a client to talk to a server. Web applications have many components; http provides those aspects of the application that are related to its communications requirements. Other aspects, such as the browser used and the viewers available to display various resource file formats, are local issues. http encapsulates all aspects of communication with a remote system and all the steps needed to invoke lower-layer network services.

In applications built on the World Wide Web, the Presentation layer's role in issues of representation of information refers to dealing with differences in the way machines represent characters, sounds, and images. In the Web, these issues are handled in a very straightforward manner. Several formats are recognized explicitly: ASCII for characters, some specific ways of representing images, sound, and animation. Each client system has some number of programs (called viewers) installed that recognize and display particular formats. If the client does not have a viewer for a format used in an object, the object cannot be displayed. Compression and encryption are also issues in the way the Web transfers information. There is no specific collection of modules called the Presentation layer in the World Wide Web. However, the responsibilities of the Presentation layer are issues of importance in developing Web applications and all other applications that will run over a network.

World Wide Web applications often require large files to travel across the network. Session layer services could be employed to assist in the recovery of interrupted transfers. The synchronization issue is dealt with by the client/server mode of operation. The client requests a file from the server, and the server sends it if possible. The client then continues with other processing. Synchronization between the client and server is not an issue in this model.

The Transport layer provides dependable transfer across intervening nodes of a network. World Wide Web applications depend on TCP to mask any problems in the network and provide the appearance of a dependable communication channel. http invokes TCP to establish a connection. The TCP connection must then carry a request from the client and a response from the server. http then closes the connection before considering the next task before it. Newer versions of http allow repeated use of the TCP connection.

The Network layer is concerned with addresses for individual machines and with finding a good route from one to another. A Web application user becomes aware of the Network layer when the domain name server fails to locate the requested server. More often, the work of the Network layer (the Internet IP for the World Wide Web applications) remains hidden. Somehow the server is found, and the data is moved between the client and server.

The Data Link layer is concerned with communication between adjacent machines. If the client is a node on a local area network, the Data Link layer controls sending and receiving data on the shared communication link. If the node is directly connected to another, the Data Link layer governs the use of the connecting line to transfer data. The user of the World Wide Web application has very little idea of what is happening at this layer. The most significant impact of the Data Link layer is the speed of the connection. If a large image is moved over a relatively slow link, the user will notice the effect. To an application developer, the potential impact of a slow connection is an issue to consider in designing the data exchange required to support the application.

The Physical layer determines the interface between the system and the media that will carry the bits. In the World Wide Web, the electrical and mechanical interface to the physical channel is rarely noticed by the user or considered by the application developer. Emerging technologies such as wireless communications promise increased accessibility to Web resources.

1.8   INTERACTIONS BETWEEN THE LAYERS

1.8.1   Services

In the OSI reference model, each layer uses services provided by the layer below it to provide services to the layer above it, except that layer 7 is the ultimate user of network services of other layers, and layer 1 is the ultimate provider. Layer 7 does provide services to the application. The concept of service is defined in the OSI model for each layer in terms of adjacent layers:

(N)-service: a capability of the (N)-layer and the layers beneath it, which is provided to (N+1)-layer entities at the boundary between (N)-layer and the (N + 1)-layer. [OSI]

Such descriptions are read by substituting the name of a particular layer for the (N) and the appropriate adjacent layer for (N + 1). Thus, for example, a transport service is a capability provided collectively by the Transport, Network, Data Link, and Physical layers

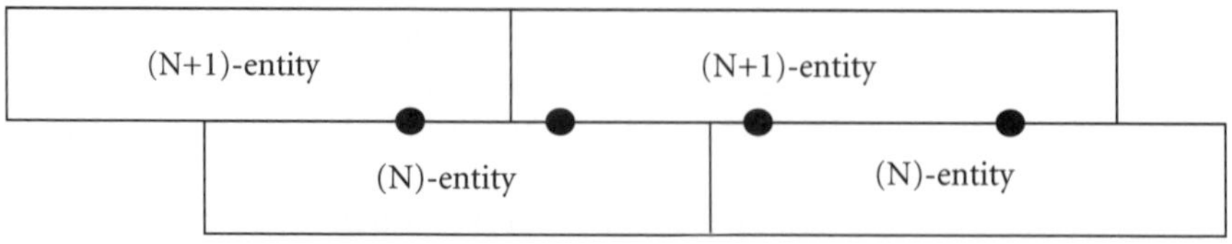

Figure 1.11. Service
access points

to session entities at the boundary between the Transport and Session layers. Entities are active elements within a layer or a subdivision of a layer that provide a particular type of capability. For example, one of the capabilities of the Application layer is establishing and maintaining an association between processes that will interoperate.

Service Access Points

Each layer is defined by the specific responsibilities assigned to it. A layer must provide services to the layer above it and can use the services of the layer below it. Each layer is implemented independently of the others, and its internal operation can be changed without affecting the others.

   Thus, a connection-oriented transport entity assures the session entity that message units are properly ordered, using any method that the implementer chooses. The Transport layer, regardless of the means it uses to order the message units, must provide the expected messages to other Transport layers, and must cooperate with the Session and Network layers in a way dictated by the standards. The contact between procedures operating in adjacent layers is called a service access point (SAP). Exchange of messages across a SAP is an important component of the protocol specifications.

   An (N + 1) entity may concurrently be attached to one or more (N)-SAPs, which are attached to the same or different (N)-entities. Similarly, an (N)-entity may concurrently be attached to one or more (N + 1) entities. A SAP connects only one (N + 1) and (N)-entity at a time, but may support connection-oriented service, connectionless service, or both concurrently. Figure 1.11 shows two layers, each containing two entities, connected at service access points. The two layers might be the Transport and Network layers, for example. In that case, the example shows one of the transport entities (layer N + 1) attached to one network service access point (N)-SAP, and the other transport entity attached to three (N-)SAPs. Each of the Network layer entities is attached to two service access points.

> The contact between procedures operating in adjacent layers is called a service access point (SAP). Exchange of messages across a SAP is an important component of the protocol specifications.

1.8.2 Data Units

Peer-layer entities cooperate to accomplish the component of interoperation assigned to their layer. This cooperation requires the exchange of information between them. (N + 1)-entities communicate with each other by using the services provided by the (N)-layer. Communication consists of control information, which is used to coordinate joint activities, and possibly data that must be delivered to the user of an entity. Two kinds of communication occur in the protocol stack: communication between adjacent layers in one system, and communication between peer layers in interconnected systems. Units of data being communicated are referred to as **service data units** or **protocol data units**, where:

A service data unit (SDU) is a unit of data exchanged between adjacent layers in a single system.

A protocol data unit (PDU) is a unit of data exchanged between peer layers in interconnected systems.

Because the only communication between peer (N)-layers in separate systems is through services offered by the (N-1)-layer, it follows that the entire PDU to be transferred to a peer layer must first be passed to the next lower layer and then to the layer below that until it is finally delivered to the end system where the peer layer resides. It must then be passed up through the lower layers to the destination. So, an (N)-PDU is given to layer N-1 as an (N-1)-SDU. Layer N-1 augments the data with control information required for its communication with its peer layer in the destination system, and passes it down the stack as an (N-1)-PDU. The control information added by layer N-1 will allow its peer to identify the layer-N user for which the data unit is intended, among other things. Figure 1.12 shows the transformation of a protocol data unit received from layer N, augmented by protocol control information by layer N-1, and passed on to lower layers.

1.8.3   Layer Operation

All protocols require the delivery of information between peer-layer protocols, using the services of the layers below them. In connection-oriented communication, there is a further requirement for establishment of a connection between the communicating peer layers before data exchange and the eventual release of the connection. Establishment of an (N)-layer connection requires the existence of an (N-1)-layer connection. Establishment of multiple layers of connection can be combined to reduce the overhead involved in initiating the data exchange. Connection release may or may not involve the loss of user data. For example, if the connection is such that two-way simultaneous communication is supported, it may happen that one (N)-entity sends a protocol data unit terminating the connection at the same time that the peer (N)-entity sends a protocol data unit containing data or some other protocol unit. The two PDUs cross paths between the (N)-entities. If the (N)-entity that terminated the connection considered that the termination took effect as soon as the

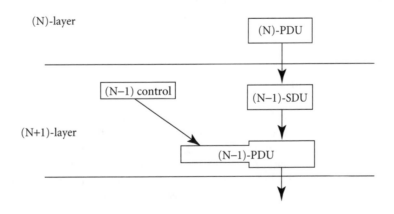

Figure 1.12. Data units moving through one system

PDU was sent, it will close its connection with the (N-1)-SAP and never receive the data that was in transit.

Normal transfer of control information and user data occurs between (N)-entities in (N)-PDUs, using (N-1) services. Though there is no limit to the quantity of user data in a PDU conceptually, pragmatism imposes limits that may require that a unit of data be fragmented into a number of smaller units for transfer over a SAP to a service provider, and reassembled at the destination before delivery to the (N)-layer user. Expedited data is processed and transferred with priority over normal data. An example of expedited data is to send a command to cancel a previous command. Suppose a user has sent a collection of commands to be executed on the remote system. Perhaps one of them is a command to display the contents of a file. Realizing that the file is much larger than expected, or is the wrong file, the user would like to cancel the command before it is executed. It would be useless to send the canceling command if it were to be taken only after the other. The user sends the command by expedited data.

Many of the choices that must be made by an application process relate to the quality of service (QOS) expected by the application from the network. In connectionless communication, QOS is specified in the same protocol data unit that carries the data. In connection-oriented communication, some give and take is possible with negotiation between peer layers and the underlying services determining the characteristics of the service provided.

1.9 SERVICE SPECIFICATIONS

Each network component is described in two forms: a **service definition** and a **protocol definition**. The service definition details the interaction of the layer with the entities of the next higher layer (or other entities in the Application layer if the service is an Application layer service). The protocol definition specifies the interaction between the cooperating peer protocols.

The definition of the service provided by a layer entity includes the relation of this layer entity to those of the higher and lower layers adjacent to it.

The definition of the service provided by a layer entity includes the relation of this layer entity to those of the higher and lower layers adjacent to it, that is, the services provided to the entity user and the services required of the next lower service provider. The services used by the (N)- entity are thoroughly described in the (N-1)-service definition, and are not repeated. In the service definition of an entity, a number of facilities may be defined. For example, a particular entity may include the three facilities: connection establishment, data transfer, and connection termination. Each facility may consist of one or several services, which in turn comprise primitives.

1.9.1 Service Primitives

In the exchange of information between peer protocol entities, one acts as a **requestor** of the service of the lower layers, and the other is a **responder** of the service. All communication in an open system thus comes down to interactions between adjacent layers in a protocol stack. A service is a capability of a service provider that is available to a service user at the boundary between them. For each service, four primitives are defined that allow the service user to access the service [OSI91]. These primitives are grouped according to

Submit Primitives that are initiated by a service user

Deliver Primitives that are initiated by a service provider

The four primitives are

request A submit primitive issued by a requestor of a service

indication A deliver primitive received by an accepter of a service

response A submit primitive issued by an accepter of a service

confirm A deliver primitive received by a requestor of a service

Requests and responses are always issued by a higher layer to a lower layer. Indications and confirms are always issued by a lower layer to a higher layer. Requests and confirms are always exchanged between a user and a service provider in the same (initiator) system. Indications and responses are always exchanged between a user and a service provider in the same (target) system.

These primitives are combined in one of three ways to provide a particular type of service: unconfirmed (with two primitives), confirmed (with four primitives), or indication only. A user that wants a service performed (that is, a requestor) issues a *request* for the service. The layer that provides the service reacts by doing any processing necessary to provide the service at its end. It then communicates with its peer on the other system (by using services of the lower layers) to gain the participation of the peer (that is, the accepter) of the requesting user. When this communication reaches the peer service provider, further processing may be required to carry out the user's request. When that processing is complete, the peer service wakes up the accepter by passing an **indication** of the request that was made. The combination of a request and an indication produces an **unconfirmed service**. The initiator of the activity has sent a request, and the service providers have delivered an indication of that request. No further communication need occur. The initiator may assume that the lower layers of the network have performed their roles, and thus the initiator does not worry about a failure to deliver the message. Figure 1.13 shows the steps involved in an unconfirmed service.

In some cases, it is not sufficient for the initiator of a communication to know that the message arrived safely. A **response** from its peer (sometimes called target) confirms that conditions have been accepted, and that the two have an agreement about how to proceed. A **confirmed** service thus has four parts: *request, indication, response,* and *confirm.* Figure 1.14 shows the steps involved in a confirmed service.

The same patterns appear at every layer. The initiator of a communication issues a request for the service at the next lower layer. That lower layer is the service provider. The service provider may do some processing as a result of the service request. The service provider will eventually invoke a service of the next lower layer to communicate the request

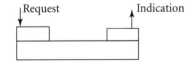

Figure 1.13. Unconfirmed service

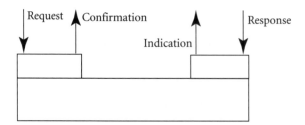

Figure 1.14. Confirmed
service

to the target system. The term used on the target system is "indication" because what arrives may not be exactly the same as what left the initiator. There may have been alterations in the request because of the processing done at lower layers. The target process responds to some types of indications, but not to others. The content of the response is returned to the initiator in a confirm primitive.

Most services are either confirmed, with four primitives, or unconfirmed, with only two primitives. However, a few services are defined with only an indication part. This means that the service provider issues a message to its user, and that message is not a reaction to a request from the user. This is needed when the service provider has information that must be given to the user, usually of an error from which no recovery is possible. Thus, a transport provider that has lost all contact with any network services cannot continue to provide the transport service and will notify the transport user that the communication must end. See Figure 1.15.

1.9.2 Time Sequence Diagrams

Time sequence diagrams are used to illustrate the interrelated actions between a service requestor and a service accepter using the service provider available to both. These diagrams not only show the service primitives used, but also the relative placement of the primitives in time. Figure 1.16 shows the general format of a time sequence diagram.

By convention, time increases down the vertical lines in the diagram so the earliest event appears at the top of the figure. Each vertical line represents a border between the service user and the service provider. Horizontal arrows show the service primitives submitted to and delivered by the service provider. The areas outside the vertical lines correspond to the requestor and the accepter of the service. The space between the lines represents the service provider. To the service user, there is no need to distinguish between the two sides of a service provider. The service user is unaware of what exists on the other side of the service access point and treats the service provider as if it were a tunnel connecting it with the peer service user at the other open system. Each arrow is labeled with the service primitive that crosses the SAP in the exchange of information between the service user and provider.

Figure 1.15. A special
case: indication only

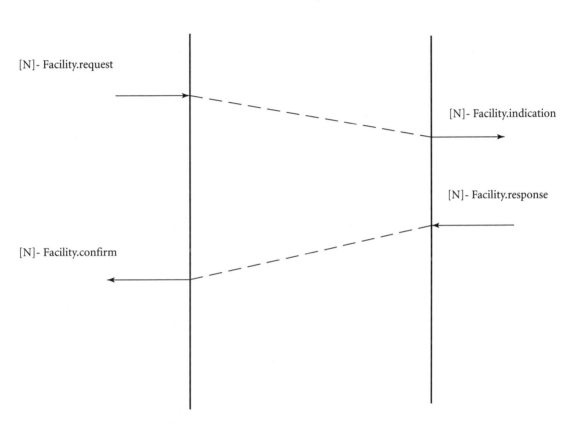

Figure 1.16. Time sequence diagrams

Dashed lines may be used to show the connection between related events. In the figure, (N)-Facility.request leads after some time to (N)-Facility.indication. More complex time sequence diagrams may show interactions involving more than two systems. In all cases, arrows to the left of a vertical line represent requestors, and arrows to the right of a vertical line represent accepters.

Something considerably more precise is required in describing how cooperating peer protocols will interact with each other. The second part of each layer entity is the **protocol specification**. The protocol specification is concerned with the interoperability of cooperating entities in different open systems. Each must be able to determine exactly what the other is doing as far as the activity relates to the interaction.[1] A layer entity is modeled as a protocol machine, a special type of finite state machine. Cooperating layer entities communicate with adjacent layers by means of service primitives, and communicate with each other by exchanging PDUs. The reception of an incoming service primitive and the generation of the resulting action are considered indivisible, atomic events.

[1]Interoperability is not limited to pairs of processes. However, for simplicity, we will refer to interactions as if they are between exactly two processes.

1.9.3 Protocol Machines

A protocol machine consists of a set of states, a set of transitions between states, and a set of labels for the transitions. The labels indicate events recognized by the protocol machine while in a particular state and events initiated by the protocol machine while in that state. In the OSI protocol specifications, the protocol machines are defined in tabular form. We will use a modification of that format, augmented with diagrams, to provide a more readable description. We begin with a simplification of a part of the Presentation Protocol Machine (PPM). We choose again to focus on connection establishment, partly because it is an activity that is easily related to familiar actions. Connection establishment proceeds very much like making a phone call. In defining the part of the presentation protocol machine that accomplishes this function, we define four states:

- Idle (no connection)
- Waiting for our call to be answered (outgoing connection pending: awaiting the arrival of a protocol data unit from the presentation protocol machine that accepts our call [Await CPA, in the real protocol specification of the Presentation layer])
- Waiting for an incoming call (awaiting the service primitive P-CONNECT.response, indicating that our protocol service user has accepted the proposed connection)
- Connected (ready for data transfer)

We will keep the illustration simple by limiting it to normal, successful operation. Figure 1.17 shows the four states and the transitions between states. We need this many states because the protocol machine will react differently to possible events, depending on the state it is in. For example, if the PPM is in the Idle state and a P-CONNECT.request arrives from the presentation service user, the PPM has a defined response. It sends a PDU to its peer presentation entity at the desired open system, requesting that a connection be established. It then waits for a reply. If the PPM is waiting for a reply, and another P-CONNECT.request were to arrive, it would be in the situation of having multiple outstanding connection requests.

The transitions between states are triggered by events that occur while the PPM is in a particular state. Figure 1.18 shows a section of a protocol stack with only the Presentation layer drawn in. To establish a connection, the presentation protocol machine waits for a P-CONNECT.request to arrive from the presentation service user. The work done by the presentation entity on receipt of the request is to send a PDU to its peer presentation entity, requesting the connection. The official name of this PDU is CP (presentation connect). In the figure, the PDU is shown in transit over the virtual connection between the presentation entities. The virtual connection is realized by invoking the services offered by the Session layer. Part of the specification of the protocol is the mapping between the PDU and the available services in the next lower layer. We will see this in more detail as we look at the individual layers, the protocols they implement, and the services they offer and use.

In the implementation of the PPM, the arrival of P-CONNECT.request and the sending of the CP PDU are considered inseparable events; nothing is allowed to interrupt the sequence. We will show the two events as labels on the transition arrow from the Idle state to the Await CPA state. Figure 1.18 shows this transition as well as the protocol stack. Meanwhile, on the protocol stack where the connection request is received, the PPM moves from the Idle state to the state Incoming connection pending when the PDU arrives.

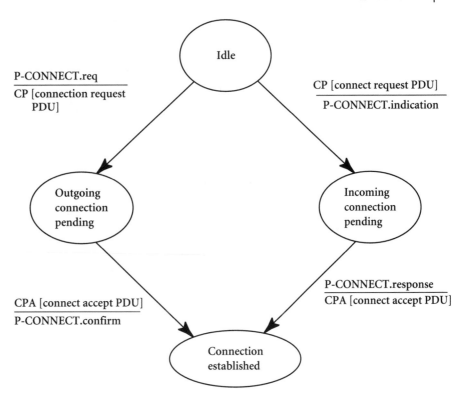

Figure 1.17. The four states of the Presentation Protocol Machine for connection establishment

In Figure 1.19, the target application entity (where the connection is requested) sends P-CONNECT.response to its presentation entity, which responds by sending the PDU CPA (Presentation Connection Accept) and moving to state Connection Established, where it awaits data transfer. On arrival of the CPA, the originating PPM issues P-CONNECT.confirm to its presentation service user and moves to state Connected, where it awaits data transfer. Figure 1.20 shows the full state transition diagram for the PPM illustrated in Figures 1.18 through 1.20.

Though state transition diagrams such as those in Figure 1.20 are useful for visualizing the actions of the PPM, a table form such as shown in Figure 1.21 is used in the protocol specifications [Pre87a]. In Figure 1.21, the leftmost column contains the names of things that can arrive—some are service primitives and some are PDUs. Across the top of the table are the states. In the body of the table are the output produced from that state on the occurrence of that arrival and also the next state. One advantage of the table form is the clear indication of all possible combinations. The empty boxes in the table correspond to undefined combinations of events and states. It is easy to see what has not been defined and to look at them for possible oversights. The table in Figure 1.21 corresponds exactly to the state transition diagram of Figure 1.20.

In addition to identifying the PDUs exchanged between the peer protocol entities and the protocol machine that defines the actions of the protocols, the protocol specification document maps each PDU to services available from the next lower layer. For example,

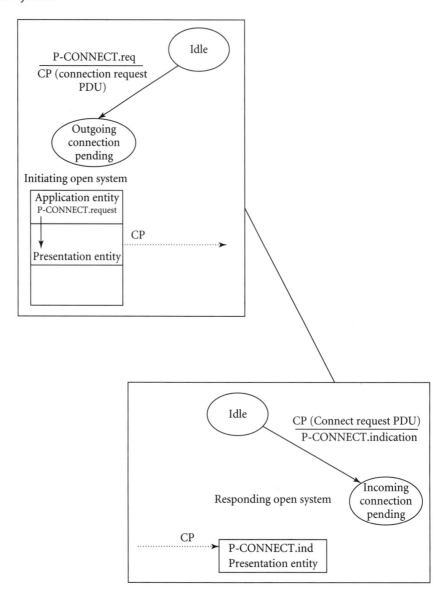

Figure 1.18. Presentation connection establishment: first step

the P-CONNECT service is provided by invoking the S-CONNECT service offered by the Session layer and using the user data parameter of S-CONNECT to carry the Presentation layer parameters that have no equivalent in the Session layer connect service.

1.10 THE MAJOR TYPES OF NETWORKS

Networks are classified as local area networks (LANs), wide area networks (WANs), and high-speed networks with intermediate distance restrictions (sometimes called metropoli-

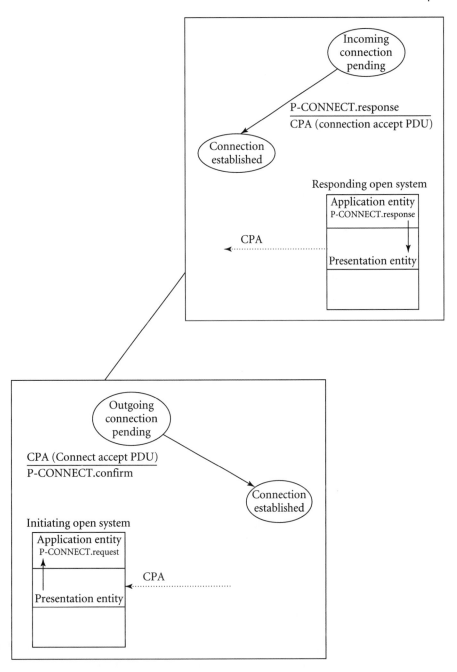

Figure 1.19. Presentation connection establishment: second step

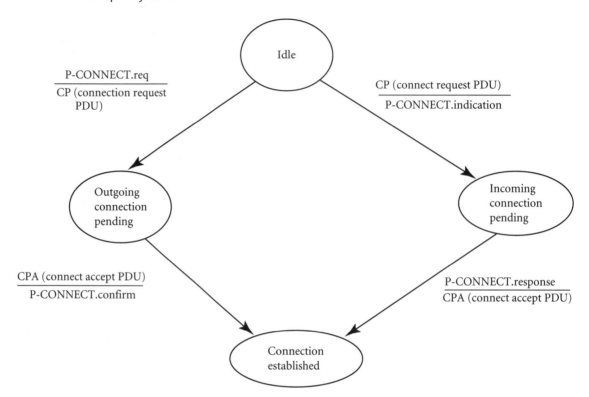

Figure 1.20. State transition diagram for the PPM: connection establishment

tan area networks, or MANs). Though the titles suggest geographic spread, the principal traits are only indirectly related to the distance covered.

Many network applications run by invoking functions of the network software, and with little or no concern about the physical characteristics of the specific network platform in use. Characteristics of the major types of network systems do intrude on application development in some cases. Furthermore, concerns such as privacy, security, reliability, response time, and accessibility often depend on the type of network platform in use.

1.10.1   Local Area Networks

Local area networks have very low error rates and propagation delay that is negligible for most purposes. Transmission in most local area networks is by **broadcast**—every station on the network receives every transmission. Thus, there are no routing decisions to make. Every packet (message unit) follows the same path, so reordering does not occur. These characteristics make LANs suitable for applications that depend on timely results, for example, interactive processing involving files or other resources located on several different systems or time-critical response to a monitoring device. The broadcast mode of operation is suitable for applications requiring message exchange among a number of stations, like checking

	State 1 Idle No Connection	State 2 Await CPA	State 3 Await P-CONNECT.rsp	State 4 Connection Established
P-CONNECT.req	CP ⇒ State 2			
CP	P-CONNECT.ind ⇒ State 2			
P-CONNECT.rsp			CPA ⇒ State 4	
CPA		P-CONNECT.conf ⇒ State 4		

Figure 1.21. Presentation Connection Establishment PPM in tabular form

individual calendars to schedule a meeting or searching for a processor able to share in a demanding computational task.

A combination of technology and the performance expectations of LANs limits the distances they can cover. A small LAN might connect a few computers in an office or in a home; a large LAN could extend over an office park or university campus, connecting computers and other devices in a number of buildings. Common speeds are 10 Mbps (megabits per second) or 16 Mbps; 100 Mbps is increasingly common and gigabit speeds are available.

Very simple network systems that allow limited sharing between two or more personal computers (for example, at home) are sold at most computer stores. The simplest of these use the computers' serial ports, standard telephone wire, and software that allows printer sharing, file transfer, and sending messages between computers [Net91]. This system has the three essential components of any network: a *communication medium* (telephone wire), an *interface* between the computer and the medium (the serial port), and *software* to send and receive on the interface. In the simple network shown in Figure 1.22, each station is connected to the next in a line. Each computer can send a message to, access a file on, or

> A small LAN might connect a few computers in an office or in a home; a large LAN could extend over an office park or university campus, connecting computers and other devices in a number of buildings.

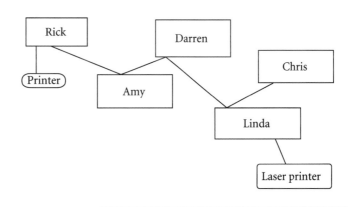

Figure 1.22. A simple serial network

use a printer on any of the other connected computers. If Rick uses the printer attached to Linda, Amy and Darren participate in the effort by passing on the messages. (This is not a broadcast type LAN since a message does not go beyond the intended destination station.)

Most local area networks are more complex than the one illustrated in Figure 1.22. Many local area networks have servers—designated stations that provide access to disk storage or printers or other resources shared by users at other stations. Regular use of the servers increases traffic on the network and suggests that individual LANs be kept small, limited to a small cluster of computers that can efficiently share a common set of resources. Communication and sharing among clusters requires that the small LANs be connected. A popular way to interconnect local area networks is to attach each to a high-speed backbone network such as shown in Figure 1.23. Though the backbone could be the same type of LAN used in the clusters, more of them are using fiber-based network technology. Fiber Distributed Data Interface (FDDI) operates at 100 Mbps. It outperforms a slower LAN in providing high data rates required to connect other LANs as a backbone. The distributed queue dual bus (DQDB) is another high-speed fiber-based network for times when high data rates are required. Because of their potential for city-wide installation, high speed fiber-based networks are sometimes called *Metropolitan Area Networks*.

All local area networks have the same components: communications medium, an interface between the computer and the medium, and software to drive the interface to send and receive transmissions. The software coexists in the computer with other hardware drivers, such as those for printers and modems, as well as with other software such as compilers and databases, text editors, and spreadsheets, as seen in Figure 1.24. All the network services we will see in this book are simply extensions to the large collection of services already offered by modern operating systems.

Local area networks are sometimes described by the topology used to connect the machines. For the most part, the topology is transparent to the user and to the application developer. Sometimes, there are implications that affect the development effort. For example, in Figure 1.22, the stations are connected in a daisy chain: each is tied to the next, and if any station is lost, the chain is broken and communication cannot continue across the break. The most popular topologies for LANs are the *bus*, the *ring*, and the *star*.

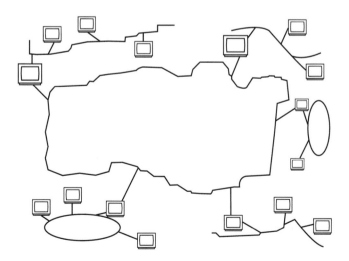

Figure 1.23. A backbone network connecting local area networks

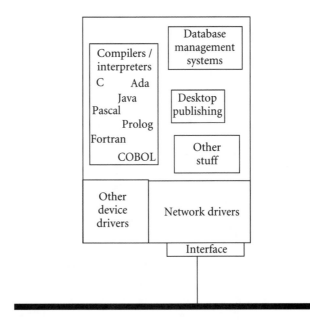

Figure 1.24. The basic components of any computer network, shown co-existing with other computing system services

In the bus topology, the stations are connected to the medium, which can be run in any convenient shape—just like Figure 1.22. The difference is that each connection is independent of the others. Individual computers attached to the network do not participate in passing each others' messages along. The way the stations share the single communication medium is similar to the way people share multiple extensions on the same phone line (listen to see if the line is in use; if so, try again later; if not, talk). See Figure 1.25(a). The rules for sharing the bus are codified in the standard IEEE 802.3, derived from and nearly identical to Ethernet [MB76].

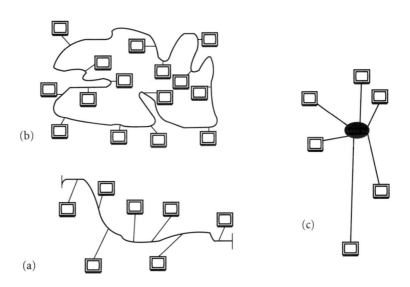

Figure 1.25. Examples of the ring, bus, and star topologies for LANs

Computer Networks and Open Systems

In the ring topology, the medium is distributed as a closed loop, as shown in Figure 1.25(b). The stations are attached to the ring and share the ring by passing a "token" that specifies whose turn it is. IEEE 802.5 defines the way the token ring operates.

IEEE 802.4 defines a special-purpose network called the token bus. It requires network stations to behave as a logical ring while connected to a physical bus. The bus is a convenient network type to install in factories and processing plants, while the token-passing method of gaining access to the transmission medium provides a guarantee for the maximum time a station must wait to receive a chance to transmit.

There are several approaches to the star topology illustrated in Figure 1.25(c). The idea is to have a central location where all troubleshooting can be done. To understand the desirability of this, suppose you are sitting at station Rick in Figure 1.22 and attempting to print at station Linda. If the print request does not succeed, there are several possible problems. Any of the stations between you and the printer may be turned off or malfunctioning. If the stations are all lined up in the same room, it is not difficult to find the problem. However, if each is locked in a separate room, and you don't have the keys, the solution is not so simple.

When the network topology is a star, every transmission goes through a central site. When trouble occurs, locating the problem requires disconnecting suspected links and trying again. When the faulty unit is located, it can be repaired and then reconnected, all from the central site. Meanwhile, the rest of the network continues to function.

The bus, ring, and star topologies are the basic building blocks of network shapes. Figures 1.26 and 1.28 show more complex figures constructed from these.

Figure 1.26 shows several ways to join bus segments to form a tree shape. The boxes shown between the bus segments are one of several types of network connecting devices. The type of connection is determined by the protocol layers at which the box participates in

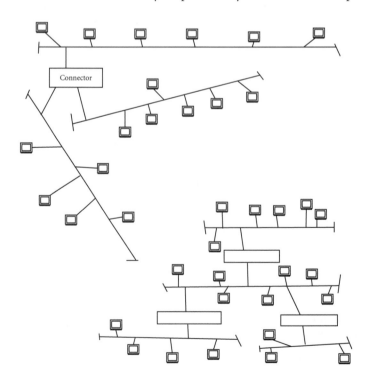

Figure 1.26. Bus segments combined in a tree shape

the network operation. Though the word *gateway* is sometimes used as a generic term for any device that connects networks, three types of connecting devices have specific names: repeaters, bridges, and routers.

If the boxes operate on only the Physical layer, they are **repeaters**; they just enhance the electrical signal that carries the communications on the networks. In that case, any transmission sent on any of the network segments arrives at all the others. Networks joined by repeaters are really one logical network.

The use of repeaters allows a network to spread over a larger distance than it could otherwise span, and also allows more flexibility in getting the cable where it is needed. Multiple port repeaters, or **hubs**, also make it easy to expand a network. A new segment can be run where the additional stations are needed, then joined to the network by connecting to a port in the repeater. When the boxes shown in the figure are repeaters, the tree shape is a wiring decision, but the network is logically a single bus. Just like a bus with only one segment, all the stations receive every message, and all the stations must share the same communications medium.

If the boxes in Figure 1.26 include network protocols implemented at the Data Link layer, they are called **bridges**. Bridges not only repeat the transmission, they also examine the packet to determine if it should be sent on to the networks on the other side of the box or confined to the network where it began. This filtering operation reduces the traffic on the individual segments of the network. Further, by keeping messages exchanged by two nodes on the same segment on that segment only, filtering provides a limited privacy function.

Routers are connecting boxes that participate in network protocols to the Network layer. Routers can decide the path a packet should take to reach its destination, can participate in distributed congestion control schemes, and can fragment large packets and reassemble them when necessary to get through intermediate networks. Routers rely on information in the data packet to determine what action to take. Initially, routers were considered protocol sensitive, that is, a separate router is needed for each protocol used on the connection, but multiprotocol routers are available.

Networks can be connected at higher layers as well. The higher the protocol layer implemented in the gateway, the deeper the gateway looks into the data that it transfers. An example of a layer 7 gateway is a mail gateway connecting two incompatible mail systems and allowing them to exchange messages. Figure 1.27 shows network connections through repeaters, bridges, and routers.

Figure 1.28 shows several star-shaped networks making a more complex structure. This arrangement is convenient when a network includes stations on several floors of a building. A wiring closet on each floor provides a convenient place to look for problems, without requiring the extensive wiring that a single hub needs. In later chapters, we will look more thoroughly into interconnecting networks, including implications for applications that span the connections.

1.10.2 Wide Area Networks

Unlike local area networks, wide area networks consist of specific point-to-point links. Messages pass from one network station to another through a communications subnet. The communications subnet consists of nodes whose function is to pass the message from its origin to its intended destination quickly and accurately. Message units, called packets, are

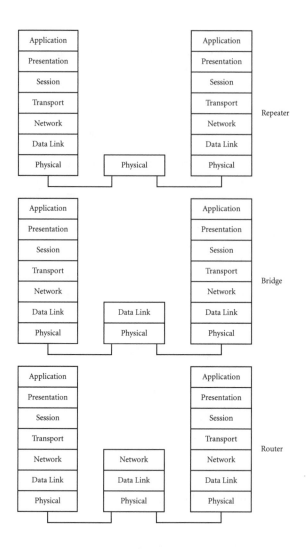

Figure 1.27. Network connections using repeaters, bridges, and routers

passed from one intermediate node to another until they arrive at the destination. Effective routing techniques are important to network performance. Packets from a single message may travel by different routes and arrive at the destination out of order. Typical transmission speeds range from 56 Kbps to 1.54 Mbps. Much higher speeds are on the horizon; emerging gigabit networks promise new opportunities for applications dependent on high-volume data movement.

Since a wide area network comprises point-to-point connections, connectivity is an important design consideration. Figure 1.29 shows some of the ways to join a set of five nodes in a communication subnet by point-to-point links. Figure 1.29(a) shows the minimum number of links to allow the nodes to communicate with each other. It is really the same topology as we saw in Figure 1.22, and consists of a simple daisy chain. Routing is easy: each station has to know only which direction to go to reach the destination. The obvious weakness is vulnerability: in case a single node (other than the ends of the chain) fail to function correctly, communication is lost across the faulty node.

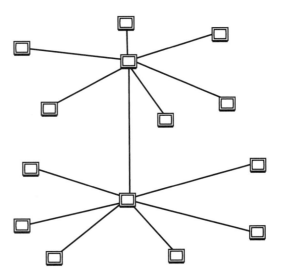

Figure 1.28. Connected stars

Figure 1.29(b) shows a fully connected configuration of five nodes. Again, routing is easy: every node connects directly to every other node. Vulnerability to failure is minimized since no node is dependent on any other. The problem here is cost. From graph theory, we know that a complete graph with n vertices has $\binom{n}{2} = \frac{n(n-1)}{2}$ edges, where $\binom{n}{2}$ is the combination of n things taken two at a time. Fully connecting 5 nodes $\left(\frac{5 \times 4}{2} = 10\right)$ might be extravagant; fully connecting 100 nodes ($\frac{100 \times 99}{2} = 4950$ links) is probably unreasonable. Networks of many thousand nodes clearly require another approach.

Figure 1.29(c) shows a compromise configuration for the five-node example. Every node has at least two connections. No single node loss would cut off any operating node from the others. On the other hand, loss of two nodes (or two links) could interrupt communication among the remaining nodes, depending on which two nodes failed. Routing is no longer obvious in this network. Since there is a direct link from node A to node B, that link is probably the best route for communications between those nodes. To get from A to E, however, a transmission could go by way of B or C, D or B, C, D. Many factors could enter the decision. One path might support higher transmission rates. Security concerns may dictate the better choice. Different costs may be involved. Even these issues would not be difficult if the best choice were always the same. Transient conditions such as heavy congestion complicate the decision process. Processes running in the nodes respond to instructions from the host computers regarding routing, but they also monitor the behavior of the network and learn what paths are best.

Often the station connected to the subnet is a gateway to a local area network. Thus, the user with access to the resources of a local network can reach out to a larger network for still more resources. Local area networks (or metropolitan area networks) connected to other networks combine to form very complex patterns with characteristics similar to point-to-point wide area networks. Similar problems concerning routing decisions, dealing with failures, temporary conditions, and so on arise. A further complication concerns the differences among the types of local area networks: the required format for transmissions, maximum lengths, conventions for acknowledging successful delivery of a packet, and so

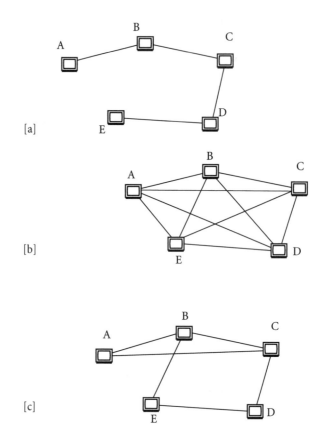

[a]

[b]

Figure 1.29. Point-to-point network topologies

[c]

on. The stations that join two or more local area networks and address these issues are called routers.

1.10.3   Metropolitan Area Networks

The term *metropolitan area networks* is often applied to the new high-speed network technologies to distinguish them from wide area and local area networks. These technologies have pushed the carrying capacity of the communication links into the gigabits range. They can be used over larger areas than LANs and are often used to connect LANs to form a greatly extended LAN environment.

Another important potential for these networks is the ability to carry information in forms that require many more bits than conventional text or simple graphics. An ordinary computer monitor screen displaying 25 lines of 80 characters contains only 2000 characters. At 8 bits per character, only 16,000 bits are needed to fill the screen. At 10 Mbps, the standard speed of LANs, only 1.6 msec would be needed to fill the screen completely. However, when that same screen displays high-resolution, bit-mapped images at 1024 by 768 bits, 786,432 bits are required to fill the screen. At 10 Mbps, the screen is refreshed every

78.6 msec. If the display includes 256 colors, 8 bits are required to represent each position on the screen. The time required to deliver the information for a full-screen display (at 10 Mbps) grows to 0.63 second—hardly suitable for smooth motion video. Clearly, the 10 Mbps LAN speeds are not adequate. LAN speeds of 100 Mbps improve the situation considerably. High-speed networks, approaching gigabits per second, are needed to provide the ability to deliver the full potential of multimedia displays to the user from a source on a different machine and to connect LANs and deliver timely access to resources.

In the later chapters of this book, we look at the high-speed network protocols to see how they overcome some of the limitations of the older LAN systems and to see the potential for increased capability in the services networks can deliver.

SUMMARY

Networks consist of individual computing devices that exchange messages and share resources. Each participating device must send and receive messages and behave according to rules known and understood by the others. Though a set of communication protocols specifically designed for the best use of an individual type of computer can make best use of that computer's characteristics, open systems used by many different types of systems provide access between the widest variety of devices.

An important collection of communications protocols follows the Open Systems Interconnection (OSI) reference model of the International Organization for Standardization (ISO). All the functions required are divided into seven layers. The model defines the responsibilities of each layer, the services each layer provides to the layer above it, and the services each layer receives from the layer below. On separate systems, peer layers cooperate by exchanging protocol data units. These messages are delivered by the lower-layer services.

Services comprise from one to four primitives: request, indication, response, confirm. Confirmed services use all four primitives and allow negotiation of expectations or requirements. Unconfirmed services include only the request and indication.

The ISO protocols provide the seven layers of network functions to allow systems to cooperate.

In the chapters that follow, network functions are presented from the top layer down, in the order in which a user process encounters them. We will look at each layer, considering the concepts involved in providing its part of the network services and at how the model is realized in the ISO network protocols. We will note issues still unresolved and areas of continuing study and development. An important goal of our efforts is to work with a computer network as a single platform for developing application programs in much the same way as we work with an operating system and its resources on a single computer system.

Though we depend on the OSI reference model to provide a context and even a language for discussing network protocols and services, we will address the ISO and the TCP/IP protocols throughout the text. We will indicate similarities and differences. We will see both approaches in the Application layer and the Transport and lower layers. Since the TCP/IP suite does not explicitly define Presentation and Session layers, the references to TCP/IP will be indirect in those chapters.

We move now to a ubiquitous network application area, the World Wide Web.

EXERCISES

1. In the Office Supplies Unlimited example, identify each of the requirements with one of the seven layers in the OSI reference model.

2. Give one advantage of an open system network over a proprietary system network. Give an advantage of a proprietary system over an open system network.

3. Differentiate between connectionless and connection-oriented modes of communication in an interconnected system.

4. Explain the roles of application entities and abstract syntax in the Application layer.

5. What is the relationship between the user data of the Presentation layer service and the user data of the Session layer service?

6. Describe the steps involved in establishing a communication with connection-oriented Application, Presentation, Session, and Transport layers.

7. In what ways are the responsibilities of the Transport and Data Link layers similar? How are they different?

8. Describe how a computerized library network would be used for resource sharing. Contrast it with a noncomputerized system. Give several advantages and several disadvantages for each from the user's point of view and from a system administrator's point of view.

9. What is the significance of the ISO-OSI reference model to networking?

10. Differentiate between the reference model and a set of protocols.

11. Describe the TCP/IP suite of protocols in terms of the OSI reference model.

12. Why are architectures and standards important in computer networks?

13. Why do the Network, Data Link, and Physical layers play a greater role in data communications than in network application development?

14. Differentiate between protocol data units and service data units.

15. Illustrate the steps in a confirmed service with a time sequence diagram.

16. Draw a finite state machine representation of the operation of an automatic toll booth assuming the toll is $0.75. To keep it from becoming too cluttered, assume that only quarters are accepted. Produce the corresponding state transition table.

17. Use a protocol machine to describe the operation of the protocol AcknowledgeAndShow described in Section 1.5.1. Show the corresponding state transition table.

18. Describe a LAN at your place of work or on your campus. Include a description of the topology, number and type of equipment, software, and length of time it has been in operation. Identify the main applications on the LAN, and indicate which ones are most frequently used. What documentation is available to users? How does a user qualify for access to the LAN? How does a user learn about the LAN and the resources it offers? If more than one network is available, are they connected? Describe.

19. Compare and contrast the use of a LAN or WAN with the use of a telephone (telecommunications) network.

20. Differentiate between a LAN and a system of terminals connected to a mainframe. List several applications appropriate for each system.

21. List several basic differences among LAN, WAN, and MAN. How are they similar?

22. Explain the difference between connection and interoperability.

23. Characterize each of the following as a LAN, WAN, neither, or "could be either." If it might be neither, explain why. If it could be either, explain the circumstances that would determine the answer.

(a) Personal computer network
(b) Telephone network
(c) International network of universities and colleges
(d) Automatic teller machine system for one bank
(e) Automatic teller machine system for all banks
(f) Airline reservation system
(g) Electronic bulletin board system
(h) Satellite communication system

24. How frequently could a computer monitor screen with 1024 x 768 bits resolution be refreshed on a 10-gigabit-per second network?

25. Assume you had access to a network that included all other students in a course and the course instructor. How might you benefit from the network? What services would you wish to have on the network?

26. Assume your computer at home or work was connected to any network, local or national, actual or imagined. List two significant activities on a local or national scale (for example, work, civic duties) that you could perform differently. Give an advantage and disadvantage of each activity in your list.

CHAPTER 2

The Internet and the World Wide Web

KEY CONCEPTS

- What Is the Internet?
- Hypertext and Hypermedia
- Protocols
- Application Development in the World Wide Web
- Information Discovery

We enter the realm of networks through a popular application environment and find that we can use applications and develop additional ones with very little knowledge of how systems actually move bits over networks. In later chapters, we will uncover the complexities of data movement in layers of programs that support network-based applications. Developing applications to run on the World Wide Web will illustrate the opportunities to do significant work before concentrating on the lower layers.

In this chapter, we introduce the World Wide Web and the associated tools for sharing information in many forms with users throughout the world. We begin this application with some background and general information about the Internet and the World Wide Web. We identify some of the principal tools of the Web: hypertext and hypermedia; a language for developing hypermedia documents; and the software to read, interpret, and present these documents. The protocols involved in moving materials between servers and clients and the importance of differences in file formats are included. Then we give examples of HTML, an introduction to metadata, and a discussion of Java as application development tools. The chapter concludes with a look at the growing collection of search engines that assist users in finding information in the World Wide Web. We will explore the general principles under which a number of search engines operate and will consider the nature of the problems they address and other problems that remain to be solved.

2.1 WHAT IS THE INTERNET?

The Internet is a collection of networks. The computers on those networks use common communication protocols that allow them to send and receive messages. Although each of the networks belongs to an organization or an individual, the complete collection—the Internet—has no owner, no central manager, and no controlling authority. The wonder of the Internet is the voluntary openness to interaction with other systems. People put resources on computers attached to networks and allow others to see those resources. People advertise their electronic addresses and respond to messages sent to them. People develop useful or interesting programs and make them available for other people to use. Technology makes it possible to send and receive communications on networks. People make it worthwhile.

The Internet originated from a U.S. Department of Defense project begun in the 1960s. Over the years, users of the Internet have developed applications, stored data, and communicated with each other through electronic mail and file transfer programs. Originally limited to researchers in laboratories and universities, access grew to include other individuals and organizations. Resources were growing, but people had difficulty finding what was available and where it was stored. The primary means of accessing material stored on network nodes was through **anonymous FTP**. The file transfer protocol (FTP) allows the movement of files between dissimilar computer systems. Anonymous FTP permits users to access remote files without identifying themselves to the system. Anonymous FTP provides easy access to information but does not help in finding the information.

The first solution to the searching problem was a program called the **Internet Archive Server, Archie**. Archie searches anonymous FTP sites and produces an index of the files found. Accessing information is then a two step process: first run Archie to discover the location of information, then use anonymous FTP to retrieve it. A complete explanation and example of the use of Archie and anonymous FTP are found in Appendix A.

Though a useful tool in discovering the location of files, Archie is not helpful in identifying collections of resources on a common theme or relationships among files at various sites. Students at the University of Minnesota addressed this deficiency by creating a tool that permits a logical organization of related resource information, which they named **Gopher** in honor of the school mascot. Gopher provides a nested list organization of information resources. The particular items included in the list depend on choices made by the organization presenting the list. Descriptions are very brief, but related information is linked to facilitate searching. The nested lists form tree structures. To find a needed resource, a user must *walk the Gopher tree* from its root to the desired leaf node. Searches or browsing in Gopherspace became an important part of information searching and also a fascinating pastime. Figure 2.1 shows the top level of the Gopher tree at the University of Minnesota.

Though a powerful tool, Gopher still restricts the presentation of search information to a tree shape. The next step was to allow a document to have any form the author chooses and to provide links to resources in logical places throughout the text. The name of this type of organization is **hypertext**. Gopher provides a limited form of hypertext. To exploit the concept more fully requires a language for designing hypertext documents. Though there are a number of languages or tools for creating hypertext documents, the language most frequently used to interconnect documents in the Internet is the **hypertext markup language (HTML)**. All the connected resources form a web pattern. The collection of all

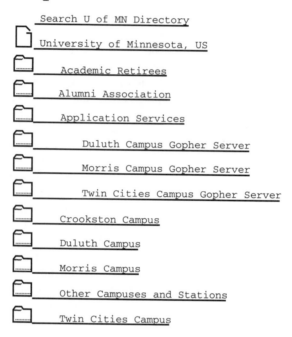

Gopher Menu

Figure 2.1. The Gopher tree at University of Minnesota

the resources connected by hypertext links in the Internet is called the **World Wide Web** (WWW or the Web).

2.1.1 The World Wide Web

What then is the World Wide Web? The Web is a distributed collection of resources in many forms (text, video, audio, graphics, even applications), a common naming system that supports searching and recognition, and a collection of protocols that allows machines to send and receive the requested resources.

The project known as the World Wide Web began in 1989 at CERN, the European Laboratory for Particle Physics, as an effort to provide access to information stored on computers all around the world. Early access to Web resources involved use of Gopher. By 1993, there were about 50 Web sites in the world, and Gopher was the principal access tool [For95]. In 1993, the National Center for Supercomputing Applications (NCSA) at the University of Illinois at Urbana-Champaign released **Mosaic**, an easy-to-use, almost intuitive, tool that made Web browsing accessible to virtually anyone who had access to a computer. Mosaic was the first of a succession of browsers with a graphical interface. All are revised frequently as the state of the art advances. Netscape and Microsoft's Internet Explorer are among the most common of the browsers, and both change frequently to improve access to Web resources.

What then is the World Wide Web? The Web is a distributed collection of resources in many forms (text, video, audio, graphics, even applications), a common naming system that supports searching and recognition, and a collection of protocols that allows machines to send and receive the requested resources. **Browsers** are programs that allow a user to explore the resources of the Web, retrieve those that are wanted, and display them on the user's system. "Display" takes on an extended meaning here: it may show an image or video, play an audio file, format and show a document, or execute an embedded application.

2.2 HYPERTEXT AND HYPERMEDIA

One of the conspicuous features of documents on the Web is the common use of hypertext. A hypertext document contains links that allow a reader to jump from one place to another, in contrast to the linear structure of traditional documents. A hypertext link might allow a reader to see the definition of a term or some background information about a part of the text, for example. The reader can either look at the supplementary information or continue with the main body of the text.

Documents accessed on the Web may have links to other parts of the same document, to other files on the same file system, or to any resource on any system accessible through the Web. Links in documents can connect the document to other text, images, sounds, video clips, applets—any resource on the Web. The concept of a "document" is changed forever.

In the remainder of this chapter, we describe basic tools for use of the Web. We focus on fundamentals and provide enough detail for useful results. We include an overview of HTML, a language for making hypertext documents, as an appendix. Here we consider the tools that allow an interaction between the user and a service provider. We conclude with some thoughts about the role of these concepts in network-based application development and distributed systems.

2.2.1 Browsers

A browser is a user's interface to information resources on the World Wide Web. All browsers allow the user to specify a resource by entering its URL. Browsers then invoke the protocol indicated in the access protocol portion of the URL to transfer the resource to the local system. Once the source material arrives on the local system, the browser displays it. The nature of the display depends on the design of the browser and on the kind of information contained in the resource.

Documents created using HTML arrive at the user's system with the HTML tags in place. The display presented to the user depends on the way the browser interprets the tags. A level-1 head tag may be displayed as 24-point Times Roman font by one viewer and as 18-point Helvetica font by another. A reader of an HTML document will not necessarily see it as the author does. Fine-tuning the appearance of a document while seeing it through one particular browser is not a meaningful exercise.

Browsers handle non-HTML files according to the content of the file. If the file contains text, the browser will display the text without any formatting. If the file contains information of another type, such as an image or sound, the browser must invoke another process to interpret the content of the file and display it.

2.2.2 Cascading Style Sheets

Many options are available in the design of a Web page. HTML, intended for simple formatting and linking in text documents, is pushed beyond its design goals when it is used to describe very creative displays. Designing a consistent presentation of a collection of pages belonging to the same organization involves repetitive entries with nonintuitive tags. In addition, when the same elements are repeated on many pages and all those pages are downloaded, the elements must be transferred many times. This congests the network and slows access to the materials.

Cascading style sheets address these issues by allowing a style definition to apply to multiple elements. CSS1 is a language for defining a cascading style sheet. It uses terminology associated with desktop publishing. The term *cascading* refers to the fact that multiple style sheets may be in effect at one time. The author of a document will define a style sheet to describe the intended presentation of the pages. The reader of the document might use a different style sheet, which overcomes local restrictions or addresses special needs. An example might be a style sheet used by a reader who requires exceptionally large type fonts. Another example of cascading style sheets is use of a global master style sheet augmented with local variations for individual groups. CSS1 specifies rules for determining which style elements dominate in case conflicts occur. In general, the style specified by the author takes precedence over the style specified by the reader, and both supersede the default styles of the browser. Imported style sheets override others in the order in which they appear. Styles specified within the local style specification override any imported style sheet specifications.

We mentioned earlier that different browsers render the same HTML elements differently. Fonts vary, as do paragraph indenting, colors, and so forth, meaning that each browser has a default style sheet. By defining style sheets explicitly, the author takes control and determines a uniform appearance for each page (unless the reader chooses to override these choices).

A full description of style sheets can be found at the Web site for the World Wide Web Consortium (W3C) at www.w3.org. The introduction provided here will give a general idea of how style sheets are specified and incorporated into HTML documents.

Defining Style

Style rules are specified by the general format:

```
selector {property: value}
```

Multiple selectors can share the same style:

```
h1, h2, h3, h4, h5, h6 {color: blue}
```

and one or more selectors can receive the same style specification:

```
h1, h2 {font-family: helvetica;
        font-weight: bold}
```

Approximately 50 properties and their legal values are defined in CSS1.

Selectors are not limited to the regular HTML tag elements such as headers, anchors, and paragraphs. Among the more interesting options are the typographical pseudo-elements: first line and first letter. First line specifies a special appearance for the first line of a paragraph; first letter allows drop caps (a special style for the first character that allows it to be several lines deep). These features are not supported by all browsers, so they might be ignored.

Connecting Style with HTML Documents

The HTML specification states how style sheets are linked to documents. There are four methods:

```
<HTML>
  <HEAD>
    <TITLE> title </TITLE>
    <LINK> REL=STYLESHEET TYPE="text/css"
           HREF="http://style.com/cool" TITLE="Cool">
    <STYLE TYPE ="text/css">
      @import url(http://style.com/basic);
      H1 (color: blue )
    </STYLE>
  </HEAD>
  <BODY>
     <H1> Headline is blue</H1>
     <P STYLE="color: green">While the paragraph is green.
  </BODY>
</HTML>
```

Figure 2.2. Four methods of specifying STYLE

- The LINK element refers to an external style sheet whose entries are to be applied to the current document
- Import reads a style specification into the document
- A STYLE element inside the HEAD element of a document defines characteristics to apply throughout the document, but is not available for inclusion in other documents
- A STYLE element inside an element in the BODY defines a characteristic to apply locally

The example in Figure 2.2 comes from the definition of CSS1 [Wor96]. All four of the style specification methods appear.

2.2.3   File Formats

Browsers recognize an HTML file by the filename with extension .htm or .html. A browser can determine that a file contains an HTML document by reading the <HTML> tag that begins the document, but not all browsers use this information if the filename does not provide the first clue.

Other file formats require separate **viewers**, processes that will be invoked as needed to read and interpret the contents of the file. Invoking a viewer requires two things: the browser must recognize the file type in order to associate it with the correct viewer, and the correct viewer must be available. Part of the configuration process for a browser is to describe the file extensions that might be encountered and to relate those to a class of application that can be displayed by a particular viewer. Figure 2.3 shows file types that might be recognized and the kind of viewer needed to display them.

Image Formats

GIF The Graphical Information Format was designed at CompuServe. The ability to display gif format images is incorporated into every browser that can display any image

File Type	File Extension		Comments
	Standard	3 Character	
html	html	htm	No extra viewer needed
audio	au snd wav		soundtool, xplaygizmo on X systems, wham, wplayany, mplayer on Windows, soundmachine on Mac
images	gif jpeg tiff	jpg jpe tif	xv on X systems, lview on Windows, gif-converter, graphic-converter, jpeg-view on Mac
video	mpeg mov	mpg mpe avi	mpeg_play on X systems, mpegplay, qtw11 on Windows, sparkle, fast_player on Mac

Figure 2.3. File formats and their viewers

at all. Hence, if an author uses only gif images, all readers will be able to see them. Some browsers can also display other image formats, but since the author cannot control the tool that a reader will use, it is safest to use only gif format for inline images.

jpeg The bitmap format used in jpeg—named for its creators: the Joint Photographic Experts Group—is compressed, addressing a problem of image files in general. Some browsers support inline jpeg images.

tiff Tagged Information File Format was designed by Microsoft and Aldus to support images produced by scanners and desktop publishing systems.

Sound Formats

Basic sound This is the most commonly available sound format, and sounds stored in this format can be played on most systems. It originated on UNIX systems and is indicated by .au or .snd extensions.

Wave The sound format for Microsoft Windows; it is not commonly accessible on other platforms.

Video Formats

mpeg Mpeg uses file compression techniques similar to those employed in jpeg files. Viewers are commonly available. The format is named for the group that designed it, the Motion Picture Experts Group.

avi This movie file format developed for Microsoft Windows is not routinely available on other platforms.

Document Formats

text Plain text files are displayed by all browsers without formatting.

HTML HTML files are interpreted and displayed by all browsers, though the effects of formatting tags may vary.

PostScript This document description language was developed to drive printers in producing very high-quality document output. A number of viewers are available to display PostScript files on a monitor.

2.2.4 Beyond HTML: XML

Nearly all linked documents on the World Wide Web in the early 21st century are described in HTML. However, HTML has limits. It was intended to describe documents of one type: simple office-style reports. Additions to HTML to allow it to meet other needs have led to incompatible formats and documents that can be read by some browsers and not others. The **Extensible Markup Language (XML)**, Recommendation 1.0, was released in February 1998. XML is a simplified version of the Simple Generalized Markup Language (SGML), the international standard language for defining document types. SGML and XML are languages for describing languages for describing types of documents. HTML is an application of SGML and describes a simple report document type. XML allows users to define other document types to meet special needs. For example, XML could be used to define a type advertising banner or mathematical proof or university approved dissertation style or musical score.

XML is not a markup language. Instead, it is a tool for defining new markup languages. The new markup languages then describe documents. Clearly, to view a document described in a new markup language requires an application, a browser perhaps, that understands the new markup language. Both Microsoft and Netscape are adding XML compatibility to their products. Other applications are likely to address special niche requirements.

2.3 PROTOCOLS

The access protocol field of a URL specifies how a browser will communicate with another system in order to retrieve a resource. The most common access protocols used in the World Wide Web are HTTP (the hypertext transfer protocol), Gopher, FTP (file transfer protocol), file, mailto, and news. Each of these access protocols invokes lower-layer network services to accomplish the movement of resources.

2.3.1 HTTP

Use of the protocol HTTP establishes a connection with an HTTP server, called a daemon process on UNIX systems, and sends a request for a specific file. The server process returns the file or a status code. Status codes allow the browser and the server to communicate in addressing the user's request. HTTP uses status codes in five classes:

- 1xx codes indicate a provisional status, suggesting progress in serving the request; more will come.
- 2xx codes indicate that the request was received, understood, and accepted.

- 3xx codes indicate further action must be taken by the client. Responses of this type include information identifying the nature of the further action required.
- 4xx codes indicate an error on the client side of the interaction.
- 5xx codes indicate the server has recognized an error condition on its own side of the interaction.

Sample status codes include:

- 101 Switching protocols
- 202 Accepted
- 307 Temporary redirect
- 404 File not found
- 500 Internal server error

The user ordinarily will not see status codes in the 100, 200, and 300 categories. The 404 code often means a URL has been mistyped. Code 500 is often accompanied by a message to contact the server's administrator about the condition that led to this status report.

We have seen a number of examples of HTTP URLs. The general format is:

```
http://machine[:port]/path/file
```

The port number is part of the connection establishment between the local process and the HTTP server process. The default port number for HTTP is 80. The port number needs to be specified only if the process is running in an unusual configuration—most likely testing of a new implementation of the server process. If the location given includes a directory but no filename, the server will look for the default filename, usually index.html. If no such file is found, the server may return a directory listing.

Here are some additional sample HTTP URLs:

```
http://www.csc.villanova.edu/~cassel
```

```
http://www.csc.villanova.edu/~cassel/netbook/authors.gif
```

2.3.2 Gopher

Use of Gopher in a URL returns a portion of a Gopher tree. The general format of a URL to access a Gopher server is

```
gopher://machine[:port]/[type[item]]
```

Again, the port number is not needed unless the server is running in an unusual configuration, perhaps for testing. The default port number for Gopher is 70. When no type or item is specified, Gopher will return the top of the Gopher tree at the specified host. The reader can follow paths through Gopherspace by choosing items from the tree presented. An example URL for Gopher access is

```
gopher://gopher.tc.umn.edu:70/
```

This is the Gopher site at The University of Minnesota. Gopher sites are less common since the use of the World Wide Web has become more readily available.

2.3.3 FTP

FTP is a file transfer protocol. It can be invoked as a standalone program, as illustrated in Appendix A, where anonymous **FTP** retrieves files identified by the Archie search engine. When the URL specifies FTP as the access protocol, the browser invokes the same FTP program accessible without the browser. Most often, the user accesses anonymous FTP, mentioned earlier in this chapter and illustrated in Appendix A. Optionally, the user may specify user id and password to gain access to private files. Passwords should never be stored in documents because of the security risk. The general form of a URL to access files through FTP is

```
ftp://[user-id[:password]@]machine/path/file
```

For example:

```
ftp://cassel:pwd4demo@tiger.villanova.edu/mnt/a/cassel/Mail/addr
```

2.3.4 File

Using `file` for the access protocol requests access to a local file. No transfer protocol is needed since the file is opened but not moved. The general form is

```
file:[//machine]/path/file
```

An example is

```
file://c:/netbook/www.tex
```

2.3.5 Mailto

The access protocol `mailto` invokes a process to send an electronic mail message to the address specified in the tag. `mailto` is often included in the <ADDRESS> ... </ADDRESS> part of a Web page to allow a reader to communicate with the page author. The general form of this feature is `mailto:username@machinename`. For example:

```
<a href = "mailto:cassel@tiger.villanova.edu"> cassel@villanova.edu</a>
```

Notice that what is highlighted (`cassel@villanova.edu`) is not necessarily the same as the address that will be used to send mail (`cassel@tiger.villanova.edu`). The highlighted part can be anything you wish. For example, this would do just as well:

```
<a href = "mailto:cassel@tiger.villanova.edu"> Send me mail!</a>.
```

Displaying the e-mail address, or some form of it, provides some information that a reader might use later. It has no effect on the way the `mailto:` access protocol works.

2.3.6 News

The news access protocol in a URL allows access to a usenet newsgroup or specific article. No host is specified because access is through a designated news server identified in the local host configuration. The user must provide identification of a newsgroup or a specific article. The general form is news:newsgroup or news:article-id.

Here is an example:

```
<a href="news:villanova.csc.networks-course">Class News Group</a>
```

2.4 APPLICATION DEVELOPMENT IN THE WORLD WIDE WEB

HTML provides the input and output portions of a general-purpose distributed application development environment.

Using hypertext documents to link resources throughout the world provides a powerful tool for information organization and access. The real power of Web tools requires another giant step, however. The next tool presented does more than respond with existing information resources. It permits the application developer to respond to a user by executing code. *HTML provides the input and output portions of a general-purpose distributed application development environment.*

2.4.1 Forms and Form Servers

Figure 2.4 shows a sample HTML form. The reader fills in the blanks, sometimes entering text, sometimes checking boxes, sometimes selecting from lists in scroll boxes. All the information gathered by the form becomes input to an executable file—a server process designed specifically to respond to the user of this form. Output from the server process goes back to the user's browser for display. Output can be presented using any HTML features. The server output can present a final result to the user, or can present another form that requests further information and invokes still another server process. The interaction can continue indefinitely. In addition to responding to the user, the server may store information in a file or invoke other processes.

Applications based on HTML forms include surveys, voting systems, registrations, database query front-ends, data manipulation and presentation, and nearly any other type of application that accepts input and produces output. Since the form and its server often reside on different systems, this is a useful tool for distributed application development.

Creating forms is a simple extension of the HTML facilities we have seen. Developing executable code to interact with the form is as simple or as complex as the application demands. The limiting factor in this type of application development is a security concern. Although the system administrator may be willing to have unknown users from around the world browse through resources on the system, he or she may feel differently about those unknown users executing code produced by people experimenting with the power of forms processing. To create processes that interact with forms, you will need permission to store those processes in areas described in the HTTP system configuration.

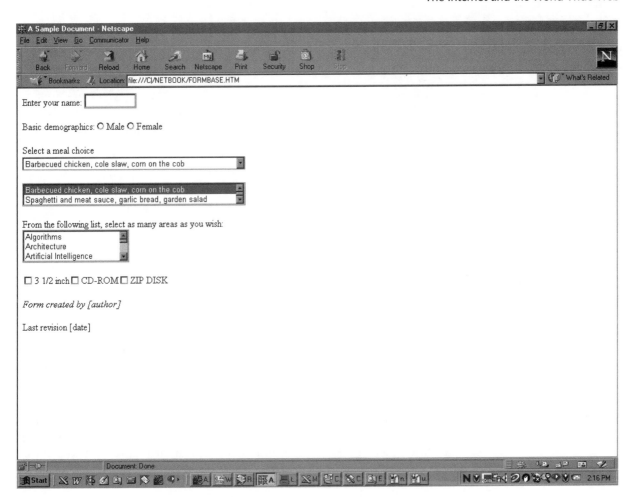

Figure 2.4. A sampling of HTML form elements

2.4.2 HTML Forms

Figure 2.5 shows the format of an HTML form. It has the same base HTML elements as any other document: <HTML>, <TITLE>, <BODY>, and a signature element <ADDRESS>; and two new elements used to define a form: <FORM> and <INPUT>. A form may use any of the elements we saw for other documents as well.

<FORM> notifies the browser that it will send data to a server process. The <FORM> tag contains two attributes:

- ACTION provides the URL for the server process that will receive and process data from the form. The server process will normally reside in the cgi-bin directory of the server.
- METHOD describes the way data will be sent from the form to its server. The choices are GET and POST. GET places the data from the form into the QUERY_STRING envi-

```
<HTML>
<HEAD>
<TITLE> A Sample Document </TITLE>
</HEAD>
<BODY>

<FORM ACTION= "http://machine/cgi-bin/file" METHOD="POST">
<INPUT TYPE="submit">
</FORM>

<ADDRESS>

</ADDRESS>
</BODY>

</HTML>
```

Figure 2.5. The basic HTML form document structure

ronment variable. POST passes the data to the process in its standard input. Limitations on the length of QUERY_STRING make POST the preferred method for data passing in large forms.

<INPUT> is one of several tags that describe the data to be entered through the form. The INPUT attribute TYPE specifies the kind of information that will go to the server process. There are a number of types defined, and there is an alternative way to collect data on a form as well. We consider these next.

Information-Gathering Tools

This section describes the HTML specifications for producing each of the form elements shown in Figure 2.4. Refer to the figure to see how each of the constructions described here is displayed by Netscape.

There are several ways to prompt a user for input in a form:

- Give a list of choices from which the user selects one.
- Give a list of choices from which the user selects any subset.
- Provide space for the user to type information.

Lists from which the user makes exactly one selection can be produced in either of two ways, depending on the length of the list. For short lists, all the choices show on the form with a "button" next to each. The user "presses" one button (clicks on the box next to the item), and all other choices become unselected. Buttons of this type are called radio buttons, after the station selector buttons on some radios.

The example radio button list of Figure 2.4 was produced by the following HTML tags:

```
Basic demographics:

<INPUT TYPE ="radio" NAME="gender" VALUE="M"> Male

<INPUT TYPE ="radio" NAME="gender" VALUE="F"> Female
```

"Basic demographics" appears on the form and serves as a label for the choices. The TYPE="radio" specifies the type of data to send. It means that the variable name, gender, will have one value. NAME="gender" defines the variable name associated with this data item. The VALUE="F" and VALUE="M" define what will go to the server if the corresponding button is selected. The text Female and Male are the labels that appear next to the buttons.

When the number of choices is large enough to consume more space on the form than can be spared, a pull-down menu or scrolling list serves the purpose. The HTML tag required to define these structures is SELECT. The following HTML description produced the meal selection pull-down menu in Figure 2.4:

```
Select a meal choice
<SELECT NAME="meal_choice">
<OPTION> Barbecued chicken, cole slaw, corn on the cob
<OPTION> Spaghetti and meat sauce, garlic bread, garden salad
<OPTION> Grilled fresh tuna steak, red skin potatoes, fresh asparagus
<OPTION> Pasta Primavera, fresh breadsticks, lettuce and tomato salad
</SELECT>
```

The user clicks on the box displayed, which is labeled with the first choice option. A pull-down menu opens, and the user selects one of the items shown. To show more than one choice in the initial display, include a SIZE attribute in the SELECT tag:

```
<SELECT NAME="meal choice" SIZE=2>
<OPTION> Barbecued chicken, cole slaw, corn on the cob
<OPTION> Spaghetti and meat sauce, garlic bread, garden salad
<OPTION> Grilled fresh tuna steak, red skin potatoes, fresh asparagus
<OPTION> Pasta Primavera, fresh breadsticks, lettuce and tomato salad
</SELECT>
```

This converts the pull-down menu to a scrolling list as shown in Figure 2.4. The first two choices show, and the scroll bar invites the user to examine other options. The SIZE specified depends on the amount of space the author wishes to give to the display of this list. A default selection can be added to either the pull-down menu or the scrolling list by adding the word SELECTED to one or more options. The following example preselects the chicken dinner in the menu choice:

```
<SELECT NAME="meal choice">
<OPTION SELECTED> Barbecued chicken, cole slaw, corn on the cob
<OPTION> Spaghetti and meat sauce, garlic bread, garden salad
```

```
<OPTION> Grilled fresh tuna steak, red skin potatoes, fresh asparagus
<OPTION> Pasta Primavera, fresh breadsticks, lettuce and tomato salad
</SELECT>
```

Many situations require the ability to select a number of items from a list of options. Pull-down menus and scrolling lists convert easily to allow multiple options. The attribute MULTIPLE in the SELECT tag makes the change. The following HTML code produced the interest area survey of Figure 2.4:

```
<SELECT NAME ="Interest areas" SIZE=3 MULTIPLE>
<OPTION> Algorithms
<OPTION> Architecture
<OPTION> Artificial Intelligence
<OPTION> Computers and Society
<OPTION> Database Management
<OPTION> Data Structures
<OPTION> Discrete Mathematics
<OPTION> Graphics
<OPTION> History of Computing
<OPTION> Information Systems
<OPTION> Image Processing
<OPTION> Knowledge-based Systems
<OPTION> Networks
<OPTION> Operating Systems
<OPTION> Performance
<OPTION> Programming Languages
<OPTION> Systems
</SELECT>
```

The OPTION tag may include a VALUE parameter. If it is present, the value parameter specifies what is sent to the form server if this choice is selected. In the absence of a value tag, the full string of the choice will be sent. Giving a short value for the form server to process simplifies parsing of input, but if the item selected will be displayed in the output of the form server, having the full text is useful.

When all the choices fit comfortably on the form, checkboxes replace radio button lists to allow multiple selections. The following HTML commands produced the disk type options in Figure 2.4:

```
<INPUT TYPE ="checkbox" NAME ="disk3"> 3 1/2 inch

<INPUT TYPE ="checkbox" NAME ="diskcd"> CD-ROM

<INPUT TYPE ="checkbox" NAME ="zip"> ZIP DISK
```

A checkbox sends to the form process the name of each choice that is checked and the value on. If the disk types 3 1/2 and CD-ROM were checked in Figure 2.4, the form would send the following stream to the form server: disk3=on&diskcd=on

Finally, some applications require text entered by the form user. A text entry location is an INPUT field, and resembles others that we have seen. The distinction is the TYPE specification.

```
<INPUT TYPE="text" NAME="responder">
```

creates a text entry field on the form. The text entered in that field goes to the form server in the variable responder. The INPUT tag includes optional attributes that allow the form designer to control the text area. To limit the size of the box presented to the user for entering text, use the SIZE attribute. Extra text entered forces scrolling in the display box. To limit the user's text, use the MAXLENGTH attribute. For example:

```
Enter your name: <INPUT TYPE="text" NAME="responder" SIZE=10 MAXLENGTH=50>
```

gives the user enough space for 10 characters in the input box, but allows the user to enter up to 50 characters. As the user types to the end of the box, the text scrolls.

One final input option allows the user to input text of more than one line. The tag TEXTAREA defines an area of specified width and height and assigns a variable name to the input from that area. For example:

```
<TEXTAREA NAME="responder" ROWS="10" COLS="40" MAXLENGTH = 40> </TEXTAREA>
```

defines an area of 10 lines each, 40 characters wide. Because the maximum line length is constrained to the box width, long lines wrap; extra lines scroll.

Submit and Clear Form Operations

The whole purpose of a form is to gather information that is input to a process. A form needs an element that lets a user indicate that the form is completed and the information can go to the form server for processing. The SUBMIT button serves this purpose. The syntax is

```
<INPUT TYPE="submit" VALUE = "Done">
```

This will produce an area on the form that the user should click on when ready to submit the form for processing. The VALUE parameter provides a label for the button. If the VALUE parameter is not used, the button will be labeled SUBMIT.

One final input type allows a user to clear a form; its syntax is

```
<INPUT TYPE = "reset" VALUE = "Clear the form">
```

Again, the VALUE parameter provides an optional label for the button; in its absence, the label is RESET.

2.4.3 Forms Processing

Data collected in a form becomes input to a process, a **form server**. A form server is an executable file stored in a location that the system administrator has made accessible to client forms. The form server can be written in a script language or a programming language.

Submitting the form causes the Web server to launch the indicated form server process. The form server has complete flexibility concerning what it does with the input data. It can manipulate the data, call other processes, or do anything any application program can do. For security reasons, the form server process may be given strict restrictions in the server configuration. The output of the form server gets to the user by means of the same protocol that allowed the user to submit the form: HTTP. The output display appears in the browser like any other Web document. To present the output with formatting, the form server will send HTML tags with the information.

Figure 2.8 shows a form server written in the Perl language. The input to this program comes from the form of Figures 2.6 and 2.7. Output appears in Figure 2.9. We cannot fully cover the Perl language in this book, but a review of the program will give an idea of the kind of processing required in a program to process forms. The program could have been written in C or Java or UNIX script, or any other programming language.

```
<html>
<head>
<title> A sample HTML form          </title>
</head>
<body>


<h3> A Sample HTML Form </h3>
<p>
<form method="post" action="/cgi-bin/cgi-bin/gen.pl">
<input type ="submit"></p>
<p> This sample form includes examples of text entry, radio buttons, and
checklists.


<input type = "RESET" VALUE = "Clear the form"><br>
<p>
Please enter your name: <input type="text" name="myName" maxlength=50> <br>


<p>
What is your favorite part of this course?
<textarea name="comments" rows=5 cols=40 > </textarea>


<p>
What is your favorite kind of pet?
<ul>
<li><input type="radio" name="petkind" value="Cats"> Cats are best
<li><input type="radio" name="petkind" value="Dogs"> I like dogs
<li><input type="radio" name="petkind" value="Chimps"> Chimpanzees!!
<li><input type="radio" name="petkind" value="Fish"> Fish are nice
<li><input type="radio" name="petkind" value="Birds"> Birds are good
<li><input type="radio" name="petkind" value="Snakes"> I like snakes
<li><input type="radio" name="petkind" value="Ferrets"> Ferrets, yes!
<li><input type="radio" name="petkind" value="None"> None of these
</ul>
```

Figure 2.6. A sample form server: part 1 of 2

```
<p>
What kinds of music do you like (check as many as you wish)?
<ul>
<li><input type="checkbox" name="jazz"> Jazz
<li><input type="checkbox" name="classical"> Classical
<li><input type="checkbox" name="rock"> Rock
<li><input type="checkbox" name="polka"> Polka
<li><input type="checkbox" name="country"> Country
<li><input type="checkbox" name="others"> Others not shown here
<li><input type="checkbox" name="none"> None of These!!!
<p>


Which of these would you choose?
   <SELECT NAME="maincourse">
      <OPTION> Fried Chicken
      <OPTION> Stuffed Flounder
      <OPTION> Mushroom Nut Pilaf
    </SELECT>


<p>  What would be your second choice?
   <SELECT NAME="second" size=2>
     <OPTION> Fried Chicken
     <OPTION> Stuffed Flounder
     <OPTION> Mushroom Nut Pilaf
     <OPTION> No second choice
    </SELECT>


<p>  Sometimes it is appropriate to have more than one selection chosen in the
list.  For example: <br>
<p>  which of the following are of interest to you?


<SELECT NAME="interests" multiple size=4>
  <OPTION> Museums
  <OPTION> Amusement Parks
  <OPTION> Movies
  <OPTION> Theater
  <OPTION> Concerts
  <OPTION> Dining Out
  <OPTION> Sports
  <OPTION> Outdoor activities
 </SELECT>
<input type="hidden" name="null" value="0">
```

Figure 2.7. Sample form server: part 2 of 2

```
#!/usr/Per15/per15.001/per1
print "Content-type: text/html\n\n";
print "<Head><Title>Survey Echo</Title></Head>n";
Print "<BODY BACKGROUND=\"/mnt/a/cassel/html/gif.files/paper12.gif\" >\n";
print "<CENTER><H3>Survey Echo</H3></CENTER><HR><BR>\n";
# Get the input
$buffer=<STDIN>;

#Split the name-value pairs
@pairs = split(/&/, $buffer);
foreach $pair (@pairs)
{

    ($name, $value) = split(/=/, $pair);
    # Un-Webify plus signs and %-encoding
    $value =~ tr/+/ /;
    $value =~ s/%([a-fA-FO-9] [a-fA-FO-9]/pack("C", hex($1))/eg;

    $FORM{$name} = $value;

}

print "<p><h4>Hello,  $FORM{myName}, thanks for filling in our survey</h4>";
print "<p><h5>Here is a summary of your responses</h5>";
print "\n\n";
print "<i>Your favorite pets are</i> $FORM{petkind}";
print "\n<p>";

print "<p> <i>In music, you like </i><br> \&\#183\; ";
foreach $pair (@pairs)

  { ($name, $value) = split(/=/, $pair);
      if ($value eq "on") {print "$name \&\#183\ ; "}};

print "\n";

print "<p> <i>Your meal choices are</i> $FORM{maincourse} <i>or</i>
                  $FORM{second}.\n";

print "<p> <i>Your interests include the following:</i> <br>";
print "\&\#183\;\n";
foreach $pair (@pairs)

  { ($name, $value) = split(/=/, $pair);
    #print "$name = $value\n";
    $value =~ tr/+/ /;
    if ($name eq "interests") {print "$value \&\#183\; "}};
print "\n";
print"<p>";

print "<i>Here is your comment:</i><p>";
print "$FORM{comments}";

print "</TR></TABLE><HR></BODY><ADDRESS>\n";
print "Comments to";
print "<A HREF=\"mailto:cassel\@tiger.villanova.edu\"> cassel\@tiger.villanova.edu </A>\n";
print "</ADDRESS></HTML>\n";
```

Figure 2.8. A form server script

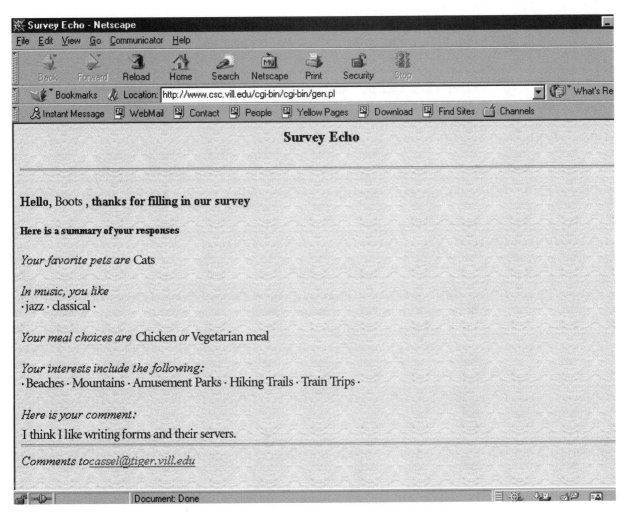

Figure 2.9. Response from a form server

The first line of the program specifies the path to the Perl interpreter. The next few lines of the program, those that start with `print`, send output from the program to the standard output. In the case of programs identified as Web form processing programs, the standard output goes back to the browser that provided the program input. In other words, the output of this program will be displayed by the browser where the form was submitted. Understandably then, the first lines of output produce the opening of an HTML document. Actually, the first line of output informs the browser to expect an HTML document. This is information it would get from the filename if it were receiving a file. The statement

```
Content-type: text/html\n\n
```

tells the browser to expect HTML codes. `\n\n` represents two new lines, one to end the `Content-type` statement and one to produce a blank line. Both these lines are required when a program sends HTML code to a browser. The next three lines send the <head> section, the tag to begin the BODY of the document, and code to produce a centered title for the page. Lines that begin with # are comments in the Perl program. $buffer=<STDIN> places the contents of standard input into the buffer. That gives the program access to the variable names and the values provided by the user of the form. Output from the form consists of name–value pairs separated by &s. For example, part of the input from the sample form might look like this:

```
petkind=Cats&jazz=on&classical=on&maincourse=Mushroom+Nut+Pilaf
```

Split separates the parts of that input at the &s, producing a list (@pairs is a list or array named pairs) containing the following items:

```
petkind=Cats
jazz=on
classical=on
maincourse=Mushroom+Nut+Pilaf
```

No spaces or special characters are allowed in the information sent from the form to the form server. All such characters are encoded for transmission. The + signs replace spaces in the data. Other nonalphabetic characters are represented by their hexadecimal codes. The loop beginning foreach $pair accomplishes three tasks. It splits the name–value pairs into a name part and a value part; it decodes any +s and hexadecimal representations; and it associates each value with the appropriate name. Without the third task, we would have a name and a value for each name–value pair. However, we would not have the value understood as belonging to a location referred to by the name. Essentially, we would have two parallel lists, one with values petkind, jazz, classical, maincourse; the other with values Cats, on, on, Mushroom Nut Pilaf. We would not have the value Cats associated with a variable named petkind. The statement $FORM{$name} = $value establishes the relationship between name and value.

Next come a set of print statements that send output back to the browser. Notice the use of <p> to define new paragraph spacing and h4 to control the size and appearance of the text. Hello, appears on the output displayed by the browser followed by the value stored in the variable $FORM{myName}. The other print statements send more text and formatting information, and the value associated with petkind. Since petkind came from the form through a radio box statement, it has only one value. The music choices were sent by a checkbox allowing multiple selections. The program examines each name–value pair. Wherever value on appears, the associated name is sent to the browser.

The other form fields are treated similarly. Finally, a set of print statements sends an <ADDRESS> ... </ADDRESS> part for the end of the page and </HTML> to complete the page description.

The example form and response is simple: the response just repeats the input. The form server is not limited to such straightforward processing. The form server process could call other processes, look up information in a database, perform complex analysis or computation—anything any program could do with this input data. The form server process is reached through a Web server. The program must reside in an area designated to hold such processes, usually a directory called cgi-bin. The application that receives input from the form and generates the response to the browser may be on the Web server or may be on another system known to and accessible by the program in the `cgi-bin` directory of the Web server.

The role of the computer system where the browser is running (the client) is limited in this exchange. The client browser presents the form to the user, sends the form data to the form server process, and displays the form server output. The next section introduces a facility for moving the work of this interchange to the client machine.

2.4.4 Java

Forms and the processes that respond to them provide an easy entry into distributed computing, but put a severe burden on server systems. A logical extension to this distribution of computing is to provide for processes that run on the client machine. Consider how such an environment would function. The application process resides on a host system somewhere in the Internet. A client requests the process. Executable code is transferred to the client system and runs there. Every time a new client requests the process, the server sends executable code and the client runs it. The server, freed from the need to run the process for each client, can respond to requests from many clients quickly.

A system in which processes retrieved over the Internet are executed on the client presents some serious challenges:

- Portability. What kind of process description can move to any of the many kinds of computer systems in the Internet and expect to execute without tailoring to the specific system?
- Reliability. What happens if a downloaded program fails during execution?
- Security. Can the client system execute a process downloaded from an arbitrary host without concern about what that process might do?
- Integration. How do such programs integrate with other Web-based services?

The programming language Java provides a tool for developing programs with these concerns in mind. Java evolved from a language designed to produce code to run in embedded systems for consumer electronics—microwave ovens, electronic schedulers, and such. The language had to produce programs to run on a variety of chips used in producing the electronic devices. It had to be simple enough to minimize errors in the code, but powerful enough to produce the results needed. James Gosling and a small team of developers at Sun Microsystems began working on a language to meet these needs in 1990. When the phenomenon of the World Wide Web burst on the scene in 1993, Gosling realized the usefulness of an architecture-independent, small, reliable programming language in the new environment. Java took on new importance at Sun. The team developed a new browser, HotJava, that supported embedded applications written in the Java language. These "applets" exist as part of a Web document.

Java applets provide a new dimension to Web documents.

Java applets provide a new dimension to Web documents. Hypertext permits a document to link to other static elements. Forms permit a client to execute a program on a server. Applets put a dynamic, interactive component into the document itself. Here are a few possibilities of what can be done with applets:

- You could look up the definition of an arbitrary word in a document. This is different from having a hypertext link to an expanded explanation of the word. In that case, the author of the document would have decided to make a link on that word to provide additional information. In the case of an applet, the reader could open a dictionary and look up any word.

- You could select some numeric values in a document and graph them. Again, the applet gives you access to the graphing capability, and you decide what figures you want to graph and what style presentation you want. The author of the document does not have to present the figures in graphical form; the reader can get a graph of any combination of figures.

- You could annotate the document—underlining, highlighting, even making margin notes.

- The author could include animation in the document—not a film clip to be played, but a process that calculates the positions and displays the moving object. This feature has been a popular choice in early demonstration applets.

The possibilities are limited only by our imaginations.

But how does Java address the issues of portability, reliability, security, and integration? Portability was an original design goal when the language was intended for embedding code in consumer electronics. Portability is provided by a two-part translation process. Java is a high-level language that resembles C/C++. Programs written in Java are compiled into an intermediate form called **bytecode** that is independent of any machine architecture. Bytecode is designed for transmission over networks. On the client machine, the bytecode is interpreted. To run a Java program, a client machine needs a Java interpreter. The interpreter executes appropriate machine-specific instructions under control of the bytecode. An interpreter must be developed for each different computer architecture that will run Java applets. The bytecode sent to each machine is identical.

Reliability cannot be guaranteed. However, the Java language was designed to reduce the probability of coding errors. Java is small and simple. The designers removed many constructions found in C/C++ that give rise to errors in programming. For example, there are no pointers in Java. Java is also object oriented. This is not an added feature; it is part of the original design of the language. With the exception of simple types for numbers, characters, and boolean values, everything in Java is an object. Java includes a large collection of classes arranged in packages. Java applets access the packages from a server as needed; packages are not stored on the client system.

Security is an essential concern for processes that will be downloaded from unknown hosts and run on client systems. Although Java is a general-purpose language and can be used for ordinary application development, special restrictions apply to applets. An applet may not read or write files on the system on which it is running. Furthermore, applets may not access the local file system to discover directories or their contents; may not create or remove files or directories; may not establish network connection with any system except the one from which the applet was loaded; may not obtain information about the user or the local system; may not create a window without a warning that it is untrusted (this prevents an applet from disguising itself as another application to trick a user into entering sensitive information); and may not create, access, or manipulate resources that would jeopardize the local system integrity. Enforcement of these restrictions is the responsibility of the local configuration. A downloaded applet must pass through a bytecode verification process to ensure that the applet conforms to the security regulations. (Even the Java compiler that produced the bytecode is not trusted.) Local configuration may relax some of the restrictions; for instance, an applet loaded from a local system or from a trusted remote system may be freed from some of the limitations placed on applets from unknown sources.

Java applets are integrated into the Web environment by embedding them into an HTML document using the <APPLET> tag. The <APPLET> tag and its parameters provide the location from which the bytecode will be loaded, the dimensions of the window in which the applet will run, and an optional text message to be displayed by browsers that are not Java-ready.

The Java language was specifically designed to meet the needs of Web-based applications. It addresses the needs of portability, reliability, security, and integration. It cannot guarantee that every applet developed in Java will run correctly and will never pose a threat to any system. It is possible to write bad code in any language. It is impossible to imagine every security threat that could ever exist and provide absolute protection against any attack. Java, in allowing a client to load and execute applets just when they are needed, provides a significant step forward in integrating the entire network into the computing system.

2.5 INFORMATION DISCOVERY

Browsing in the World Wide Web is fun and interesting, and often yields useful or important results. However, the size of the Web and its growth rate preclude complete searches by an individual. To get a reasonably complete report of what is available on any particular topic requires help from a computer-based service. A number of tools are available to do the searching, and more are emerging. In this section, we review some of these search engines and their distinguishing characteristics. More important, we describe the distinguishing characteristics so that new search tools can be categorized and evaluated for their appropriateness to various needs.

The goal of search tools is easy to state: help the user find the resources that meet a need. Realizing the goal is difficult. The sheer volume of material stored and the number of different locations where parts of any collection of information reside is overwhelming. A person cannot search it all; search tools cannot search it all in response to each request either. Search tools compromise on the need to have up-to-date information available to give to users in a reasonable amount of time by doing the searching on a periodic basis and storing locally a description of what was found. The differences among the various search tools include what locations they search, how frequently they update the local descriptions, and the nature of the descriptions they maintain.

The goal of search tools is easy to state: help the user find the resources that meet a need. Realizing the goal is difficult.

2.5.1 Anonymous FTP and Archie

Anonymous FTP was the first commonly available method to access files stored in the Internet and available for public use. Archie, the Internet Archive Server, was the first search tool. Archie is a service provided by about two dozen host systems in the world. Access to any of these servers will yield the same result except for minor variations due to catching one just after an update of its records and another just before the update. Archie searches for directory names and filenames that match the search string provided by the user without considering the content of the files, only the filename. Archie reports all the locations where a particular file resides and is available through anonymous FTP. The user must then choose from which location to retrieve the file and decide if any of the files listed sound promising for the purpose. If you want a particular file and you know its name, Archie is a very useful tool for finding it. If you want material on a particular topic, the response from Archie may help you find it, but will be more difficult to use than if you were searching for a particular file. For that reason, other search engines have preempted Archie as a tool for searching the resources of the Web. Appendix A illustrates the use of Archie and anonymous FTP.

2.5.2   Gopher and Veronica

Gopher servers, introduced in section 2.1, make information available by subject rather than by filenames. The interface is a menu, and the user selects paths to follow from the short descriptions provided. The number of Gopher servers exceeds 1000 [Com95]. To follow every link and search every machine for information on a topic of interest would be prohibitive. **Veronica** is a search tool that performs the search of Gopherspace in response to a user query. A user will find Veronica listed as an option on many Gopher menus. Choosing the Veronica service causes the server to ask for a search string. The user enters the words to be used in the search. Veronica then searches Gopher menus for matches. If the user wishes to search for vision, for example, Veronica will search all Gopher menus for the word vision. Veronica accepts more complex search strings than single words. If several words appear in the search string, Veronica will search for menu items that contain all the words. If the user wishes to search for menu items that contain any substring of the words in the search string, the words must be separated by or. For example, the search string fun games would match menu items that contain both the word fun and the word games. The search string fun or games would return all menu items that contain either the word fun or the word games. A string containing the word not will exclude menu choices that contain the word following not. For example, a search string vision not computer would exclude items about computer vision in the result. Like Archie, Veronica works by periodically contacting servers and accumulating information about resources available. Whereas Archie contacts all sites that provide anonymous FTP service, Veronica contacts all Gopher servers. Archie stores filenames; Veronica stores Gopher menu items.

2.5.3   Web Searchers and Indexing

Automatic searching of filenames and menu entries relieves the user of a formidable task in finding a desired resource. However, each requires that users judge whether a given resource is what they want based on minimal information—the filename or a short menu item description. What is the possibility of knowing the *contents* of a file before retrieving it?

Many search engines explore links found in the Web and summarize what they find. The search tool produces an index into a database of descriptive information about Web sites it has found. These databases are invaluable tools to users searching for specific Web

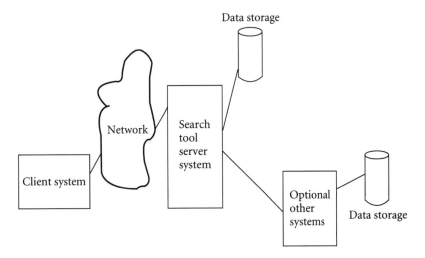

Figure 2.10. Client/ server interaction in a Web search

resources. Instead of searching the Web itself, the user sends a query to the search tool server site. The search tool uses the query to access its database of Web page descriptions. Figure 2.10 illustrates the general method.

The search engine builds and maintains the database completely independent of any user searches. As an independent process, the search tool looks for links to follow and collects pages to populate the database. The programs that go from site to site indexing pages are called **spiders** or **robots**. The information stored in the database varies from one search engine to another. Most tools extract the title of the page. Many store the first few lines of the page. All tools record the page's URL so a user of the search tool can access the page. Some tools retain all the text found on a page.

When a user sends a query to the search tool, the keywords entered become a query into the database. Some tools attempt to judge how well a particular page matches the search query entered by a user. Since most search tools do not have the actual page, it must base its judgment of the quality of the match on information about the page. Deciding what to store in order to make decisions related to the content of the page is a significant problem in the design of search tools. Another problem is knowing how to interpret what is retained from the page. What can an automatic search tool possibly tell us about the content of a page we might like to retrieve?

Knowing the contents of a file or document before retrieving it would be wonderful if we have a meaningful interpretation of *knowing*. Douglas Comer presents a description of the perils of searching for resources based on the words they contain [Com95]. In a particularly striking illustration, he notes that a document containing the sentence

```
This document has absolutely nothing to do with a bicycle, India,
or fishing.
```

would be retrieved by a search on any of the words bicycle, India, or fishing. The problem is that computers that make it possible to look at all the words in a document do not understand the words. A string match is a string match. Assuming that we have computers available that actually scan the contents of documents, how do we effectively select the documents meaningful in a particular context?

The Wide Area Information Servers (WAIS) use a three-tiered approach. First, a user must select a document collection to be used in searches. This narrows the field somewhat and increases the probability of getting useful results. Fortunately, users may invoke WAIS to search the list of document collection descriptions to find those that match an initial search string. Once the user has selected some document collections to search, he or she enters a search string for the document contents. The list of documents that contain the words in the search string will often be long. Seeing the list of titles may help the user refine the search string. Another search ensues, and a new list of documents is presented. This process may be repeated indefinitely. WAIS also provides a service that searches for other documents that it judges to be similar to one or more that the user selected. This is accomplished by comparing the words and their frequency of occurrence in the documents.

Like other search tools, WAIS searches locally stored information about the documents, not the documents themselves, to answer a user's query. Since the whole document, not just the title or a brief menu description, is subject to the WAIS search, some preprocessing of the document is required. WAIS stores a list of words from the document and a count of occurrences of each word. This allows WAIS to respond with the fact of a match and also the number of times the word occurs in the document. WAIS presents the search results ordered by the occurrence of the words in the search string. This storage greatly compresses the document, makes it easier to retrieve the information relative to the search, and facilitates the comparison of documents in terms of similarity of the words used. Of course, this method precludes searches on phrases since words are stored individually.

Word count can be expanded to include information about the expected frequency of a word. Advanced techniques for evaluating good matches of keywords with documents look at the relative frequency of the word in the document and compare that to a base standard body of text. If the word appears no more often in the target document than it does in the standard text, the target document is not a particularly good match for the word. If the word appears significantly more often in the target document than it does in the standard text, we presume that the target document is more relevant to a search on that word.

The number of search engines is growing rapidly. Some focus on particular kinds of Web sites; others try to be inclusive. Keeping the index and page descriptions up to date is a challenge. Some tools require Web page authors to notify them to become indexed; others search for new pages to enter into their lists. It is not uncommon to receive an e-mail message from someone who has discovered a page you have produced. If the page is accessible through the Web, it is almost certainly indexed somewhere.

A number of interesting problems remain to be solved in this area. The Web is a wonderful place to explore; "surfing" almost always yields pages worthy of discovery. The problem comes when you want to find something in particular or discover all that is accessible on a particular topic. A search limited to the engines that do the best possible matching of keywords to documents may miss very useful sites. If you use other search tools and learn about a much larger set of pages, you will often be overwhelmed with the number of responses—and most of the responses will be useless to you. More tools are needed to filter what is found and give you only the best resources to meet your needs. Researchers are working on intelligent agents—software that will act on behalf of a user to judge the quality of a resource, and will act independently of the user to find new materials and notify the user when they arrive. Imagine the day you find a message on your screen that says

A search limited to the engines that do the best possible matching of keywords to documents may miss very useful sites.

"Agent AUTOS reporting. I've found a new site that deals with ELECTRIC CARS and their PERFORMANCE. I judge the probability that it will interest you to be 78%. The URL is http://www.newcars.com/ electric/." Of course, the URL will be a link you can click on, or perhaps your agent will add the URL to a structured document that is your personal index to the Web. You will have other agents researching other topics as well. Your agents will update your indices to indicate when a page has changed or moved or disappeared.

The possibilities are great, and the work to be done will keep researchers and developers busy for a long time.

2.5.4 Metadata

Efforts to make machines understand the contents of Web pages sufficiently to match them to the needs of human users and programs are ongoing. One approach continues to advance the effectiveness of algorithms for this purpose; another effort approaches the problem from a different direction. Instead of developing ways to analyze the content of a page, this second approach requires that descriptive information be included in the page itself. The descriptive information resides in special tags and is called **metadata**.

Metadata facilitates searching by descriptive labels on pages. However, that is just the beginning of the possible uses of metadata. Metadata also encodes information about documents so that programs can read the metadata and make decisions about the documents. In addition to aiding searching, this allows automated agents to explore the Web interacting with various sites on behalf of a human user. For example, an agent might be set to find the best price for a particular product. Metadata could give the agent the information it needs so it does not have to interpret all the contents of a page trying to extract the product description and price from the other text and images. The effect of metadata for this kind of application is to change searching the Web from a machine-readable to a machine-understandable process.

Metadata architectures are under development for a number of applications. The overriding architecture is the **Resource Description Framework (RDF)**, a specification that is an ongoing effort within the W3C Metadata activity. A draft of the foundation for processing metadata was made public in February 1998. The encoding syntax is XML. After four more drafts, W3C RDF Model and Syntax Proposed Recommendation was released in January 1999. Current status of this work can be found at `http://www.w3.org/Metadata`. Expectations for this application of metadata include more focused searching, increased facility for automated agents to search or transact business for a user, and transformation of the Web to a more manageable and useful entity. RDF does not contain its own vocabulary for authoring metadata, but allows vocabularies for specific applications. For example, the **Platform for Internet Content Selection (PICS)** is a mechanism for communicating ratings of Web pages, and the **Dublin Core** is a digital library vocabulary. Consistent with the Dublin Core, the **Instructional Management System** project of EduCAUSE defines fields suitable for identifying education-oriented materials on the Web. A list of metadata fields from the IMS set appears in Figure 2.11, and the attributes associated with each field description appear in Figure 2.12.

Metadata will only add to the chaos on the Web unless the definition of metadata categories and tags is coordinated and well understood. Another important factor in the effect of metadata will be the acceptance by the communities the tags intend to serve. If authors

Author or Creator	Title	Pedagogy
Coverage	Agent	Platform
Date	Availability Date	Prerequisites
Description	Concepts	Presentation
Format	Container Type	Price Code
Language	Expiration Date	Publication Date
Other Contributors	Granularity	Role
Publisher	Interactivity Level	Scheme
Relation	Keywords	SizeOf
Resource Identifier	Last Modified Date	Structure
Resource Type	Learning Level	Use Rights
Rights Management	Location	Use Time
Source	Meta-Meta-data	Version
Objectives	User Support	
Subject (note: Dublin Core refers to this as Subject and Keywords)		

Figure 2.11. IMS fields for educational materials

Full desriptions and explanations of these fields are available at the IMS project Web site: `http://www.imsproject.org/textdictionary.html`

Name: the name of the field.

Definition: a description of what the field represents.

Obligation: an indication of whether or not the field must have a valid value. A "mandatory" obligation means that the field must have a value; a "conditional" obligation means that the presence of a value depends upon the context; an "optional" obligation means that the field does not need to have a value. If the obligation is "mandatory," then a default value must be indicated. *NOTE: The obligation attribute refers to the obligation of the field's value not to the field itself. Obligation in this dictionary refers to the base type metadata set.

Datatype: a description of the digital format in which the field value is stored (string, alphanumeric, etc.). Some fields may have structured datatypes.

Length: number of characters or bytes.

Default: the field value to be used if the metadata cataloger enters no value.

Permitted values: a description of the values that are consistent with the field definition and the datatype. Some fields will include a defined vocabulary list of permitted values. The vocabulary list will be given here. This attribute also indicates if there can be more than one value for a given field.

Comment: Helpful explanation of the field and its values may be optionally provided. This may include the purpose of the field's value. Examples of the field may be provided here.

Figure 2.12. ISO 11179 standard attributes for each field in the IMS metadata set do not use the tags to describe their pages, the beneficial effects will not occur. The primary motivation to include the tags in a page is the possibility of more searchers finding the page. As the tags become more integral to search engine strategies and the design of autonomous agents, there will be increasing motivation to include the tags in pages. Searchers will find pages that match their needs—or at least will find pages whose tags indicate that they match the need. Unfortunately, unscrupulous authors will deliberately mislabel pages in order to get more attention. Dealing with this human issue remains a challenge.

SUMMARY

In this chapter, we introduced the World Wide Web: a network-based application that is widely available and easy to use. We identified the principal features of HTML, a language for describing hypertext documents, and observed the role of a browser in displaying HTML documents. We learned that an HTML document may contain links to other documents, and to other types of resources—images, video, sound, and embedded applications called applets. We briefly looked at several protocols used to transfer resources from one system to another. We also learned about the use of forms and form servers for general application development.

We introduced the application-dependent tool, metadata, that has an increasing number of uses. In particular, metadata facilitates the search on descriptive labels that are distinct from, but intimately related to, the contents of a document. With metadata, it is no longer necessary to search for the appearance of one or more words or phrases in a document. Rather, the search can be on a description of content.

The key element in all this is HTTP—an application layer protocol that deals with the communication requirements of applications built with HTML. Though HTTP was initially built on top of network services from the TCP/IP family, it can just as well run over the ISO protocol stack or any other. By the same token, users of HTTP and the applications it supports are insulated from the complexities of lower-layer network operation.

In the chapters that follow, we will look at other applications built on networks: electronic mail, virtual terminals, remote file access, and directory services. Before we look at those applications, we will consider the common characteristics and widely recognized model of network software, the OSI reference model. We follow that with a language, ASN.1, for describing the information exchanged between cooperating applications, and then introduce some very common components of network software. We jump-started our study of network application development by introducing the World Wide Web and the resources it offers. As we get into the details of what is needed to make network-based applications work, keep in mind the Web and what it offers. It will be enough to keep your motivation high.

EXERCISES

1. Using a system connected to the World Wide Web and a browser, find Web pages with the following items. Look at the source document for the pages and see if you find an HTML code that you do not recognize. Can you determine from the context and from the effect you see in the page what the meaning of the tag is? Can you use the tag on a page of your own?

- An image of a famous artwork
- Words to a song
- A historical document
- Material about a current news story
- A poem
- Principal exports of some country
- A London or New York theater guide
- Images from space
- Information about rain forests
- Recent Supreme Court decisions

2. Create your own list of things to search for, using those in Exercise 1 as a starting point. Exchange lists with someone else, and challenge each other to find the items on the lists. Use these exercises (1, 2) to evaluate search tools available. What characteristics of search tools can you detect? Can you identify specific weaknesses? surprising capabilities?

3. Make a Web page for yourself. Include a variety of information about yourself and appropriate links to other Web pages. Some examples: identify your hometown and link to a page that describes that town or city. Say what sports you like to play or teams you follow and include a link to related Web pages. Identify an issue about which you feel strongly and link to further information on the topic. Indicate what organizations you belong to and link to their Web pages.

4. Modify the form in Figure 2.4 to show

```
Basic demographics: O Male O Female
```

on separate lines.

5. Create a simple survey form and a process to receive the data. Return to the form user a summary of the data on the form.

6. Create an application to support voting. Require each voter to provide identification and a password. Tally the votes and generate a current status report.

7. Create an application that uses an HTML form to provide an interface to a database. (You will need an existing database. Your form will present options or text input areas. Your server process will receive data from the form, make a query to the database, receive the result, and send it back to the form user.)

8. PICS (Platform for Internet Content Selection) is an infrastructure for associating labels with Web material. Originally intended to support parents and educators who wished to restrict access to some kinds of sites, PICS has become useful for privacy and authentication use. Investigate PICS and associated filtering tools, and report on their current status. There is debate about the definition and use of tools for blocking access to categories of sites. One side says it is appropriate for parents and schools to control the kinds of material children access and that others should be able to avoid the kinds of material they don't want to see. Others say that by making restrictions possible, such systems support censorship by allowing countries to lock out material they don't want their people to see. Take a position and research the topic. Defend your position in light of possible arguments on the other side. Challenge someone with the other view to a debate on the topic. Find information about PICS at the World Wide Web Consortium (W3C) Web site: www.w3c.org.

9. Install and configure a Web server. You can learn a lot about how Web-based applications work by seeing the details of a Web server. Acquire a copy of a Web server such as Apache

(www.apache.org), and install it on a PC running Windows. (You don't need any special kind of computer to install a Web server. A direct network connection with a permanent IP address will be needed to allow others to connect to your server, but you can install it on any system.) Look through the files downloaded from the Apache site. Print out the files in the config directory and look through the choices required for installation. There are default values for almost every entry. Decide how you would like your server to work. Will you restrict Web documents to certain directories or give visitors access to all of your system? Will you allow processes that respond to forms to have general user privileges? What other choices can you make? Are you inclined to the widest possible access, or are you primarily concerned with system security?

CHAPTER 3

ASN.1

KEY CONCEPTS

- Purpose of ASN.1
- Example
- Abstract Syntax Notation

One of the fundamental problems confronting users communicating with different systems is the efficient transfer of data in such a way that the data received is the same data transmitted. In the OSI model, the representation of data types and structures to facilitate this transfer is a function of the Application layer; the encoding of the data into a specific sequence of bits for transfer is attributed to the Presentation layer. This separation of functions enables the Application layer to deal only with the content and structure of the data, leaving the choice of representation to the Presentation layer. Consistent with that separation, we introduce an abstract notation for data values and structures in this chapter, prior to examining the Application layer services in the next group of chapters. The notation introduced is called **ASN.1 (Abstract Syntax Notation One)**. We defer discussion of the standards for converting ASN.1 described data, the Basic Encoding Rules (BER), until Chapter 10.

This chapter begins by identifying the purpose of ASN.1 and illustrating why it is used by means of an example. We introduce the basic unit of ASN.1, the module, and include significant aspects of ASN.1 syntax, primarily through examples. Additional examples will appear in later chapters. You will discover that learning ASN.1 is similar to learning the syntax of a high-level programming language.

3.1 PURPOSE OF ASN.1

ASN.1 is a fundamental tool for use by applications. It provides the ability to describe the information that will be exchanged independent of the way that information is represented on each of the communicating systems.

ASN.1 provides application and protocol developers a high-level tool, essentially a data definition language, for defining protocol syntax and the information that an application exchanges between systems. The ASN.1 description of data is converted into data definitions in the language used locally for the application development. The syntax of ASN.1 has much in common with the declaration part of a programming language in defining, declaring, and assigning values to data types and for creating complex types from simple ones.

3.2 EXAMPLE

The inventory example in Chapter 1 presents an appropriate environment to illustrate the situation. Suppose data on specific items in store A are sent to store B, which uses a different system and possibly a different programming language. Each system might be flexible and large enough to handle the communication by translating each representation of the data into the representation in the other system. However, this approach would become untenable as the number of stores with different systems increased or as systems changed at individual stores over time. A better solution is to make communication independent of change. This can be achieved by using a defined set of rules, an **abstract syntax**, for representing the data types and structures of the items stored in the inventory database, and another set of rules for transmitting the data, a **transfer syntax**. These sets of rules would be common for all systems. Each system would then require the capability to translate the abstract representation into a realization for the system.

More specifically, assume the item can be represented by the four-tuple [PN, Q, WP, SP], for Part Number (a string), Quantity (an integer), Wholesale Price (a real), and Sale Price (a real), respectively. Assume also that an abstract syntax has been defined for these variables and their data types. A C program in store A's system and a Java language program in store B's system include references to the item. Before the program is run, a compiler in store A's system translates the abstract representation into a concrete syntax consisting of a C structure (as if it were part or all of the declaration section) and a set of encoding/decoding procedures. A corresponding application process is established in store B's system using Java.

When the data are sent from store A, the encoding procedure is called and produces an encoded version to send to store B's system. There, the decoding method is called and the Java structure is stored. Although programmers in stores A and B could develop their own syntax and encoding rules, they would be better off using the ASN.1 abstract syntax and BER transfer syntax, established as international standards.

3.3 ABSTRACT SYNTAX NOTATION

ASN.1 (Abstract Syntax Notation One) is the international standard for representing data types and structures. CCITT published the first version of the standard as X.409 in 1984 after approximately four years of effort. A newer version of ASN.1 resulting from a cooperative venture of CCITT and ISO is specified in X.208 (1988) of CCITT and ISO 8824 (1990). There are also amendments (ISO 8824 PDAM 2) titled Part 1: Basic ASN.1, and three additional parts: Information Object Specification, Constraint Specification, and Parameterization of ASN.1. Enhanced versions are being drafted.

The standards documents contain detailed specifications of ASN.1, including definitions given as productions in Backus-Naur Form (BNF). The most common features of the abstract syntax are included in the following sections.

3.3.1   Modules and Assignments

Modules

The fundamental unit of ASN.1 is the **module**. The sole purpose of a module is to name a collection of type definitions or value definitions (assignments) that constitute a data specification. A **type definition** is used to define and name a new type by means of a **type assignment** and a **value definition** is used to define and name a specific value, when it is necessary, by means of a **value assignment**. The only format constraint on type or value assignments in a module is that each must be on a new line.

Figure 3.1 contains an example module. It is defined as a *module reference* InventoryList, followed by an optional *object identifier* value 1 2 0 0 6 1 (see section 3.3.2.), followed by the keyword DEFINITIONS, followed by the optional *tag default* (not included in the example), followed by the assignment character sequence ::= , followed by the keywords BEGIN and END bracketing the *module body*.

Type Assignment

A type assignment consists of a **type reference** (the name of the type), the character sequence ::= ("is defined as"), and the appropriate type. Each of the components must be separated by at least one space. The type reference must be a character string consisting of only uppercase and lowercase letters, digits 0 to 9, or a hyphen (-). None of the other ASN.1 characters : ; = , ¡ . ( ) [ ] ' " may be used. A type reference must begin with an uppercase letter, not end with a hyphen, and not contain two consecutive hyphens. Comments in ASN.1 begin with two consecutive hyphens and end either with two consecutive

```
InventoryList {1 2 0 0 6 1}  DEFINITIONS  ::=
  BEGIN
    {
      ItemId    ::=  SEQUENCE
        {
          partnumber              IA5String,
          quantity                INTEGER,
          wholesaleprice          REAL,
          saleprice               REAL
        }
      StoreLocation    ::=    ENUMERATED
        {
          Baltimore    (0),
          Philadelphia    (1),
          Washington    (2)
        }
      }
  END
```

Figure 3.1. Example of an ASN.1 module

hyphens or the end of a line. In the module body in Figure 3.1, the name ItemId has type SEQUENCE and StoreLocation has type ENUMERATED. There are four component values in the sequence: partnumber, quantity, wholesaleprice, and saleprice. StoreLocation has the three component values Baltimore, Philadelphia, and Washington.

Value Assignment

A value assignment consists of a **value reference** (the name of the value), the type of the value, ::= ("is assigned the value"), and a valid value notation. A value reference must begin with a lowercase letter, but otherwise has the same syntax as a type assignment. For example,

```
gadget  ItemId  ::=
  {
    partnumber       "7685B2",
    quantity         73,
    wholesaleprice   13.50,
    saleprice        24.95
  )
```

defines gadget as a value of type ItemId.

3.3.2 Built-in Types

ASN.1 has built-in types that are **simple** and **structured**. Structured types are comprised of **component types**, each of which is a simple or structured type. A **user-defined** type is comprised of simple and structured types. ASN.1 also has another category of types called **useful**, which provide standard definitions for a small number of commonly used types.

Simple Types

ASN.1's built-in simple types are shown in Figure 3.2. The universal class number (tag) and a typical use of each type are also included.

Type BOOLEAN takes values TRUE and FALSE. Usually, the type reference for BOOLEAN describes the true state. For example, Female ::= BOOLEAN is preferable to Gender ::= BOOLEAN.

Type INTEGER takes any of the infinite set of integer values. Its syntax is similar to programming languages such as C or Pascal. It has an additional notation that names some of the possible values of the integer. For example,

```
ColorType ::= INTEGER
    {
        red     (0)
        white   (1)
        blue    (2)
    }
```

indicates that the ColorType is an INTEGER and its values 0, 1, and 2 are named red, white, and blue, respectively. The ColorType could also have any of the other valid integer values, such as 4 or −62.

Simple Types	Tag	Typical Use
BOOLEAN	1	Model logical, two-state variable values
INTEGER	2	Model integer variable values
BIT STRING	3	Model binary data of arbitrary length
OCTET STRING	4	Model binary data whose length is a multiple of eight
NULL	5	Indicate effective absence of a sequence element
OBJECT IDENTIFIER	6	Name information objects
REAL	9	Model real variable values
ENUMERATED	10	Model values of variables with at least three states
CHARACTER STRING	$\star$	Model values that are strings of characters from a specified character set

Figure 3.2. Simple types in ASN.1, their universal tags, and uses; a * indicates more than one tag

Type BIT STRING takes values that are an ordered sequence of zero or more bits. The bit sequence is either a binary or hexadecimal string delimited by single quotes followed by B or H, respectively. For example, '11010001'B or '82DA6'H are valid values of BIT STRING. The length of the string of bits must be a multiple of four when hexadecimal is used. BIT STRING also has a form similar to INTEGER, but the numbers in parentheses indicate location in the string of bits. For example, the type notation

```
Occupation  ::=  BIT STRING
     {
         clerk      (0)
         editor     (1)
         artist     (2)
         writer     (3)
     }
```

names the first bit clerk, the second bit editor, and so on. Strings of bits can then be written by listing the named bits that are set to 1. For example, (editor, artist) and '0110'B are two representations for the same value of Occupation.

Type OCTET STRING takes values that are an ordered sequence of zero or more 8-bit octets. The sequence is written in the same form as a BIT STRING sequence. Thus, '1101000100011010'B and '82DA'H are valid values of OCTET STRING.

Type NULL takes only one value, NULL. It can be used as a place marker, but other alternatives are more common.

Type OBJECT IDENTIFIER names information objects (for example, abstract syntaxes or ASN.1 modules). The type notation requires the keywords OBJECT IDENTIFIER. The named information object is a node on an **object identifier tree** that is managed at the international level. ISO, CCITT, or any other organization is allowed a subtree that the organization defines. On each level j of the object identifier tree, nodes are numbered $0, 1, 2, \ldots, k_j$. A list of positive numbers, enclosed in braces and ordered by level starting from the root, uniquely identifies an information object at a node of the tree. This

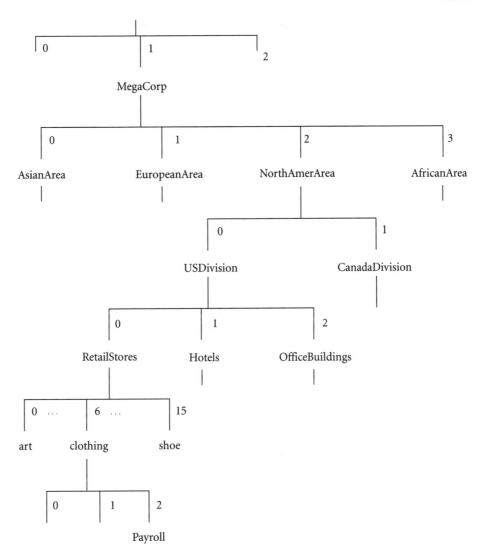

Figure 3.3. Sample object identifier tree

ordered list of positive numbers delimited by braces is the value notation for type OBJECT IDENTIFIER. Figure 3.3 illustrates the concept of an object identifier tree. For example, in the subtree with root RetailStores, the information object payroll has local value 0 6 2. More formally, if

```
ClothingType   ::=   OBJECT IDENTIFIER
```

then

```
payroll  ClothingType  ::=  {0 6 2}.
```

If the retail stores are considered as part of an international MegaCorp, then 1 2 0 0 6 2 uniquely identifies payroll.

Type REAL takes values that are the machine representation of a real number, namely, the triplet (m, b, e), where m is the mantissa (a signed number), b the base (2 or 10), and e the exponent (a signed number). For example, the representation of the value 3.14 for the variable Pi, declared as Pi ::= REAL, can be (314, 10, -2). Three special values, PLUS-INFINITY, 0, and MINUS-INFINITY, are also allowed.

Type ENUMERATED is similar to the INTEGER type, but names specific values only. For example,

```
ColorType ::= ENUMERATED
    {
        red      (0)
        white    (1)
        blue     (2)
    }
```

has the same interpretation as in the type INTEGER example near the beginning of this section, except that ColorType can take only the values specifically in the list, that is, no other values than 0 for red, 1 for white, or 2 for blue.

Type CHARACTER STRING takes values that are strings of characters from some defined (ISO- or CCITT-registered) character set. Type references and specifications of the characters in their strings are given in Figure 3.4. Also included are short labels, called tags, that are assigned to character string types for machine readability. The value notation for each character string type is a string of characters from the corresponding character set delimited by double quotation marks. For example, if Address is of type PrintableString, then Villanova, PA 19085 is an Address value.

Structured Types

ASN.1's built-in structured types are shown in Figure 3.5. The universal class number (tag) and a typical use of each type are also included.

Character String Type	Tag	Character Set
NumericString	18	0,1,2,3,4,5,6,7,8,9, and space
PrintableString	19	Uppercase and lowercase letters, digits, space, apostrophe, left and right parentheses, plus sign, comma, hyphen, full stop, solidus, colon, equal sign, question mark
TeletexString (T61String)	20	The Teletex character set in CCITT's T61, space, and delete
VideotexString	21	The Videotex character set in CCITT's T.100 and T.101, space, and delete
VisibleString (ISO646String)	26	Printing character sets of international ASCII, and space
LA5String	22	International Alphabet 5 (International ASCII)
GraphicString	25	All registered G sets, and space
GeneralString	27	All registered C and G sets, space, and delete

Figure 3.4. Character string types

Structured Types	Tag	Typical Use
SEQUENCE	16	Model an ordered collection of variables of different types
SEQUENCE OF	16	Model an ordered collection of variables of same type
SET	17	Model an unordered collection of variables of different types
SET OF	17	Model an unordered collection of variables of the same type
CHOICE	★	Specifies a collection of distinct types from which to choose one type
SELECTION	★	Select a component type from a specified CHOICE type
ANY	★	Enable an application to specify the type

Figure 3.5. Structured types in ASN.1, their universal tags, and uses; * indicates more than one tag

Type SEQUENCE is an ordered list of zero or more component types. The type notation requires braces around the list and permits a local identifier preceding the list to act as the name of the sequence type. The identifier increases readability. There are two ways to specify that a component type is optional in the ordered list: using OPTIONAL after the component type and using DEFAULT followed by a value after the component type. When DEFAULT is used, the specified value is assumed whenever the type is absent from the list. Any of the component types can be an embedded sequence, in which case COMPOSED OF precedes the embedded sequence. The value notation for each sequence type is the list of component values within braces. For readability, it is recommended that the component identifier precedes each ordered list of values. For example,

```
{
 airline    "American",
 flight     "1106",
 seats      { 320, 107, 213 },
 airport    { origin  "BWI", destination  "LAX" },
 crewsize   10
 }
```

or

```
{
 "American", "1106", { 320, 107, 213 }, { "BWI", "LAX" }, 10
}
```

represents the same instance of the sequence type

```
AirlineFlight  ::=  SEQUENCE
   {
     airline   IA5String,
     flight    NumericString,
     seats     SEQUENCE
                  {
                    maximum    INTEGER,
                    occupied   INTEGER,
                    vacant     INTEGER
                  },
```

89

```
airport    SEQUENCE
               {
                 origin                 IA5String,
                 stop1         [0]      IA5String  OPTIONAL,
                 stop2         [1]      IA5String  OPTIONAL,
                 destination            IA5String
               },
    crewsize ENUMERATED
               {
                   six      (6),
                   eight    (8),
                   ten      (10)
               },
    cancel    BOOLEAN      DEFAULT FALSE
   }.
```

This instance of AirlineFlight indicates that American Airlines flight 1106 flies nonstop from Baltimore–Washington Airport to Los Angeles. The airliner requires a crew of 10 people, has 320 seats, of which 107 are filled and 213 are empty. The flight is not canceled. Two components, Stop1 and Stop2 of the sequence type airport are tagged with the context-specific tags [0] and [1] (see section 3.3.3) to avoid ambiguity due to consecutive optional components not having distinct types. Without the tags, the definition of airport would be invalid in ASN.1.

Type SEQUENCE OF is similar to SEQUENCE, except that all values in the ordered list must be of the same type. For example, the seats type in the example could be SEQUENCE OF INTEGER instead of SEQUENCE.

Type SET takes values that are unordered lists of component types. The type and value notations for SET are similar to SEQUENCE, except that the type of each component must be distinct from all others and the values can be in any order. For example,

```
{"Maggie", 4, TRUE}   {TRUE, "Maggie", 4}   {4, TRUE,"Maggie"}
```

are three representations of the same instance of

```
Person  ::=   SET
    {
      name       IA5String,
      age        INTEGER,
      female     BOOLEAN
    }.
```

In the type SEQUENCE example, using SET instead of SEQUENCE for the seats type would be invalid in ASN.1 because at least two of the components (all of them in this case) are of the same type. In particular, if the type were SET, then 180, 0, 180 and 180, 180, 0 would be the same value and the receiving system could not determine whether all seats were filled or empty.

Type SET OF takes values that are unordered lists of a single type. The SEQUENCE type example above would be valid if the seats type were SET OF INTEGER instead of SEQUENCE, but would be ambiguous in some instances, such as in the example of the preceding paragraph.

Type CHOICE takes one value from a specified list of distinct types. The alternative types are contained in braces and may be preceded by local identifiers. The value notation is that for the type chosen. For example, each of the three values,

```
(1) nothing  TRUE,   (2) car   "Lincoln",   (3) cash  25000
```

is a valid instance of

```
Prize  ::=  CHOICE
  {
   car         IA5String,
   cash        INTEGER,
   nothing     BOOLEAN
  }.
```

Type SELECTION enables the user to choose a component type from a specified CHOICE type. The less than symbol < must precede the name of the CHOICE type. For example, the component cash of CHOICE type Prize can appear in a specified SEQUENCE type

```
Winner  ::=  SEQUENCE
  {
   lastName    VisibleString,
   ssn         VisibleString,
   cash   <    Prize
  }
```

with value notation

```
{
 lastName     'AUSTING',
 ssn          '222334444',
 cash         5000
}
```

Type ANY, without further specification, is incomplete. It must be supplemented by any valid ASN.1 type defined in another module. ANY can be used, for example, in a user data field definition within a PDU. The application then specifies the type. The value notation for the type notation ANY is the specified type followed by its value. For example,

```
{
  author       "Austen",
  reference    IA5String   "ISBN0669123757"
}
```

and

```
{
  author       "Shakespeare",
  reference    INTEGER     1988
}
```

are two possible values of

```
Novel  ::=  SEQUENCE
   {
     author       IA5String,
     reference    ANY
   }
```

The ASN.1 standard allows an alternative, ANY DEFINED BY, within type SEQUENCE or SET only. The type notation is ANY DEFINED BY followed by an identifier, a nonoptional component of the SEQUENCE whose type is either INTEGER or OBJECT IDENTIFIER. The identifier acts as a pointer to where the type is defined. For example, the definition

```
Novel  =  SEQUENCE
   {
     author            IA5String,
     CitationType      INTEGER,
     reference         ANY DEFINED BY CitationType
   },
```

requires a list of CitationTypes defined elsewhere that specifies the ASN.1 type for each permitted value of INTEGER. In particular, if the list defined 0, 1, and 2 as IA5String, INTEGER, and PrintableString, respectively, then novel could have values such as

```
{
 author          "Austen",
 CitationType  0,
 reference  IA5String   "ISBN0669123757"
}
or
{
 author          "Austen",
 CitationType  1,
 reference  INTEGER  1988
}
or
{
 author          "Austen",
 CitationType  2,
 reference  PrintableString   "Jones & Bartlett"
}
```

3.3.3 Tagged

Type TAGGED is used to enable the receiving system to correctly decode values from several data types that a protocol determines may be transmitted at any given time. TAGGED has no value notation of its own. Its type notation consists of three elements: a user-defined tag, possibly followed by IMPLICIT or EXPLICIT, followed by the value notation of the type being tagged.

The user-defined tag consists of a **class** and **class number** contained in braces. Class is UNIVERSAL, APPLICATION, PRIVATE, or CONTEXT-SPECIFIC. The UNIVERSAL class is restricted to the ASN.1 built-in types (see Figures 3.2 and 3.5). It defines an application-independent data type that must be distinguishable from all other data types. The other three classes are user defined. The APPLICATION class distinguishes data types that have a wide, scattered use within a particular presentation context. PRIVATE distinguishes data types within a particular organization or country. CONTEXT-SPECIFIC distinguishes members of a sequence or set, the alternatives of a CHOICE, or universally tagged set members. Only the class number appears in braces for this data type; the term CONTEXT-SPECIFIC does not appear.

For example, suppose seats in AirlineFlight of section 3.5 were of type SET rather than sequence. Three different ways to specify seats by tagging and one (invalid) way without tagging are shown in Figure 3.6.

As we indicated in the discussion of type SET, the representation in (a) is invalid in ASN.1 because its instances can be ambiguous. The tagging in representations (b), (c), and (d) overcome the problem and allow instances to be transmitted uniquely. IMPLICIT in (c) indicates that an original tag is replaced by any of the three user-defined tags. EXPLICIT tagging would be appropriate when strong-type-checking is more important than compact representation; it can be used when the original tag is accompanied by a user-defined tag.

```
a)      seats SET
        {
        maximum             INTEGER,
        occupied            INTEGER,
        vacant              INTEGER
        }


b)      seats SET
        {
        maximum             [APPLICATION 0]  INTEGER,
        occupied            [APPLICATION 1]  INTEGER,
        vacant              [APPLICATION 2]  INTEGER
        }


c)      seats SET
        {
        maximum             [APPLICATION 0]  IMPLICIT  INTEGER,
        occupied            [APPLICATION 1]  IMPLICIT  INTEGER,
        vacant              [APPLICATION 2]  IMPLICIT  INTEGER
        }


d)      seats SET
        {
        maximum             [0]  INTEGER,
        occupied            [1]  INTEGER,
        vacant              [2]  INTEGER
        }
```

Figure 3.6. Using tagging to specify SET components; note that (a) is invalid

The context-specific tagging in (d) is similar to the APPLICATION class tagging in (b) except that the class of the tag is not specifically transmitted.

3.3.4 Useful Types

Date and time data are commonly transferred along with other data types. Rather than have the user define a type to model date and time data, ASN.1 provides a standard syntax. This standard notation is not only useful, but also ensures uniformity. ASN.1 defines two **useful types** for transferring time and date data, **GeneralizedTime** and **UTCTime**. Two other useful types, **ObjectDescriptor** and **EXTERNAL**, were added to the standards in 1988. Type ObjectDescriptor is used with the OBJECT IDENTIFIER type and takes values that are human-readable strings delimited by quotes. The type has seldom been implemented, and will not be discussed further.

Time

Consistent representations of time often are critical to effective interoperation between distributed sections of an application. The formats GeneralizedTime and UTCTime define two representations, which vary in the level of detail provided.

Type GeneralizedTime takes values of the year, month, day, hour, time, minute, second, and second fraction in any of three forms:

1. Local time only. YYYYMMDDHHMMSS.fff, where the optional fff is accurate to three decimal places.
2. Universal time (UTC time) only. YYYYMMDDHHMMSS.fffZ.
3. Difference between local and UTC times. YYYYMMDDHHMMSS.fff+-HHMM.

The type notation is the keyword GeneralizedTime. For example, if

```
CurrentTime  ::=  GeneralizedTime
```

then any of the following three values of CurrentTime are valid: 19991231235959.999 is 1/1000 second before the end of the 20th century local time; 19991231205959.999Z is the universal time three hours different from the above local time; and 19991231235959.999 + 0300 indicates the local time is three hours ahead of universal time.

Type UTCTime takes values with the same three forms as GeneralizedTime, except the accuracy is to one minute or one second. Thus, UTCTime has no fff, and the SS is optional in the three forms. The value notation is the keyword UTCTime. For example, if

```
NewTime  ::=  UTCTime
```

then 199912312359 or 19991231235959 is a valid local time value of NewTime.

EXTERNAL

Type EXTERNAL takes values that communicate both data and how the data should be interpreted. The type of the data need not be an ASN.1 type. EXTERNAL is used, for example, in the Association Control Service Element (ACSE) that is common to all OSI applications (see Chapter 4) to model a variable whose type is either unspecified or specified elsewhere. There is no restriction on the notation to specify the type.

ISO 8824 contains the following definition of the EXTERNAL type:

```
EXTERNAL   ::=   [UNIVERSAL 8] IMPLICIT SEQUENCE
   {
    direct-reference  OBJECT IDENTIFIER OPTIONAL,
    indirect-reference  INTEGER OPTIONAL,
    data-value-descriptor  ObjectDescriptor  OPTIONAL,
    encoding  CHOICE
               {single-ASN1-type  [0] ANY,
                octet-aligned     [1] IMPLICIT OCTET STRING,
                arbitrary         [2] IMPLICIT BIT STRING}
   }
```

Because abstract syntax names are transferred as OBJECT IDENTIFIER names and Presentation Context Identifiers (PCI) as INTEGER names, Presentation layer negotiation makes at least one of direct-reference or indirect-reference mandatory. Each abstract syntax name identified by the calling P-user (sender) is given a PCI. Its transfer syntax is then negotiated, connection is established, and data values and their PCIs (for interpretation of the data values) are then transmitted.

When the data value is an instance of a single ASN.1 data type, the standard encoding rules for that data type apply. Otherwise, the sender has a choice of octet-aligned or arbitrary if the data value is an integral number of octets, but can use only arbitrary if the data value is not an integral multiple of octets.

For example, suppose that, during negotiation, the PCI of 7 is assigned to a string type defined by a nonASN.1 standard and that

```
String  ::=  EXTERNAL
```

is a definition in ASN.1. Then an instance of String is

```
{
 indirect-reference   7,
 encoding    arbitrary   BIT STRING
    '27ABC63'H
}
```

where arbitrary is chosen for encoding, and the hexadecimal string is a representation of the actual string transmitted.

3.3.5 Additional Features

ASN.1 defines a **subtype** notation and value sets, a method for handling recursion in data types, and a macro facility. Subtypes and recursion are used more frequently than macros. We include macros because of their role in common service elements of the Application layer discussed in Chapter 4.

Subtype Notation and Value Sets

Frequently, we encounter situations where only a portion of a finite set or sequence is of concern. For example, we may be interested only in the divisors of 24, values between two

Subtype Form	Example
SingleValue	Divisors_of_6 :: = INTEGER (1| 2| 3| 6)
ContainedSubtype	Divisions_of_18 :: = INTEGER (INCLUDES Divisors_of_6 | 9 | 18)
ValueRange	TeenAgeYears :: = (11 .. 19)
PermittedAlphabet	Boolean Value :: = LA5String (FROM ("T"| "F")
SizeConstraint	BaseballTeamRoster :: = SET SIZE (1..25) OF PlayerNames

Figure 3.7. Examples of ASN.1 subtypes

integers, or the first 9 people in a queue. ASN.1 allows **subtyping**, which enables a user to specify values within the range of values of a type, in much the same way as the syntax of a high-level programming language. The value notation of a subtype is that of the parent type. The type notation is the union of the value sets within parentheses and separated by the symbol |, which has the same meaning, "or", as in BNF.

ASN.1 defines six forms of notation for value sets. Examples of five of them—*SingleValue, ContainedSubtype, ValueRange, PermittedAlphabet*, and *SizeConstraint*—are in Figure 3.7. The sixth form, *InnerType*, is discussed separately.

The keywords INCLUDES, FROM, and SIZE are required in the subtype syntax. INCLUDES must be followed by the value set of the parent type. In the example, the divisors of 18 are 18, 9, and all the divisors of 6 (namely, 1, 2, 3, and 6 specified in the example of SingleValue). FROM must be followed by a subset of the specified character string. SIZE must be followed by the lower- and upper-end values of an interval. Values of MIN or MAX indicate that the range extends as far in that direction as the parent type allows. The interval is closed unless the symbol < follows the lower-end value and precedes the upper-end value, in which case the interval is open.

InnerType constrains the value ranges of structured types. In particular, it can change an OPTIONAL component of a structured type into one that is always PRESENT or always ABSENT. The type notation requires the keywords WITH COMPONENTS followed by the components of the structured type, each component with or without a constraint. For example, if AirlineFlight is the SEQUENCE structured type defined in section 3.3.2, then the following definition allows only those flights of American and Delta Airlines that are nonstop to Los Angeles (LAX), have no more than 200 passengers, and are at least half filled:

```
NonStopFlights ::= AirlineFlight
                ( WITH COMPONENTS
                  {
                   airline ("American" | "Delta"),
        flight,
        nonstopseats ::= seats
                ( WITH COMPONENTS
                  {
                   maximum   (0..200),
                   occupied  (100..200),
                   vacant    (0..100)
                  }
                ),
```

```
nonstopairport ::= airport
                ( WITH COMPONENTS
                 {
                  origin,
                  stop1          [0]     ABSENT,
                  stop2          [1]     ABSENT,
                  destination            ("LAX")
                 }
                ),
      crewsize,
      cancel
      }.
```

Figure 3.8 displays the subtype value sets that can be applied to specified ASN.1 built-in types. A Y entry indicates that the notation of the value set named in the column header can be applied to the parent type named in the row header or to a type derived from that parent type by tagging.

Recursion

Recursion, a common feature in high-level languages, is also a feature in ASN.1. Data types, such as a set of sets, records with one or more components being a record, linked lists, and trees, are better understood when viewed as recursive structures. ASN.1 allows definitions of these kinds of data types and values to include recursion. For example, the linked list of integer values, each of whose nodes can be a linked list of integer values, is specified

```
LinkedList  ::=  SEQUENCE
        {
        label      IA5String,
        value      CHOICE
```

Type	Single Value	Contained Subtype	Value Range	Size Range	Alphabet Limitation	Inner Substring
Boolean	Y	Y	N	N	N	N
Integer	Y	Y	Y	N	N	N
Enumerated	Y	Y	N	N	N	N
Real	Y	Y	Y	N	N	N
Object Identifier	Y	Y	N	N	N	N
Bit String	Y	Y	N	Y	N	N
Octet String	Y	Y	N	Y	N	N
Character String	Y	Y	N	Y	Y	N
Sequence	Y	Y	N	N	N	Y
Sequence-of	Y	Y	N	Y	N	Y
Set	Y	Y	N	N	N	Y
Set-of	Y	Y	N	Y	N	Y
Any	Y	Y	N	N	N	N
Choice	Y	Y	N	N	N	Y

Figure 3.8. Applicability of ASN.1 subtype value sets

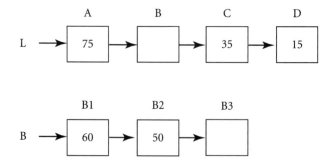

Figure 3.9. Instance of a linked list of linked lists

```
{nodevalue       INTEGER   OPTIONAL,
 node            SEQUENCE OF LinkedList OPTIONAL
 }
}
```

Assume L, shown in Figure 3.9, is an instance of LinkedList consisting of four nodes labeled A, B, C, D, where B is a linked list of three nodes B1, B2, B3, and B3 is a linked list of two nodes B31, B32. Header nodes are not included in this example. Then, the instance can be represented

```
{
 label     "L",
 value     node
   {
      {label      "A", value nodevalue 75},
      {label      "B",
       value      node
         {
            {label    "B1", value nodevalue 60},
            {label    "B2", value nodevalue 50},
            {label    "B3",
             value    node
               {
                  {label    "B31", value nodevalue 48},
                  {label    "B32", value nodevalue 46}
               }}
         }}
   }
      {label    "C", value nodevalue 35},
      {label    "D", value nodevalue 15}
   }
```

Macros

Macros in ASN.1 are similar to macros in application software: they provide the capability of defining types and values that are not included in the standard repertoire. This capability is not commonly implemented in ASN.1, however, because all the macros' grammatical rules must be known by a compiler before it can compile the module containing the macros. Their definition is found in Annex A of ISO 8824, but discussions are underway to replace macros with built-in data types.

Macros can be reduced to ASN.1 types (another reason why macros are not common) even though macros are not themselves types. One significant use of ASN.1 macros is in OSI application protocol standards, specifically for defining remote operations and object classes. In this section, we include two macros, ERROR and OPERATOR, that appear in the common service elements in Chapter 4.

The template for an ASN.1 macro is

```
<macro name> MACRO ::=
BEGIN
   TYPE NOTATION    ::=    <user-defined type notation>
   VALUE NOTATION   ::=    <user-defined value notation>
<supporting syntax>
END
```

where MACRO is the keyword that indicates a definition of the macro named <macro name>; BEGIN and END delimit the body of the macro definition; TYPE NOTATION and VALUE NOTATION, respectively, introduce the production rules for the user-defined types and their values; and <supporting syntax> gives details about the types in the body of the macro.

The following ERROR macro defined in X.219 provides a specific instance of the general template:

```
ERROR   MACRO   ::=
BEGIN
   TYPE NOTATION    ::=    Parameter
   VALUE NOTATION   ::=    value (VALUE CHOICE
                                 {
                                    localValue    INTEGER,
                                    globalValue   OBJECT IDENTIFIER
                                 })
   Parameter        ::=    ''PARAMETER'' NamedType | empty
   NamedType        ::=    identifier type | type
END
```

In this definition, details of Parameter and NamedType are in the supporting syntax. Parameter consists of the keyword PARAMETER followed by a named type; it may not have an entry. The value notation is a choice of INTEGER or OBJECT IDENTIFIER. The definition allows users to define operation errors. For example, the ERROR macro is used in the Remote Operations Service Element (ROSE) of Chapter 4 to define BadQueueName as follows:

```
BadQueueName    ERROR
                PARAMETER    QueueName
                  ::= 0
```

BadQueueName has type ERROR, one parameter QueueName (identified elsewhere as type IA5String), and value 0. In the remote operation, only the value 0 is transmitted; the other terms in the definition are for the user's benefit.

As a second instance of the macro template, we consider the following OPERATION macro definition, used by application protocol designers to define remote operations:

```
OPERATION  MACRO    ::=
BEGIN
  TYPE NOTATION      ::=    Argument Result Errors LinkedOps
  VALUE NOTATION     ::=    value (VALUE CHOICE
                              {
                                  localValue   INTEGER,
                                  globalValue  OBJECT IDENTIFIER
                              })
  Argument           ::=    ''ARGUMENT'' NamedType | empty
  Result             ::=    ''RESULT'' ResultType | empty
  ResultType         ::=    NamedType | empty
  Errors             ::=    ''ERRORS'' ''(ErrorNames)'' | empty
  LinkedOpts         ::=    ''LINKED'' ''(LinkedOpNames)'' | empty
  ErrorNames         ::=    ErrorList | empty
  ErrorList          ::=    Error | ErrorList'',''Error
  Error              ::=    value(ERROR) | type
  LinkedOptNames     ::=    OperationalList | empty
  OperationList      ::=    Operation | OperationList'',''Operation
  Operation          ::=    value(OPERATION) | type
  NamedType          ::=    type | identifier type
END
```

In this definition, TYPE NOTATION has four production rules, each of which is refined in the supporting syntax. We note that each of them may or may not be present in a specific instance. As in the definition of the ERROR macro, there is a choice for value notation, either INTEGER or OBJECT IDENTIFIER.

In the following example, the OPERATION macro is used to define getcount as type OPERATION with three parameters and value 0:

```
getcount OPERATION
              ARGUMENT    QueueName
              RESULT      Count
              ERRORS      {BadQueueName, QueueNotAvailable, Other}
                ::= 0
```

SUMMARY

The abstract syntax notation, ASN.1, is a data definition language that provides a syntax for specifying Application-layer protocols and information in open systems. The basic unit in ASN.1 is the module. It consists of types and value definitions that are used, respectively, to define and name new types and values. Syntax for built-in simple and structured types is specified and exemplified. Tagging enables the receiver to distinguish and correctly decode values from various data types. Additional features of the notation allow specification of subtypes, handling of recursion, and defining new types and values with macros.

In the next chapter, we use ASN.1 to define one of the Application layer's common service elements, ACSE (Association Control Service Element). Further, an example is included of an ASN.1-defined application protocol to check the number of entries in a remote system's print queue.

EXERCISES

1. Given the definition

```
company   ::=   SET
              {
                name            [0]   IA5String,
                zipcode         [1]   IA5String,
                CitationType          INTEGER,
                other                 ANY DEFINED BY CitationType
              }
```

where the INTEGER value of CitationType can be 0 = INTEGER, 1 = REAL, or 2 = BOOLEAN, which of the following values are valid? Assume tagging has been done accurately.
   (a) "CyberReal", "20742-1911", 0, TRUE
   (b) "60603", "Villaland", 1, 500000.00
   (c) 0, 450, "HomeNet", "12345"
   (d) "SitCom", 1, 70000.00

2. Write a module that identifies DaysOfWeek as a BIT STRING consisting of 7 bits, one for each day of the week and the first of which represents Sunday. Write a value of the string that represents (Monday, Wednesday, Saturday).

3. Rewrite the Inventory Record of section 1.6.4 using correct ASN.1 syntax.

4. Differentiate between the following two representations:

```
a.   HouseType   ::=   INTEGER          b.   HouseType   ::=   ENUMERATED
       {                                       {
         Ranch        (1)                        Ranch        (1)
         SplitLevel   (2)                        SplitLevel   (2)
         Colonial     (3)                        Colonial     (3)
         TownHome     (4)                        TownHome     (4)
       }                                       }
```

5. Assume that an Employee record has the following components: hire date, job title, age, salary, and office location (a city name). Write an ASN.1 notation for Employee. Give a valid representation (set of example values) of Employee.

6. You are writing a program to track the results of the NCAA playoffs. This is a distributed application, running at the site of each game. The various hosts regularly exchange information to

keep each other up to date on the status of the teams. Decide what information you will need to exchange and write the ASN.1 definitions of the information.

7. Distinguish among the various kinds of tagging in ASN.1. Use an example to illustrate the distinctions. Indicate the effects of IMPLICIT and EXPLICIT.

8. Differentiate among SEQUENCE, SET, ENUMERATED, and WITH COMPONENTS. In your discussion, use the following structures as examples to illustrate differences:

```
(a)  airport ::= SEQUENCE
                {
                    origin       [0]   IA5String,
                    stop         [1]   IA5String   OPTIONAL,
                    destination  [2]   IA5String
                }

(b)  airport ::= SET
                {
                    origin       [0]   IA5String,
                    stop         [1]   IA5String,
                    destination  [2]   IA5String
                }

(c)  airport ::= ENUMERATED
                {
                    origin       [o],
                    stop         [s],
                    destination  [d]
                }

(d)  airport_list ::= airport
                ( WITH COMPONENTS
                    {
                        origin       [0],
                        stop         [1],
                        destination  [2]
                    }
                )
```

9. Give an instance of the AirlineFlight example in section 3.3.2 that includes a stop in the Dallas–Fort Worth (DFW) airport.

10. For each of the following examples, name an appropriate ASN.1 data type and write the corresponding ASN.1 definition:
    (a) An alphabetized list of employees
    (b) One of a movie, play, or sport event
    (c) Prime numbers between 0 and 15
    (d) 110010001111000011111100
    (e) The local time in hours, minutes, and seconds
    (f) A sentence of text
    (g) Number of cars delivered, sold, leased, and on hand

11. The following data structures are written in C. Write each structure in ASN.1.

(a) struct calendar birthday[2] =
    { { {'O', 'C', 'T'}, 2, 1948 }, { {'A', 'P', 'R'},
      14, 1955 } }

where "calendar" is a structure defined by

```
struct  calendar
  {
  char  name[3];
  int   date:
  int   year;
  };
```

(b) struct time depart_time, arrive_time;

where "time" is a structure defined by

```
struct  time
  {
  int  hour;
  int  minute;
  int  second;
  };
```

(c) char array[7] = "NETWORK"

(d) struct entry
```
    {
    char  *word;
    int   *page_number;
    } index[50] =
        {  {"ARPANET", 105}, {"ASN.1", 328}  };
```

12. Write, in a high-level language different from C, each of the ASN.1 representations you produced in the preceding exercise.

13. Case: Stores in Philadelphia and Washington, but not Baltimore, carry colonial flags. The stores obtain the flags for $13.20 each and offer them to customers for $25.99 each. The identification number for colonial flags is cf1783. The Philadelphia store has 14 flags on hand, and the Washington store has 10. Write the ASN.1 representation(s) for this case using the module in Figure 3.1.

14. Write a definition of NonStopFlights in section 3.3.5 with the following additional conditions: include United Airlines and allow both nonstop flights and those that stop in Dallas–Fort Worth (DFW).

15. Consider the entries in the table of contents for this chapter as records in "ASN.1".

    (a) Which main section headings represent simple records, and which represent structured records?

(b) Write an ASN.1 recursive definition that specifies a record such as ASN.1.

(c) Write the table of contents of Chapter 3 as an instance of the record definition.

16. Write an ASN.1 recursive definition of a binary tree.

17. Use your definition of a binary tree in the preceding exercise to represent the following instance:

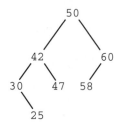

PART TWO

The Application Layer

In this part of the book, we focus on the Application layer. This is where most people, both users and developers, interact with computer networks. We begin in Chapter 4 with some utility building blocks, application service elements that will be incorporated into many application entities. These are tools of general use, but only as they are combined with other tools and with specific application service elements. They are not useful independent of a larger context. Many such elements exist, and others are under development. We select a few to illustrate the nature of these services and to provide a set of common building blocks to use in construction of new applications.

In the remaining chapters of this part, we examine a selection of the most popular specific application service elements. Each serves a particular purpose—electronic message handling, file access, virtual terminal access, and directory service. Unlike the utilities of Chapter 4, each of these serves a meaningful purpose in its own right. We can use an e-mail service directly, for example. Like the utilities, however, each can also be incorporated into other applications as needed. We may, for example, develop applications that include a requirement to access remote files. Those applications do not have to recreate the file access service; they call on the specific application service element defined for file access, using whatever features of that service that are needed for the current application. As in the case of the common tools of Chapter 4, many services are defined and more are under development. We choose four of the most important ones to treat here in depth: Message Handling Service (X.400); virtual terminal; File Transfer, Access, and Management (FTAM); and the Directory (X.500).

There is a difference in philosophy and approach between the OSI model and the TCP/IP environment. Both paradigms are important, and we give a lot of attention to each.

The term *application service element* is part of the OSI model. There is a difference in philosophy and approach between the OSI model and the TCP/IP environment. Both paradigms are important, and we give a lot of attention to each. We talk about the differences and the ways in which they are similar. The distinction is most evident at the top layers of network software. Where the OSI model includes Application, Presentation, and Session layers and further modularizes aspects of the Application layer, the TCP/IP approach treats everything above the Transport layer as "application." That does not mean that the functionality of the upper layers is absent from the TCP/IP environment. Rather, the approach is to leave such issues to each application to include as appropriate. Current work in the area of *middleware* addresses these application support needs. To date, there is no widespread deployment of tools or service elements corresponding to the OSI resources. In the chapters of this part, we address the Application layer from both the OSI and the TCP/IP view.

The treatment cannot be exactly parallel because of the differences in approach by the two models.

Terminology used throughout this part is heavily dependent upon the background established in Chapter 1. Some examples and explanations depend upon the ASN.1 notation introduced in Chapter 3.

CHAPTER 4

The Application Layer: Common Elements

KEY CONCEPTS

- Common Needs of Applications
- Association and Shared Context
- Remote Operation of Instructions
- Reliable Transfer of Information
- Commitment, Concurrency, and Recovery
- Some Common Tools from the TCP/IP Environment

Many applications distributed over networked computers share common needs. In this chapter, we identify four of these, discuss why these needs arise and what facilities are needed to address them, and introduce standard services and protocols designed to meet these requirements. The issues introduced in this chapter are

- The need to establish a context for communication between separated processes
- The need to execute instructions on a remote system
- The need for reliable transfer of large data volumes
- The need to coordinate components of a distributed application to avoid inconsistencies of state in shared data

Each section of this chapter begins by considering a problem inherent in distributed application development. Description of the OSI service and protocol designed to address the problem follows. Where appropriate, we identify the corresponding approach in the TCP/IP suite.

4.1 COMMON NEEDS OF APPLICATIONS

Separate components of a distributed application have an association that provides context to their interactions. The need to establish context goes beyond the connection established between machines by the transport service. Application context includes understanding the components of the application and how they will communicate with their peers on the remote system. Establishing an association between processes can be compared to what happens during a phone call. A caller dials a number, and phone utility services establish contact between the phones at two ends of the communication. After this connection is established, someone answers the phone and says "Hello." Then the caller says who he or she is calling and whether he or she is willing to talk to someone else if the requested party is not available. Establishing a context and completing an association between two processes requires similar effort to identify the communication partner needed or a suitable substitute and also includes establishing the semantics of the information exchanged over the connection. This requirement is common to all connection-oriented applications and is addressed by the OSI Association Control Service Element (ACSE). In the TCP/IP suite, it is considered to be an application-specific problem.

Executing instructions on a remote system requires a paradigm shift from the execution of local operations. It involves reconsideration of what is known about the data used in an operation and what the initiator knows about the results of the operation. The Remote Operation Service Element (ROSE) of the OSI services addresses these issues.

At the Application layer, reliable transfer of bulk data means that the *application process* has received the data. In the event of interruption to network services, some mechanism holds the data and continues the transfer when services are resumed. The OSI Reliable Transfer Service Element (RTSE) provides this facility. The TCP/IP approach considers the requirement to supplement the services of the Transport layer to be application specific.

Distributed applications also face complexities in maintaining a consistent state in shared resources. Since multiple processes could use the same data independently and no single process coordinates their access, the potential exists for lost transactions. In addition, when parts of an operation execute independently on separated machines, failure of part of the process could leave the operation in an incomplete state not known to the initiator of the operation. The OSI Application Service Element commitment, concurrency, and recovery (CCR) provides tools for protecting applications from this situation.

In addition to the OSI services, we introduce two simple tools available in the TCP/IP suite: PING and TRACEROUTE. These may be invoked by an application or may be used independently. Though they are different in form and use from the ASEs of the OSI suite, we include them in this chapter because they provide useful services that can be included in application development. Other tools of the TCP/IP suite will appear in later chapters where specific services such as message handling and remote file access are discussed.

4.2 ASSOCIATION AND SHARED CONTEXT

In section 1.5.3, we noted the difference between connection-oriented and connectionless modes of communication between processes. Connection-oriented communication re-

Connection-oriented communication requires establishment of an association between the processes prior to exchange of information.

quires establishment of an association between the processes prior to exchange of information. All OSI Application Service Elements (ASEs), whether the common type described in this chapter or the more specialized ones of Chapters 5 through 8, are connection-oriented. All require that an association be established between a process that is the **initiator (client)** and another that is the **responder (server)**. An application that is distributed over multiple machines may require an association among its elements for successful operation. That association consists of shared state information and a common view of required resources. An Application Association can be built over various types of services at lower layers. Thus, connectionless network communications may well provide suitable physical connection to support the Application Association. For example, a contract negotiation might occur through postal mail communication, a connectionless service, rather than ongoing telephone linkage, a connection-oriented service.

4.2.1 Association: Concepts and Processes

Association establishment requires a mechanism to locate a partner for the application process. It also involves establishing a context for the communications that will occur between cooperating peer application entities. Both parties to the association must know what semantics to attach to the data that flows between them. Both must know what level of service to expect from the network. Each party to the association must consist of elements able to communicate with the other. For example, if one process expects to send requests for remote operation of commands, the other must include a component that can interpret these requests and respond correctly.

During association establishment, the Application Entity (AE) (the particular collection of ASEs that will cooperate to provide service to the application process) must be identified. The exchange of information during association establishment also serves to define the relationship between the Application Entity and the Presentation service and the expected quality of service (QOS) to be provided by underlying network layers.

Establishing an association means gathering descriptions of components of an application's communication environment and establishing a link with a peer application on another system that has a compatible communication environment.

4.2.2 ACSE: The Service

A component of every connection-oriented application entity in the OSI model is the service element that establishes application-to-application association, the **Association Control Service Element (ACSE)**. ACSE offers two types of service to its user: association establishment and association termination. Association establishment is provided by the A-ASSOCIATE service. Association release is provided by three services:

- A-RELEASE is an orderly termination of an association.
- A-ABORT is an unconfirmed, user-initiated termination of an association with the risk of loss of data in transit.
- A-P-ABORT is an indication by the ACSE service provider that a nonrecoverable error, such as loss of underlying services, has occurred.

109

Association Establishment

The first step toward establishing an association between an initiator and a responder is taken when an application program invokes the service A-ASSOCIATE. In the parameters of A-ASSOCIATE, a user proposes a set of desired characteristics, the context, for the association. These characteristics include the environment in which this application will run; specifically, what application service elements will be active in the cooperating systems. This is the only application-related parameter that is required to establish the association. Other required parameters identify the **Presentation Service Access Point (PSAP)** of both ends of the association and define the **Presentation Context**.

A PSAP is a concatenation of the network address of the host and selectors for entities at the Transport, Session, and Presentation layers. The PSAP on the initiating system is obtained by a call on a system service and is not something that a user or an application developer needs to construct. The PSAP of the responding system must be obtained from a database of applications and their locations. Commonly used remote applications may be listed in a local database. To establish an association with a remote process not listed locally, an application process may query a global database using a service such as the Directory discussed in Chapter 8. The closest analogy to the OSI PSAP in Internet terms is the port number. Since the Internet suite (TCP/IP protocols) do not explicitly include a Session or Presentation layer, a single identifier (port number, for example) connects the Transport layer to the appropriate Application process.

The Presentation Context allows the Presentation layer in the initiator system to inform its peer in the responder system what type of information to expect over this connection and how it will be encoded. To do this, the Presentation layer needs to know what information forms the application entity will use as well as any special requirements for encoding information in transit. Thus, the AE might specify to the Presentation layer that it will use the abstract syntax known as "PersonnelData" and wishes the information to be conveyed in encrypted form. This is done by specifying a simple identifier, a small integer, that selects this choice of abstract syntax and transfer mode from a collection of available combinations stored locally.

For example, suppose that the local set of abstract syntaxes and associated transfer modes is the following:

{1{PersonnelData,Encrypted},2{AnnualReport,Compressed},3{AnnualReport,Basic}}

The numbers serve as identifiers for the various combinations of information and transfer modes. To request communication of the annual report using basic encoding, the AE would specify the presentation context identifier 3 in the presentation context definition list of the ACSE parameters.

Among the optional parameters of A-ASSOCIATE.request is user data. User Data, in this first communication between the cooperating applications, allows data delivery to occur even before the association is established. A reasonable use of this option is to carry authentication information, such as login name and password. Finally, the parameters of A-ASSOCIATE include an opportunity for the user to specify the quality of service expected in this session.

Closing the Association

A-RELEASE is the ordinary, orderly release mechanism used to end an association. It is a confirmed service that protects against loss of data, a possible result if one side began the process of closing the association while the other side was still sending data. A-ABORT is an unconfirmed service that corresponds to an abrupt termination of the association, usually because of an error condition. Loss of data could occur as a result. The time line of Figure 4.1 illustrates the orderly and abrupt termination situations. P-DATA is the basic data transmission service; it is available only while the association is in effect.

We can think of this process of orderly closing of the association in terms of the usual "protocol" for terminating a telephone conversation. Ordinarily one party to the call says "Goodbye," then waits for the other party to say "Goodbye," then both hang up. If Colleen and Maggie are talking, and Colleen says "Goodbye" and hangs up without waiting for Maggie to respond, and if just after Colleen says "Goodbye" Maggie says "Oh, wait, I found that book you are looking for; I'll leave it on my desk for you to pick up," Colleen will never get the information. If Colleen had waited for Maggie to say "Goodbye," she would have heard the message about the book before Maggie's "Goodbye" ended the conversation. The effectiveness of this protocol depends on reliable communication service. We assume that the protocol data units ("Goodbye" in this case) will arrive. At the Application layer, protocols depend on the reliable delivery of messages by lower-layer network services.

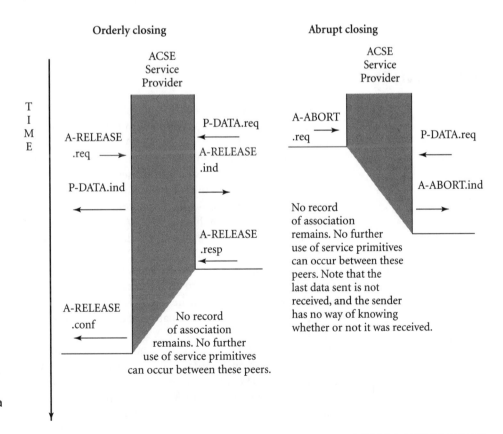

Figure 4.1. Orderly versus abrupt termination of an association, including possible data loss

A-ABORT may be issued by either participant in the association. When one side issues an A-ABORT.request, an A-ABORT.indication is delivered to the peer application entity. There is no response issued, all record of the association is deleted, and no further exchange can occur. The parameters of A-ABORT include an optional **user data** field and a required **abort source** carried only in the indication primitive. The user data field, if present, is delivered to the ACSE user and is likely to provide termination information for the user process. The abort source, carried in the indication, differentiates between an abort that originates with the ACSE user issuing A-ABORT.request and one that originates with the ACSE service provider without a request ever used. This latter case would occur if the ACSE service provider detected an error and issued an indication of association termination (A-ABORT.indication) to both ACSE service users.

A-P-ABORT is a service that contains only an indication primitive. It is issued by the ACSE service provider to notify its users that a nonrecoverable error has occurred. Its only parameter is the reason for this drastic action. The reason is provided by underlying service providers that detected the condition leading to termination of the association. Notice that the ACSE service provider has two vehicles for notifying its users of an error state that requires termination of the association: A-ABORT.indication generated by the ACSE service provider and A-P-ABORT.indication. The difference is that A-ABORT.indication notifies the user of an error detected or encountered by the ACSE service provider. A-P-ABORT.indication allows ACSE to convey to its user the information that the connection with the remote process has been broken by the lower-layer service providers. It is a way of passing on to the ACSE user the information given to the ACSE provider by the presentation service provider.

4.2.3   ACSE: The Protocol

The ACSE protocol is very closely related to the ACSE services. A-ASSOCIATE, A-RELEASE, and A-ABORT each has a corresponding protocol data unit (PDU) conveyed to the ACSE peer service provider. The ACSE protocol machine is shown in Figure 4.2, using the format and notation conventions introduced in section 1.9.2.

Receipt of A-ASSOCIATE.request causes the ACSE service provider to send the ACSE PDU AARQ to its peer on the responding machine. AARQ carries as parameters the information required by its ACSE peer to perform the work expected of ACSE. This information is contained in four of the A-ASSOCIATE.request parameters: the Application Context Name, the calling AE information, the called AE information, and user data.

All the other A-ASSOCIATE.request parameters go to the lower-layer service providers to be used in establishing the type of connection required to support the association. Figure 4.3 shows the distribution of the parameters received in A-ASSOCIATE.request between the APDU AARQ and the P-CONNECT.request. Note that user data provided in A-ASSOCIATE.request becomes part of the parameter list of AARQ; it is used to communicate between ACSE users. There is still a user data parameter in P-CONNECT.request, however. This user data carries communication between the peer ACSEs. In particular, it is this user data parameter that actually carries AARQ from the initiating ACSE to the responding ACSE. The other parameters constitute communication between ACSE (on behalf of its service user) and the lower-layer service providers (the Presentation entity and through the Presentation entity to the Session entity).

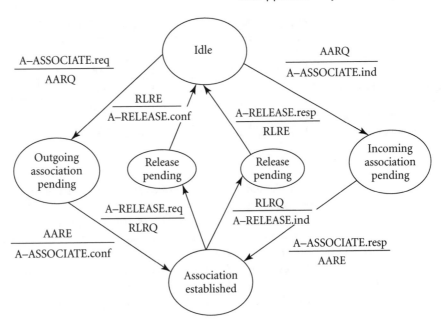

Figure 4.2. ACSE protocol machine showing association establishment and normal release

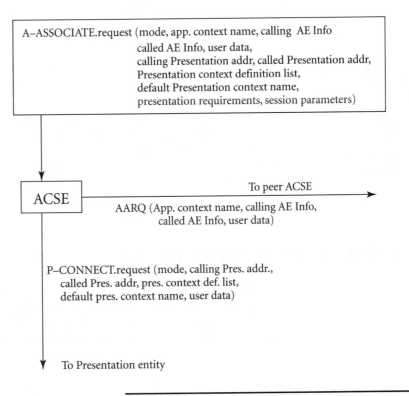

Figure 4.3. Distribution of parameters provided in A-ASSOCIATE.request

ACSE primitive invoked	Resulting APDU	Carrier Presentation Primitive
A–ASSOCIATE.req	AARQ	P–CONNECT.req
A–ASSOCIATE.resp	AARE	P–CONNECT.resp
A–RELEASE.req	RLRQ	P–RELEASE.req
A–RELEASE.resp	RLRE	P–RELEASE.resp
A–ABORT.req	ABRT	P–U–ABORT.req

Figure 4.4. Mapping ACSE primitives, APDUs, and Presentation primitives

ACSE and its users are not conscious of a separation of function between the Presentation and Session entities. They are aware only of the type of connection needed with their peers, and they provide the necessary descriptive information so that connection can be established and maintained by the appropriate service providers.

Other APDUs are similarly closely related to ACSE service primitives. AARE goes from the responding ACSE to the initiating ACSE when A-ASSOCIATE.response arrives from the responding ACSE user. It carries information needed by the peer ACSEs and optional user data to be delivered to the initiating ACSE service user. It is carried in the user data field of the P-CONNECT.response primitive. RLRQ is the APDU sent from initiating ACSE to responding ACSE to request a release of the association. The response is RLRE. ABRT is the APDU sent from one ACSE to its peer to demand immediate termination of the association, in response to A-ABORT.request. Each of these APDUs is carried as user data in an appropriate Presentation service primitive. The complete mapping is shown in Figure 4.4. There is no APDU corresponding to the A-P-ABORT service, because there is no exchange between the ACSE service providers involved in this service. Instead, an indication is received from the Presentation entity that the connection is irretrievably lost, and the word is passed to the ACSE user. No protocol data units are involved.

Many OSI protocols and a number of the newer protocols in the TCP/IP suite are specified using ASN.1. Figures 4.5 and 4.6 show the ASN.1 definition of ACSE.

This section introduced the cornerstone of all connection-oriented Application-layer protocols. Once ACSE has done its job, cooperating peer Application processes have agreed to interact and have established a context to give meaning to their communications. In the remaining sections of this chapter, we address some of the most basic needs of cooperating processes executing on separated systems. The next section provides the ability to cause a remote system to execute a specified instruction and return a result or an error message.

Once ACSE has done its job, cooperating peer Application processes have agreed to interact and have established a context to give meaning to their communications.

4.3 REMOTE OPERATION OF INSTRUCTIONS

Remote operation of instructions allows an application process to call for the execution of an operation on a remote system, while retaining a separation between the process invoking the operation and the internal characteristics of that operation. This form of interaction between remote processes complements the message-passing paradigm, increases the flexibility, and contributes an important tool in construction of network-based applications.

```
ACSE-1 DEFINITIONS  ::=
BEGIN
ACSE-apdu  ::=  CHOICE
        {   aarq            AARQ-apdu,
            aare            AARE-apdu,
            rlrq            RLRQ-apdu,
            rlre            RLRE-apdu
        }
AARQ-apdu  ::= [APPLICATION  0] IMPLICIT SEQUENCE
        {   protocol-version                    [0] IMPLICIT BIT STRING
                                                    {version 1 (0)  }
                                                    DEFAULT {version 1},

            application-context-name            [1] Application-context-name,
            called-AP-title                     [2] AP-title                OPTIONAL,    {version 1}
            called-AE-qualifier                 [3] AE-qualifier            OPTIONAL,
            called-AP-invocation-indentifier    [4] AP-invocation-indentifier OPTIONAL,
            called-AE-invocation-indentifier    [5] AE-invocation-indentifier OPTIONAL,
            calling-AP-title                    [6] AP-title                OPTIONAL,
            calling-AE-qualifier                [7] AE-qualifier            OPTIONAL,
            calling-AP-invocation-indentifier   [8] AP-invocation-identifier  OPTIONAL,
            calling-AE-invocation-indentifier   [9] AE-invocation-identifier  OPTIONAL,
            implementation-information          [29] IMPLICIT Implementation-data OPTIONAL,
            user-information                    [30] IMPLICIT Association-information OPTIONAL,
        }



AARE-apdu  ::=  [APPLICATION 1] IMPLICIT SEQUENCE
        {   protocol-version                       [\0] IMPLICIT BIT STRING
                                                        {version 1  (0)       }
                                                        DEFAULT {version 1},

            application-context-name               [1] Application-context-name,
            result                                 [2] Association-result,
            result-source-diagnostic               [3] Association-source-diagnostic,
            responding-AP-title                    [4] AP-title                OPTIONAL,
            responding-AE-qualifier                [5] AE-qualifier            OPTIONAL,
            responding-AP-invocation-identifier    [6] AP-invocation-indentifier  OPTIONAL,
            called-AE-invocation-indentifier       [7] AE-invocation-indentifier  OPTIONAL,
            implementation-information             [29] IMPLICIT Implementation-data  OPTIONAL,
            user-information                       [30] IMPLICIT Association-information OPTIONAL,
        }



RLRQ-apdu  ::=  [APPLICATION 2] IMPLICIT SEQUENCE
        {   reason                       [0 ] IMPLICIT Release-request-reason OPTIONAL,
            user-information             [30] IMPLICIT Association-information OPTIONAL,
        }


RLRE-apdu  ::=  [APPLICATION 3] IMPLICIT SEQUENCE
        {   reason                       [0 ] IMPLICIT Release-response-reason OPTIONAL,
            user-information             [30] IMPLICIT Association-information OPTIONAL,
        }


ABRT-apdu  ::=  [APPLICATION 4] IMPLICIT SEQUENCE
        {   abort-source            [0] IMPLICIT Abort-source,
            user-information        [30] IMPLICIT Association-information OPTIONAL,
        }
```

Figure 4.5. ASN.1 specification of ACSE: the APDUs

```
Application-context-name          ::= OBJECT IDENTIFIER
AP-title                          ::= ANY
AE-qualifier                      ::= ANY
AE-title                          ::= SEQUENCE {AP-title, AE-qualifier}
AE-invocation-identifier          ::= INTEGER
AP-invocation-identifier          ::= INTEGER
Association-result                ::= INTEGER {accepted(0),
                                                  rejected-permanent(1),
                                                  rejected-transient(2)}

Association-source-diagnostic     ::= CHOICE
    {acse-service-user[1]              INTEGER
        { no-reason-given -                              (1),
            application-context-name-not-supported       (2),
            calling-AP-title-not-recognized              (3),
            calling-AP-invocation-identifier-not-recognized    (4),
            calling-AE-qualifier-not-recognized          (5),
            calling-AE-invocation-identifier-not-recognized    (6),
            called-AP-title-not-recognized               (7),
            called-AP-invocation-indentifier-not-recognized    (8),
            called-AE-qualifier-not-recognized           (9),
            called-AE-invocation-identifier-not-recognized     (10)
        }

    acse-service-provider [2] INTEGER
        { null                        (0),
          no-reason-given             (1),
          no-common-acse-version      (2)
        }
    }

Association-information           ::= SEQUENCE OF EXTERNAL
Implementation-information        ::= GraphicString
Release-request-reason            ::= INTEGER
        {normal                       (0),
          urgent                      (1),
          user-defined                (2)
        }
Release-response-reason           ::= INTEGER
        {normal                       (0),
          not-finished                (1),
          user-defined                (2)
        }
END -- of ASCE-1 Module
```

Figure 4.6. ASN.1 specification of ACSE: supporting definitions

- What do we know about the data to be operated on? Is it local to the initiator's system and so must be sent to the responder? Does it exist on the responder's system? Will the responder's system understand the data in the same way that the initiator's system does?

- How will the initiator know when the remote operation is completed? If a result is expected but has not arrived, it may mean that the remote system is still executing the instructions or that the remote system has crashed.

- If the remote system crashed before carrying out the operation requested, is it safe to repeat the request when the system recovers? For example, suppose the operation was to deduct the cost of a purchase from an account balance. If the amount was deducted before the system crashed, then reissuing the remote operation request would cause the deduction to be made twice.

Figure 4.7. Questions in remote operations

- What does the initiator do while the remote system responds to its request? Does it stop and wait or go on with other work?

4.3.1 Concepts and Processes

The concept of remote execution of some instructions raises important questions, itemized in Figure 4.7. The first set of these questions is dealt with by the use of abstract syntax as introduced in Chapter 3. Data to be accessed by the remote operation is described with abstract syntax notation such as ASN.1 and rules that specify how the abstract syntax is converted to a concrete representation (a string of octets). The basic encoding rules (BER described in section 10.1.2) provide that service. Some UNIX systems provide an alternative encoding scheme called **external data representation (XDR)**. Operations are then defined in terms of the behavior of an instance of the abstract data type defined by the abstract syntax when the operation is applied to it. This is defined in OSI by the **Remote Operation Service Element (ROSE)**.

The second set of questions can be addressed in part by making sure that every operation returns some result, even if it is a simple indication of completion. Then the initiator will know when the operation is complete.

The third question set is addressed by using an additional Application layer common service: Commitment, Concurrency, and Recovery (CCR), which appears in section 4.5. If an operation can be performed repeatedly without adverse effect, it is called **idempotent**. An example of an idempotent operation is to return a count of the number of users currently logged in to the remote system. Repeated execution of that operation may return different results but will have no effect on the status of any data or process. An example of an operation that is not idempotent is incrementing a counter. Repeating such an operation results in errors.

The fourth set of questions depends on the execution mode selected by the invoking process: synchronous or asynchronous. In synchronous operation, the requestor issues the remote operation request and then blocks until a response arrives. In asynchronous operation, the requestor issues the remote operation request, then goes about its other work. If the request is not rejected, then some time later the responder will notify the initiator of a result of the operation or of an error.

4.3.2 ROSE: The Service

The Remote Operation Service Element (ROSE) provides the mechanism for an application entity to cause some operation to be performed remotely, possibly receiving a result from that operation.

ROSE forms a part of an Application entity, a particular combination of Application service elements and a control function that determines how they interact. ACSE will always be a part of that application entity also. Other ASEs can be included, depending on the requirements to be met by this application entity.

The services offered by ROSE allow an operation to be invoked (RO-INVOKE), a result or error to be returned (RO-RETURN-RESULT and RO-RETURN-ERROR), and the remote system or the ROSE service provider to reject the operation invocation (RO-REJECT-U and RO-REJECT-P). It is worth noting the basic difference between the usual connection-oriented communication between cooperating processes in the OSI environment and the remote operation approach. Although ROSE uses the context established by ACSE, it provides its user the opportunity to interact with another OSI system while maintaining minimal state information. All ROSE services are unconfirmed. That means there is no initial setup stage, no negotiated end to the contact. ROSE defines five classes of operation based on these two modes: synchronous or blocking operation, and four variations on asynchronous operation. Asynchronous operation can expect reporting of both results and errors, errors only, results only, or neither results nor errors.

Parameters of the service invocations specify the operation the remote system must execute and any argument needed for the operation. An invocation identifier matches a result with the right request. Not all operations have results. For example, an operation to delete a file from a remote system does not generate a result. However, good practice suggests that the initiator of the request must get feedback on the operation. The responder uses RO-RESULT to return a result or simply to notify the initiator that the operation is complete. In synchronous operation mode, RO-RESULT or RO-ERROR must follow RO-REQUEST. In asynchronous operation mode, RO-RESULT or RO-ERROR will follow RO-REQUEST unless the option of no reporting was specified. Figure 4.8 lists user-generated rejections returned in RO-REJECT-U.

A responder may fail to execute an instruction if a problem occurs. An error may be caused by a local condition at the responder's system, such as a resource unavailable or a file not found. On the other hand, an "error" is sometimes the correct and expected result of an operation. For example, before writing a new database entry with a key value that is supposed to be unique, a process will first attempt to read the entry with that key value. The expected "error" reply, "No such entry," is exactly what is required to allow the process to write the new entry. The Presentation Context for an application needing this response would include the following entry in its abstract syntax definition:

```
-- error definitions
noMatchingKeyFound ERROR ::= 0
```

When an initiator requests a read with a specified key value, the responder returns RO-ERROR with parameter error-value = 0. The user of ROSE receives this expected result and issues a request to write the new entry into the database.

If the database read operation yields an RO-RESULT (the normal "successful" conclusion of the read operation) with the content of an entry in the database with the new key,

Problem Occurred in	Rejection Reason
Invocation	Duplicate invocation identifier Operation number not recognized Argument type is incorrect Required resource not available A–RELEASE.req had been issued Linked identifier not recognized Linked response unexpected Unexpected child operation
Result	No matching invocation identifier Result response not expected Result type is incorrect
Error	No matching invocation identifier Error response not expected Error value not recognized Error value not expected Parameter type not correct

Figure 4.8. Reasons for ROSE service user-generated rejections

then the initiator process will be unable to write its new entry with the key it had calculated. RO-REJECT-U provides an opportunity for another stage in this conversation. Suppose the read operation yields RO-ERROR with error value indicating "Duplicate entries for this key value," the initiator can respond with RO-REJECT-U with reason equal "Unexpected error." The responding application entity would then have notice of an error in the database. If no RO-REJECT-U were issued, the error condition would continue undetected. The application process that uses ROSE determines what error or result to convey; ROSE itself defines the rejection by providing reasons.

4.3.3 ROSE: The Protocol

ROSE delivers the information required to cause a remote execution of an operation and to return a result or error response.

The simplicity of the ROSE protocol underscores the role of the service provided. ROSE delivers the information required to cause a remote execution of an operation and to return a result or error response. The responsibility to execute an operation rests with the remote peer of the ROSE service user. Since the services provided by ROSE are all unconfirmed and require no state information kept by ROSE, the protocol machine is very simple. Each service maps to a corresponding PDU, which in turn requires a service to provide delivery. Two types of delivery service are called for—one for ordinary data delivery and one for reliable transfer of bulk data. The Presentation layer provides access to ordinary data delivery; the common application service, RTSE, offers delivery of bulk data.

4.3.4 An Example Using ROSE

We conclude this section with an example application protocol built with ACSE and ROSE. The example protocol will simply check the number of entries in the print queue of a remote system. The protocol is defined using ASN.1 and appears in Figure 4.9. Notice that the

```
QueueCount  DEFINITIONS  ::=
BEGIN
    --  Definition of a simple protocol to return the size of a print
    --  queue on a target system

    --  operations
    getcount OPERATION
         ARGUMENT      QueueName
         RESULT        Count
         ERRORS        {BadQueueName,  QueueNotAvailable, Other}
         ::= 0

    --  error definitions
    BadQueueName      ERROR
                      PARAMETER QueueName
                         ::= 0

    QueueNotAvailable     ERROR
                          PARAMETER QueueName
                             ::= 1

    Other       ERROR
                PARAMETER Explanation
                   ::= 2

    --  Supporting Definitions
    QueueName    ::= IA5String
    Explanation  ::= IA5String
    Count        ::= INTEGER
END --  QueueCount Module
```

Figure 4.9. ROSE example: Queue Count

definition of this protocol does not include the implementation details. The definition specifies that an operation (getcount) exists and takes the argument QueueName and provides a result, Count, or one of three error indications: BadQueueName, QueueNotAvailable, or Other. Each error indication is assigned a unique identification number. Error Other carries a parameter Explanation as well. To complete implementation of this example, application programs must be developed to run in the initiating side and in the responding side. The initiator uses ROSE services to invoke execution of this operation on the responder. The responder uses ROSE services to receive the invocation and to respond with a result or error notification.

The ASN.1 specification of this protocol includes an operation called getcount, which is assigned the identifier value 0. The operation takes as its argument the name of the queue to examine. Three error cases are specified, and each is assigned a value. The error case "other" allows a free form string to be returned when an error occurs that is not of the predefined types. This protocol specification does not say how the operation will be implemented on a remote host. It defines what is needed between cooperating application entities using this service. An initiator would invoke the service by establishing an association with the remote system through use of A-ASSOCIATE.req with an Application Context that includes ACSE, ROSE, and QueueCount. Assuming we require no special coding for the information exchanged in using this protocol, we would specify a Presentation Context corresponding to using ACSE, ROSE, and QueueCount and BER for the transfer syntax.

With the association established, a user on the initiating side would invoke the ROSE service RO-INVOKE with the operation-value parameter = 0 (the only value defined in this application context) and argument equal the name of the remote print queue. The peer service on the responding system would receive the request and issue a local command to check the contents of the print queue, count the entries, and then use RO-RESULT to return the integer value result. If the remote system finds that the queue name provided does not exist, it will use RO-ERROR with error-value parameter = 0.

Note that the application programs for both the initiator and responder must be implemented and installed on the appropriate systems. The ASN.1 specification of the protocol does not say what language will be used to implement the programs; nor does the specification say how the responding application will obtain the information needed to satisfy the request. The specification does describe the expected response and provides a short numeric code for each of the anticipated error cases. In this example, there is also an open-ended error response possible.

Information exchanged in this example is short—integer identifiers or brief strings. Other remote operations might require significant data movement, perhaps transfer of a large file. Then the reliable transfer of that data becomes an important consideration.

4.4 RELIABLE TRANSFER OF INFORMATION

When an application needs to move a large quantity of information, it may wish protection from data loss due to various types of failure. We have noted that it is the responsibility of the Transport layer to provide reliable data flow from end to end over a network connection. Why should anything further be required? Given a strong transport protocol, what is the purpose of a reliable transfer protocol in the Application layer?

Even if we assume that the Transport service never fails, it delivers data to the destination machine; the Transport layer cannot protect against failures that occur after the data is delivered, but before the application has completed its use of the data. For example, consider an application that copies a file from a remote system to a local floppy drive. Suppose that after the data arrives at the local machine, a disk access error occurs in writing the data to the floppy drive. The transport service has done its job, but the application's need for reliable transfer has not been met. This situation illustrates one need for the additional reliability tools available to the application through use of Session-layer services.

4.4.1 Reliable Transfer: Concepts and Processes

We will return to the services provided by the Session layer. Here we restrict our attention to the particular requirements of reliable bulk transfer. Applications such as simple file transfer, message handling, directory queries, or remote video screening might use such a facility.

Given the availability of reliable machine-to-machine transport, what must a reliable transfer service add? The reliable transfer service must deal with possible application failures. In the example of a failed disk access, the application needs to pause while a new disk is inserted, then restart. In the restart, the application must resend data that was lost on the bad disk. The service must provide a means to note when the application has finished with some data so the sender can clear it from its buffers. It must also provide a means for the receiver to request retransmission of information that was lost or corrupted *in the application*.

In the file transfer example, data flows in one direction only. Some applications require two-way communication. A reliable transfer service should provide a mechanism to coordinate sending and receiving and to prevent one side from closing the association before the other has finished sending data.

The **Reliable Transfer Service Element (RTSE)** provides for dependable transfer of application protocol data units (APDUs) of substantial length. RTSE invokes the services of the Session layer on behalf of the application process, providing a simpler interface to those services.

4.4.2 RTSE: The Service

The services offered by RTSE fall into three categories: association establishment, data transfer, and association termination. RT-OPEN provides for association establishment. RT-TRANSFER, RT-TURN-PLEASE, and RT-TURN-GIVE support data transfer. RT-CLOSE, RT-U-ABORT, and RT-P-ABORT provide for termination of the association. RTSE opens and closes an association by using the services of ACSE. Thus, when the Application Context includes RTSE, it is RTSE that uses ACSE.

Association Establishment

RT-OPEN simply invokes A-ASSOCIATE to establish an association with a peer application entity. The service provided by RTSE is closely related to the session preservation and restoration services provided by the Session layer. The relevant services of the Session layer control the **dialog mode** between the two entities. The dialog may be *monologue* or *two-way alternate*, depending on whether the data will move only from one side or from both directions by turns. An *initial turn* parameter specifies which side will send data if the dialog is monologue, or which will send first if the dialog is two-way alternate.

Data Transfer

The central data transfer service of RTSE is RT-TRANSFER, a confirmed service invoked by the application entity that wishes to send data. Its parameters specify the data to be sent and a maximum time permitted for completion of the transfer. If two-way data transfer occurs, each side must take its turn. Two services participate in giving a turn to a would-be sender. RT-TURN-PLEASE, an unconfirmed service, allows an application entity to request the right to send data. Only one parameter appears with this service: an integer-valued priority that suggests how the system should allocate resources in case of service problems. An application entity yields the turn by invoking RT-TURN-GIVE, an unconfirmed service with no parameters. RT-TURN-GIVE can be used to respond to the arrival of RT-TURN-PLEASE.indication, or it can be used in anticipation of a need to send by the peer process, without a prior RT-TURN-PLEASE.

Association Termination

RT-CLOSE, a confirmed service, maps directly to A-RELEASE to provide orderly release from an association. The side of the association wishing to use RT-CLOSE must be the one whose turn it is to transmit data. Since only the one entitled to send data is allowed to initiate the process of closing the association, there will be no chance of data sent by the other side crossing the close request in transit. RT-CLOSE cannot be invoked while an RT-TRANSFER is in an incomplete phase (RT-TRANSFER.request has been issued, but RT-TRANSFER.confirm has not arrived). RT-U-ABORT maps directly to the A-ABORT service of ACSE to provide a prompt termination with the possibility of lost data. RT-P-ABORT is issued by the RTSE service provider to notify its user of a failure from which recovery is not possible. It will most often happen as a result of RTSE receiving an A-P-ABORT from ACSE.

4.4.3 RTSE: The Protocol

RTSE establishes an association with a peer system on receiving RT-OPEN.request. This is accomplished by using the A-ASSOCIATE service of ACSE. Turn management is provided by invoking the token control services offered by the Presentation layer on behalf of the Session layer.

RTSE provides for the reliable transfer of bulk data by transforming the data into a string of octets, then breaking the string into segments and handing each segment to the Presentation layer for delivery. Checkpoints are established between segments. Through the services of the Presentation layer, RTSE uses the activity management services of the Session layer to manage the transfer of the collection of segments that makes up the bulk data. Activity and minor synchronization facilities of the Session layer support interruption and possible resumption of data transfer if the underlying network connection is lost. We will examine these services in section 10.2.

RTSE is used in the X.400 Message Handling Service (MHS) and is available for use by ROSE when remote operations require reliable transfer. Because of its use in X.400, RTSE is widely available.

4.4.4 Services Required by RTSE

RTSE requires a basic data delivery service, which it obtains by invoking P-DATA from the Presentation layer. RTSE also requires synchronization services provided by the Session layer. The user of RTSE requires very little knowledge of the Session layer, only that it provides for one-way or two-way-alternate communication modes. RTSE itself will invoke other Session-layer services to provide for protection against data loss. Specifically, RTSE requires tools to distinguish between data that has been delivered safely to the destination application and data that is not yet known to be secure. It also needs to be able to request the retransmission of data that did not make it to its intended destination. We will investigate those services in detail when we discuss the Session layer, and we will also discuss why we need these additional services on top of the reliable transport service offered in the Transport layer.

RTSE addresses a limited set of potential failures on a remote system. In distributed application development, many types of conflicts and inconsistencies can arise if cooperating processes are not carefully coordinated. In the next section, we consider problems and approaches to addressing those problems.

4.5 COMMITMENT, CONCURRENCY, AND RECOVERY

Applications developed on a network, such that more than one autonomous processor is used, present special challenges. There is the potential of conflicting concurrent access to a resource by other applications, and the potential of partial failure—one or more of the processors involved in the distributed application fails while others continue to operate.

Problems arising from these causes occur infrequently: the probability that more than one process will seek to update the same database entry at the same time is low. Similarly, it is unlikely that during a funds transfer, one process will record the deposit but the other will fail before recording the withdrawal. Most applications would execute successfully most of the time without any special provision for these special cases.

However, those applications that must make provision for these cases must address the following:

- Commitment: assurance from a server process that it will carry out a requested task regardless of difficulties that might arise.

- Concurrency: protection from the intrusion of interleaved operations that interfere with correct completion of a requested task.

- Recovery: establishment of procedures to overcome failures by one or more participating processes during execution of a distributed application.

Methods to deal with these requirements form the subject of this section. The OSI service element designed to meet this need is called **CCR** for **commitment, concurrency, and recovery**.

4.5.1 CCR: Concepts and Processes

The complications associated with applications distributed over networked computers include the possibility that more than one process, each without any knowledge of the others, will attempt to make use of an unsharable resource at the same time.

The complications associated with applications distributed over networked computers include the possibility that more than one process, each without any knowledge of the others, will attempt to make use of an unsharable resource at the same time (for example, updating the same data item). Figure 4.10 illustrates an example of a common conflict pertaining to an entry in a database. Each process wishes to update the credit remaining in an account when more than one person has access to the account. Two valid transactions, each executing without knowledge of the other, collide. The result is that one transaction is canceled by the other. The problem illustrated in the figure is the interleaving of the reads and writes to the database. The result is called the *lost transaction problem*. Concurrency controls would prevent this from happening if both access attempts were under the control of the same multitasking operating system. However, since these processes are not subject to a common control, a valid transaction is lost.

In addition to the concurrency problem, distributed applications are further complicated by the fact that more than one processing unit is involved, and one may fail while the other continues to function normally. What should happen when one application process requests that another perform some activity and then one or the other of the processes crashes? What must happen when the failed system restarts? These are the types of

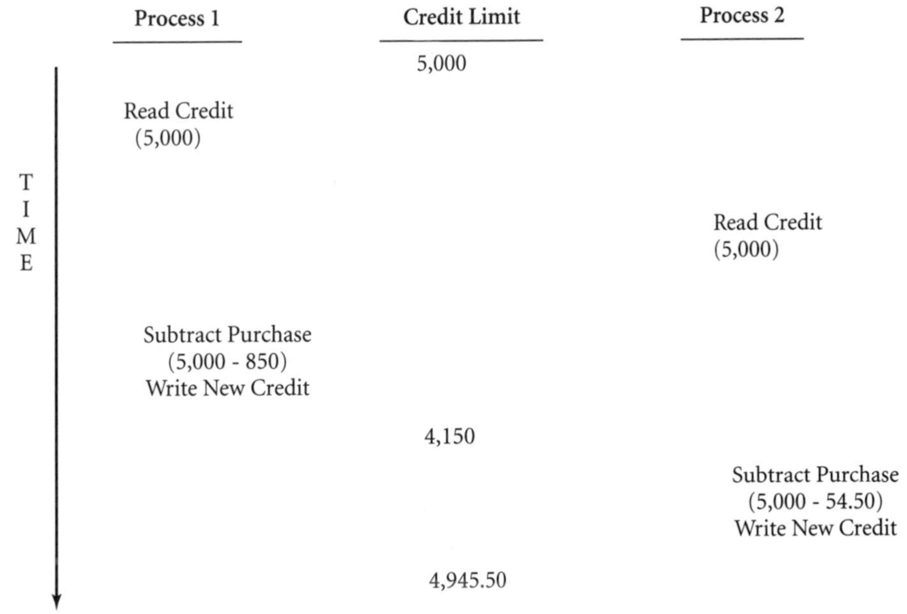
Process 1
Credit Limit
Process 2
5,000
Read Credit
(5,000)
T
I
M
E
Read Credit
(5,000)
Subtract Purchase
(5,000 - 850)
Write New Credit
4,150
Subtract Purchase
(5,000 - 54.50)
Write New Credit
4,945.50

Figure 4.10. Conflict in resource access: the lost transaction problem

questions addressed by the Application Service Element Commitment, Concurrency, and Recovery (CCR).

The central concept in a distributed application is the notion of an **atomic action**. An atomic action is a sequence of operations such that either

- All the operations are performed successfully with no other operations interleaved with them (this problem is demonstrated in Figure 4.10), or
- All the operations are terminated in such a way that the state of the system and all data retain no effect of any of the operations having been executed. (An example of this problem is the funds transfer. If the operations cannot be completed successfully, then neither the deduction from one account nor the addition to the other account occurs.)

The concept of an atomic action is familiar from the study of operating systems. However, it is complicated in distributed systems by the separation and independence of the processors. Since no single process controls scheduling and access for all the processes active in the network, control requires a distributed effort shared by separate processes that may be unaware of each other's existence.

Processes built from atomic actions are called **transaction** processes. A transaction is initiated by a **client** and carried out by a **server**. For the server, a transaction consists of two phases. During phase 1, the server receives a description of the atomic action (the sequence of operations) and makes arrangements to carry out the atomic action. (The server may carry out the requested operation but retain the ability to return to its state before the action, or it may record the desired action pending final instruction to do it.) When the atomic action is fully defined, phase 2 begins. During phase 2, the server *commits* to successful completion of the transaction if possible; otherwise, the server aborts the transaction and reports failure to the client.

Once the server is committed, it must complete the requested operations regardless of any failures it may encounter. If the server crashes during execution of the operations that constitute the transaction, it must resume processing upon restart. Once the server has committed to carry out the transaction, neither the server nor the client can abort the processing.

4.5.2 CCR: The Service

CCR provides services

- To bracket a sequence of operations that form an atomic action (C-BEGIN and C-PREPARE)
- For a server to tell the client it is ready to undertake the transaction (C-READY)
- For a server to tell the client it is not going to undertake the transaction (C-REFUSE)
- For a client and server to agree to enter phase 2 of the transaction processing, in which the server executes the operations of the transaction (C-COMMIT)
- For a client to tell a server not to carry out a transaction (C-ROLLBACK)
- For a client or server to initiate a backup to a prior known state (C-RESTART)

Figure 4.11 shows normal use of the services provided by CCR, labeled with *client* or *server* to indicate which side of the communication connection uses that service. The point of the tree-shaped sequence of actions is to show that from the time C-BEGIN is issued until the interaction ends, only a limited number of results are possible. In particular, either the atomic action is carried out or no effect of the action occurs. The loop back to sending C-COMMIT is needed to account for the possibility of a failure at the server after it issues C-READY. Keep in mind that more than one server might be involved in the transaction. If the client requires that all the servers participate in the transaction, then receiving one C-REFUSE will cause the server to issue C-ROLLBACK to all the servers that sent C-READY. The server that sent C-REFUSE does not need C-ROLLBACK since it has already declined to participate. C-ROLLBACK is needed to tell other servers to cancel the transaction.

An example of a transaction involving more than one server process appears in Figure 4.12. Bank C, the client, initiates a transfer from an account in Bank A to Bank B. Clearly, either both Bank A and Bank B must complete their portions of the transaction, or neither must do its part if the accounts are to remain in a consistent and correct state. The figure shows a successful transfer of funds. Figure 4.13 shows a failure to complete the transaction, but a final correct balance (excluding the desired transfer) remaining in both accounts. Since Bank A has no direct knowledge of Bank B's involvement in the transaction, Bank C must issue C-ROLLBACK to tell Bank A to cancel the transaction.

Delineating the Transaction

CCR provides the services C-BEGIN and C-PREPARE to mark the beginning and end of a sequence of steps to be treated as a single transaction. C-BEGIN includes the four prim-

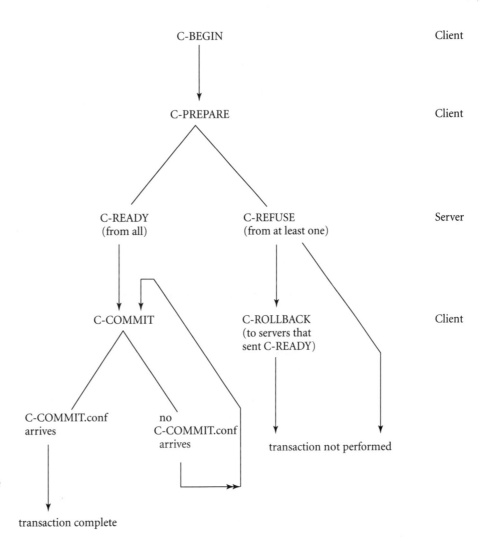

Used by

C-BEGIN   Client

C-PREPARE   Client

C-READY (from all)   C-REFUSE (from at least one)   Server

C-COMMIT   C-ROLLBACK (to servers that sent C-READY)   Client

C-COMMIT.conf arrives   no C-COMMIT.conf arrives   transaction not performed

transaction complete

Figure 4.11. Sequence of CCR service invocations in an atomic action

itives of a confirmed service; an application may elect to use either the confirmed or unconfirmed form. An application initiating a transaction (the client) follows C-BEGIN with a list of operations that it wishes the responding application (the server) to perform. In some applications, the end of the list may be clearly indicated, in which case C-PREPARE is not necessary. Otherwise, the initiating application sends C-PREPARE to define the end of the transaction definition and to request the responder to indicate its ability to commit to completing the transaction.

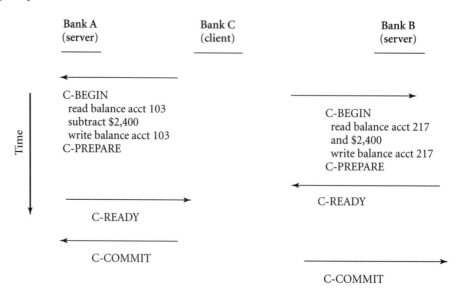

Figure 4.12. Multiple servers participate in a transaction

Response to a Request for a Transaction

The server uses C-READY or C-REFUSE to agree or refuse to participate in a transaction. When a server invokes C-READY, it declares itself able to complete the transaction, but also able to return to conditions that existed before the transaction arrived. The server waits for final word from the client before carrying out a transaction or returning to its prior state.

A server that invokes C-REFUSE declares that it will not carry out the transaction and no change to the local conditions results from the transaction request. No further communication from the client is expected.

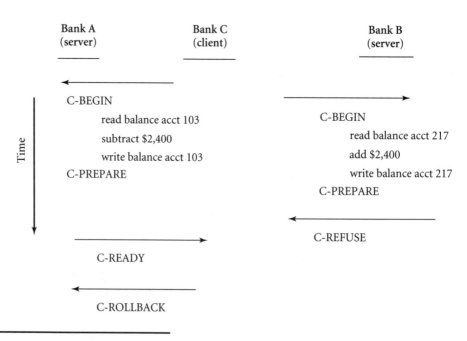

Figure 4.13. Canceling a failed transaction

Complete or Cancel the Transaction

C-COMMIT and C-ROLLBACK are confirmed services that provide the client CCR user the capability to lock into completing a transaction or to cancel and return to the state that preceded the use of C-BEGIN. The CCR service user decides whether to cancel or to go ahead with a transaction after hearing from all the servers expected to participate.

C-RESTART provides facility to deal with several types of failure. It can be used by a server at any time before it uses C-READY to notify the client that it must return data involved in the transaction to a prior state. C-RESTART can be used by a client when a failure in the communication system or at the server leaves the client unsure about the state of the server. Using the parameter of C-RESTART, the client may request the server return to the beginning of the atomic action or return to the latest commit or rollback point.

In the funds transfer example, participation by both servers is required. If either refuses, the transaction is canceled. In another case, refusal from one server may lead the client to enlist the participation of an alternative server. To continue with the bank example, suppose Bank C has received a check on a customer account in Bank A and the account does not have sufficient funds. Assuming that prior authorization has been made, Bank C initiates the fund transfer from another account of that customer, which is in Bank B. If Bank B is not able to transfer the funds, but another account is known, the refusal from Bank B will cause Bank C to send a transaction request to Bank D. Bank A continues to wait for the instruction to commit or to rollback. If Bank D sends C-READY, Bank C sends C-COMMIT to both and the transaction completes.

In another case, receiving C-READY from a subset of the servers might be sufficient to have the client issue C-COMMIT. The servers that refused were not needed for valid completion of the transaction. For example, a client seeking to arrange a meeting sends a query to an electronic calendar for each committee member to set a time. If some responses are refusals to schedule the meeting at the suggested time, but a quorum accepts the time, the client may proceed to schedule the meeting.

Note that procedures for correct implementation of distributed applications with respect to these complications remain the responsibility of the application process or a specific application protocol; CCR provides the necessary tools.

4.5.3   CCR: The Protocol

CCR services allow a client and server to communicate information that is important in coordinating their actions. All the actions undertaken as a result of using CCR are local to the client and server processes and are separate from the CCR protocol. Thus, there is little to say about the CCR protocol itself. C-BEGIN uses a Presentation layer service to reach a Session layer service that establishes a synchronization point. We will look at this facility in detail later. Its significance to CCR is that it marks a place in the information exchanged between the client and the server, and indicates that the client must retain this information and all that follows it until it is told it may abandon it. Thus, the atomic action is kept intact at the client until there is an indication that it has been conveyed successfully to the server. C-REFUSE, C-ROLLBACK, and C-RESTART each serve to mark the end of information retention requirement. Any of them gives permission to abandon what has been kept. C-PREPARE and C-READY use special facilities of the Presentation layer to convey data without regard to any flow control constraints that might be in place (P-TYPED-DATA).

In summary, the CCR protocol is used to convey coordination information between a client and a server. It is up to the client and the server to use the information correctly.

This concludes our discussion of OSI ASEs. We now turn our attention to the TCP/IP environment. The tools introduced in the next section do not have the same kind of use as the OSI ASEs, but that is because the TCP/IP protocols leave such requirements to each application to develop as needed.

4.6 SOME COMMON TOOLS FROM THE TCP/IP ENVIRONMENT

The TCP/IP protocol suite does not distinguish common and specific application service elements or Presentation and Session Layers. The components that make up these parts of the OSI environment are considered application specific in the TCP/IP approach to networking. Thus, we do not have a comparable set of common services and protocols to present in this chapter. The TCP/IP environment does include some tools that are considered useful and available to use within applications as needed. Some of these fit the general theme of this chapter: recognition of common problems and identification of useful tools to address the problems. These tools may also be invoked from a command line or other interface not included in an application, which makes them different from the ASEs of the OSI suite. Because they can be incorporated as useful modules within an application, we present a few of them here.

4.6.1 PING

PING sends a probe message across the network to determine if a particular remote host is available and to estimate the round-trip time required to communicate with that host. PING requires a host name or address. Each host running the TCP/IP protocol suite has a service called Echo, which will receive a message and send it back to its source. PING invokes this echo service. If used with only a host identifier, PING sends a 64-byte message, waits for its return, and responds to its user with notice that the destination host is alive. If the destination does not respond, PING will notify the user that the host is down after it times out. Options to PING allow the user to request

- That a message of a particular size be sent rather than the default 64 bytes
- That messages be sent every second rather than only once
- That the number of messages sent be limited to a fixed number rather than continuing until the request is canceled

Figure 4.14 shows the response from PING when a single message request is made and when 15 messages, each of size 100 bytes is requested. PING allows a user to determine if there is a significant delay in communication between the local host and a desired communication partner as well as an indication of packet loss probability in the communication. (Messages that do not return are lost packets.) This information could be incorporated into an application for setting timers and retry counters.

```
Command:  ping bbn.com
Response: bbn.com is alive

Command:  ping -s acm.org 100 15
Response: PING acm.org: 100 data bytes
          108 bytes from ACM.ORG (192.135.174.1): icmp_seq=0. time=165. ms
          108 bytes from ACM.ORG (192.135.174.1): icmp_seq=1. time=222. ms
          108 bytes from ACM.ORG (192.135.174.1): icmp_seq=2. time=173. ms
          108 bytes from ACM.ORG (192.135.174.1): icmp_seq=3. time=198. ms
          108 bytes from ACM.ORG (192.135.174.1): icmp_seq=4. time=169. ms
          108 bytes from ACM.ORG (192.135.174.1): icmp_seq=5. time=207. ms
          108 bytes from ACM.ORG (192.135.174.1): icmp_seq=7. time=207. ms
          108 bytes from ACM.ORG (192.135.174.1): icmp_seq=8. time=207. ms
          108 bytes from ACM.ORG (192.135.174.1): icmp_seq=9. time=188. ms
          108 bytes from AMC.ORG (192.135.174.1): icmp_seq=10. time=173. ms
          108 bytes from AMC.ORG (192.135.174.1): icmp_seq=11. time=192. ms
          108 bytes from AMC.ORG (192.135.174.1): icmp_seq=12. time=179. ms
          108 bytes from AMC.ORG (192.135.174.1): icmp_seq=13. time=181. ms
          108 bytes from ACM.ORG (192.135.174.1): icmp_seq=14. time=192. ms


          ----ACM.ORG PING Statistics----
          15 packets transmitted, 14 packets received, 6% packet loss
          round-trip (ms) min/avg/max = 165/189/222
```

Figure 4.14. PING
example

4.6.2   TRACEROUTE

TRACEROUTE is a tool in the TCP/IP suite that allows a user to determine the path followed by a message from the local system to a specific destination. The information is useful in analyzing network problems and may be significant in applications that wish to know where the information travels in the network.

TRACEROUTE sends data units toward a specified host using an invalid location at the remote host as the final destination. Since the destination is invalid, a failure to deliver message will be returned to the sender. To determine the route taken by the message, the data unit is sent repeatedly, each with a larger number indicating how many times the data unit may be forwarded. The first attempt allows only one step; if the destination is not reachable in one transmission, a failure notice will come back from the first intermediate node that handles it. The data unit is then sent with a permission to forward it one more time. If that is not enough to get the message to the destination machine, another failure response will result. The process continues, incrementing the number of steps allowed, until a failure arrives from the desired destination host or a maximum number of tries is exceeded.

The format of the command invoking TRACEROUTE follows [KS94]. TTL (Time To Live) is the measure of the number of times the message may be forwarded. UDP (User Datagram Protocol) is the specific Transport-layer service used to send the message.

```
TRACEROUTE [-m #] [-q #] [-w #] [-p #] {IP_address | host_name}

where -m  is the maximum allowable TTL value, measured as the
          number of hops allowed before the program terminates
          (default = 30);
```

```
-q  is the number of UDP packets that will be sent with each
    time-to-live setting (default = 3);
-w  is the amount of time, in seconds, to wait for an answer
    from a particular router before giving up (default = 5);
-p  is the invalid port address at the remote host (default
    = 33434).
```

SUMMARY

In this chapter, we begin the detailed investigation of requirements for successful network-based application development by examining services that are common to all connection-oriented applications.

Because all application service elements are connection-oriented, there must be an association between initiator and responder processes. Association means establishing a context that provides meaning to the communication undertaken by other application components. The OSI Association Control Service Element (ACSE) establishes the association by means of the A-ASSOCIATE service, and releases the association by one of three services: A-RELEASE, A-ABORT, and A-P-ABORT.

A second common service element allows an application process to call for the execution of operations on remote systems. Issues that arise in remote operation include knowing where the needed data resides and how it will be interpreted, how the initiator knows when the operation is completed, whether or not it is safe to repeat an operation after a crash, and whether the initiator can continue with other work while waiting for a result. The mechanism for an application entity to cause an operation to be performed remotely is called the Remote Operation Service Element (ROSE). ROSE provides four services relative to the operation: invoke it (RO-INVOKE), return a result (RO-RETURN-RESULT) or error (RO-RETURN-ERROR), and reject it (RO-REJECT-U, if rejection comes from the user service, and RO-REJECT-P, if rejection is from the provider service). ROSE services are unconfirmed. They use the ACSE context in allowing user interaction with a different OSI system.

The third common service element is reliable transfer of long application protocol data units (APDUs). Transfer of bulk data requires continuing an interrupted transmission rather than retransmitting as in short messages. Using ACSE, the Reliable Transfer Service Element (RTSE) handles the association establishment (RT-OPEN) and association termination (RT-CLOSE, RT-U-ABORT, and RT-P-ABORT). RTSE invokes services of the Presentation and Session layers to accomplish reliable data transfer (RT-TRANSFER, RT-TURN-PLEASE, and RT-TURN-GIVE).

The common service element of commitment, concurrency, and recovery (CCR) provides tools to handle infrequent, but important, problems such as conflicting concurrent accessing of a resource or one or more processors failing while others continue to operate.

Finally, we introduced some handy tools of the TCP/IP environment: PING, which allows a user to determine if a remote system is available and to discover the round-trip time to that system; and TRACEROUTE, which allows a user to determine the route that messages travel in reaching a specific remote system.

All the service elements considered in this chapter have a common theme: each is meaningful in the context of some larger task. They provide tools to accomplish some final result.

In the chapters that follow, we will consider application service elements that are useful in building other applications, but that also provide an endproduct in their own right. These specific application service elements include an electronic mail facility (MOTIS), remote file access and management (FTAM), and a directory service (X.500).

EXERCISES

1. Looking at Figure 4.11, consider every instance of a failure by one processor that you can think of and determine if a problem will occur in executing the transaction. For example, if the client fails between issuing C-BEGIN and C-PREPARE, the transaction will not be executed by a server since it was not completely specified and no C-COMMIT arrived.

2. In your system, find two examples of data delivery (transfer) facilities that perform the function offered by RTSE.

3. What dialog modes would you associate with use of a walkie-talkie? With calls answered by an answering machine?

4. Assume that you have available the services described in this chapter, plus one other: P-DATA. P-DATA takes data provided by a user process and delivers it to the user's peer at another open system. Using these services, sketch a solution to each of the following problems. For each, show a time sequence diagram that displays the use of services on each participating open system. For each problem, describe the services required and the OSI Application Service Element that provides the service.

   (a) Obtain a list of users currently logged in to system A.

   (b) Query the inventory file on system A to find the quantity of widgets in stock. (Assume you know the necessary information to access the file.)

   (c) Schedule a meeting at 2 p.m. next Tuesday to involve Mary, Joe, and Chris by writing the meeting into their calendar files if everyone is available.

5. Using ASN.1 and the services of ROSE, specify a protocol to return the current time on a remote system.

6. You are developing applications using ROSE. What operations and errors would you define for each of the following protocols:

   (a) Return the ratio of print queue length to number of users logged in.

   (b) Return the process identifier of the longest running process on the system.

   (c) Return directory information about a specified file (for example, the creation date, length, owner).

7. Draw the protocol machine to describe operation of ROSE or RTSE. Use Figure 4.2, the protocol machine for ACSE, as an example.

8. If you have access to a system with the TCP/IP protocols, use PING to discover the round-trip time between your host and some other host known to you.

9. If you have access to a system with the TCP/IP protocols, use TRACEROUTE to determine what machines participated in sending your message from your machine to a designated other host.

10. In Figure 4.14, which message was lost?

CHAPTER 5

Applications: Electronic Messaging Systems

KEY CONCEPTS

- A Model for Electronic Messaging
- The Mail Access Environment
- Dealing with Addresses
- Retaining and Discarding Messages
- The System Components
- X.400 Messaging System

For many people, electronic mail is the introduction to network use and quickly becomes an integral part of their business and personal communications. You have probably sent and received e-mail using some system. In this chapter, we examine networking concerns that provide the capability of sending and receiving e-mail within a system and across different systems. We examine these facilities from three levels of interest: the perspective of a user of an electronic mail service; the perspective of the network administrator who must install, configure, and maintain the service facility; and the perspective of a developer of new mail services.

The functional model of electronic message-handling systems in ISO/ITU Recommendation X.400 provides a map guide to our detailed exploration. Using the terminology included in the X.400 model, we will separate what the user sees and works with from the system aspects that provide the functionality needed. Although we address the needs of an electronic messaging system in general terms, we will illustrate the implementation of real systems using both the TCP/IP messaging protocol (the message format defined in RFC 822 and the Simple Mail Transport Protocol, SMTP, defined in RFC 821) and the ISO/ITU approach (X.400).

5.1 A MODEL FOR ELECTRONIC MESSAGING

Figure 5.1 illustrates the functional model of a message-handling system. Though the terminology is from the definition of X.400, the model provides a useful reference for discussion of electronic messaging in general. We use this model throughout the chapter to describe the requirements of a message system and to distinguish the components of such a system. The figure identifies the section in which the components are introduced.

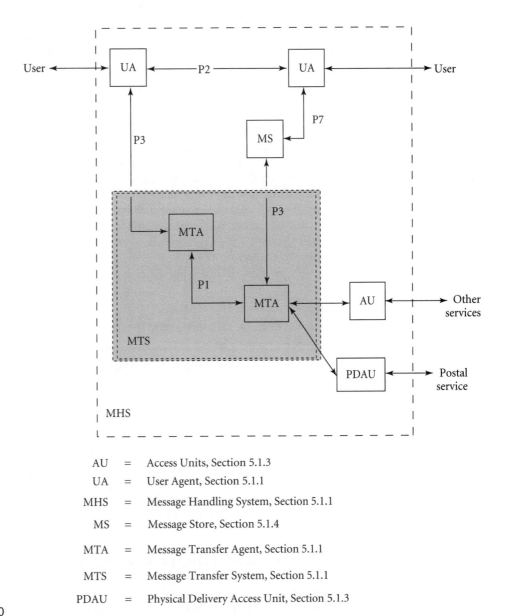

AU	=	Access Units, Section 5.1.3
UA	=	User Agent, Section 5.1.1
MHS	=	Message Handling System, Section 5.1.1
MS	=	Message Store, Section 5.1.4
MTA	=	Message Transfer Agent, Section 5.1.1
MTS	=	Message Transfer System, Section 5.1.1
PDAU	=	Physical Delivery Access Unit, Section 5.1.3
P1, P2, P3, P7	=	Protocol Units, Section 5.1.5

Figure 5.1. The X.400 functional model

Message is a generic term and can take many meanings. Still the most common form of message is mail from one person to another. In the X.400 model, this type of message is called an **inter personal message (IPM)**.

5.1.1 User Agents

In the functional model of the **Message Handling System (MHS)**, the user may be either a person or an application process interacting with the message handling system. A **User Agent (UA)** provides the interface between the user and the **Message Transfer System (MTS)**. The MTS consists of some number of **Message Transfer Agents (MTA)** collectively charged with the responsibility of moving messages from the originator to the recipient. Since a large portion of what the user agent does is unrelated to network communication, a variety of designs are possible.

The UA is the interface between the e-mail system and its user. Examples of popular UAs include Netscape mail, Microsoft Exchange/Outlook, Lotus, and Eudora. Much of the UA is concerned with matters not affecting communication and is thus part of the application process that is strictly local and not regulated by communications standards. Examples include allowing the user to compose a message, searching the local file system for a file to be attached to a message, interacting with the file system to store and retrieve messages that the user wishes to retain, and other such local functions. The parts of the UA that require common treatment of messages based on the content of the header are subject to standards. For example, the UA must construct headers for the message that will be understood by the MTA and by the recipient's UA.

The UA provides the following abilities:

- Execute mail system operations
- Compose or access the message that is to be sent
- Provide the destination description the mail system requires to deliver the message
- Know about and retrieve incoming messages
- Present incoming messages to the user with a display suited to the message content

In sections 5.2 through 5.4.3, we examine issues related to providing mail services to the user. In particular, we look at accessing the mail system, message creation and presentation, dealing with addresses, retaining and discarding messages, and knowing about mail delivery or failure. We use examples from the Internet mail service, including addressing conventions and the operation of SMTP because of their widespread availability and common use. We will also include descriptive information about the X.400 protocols and compare their features to those of SMTP.

5.1.2 Message Transfer Agents: X.400 MTA and Internet SMTP

Message Transfer Agents are completely constrained by protocols that govern their interaction with other entities. SMTP and X.400 MTAs differ in the way they interact with user agents and in the way they interact with their partners in a message transfer system. In particular, Figure 5.2 shows how these two facilities differ in the way they view the parts of a message. X.400 recognizes three parts: the envelope, the header part, and the body of the message. The envelope is significant to the MTAs; the header and body are significant to the sender and receiver UAs. SMTP recognizes only two parts of a message: a header part and a message body. However, SMTP MTAs ignore any header fields they do not recognize. This gives great flexibility in defining new headers as needed without interfering with proper functioning of the MTA. The disadvantage of this approach is that the MTA does not know in advance that there are headers it should ignore, and looking at headers unrelated to message transfer adds to the overhead of MTA operation.

The X.400 envelope, like the envelope used for postal mail, contains information needed by the message transfer system to move the message from its source to its destination. En-

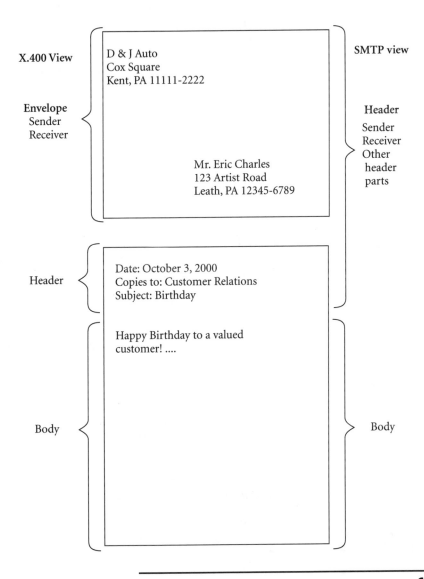

Figure 5.2. Correspondence between the message header and body in e-mail and the envelope and its contents in postal mail

velope fields include an identifier for this message (Message Protocol Data Unit or MPDU), the address of the message originator, original message format (for example, text, teletex, and so on), content type (for example, IPMs), UA Content ID (set by the UA when a message is delivered to the MTS; subsequent reports on the fate of that message carry the same ID), priority, flags specifying permitted operations, delivery deadline, information for management domains through which the message passes, information about intended recipients of the message, and trace information (path taken by a message and statements about actions undertaken by MTAs). Some of the fields are optional (original message format, UA Content ID, delivery deadline, information for management domains), and others have default values (priority defaults to normal, operations flags default to no value set). In addition to the address of each recipient, recipient information includes a "responsibility flag" (which instructs an MTA to deliver the message or determine that the message cannot be delivered, or transfer the message to another MTA for processing) and information about delivery reports required.

The X.400 header contains information about the message; some of it is relevant to the final recipient of the message, and some is useful to the UA and the message store. Figures 5.3 and 5.4 show the header fields defined in X.400 interpersonal mail and SMTP.

Originator Authorizing users	Message originator Who authorized sending this message (This is information only. The MTS makes no guarantee that the authorization is legitimate)
Primary recipients Copy recipients Blind copy recipients	To whom the message is addressed Who also receives a copy of the message Who receives a blind (secret) copy of the message
Reply time Reply to users	A time and date after which the message originator considers a response to be useless Users to whom a reply should be sent
IPM identifier Replied to IPM Obsoleted IPMs Related IPMS	An identifier for this IPM Identifies a message to which this is a reply What previously sent IPMs are made obsolete by this message What other IPMs are related to this one
Subject Importance Sensitivity	The subject of this message Priority of this message Indicates a degree of confidentiality — public, private, group limited, etc.
Auto forward Expiry time	Whether or not this message should obey automatic forwarding that might be set by the recipient A time and date after which the message originator considers this IPM will be invalid or useless

Figure 5.3. Interpersonal message (IPM) headers

(Remember that SMTP does not distinguish an envelope, so the complete correspondence between the two systems requires looking at the X.400 envelope fields and header fields.)

The body is the message itself and is meaningful to the recipient, but not to any other aspect of the MHS. The body of the message may consist of several parts, each of which may be of a different type. X.400 includes 12 predefined types for use in a message body: these include several different alphabets from which a text message can be constructed, voice type, videotex, encrypted (without further specification in X.400), and a "simple format-table document" type allowing a representation of text documents, including information to allow the text to be displayed on the output device available at the destination. The corresponding facility for defining content types for a message in SMTP is known as the **Multipurpose Internet Mail Extensions (MIME)** extension.

Internet mail is governed by conventions first described in RFC 822, which specifies a format for text messages. The mail format initiated in RFC 822 now governs mail systems well beyond its originally intended scope, and its limitations are evident. Unlike the variety of message types recognized by X.400, mail conforming to RFC 822 is limited to plaintext in the US-ASCII character set.

MIME [BF96] extends the Internet electronic mail specifications in RFC 822 to allow other than plain text to be transmitted as the message body. In particular, MIME allows a

MIME [BF96] extends the Internet electronic mail specifications in RFC 822 to allow other than plain text to be transmitted as the message body.

```
message      = fields *( CRLF *text )        ; Everything after first null
                                             ; line is message body

fields       = dates                         ; Creation time,
                   source                    ;   author id & one
                   1*destination             ;   address required
                   *optional-field           ;   others optional

source       = [ trace ]                     ; net traversals
                 originator                  ; original mail
                 [ resent ]                  ; forwarded

trace        = return                        ; path to sender
                 1*received                  ; receipt tags

return       = "Return-path" ":" route-addr  ; return address

received     = "Received"       ":"          ; one per relay
                   ["from" domain]           ; sending host
                   ["by"   domain]           ; receiving host
                   ["via"  atom]             ; physical path
                   *("with" atom)            ; link/mail protocol
                   ["id"   msg-id]           ; receiver msg id
                   ["for"  addr-spec]        ; initial form
                   ";"     date-time         ; time received

originator   = authentic                     ; authenticated addr
                 ["Reply-To" ":" 1#address])

authentic    = "From"        ":"   mailbox   ; Single author
             / ("Sender"     ":"   mailbox   ; Actual submittor
                 "From"      ":"   1#mailbox ; Multiple authors
                                             ;   or not sender

resent       = resent-authentic
                 [ "Resent-Reply-To" ":" 1#address] )
```

Figure 5.4. Header entries defined in RFC 822: part 1

```
              resent-authentic =

                          =    "Resent-From"              ":"     mailbox
                          / ( "Resent-Sender"             ":"     mailbox
                              "Resent-From"               ":"   1#mailbox  )


          dates           =    orig-date                  ;  Original
                               [ resent-date ]            ;  Forwarded



          orig-date       =  "Date"             ":"     date-time


          resent-date     =  "Resent-Date" ":"     date-time


          destination     =  "To"             ":"   1#address  ;  Primary
                          /  "Resent-To" ":"   1#address
                          /  "cc"           ":"   1#address  ;  Secondary
                          /  "Resent-cc" ":"   1#address
                          /  "bcc"          ":"   1#address  ;  Blind carbon
                          /  "Resent-bcc"":"   1#address


          optional-field  =
                          /  "Message-ID"          ":"  msg-id
                          /  "Resent-Message-ID" ":"  msg-id
                          /  "In-Reply-To"         ":"  *(phrase / msg-id)
                          /  "References"          ":"  *(Phrase / msg-id)
                          /  "Keywords"            ":"  #phrase
                          /  "Subject"             ":"  *text
                          /  "Comments"            ":"  *text
                          /  "Encrypted"           ":"  1#2word
                          /  extension-field           ;  To be defined
                          /  user-defined-field        ;  May be pre-empted


          msg-id          =   "<" addr-spec   ">"          ;  Unique message id


          extension-field =

                          <Any field which is defined in a document
                          published as a formal extension to this
                          specification; none will have names beginning
                          with the string "X-">

          user-defined-field =

                          <Any field which has not been defined
                          in this specification or published as an
                          extension to this specification; names for
                          such fields must be unique and may be
                          pre-empted by published extensions>
```

Figure 5.4. Header entries defined in SMTP: part 2

message to include more than one object; to represent text in character sets other than US-ASCII; to represent formatted text with multiple fonts, font sizes, and emphasis; to include nontext objects such as images, audio fragments, and video clips; and to handle other mail types as they are defined.

MIME does not change the restriction that Internet e-mail headers must be in US-ASCII characters. It does extend the options for the body of the e-mail message. MIME addresses two major restrictions in 822 mail: the limitation to US-ASCII code requires a restriction of 7-bit codes for characters, and lines are limited to 1000 characters. Users wishing to send other types of material through 822-based mail systems must encode the content into 7-bit ASCII characters before presenting the message to a user agent. Uuencode is one such scheme for making nontext data compatible with Internet mail systems. The limitations of the original Internet mail are especially apparent when messages must pass through a gateway to an X.400 mail system. X.400 allows messages to have multiple parts and to include many types of data. MIME extends Internet mail standards to allow similar flexibility. A gateway may move mail from an 822-based environment to an X.400 environment or may tunnel through one environment on its way between compatible end systems. In any case, the need to recode the content of an X.400 message on every entry to an 822 environment causes inefficiency and possible loss of information.

In the MIME version of Internet mail, a message still consists of a header and a body. However, now a body can be of type message and consist of a header and a body as well. The body of a message can be multipart with each part having a header and a body. In addition to the standard 822 headers shown in Figure 5.4, mail headers for a MIME message include the following:

- A MIME version header field that allows coordination between mail-processing agents handling the message.
- A Content type header field, which specifies the type and subtype of the data in the body of the message. The purpose of this header is to allow the receiving user agent to process the message body content correctly and to present it to the human receiver in a meaningful way. This might mean invoking a display agent for a specific word processor or spreadsheet or beginning a player to show a video clip or an audio file.
- A Content-Transfer-Encoding header field that specifies encoding that has been applied to the body of the message. Such encoding might be required to pass the message through a message-handling agent that has coding restrictions.
- Content-ID and Content Descriptor header fields may be used to further describe the content of the message body.

MIME header fields may occur in a message header or in the header part of a message contained within a message. The desire for compatibility with existing mail systems determined a number of choices made in the creation of MIME.

The Content Type Header field is the heart of MIME. It allows communication between a sending UA and a receiving UA about the type of the data contained in the message body. When only US-ASCII text was recognized, this communication was not necessary. To take advantage of the range of possibilities of message exchange, this communication between sender and receiver is essential.

The Content Type Header field specifies the media type of the message body, a subtype, and any parameters required for correct presentation of the message to the user. The default type is the standard message type when MIME is not used. The following example MIME header is typical for an ordinary message containing plaintext:

```
MIME-Version: 1.0
          To: Boots at Erols account <lcassel@erols.com>
     Subject: Foundation support for private colleges
Content-Type: text/plain; charset=us-ascii
Content-Transfer-Encoding:  7bit
```

A forwarded message generally contains two parts: the message that is forwarded and a possible introductory note from the person who forwarded it. The following is a typical MIME header for a forwarded message:

```
MIME-Version: 1.0
          To: Boots at Erols account <lcassel@erols.com>
     Subject: [Fwd: FW: ACTC'98 Conference -
              Registration details of 22/05/98]
Content-Type: multipart/mixed;
              boundary="-----------E84033BF21606545DB1F600A"
```

In addition to text and multipart, defined Content-Types include message (the body of the message is another message with its own header and body parts), image, audio, video, and application. Application refers to a type of data that is associated with some particular application program. The receiving user agent may invoke the application program to display the data or save the body of the message as a file for the user to open with the application.

The following is an example of a message containing application-specific data:

```
          To: lcassel@erols.com
Mime-Version: 1.0
     Subject: New version of Excel file
Content-type: multipart/mixed; boundary="part0_888200161_boundary"
    X-Mailer: AOL 3.0 for Windows 95 sub 64
      X-UIDL: 978e7a12f0
X-Mozilla-Status: 8001

Dr LC:
     Attached is a new version of my study attachment.
The new file has TWO SHEETS (Attachments A & B).
Regards, Russ


NETPERF.XLS Content-ID: 0_888200161@inet_out.mail.aol.com.2>
          Content-type: application/octet-stream; name="NETPERF.XLS"
          Content-transfer-encoding: base64
          Content-disposition: inline
```

The main message header shows the body as multipart and mixed types. There is a text message explaining the attachment. The attachment has its own MIME header fields. The type of data is octet-stream. The name of the attached file includes the extension XLS, which clues the UA to the specific application to use to read the data.

5.1.3 Access Units

In addition to a user agent, the functional model of the message-handling system includes an access unit (AU), which provides access to the mail system by other services such as telex and teletex. A particular class of access unit, the **Physical Delivery Access Unit (PDAU)** provides a gateway between X.400 and postal delivery systems. Though two-way communication between an electronic message delivery system and a conventional postal system is possible, only delivery from the MHS to the postal system is defined in X.400 (1988). The Internet mail system includes access to facsimile machines through procedures defined in RFC 2305, *A Simple Mode of Facsimile Using Internet Mail* [TOMW98]. This allows a distribution list to consist of a combination of e-mail addresses and fax numbers.

5.1.4 Message Store

The MHS object **message store (MS)** addresses two difficulties associated with message handling. First, the UA to which a message is traveling might not be online when the message arrives at the connecting MTA, so the message delivery fails unless the MTA includes a facility for storing the message until it can be delivered. The message store, a part of the MHS, addresses this problem by allowing the MTA to deposit the message and to report successful delivery to the message originator. The message will be accessible to the user agent whenever the user agent (often in a PC or workstation) becomes available. The second difficulty addressed by the message store is the problem of transparent access to archived messages by a particular user when that user moves from one user station to another. Since the message store is part of the MHS, it is accessible from many locations. Message storing and access is thus transparent to the user.

Some of the services of a message store are provided through the **Post Office Protocol (POP)** [Ros96]. A POP3 (version 3 of the Post Office Protocol) server receives mail from an MTA on behalf of some number of users and retains the mail until a UA requests the mail. Many Internet Service Providers (ISPs) operate a POP server on behalf of their clients. Mail resides in disk space maintained by the ISP until downloaded to the user's machine. An option allows mail to be retained on the server and a copy sent to the UA; generally, mail is removed from the server and deposited on the machine running the UA. This allows the ISP to serve many users without needing large amounts of storage. Access to the retained mail messages comes under control of the local UA.

5.1.5 The Protocols

In Figure 5.1, P1, P2, P3, and P7 represent protocols. Notice that no protocol governs the interaction between a user and the UA, between the AU and other services, or between the PDAU and the postal service. Because none of these interactions require communication with a remote peer, their design is unrelated to the functioning of the electronic messaging system. Local definitions that address local needs and preferences are sufficient. The protocols govern communication between cooperating entities:

P1 defines the communication between message transfer agents. A message transfer agent accepts a message from its originator and delivers it to another message transfer agent for eventual delivery to the intended recipient. P1 defines the equivalent of the envelope of postal mail—the information required for delivery of the message to the message transfer agent that serves the user agent of the intended recipient.

P2 defines the (virtual) interaction between the sending and the receiving user. P2 defines the header component of a message—the part that describes the content of the message sufficiently to allow local processing.

P3 defines the interaction between a UA or an MS and its associated MTA. P3 has three components: submission of messages to the MTA, delivery of messages by the MTA, and an administrative function.

P7 defines the interaction between a user agent and its associated message store. P7 has three components: indirect submission (messages are given to the MS to pass to the MTA), retrieval of messages in the MS, and an administrative function.

Although the protocol names and descriptions refer to the functional model of the X.400 message-handling system, they indicate the kinds of communication that must occur between and among the components of any functioning message exchange system.

5.2   THE MAIL ACCESS ENVIRONMENT

The user interface of most mail systems involves running a program that puts the user into an environment where mail-related options are presented. Often, the mail program presents a set of nested menus or icons to guide you. You do not have to remember how to invoke any specific function. A *help* function lists the features provided by the mail system and tells how to access those features. Figures 5.5 and 5.6 show typical mail program interfaces. The guidance available in mail environments helps new users particularly and encourages people who do not use computers extensively by making electronic mail self-explanatory.

Some mail systems, such as the UNIX[1] MH (message handler), consist of several separate programs, each of which provides some mail system function and benefits users who choose to intersperse their mail operations with other activities. For example, in a typical session a user reads a message, runs a program to process some data, replies to the message, forwards the message to colleagues, checks the calendar, sends a message to someone to propose a meeting, checks to see who is currently logged onto the system, enters *talk* mode to chat with someone, and so on. MH functions in this way. There is no mail environment. Each command is entered separately as needed. The commands can also be called from within a program, which makes it easy to build applications based on mail services. Figure 5.7 gives a brief description of the principal MH commands as found in the UNIX manual pages. Figure 5.8 is a complete list of MH commands. These include some functions that are used by other functions to produce the mail service. For example, the command *whatnow* is used by *send, repl,* and *forw* on exit from the editor to allow you to choose to continue and release the message or make a change or cancel. Though these functions are not available to a person to execute directly, they can be invoked by a program that has

---

[1] UNIX is a trademark of UNIX Systems Laboratories.

```
& ?
   Mail Commands
t <message list>            type messages
n                           goto and type next message
e <message list>            edit messages
f <message list>            give head lines of messages
d <message list>            delete messages
s <message list> file   append messages to file
u <message list>            undelete messages
R <message list>            reply to message senders and all recipients
r <message list>            reply to messages go back to /usr/spool/mail
pre <message list>          make messages go back to /usr/spool/mail
m <user list>               mail to specific users
q                           quit, saving unresolved messages in mbox
x                           quit, do not remove system mailbox
h                           print out active message headers
!                           shell escape
cd [directory]              chdir to directory or home if none given

A <message list> consists of integers,
ranges of same, or user names separated
by spaces. If omitted, Mail uses the last
message typed.

A <user list> consists of user names or aliases
separated by spaces.
Aliases are defined in .mailrc in your home directory.
&
```

Figure 5.5. Basic UNIX Mail

need of the function. In windowed multitasking environments, the ability to access individual programs from other programs becomes more significant than interspersing nonmail activities with mail-related actions.

Since electronic mail has become a nearly universal computer application, there are now many different styles of interfaces to the mail function. Many use the Windows style and allow actions to be specified by pressing a button. The best mail program for a given application depends upon who will be using it and how it will be used. If you are building a new application that must invoke mail services, you will want a mail system that allows you to call its individual functions. If you are using the mail system to send and receive mail, you need to consider the kind of functionality that matters to you. The most basic operations of the mail system, as the user sees it, include the ability to construct a new message for handoff to the mail delivery system and the ability to display a message that arrives from the mail delivery system.

As you evaluate mail packages, be sure to look beyond the surface to the actual services offered. Mail systems should support the user in constructing messages, displaying received messages, retaining messages in a well-organized collection from which it is easy to retrieve what is needed; they should support all the addressing methods the user needs and make it easy to give aliases to frequently used addresses and groups of addresses. The mail system interface should make it easy for the user to respond to a message by putting comments into a copy of the original message. The mail system should allow you to resend a message that arrived in one place and should be somewhere else. Resend is not the same as forward: when a message is resent, it goes to a new destination looking as though it arrived there in the first place, without the detour. Only close examination of the message header will determine that there was an extra step along the way. A mail system should allow you to

Mail systems should support the user in constructing messages, displaying received messages, retaining messages in a well-organized collection from which it is easy to retrieve what is needed; they should support all the addressing methods the user needs and make it easy to give aliases to frequently used addresses and groups of addresses.

145

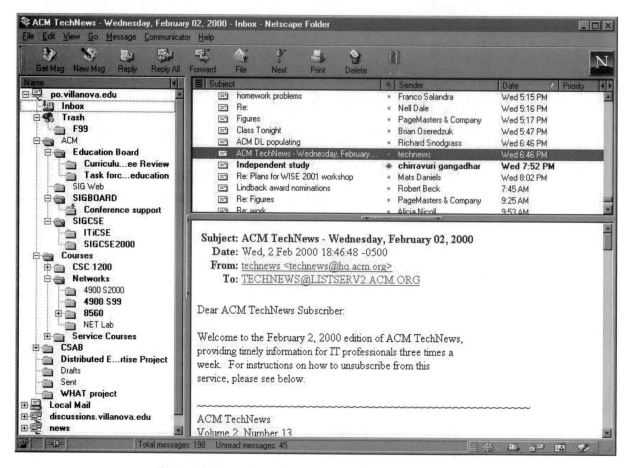

Figure 5.6. A Windows-based mail interface

append a signature to each of your messages without having to type it each time. Of course, displaying a message means handling information in any of a number of formats: text, voice, image, and so on. Some mail systems automatically display any URL as a link and will open your default browser program to display the indicated page if you click on the link in the mail message. Some include full browser capability and can display messages that include HTML code.

In the sections that follow, we look more closely at what the user can expect in the interface and what must happen behind the scenes to make those services available. We will not go into detail of the configuration of mail systems to make them provide these services because the configuration details vary greatly from one system to another. Our goal is to point out the issues that must be addressed.

inc   moves mail from your system maildrop into your MH `+inbox' folder, breaking it up into separate files and converting it to MH format as it goes. For each message it processes, it prints one line containing the from field, the subject field, and as much of the first line of the message as will fit. It leaves the first message it processes as your current message. You will need to run inc each time you wish to incorporate new mail into your MH file.

Scan   Prints a list of the messages in your current folder.
The commands **show**, **next**, and **prev** are used to read specific messages from the current folder. **show** displays the current message, or a specific message, which may be specified by its number, which you pass as an argument to show. **next** and **prev** display, respectively, the message numerically after or before the current message. In all cases, the message displayed becomes the current message. If there is no current message, show may be called with an argument, or next may be used to advance to the first message.

rmm   (remove message) deletes the current message. It may be called with message numbers passed as arguments, to delete specific messages.

repl   is used to respond to the current message (by default). It places you in the editor with a prototype response form. While you are in the editor, you may peruse the item to which you are responding by reading the file @. After completing your response, type l to review it, or s to send it.

comp   allows you to compose a message by putting you in the editor on a prototype message form and then lets you send it.

All MH commands may be run with the single argument `-help', which causes them to print a list of the arguments they may be invoked with.

Figure 5.7. MH mail command summary

5.2.1   Message Creation and Presentation

Once the mail program is entered or the set of mail-related programs is available, the user wants to send mail or view mail that has arrived. Entering a text message usually requires invoking an editor. Alternatively, the text may be brought in from a file or entered with a scanner. Increasingly, the message is not simply text. Voice mail allows an audio clip to be sent. You might want to send a spreadsheet—not just a text representation, but the actual spreadsheet format, including formulas in the cells and definitions of graphs. You might want to send a PostScript file, which is a way to send a formatted file directly to compatible printers. Your message might be multimedia, including video, high-resolution images, audio, and hypertext. Knowing the format of the message contents, you can select the most suitable method for capturing it and packaging it for the mail system to transmit. Once the message is handed off to the MTA, its content is not significant. The MTA takes whatever it is given and delivers it to the intended destination.

The situation at the receiver's side is somewhat different. By previous agreement, the user agents have chosen to use the same format for information in the message header. Thus the user agents can communicate with each other about where the message comes from and where it must be delivered. Presenting the message to the user can be a complex

Command	Description	Command	Description
ali	List mail aliases	anno	Annotate messages
burst	Explode digests into messages	comp	Compose a message
dist	Redistribute a message to additional addresses	folder	Set/list current folder/message
folders	List all folders	forw	Forward messages
inc	Incorporate new mail	mark	Mark messages
mhl	Produce formatted listings of MH messages	mhmail	Send or read mail
mhook	MH receive-mail hooks	mhpath	Print full pathnames of MH messages and folders
msgchk	Check for messages	msh	MH shell (and BBoard reader)
next	Show the next message	packf	Compress a folder into a single file
pick	Select messages by content	prev	Show the previous message
prompter	Prompting editor front-end	rcvstore	Incorporate new mail asynchronously
refile	File messages in other folders	repl	Reply to a message
rmf	Remove folder	rmm	Remove messages
scan	Produce a one line per message scan listing	send	Send a message
show	Show (list) messages	sortm	Sort messages
vmh	Visual front-end to MH	whatnow	Prompting front-end for send
whom	Report to whom a message would go	mh-alias	Alias file for MH message system
mh-format	Format file for MH message system	mh-mail	Message format for MH message system
mh-profile	User customization for MH message system	ap	Parse addresses 822-style
conflict	Search for alias/password conflicts	dp	Parse dates 822-style
install-mh	Initialize the MH environment	post	Deliver a message

Figure 5.8. MH mail complete command list

problem when so many choices are available. In the OSI approach, these problems are in the domain of the Presentation layer. Isolating presentation complexity relieves the mail system developer of them and allows the treatment of presentation problems for mail systems to benefit from the treatment of similar problems in other contexts. Thus, the mail system developer is freed to concentrate on issues more closely related to mail. Since TCP/IP does not separate out presentation functions, the mail programs must deal with the complexities. The MIME extensions to Internet mail provide functionality that would belong to the Presentation layer in the OSI reference model. The difference is that these extensions are built into the particular application—mail—and do not transfer immediately to other situations where communications between processes include multiple formats.

5.3 DEALING WITH ADDRESSES

In electronic mail, as in postal mail, the sender must provide the address of the intended receiver of a message. Addresses for postal mail include information essential to delivery of the mail. In most countries, mail addresses provide decreasing levels of detail from the top line of the address to the bottom. The address starts with the name of a specific person, continues with a department and company name if appropriate, continues with a street address, then specifies the city, state, and zip code in the United States, or other information relevant to a particular country. All the information has to go on each piece of mail.

Electronic mail systems also have requirements about the form and content of an address. An address specifies enough information for the mail system to deliver the message. The mail system requires that the format of the information conform to some requirements. If we addressed a letter to someone with only "Albany, In the Empire State," chances are that it would come back to us marked "Insufficient Address." (The post office has dealt successfully with stranger things, however.) An electronic mail system requires that the user provide needed information in an expected form.

Let us consider two classes of addresses, local and remote. A local address calls for delivery to another user in the local mail system. The address is anything the local mail system recognizes, which commonly is the same as the login name. Its purpose is to tell the mail system where to deposit the mail. On a small network with few users, first names are sometimes used. Although attractive in a small group, this practice quickly brings problems if the group grows or is linked to other groups. Some systems offer use of a full name, such as Mary_Tempe or John.Q.Jones. It is particularly useful to have a predictable pattern used as the login so that people can guess at the login name of someone else instead of looking up each different user. Possibly the most common form of login name is first initial followed by last name for a maximum of eight characters.

Access to a local user requires only use of the local name. When the message must leave the local system, the address must conform to a standard accepted by all the systems that might receive it. Incomplete or unrecognized e-mail addresses cause the message to be returned to the sender.

5.3.1 Making Two Different Mail Systems Talk to Each Other

What happens when users who select different mail systems want to exchange mail? The degree of difficulty depends upon the nature of the differences between the systems. If the mail systems provide very different user interfaces, but use the same or compatible MTAs underneath, the exchange of messages proceeds easily. Many mail systems are built on top of SMTP. Any user agent can be used to generate the message handed over to SMTP. (SMTP does not define the steps for delivery of local mail, mail that does not leave the sender's machine. The local mail system can handle that any way it wants.) SMTP does establish a connection with its corresponding program on the destination machine. It passes the message to the destination SMTP, which makes it available to the local user agent for notification of the recipient. SMTP also generates messages when failures occur in the message transfer process. SMTP, in turn, uses TCP/IP protocols to carry out the message delivery.

If the two mail systems do not use the same underlying message transfer protocols, then they cannot work together. One will not know how to contact the other, or what control codes to send it if it could make contact. Header fields will vary, and the correspondence will not be clear. There are several ways to approach establishing cooperative communication between such systems.

First, each message transfer agent could be programmed with the methods needed to communicate with the other. Then, when mail system A wants to send a message to a user of mail system B, A is careful to use B's protocol. Though that approach may be practical if only a small number of protocols are attempting to communicate, it quickly becomes unwieldy. If A has messages for users of systems B, C, D, and so on, it will spend a great deal of time making all the necessary protocol conversions.

A second approach is to identify a machine that does understand both protocol A and B. That machine takes in messages in format A, converts them to format B, and sends them to the destination. It also converts from B to A for messages going the other way. Such a machine is called a *mail gateway*. Mail gateways provide an important link between very different mail systems and allow much broader access than would be possible if each user were restricted to mail systems that used the same protocol.

A third approach to handling incompatible mail systems is to define a universal standard that all systems understand. When mail is exchanged between two type A mail systems, no conversions are needed, and the transfer is quick and efficient. However, when mail system A wishes to send to any other type of mail system, it does not attempt to convert to that system. Instead, it converts to a universal standard, say, mail system X, and sends the message. It knows that the other host does not understand system A, but does understand X. The destination system will receive the converted message in the X standard and process it correctly.

It might seem that if we can define a universal standard, there is no need for mail system A, B, and C to exist at all. Everyone should just use the standard. Though sensible in many ways, this solution is unlikely to occur. First, the users of system A, and so on, may be convinced that system A is far superior to the universal standard and may not want to give it up. Second, in the context of some particular use, system A *is* better than the universal standard X. By its very definition, X must meet every need that anyone can identify for a mail system. That makes it complex and much more cumbersome than what is needed for simple mail transfer in most cases. For these and other reasons, the individual mail systems will continue to exist. The advantage of the universal system is that even those who do not choose to use it for most cases can use it to communicate with other special systems. The concepts of mail gateways and use of a universal standard as a middle ground are combined in systems where the mail gateway converts from a local system to the universal standard and then transfers the mail to another gateway that does the reverse conversion, from the universal system to a different local system. X.400 is often used as this universal mail standard.

5.3.2   Internet Domain Name Addresses

By far the most common type of nonlocal address is the domain addressing format defined in RFC 822 [Cro82] and used in the Internet. Domain addresses consist of two parts: the local address part and the domain. The two parts are separated by the @ symbol, as *local@domain*.

The local address part tells the local mail system where to deposit the mail. The domain part tells other mailers where the local part is. The domain part may be subdivided into several subdomains, depending on how incoming mail is handled at the destination site.

For example, suppose we have mailboxes located on each of five local hosts or servers: dddddd, mmmmm, kkkkkk, cccccccc, and ppppp. To send a message from Sue_Worth to Tom_Peters, when both have mailboxes on dddddd, only a local address is needed. Sue might type *mail Tom_Peters* to enter the mail program and start a message to Tom. To send a message to Clare_Lancy, whose mailbox is located on mmmmm, Sue would type *mail Clare_Lancy@mmmmm*. Because the mail system on dddddd recognizes mmmmm as the name of another local system, dddddd's mailer can deliver the mail to mmmmm, and mmmmm's mail system will receive it and deposit it in Clare's mailbox.

5.3.3 Resolving Addresses: Domain Name Service

To send mail to a machine not known to the local mailer, the mail system must have additional information. The address *Bob_Beann@stateu.edu* includes a two-level domain. It identifies *stateu* as a destination in the collection of destinations jointly designated *edu*. Part of the configuration of an SMTP-based mail system is identification of a set of **Domain Name Servers (DNS)**. A DNS is a service that accepts queries concerning name-to-address mapping in a particular domain. A DNS for the *edu* domain receives a query for the address associated with stateu and returns a network address associated with that domain. Since this example contains only a two-level domain, the network address of stateu is the location to which this mail must be delivered. SMTP then opens a session with its peer at the address associated with stateu. The process appears in Figure 5.9. If the session is successful, the mail will be passed to the SMTP process at the stateu machine. Some addresses

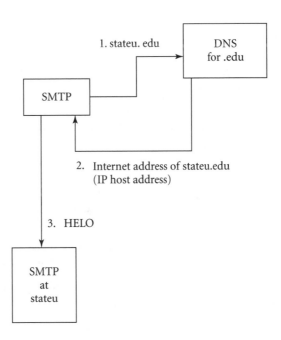

Figure 5.9. Querying the domain name server and transferring a message

.uk	United Kingdom
.fr	France
.mx	Mexico
.ca	Canada
.us	United States

Figure 5.10. Sample country codes

contain more subdomains. To deliver mail to *tiger.villanova.edu*, the SMTP process would query the *edu* domain server to get an address for villanova. It would then query the server for the domain villanova to obtain an address for tiger. Finally, SMTP would establish a session with its peer on tiger and the mail would be delivered.

Surprisingly, some modern electronic mail systems assume that nearly all mail will be local and make the user treat nonlocal mail in a special and inconvenient way. The effect of this is to make the user do extra work in order to invoke the DNS process associated with the mail system. Such mail systems are poorly designed and should be avoided. The user should be able to enter any properly constructed address. It is the responsibility of the mail system to understand the kind of address it sees and to invoke the processes required to handle it.

In the Internet DNS, there are three types of top-level domain names: countries, networks, and organizational designations used in the United States and Canada. The full set of country designations is found in [Cou]; Figure 5.10 shows a sample. The network top-level domains are a temporary convenience for providing access between networks that use the domain name addresses and those that do not. For example, addresses used in BIT-NET, EARN, and NetNorth have a format different from the domain naming scheme. To pass mail to a mailbox on one of those networks, an address translation must be done in a gateway connecting the networks.

> It is the responsibility of the mail system to understand the kind of address it sees and to invoke the processes required to handle it.

Figure 5.11 describes the organizational designations used in the United States and Canada. These designations really should be subdomains of a top-level domain *us* or *ca*, but survive for historical reasons as domain names in their own right. Some networks have begun to use the *us* domain modified by host, organization, city, and state, so you might see an address such as

```
cassel@tiger.villanova.villanova.pa.us
```

to mean Cassel on host *tiger* at Villanova University (villanova) in Villanova, Pennsylvania, USA. For such an address form to work, there must be a domain server system that translates an address of this form to a particular machine address. This requires that domain servers exist for the domains us, pa, villanova, and vu. In other words, a sender must be able to query a domain server that resolves the next level of domain address and returns the necessary information for contacting the destination.

Each host that is accessible through any network, or interconnected collection of networks, must be associated with a unique network address. In mail systems that run over

.edu	Educational institutions
.com	Commercial sites
.gov	Government sites
.net	Sites with special relationship to the network
.org	Other organizations
.mil	Military sites

Figure 5.11. Organizational domain designations

the TCP/IP protocols, the host has an IP address. Within that host, the incoming communication is handed to the TCP process. TCP hands the message to its SMTP client, identified by a **TCP port number**. SMTP in turn gives the message to the user agent that requests incoming messages on behalf of a particular user. All told then, the user is located by the combination of a host IP address, the TCP protocol process, the SMTP process, and a particular user agent. In X.400, a similar mapping must occur. The terms used to describe the parts of the system are different, but the effect is the same. A network address identifies a particular machine. The transport, session, and presentation process identifiers connect to the particular user agent that receives mail for the user.

5.3.4 X.400 O/R Addresses and the Directory

X.400 also includes a procedure for mapping a name to a machine destination. The addresses used in X.400 consist of attribute/value pairs. For example, surname = cassel, common name = kevin, organization = campus corner, organization unit = transportation, country = us, state = pa identifies a particular employee of a particular organization. This attribute/value pairing is well suited to look up in a directory database. Chapter 8 considers the directory service used by X.400. The end result is the same as in the DNS lookup: the MTA learns where to deliver this message.

Originator/Recipient Address

MHS delivers a message from a submitting user to an intended recipient user. The recipient must be unambiguously specified. Ultimately, the recipient is identified by a PSAP, the place where the recipient's user agent is attached to the communications system. The fully specified PSAPs at which the sender and recipient are reached is called an **O/R address** (for originator/recipient). The O/R address consists of a network address, a selected transport entity, a selected session entity, a selected presentation entity, and an association active in the presentation entity. This complex address is not convenient for users to remember or to provide; moreover, it could change from one contact to another. It is more efficient, therefore, for the originator to specify a name for the intended recipient in a form that can be found in a directory. The directory service associated with an MTA provides the O/R address when presented with a suitably formatted name.

5.3.5 Aliases and Distribution Lists

Some addresses are simple and easy to remember. Others are long and cumbersome and very difficult to recall. A shortened, more intuitive form of the address, that is, an alias, saves time and reduces errors. For example, when Dave and Chris learn to bypass the postal system and communicate by electronic mail, Chris might tire of typing

```
Dave_Morris@stonehenge.schoolname.edu
```

and define an alias such as

```
Dave: Dave_Morris@stonehenge.schoolname.edu
```

She would then use "Dave" in the address part of all e-mail messages. Most mail systems have some facility for making aliases. An alias is just a private designation for an official address.

In addition to simplifying unwieldy addresses, an alias can represent a collection of addresses often used together. Thus, a project leader might establish an alias that includes all members of the project team. Mail intended for every member in the team carries just the alias: *mail projectteam*, for example. The alias *seminar* in Figures 5.12 and 5.13 simplifies message exchange among a group of people participating in a study group. An alias for a group of addresses is called a **distribution list**. Some mail systems distinguish between aliases and distribution lists, and keep them separate.

Aliases are stored in a file that is known to the mail system. The format is a component of the user environment provided by a particular mail system. For example, the standard UNIX mail program uses a file called .mailrc to hold aliases and other information that customizes the mail program behavior for a particular user. Figure 5.12 shows a typical .mailrc file. The first three lines in the file define options for the mail program. *set askcc* tells the mail program to prompt the user for who should receive courtesy copies of the message. *ask* requires the mail program to prompt for a subject line. *set EDITOR vi* specifies that this user chooses to use vi (the UNIX *visual* editor) whenever an editor is needed. The first alias shown in the file is the one we defined for Dave Morris, but it is formatted correctly for this system (the word *alias*, then the short name, then the full address). The address *cscfaculty* shows the format required for a group address. The MH mail system uses a file, which the user can name, containing only aliases. Figure 5.13 shows a sample alias file. Some graphical mail systems, such as the Netscape mail system, call the alias file the **address book**. An example Netscape address book appears in Figure 5.14. An example individual entry and a group entry from the address book file appear in Figure 5.15.

Usually, an alias cannot contain another alias. Thus in Figures 5.12 and 5.13, the alias for Dave cannot reappear in the group alias for "seminar"; the full address is repeated. In the case of Netscape mail, an address must first be entered into the address book before it

```
set askcc
set ask
set EDITOR vi
alias Dave Dave_Morris@stonehenge.schoolname.edu
alias cscfaculty beck@ucis,\
          brooks@ucis,\
          ching@ucis,\
          fleischma@ucis,\
          goelman,\
          gormley@ucis,\
          joyce@ucis,\
          nadi,\
          cassel
alias seminar Dave_Morris@stonehenge.schoolname.edu
          beck@vaxcom,\
          brooks@vaxcom,\
          map@vaxcom,\
          joyce@vaxcom,\
          goelman, cassel
```

Figure 5.12. Aliases in a UNIX mail system

```
Dave: Dave_Morris@stonehenge.schoolname.edu
cscfaculty: beck@ucis,\
             fleischma@ucis,\
             goelman,\
             gormley@ucis,\
             joyce@ucis,\
             levitin@ucis,\
             map@ucis,\
             soong@ucis,\
             nadi,\
             cassel
syl: Jackson@brahms.udel.edu
kevin: "KEVIN CASSEL" <256686673@ucis>
david: 223482770@ucis
dick: austing@cs.umd.edu
Seminar: beck@ucis,\
             map@ucis,\
             Dave_Morris@stonehenge.schoolname.edu,\
             joyce@ucis,
             goelman,cassel
```

Figure 5.13. Aliases in the MH mail system

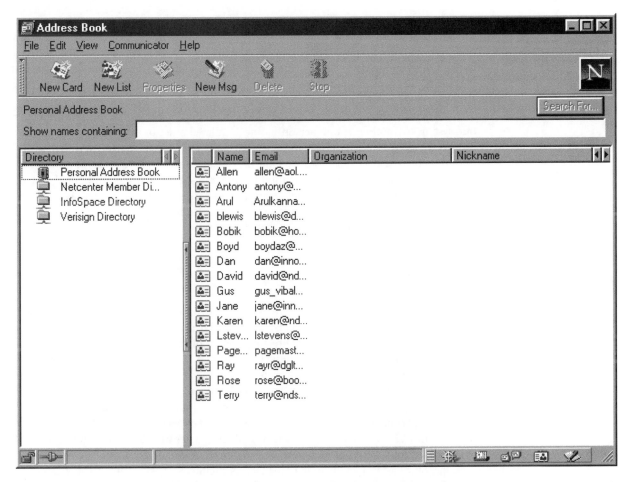

Figure 5.14. An address book defined in Netscape mail

```
dn:   cn=Bill Cassel, mail=wcassel@corp.com
cn:   Cassel, Bill
sn:   Cassel
givenname:  Bill
objectclass: top
objectclass:  person
mail: wcassel@corp.com
xmozillanickname:  bill
xmozillausehtmlmail:    FALSE
xmozillauseconferenceserver: 0


dn: cn=Household family
cn: Household family
objectclass:  top
objectclass:  groupOfNames
member:  cn=Bill Cassel, mail=wcassel@corp.com
member:  cn=David and Dawn Cassel, mail=ddcassel@isp.com
member:  cn=Eric Cassel, mail=whtcstl@postoffice.isp.net
member:  cn=Kevin Cassel, mail=kcassel@isp.com
xmozillanickname: family
```

Figure 5.15. An individual and a group entry in the Netscape mail address book file

can be included in a list. Once the address enters the address book, it can be changed in any one place and automatically becomes updated in all lists where it appears. See the reference to Bill Cassel in the `Household family` entry in Figure 5.15. The restriction against lists inside lists prevents loops from forming in aliases (as, for instance, when two group addresses each refer to the other by alias name).

Note that although most mail systems allow definition of aliases, the format varies from one system to another. If one person has accumulated a list of mail addresses, such as a group of people with a common interest, sharing it with someone using a different mail system is not easy. The person receiving the list must reformat it. Because some groups have hundreds of members, this incompatibility constrains alias sharing. Some mail systems will allow lists to be constructed only from the addresses known to a systemwide address list. This is not convenient for people whose lists include people from client companies, suppliers, and perhaps personal contacts, such as doctor's offices.

5.3.6   Distribution Lists in X.400

Multiple recipients are specified in X.400 systems by listing their names or addresses, or by providing a list name, a Distribution List (DL). The DL is in a format suitable for looking up in the Directory. DL entries in the Directory consist of several components (attributes, in directory terminology): the first attribute is the list of names of members of the distribution list (some of which may be names of distribution lists themselves); the second attribute is an O/R address associated with the DL. The DL owner and the DL submit permission attributes may also be stored. The owner has rights to modify the content of the DL, while the submit permission attribute identifies users who are permitted to send messages using the DL. The O/R address corresponding to a DL designates the MTA where the address will be expanded into the set of individual destination O/R addresses for use in delivering the message. Since a DL may include other DLs as members, it is possible for the same end user to be addressed more than once in a fully expanded DL. The MTA is not responsible for noticing and eliminating duplicates bound for the same destination. Such service could be provided by the recipient's UA or as a function of the MS. More serious than duplicate copies is the possibility of a loop in the expansion. Prevention of such loops is a function of the MTS.

5.4 RETAINING AND DISCARDING MESSAGES

Once delivered, a mail message can be kept or deleted. When the user keeps a message for later reference, it should be stored with others that share a common characteristic. Most mail systems use a term like *folder* or *mailbox* for the collection of messages. We will use the term *folder*.

5.4.1 Folders

A *folder* acts like a file folder found in file cabinets. File folders hold paper documents that have a common characteristic. A mail folder is a type of file that contains mail messages. The mail system user accesses messages in any folder in the same way that he or she accesses new mail. Using the mail system, the user can display the sender name and subject line of all messages in the folder, display any message, reply to messages, delete, or forward any of them. The user organizes folders any way that is convenient: by subject, by group of people or individual, or by project, for example.

Two common problems with mail system folders are similar to problems with any storage facility. Once the message is filed, it can be easily forgotten. Folder names must suggest their contents. Further, old messages accumulate and occupy storage space. Periodic review and purging of folders releases space occupied by old messages. Some UA and MS implementations include automatic deletion of obsolete messages. In some mail systems, a message can be filed in more than one folder. Only one copy of the message exists. Each folder lists the message and contains a pointer to the one copy. Many systems include search functions that allow a user to search through stored messages, either restricted to a folder or throughout the whole system, for a particular message. Searching can be done by subject, sender, date, or full text search of the message body.

The mailbox in which mail is delivered to the user is just a folder of unread mail. This is the default folder for all mail system commands. One message in the folder is the *current* message—usually the most recently displayed or the first in a set of newly arrived messages. Commands such as *delete* and *reply* refer to the current message unless some other message identifier is given. A message in any folder can be read or moved to a different folder. Once stored, the message can be moved again, even back to the mailbox to be treated as new mail.

5.4.2 Message Storage and Retrieval

One constant in the descriptions of folders and the user's access to them is the need for the user agent to have access to the folder. On a large, multiuser system, this is straightforward. A user agent running on a personal computer presents several difficulties to the MHS. First, a personal computer may not always be accessible to an MTA for delivery of messages. If the personal computer is turned off or if the UA is not running, the MTA is unable to deliver incoming messages. The MTA must hold the messages, waiting for the user agent to become available. If the user agent remains unavailable for some time, perhaps as little as 24 hours, the MTA will return a message to the sender indicating that the mail was undeliverable.

The MS addresses these limitations by separating the tasks of receiving, storing, and accessing messages from the other responsibilities of the UA. The message store resides on a system that is usually accessible, provides substantial storage, and is routinely and dependably backed up.

The MS is defined as an abstract service, as illustrated in Figure 5.16. The MS accepts delivery of messages from the MTS on behalf of a single MHS end user and retains messages for subsequent retrieval by the end user's UA. The MS also accepts messages from a UA and submits those messages to the MTS on behalf of the UA. Both UAs and MSs are associated with a single user. Of course, a single file server or host system may support the message store of many users, and many users may use the same mail program, giving them identical UAs.

The MS provides retrieval, indirect submission, and administration services to its user (a UA). Although submission and administration functions are available to users of the MTS (through the services of a UA) when interacting directly with an MTA, the retrieval service is available only between the MS user and the MS. This service allows the user to gather information about messages stored in the MS and to retrieve or delete specified messages. The MS can also perform other functions, such as autoforwarding and alerting.

To retrieve messages, parts of messages, and information about messages received, the MS provides an information base. An information base is a database containing entries representing objects of a particular category or categories. In particular, the **stored messages information base** holds information about message and report deliveries. The information base consists of entries, each of which is made up of attributes. An attribute consists of a type and values. This is the same form as the entries in the Directory, which we consider in more detail in Chapter 8. It is similar to the format of the entries in the Netscape address book file.

Some attribute types are internationally standardized; others are defined locally in national or private administrative domains. Figure 5.17 contains the general-purpose attribute types defined in ITU Standard X.413.

The concept of the MS is an important contribution of the X.400 message handling system. This section contains some details of the MS for those who wish a fuller understanding of its definition and function.

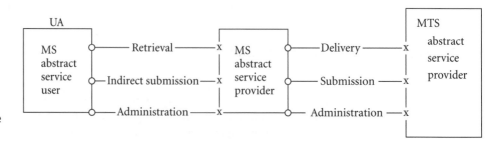

Figure 5.16. Message store abstract service

Attribute-Type Name	Single/ Multivalued	Support Level by MS and Access UA	Presence in Delivered Message Entry	Presence in Delivered Report Entry	Presence in Returned Content Entry	Available for List, Alert	Available for Summarize
Child-sequence numbers	M	M	C	C	C	Y	N
Content	S	M	P	—	P	N	N
Content-confidentiality algorithm-identifier	S	O	C	—	—	Y	N
Content-correlator	S	O	—	C	—	Y	N
Content-identifer	S	O	C	C	—	Y	N
Content-integrity-check	S	O	C	—	—	Y	N
Content-length	S	O	P	—	P	Y	Y
Content-returned	S	O	—	P	—	Y	Y
Content-type	S	M	P	C	C	Y	Y
Conversion-with-loss-prohibited	S	O	C	—	—	Y	N
Converted-EITs	M	O	C	—	—	Y	N
Creation-time	S	M	P	P	P	Y	N
Delivered-EITs	M	O	P	—		Y	N
Delivery flags	S	O	P	—	—	Y	N
DL-expansion history	M	O	C	C	—	Y	N
Entry status	S	M	P	P	P	Y	Y
Entry type	S	M	P	P	P	Y	Y
Intended recipient name	S	O	C	—	—	Y	N
Message delivery envelope	S	M	P	—	—	N	N
Message delivery identifier	S	O	P	—	—	Y	N
Message delivery time	S	O	P	—	—	Y	N
Message origin authentication check	S	O	C	—	—	Y	N

Figure 5.17. General attribute types for stored messages: part 1 of 2

Attribute-Type Name	Single/ Multivalued	Support Level by MS and Access UA	Presence in Delivered Message Entry	Presence in Delivered Report Entry	Presence in Returned Content Entry	Available for List, Alert	Available for Summarize
Message security label	S	O	C	C	—	Y	N
Message submission time	S	O	P	—	—	N	N
Message token	S	O	C	—	—	Y	N
Original EITs	M	O	C	C	—	Y	N
Originator certificate	S	O	C	—	—	Y	N
Other recipient names	M	O	C	—	—	Y	N
Parent sequence number	S	M	C	C P	Y	N	
Per recipient report delivery field	M	M	—	P	—	Y	N
Priority	S	O	P	—	—	Y	Y
Proof of delivery request	S	O	C	—	—	Y	N
Redirection history	M	O	C	—	—	Y	N
Registration indication	S	O	C	—	—	Y	N
Report delivery envelope	S	M	—	P	—	N	N
Reporting DL name	S	O	—	C	—	Y	N
Reporting MTA Certificate	S	O	—	C	—	Y	N
Report origin authentication check	S	O	C	C	—	Y	Y
Security classification	S	O	C	C	—	Y	Y
Sequence number	S	M	P	P	P Y	N	
Subject submission identifier	S	M	P	—	Y	N	
This recipient name	S	O	P	—	—	Y	N

Figure 5.17. General attribute types for stored messages: part 2 of 2

The MS creates and maintains an *entry status* for each entry:

New The message has been neither listed by a UA nor automatically processed by the MS.

Listed The UA has obtained information about the entry through use of either a list operation or a fetch operation, but the message has not yet been fully processed.

Processed Either the MS has performed some automatic action (forward or delete, for example) or the UA has performed some operation that is defined as "completely fetched," the meaning of which is content specific.

The UA's retrieval access to the MS includes the operations *summarize, list, fetch, delete, register-MS,* and *alert.* The operations can be constrained by use of a *range, filter, selector, entry information selection,* or *entry information.*

A range can specify a minimum and maximum sequence number or a range of creation times. Thus, the user can retrieve messages numbered 38 through 55 or messages with creation times from 0001 January 1, 1994 through 2400 January 5, 1994, for example. Either type of range can be specified with no lower bound, resulting in the retrieval of all messages before the upper limit specified.

A filter differs from a range in that it specifies a test to apply to entries. The entry is returned if it satisfies the test. A filter could be used to retrieve entries with Originator-name = Jones and Priority = URGENT, for example.

A selector includes three stages: first a range limits the selection, then a filter further restricts the entries accessed, and finally a limit is imposed on the number of entries returned. Entry information selection further specifies the information from an entry (rather than a complete entry) to be returned.

The summarize operation returns summary counts of selected entries along with a count of the entries selected and the lowest and highest sequence numbers of the selected entries. The register MS operation sets or unsets information in the MS. The user can register a list of autoactions, a default list of attribute types, new credentials, or a new set of user security labels.

In general, the MS offers the user of MHS a powerful tool for storing and retrieving messages and reports that come from the MTS. A user can retrieve messages by subject, by sequence number, by time, by originator, and even by information contained in the message content. The user agent stands between the end user and the MS, and thus the view of the MS available to the user will be determined by the UA through which it is seen. The capabilities made possible by the standard MS present a wide range of possibilities for time-saving services to the user.

5.4.3   Knowing About Mail Delivery or Failure

The amount of information given to the mail user about the delivery of outgoing mail varies. Some mail systems offer options of silent or verbose delivery. Verbose delivery describes all the steps that occur in the process of moving the mail through the networks.

The mail system operation shown in Figure 5.18 is UNIX mail with the verbose option set. The address given, cassel@tiger.villanova.edu, indicates an Internet destination. The UNIX mail system connects to the mail service at tiger and delivers the mail. In

```
cassel@tiger.villanova.edu... Connecting to tiger.csc.villanova.edu. via ether...
220 tiger.villanova.edu Sendmail 5.51/jtc ready at Sat, 17 Aug 96 17:01:45 EST.
>>> HELO tove.cs.UMD.EDU
250 tiger.villanova.edu Hello tove.cs.UMD.EDU, pleased to meet you
>>> MAIL From: <austing@cs.UMD.EDU>
250 <austing@cs.UMD.EDU>... Sender ok
>>> RCPT To: <cassel@tiger.villanova.edu>
250 <cassel@tiger.villanova.edu>... Recipient ok
>>> DATA
354 Enter mail, end with "." on a line by itself
>>>.
250 Ok
cassel@tiger.villanova.edu... Sent (Ok)
Closing connection to tiger.csc.villanova.edu.
>>> QUIT
221 tiger.villanova.edu closing connection
```

Figure 5.18. Mail delivery: verbose mode

the first line of the communication, the local mail server notes that it is connecting to tiger.csc.villanova.edu. The lines that follow form a conversation between the sending UNIX machine, tove.cs.UMD.EDU, and tiger. This conversation is an example of the SMTP operating at both the sender (client) and receiver (server) machine. The lines that begin with the symbols >>> come from the client machine; those that begin with numbers show the server side of the exchange. The opening and closing of the connection indicated at the first and last lines of the figure refer to the transport (TCP) connection between these two processes. (Remember that there is no Presentation or Session layer in this protocol stack.) The SMTP software takes the message from the local mail system and delivers it to its peer at tiger. It will be up to a local mail server on tiger to notify the intended recipient that the mail has arrived.

Although sometimes interesting, this amount of information is distracting when the user wants to do other work. On the other hand, launching a message into the interconnected networks of the world and never hearing about it again may leave you wondering if the message was lost along the way. Something between these extremes serves most purposes. The usual compromise provides notification to the sender only if the system fails to deliver the mail. The failure message comes from the local mail system if it was unable to decide what to do with the message. If the message was forwarded, the failure message comes from the first mail handler that could not proceed with the processing. The failure message may be almost immediate or may take days, depending on whether the error was encountered by the local mailer or a remote mailer and how long a mailer continues trying to deliver the message before reporting failure. When the message takes many days, the problem is that repeated efforts to deliver the message have failed. The error in that case is that a mail system cannot be reached. The mailer will try repeatedly, but will eventually give up. Often, the sender can resend the message, and it will be delivered because the mail service has been restored.

Mail systems offer options about the amount of information to provide concerning successful mail delivery. Some notify the sender when the mail arrives safely at the mailbox to which it was addressed. Others even notify the sender when the recipient has displayed the contents of the message. (These sometimes say they notify the sender when the message has been *read,* but of course there can be no guarantee that the intended receiver actually saw and read the message.)

Some messages from the mailer are easy to understand. For example, the message *unrecognized host name* is clear enough; it usually means that the host name is mistyped.

A failure notice from a mailer often also includes messages that are not clear. Usually, there is enough information in the clear part of the notice to allow the user to solve the problem. The cryptic parts are meaningful to the person who maintains the mail system and are useful in tracking down unusual problems. Most users can ignore these and correct the clearly described problems. If the mail is still not delivered, the user will generally seek help from the mail system administrator of the local system or from the "postmaster" of the system that generated the message.

The postmaster is a human being at each mail site who receives messages addressed to *postmaster@address.* When a message comes from a particular site, indicating that it was not able to deliver mail, and the user cannot determine the problem from the notice, the user can forward the failure notice to the postmaster at the site and request further information about the failure. Figure 5.19 shows a typical failure notice from the mail system. The From

```
(Message inbox:25)
Return-Path:
Received: from wild.ucis.villanova.edu by tiger.villanova.edu id
    <AA12881@tiger.villanova.edu>;
            Sat, 17 Aug 96 09:13:32 EST
Message-Id: <9608171413.AA12881@tiger.villanova.edu>
    Site IP: [153.104.7.161]
Date: Sat, 17 Aug 1996 09:30 EST
From: Postmaster@wild.ucis.villanova.edu (SMTP-OpenVMS Mailer Agent)
To: cassel@tiger.villanova.edu
Subject: Undeliverable Mail
Encoding: 7 Text, Message


Your message cannot be delivered to its destination, and has been returned
to you by the SMTP-OpenVMS delivery agent for the following reason(s):

Error sending mail to <austing@wild.ucis.villanova.edu>:
No such user AUSTING at node WILD


==================:   TEXT OF RETURNED MESSAGE   ==================

Received: from tiger.villanova.edu [153.104.7.161] by ucis.villanova.edu
            with SMTP-OpenVMS via TCP/IP; Sat, 17 Aug 1996 09:30 EST
Received: by tiger.villanova.edu id <AA12875@tiger.villanova.edu>;
    Sat, 17 Aug 96 09:13:24 EST
Date: Sat, 17 Aug 96 09:13:24 EST
From: cassel@tiger.villanova.edu
Message-Id: <9608171413.AA12875@tiger.villanova.edu>
    Site IP: [153.104.7.161]
To: austing@wild.ucis.villanova.edu
Subject: Demo message
```

Figure 5.19. Mail system error messages

```
This will produce a failed mail message.
```

line of the failure message identifies the source of the notice—in this case the postmaster at ucis.villanova.edu. The message was generated automatically, not constructed and sent by the person who fills the role of postmaster on that system. The reason for the failure to deliver the mail is stated: No such user AUSTING at node WILD.

5.5 THE SYSTEM COMPONENTS

The user/system interface discussed in section 5.1.1 is an important part of any mail system because it affects how easily you can get access to the services that make electronic mail an important communication tool. The system components of a mail system represent the "behind-the-scenes" activity that provides the services. In this section, we will look at the system tasks that support electronic mail: parsing the envelope/header, recognizing addresses, receiving mail, and delivering mail. Remember that X.400 distinguishes an envelope, header, and message body. SMTP recognizes only a header and message body.

5.5.1 Parsing the Mail Envelope/Header

When a mail message is ready to send, the user agent hands it over to the message transfer agent.

The two most basic entries in the message header are the `To:` and the `From:` lines. These lines contain the addresses of the message's destination(s) and the message's sender. Section 5.3 looked at addresses used in these entities. Additional header fields that contain addresses include the `cc:` line, which lists recipients of a "courtesy copy" of the message. Listing a destination in the `To:` line or the `cc:` line is a matter of the sender's choice. The message looks the same in either case. Any number of recipients can be listed in either place. A different type of destination line is introduced by the `bcc:` line. The "blind copy" indicates that the listed addresses will receive a copy of the message, but their addresses will not appear in the copies sent to others.

Figure 5.20 shows an ordinary message header. In addition to the addresses of the sender and the recipients, the header includes the current date and time, and a message identifier.

```
(Message mail:17)
Return-Path: maylor@csvax.csc.lsu.edu
Received: from csvax.csc.lsu.edu by tiger.villanova.edu id
          <AA14610@tiger.villanova.edu>; Wed, 22 Apr 92 15:43:04 EST
Received: by csvax.csc.lsu.edu (5.61/1.34)
    id AA29261; Wed, 22 Apr 92 14:45:11 -0500
Date: Wed, 22 Apr 92 14:11 -0500
From: maylor@csvax.csc.lsu.edu (Harriet G. Maylor)
Message-Id: <9204221945.AA29261@csvax.csc.lsu.edu>
To: cassel@tiger.villanova.edu
Subject: Conference
```

Figure 5.20. An ordinary message header

```
Boots

I received your message...
```

The identifier is useful if delivery fails and the message must be traced. As the message moves through whatever systems it must traverse, the message is "stamped." When it arrives at the final destination, the message header shows the path it has traveled and the time spent at various places along the way.

When a message arrives, the receiving message transfer agent must parse the header, extracting and reacting to the information contained there. If one of the addresses is that of a local user, the message transfer agent deposits the message in a place where a user agent can get to it.

5.5.2 Receiving Mail

From a Local User

In this section, we consider what the mail system must do when mail arrives. We begin with mail arriving from a local user. Mail coming from one user and going to another with a login on the same computer system requires minimal processing. The mail message exists as a temporary file in the sender's file space until the mail system takes it. The message transfer agent of the mail system moves the message file to the file space of the recipient and generates a notice to the recipient that mail has arrived. The message transfer agent needs file access privileges to allow it to delete the temporary file in the sender's file space and to write the arriving message in the receiver's space. Alternatively, all the messages can be written in a special storage area to which only the MTA and UAs have access. The user agent provides the user with an interface to the mail system to make it convenient to produce a message and turn it over to the message transfer agent. In delivery between local users, the message transfer agent has an easy task.

There are some potential problems even in a completely local exchange of electronic mail. Many different mail programs have features that appeal to their users. If two or more co-exist on the same system, each must be able to deliver mail that the other can receive. To do so, they must understand each other's mailbox names and locations. They must recognize and respond to the same header fields. (If one mail system produces a header field called ReturnReceiptRequested, and the other does not recognize the field, the sender probably will not get the requested response when the message is read.) The most serious conflict in local mail systems is the possible difference in mailbox conventions. Suppose that mail system A delivers mail to a recipient by depositing into a file called Firstname_Lastname that is located in the system storage area. If the recipient uses mail system B, which looks in a file called Mail_xxxx in the user's area, the two users may not be able to communicate.

From a Remote System

Mail arriving from a remote site requires more processing. The mail program must be active and receive the incoming packets. If the site has only a single domain, such as user@school.edu, the system must listen for queries from remote mail systems seeking to establish a connection and deliver mail. If the site has multiple domains, such as user@host.dept.school.edu, it must maintain a domain server to allow external sites to find individual hosts. Domain servers that manage addresses ending in edu will know the location responsible for subdomains in the school domain. When an MTA wishes to connect to host.dept.school.edu, it will first query the edu server and get an address for the domain server for school. The MTA will then send another query to find the location of dept within the school domain. It will receive the address of a domain server for dept, which in turn will provide the IP address for the machine host.dept.school.edu. The MTA wishing to transfer a message will then send a message to the MTA residing on host.dept.school.edu to establish a connection and transfer the message. It is not necessary to have so many steps involved. The mail system could be configured so that a query to school.edu will return the Internet IP address of host.dept.school.edu without further effort. The best configuration will depend upon the size of the institution and the degree of separation desired among the subdomains.

If the message is addressed as this:

user%hostb.otherschool.edu@hosta.school.edu

the mail program running at the machine known as school treats it like any other mail to deliver to hosta. When the message is received by the mail program at hosta, the following processing is required:

- hosta deletes all the address from the @ sign to the right end.
- hosta then examines what remains with the intention of depositing the mail in a user's mailbox.
- Not finding a user id, but finding another complete address instead, hosta treats the message as if it had originated locally. It looks for hostb.otherschool.edu in its local host file. If it does not find hostb.otherschool.edu, it sends a query to a name server for the .edu domain to resolve the address. It receives the address of the domain server for otherschool, then queries that server for hostb's address. When the IP address comes back, hosta sends the message on to hostb.

5.5.3   Delivery of Mail Messages

We have seen what the mail system must do to receive a mail message and deliver it to the intended recipient. In this section, we consider what the mail system does when it receives a message from a local user and must send it out to another host. Actual movement of the message from one machine to another is provided by lower-layer network services. At this time, we simply assume those services are there and working properly. In later chapters, we will look at those services, how they do their job, and how applications such as mail invoke those services.

Constructing Addresses

The Sender's Address in Messages Sent out of the Local Site.   When a message is sent, the mail system attaches the sender's address to it. When a message goes from one user to another on the same host, the address of the sender can be simple—just the local name. For example, mail sent from user Brooks to user Cates, both on the system tiger.villanova.edu, could have the following addresses in the headers:

```
To: Cates
From: Brooks
Subject: ...
```

If a message from Brooks goes to Drampt on jaguar.villanova.edu, some further qualification is needed. The mail header should now look like this:

```
To: Drampt@jaguar
From: Brooks@tiger
Subject: ...
```

A message from Brooks to Eliason at University of Maryland, needs even more detail, and looks like this:

```
To: Eliason@walrus.umd.edu
From: Brooks@tiger.villanova.edu
Subject: ...
```

Notice that the address that the mail system generates for the sender resembles the address that is used for the recipient of the message. The correspondence need not be so close; if the destination address is complex and involves special steps in the delivery process, the mail system will not attempt to duplicate all the construction in what it generates as the sender's address. It will, however, produce a fully qualified version of the sender's address to aid the recipient's mail system in constructing a reply address if needed.

If Brooks constructs an address for a colleague at a site whose address cannot be resolved locally (that is, the local mail system does not know a domain name server for the domain com) the mail header might look like this:

```
To: Fatih%dogwood.uln.com@mailgate.stateu.edu
From: Brooks@tiger.villanova.edu
Subject: ...
```

The assumption is that the recipient's mail system will be able to generate an address that gets back to tiger. Senders outside the villanova domain require the full domain information for tiger.

The Receiver's Address in Replies. When any of the messages shown arrive at their destination, the receiver may wish to reply. The mail system must then generate the address of the destination of the reply—which is the address of the original sender, but in a form that is recognized on the system that received the original message.

In the first of the examples shown (Brooks to Cates), the mail system's job is simple. It takes the address found on the `From:` line of the original message and places it on the `To:` line of the response. It also takes the address of the `To:` line in the message and makes it the new `From:` line. The second example (Brooks to Drampt) and the third (Brooks to Eliason) work exactly the same way. Whatever was appropriate in the `From:` line of the message that came in works well in the `To:` line of the message that goes in reply.

In the fourth example (Brooks to Fatih), the `From:` line and the `To:` line are constructed according to different rules. A good mail system should recognize a special situation. If the sender address cannot be resolved by the responding mail system, the path used in the `To:` line of the incoming message suggests a possible path for the return. Since the sender routed the message through mailgate.stateu.edu, perhaps we can construct a return path through that same gateway. The mail system first checks to see if the edu domain can be resolved. If not, the return address is constructed as follows:

```
To: Brooks%tiger.villanova.edu@mailgate.stateu.edu
From: Fatih%dogwood.uln.com@mailgate.stateu.edu
Subject: Re: ...
```

By retaining the same form of address in the `From:` field as the sender used in the first place, the mail system makes it easier for the other mailer to reply to us again. Notice, too, that the mail system produces the `Subject:` line in the reply, taking the subject in the original message and putting `Re:` in front of it. This automatic generation of the subject line allows the correspondents to identify easily which messages are part of an ongoing conversation. Often, the mail system generates the subject line, but allows the user the opportunity to modify the line to whatever he or she chooses.

The mail system encounters a more complex problem when a message is sent to a number of people on different sites. Consider the following example:

```
To: Cates, Drampt@jaguar, Eliason@walrus.umd.edu,
    Fatih%dogwood.unl.com@mailgate.stateu.edu
From: ???????
Subject: ...
```

What should the mail system put in the `From:` line? It could make a different `From:` line for each copy of the message that is sent and construct the address appropriately for each. More often, however, the mail system uses the form of the address that satisfies most cases.

In this example, such a mail system would produce the following:

```
To: Cates, Drampt@jaguar, Eliason@walrus.umd.edu,
    Fatih%dogwood.unl.com@mailgate.stateu.edu
From: Brooks@tiger.villanova.edu
Subject: ...
```

That is a bit of overkill for Cates and Drampt's copies of the message, but it is just right for Eliason and all that Fatih can reasonably expect. Many mail systems make no attempt to form the most appropriate version of the address, but just use the one version that works in the largest number of situations.

The question of the destination addresses remains an issue. Though the sender will likely use the short forms shown in the example, the mail system must transform those addresses, providing enough information to allow all the recipients to reply to all the others.

Errors in constructing the sender's address (the return address for the message) or the address of someone receiving a copy of the message, occur commonly in improperly configured systems. If the message goes to a local destination and also to someone on a remote system, many mail servers will fail to expand the address of the local recipient. When the remote receiver attempts a reply intended for all recipients of the original message, a failure message will show that the address of the people who were local to the system where the message originated was not properly formed. Figure 5.21 shows an example where a message bounced back and forth between two mail servers at a site because the address was not recognized. There are two problems here. First, the original message did not expand the addresses of recipients local to the system from which the mail was sent. Then the remote mail system where one person received the message tried to construct a valid address by inserting fields it knew about.

```
Return-Path: <>
 Received: from mailman.site.org (mailman.site.org [110.133.11.2])
     by notel.site.org (8.8.8/8.8.8) with ESMTP
     id 0AA128946; Tue, 30 Jun 1998 14:44:40 -0400
Received: from beta.site.org (baker.site.org [110.133.1.5.])
     by mailman.site.org (8.8.4/8.8.4) with ESMTP id
     OAA22084; Tue, 30 Jun 1998 14:44:49 -0400
Received: by beta.site.org; id OAB01017;
     Tue,30 Jun 1998 14:45:09 0400 (EDT)
  Date: Tue, 30 Jun 1998 14:45:09 -0400 (EDT)
  From: Mail Delivery Subsystem <MAILER-DAEMON@beta.site.org.>
  Subject: Returned mail: Too many hops 21 (20 max):
     from <lcassel@site.org> via localhost, to <local2@email.site.org>
  Message-ID: <199806301845.OAB01017@beta.site.org>
 To: <lcassel@site.org>
 To: postmaster@beta.site.org
 Auto-Submitted: auto-generated (failure)
 X-UIDL: 31d4b4493b23bdbca15a3562978f102c
 Status: U
X-Mozilla-Status: 8001


The original message was received at Tue, 30 Jun 1998 14:45:07 -0400 (EDT)
from uucp@localhost


----- The following addresses had permanent fatal errors -----

<local2@email.site.org>

<local1@email.site.org>


----- Transcript of session follows  -----

554 Too many hops 21 (20 max): from <lcassel@site.org>
via localhost, to <local2@email.site.org>


----- Original message follows -----

Return-Path: <lcassel@site.org>
Received: by beta.site.org; id OAA01017; Tue, 30 Jun 1998 14:45:07 -0400 (EDT)
Received: from mailman.site.org (110.133.11.2])
  by beta.site.org via smap (3.2) id xma000613; Tue, 30 Jun 98 14:44:33 -0400
Received: from beta.site.org (baker.site.org [110.133.1.5])
  by mailman.site.org (8.8.4/8.8.4) with ESMTP id OAA14594; Tue, 30 Jun 1998 14:44:11 -0400
Received: by beta.site.org; id OAA00561;
  Tue, 30 Jun 1998 14:44:31 -0400 (EDT)
Received: from mailman.site.org(110.133.11.2)
  by beta.site.org via smap (3.2)id xma000224; Tue, 30 Jun 98 14:43:59 -0400
Received: from beta.site.org (baker.site.org [110.133.1.5])
  by mailman.site.org (8.8.4/8.8.4) with ESMTP
        id OAA14801; Tue, 30 Jun 1998 14:43:28 -0400
```

Figure 5.21. Mail delivery failure due toincorrect address construction by the mail servers

```
Received: by beta.site.org; id OAA29888; Tue, 30 Jun 1998 14:43:48 -0400 (EDT)
Received: from mailman.site.org(110.133.11.2) by beta.site.org via smap (3.2)
         id xma029700; Tue, 30 Jun 98 14:43:18 -0400
Received: from beta.site.org (baker.site.org [110.133.1.5])
           by mailman.site.org (8.8.4/8.8.4) with ESMTP
           id OAA17581; Tue, 30 Jun 1998 14:42:56 -0400
Received: by beta.site.org; id OAA29637; Tue, 30 Jun 1998 14:43:15 -0400 (EDT)
Received: from mailman.site.org(110.133.11.2) by beta.site.org via smap (3.2)
         id xma029272; Tue, 30 Jun 98 14:42:41 -0400
Received: from beta.site.org (baker.site.org [110.133.1.5.])
           by mailman.site.org (8.8.4/8.8.4) with ESTMP
           id OAA22170; Tue, 30 Jun 1998 14:42:19 -0400
Received: by beta.site.org: id OAA29199;
   Tue, 30 Jun 1998 14:42:38 -0400 (EDT)
Received: from mailman.site.org(110.133.11.2)
   by beta.site.org via smap (3.2)
         id xma028924; Tue, 30 Jun 98 14:42:09 -0400
Received: from beta.site.org (baker.site.org [110.133.1.5])
           by mailman.site.org (8.8.4/8.8.4) with ESMTP
           id OAA15447; Tue, 30 Jun 1998 14:41:46 -0400
Received: by beta.site.org; id OAA28878;
   Tue, 30 Jun 1998 14:42:06 -0400 (EDT)
Received: from mailman.site.org(110.133.11.2)
           by beta.site.org via smap (3.2)
           id xma028667; Tue, 30 Jun 98 14:41:40 -0400
Received: from beta.site.org (baker.site.org [110.133.1.5])
           by mailman.site.org (8.8.4/8.8.4) with ESMTP
           id OAA14642; Tue, 30 Jun 1998 14:41:18 -0400
Received: by beta.site.org; id OAA28587;
   Tue, 30 Jun 1998 14:41:32 -0400 (EDT)
Received: from mailman.site.org(110.133.11.2)
   by beta.site.org via smap (3.2)
         id OAA028450; Tue, 30 Jun 98 14:41:07 -0400
Received: from site.org (ehr0229.ehr.site.org [110.133.138.238])
           by mailman.site.org (8.8.4/8.8.4) with ESMTP
           id OAA18402; Tue, 30 Jun 1998 14:40:46 -0400
Message-ID: <35993133.DB87D4A8@site.org>
Date: Tue, 30 Jun 1998 14:40:52 -0400
From: lcassel <lcassel@site.org>
Organization: National Science Foundation
X-Mailer: Mozilla 4.04 [en] (Win95; U)
MIME-Version: 1.0
To: beck@compsci.csc.vill.edu
CC: local2@email.site.org, local1@email.site.org
Subject: Re: Computer Science accreditation
References: <MAILQUEUE-101.980630141209.480@compsci.csc.vill.edu>
Content-Type: text/plain; charset=us-ascii
Content-Transfer-Encoding: 7bit

I can affirm Bob's ...
```

Figure 5.21. (Continued) Mail delivery failure due to incorrect address construction by the mail servers

5.6 X.400 MESSAGING SYSTEM

We have discussed X.400 Message Handling Systems in parallel with SMTP. In this section, we return to the X.400 model and fill in details of this OSI message handling system that do not have corresponding features in SMTP. You may want to refer to Figure 5.1 throughout the study of X.400 capabilities.

5.6.1 Management Domains

An effective message-handling system must reach users at locations around the world. The number of potential users and the different regulatory environments under which they might live makes management by a single global authority infeasible. The full X.400 facility is thus divided into a number of *management domains,* each consisting of at least one MTA, zero or more UAs, zero or more MSs, and zero or more AUs. Management domains operated by an administration such as a PTT or a telephone company are called Administrative Management Domains (ADMDs).

5.6.2 X.400 in the Application Layer

In this section, we address the X.400 message handling system in its position as an application in the OSI reference model. As an OSI application, X.400 contains elements that concern communications between cooperating systems. There are also aspects of message handling that are not concerned with communications and can be handled locally without need for standardization. In particular, the interface between the user and the user agent is a matter of local design. The MHS application entity (MHS-AE) includes both general-purpose and MHS-specific application service elements. An application context for message handling consists of a combination of ACSE, ROSE, possibly RTSE (all described in Chapter 4), and appropriate members of the following set of service elements:

Message Administration Service Element (MASE) provides for registration of consumers (UA, MS, AU) with a supplier (MTA, MS) and for the exchange of data for the purpose of authentication.

Message Delivery Service Element (MDSE) includes operations for the delivery of messages and reports and control of the delivery process.

Message Retrieval Service Element (MRSE) includes operations for accessing the message store. Operations include *summarize, list, fetch, delete, register,* and *alert.* Alert is used by the message store to notify the user agent of the arrival of a message.

Message Submission Service Element (MSSE) provides operations for submitting messages and reports and for controlling the process of submission.

Message Transfer Service Element (MTSE) allows MTAs to establish associations and send messages, probe messages, and reports.

A number of different implementations of protocols (P1, P2, P3, and P7) are possible using different combinations of the ASEs. For example, an application context corresponding to protocol P7 might or might not guarantee reliable message transmission. If the RTSE ASE is included in the application context, reliable transmission is guaranteed. If RTSE is absent, there is no such guarantee.

There are four application contexts for P3. Each provides access to an MTA by a UA or MS. Access may be initiated by the MTS, thus forcing delivery of a message to the user agent, message store, or access unit, or initiated by the consumer of the messages. Each version can include reliable transmission or not, thus providing the four options. The application context established between the service and destination sides of the communication serves to establish which ASEs exist in application entities attempting to cooperate.

Protocol P1 specifies cooperation between message transfer agents. Different versions of P1 include implementations of the 1984 version of X.400. There are three application contexts for P1: *MTS-transfer-1984* uses the 1984 specification of X.400; *MTS-transfer-protocol* uses the same protocol architecture as MTS-transfer-1984 but includes functions added in X.400 in 1988 (this is accomplished by using the MTSE of X.400 1988 with special versions of RTSE and ACSE that are compatible with X.400 1984); finally, *MTS-transfer* is the 1988 version of the P1 protocol. Because of the existence of these variations on the MTA protocol, gateways are needed not only between X.400 message-handling systems and non-OSI systems, but also between 1984 X.400 and 1988 X.400.

5.6.3 Services

The service elements of MHS provide a collection of services that collectively allow a message to travel from one user to another. Exchange of messages between user agents involves several distinct interactions:

Submission is the interaction by which an originating user agent or message store transfers to a message transfer agent the content of a message and the submission envelope. The submission envelope contains the information known by the UA or MS and required by the MTA to provide the requested service.

Delivery is the interaction by which an MTA transfers the message content and its delivery envelope to the recipient UA or MS. The delivery envelope contains information relative to the delivery of the message.

Transfer is the interaction occurring between MTAs in the process of passing the message and a transfer envelope from the originator's MTA to the recipient's MTA. The transfer envelope contains information concerning the operation of the MTS and information required by the MTS to provide the service requested by the originator.

Notification is the interaction by which the MTS provides notification of delivery or nondelivery to the originating user after submission of a message or a probe.

5.6.4 Message Format

The MTS can carry three types of communications: *messages, probes,* and *reports*. Messages are the ordinary submissions by a user for delivery to an intended recipient. Probes are submitted by a user for the purpose of determining whether delivery is possible. A probe resembles a message except that it has no content; it receives processing from the MTS but is not delivered. A report is a communication initiated by the MTS because of a user request. A report conveys information about an attempt to deliver a message or to process a probe.

The message content includes whatever the originating UA submits for delivery to a destination UA. The MTS is not concerned with the content. Content of an interpersonal message includes a header and body. The header of an interpersonal message user agent protocol data unit (IM-UAPDU) is used by the UA to process messages, including constructing the envelope. The IM-UAPDU header entries appear in Figure 5.3.

Including these fields in formatted entries in the message header allows UAs to use the information included. Thus, a UA could send a notice to a user that some set of messages are approaching the Reply By deadline. Cross Reference and Obsoletes and In Reply To fields could be used to retrieve automatically all the messages that are related. The Reply To field allows the user agent to construct the address for a reply message. The Subject field, in addition to helping a user know what the message is about, could be used to sort messages or to retrieve all messages that deal with a particular subject from the message store.

5.6.5   Security

Message exchange is subject to a number of types of security threats. X.400 specifically identifies the following:

Access threats   Use of the MHS by invalid (unauthorized) users.

Intermessage threats   Improper treatment of messages resulting from access by unauthorized agents. Examples include the following:

masquerade, in which a user is misled into revealing sensitive information by an agent pretending to be a legitimate communication partner.

message modification, in which a real message has been altered by an unauthorized agent before delivery.

replay, in which a legitimate message is captured and replayed at a later date. This could cause duplicate actions or confused operation.

traffic analysis, in which no visible signs of interference are present, but an intruder is aware of message exchange. Even if encryption succeeds in keeping the content of the message secret, useful information can often be obtained from knowing that the exchange occurred.

Intramessage threats   Security threats contained within the original message. Examples include the following:

repudiation means that one of the parties to a communication denies having participated. This is significant in the case of contracts or agreements that have legal consequences.

security level violation means enforcing the security clearance levels implemented in an MTS.

Data store threats   Vulnerability of the many message stores included in the MHS.

Elements of Service	Originating MTS User	MTS
Message origin authentication	P	U
Report origin authentication	U	P
Probe origin authentication	P	U
Proof of delivery	U	M
Proof of submission	U	P
Secure access management	P	U
Content integrity	P	M
Content confidentiality	P	M
Message flow confidentiality	P	M
Message sequence integrity	P	M
Nonrepudiation of origin	P	—
Nonrepudiation of submission	U	P
Nonrepudiation of delivery	U	M

Figure 5.22. Provider (P) and User (U) of Secure Messaging Elements in MHS

The MHS security capabilities are summarized in Figure 5.22. The issue of security in data exchange is further addressed in Chapter 9, which includes encryption and digital signatures.

SUMMARY

Electronic mail represents a common encounter with networks for computer users. Typical functions of e-mail systems were introduced that enable a user to communicate with others in the same network or over interconnected networks. A sampling of the diversity of form and features of mail systems was given. Even though one system may present more commands and options than another, or one may use a colorful graphical interface whereas another is accessed from a command line, the distributed message-handling system is not affected—only a user's view of it.

Specific formats and examples from different e-mail systems were included rather than a full set of details on one particular system. This approach empowers you to be a more sophisticated user of e-mail systems over networks.

We chose the X.400 Message Handling System as the functional model for electronic messaging because it provides a convenient format for general discussion of the many facets of the topic. One of its components, the user agent, plays a significant role in separating the function of providing a service from the user's interface to the service. The UA serves two purposes:

- It simplifies access to the service, masking most of the complexity that is not clearly related to meeting the user's needs.

- It provides a view of the service tailored to the specific needs of the particular users it serves.

Other components of the model include message transfer agents, access units, message store, and protocols. Differences in viewing messages between the MTA of the X.400 model and the SMTP of the TCP/IP stack were identified.

When considering the environment for accessing mail systems, the developer is presented with options. Major functions include creating and presenting messages, address handling, and establishing aliases and distribution lists. Examples from UNIX and the Internet illustrated these functions. Additional important concerns pertain to retaining and discarding messages. The importance of folders to collect mail and a message store to handle messages that cannot be read at time of delivery is indicated. Examples of mail delivery and failure illustrate the developer's options.

A knowledge of system components, such as parsing headers, recognizing addresses, receiving and delivering messages, and making different systems communicate with each other not only makes you an informed user of electronic mail systems but also helps you perform some of the functions of a mail system administrator. Later chapters will explore more topics relevant to this role. In the next chapter, you will experience a second application, sharing and accessing files over networks.

EXERCISES

1. Establish an alias that will allow you to send a message to all students in your class.

2. If you have a login on more than one computer system, investigate one of the mail systems and find out how to have it forward all the mail that comes to your address on the other.

3. What can you say about each of the following addresses? Identify recipient/sender, domain, network, path, how the addressed is parsed, and so on.

   (a) cassel@vuvaxcom.bitnet
   (b) pucc!duvm!vuvm!tiger!monet!cassel
   (c) cassel
   (d) 12345.6789@compuserve.com

4. Look at the following mail failure messages. Where did the trouble occur? If the error might be the sender's, what should he or she do to decide and to correct it if it is? If the failure is not the user's, whom should the user contact about the problem?

```
Return-Path: MAILER@msu.edu
Received: from [35.8.2.2] by tiger.villanova.edu
     id <AA09622@tiger.villanova.edu>;
          Tue, 22 Sep 92 13:16:40 EST
Message-Id: <9209221816.AA09622@tiger.villanova.edu> Site IP: [153.104.7.161]
Received: from MSU.BITNET by msu.edu (IBM VM SMTP R1.2.2MX) with BSMTP
          id 1060; Tue, 22 Sep 92 13:19:34 EDT
Received: from MSU.BITNET by MSU.BITNET (Mailer R2.08 PTF008) with BSMTP
   id 7245; Tue, 22 Sep 92 13:19:33 EDT
Date: Tue, 22 Sep 92 13:19:32 EDT
From: Network Mailer <MAILER@msu.edu>
To: cassel@tiger.villanova.edu
Subject: mail delivery error

Batch SMTP transaction log follows:
```

```
220 MSU.BITNET Columbia MAILER R2.08 PTF008 BSMTP service ready.
050 HELO CUNYVM.BITNET
250 MSU.BITNET Hello CUNYVM.BITNET
050 TICK 2163
250 2163 ... that's the ticket.
050 MAIL FROM:<cassel@tiger.villanova.edu>
250 <cassel@tiger.villanova.edu>... sender OK.
050 RCPT TO:<21874BJK@MSU.bitnet>
250 <21874BJK@MSU.bitnet>... recipient OK.
050 DATA
354 Start mail input. End with <crlf>.<crlf>
554-Mail not delivered to some or all recipients:
554 No such local user: 21874BJK
050 QUIT
221 MSU.BITNET Columbia MAILER BSMTP service done.

Original message follows:

Received: from CUNYVM.BITNET by MSU.BITNET (Mailer R2.08 PTF008)
   with BSMTP id 7244; Tue, 22 Sep 92 13:19:32 EDT
Received: from CUNYVM by CUNYVM.BITNET (Mailer R2.08) with BSMTP id 2163;
   Tue, 22 Sep 92 13:17:59 EDT
Received: from tiger.villanova.edu by CUNYVM.CUNY.EDU (IBM VM SMTP V2R2)
   with TCP; Tue, 22 Sep 92 13:17:16 EDT
Received: by tiger.villanova.edu id <AA09565@tiger.villanova.edu>;
   Tue, 22 Sep 92 13:11:36 EST
Message-Id: <9209221811.AA09565@tiger.villanova.edu>
   Site IP: [153.104.7.161]
To: austing@cs.umd.edu, durton@cpswh.cps.msu.edu, 21874BJK@MSU.BITNET
Subject: Airline settlement
Date: Tue, 22 Sep 92 13:11:35 EST
From: Boots Cassel <cassel@tiger.villanova.edu>

For your information
......
```

5. Evaluate two e-mail systems, including one that is unfamiliar to you. Using a column for each mail system, make entries for all the features you can find on either system. In the column for each mail system, describe that feature or note that it is not available. Your description of a feature should include any restrictions or advantages in its use.

6. Try an e-mail system you have not used before. Keep a log of your experiences in learning its use and setting up special characteristics (which editor to use, where to store old messages, and so on) while learning its use. Write an evaluation of that system as a package to recommend (or not) to inexperienced computer users.

7. A number of commercial, shareware, and freemail e-mail systems are available on PC-based local area networks and have been described and reviewed in popular computing magazines. Choose one or more of these systems (Oracle Office, Lotus, Eudora, Netscape mail, Outlook or Outlook Express, Pegasus, and so on) and research its special features. Include both strengths and limitations. Compare one of them to a mail system found on a larger host, such as the Vax Mail system, UNIX mail, or MH.

8. How would you address the following problem? You are systems administrator for a company with approximately 10,000 employees who have computer systems and need electronic mail access. The employees are distributed over 25 departments in 8 divisions. The sizes of the divisions vary from one that has 2 departments and a total of 50 employees to one that has 7 departments and a total of 3000 employees. The company has been using a mainframe-based mail system and has decided to replace it with one that has a Windows type interface. It is your job to recommend a total electronic mail configuration. Include all the company-based elements of the mail system as described in Figure 5.1. Is it necessary for all employees to use the same UA? Where is uniformity required, and where can individual preferences be accommodated?

9. Within your organization, a special type of file is frequently used. It is a proprietary file type with special meaning in the organization. People want to be able to exchange files of this type and have them displayed properly directly from the e-mail system. How can you address this need, assuming that the organization mail systems are compatible with MIME? Make up such a file format (or use a standard one such as a particular spreadsheet format or a particular word processor format). Make your MIME-compatible mail system properly display the files of this type. Note that there are no specific instructions in this chapter that allow you to do this. You will need to investigate the options of your mail system and learn something about MIME. See RFC 1341 for the MIME specification.

10. (Programming Assignment) Write a program to parse an address and respond as described in section 5.5.2. If the address represents an end user, output the line

```
Mail deposited in Mailbox: <userid>
```

If the address represents another mail machine, output the line

```
Mail sent to address: <new address>
```

where <new address> is the result of this round of parsing. For example, if the original address is user%host.place.domain@otherhost.otherplace.otherdomain, then the <new address> will be user@host.place.domain. Make no restrictions on the number and depth of nesting of addresses.

11. Obtain the specification of the X.400 PDAU standard and implement it, providing delivery of printed messages to users who cannot or choose not to receive electronic messages. (Alternatively, design a specification for a similar service and implement that, including an interface to SMTP.)

12. What AUs can you envision in addition to the PDAU?

13. (Programming Assignment) Assume that your mail system is rather limited. Any mail message going off the local machine must be sent to another machine called mailserver. Unfortunately, the local mail system does not do this automatically. It sends only messages that are explicitly directed to mailserver. Write a program to modify the header of any mail message and change any nonlocal address so that it will go to mailserver. For example, if the mail is addressed to austing, it will be deposited in the local mailbox for austing. If the address is of any other form, such as austing@cs.umd.edu, it must be modified to be of the form austing%cs.umd.edu@mailserver.

14. (Programming Project) Consider the following scenario: You work for a small company that has internal mail functioning, but has no access to mail outside the company. To overcome this deficiency, the company has obtained access to a commercial network that does provide electronic mail. The problem is that there is a charge for connect time to the network. Thus if a company employer gets mail and spends a lot of time reading it, thinking about it, constructing and sending replies, then the charges become substantial. You have been asked to solve the problem by developing software that allows the company employees to benefit from access to the

network mail, but keeps the cost to a minimum. Your software is to present the mail user with an easy-to-use interface that allows the usual mail functions (read, send, reply, forward, keep a copy of a message). The software is to provide this capability with minimal connect time to the commercial network. When your software is executed, for example, it could present options to the user. If the user selects the option *Check for incoming mail*, the software would connect to the commercial network and retrieve any incoming mail messages for that user. The mail would be downloaded to the user's workstation, and the connection to the commercial system would be terminated. The user can then read and respond to the messages without incurring connect charges. When ready, the user would select the option *Send outgoing mail*. The software would then connect to the commercial network and deliver all the user's mail to the message transfer agent of the network. Write such software, using your PC or other workstation as the user's machine, a dial-up connection, and the host on which your mail system resides. Note that these features have been incorporated into some modern mail systems; examine the mail system built into Netscape, for example. Begin by observing what has been done. Evaluate it and decide what you would do differently.

15. Obtain a copy of a host mail system configuration file and determine the following:

    (a) What is the address of the system that resolves .edu domains? .org domains? .es (Spain) domains?

    (b) What other functions can you identify?

    How would you modify the file (or a different but related file) to filter out all mail from a specific address? (This chapter does not contain detailed information about these files because they are different for each type of mail system/operating system combination.) This exercise requires that you research the system to see what you can learn about it. Keep track of what is open to casual browsing and what is restricted. What security considerations are involved?

16. Your organization is about to make a transition from one mail system to another. One of the problems that many people will face is the need to move their existing aliases and distribution lists to the new system. Using two systems to which you have access, develop a process for making that transition. For example, if you are moving from the simple UNIX mail system described in this chapter to the Netscape mail system, how would you reformat and move the alias information to make it accessible to Netscape mail?

17. In changing over from one mail system to another, most users will want to keep access to the mail folders they made under the old system. Using two mail systems accessible to you, develop a scheme for transferring retained mail in folders from one system to the other.

18. Obtain a copy of the sendmail daemon (anonymous ftp from ftp.cs.berkeley.edu directory ubc/sendmail). Install and configure the daemon.

Virtual Terminals

Electronic mail, considered in detail in Chapter 5, is an application that gives a user access to the message-passing capability of networked computers in an obvious way. The message is passed between two users on separate systems, both using services of the network. In electronic mail communication, processes running on the user systems require minimal coordination. Headers must conform to standards that support communication with the message-handling system and that permit the receiving mail system to deliver the message correctly. The mail process supporting the sender does not need to know what kind of system the receiver uses.

In this chapter, we begin to explore more direct interaction between distributed computing systems. First, we consider the case in which a user of one computer system wishes to interact directly with another computer system by using the local system as a terminal to the remote system. In Chapter 7, a process running on one system will need to interact directly with the filestore on another system. The two cases are similar: a process running on one computer system must interact with devices that are part of an entirely separate system. Moreover, the process will interact with different systems at different times. The problem is knowing the features of that remote system in order to interact correctly. The solution is a **virtual device interface**.

6.1 VIRTUAL DEVICE INTERFACE

Figure 6.1 represents the environment in which interoperating systems are interacting with remote devices with unknown characteristics. If it were necessary for every system to know the details of every end system with which it might work, interoperability would be severely constrained. If, instead, each application entity interacts with a common image of that class

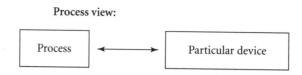

Process view:

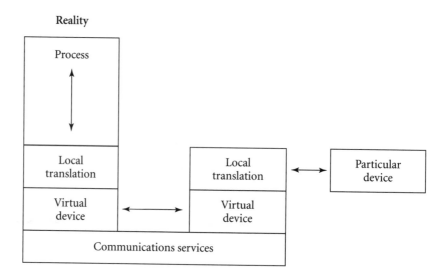

Reality

Figure 6.1. Virtual devices

of device, the problem is reduced to mapping the common image to each possible real end system.

In general, if there are n different types of end system devices (n types of computer systems, each with its own definition of a terminal, for example), then there are n^2 different types of interactions for each process to implement. If there is one common form of the device (a generic terminal, for example), then each of the n systems must interact with only one type of terminal and must translate only between its local characteristics and the generic (virtual) device. The problem is reduced to only $2n$ translations in total; each system talks to the virtual terminal and the virtual terminal is mapped to each real terminal, with each system perhaps using only one pair of them.

The problem then becomes one of defining a suitable virtual device that must permit access to simple devices without adding unreasonable complexity. At the same time, it must encapsulate the properties of very sophisticated devices so that they are also accessible. Virtual terminals, the subject of this chapter, and virtual filestores, the subject of Chapter 7, fill this need.

Translation between the characteristics of a local system and the features of a virtual device is a matter for local implementation, not for the standards process. This is because the standards products deal with system-independent aspects of communication, not with local matters. The only impact of the standards work on the local translation is definition of the interface to the virtual device. Various companies can produce new devices and have them immediately accessible from all interoperating, standards-conforming processes by providing a mapping between the new device and the virtual device to which the processes

Various companies can produce new devices and have them immediately accessible from all interoperating, standards-conforming processes by providing a mapping between the new device and the virtual device to which the processes communicate.

communicate. The communication is provided through a virtual terminal (VT) between the two communicating systems. Each system must be programmed or manufactured to interact with the VT.

6.2 TERMINAL EMULATION

A terminal is a user's tool for interacting with a remote system. The terminal sends and receives characters and display images making remote system access possible. Because no common terminal implementation is universally accepted by manufacturers, applications cannot be designed to interact with a particular type of terminal without limiting the ability of users to interact with them. Three general solutions to this difficulty exist:

- The user's terminal emulation software can have the ability to imitate the type of terminal expected by the application.
- The application can include knowledge of many types of terminals and interact with the particular type the user has.
- Both the user's terminal and the application can assume a common set of terminal characteristics with possible negotiation of special properties as needed.

In this section, we will look at commonly available implementations of each of these solutions: Kermit for terminal imitation, UNIX termcap for matching the application to the user's terminal type, and telnet for negotiating terminal properties. In Section 6.3, we will look at a more complex virtual terminal definition defined in OSI.

6.2.1 Terminal Imitation with Kermit

Kermit, as we will see in Chapter 7, is principally a file transfer protocol. However, the Kermit program allows a user of a computer, usually a microcomputer, to connect to and log into another computer; thus, Kermit allows a computer to play the part of a terminal. There are many terminal emulation programs. We consider Kermit because it is commonly available and typical of such software. Kermit emulates certain very common terminal types, so it presents to the application running on a different computer the type of terminal the application expects [CG89].

The emulation is accomplished by mapping the keys of a user's keyboard to that of the application. Figure 6.2 shows part of the definition of key mappings that Kermit provides to allow the standard 101-key PC keyboard to be used as a VT300 terminal, one of the DEC VT family of terminals. With these mappings defined, the Kermit program will send the code expected by the remote application when the appropriate key is pressed. For example, the DEC VT300 keyboard includes a key labeled *Help*. There is no such key on the 101-key PC keyboard. The line

```
set key \2412 \kdechelp   ; Alt-F5              Help (F15)
```

tells Kermit to send the code associated with the DEC *Help* key when the user holds down the Alt key and presses the function key F5. Kermit, using these mappings, will "look like" a

```
:kb101
echo VT300.INI: IBM-101 Extended Keyboard Setup...
;
; ***************** IBM-101 Extended Keyboard Definitions ****************
;                              IBM KEY                    DEC KEY
set key \2411 \kdecF14      ;Alt-F4                      F14
set key \2412 \kdechelp     ;Alt-F5                      Help (F15)
set key \2413 \kdecdo       ;Alt-F6                      Do (F16)
set key \2414 \kdecF17      ;Alt-F7                      F17
set key \2415 \kdecF18      ;Alt-F8                      F18
set key \2416 \kdecF19      ;Alt-F9                      F19
set key \2417 \kdecF20      ;Alt-F10                     F20

;Cursor Keypad
set key \4434 \kdecinsert   ;Gray Insert                DEC Insert Here
set key \4435 \kdecRemove   ;Gray Delete                DEC Remove
set key \4423 \kdecFind     ;Gray Home                  DEC Find
set key \4431 \kdecSelect   ;Gray End                   DEC Select
set key \4425 \kDecPrev     ;Gray Page up               DEC Prev Screen
set key \4433 \kDecNext     ;Gray Page down             DEC Next Screen
```

Figure 6.2. Part of the key mappings that make a 101-key PC keyboard behave like a VT300 terminal

VT300 terminal, and thus will interact correctly with an application designed to work with that type of terminal.

Applications running on an IBM host frequently expect an IBM-type terminal, which uses a different set of codes to represent the function keys than does a VT300-type terminal. Figure 6.3 shows key mappings that you can add to the Kermit definitions to allow a Kermit connection to an IBM host to send the expected signals when the function keys are used.

Other terminal emulation programs also come with some predefined characteristics to mimic common terminal types. Some of them, like Kermit, allow a knowledgeable user to specify the details of an additional mapping between the PC keyboard and the expectations of the host system applications.

6.2.2   Terminal Conformance with UNIX Termcap

UNIX termcap (terminal capability) is an example of a facility that allows application programs to conform to terminal characteristics rather than having the terminal emulation mimic the type of terminal that the application expects. The file /etc/termcap provides a description of the control codes used by each terminal manufacturer to position the cursor on a display screen and to control features such as blinking characters and reverse video. A small section of the termcap file is shown in Figure 6.4 to give a sample of the definitions available. Each entry has an associated name or alias that allows that description to be matched to the type of terminal specified at the beginning of the session. The remainder of the entry consists of a two-character symbol for each terminal capability and the associated control code. Entries are separated by a colon (:). For example, the first entry in the termcap segment is named Mu with alias sun and Sun Microsystems Workstation console. It is defined to have 34 lines (li#34) and 80 columns (co#80). Some control codes are defined both for application to terminal and for terminal to application. In the example, the control code to move the cursor up one line is defined as up=\E[A to tell the application what code to send to the terminal, and as \sf ku=\E[A to tell the application what to expect from the terminal when a user presses the up arrow key. Some capabilities are boolean. For

;	PC Keyboard	IBM Host
set key \318 \270w	;F4	PF4
set key \319 \270x	;F5	PF5
set key \320 \270y	;F6	PF6
set key \321 \27To	;F7	PF7
set key \322 \270u	;F8	PF8
set key \323 \270v	;F9	PF9
set key \324 \270q	;F10	PF10
set key \389 \270r	;F11	PF11
set key \390 \270s	;F12	PF12
set key \852 \27-	;shift F1	PF11
set key \853 \27=	;shift F2	PF12
set key \854 \27!	;shift F3	PF13
set key \855 \27@	;shift F4	PF14
set key \856 \27#	;shift F5	PF15
set key \857 \27$	;shift F6	PF16
set key \858 \27%	;shift F7	PF17
set key \859 \27^	;shift F8	PF18
set key \860 \27&	;shift F9	PF19
set key \861 \27*	;shift F10	PF20
set key \271 \27\270C	;Tab	Tab
set key \783 \27\270D	;shift Tab	Back Tab
set key \4435 \270M	;Gray Delete	Clear
set key \4424 \270A	;Up arrow	Up arrow
set key \4432 \270B	;Down arrow	Down arrow
set key \4427 \270D	;Right arrow	Right arrow
set key \4429 \270C	;Left arrow	Left arrow

Figure 6.3. Key mapping for using Kermit with an IBM host

```
Mu|sun|Sun Microsystems Workstation console:\
      :li#34:co#80:cl=^L:cm=\E[%i%d;%dH:nd=\E[C:up=\E[A:\
      :am:bs:km:mi:ms:pt:\
      :ce=\E[K:cd=\E[J:so=\E[7m:se=\E[m:rs=\E[s:\
      :kd=\E[B:k1=\E[D:ku=\E[A:kr=\E[C:kh=\E[H:\
      :k1=\EOP:k2=\EOQ:k3=\EOR:k4=\EOS:\
      :a1=\E[L:d1=\E[M:im=:ei=:ic=\E[@:dc=\E[P:\
      :AL=\E[%dL:DL=\E[%dM:
v2|xterms|vs100s|xterm terminal emulator (small) (X window system):\
      :co#80:li#24:tc=xterm:
dQ|qvss|VCB01/02/GPX on MORE/bsd:\
      :am:cr=^M:nl=^J:do=^J:le=^H:bs:cl=^L:co#128:li#54:up=^K:pt:\
      :cm=\E%dV\E%dH:ch=\E%dH:ch=\E%dV:sr=\023\EV\013\022:
vs|xterm|vs100|xterm terminal emulator (X window system):\
      :cr=^M:do=^J:nl=^J:bl=^G:le=^H:ta=^I:ho=\E[H:\
      :co#80:li#65:cl=\E[H\E[2J:bs:cm=\E[%i%d;%dH:nd=\E[C:up=\E[A:\
      :ce=\E[K:cd=\E[J:so=\E[7m:se=\E[m:us=\E[4m:ue=\E[m:\
      :md=\E[1m:mr=\E[7m:me=\E[m:\
```

Figure 6.4. A section of UNIX termcap

example, the entry bs indicates that this type of terminal does have the ability to backspace (the terminal is a display screen rather than a printing terminal).

In a program for an application that intends to make use of the terminal's characteristics, the programmer includes code to read the termcap file so that the application performs correctly with the terminal. A collection of library routines called *curses* [Str91] is available to make this easier. Other operating systems have similar facilities for defining the characteristics of the terminal in use so that the user can communicate effectively with the system. Because there are many types of terminals with very different characteristics, this solution to compatibility between the application and the terminal is not very satisfactory for general use; however, it does provide the only solution when a real terminal, rather than a software emulation, is used.

6.2.3   Terminal Characteristics Negotiation with Telnet

Telnet is an example of software that runs on both the user's system and the remote host and permits cooperation between them in defining the characteristics of a virtual terminal to be used. Telnet is the virtual terminal protocol of the TCP/IP suite. Figure 6.5 shows telnet and its place relative to the other ARPA protocols. Telnet was defined in RFC 764 in 1980 and subsequently refined by RFC 854 [PR83] in 1983. Three key ideas were involved in the definition of telnet:

- The notion of a network virtual terminal
- The principle of negotiated options
- A symmetric view of terminals and processes

The notion of the network virtual terminal (NVT) is a way to avoid very large numbers of potential combinations of host and terminal characteristics. NVT is a particular set of terminal characteristics and behaviors that provides a standard facility with which all hosts can interact. When a telnet session is established, each side of the connection maps its local device characteristics and conventions as if dealing with an NVT and knows that the other side is doing the same thing. Although this provides the convenience of a common terminal interface, it would shortchange users with sophisticated or specialized terminals who require more features than can be defined in the NVT.

The principle of negotiated options addresses this problem by allowing the two sides of the session to establish a common set of extra capabilities. The protocol for establishing these extra capabilities is called *DO, DON'T, WILL, WON'T*. An option can be requested

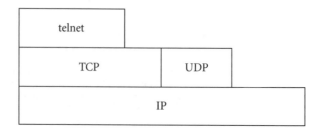

Figure 6.5. Telnet in the TCP/IP protocol suite

by either side of a session. For example, let's use the term *user's side* to indicate the side of the session where the user is and the term *server side* to indicate the location of the responder to the user. The user side of the session, wishing, for example, to enter into binary data transfer mode, would request this change of the server side by sending one of the following messages: WILL TRANSMIT-BINARY, which indicates that the user intends to send binary data, or DO TRANSMIT-BINARY, which indicates that the user wants the server to send binary data. When the server receives the WILL command, it will respond either with DO TRANSMIT-BINARY, which means that it is ok, go ahead, or with DON'T TRANSMIT-BINARY, which means it demands that transmission be in ASCII characters. The server responds to DO with either WILL TRANSMIT-BINARY, which confirms that it will now transmit in binary, or WON'T TRANSMIT-BINARY, which refuses the request to send binary.

The basic terminal assumed by the NVT consists of a keyboard for entering data and a display for receiving output. The default configuration does not echo characters on the display over the network (characters entered locally are also displayed locally). Data exchange is in 7-bit ASCII code, in line-buffered mode. Other options are requested and either confirmed or refused as in the binary transmission example. Options include echoing characters back to the sender, suppression of a go-ahead signal (used to control synchronization), sending status information, and others. The following exchange selects the use of IBM 3270-type full-screen display:

```
   IAC DO TERMINAL-TYPE                        (Do you negotiate terminal type?)
>> IAC WILL TERMINAL-TYPE                      (Yes, I negotiate terminal type.)
   IAC SB TERMINAL-TYPE SEND IAC SE            (Send your terminal choice.)
>> IAC SB TERMINAL TYPE IS IBM-3278-2 IAC SE   (IBM 3270-type terminal)
```

IAC means to interpret what follows as a command. SB is the signal that subnegotiation of options follows. SE indicates the end of parameters of the subnegotiation. In most cases, this negotiation of terminal characteristics is transparent to the user because it has been incorporated into the login process.

The flexibility provided by the use of telnet allows one system to act as a terminal to any other as long as both implement the telnet protocol. This is particularly important in the environment of increasingly interconnected networks. Many types of systems offer a wide range of services. To obtain access to these requires common understanding of interaction between hosts and terminals

6.3 THE OSI VIRTUAL TERMINAL

In Section 6.2, we introduced a number of aspects of virtual terminals in discussing different characteristics of terminals and the difficulties involved in developing applications that interact correctly with any terminal that might be in use. We now turn our attention to the OSI Virtual Terminal Service (VTS). Standards for the OSI VTS model are detailed in ISO 9040. VTS contains many more options for access to terminal characteristics by a remote process than the examples we have seen previously. The overview of VTS given here is intended to illustrate some of the terminal access services available and what is needed to provide them.

6.3.1 VT Classification

The ISO standard classifies virtual terminals as basic, image, graphic, and mixed mode. Basic, image, and graphic class VTs have character, photographic, and geometric data elements respectively. Mixed mode VTs (for example, workstations) have all three kinds of data elements. Fax is an example of an image class VT. ISO 9040 pertains only to basic class VTS.

Three types of terminals in the basic class are scroll mode, page mode, and form mode. Scroll mode terminals (for example, TTYs) receive and display characters in a line, and scroll the lines, but have no built-in microprocessors. They cannot communicate in networks using standard protocols without the assistance of an auxilliary device, a packet assembler/disassembler (PAD). Page mode terminals allow screen editing and a number of additional features, such as color, with cursor addressing, not available on scroll mode terminals. ITU supports only scroll mode terminal, and has defined standard PAD interfaces in the "triple X" recommendations X.3, X.28, and X.29. Users must establish contact with a PAD by setting up parameters before they can communicate through a network; thus, a PAD is essentially a "black box" sitting between a user and the network, and is not really a virtual terminal.

Form mode terminals contain built-in microprocessors. The microprocessors can check syntax of forms downloaded from application software (for example, airline reservation systems or databases) and upload the data across a network. The OSI VTS model most closely resembles the form mode terminal.

VTS basic class supports synchronous and asynchronous operations. Synchronous (S-mode), exemplified by the IBM 3270 terminal, allows only one entity (the process running on the remote system or the process running on the local microprocessor) to perform an update at any time. Asynchronous (A-mode) operation, exemplified by the DEC VT100 terminal, allows both entities to read/write at the same time.

6.3.2 The OSI Virtual Terminal Service Model

Figure 6.6 shows the model when the user and application are associated with the same host. At this level of detail, the same model applies whether or not the user and the application, or two users, are in the same open system or in different ones.

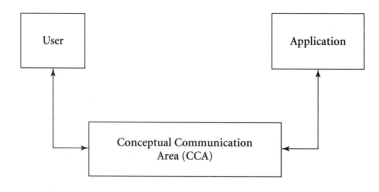

Figure 6.6. Single-system VTS communication

Conceptual Communication Area

The heart of VTS is the Conceptual Communication Area (CCA). These data structures characterize the VT in a specific communications process. Input and output exchanged between the user system and the application pass through a nonphysical entity called the **conceptual communication area (CCA)**. In particular, the application program is developed to interact with the conceptual communication area rather than with an actual display terminal. A user at any terminal that can interface with the CCA can then use the application program.

Conceptual Data Store   The Conceptual Data Store (CDS) contains **display objects**, one of the key abstract information structures in the CCA. Display objects are one (single-line)-, two (single-page)-, or three (multipage)-dimensional arrays of elements that represent on the virtual device activities on the real device. Each element has a unique x, $xandy$, or $xandyandz$ coordinate that is assigned a primary attribute or character value called a **character box graphic element** and a secondary attribute (for example, foreground/background color, bold, underline, font) from the acceptable alphabets and attributes that are negotiated at the time the connection is established.

An element is identified by a pointer, such as a cursor; addressing operations move the pointer. The pointer determines where text can be entered or deleted; attributes of an element identified by the pointer can be changed. Figure 6.7 illustrates a sampling of possible operations on array elements.

Two capabilities, defining a window and downloading a form, constrain the action of a pointer. A window definition limits the movement of a pointer to elements within the dimensions of the window. When an insertion is attempted outside that edge, the window moves, giving the effect, for example, of scrolling. A form definition can be downloaded into a terminal, providing a combination of read-only text fields and blank fields that can be filled in by the user.

S-mode operation, illustrated in Figure 6.8, is characterized by a single representation for the display object (though that single representation is repeated in the CCA and the host

A window definition limits the movement of a pointer to elements within the dimensions of the window. When an insertion is attempted outside that edge, the window moves, giving the effect, for example, of scrolling.

Operation Type	Description
Addressing: implicit	Increments pointer's x-coordinate value by one when a character is entered
Addressing: explicit	Moves pointer to an absolute position, a home position, or by a relative amount
Update text	Enters a character into the current array element. Invokes implicit addressing
Repeat text	Repeats the text operation—enters a string of characters into a range of array elements
Attribute	Assigns a designated value to a selected secondary attribute of a set of array elements
Erase	Deletes the character in a set of array elements

Figure 6.7. Sample operations on a display object

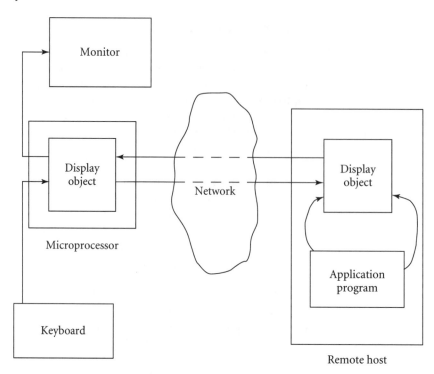

Figure 6.8. VT association in S-mode

where the application runs). Since there is only one place to write updates to the display object, only one process can write at any one time. For example, output from User A's keyboard may be written into the display object and then read by User B. Then User B can write to the display object for reading by User A. In A-mode, shown in Figure 6.9, there are two display objects at each end of the VT association, one for input and one for output. Since there are two separate locations for processes to read/write updates to the display object, both can read/write at the same time.

In both S- and A-modes, the mapping of display object information onto the real device is stored in a **device object**, one of the CCA components whose purpose is to model the real device characteristics.

The primary VTE parameters for a display object (DO) and its values are displayed in Figure 6.10. The purpose of these parameters is to establish the display object structure and each array element attributes. Parameter values are assigned through negotiation.

Several of these parameters (display-object-name, dimensions, and erasure-capability) are self-defining. DO-access refers to access token control (see next section). The block (field)-definition-capability applies only if the corresponding functional unit Block (Field) has been selected; it enables a limit to be set on the number of blocks (fields) defined on any single Y-array. The repertoire (foreground- or background-color) capability specifies the number of different repertoire (color) values that may be used. Other, secondary, parameters define the actual values of individual attributes. Their definitions are in ISO 9040. A repertoire, in the usual case for BCVT, consists of a set of displayable character-box graphic elements referred to as a graphic character set.

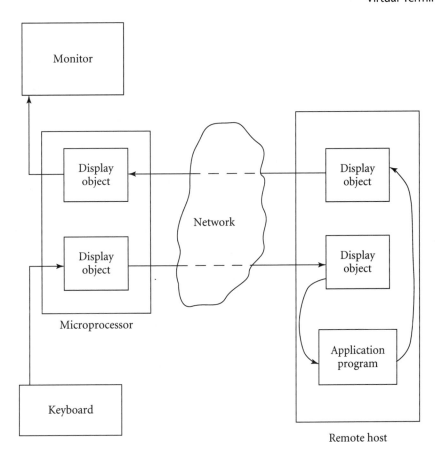

Figure 6.9. VT association in A-mode

Parameters are illustrated in Figure 6.11 for the two A-mode telnet-profile display objects. They are both two dimensional. One display object, D, models the display for data from an applications program or peer VT user. Because the DO-access for D is "WACA," it may be updated only by the VT user that accepted the VT association. The second display object, K, models the VT user's keyboard. K's access is "WACI," which means that it may be updated only by the VT user that initiated the VT association. Each DO is a

Parameter	Value
display-object-name	character string of type Printable String
DO-access	"WACI", "WACA", "WAVAR"
dimensions	"one", "two", "three" (default="two")
erasure-capability	"yes", "no" (default="no")
block-definition-capability	"yes", "no" (default="no")
field-definition-capability	"yes", "no" (default="no")
repertoire-capability	1..N (default=1)
foreground-color-capability	1..N (default=1)
background-color-capability	1..N (default=1)

Figure 6.10. Display object parameters

```
Display-objects *(double occurrence)*=
{ {display-object-name = D, *(Display)*
   DO-access = "WACA",
   dimensions = "two", *(default value)*
   x-dimension =
   {   x-bound = "unbounded", *(default value)*
       x-addressing = "no constraint",
       x-absolute = "no", *(default value)*
       x-window = profile-argument-r1, *(a negotiated value)*
   y-dimension =
   {   y-bound = "unbounded", *(default value)*
       y-addressing = "higher only",
       y-absolute = "no", *(default value)*
       y-window = 1
   },
   erasure-capability = "yes",
   repertoire-capability = 2,
   repertoire-assignment = profile-argument-r2, *(a negotiated
value)*
   repertoire-assignment =$<$ESC$>$2/5 2/15 4/2
 }
 { display-object-name = K, *(Keyboard)*
   DO-access = "WACI",
   dimensions = "two", *(default value)*
   x-dimension =
   {   x-bound = "unbounded", *(default value)*
       x-addressing = "no constraint",
       x-absolute = "no", *(default value)*
       x-window = profile-argument-r1, *(a negotiated value)*
       },
   y-dimension =
   {   y-bound = "unbounded", *(default value)*
       y-addressing = "higher only",
       y-absolute = "no", *(default value)*
       y-window = 1
   },
   erasure-capability = "yes",
   repertoire-capability = 2,
   repertoire-assignment = profile-argument-r2, *(a negotiated
value)*
   repertoire-assignment = $<$ESC$>$2/5 2/15 4/2
       },
   },
```

Figure 6.11. A-mode telnet VTE profile display objects

two-dimensional array of elements x and y. The values of the VTE addressing parameters x-bound, x-addressing, x-absolute, and x-window indicate, respectively, that there is no upper bound of the x dimension, the display pointer can be changed to a higher or lower x value, the pointer cannot be assigned a new value by absolute addressing, and the update window size is negotiated. The y-addressing value indicates that the display pointer can be changed only to a higher value. The update window size is 1 in the y direction. Each DO has the capability of erasing the character assigned to an array element. Two attribute values are defined by the assignment parameters, one negotiated and the other an 8-bit transparent character set. For S-mode operation, the telnet profile also has one display object.

Control, Signaling, and Status Store   The Control, Signaling, and Status Store (CSS) contains *control objects*, another of the key abstract information structures in the CCA. A control object consists of a number of parameters that enable a user (or application) to transmit control information to another user. A control object may be *simple*—one data element that is either a scalar value or a character, boolean, or bit string—or *structured*—a combination of data elements possibly of different types. A structured control object can be either *parametric* or *nonparametric* depending on whether changes to the data elements can be negotiated or not. Control objects are mapped to real control devices (for example, a bell or buzzer) and are negotiated when a connection is established. The mapping is stored in a device object. Each device object has an associated default control object, but can also have other control objects, for example to notify a VT user whether input updates will be echoed locally, whether the peer VT user will be automatically signaled, or whether data entry can be started.

The only operation on a control object is updating. Access to updating may be controlled. In S-mode, a *Write-Access-Variable* (WAVAR) token is used to control access to updating and only the user with the WAVAR token can update the control object. In A-mode, control of access to control objects is optional. One user has a *Write-Access-Connection-Initiator* (WACI) token; the other user has a *Write-Access-Connection-Acceptor* (WACA) token. If access control is specified, then the CO-access parameter indicates whether the user with the WACI or the WACA has access to updating. The CO-trigger parameter indicates whether a *trigger* mechanism is selected. Selection of a control object trigger enables the following actions: the user with the token giving access rights can update the control object contents; the corresponding display object is then updated; and, if in S-mode communication, access rights are passed to the peer user. Additional parameters include the name of the control object, priority, type, and size. Figure 6.12 lists the control object parameters and their values.

The following parameter specifications define the control object SY (SYNCHRONIZE), one of six control objects in a telnet profile:

CO-name: SY
CO-access: "NSAC"
CO-category: "symbolic"
CO-size: 1
CO-priority: "urgent"

Using either of two delivery control mechanisms provided by the BCVT service, a VT user can mark the end of a sequence of updates to display or control objects, initiating delivery of the stored data to a peer VT user. *Simple delivery control* enables the VT user to place an explicit mark and optionally request acknowledgment. The VT service provider can also deliver the updates independent of the VT user's marking. *Quarantine delivery control* restrains the VT service provider from the independent delivery of updates. The BCVT also provides a third way to control delivery, *no delivery control*, which prevents a VT user from marking the end of the update sequence. How the VT service provider implements delivery is not specified in the BCVT standard. Only in quarantine delivery control can the VT service provider accumulate the updates by concatenating them. This process, referred to as *net-effecting* can result in earlier updates being eliminated by later ones.

Parameter	Value
CO-name	Character string of type PrintableString
CO-type-identifier	Character string of type ASN-1 PrintableString or a value of ASN-1 OBJECT IDENTIFIER (specifies the source of semantic definition for the CO)
CO-structure	"non-parametric", number of data elements 1..N (default-1)
CO-access	"NSAC", "WAVAR", "WACI", "WACA", "WAVAR" and "WACI", "WAVAR" and "WACA", "no-access" (default="NSAC")
CO-priority	"normal", "high", "urgent" (default="normal")
CO-trigger	optional: "not selected", "selected" (default="not selected")
CO-element-id	conditional: integer (required if there is more than one data element)
CO-category	"character", "boolean", "symbolic", "integer", "transparent" (default="boolean")
CO-repertoire assignment	Each instance designates one discrete repertoire
CO-size	Data element's data storage capacity

Figure 6.12. Control object VTE parameters

A VT user can assign to control objects an *update priority* of "normal," "high," or "urgent," indicating to the VT service provider the relative importance of notifying the peer VT user of updates. Delivery control does not apply to control objects with high or urgent update priority. Normal refers to first-in-first-out delivery of updates. Delivery of high-priority updates is possible when normal updates are held in quarantine delivery control.

Device Objects   Each real device has one associated device object, which, in turn, has one associated display object and at least one control object. The parameters in a device object are set by the user. They may indicate events or conditions under which an update can occur; buffer capacity (for example, for a display terminal); the state of an on-off switch; associated control objects; and specified default conditions. Device objects are not technically a separate component of the CCA; their definitions are part of the Data Structure Definition component. Figure 6.13 lists the general device object VTE parameters and their values. There are also parameters for attributes and termination defined in ISO 9040.

Figure 6.14 illustrates a set of parameters specified in the definition of the two telnet VTE-profile device objects DISPLAY and KEYBOARD. Only the THREE control objects SY, DI (DISPLAY-SIGNAL), and KB (KEYBOARD-SIGNAL) are included in this example. Additional ones, such as NI (NEGOTIATION BY INITIATOR), NA (NEGOTIATION BY ACCEPTOR), and GA (GO-AHEAD) could be inserted. Further, device-display-object parameter values corresponding to DO-name values are not included; one value for each DO-name would normally appear.

The parameters in a device object are set by the user. They may indicate events or conditions under which an update can occur; buffer capacity (for example, for a display terminal); the state of an on-off switch; associated control objects; and specified default conditions.

Parameter	Value
device-name	Character string of type PrintableString
device-default-CO-access	Any valid value for CO-access (default="NSAC")
device-default-CO-priority	"normal", "high", "urgent" (default="normal")
device-default-CO-trigger	"selected", "not-selected" (default="not-selected")
device-default-CO-initial-value	Initial values for the eight boolean values in the default control object for the device object (default="false")
device-minimum-X-array-length	Integer value (the shortest agreed X-array length negotiated by both VT users when display object data is mapped to this device)
device-minimum-Y-array-length	Integer value (the shortest agreed Y-array length negotiated by both VT users when display object data is mapped to this device)
device-control-object	CO-name-value for each control object
device-display-object	Identical to one of the DO-name VTE parameter values

Figure 6.13. Device object VTE parameters

```
Device-object *(double occurrence)*=
{
  {
  device-name = DISPLAY-DEVICE,
  device-display-object = D,
  device-default-CO-initial-value = 1,
  device-minimum-X-array-length = 1,
  device-minimum-Y-array-length = 1,
  device-control-object = SY,
  device-control-object = DI,
  device-default-control-access = "WACA",
  device-control-CO-priority = "normal",
  }
  {
  device-name = KEYBOARD-DEVICE,
  device-display-object = K,
  device-default-CO-initial-value = 1,
  device-minimum-X-array-length = 1,
  device-minimum-Y-array-length = 1,
  device-control-object = SY,
  device-control-object = KB,
  device-default-control-access = "WACI",
  device-control-CO-priority = "normal",
  }
},
```

Figure 6.14. telnet VTE-profile device objects DISPLAY and KEYBOARD

Access Control Store and Data Structure Definition.   The other two components of the CCA are the Access Control Store (ACS) and the Data Structure Definition (DSD). The ACS contains the current token (WAVAR, WACI, WACA) assignment. The DSD contains parameter definitions associated with the display, control, and device objects.

Virtual Terminal Environment

User or application data and control information is transmitted through the CCA via the Virtual Terminal Environment (VTE) that is negotiated when communication is initiated. The VTE consists of parameters that describe display, control, and device objects as well as the communication mode (synchronous or asynchronous) and its tokens (WAVAR, WACI, or WACA). Depending on what VT service elements are available, the VTE may be modified or replaced, but only one VTE exists at any given time. Predefined self-consistent parameter sets are available in named and registered *VTE profiles*, for standard terminals, for example, to simplify establishment of the VTE. Examples of defined VTE profiles are given in Figure 6.15. Users can select a profile and then negotiate additional parameters, called *arguments*, not already defined in the profile. Both the profile and the arguments constitute a full VTE.

Annex A of ISO 9040 defines a default VTE profile for S-mode and for A-mode communication. Neither default profile contains arguments. The profile applies in the event that the VT ASSOCIATE service parameter VTE profile-name is empty and the parameter VT mode has value 'A-mode' or 'either-A'. The A-mode default VTE profile definition is specified in Figure 6.16. It includes two display objects, two device objects, and an echo control object. The two control objects that are also required in A-mode communication are not explicitly included in the definition because default control objects are assumed. Some of the parameters for display, control, and device objects are in the definition. The default VTE profile does not allow any emphasis attribute control.

In the definition, the display object named DA (DB) may be updated by the user process owning the write access token WACA (WACI). Each of the display objects is a two-dimensional sequence of 80 character lines. Because the window size is 0 and the *x*-addressing is "higher only" (the default value), the display pointer movement is restricted to forward on the same line or to the next line. The default "no" is assumed for the erase

Profile Name	Array Dimension	Purpose
Forms	3	Local data entry and validation in forms-based applications
Scroll	2	Line-at-a-time interaction between VT user and remote host Includes both forward and backward scrolling
S-mode page	2	Interactions involving full-screen display of data
telnet	2	Character-or line-at-a-time dialogues between VT users
Transparent	1	Simultaneous two-way exchange of uninterpreted character sequences
X3	1	Similar to PAD recommendations in ITU implementations

Figure 6.15. VTE profiles

```
Display-objects *(double occurrence)*=
{{ display-object-name = DA,
   DO-access = "WACA",
   dimensions = 2 *(default value)*,
   x-dimension =
   {  x-bound = 80,
      x-window = 0
      *(x-addressing and x-absolute assume default values)*
      },
   y-dimension =
   {*(y-bound, y-addressing, y-absolute and y-window all assume default values)*
      }
   },
 { display-object name = DB,
   DO-access = "WACI",
   dimensions = 2 *(default value)*,
   x-dimension =
   {   x-bound = 80,
       x-window = 0
       *(x-addressing and x-absolute assume default values)*
       },
          '
   y-dimension =
   {*(y-bound, y-addressing, y-absolute and y-window all assume default values)*
      }
   }
   },
 Control-object =
 { CO-name = E,
   CO-type-identifier = vt-b-sco-echo, *(echo control object)*
   CO-access = "WACA"},
 Device-object *(double occurrence)* =
{{ device-name = DEVICE-1,
   device-default-CO-initial-value = 1. "true",
   *(this is the on/off switch, where "true"="on" and output
       from the display object is being mapped to the device)*
   device-minimum-X-array-length = 1, *(no constraint)*
   device-minimum-Y-array-length = 1, *(no constraint)*
   device-display-object = DA,
   device-termination-event-list =
   {<<1,<CR>>, "null">,<<1,<LF>>, "null">,
    <<1,<FF>>, "null">,<<1,<VT>>, "null">},
   device-termination-length =<80, "null">
   *(other device parameters assume default values or are not required)*
      },
   {device-name = DEVICE-2,
   device-default-CO-initial-value = 1."true",
   *(this is the on/off switch, where "true"="on" and output
       from the display object is being mapped to the device)*
   device-minimum-X-array-length = 1, *(no constraint)*
   device-minimum-Y-array-length = 1, *(no constraint)*
   device-display-object = DB,
   device-termination-event-list =
   {<<1,<CR>>,"null">,<<1,<LF>>,"null">,
    <<1,<FF>>,"null">,<<1,<VT>>,"null">},
   *(1=default repertoire assignment; CR=Carriage Return; LF=line
       Feed; FF=Form Feed; VT=vertical Tab; null=no operation)*
   device-termination-length = <80,"null">
   *(other device parameters assume default values or are not required)*
      },
   }.
```

Figure 6.16. A-mode default VTE profile definition

capability. The user process owning the WACA token has control of the enabling of echo by the peer VT user, where echoing refers to updates appearing on a user's screen. A device-termination-event-list is a set of pairs of the form <event, event-id>. The pairs specify the conditions under which the VT user should cause notification to the peer VT user of previous updates to the associated display and control objects. The device-termination-length indicates that the termination condition should be caused after 80 updates (that is, after 80 updates the corresponding objects must be updated) if none of the conditions in the device-termination-event-list occurs.

6.3.3   Using VT Services: Some Examples

The basic class VT application context involves only the ASEs associated with the BCVT and the ACSEs. ISO 9041 defines the set of procedures for communication between two VT protocol machines (VTPM) in either S-mode or A-mode. We will illustrate only the portion of the standard that establishes and terminates an association between two VT users, and that negotiates parameter values in multiple interaction negotiation, a multistep process.

Establishing and Terminating an Association

Figure 6.17 illustrates the sequence of steps to establish communication between two VT users (or a VT user and an application on a remote host). The initiating VT user issues a VT-ASSOCIATE.request. The initiating VTPM accepts and sends its A-ASSOCIATE.request (one of the ACSE primitives) to the peer VT user (through its VT). The target VTPM can accept or not accept. Upon accepting, it issues an A-ASSOCIATE.indication. The peer VT user receives the A.ASSOCIATE.indication and responds (VT ASSOCIATE.respond) with VT result = "success." The VTPM then issues an A-ASSOCIATE.response that is accepted by the initiating VTPM, which issues an A-ASSOCIATE.confirm to the initiating VT user. The VT user receives the A-ASSOCIATE.confirm, and the association is established. The VT user can then issue a VT START-NEG.req to begin negotiating the VTE profile and any arguments required to establish a full-VTE.

Communication is terminated in an agreed release procedure through the same sequence of steps as followed when establishing the association, except that RELEASE replaces ASSOCIATE in each primitive (see Figure 6.18). In this procedure, the following

VT user	VT	VT	VT user
VT-ASSOC.req			
	A-ASSOC.req		
		A-ASSOC.ind	
			VT-ASSOC.ind
			VT-ASSOC.resp
		A-ASSOC.resp	
	A-ASSOC.conf		
VT-ASSOC.conf			

Figure 6.17. Connection establishment

VT user		VT		VT		VT user
VT-RELEASE.req						
		A-RELEASE.req				
				A-RELEASE.ind		
						VT-RELEASE.ind
						VT-RELEASE.resp
				A-RELEASE.resp		
		A-RELEASE.conf				
VT-RELEASE.conf						

Figure 6.18. Agreed release

assumptions are included: the initiating VT user holds the token; data is forwarded and delivered according to data transfer procedures; and no collisions occur. ISO 9041 contains appropriate procedures when any of these assumptions are changed.

Negotiating Parameter Values

We illustrate only one of the ways to negotiate parameters, namely, through Multiple Interaction Negotiation (MIN). After the association is established, MIN occurs in three phases: establishment, negotiation, and termination, as shown in Figure 6.19. During these phases, the Presentation-layer service primitives P.DATA.request and P.DATA.indication transform the syntax of message data as it is transferred between VT users through each VT and ACSE. Chapter 10 contains more detail on these Presentation-layer primitives. We do not include them in the following discussion.

The establishment phase begins when the initiating VT user issues VT-START-NEG. request. After receiving a VT-START-NEG.indication, the peer VT user issues a VT-START-NEG.response (with VT-result = "success") that is accepted by the initiating VTPM. The initiating VT user then receives a VT-START-NEG.confirm.

Parameter value negotiation begins with the initiating VT user proposing parameters (VT-NEG-OFFER.request) or inviting the peer VT user to propose parameters (VT-NEG-INVITE.request). We assume one or more parameter values are offered by the initiating VT user. If the peer VT user accepts (VT-NEG-ACCEPT.request) or rejects (VT NEG-REJECT.request), an indication is received by the initiating VT user, negotiation is completed, and the sequence ends. In either response, the same parameter values as initially proposed are included with the primitive. Instead, the peer VT user could make a counter offer by issuing a VT-NEG-OFFER.request that is received by the initiating VT user as a VT-NEG-OFFER.indication with acceptable parameter values. The initiating VT user issues a VT-NEG-ACCEPT.request or a VT-NEG-REJECT.request that is received by the peer VT user, ending the negotiation sequence. If, instead, the initiating VT user issues a counter offer, negotiation continues until one user accepts or rejects a set of parameter values.

Although negotiation of each parameter is independent of any other parameters, a protocol element may contain more than one parameter; thus, either VT user could accept some parameters and reject others in the same transmission. Further, more than one sequence can be in progress at any given time, and a single sequence could split into multiple, independently operating sequences.

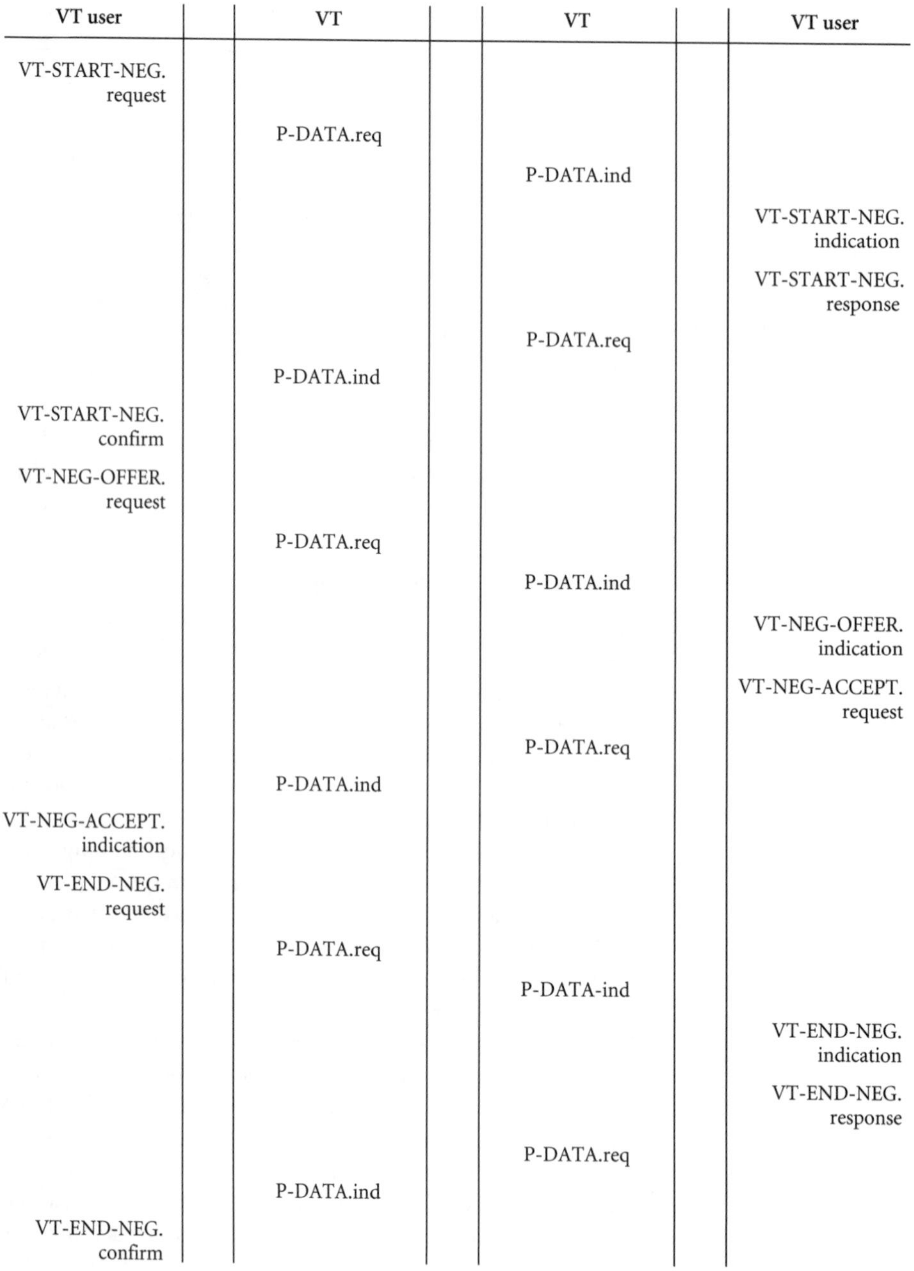

VT user	VT	VT	VT user
VT-START-NEG. request			
	P-DATA.req		
		P-DATA.ind	
			VT-START-NEG. indication
			VT-START-NEG. response
		P-DATA.req	
	P-DATA.ind		
VT-START-NEG. confirm			
VT-NEG-OFFER. request			
	P-DATA.req		
		P-DATA.ind	
			VT-NEG-OFFER. indication
			VT-NEG-ACCEPT. request
		P-DATA.req	
	P-DATA.ind		
VT-NEG-ACCEPT. indication			
VT-END-NEG. request			
	P-DATA.req		
		P-DATA-ind	
			VT-END-NEG. indication
			VT-END-NEG. response
		P-DATA.req	
	P-DATA.ind		
VT-END-NEG. confirm			

Figure 6.19. Multiple Interaction Negotiation

The termination phase of MIN follows the same sequence of steps as in the establishment phase, except that END replaces START in each primitive. Termination includes agreement on whether or not the negotiated VTE is retained as well as whether the data-handling phase is entered.

SUMMARY

Terminal emulation software extends a user's contact with a remote system to something more direct than the use of electronic mail; it provides direct involvement with the remote system. Terminal emulation allows one system to act like a simple terminal to the other. The software mimics a particular type of real terminal so that the application running on a remote system can interact with the user's system and both receive input and send output correctly.

An important technique for interoperability among processes designed for different types of systems is interaction with a virtual device. That is, a generic version of the type of device that is needed is designed and made accessible to many real processes. The accessibility is made possible by translating between the real device and the virtual device the processes perceive. In this chapter, we have seen this technique employed to give widespread access to terminals through the ISO protocol VT (virtual terminal). In the next chapter, the technique will be used for access to file systems through the ISO protocol FTAM (File Transfer, Access, and Management).

EXERCISES

1. Compare the three approaches to terminal and application compatibility discussed in this chapter. Describe the advantages and disadvantages of each. When would each be the most appropriate choice?

2. You are to develop an application in which data is entered to your program through a form displayed on the user's terminal. Users will access your program by connecting from their own computer to a server where your program will run. You will display a form on their screen. Only valid entries will be accepted in the form. Answer the following questions in the context of this problem statement:

    (a) What programming language would you choose for this application, if the choice were up to you? What features of the language led to that choice?

    (b) What facility do you expect to have available on the user's machine? (Do you expect any software to be running there? Does it matter how the user connects to the server where your program runs?)

    (c) Would it be desirable to have the validity of form entries checked on the user's machine, or should that be part of your server process? How would you provide the appropriate code in either case?

    (d) What do you need to know about the machine the user is using? Do you need to know the size of the screen? The colors available? Fonts? If the user gets a newer machine, will that cause problems in your application?

    (e) Can you bypass all the difficulties described in this chapter by using HTML forms? Is there anything about this application that you cannot do with HTML forms? Is there a way around any problems?

3. Look at the most current information you can find about the VT protocol and service and about telnet. Compare the features of the two approaches.

CHAPTER 7

File Access and Transfer

KEY CONCEPTS

- File System Characteristics
- File Transfer Modes and Options
- Issues in Network-Based File Systems
- File Transfer, Access, and Management

Files of many types are available for access over networks. A file may be a document, a spreadsheet, a database, extensive documentation for a software package, a program or large collection of programs, or anything else that can be stored in a computer system. The file could contain plain text represented in a common form such as ASCII, executable code for a particular family of computers, graphical images, video and audio segments, or a complex collection of media representations. In many cases, the file was created and stored without consideration of its transfer to other types of computer systems.

The file may be stored on a system designed to provide access to many users working on many types of computers, or it may be stored on a system designed to work alone without consideration of access by users on a network. The problems to be solved in providing access to the file are naturally different in these two cases.

This chapter begins with a review of file system characteristics. We then consider the opportunities for access to files, the potential difficulties, and options for overcoming the difficulties and realizing the potential of the vast resource of electronically stored information.

In particular, we examine a specific application service that has a goal in common with the virtual terminal: providing access by remote systems to a device whose characteristics are not known to the initiating system. Note the similarity between this problem and the problem of interacting with a terminal of unknown type, discussed in Chapter 6. We illustrate the ideas involved in distributed file access by examining both the Internet file access application, **File Transfer Protocol (FTP)** and the OSI version **File Transfer, Access, and Management (FTAM)**.

Prior to looking at these file access services, we consider the attributes and structure of a virtual filestore. The chapter concludes with several examples of file access.

7.1   FILE SYSTEM CHARACTERISTICS

File systems are integral parts of computer systems: they store programs that will be copied into memory when needed, source code for some programs that may be modified and re-compiled, and data for the programs to manipulate. Files even store information about the file system itself: the names of files, where they are located, and other important information such as the length of the file, when it was created, and who has what access rights to it.

Some files are kept online, stored on disks accessible whenever the computer is running; others are offline, stored on media such as tape, floppy disks, or CDs that must be loaded before they can be used.

Files are accessed through a set of programs that are part of the computer's operating system. By requiring that all users access files through these programs, the computer system makes it easier to use the files (the user does not need to know the tedious details of the file system to obtain the file) and also protects the files (the user is unable to make many types of errors that would threaten file integrity).

A file access system is part of every significant operating system and is an important characteristic of a computer system. As long as all access to the files comes through a single operating system, the problems involved are relatively simple. Extending the opportunity to use the system's files to users of a network, and by extension, to all users connected to any network that can access the local network on which the files reside, changes the nature of the problems to be addressed.

All file access involves three characteristics of files:

Structure refers to the logical and physical organization of data in the file, whether a contiguous string of bytes or a complex, indexed, paged structure.

Attributes are the descriptive terms applied to a file that provide information about the file such as when it was created and how large it is.

Operations are the functions that may be applied to the file, its attributes, or its contents.

When the file is created and accessed exclusively by the same file system, these characteristics are well understood. When a remote file is accessed, these characteristics must be discovered and accommodated. The degree to which a file system can accommodate these differences determines how effectively it can access a "foreign" file.

7.1.1   Structure

The structure of a file is the way the elements contained in the file are identified and related to each other. The individual elements may be bytes, collections of bytes identified as fields and records, collections of records joined as physical records or blocks, or even the entire file itself. At one extreme are UNIX files, which are composed of individual bytes and have no other structure; at the other extreme, a file containing executable code may have no reasonable subdivision and the whole file is the basic element. Regardless of the logical

At one extreme are UNIX files, which are composed of individual bytes and have no other structure; at the other extreme, a file containing executable code may have no reasonable subdivision and the whole file is the basic element.

structure of the data in a file, the file access system may or may not be able to recognize and accommodate the structure.

We will use the term **local file system** to refer to the file access system that resides in the operating system of the computer where the file is stored. We will use the term **remote file system** to refer to the file system where the access to the file is initiated. The local file system knows the structure of its local files and can access each file completely. A remote file system, on the other hand, may have limited access to a file because it is unable to accommodate all the characteristics of the local file.

Between the extremes of file systems that are accessed by individual bytes and those that are accessed only as a complete file, there are differences in the structure of files. A simple extension of a file accessed by bytes is a file accessed by fixed-length records arranged in a linear relationship. In this kind of file, individual records are accessible by specifying their relative location in the file. A number of consecutive records can be obtained by specifying a starting location in the file and the number of records wanted.

At another level of complexity, many data files are stored with a hierarchical structure, usually in a tree shape. The tree consists of a root node, internal nodes, leaf nodes, and links between pairs of nodes. A strict tree structure does not allow more than one path of nodes and links to connect any one node to the root. Some file structures violate that restriction to provide a more efficient movement through the file. Each node except the leaves contains information about the nodes lower in the tree. Some of the internal nodes may contain data also. An example of a modified B-tree structure as a file storage method is shown in Figure 7.1.

Transfering a particular part of a hierarchical file requires a method to traverse the structure, reaching each node exactly once. The depth-first search algorithm shown in Figure 7.2 is one standard way to accomplish this, visiting each node in the order shown by the numbers labeling the nodes in Figure 7.1. More detailed descriptions of these structures and the

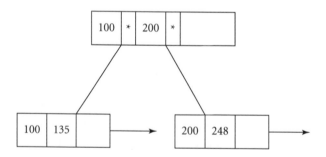

Figure 7.1. A modified B-tree as a hierarchical file structure

A B+ tree with a root node and two leaf nodes. The values in the root node index the leaf nodes. The values in the root nodes are the index values associated with a record.

Figure 7.2. Depth-first search algorithm

```
dfs{root}
    visit the root
    dfs{leftmost child}
    dfs{next right sibling}
```

operations performed in them can be found in file systems or data structures texts (see, for example, [AC88]).

7.1.2 Attributes

The collection of attributes that define a file vary in number, in type, and in the ways they are represented. Among the most common attributes a file may have are a name, size, and date created. An indication of the type of the contents may also be recorded. A file created and stored on a single user system needs no other attributes. These are displayed when a directory listing is requested, and may be used to select a particular file.

In a multiuser system, each file must also have an owner and perhaps a designation of access rights to the file for others. An account identifier allows charges for storage or other use of system resources to be allocated correctly.

In a system with not only multiple users, but also the possibility of simultaneous access, the question of file availability arises. If the file is simultaneously available for multiple users to write, the integrity of the file is jeopardized. The time when the file was last accessed, whether for reading or for writing, is a useful attribute in algorithms that protect the file from conflicts arising during simultaneous access. These times are combined with the identity of the last user process to access the file for reading or for writing.

Figure 7.3 lists the attributes identified in the OSI virtual filestore description of a general file, and some characteristics of the attributes. Certain attributes, such as the length, maximum future length, or availability of the file are changed as needed. Inserting a new section into a report, for example, increases the size of the report file. The time and identity of the last change may be stored as well.

Attribute	Type
Filename	String
Allowed operations	Bit map
Access control	List
Account number	Integer
Date and time of file creation	Time
Date and time of last file modification	Time
Date and time of last file read	Time
Date and time of last attribute modification	Time
Owner	User id
Identity of last modifier	User id
Identity of last reader	User id
Identity of last attribute modifier	User id
File availability	Boolean
Contents type	Object id
Encryption key	String
Size	Integer
Maximum future size	Integer
Legal qualifications	String
Private use	String

Figure 7.3. The OSI virtual filestore attributes

Operation	Applies to
Create file	Whole file
Delete file	Whole file
Select file	Whole file
Deselect file	Whole file
Open file	Whole file
Close file	Whole file
Read attribute	Whole file
Change attribute	Whole file
Locate a record	Contents of file
Read data from file	Contents of file
Insert new data	Contents of file
Replace data	Contents of file
Extend some record	Contents of file
Erase a record	Contents of file

Figure 7.4. The OSI virtual filestore operations

7.1.3   Operations

In addition to its structure and attributes, a set of allowed operations distinguishes a file. Operations apply to a file as a whole or to some subset of the file, such as a record. Figure 7.4 lists the virtual filestore operations defined in OSI. Operations that apply to the whole file include file creation and deletion, selection and deselection of a file (which allow access to the attributes of the file, but not to its contents), open and closing (which allow access to the contents of the file), and reading and writing file attributes.

Operations on the individual records of a file include locating a particular record, reading, inserting or replacing a record, extending the contents of a record, and deleting records. Your process may have some access rights to the records of a file, but not all. For instance, you may have read access but not the ability to write or to delete.

7.2   FILE TRANSFER MODES AND OPTIONS

A number of issues enter into selecting a suitable file transfer protocol. We describe some of the issues and then characterize a number of popular file transfer protocols.

File transfer issues:

character or image   The American Standard Code for Information Interchange (ASCII) is a 7-bit code. The 8th bit of each byte may be set to make the parity (number of ones in the byte) even or may be used to implement an expanded code. Some data communication equipment does not function properly if attempting to send or receive 8 bits per byte. Set in image (binary) mode, the equipment will transmit the bits without attempting to verify that any particular content is correct. In other words, it will not attempt to verify parity. A file that consists of only ASCII characters can be transferred in text or ASCII mode. A file containing binary-encoded information, such as executable programs; files produced by word processors, spreadsheet, or database programs; or binary output from any program must be sent in binary mode.

block size Some amount of data is transmitted as a block or continuous collection of bits. The sender and receiver must agree to allocate storage space for the block so that it can be stored when it is received. A typical transmission block size is 1K (1024 bytes).

error detection Each block may be checked for accuracy during transmission. This is done by appending some other bits to the transmission. The extra bits are determined by making a computation based on the bits in the real block of data. The sending software must compute the extra bits and append them to the block. The receiving software must recompute the extra bits in the same way and verify that the block arrived without transmission error.

error correction If an error is detected, the sender and receiver need an agreement about the way to correct the error. Usually this means notifying the sender that an error block has arrived (a negative acknowledgment or NAK) and retransmission of the bad block by the sender.

dialog control Transfer of a file requires communication both ways between the sender and the receiver. There is the movement of the data of the file itself, but also control information between the two sides. If two connections are open between the two sides, information can flow in both directions at the same time (full-duplex mode). If only one connection is open, communication can occur in only one direction at a time (half-duplex mode).

flow control To keep a fast sender from sending more than a slow receiver can manage, a method is needed to stop the sender when the receiver needs to catch up. The two sides must understand the same control messages to tell each other when to stop sending and when to start again.

Transfering a file from one location to another requires that the sending and receiving software have a common understanding about the bits they are moving. A number of file transfer protocols address that need, particularly for use with personal computers communicating with each other or with larger systems. They differ in approach to selection and implementation issues. Some of the protocols listed as options in various communications packages are briefly described next [Pro91]:

XMODEM A public domain 8-bit error-checking protocol that uses a 128-byte data block and half-duplex mode. XMODEM first tries to apply the cyclic redundancy code (CRC) as its error detection method. (We will consider the CRC in detail in Chapter 15). If that does not succeed after three tries, it shifts to a different method, the checksum. If a sender uses checksum on the first attempt to transmit, the receiver's error-checking routine will report an error and request a retransmission. This may be repeated several times before sender and receiver are coordinated.

Kermit We will discuss Kermit more thoroughly in the next section. As a communication protocol, however, it has found its way into many communications packages and is one of the most universally available of all file transfer methods. Kermit is block oriented, commonly sending blocks of 1K bytes. It uses 7- or 8-bit transmission. Kermit supports full-duplex mode communication, allowing it to send a continuous stream of data and receive responses at the same time.

ASCII ASCII mode transfer as implemented in communications software provides only minimal control (and minimal overhead). There is no error checking, and each byte is sent individually. XON/XOFF (Ctrl-Q and Ctrl-S) may be used to stop and start transmissions if both sides have the ability enabled. This transfer method requires that only plain text files be sent. Even parity may be selected in the setup of the communications software. The 8th bit is set to guarantee an even number of ones in each byte. This is the only type of error checking that will occur. The 8th bit is then stripped off at the receiver and not stored. The software should also be set for 7-bit transfer and for one stop bit. The stop bit is used to mark the beginning and end of each byte so that if an error occurs in transmission, the start of a new byte can be distinguished and the rest of the transmission can continue.

YMODEM YMODEM is a variation of XMODEM allowing 1K blocks and multiple files to be sent in one transfer (batch mode). The first packet sent is numbered 0 and contains the filename and size of the file. At the end of the transmission of the first file, a new packet number 0 is generated with the name and size of the next file. When all the files have been sent, the sender transmits another packet numbered 0 with a blank filename field to tell the receiver that the operation is completed.

ZMODEM ZMODEM is popular on bulletin board systems and has features suitable for dealing with noisy telephone lines. It permits restarting of interrupted file transfers and supports both 16-bit and 32-bit CRC error checking.

Several of the protocols mentioned have variations that provide no software error detection or recovery since they assume that will be done by the sending and receiving hardware. All these protocols are designed primarily for personal computer to personal computer transfers, usually over telephone lines that may not be dependable for a time sufficient to complete the transfer without error. Each has its supporters and its advantages in some environments.

7.2.1 Kermit

The Kermit (yes, the name comes from the Muppet) protocol transfers files over ordinary terminal connections. Versions of the Kermit program exist for many different computers and allow transfer of sequential files between any two computers running the program. Kermit was developed at the Columbia University Center for Computing Activities in 1981–1982 by Bill Catchings and Frank da Cruz initially to allow users of time-sharing systems to store files on floppy disks on CP/M-80 microcomputers.

Many people have contributed to the effort to implement Kermit on a variety of computers. When a new implementation was completed, the developers sent it to Columbia to be made available to others with the same type of system. Of course, with more systems able to use Kermit, more potential file transfer partners exist for other Kermit users. Kermit development continues, with Columbia serving as a clearing house and distribution center [Col99]. Kermit is also distributed by user groups, computing centers, and individuals. Though freely distributed, Kermit is not in the public domain. Columbia University and various contributors are protected by copyrights from having their work sold as a product by others. However, the Kermit transfer protocol is incorporated by permission into many commercial communications packages [CG89].

Figure 7.5. Kermit packet format

MARK	LENGTH	SEQUENCE	TYPE	DATA ...	CHECK

Capability

Kermit was originally developed to work over a dial-up line through a modem. Beginning with version 3.11, Kermit also runs over TCP/IP between computers on networks as well as over serial lines. Files are transferred in blocks up to 1K in length. Provision is made for protecting files from being overwritten: if Kermit detects the presence of a filename matching that of an incoming file, it modifies the incoming filename to prevent conflict and notifies the user by displaying the new name. Kermit also includes provision for character set to character set transfers for international language documents [Dou91].

Kermit transfers files by enclosing data in an envelope of control information. The format of a Kermit packet is shown in Figure 7.5. The MARK is a control byte used for synchronization—to prepare the receiver to begin accepting bytes. The LENGTH field tells how many bytes follow in the packet. SEQUENCE is used to detect lost or duplicated packets; lost packets are retransmitted, and duplicates are discarded. TYPE distinguishes data from control packets. CHECK is computed by the sender and again by the receiver from the contents of the other fields to determine whether transmission errors have occurred. DATA is up to 90 bytes in the common serial version of the protocol.

There are many versions of Kermit, some specific to machines or operating systems, some varying in age and features that were implemented. All these should be able to work together to move a file. The two Kermits begin a session by determining what features they share and agreeing to use as many as possible. Data compression, packet lengths, encoding, and checking options are among the choices.

7.2.2 FTP

Kermit and similar protocols extend the reach of a user beyond a local file system. The user, however, must know exactly where the file is, what its name is, and enough about its contents to specify ASCII or binary transfer mode. If there are redundant copies or if the copy the user accesses is not up to date, there is nothing in the Kermit function that can help. The only authentication provided is physical access to the communications system.

In many ways, the file transfer protocol (FTP) developed for the ARPAnet and defined in RFC 765 [Pos80] is similar to Kermit. Like Kermit, it extends the user's reach beyond the local system, in this case to any other system that can be reached through the Internet protocols TCP/IP. FTP runs over TCP, the dependable transport protocol of the Internet, and uses telnet, its virtual terminal protocol. Figure 7.6 shows the FTP model as presented in RFC 765.

In the figure, the user FTP represents the initiator of the FTP session and the server FTP is the responder. Two connections are used, one to carry control information and the other to transfer data. The user protocol interpreter (user PI) establishes a telnet link with the server system in response to user commands. The server PI issues standard FTP replies to the user PI over the telnet connection. Among the functions of the telnet connection is establishing the right of access to the file by the user. A login of the user to the server system begins the session. The peer data transfer protocols (DTP) operate over a separate connec-

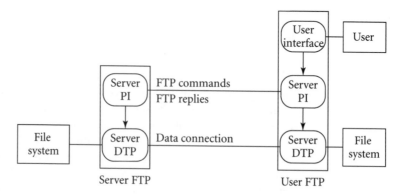

Figure 7.6. FTP model

tion and concurrently with the exchange of control information over the telnet connection. In fact, the data connection need not be to the same host as the control connection. Figure 7.7 illustrates a transfer occurring between servers A and B under control of a user at host C.

7.2.3 Network File System

Many local area networks, particularly those consisting primarily of personal computers or workstations, designate one or more of their stations as *file servers*. A file server is a computer with a large volume of disk storage space and software that allows multiple users to share that storage. Keeping most or all of the disk space in a pool shared by all users is an efficient way to provide for the varying storage requirements of users. Space can be allocated on the basis of need and reassigned as needs change. A user can get access to his or her files from any station in the network. At the same time, shared file space introduces considerable complexity to file access procedures.

A natural extension of a collection of accessible file servers is the idea that every station is a file server as well as a potential file client. A de facto standard in such distributed file systems is the Network File System (NFS) announced by SUN Microsystems in 1984. NFS permits sharing of files by users at stations with the same or different hardware and software architecture [Sch88]. All the disks in the NFS network make up a virtual extension of the local hard disk [Sou89]. NFS has become part of the suite of Internet (TCP/IP) network protocols.

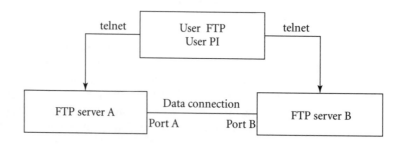

Figure 7.7. FTP with separate data and control connections

The burdens imposed on a shared or distributed file system include verification of access rights of a user, protection from conflicting concurrent access by multiple processes, protection of the integrity of the file if the client or server crashes during access, and keeping redundant file copies up to date. Dealing with these requires interaction between the server and client in addition to the actual transfer of file content. The Network File System sits as a layer of software above the normal file access facility. When a system call results in access to a file, the virtual file server interprets the call. If the file requested resides in the local file system, the call is passed to the normal file access modules of the operating system. If the requested file is remote, NFS cooperates with its peer on the system where the file resides in order to provide access.

An important distinguishing feature of file client and server implementations concerns which side keeps what information about the interaction, for how long, and to what purpose. For example, when a client reads a file sequentially beginning at some record and continuing for some number of records, some entity needs to keep track of where the file is located, who is using it, and how much of the transfer is complete at any time. If the server keeps track of what client is using which file and where in the file the next access will occur, then the server is keeping track of the state of this interaction. If the server goes down and comes up again, the state information will be lost. On the other hand, if this information is kept by the client and not by the server, then each successive access to the file must be accompanied by a complete set of access information, including file id, user authentication, and position in the file.

NFS is a stateless file system in general, which means that the state information is kept by the clients. However, a compromise is required when a file is locked to prevent conflicting concurrent access. Then the server must know who holds the lock so that it can both permit access by the lock holder and clear locks if the client crashes.

The Network File System sits as a layer of software above the normal file access facility. When a system call results in access to a file, the virtual file server interprets the call.

7.3 ISSUES IN NETWORK-BASED FILE SYSTEMS

Networks extend the reach of a user to many other systems and make available a larger number of files than would be stored on any one single system. This same facility makes it necessary for file systems to protect against a large number of new potential problems.

In [SM89], M. Satyanarayanan provides a taxonomy of design issues related to file systems in various environments from individual, single-user systems through file systems distributed over a number of machines and accessed by multiple users. These are summarized in Figure 7.8. In each of four levels of file system complexity, all the design issues of lower levels remain important and new concerns become significant.

In the first and simplest level, one computer serves a single user. The most basic elements of a file system appear immediately:

Naming A file that is stored on and retrieved from a file system requires a name; part of the design of a file system includes rules for naming files. A file naming system can be flat, in which case each file must have an individual and unique name, or hierarchical, like the directory and subdirectory systems of UNIX and MSDOS. If the naming system is hierarchical, it may be restricted to tree structure or may allow links between branches, possibly even cycles. Filenames may imply characteristics of the file, as *.exe* indicates an executable file. Multiple versions of a file may be allowed, with some naming conven-

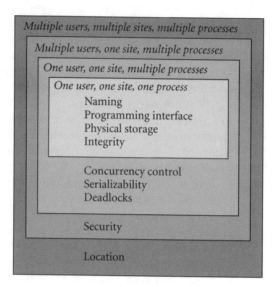

Figure 7.8. A taxonomy of file system issues

tion for distinguishing among them, such as the Vax VMS version number attached to filenames. There may be a limit to the number of characters allowed in a filename or to the number of extensions permitted.

Programming interface How does the user process gain access to a file? In most cases, the program invokes file operations that are part of the operating system. The user remains removed from the details of the physical storage. In a single-user system, the user may be aware of the location of files, at least to the extent of knowing which storage device contains a particular file. In some systems, the user may not know where the file resides, how many copies of it exist, how many other users access the file, or what means are used to guard against conflicting access by multiple users. All this may be hidden in the programming interface.

Physical storage All programs deal with an abstraction of the actual storage device. The file system, however, must map the abstraction to the physical reality. The advantages of large physical blocks in transfers of the data must be balanced with the cost of fragmentation in large blocks.

Integrity Power failures and other threats to the integrity of storage devices raise the question of preserving the integrity of data storage. What happens when the power fails while a file access proceeds? Is it possible to recover data that was deleted by mistake?

The next level in the taxonomy allows a single user to execute more than one process at a single site. Windowing systems and concurrent execution of programs makes this an increasingly common model.

Concurrency control When more than one process can be active concurrently, the file system must protect against conflicting access to data. For example, if two processes each read the same data value, then update that value and write it back to the file, only the last write will have any effect; the other operation is lost entirely. The file system must enforce synchronization policies that prevent such lost activities from occurring.

Questions that arise pertain to the granularity of file protection. If a process is accessing a file, must all that file be locked to any other process that wishes to use it? Can the protection be enforced at the level of individual data item? Can many processes read the same data item without writing? Must a process that wants to write a data value wait for all possible readers to finish? Whenever a resource is locked, the potential for deadlock arises and must be addressed. Will the file system prevent deadlock from occurring, with the accompanying cost associated with such methods; or will the system allow deadlocks to occur but recognize and correct them? How are processes selected for preemption in deadlock avoidance or recovery?

At the third level of file system taxonomy, multiple users and multiple concurrent processes may access the file system. This is the familiar time-sharing model. In addition to the concerns associated with the lower levels, the system now must protect users' files from other users.

Security Users must be identified now and their files associated correctly with each. Permission to access files belonging to another user must be accommodated. Who may grant permission to access a user's files? How can users be grouped to share some files while retaining private access to others?

At the final level of the taxonomy, we find many users, concurrent processes, and multiple computers. In one view, this is a natural extension of the previous level. The same concerns exist, but now there is the question of efficiency of the access techniques. The need to access files on a remote system involves time considerations and emphasizes the need for efficient access techniques. A new concern exists at this level of the taxonomy also:

Location In all single-system cases, the question of where to find the required file is limited to the domain accessible by the local file system. When files are located in any of a number of sites in a distributed file system, the question of location is significant. If the user is to be isolated from the effects of the network-based implementation of the application, the file access facility must be able to find a copy of the file without complete specification from the user. An advantage of a network is that a number of copies of the file may exist, thus allowing access to the file even if a particular file server is not available. The cost of this advantage is the need to determine whether a particular copy of the file is current. In addition, any changes made to a copy of the file must be propagated to other copies as well. The file system must also prevent inconsistent changes from being made to various copies of the file.

7.4 FILE TRANSFER, ACCESS, AND MANAGEMENT

As in other application areas, the OSI model and the defined services and protocols give a very thorough description of the problems involved in File Transfer, Access, and Management (FTAM). Though the OSI solution is not commonly available, the elments it defines are worth consideration. The principles developed for FTAM are useful as a general approach to distributed file systems. In this section, we look at FTAM as a way of understanding the distributed file access problem. We describe the **virtual filestore**, which provides access to any type of file from any process, and the services that define the OSI facility, **File Transfer, Access, and Management.**

7.4.1 A Virtual Filestore

The virtual filestore is a common view of a file that is general enough to be applied to any file system.

Truly accessible files, independent of location and local file system, are a significant component of distributed applications. The OSI FTAM approach to general file access, without each user process knowing the nature of the file system with which it interacts, is through a *virtual filestore*. The virtual filestore is a common view of a file that is general enough to be applied to any file system. All FTAM services refer to the virtual filestore. To accomplish real interaction with a real file system, the services must be translated into actions in the local file system by a translation facility. It is only necessary, however, for one translation to exist for each real file system in order to support interoperability from any partner.

The virtual filestore defines a file in terms of several elements, specifically:

- Single, unique, unambiguous filename
- Attributes (properties) both administrative, such as ownership, and structural, such as the structure and size of the content of the file
- Data elements, if any, called data units (DUs)

Attributes

Attributes are associated with files and with activities. File attributes are associated with the file itself and retain the same value over time until explicitly changed. File attribute values span associations and access-oriented activities. Filename and file size are examples of file attributes; the complete set of file attributes is listed in Figure 7.9.

Activities also have attributes; these are listed in Figure 7.10. Activity attributes are transient properties, related to a particular association, and have no meaning outside that association.

Attributes are grouped for convenience into four collections: the kernel group, the storage group, the security group, and the private group. Each activity is associated with its grouping in Figures 7.9 and 7.10. The kernel group must always be supported. For the other groups, either the entire group is supported or each attribute in the group is either

Attribute Name	Attribute Group
Filename	Kernel
Storage account	Storage
Permitted actions	Security
File availability	Storage
File size	Storage
Private use	Private
Access control	Security
Contents type	Kernel
Future file size	Storage
Date and time of creation	Storage
Identity of file creator	Storage
Date, time, initiator of last modification	Storage
Date, time, initiator of last read access	Storage
Date, time, initiator of last attribute modification	Storage

Figure 7.9. File attributes

Attribute Name	Attribute Group
Access request	Kernel
Access passwords	Security
Account	Storage
Active contents type	Kernel
Legal qualification	Security
Location	Kernel
Locking style	Storage
Initiator identity	Kernel
Calling application entity title	Kernel
Responding application entity title	Kernel
Concurrency control	Storage
Processing mode	Kernel

Figure 7.10. Activity attributes

supported or partially supported. When interrogated, the service provides a meaningful response or "no value available."

Structure

The structure of a file is defined in the virtual filestore as a general hierarchical structure, as illustrated in Figure 7.11. The structure consists of nodes and links between a node and its children. Each node may have an associated data unit and a name. Each node is in the

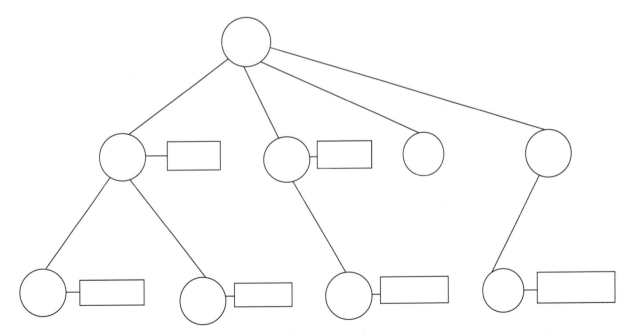

Figure 7.11. The virtual filestore as general hierarchical structure

Figure 7.12. An unstructured file represented in the virtual filestore general hierarchical structure

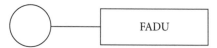

tree at a specific level, and the child of a node is not necessarily at the next lower level. The individual data units, found at nodes in the tree, are the smallest identifiable elements of the file, as far as FTAM is concerned. Each node with any associated data unit, a possible name, and all its descendants constitute a **file access data unit** (**FADU**). Just as a DU is the basic unit of the file for data transfer purposes, the FADU is the basic unit of location within the file.

The general hierarchical structure is a powerful tool for representing various file organizations. For example, an unstructured file is modeled by the general hierarchical structure as a single node with an attached DU containing all the data of the file. There is only one FADU in such a file, as seen in Figure 7.12. There is also only one DU, and it is the same as the FADU. In other words, there is no structure to separate elements of the file. Access is to the complete file as a single entity.

A flat file is modeled with two levels in the tree: a root and a number of children from the root equal to the number of data units in the file. If the nodes are not named, access must proceed in the order generated by the depth-first search—sequential order from left to right as shown in the figure. With names assigned to the nodes, access can be made directly to FADUs in any order. Figure 7.13 shows a flat file in the virtual filestore structure. Two data units are shown in this file though there is indication that many more may exist. In the limited structure shown, there are three FADUs; each is composed of a numbered node in the diagram and all the descendents of that node. Thus, the FADU centered at node 1 includes nodes 2 and 3 and any data associated with them. The FADU centered at node 2 consists only of node 2 and its DU, and so on.

Finally, a general indexed structure, such as the IBM VSAM file structure, maps to the hierarchical general filestore structure by making the interior nodes play the role of the index pointers and the leaf level nodes and their data units represent the data control intervals. Figure 7.14 represents the relationship between the structures.

Figure 7.13. A flat file as an instance of the virtual filestore general hierarchical structure

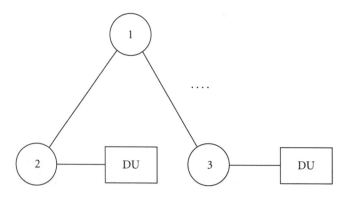

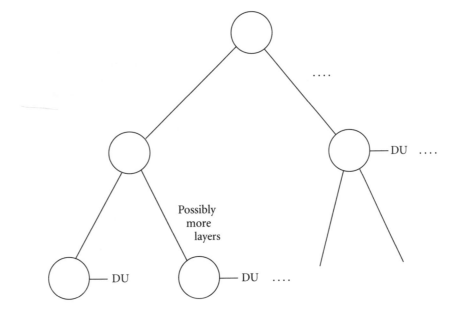

Figure 7.14. A general indexed file structure as an instance of the virtual filestore general hierarchical structure

7.4.2 FTAM Service Elements

Operations on the virtual filestore are expressed in terms of the FTAM services. The services can be grouped in a number of ways: Figure 7.15 classifies operations by what they operate on (the whole file and its attributes or the file contents); Figure 7.16 groups the operations according to **functional unit** (**FU**). Each FU contains the service elements related to a specific aspect of file service.

Functional Units and Service Classes

FTAM service elements are grouped into functional units to allow peer FTAM processes to interact efficiently. In order for FTAM processes to work together, each must support the same set of services. Because there are so many services, it is unreasonable to require every implementation to provide all possible services. However, if implementers were free to select any subset of services to include in their products, the result would be a very large number of variations on the FTAM service, most of which would be unable to interoperate. This would clearly be contrary to the purpose of the virtual filestore and common access methods.

To allow flexibility in implementing subsets of FTAM and still make interoperability generally possible, the FTAM standard groups services into functional units with a requirement that a given implementation provide all the services in any functional unit it claims to provide. At the time of association establishment, the FTAM initiator and responder negotiate the set of functional units that will be available during the interaction.

FTAM functional units and their associated FTAM service elements are shown in Figure 7.16. Some service elements appear repeatedly; both the read and write functional unit require the data transfer capability provided by F-DATA, for example. The particular functional units active during an FTAM association depend on the requirements of the cooper-

If implementers were free to select any subset of services to include in their products, the result would be a very large number of variations on the FTAM service, most of which would be unable to interoperate.

Service	Purpose
CREATE	Create a new file
SELECT	Choose a particular file for subsequent access
CHANGE ATTRIBUTES	Modify the attributes of a file
READ ATTRIBUTES	Read the value of specified attributes
OPEN	Make available the contents of a selected file
CLOSE	Terminate access to the contents of a file
DELETE	Delete (and deselect) a file
DESELECT	Terminate access to a file

Operations on a File and its Attributes

Service	Purpose
LOCATE	Find a particular FADU for further access
ERASE	Delete an FADU and its associated data units
READ	Establish data transfer access to a DU from the responder to the initiator
WRITE	Establish data transfer access to a DU from the initiator to the responder
DATA	Transfer of data as arranged by a previous READ or WRITE
DATA-END	Indication of the end of data transfer as arranged by a previous READ or WRITE
TRANSFER-END	Termination of the READ or WRITE access

Figure 7.15. FTAM services grouped by operand

Operations on the Contents of a File

ating processes. There are, of course, many potential combinations of functional units, not all of which are meaningful. For example, to choose exactly the set of FUs {Kernel, Grouping, Recovery} is not meaningful. To make it easier to choose a meaningful set of FUs, the FTAM standard defines common **service classes**, each of which is composed of some set of FUs. Each service class contains some required FUs, some optional FUs, and possibly the specific exclusion of other FUs. The service classes and their associated FUs are shown in Figure 7.17.

7.4.3 FTAM Regimes

Over time, an FTAM interaction progresses through a number of phases, which are called **regimes**. A regime is entered by invoking a particular service. During a regime, some collection of operations are permitted. A regime also carries an implication of access rights that must be established upon entering the regime. Once inside the regime, the rights are assumed and certain operations that depend on those rights are permitted. For example, the **association regime** assumes access by the initiating FTAM process to the filestore at the responding FTAM process location. To enter the association regime with that responder, the initiator must provide identification and be validated for access by the responder.

The information necessary to establish access rights to the filestore is carried in the parameters of F-INITIALIZE. Successful completion of the F-INITIALIZE service leaves the

Functional Unit	Service
Kernel	F-INITIALIZE
	F-TERMINATE
	F-ABORT
	F-SELECT
	F-DESELECT
Read	F-READ
	F-DATA
	F-DATA-END
	F-TRANSFER-END
	F-CANCEL
	F-OPEN
	F-CLOSE
Write	F-WRITE
	F-DATA
	F-DATA-END
	F-TRANSFER-END
	F-CANCEL
	F-OPEN
	F-CLOSE
File access	F-LOCATE
	F-ERASE
Limited file management	F-CREATE
	F-DELETE
	F-READ-ATTRIBUTE
Enhanced file management	F-CHANGE-ATTRIBUTE
Grouping	F-BEGIN-GROUP
	F-END-GROUP
Recovery	F-RECOVERY
	F-CHECK
	F-CANCEL
Restart data transfer	F-RESTART
	F-CHECK
	F-CANCEL

Figure 7.16. FTAM services by functional units

processes in an FTAM association called the association regime. Activities that can be undertaken while in the association regime, but not in any other regime, relate to the filestore itself, not to any particular files. These might be referred to as general filestore management activities. No such activities are currently defined in the standard, but the ability to add them at a later time exists.

FU	Service Classes					
	Transfer	Management	Transfer & Management	Access	Transfer & Access	Unconstrained
Kernel	M	M	M	M	M	M
Read	Note 1	No	Note 1	M	M	O
Write	Note 1	No	Note 1	M	M	O
File access	No	No	No	M	M	O
Limited file management	O	M	M	O	O	O
Enhanced file management	O	O	O	O	O	O
Grouping	M	M	M	O	M	O
Recovery	O	No	O	O	O	O
Restart data transfer	O	No	O	O	O	O

Key:

- M: Mandatory
- O: Optional
- No: Not available
- Note 1: Read, Write, or both FUs required

Figure 7.17. FTAM service classes

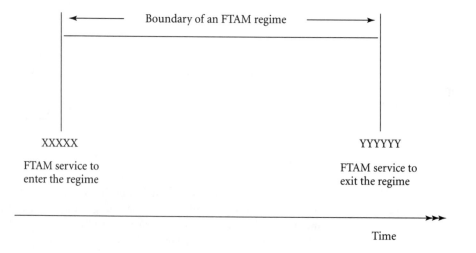

Figure 7.18. Format of FTAM regime diagrams

The regime of a pair of FTAM processes is usually diagramed as illustrated in Figure 7.18. In this representation, time is shown progressing from left to right. A vertical line labeled with a service indicates the border between one regime and another. Some regimes are nested within others (the association regime giving access to the filestore must exist during any regime giving access to a file in that filestore, for example).

Entry into the association regime also determines which functional units will be available during the association. That, in turn, determines which regimes can be active during the association regime, and the services available during the regimes. Figure 7.19 shows the association regime and the activities available within it. In particular, there are still undefined filestore management functions that do not cause a new regime to be opened, and the F-SELECT and F-CREATE services that cause entry into a nested regime, the *file selection regime*. The file selection regime is ended by use of F-DESELECT or F-DELETE and the processes return to the enveloping FTAM association regime, where filestore management operations would still be available.

The use of F-SELECT or F-CREATE connects this process with one particular file (only one file can be available in a single FTAM association). Within the file selection regime, all operations are interpreted as relative to that file. Operations within the file selection regime that do not cause a new regime to be entered are those that access the attributes of the file, but not the contents of the file. These activities are provided by the F-READ-ATTRIBUTE and F-CHANGE-ATTRIBUTE services. Use of the F-OPEN service establishes the right of the initiator to access the contents of the file and establishes a new regime—the file open regime—during which operations on the file contents are permitted. Figure 7.20 shows the file selection regime.

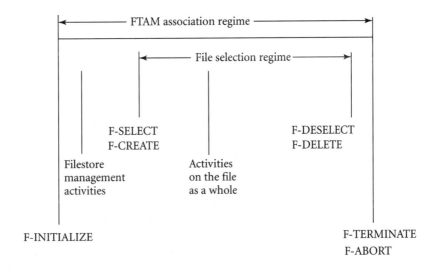

Figure 7.19. The FTAM association regime

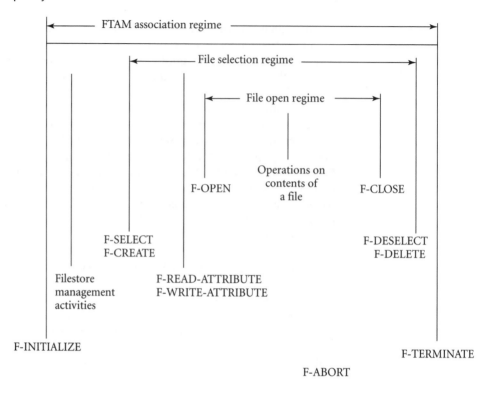

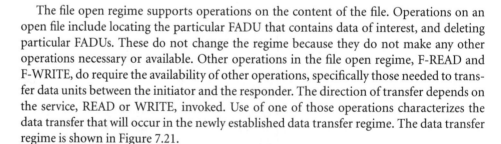

Figure 7.20. The FTAM file selection regime

The file open regime supports operations on the content of the file. Operations on an open file include locating the particular FADU that contains data of interest, and deleting particular FADUs. These do not change the regime because they do not make any other operations necessary or available. Other operations in the file open regime, F-READ and F-WRITE, do require the availability of other operations, specifically those needed to transfer data units between the initiator and the responder. The direction of transfer depends on the service, READ or WRITE, invoked. Use of one of those operations characterizes the data transfer that will occur in the newly established data transfer regime. The data transfer regime is shown in Figure 7.21.

Within the data transfer regime, the DUs that are part of the FADU identified in the READ or WRITE operation can be transferred. Use of READ or WRITE determines the direction of the data transfer: initiator to responder for WRITE, or responder to initiator for READ. It is helpful to use the terms *sender* and *receiver* to distinguish the ends of a data exchange. For a WRITE operation, the initiator is also the sender. For a READ operation, the initiator is the receiver. A WRITE operation also requires permission to replace existing data units or to extend the file by adding new data units.

The READ and WRITE operations are confirmed services, allowing the processes to agree on the nature of the exchange. Data units are then transferred using the unconfirmed

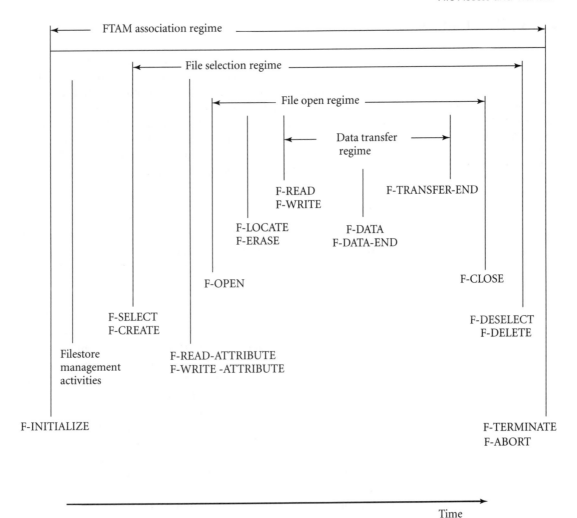

Figure 7.21. The FTAM file open and data transfer regimes

F-DATA service. The sender uses F-DATA-END to signal the end of data—where the sender is responder for a READ service or the initiator of a WRITE service. The initiator uses F-TRANSFER-END to signal that transfer of data is complete. Receipt of the F-TRANSFER-END.indication by the responder is notification that no further error-recovery steps will be required. F-TRANSFER-END.confirm serves the same purpose for the initiator. The sender of data, whether the initiator (as in the case of F-WRITE activity), or the responder (in F-READ activity), can then free the buffers in which it retained copies of data for retransmission if required. This confirmation of complete and correct conclusion of a data transfer activity is above and beyond whatever protection and verification is provided by lower-layer services at the request of the FTAM user and provides protection against possible lower-layer failures.

7.4.4   The FTAM Services

FTAM defines services to provide full access to a file and its contents. The list of services is much more extensive than in other file transfer systems.

In this section, we describe the services provided by FTAM as they contribute to the ultimate goal of a file access and management facility: transparent access to local and remote files regardless of the file system characteristics of the initiating and responding systems.

Unlike protocols designed principally to transfer files from one place to another, FTAM defines services to provide full access to a file and its contents. The list of services is much more extensive than in other file transfer systems. The regimes introduced in section 7.4.3 divide the services into groups, denote the degree of connectivity with the file system, and provide the mechanism to define various levels of access rights.

Initialization

F-INITIALIZE causes A-ASSOCIATE to be invoked, establishing the association that permits coordinated effort involving two independent systems. Parameters *service class, functional units,* and *attribute groups* convey information between the initiating and responding FTAM service elements. The initiator lists the set of services classes it supports; the responder selects one service class to be used during this interaction. The initiator lists the functional units it will need, and the responder agrees to provide the requested service. (If the responder is unable to provide the requested services, the initialization fails.) Similarly, the requestor lists the attribute groups needed for this interaction, and the responder accepts the request. F-INITIALIZE is a confirmed service; all the requests are made, and responses are provided in one exchange of messages. An *initiator identity* and *filestore password* allow the initiator to establish rights to access the requested file system.

The parameters of F-SELECT include *requested access* and *concurrency control*. Requested access is a list of actions selected from among {read, insert, replace, extend, read attribute, change attribute, delete file}. This list describes the maximum access to the file the initiator expects. If any of the requested actions are not permitted, the select regime is not established. Concurrency control is a vector of values for each of the access list entries; it specifies what type of lock is required during this action to avoid conflict with other processes. Example values are "shared," which indicates that others may access the file during an operation such as read, and "exclusive," which indicates that an operation such as write may be performed by one process at a time.

The most interesting aspect of FTAM is the ability to access the contents of a file, independent of the file system of the initiator or the file system on which the file is stored. The service primitives and parameters necessary to achieve this access are the subject of the next section.

Access to File Contents: The Bulk Data Transfer Primitives

Access to the content of a file comes from the services F-READ, F-WRITE, F-DATA, F-DATA-END, and F-TRANSFER-END. The F-READ or F-WRITE service invocation specifies what data will be transferred. Subsequent F-DATA service invocations carry data values until the transfer is complete. F-DATA-END marks the end of the data transfer initiated by the F-READ or F-WRITE. F-TRANSFER-END marks the end of the transfer of data and notifies the sender of data that no further error-recovery actions will be required for that bulk data transfer. F-DATA-END is always sent by the sender of data; this is the initiator for a write operation or the responder for a read operation. F-TRANSFER-END, on the other hand, is always issued by the initiator. Either side can end a data transfer activity by using F-CANCEL. F-TRANSFER-END and F-CANCEL are confirmed services. The others are unconfirmed.

F-READ and F-WRITE each carry a single mandatory parameter, the *bulk data transfer specification*. The bulk data transfer specification parameter consists of three subparameters: the file access data unit (identity for a read or operation for a write), access context, and FADU lock. F-DATA carries the mandatory parameter *data value*. The data are transferred as values of known data types, using the underlying presentation services—either through use of presentation management or through information in the contents list given in F-INITIALIZE.

The FADU identity specifies a location within the virtual filestore. Permitted identity specifications follow:

first refers to the first FADU in a preorder traversal of the file structure referenced, for which a data unit exists.

last refers to the last FADU in the preorder traversal of the file structure referenced.

previous refers to the FADU immediately preceding the current FADU in a preorder traversal of the file structure referenced.

current specifies that no change of location within the file structure is needed.

next refers to the FADU immediately following the current FADU in a preorder traversal of the file structure referenced.

begin is defined so that subsequent use of *next* will yield the first FADU.

end is defined so that subsequent use of *previous* will yield the last FADU.

node name is the identifier associated with a particular FADU. Search for a particular node name is restricted to children of the current FADU.

sequence of node names provides a path of FADU identifiers from the root to the FADU desired. An empty sequence of node names indicates the root.

node number identifies the desired node by its number in the sequence generated by preorder traversal of the file structure. The root node is node number 0.

Consider the structure of Figure 7.22. Each node is assigned a name in this structure and is also numbered from preorder traversal. Assume that the vertices marked with ## contain data. If access to the structure is currently pointing to the node labeled E, then the results of applying the FADU values would be as follows:

- `first` yields node D, the first that contains data
- `last` yields H
- `previous` yields G, which is previous to E in preorder traversal
- `current` yields E
- `next` yields C
- `begin` sets conditions such that `next` will yield D which is the same as the result of first
- `end` is such that a subsequent use of `previous` yields H

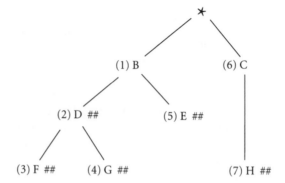

Figure 7.22. A sample filestore structure

- node name C yields C
- sequence of node names B E yields E as a path from the root to E
- node number 6 yields C

7.4.5 Using FTAM for File Access: Some Examples

Let's tie together the FTAM services by considering some examples. We start with a simple file transfer: copy a file from one system to another. We then show remote access to a file, both for sequential access to the entire file and for random access to particular file entries. The examples are first presented in terms of the FTAM service primitives and then as implemented in ISODE, a version of the upper-level ISO protocols designed to run over TCP/IP for the transport and network services.

We saw in section 4.2 that a large number of parameters must be specified to establish an association. Many of the parameters are passed down to lower layers of the network software to describe the particular types of service required by this application. We summarized those and put off describing the details until we consider those lower-layer services. We continue that policy here. As we will see, many of the details of these parameters can be generated by the environment through which we gain access to the services. In other words, many of them do not have to be provided explicitly by the user. The steps required to obtain the particular information needed for the many parameters of the various layers of network services that support this operation depend on the implementation of the OSI services used. Remember that the interface to the open systems environment seen by the user and user processes will vary considerably, depending on the agents selected to provide that interface. Thus, in these examples, we show only a generic representation of the parameters required. In the implementations-specific versions of these examples that follow, we see how the parameter values are obtained and the service calls are constructed using the ISODE implementation.

The interface to the open systems environment seen by the user and user processes will vary considerably, depending on the agents selected to provide that interface.

Example: File Copy to a Remote Site

The problem: Transfer a particular local text file to a remote system.

Parameters:

Local filename	ARTICLE
Contents type	ASCII Text
Structure	Unstructured
Local host (initiator)	monet.villanova.edu
Remote host (responder)	renoir.villanova.edu
Remote filename	DRAFT1

We identify the particular functional units of FTAM that we need to complete this task:

- Kernel

   Always required
   INITIALIZE allows establishment of the association with the remote filestore
   DESELECT releases contact with the remote file after it is written

- Limited file management

   CREATE allows establishment of a new file

- Write

   OPEN and CLOSE provide access to the file contents
   WRITE establishes the ability to write in the new remote file
   DATA and DATA-END allow transfer of the file contents
   TRANSFER-END completes the data transfer regime

Figure 7.23 is a time-sequence diagram of the FTAM service primitives used in the transfer of the file from an initiating host to a responding host. The transfer here is of an entire file, which will become a new file on the remote system.

The sequence of steps used to transfer a file becomes the following, with appropriate responses required between steps:

1. F-INITIALIZE.req(dest,user-id,functional-units,<options>)
2. F-CREATE.req(draft1,<options>)
3. F-OPEN.req
4. F-WRITE.req
5. F-DATA.req(article)
6. F-DATA-END.req
7. F-TRANSFER-END.req
8. F-CLOSE.req
9. F-DESELECT.req
10. F-TERMINATE.req

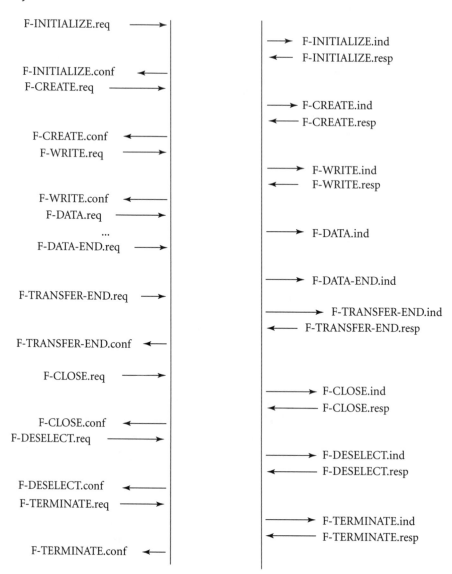

Figure 7.23. File transfer using FTAM services

Because the file transfer is going from the initiator of the FTAM use to the responder, the initiator is also the sender and invokes F-DATA, F-DATA-END, and F-TRANSFER-END.

Example: Application Using a Remote File for Sequential Access

Problem: An application process accesses a file stored on a remote system. The application reads the file sequentially, using all records in order. No writing is done to the file.

In this example, the file has a structure in the form of "records," which are called *data units* in FTAM terminology. In ordinary programs accessing local files, we expect to see the records described in the program accessing the file. The description provides names for fields in the file and specifies the type of data for each field. For example, a record description might look like this:

record

customer-id:	string(5);
customer-name:	string(25);
item-desc:	string(25);
item-cost:	real;

end;

In an open system environment, access to the content of a file is independent of programming language and of local representation of data. We explored this issue more completely in Chapter 3 and will return to it in Chapter 10. There still must be a description of what the program expects to find in the data unit it fetches. The description will be submitted to the virtual filestore as an abstract syntax. The Presentation layer will manage the task of communication between the remote system where the file is stored and the system on which the application process is running. The presentation service will identify appropriate representations for the data in transit between the systems and for storage locally. We will ignore these issues for now, and concentrate on the steps required for establishing contact with the remote filestore and obtaining access to all the data units required in the orderly fashion demanded by the application process.

Many of the operations required for access to the remote file are similar to operations required for ordinary access to a local file. Figure 7.24 lists the steps required and provides a comparison. Figure 7.25 is a time-sequence diagram of the interaction between the initi-

Operation	Local File Access	FTAM Remote File Access
Establish association		F-INITIALIZE
Select file	File declaration	F-SELECT
Open file	OPEN	F-OPEN
Locate next data unit	Implicit for sequential access; explicit for direct access	F-LOCATE NEXT for sequential access; F-LOCATE <node name> for direct access
Establish read or write access	Language dependent; usually part of OPEN	F-READ or F-WRITE
Get or put a record	READ or WRITE	F-DATA
Notify of end of data	EOF condition	F-DATA-END
Notify of end of data transfer activity		F-TRANSFER-END
Close file	CLOSE	F-CLOSE
Release the file	CLOSE	F-DESELECT
End association; compute charges		F-TERMINATE

Figure 7.24. Comparison of local file access and FTAM remote file access steps

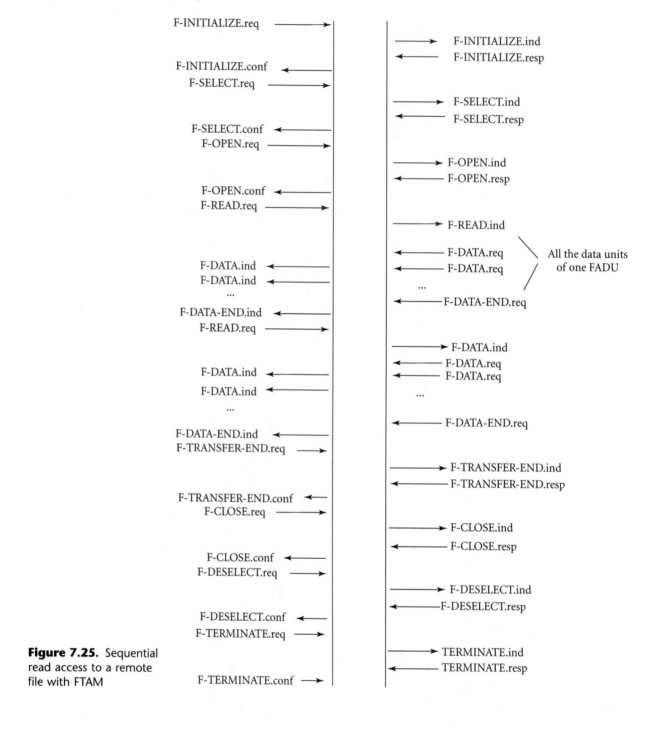

Figure 7.25. Sequential read access to a remote file with FTAM

ating and responding FTAM service providers in stepping through the file. We keep these examples simple by neglecting the potential for error and the error-recovery services available from FTAM. Recall, however, that the underlying network services are still providing a high level of service. Error recovery in the Application layer is available to protect against possible failure in lower layers.

ISODE File Transfer

The file transfer in this example is accomplished by invoking the ISODE FTAM in interactive mode.

The FTAM program is invoked from the command prompt:

```
45 /mnt/a/cassel> ftam
```

At the ftam> prompt, the user selects the destination host, and is prompted for login information:

```
ftam> open renoir
user (renoir:cassel):         % The user name defaults to the current login
password (renoir:cassel):     % name, accepted by hitting <CR>.  The password
                              % must be provided and is not displayed.

renoir... connected           % Association is established with ftam on renoir
renoir> ?                     % The new prompt identifies the remote machine.
                              % The ? requests information on the current session

Operations:
append  close   fdir    help    mkdir   put     rm
cd      dir     fls     lcd     mv      pwd     set
chgrp   echo    get     ls      open    quit    status

version info:    ftam 8.0 #1 (monet) of Wed Feb 10 19:44:38 EST 1993
        isode 8.0 #1 (monet) of Tue Feb  9 15:40:38 EST 1993


renoir> put article           % put sends a file from the local file system
                              % to the remote system
destination: draft1           % FTAM requests a name for the new file
ftam: 51 bytes sent in 0.01 seconds (4.98 Kbytes/s)
```

The transfer is complete. All the FTAM operations are hidden in the simple operation *put* for the user.

The *status* operation gets some additional information about the FTAM association:

```
renoir> status
associated with virtual filestore on "renoir"
  at '0103'H/Internet=153.104.7.174
  as user "cassel"
application-context: "iso ftam"
service class: transfer-and-management, ftam-QoS: no-recovery
functional units: 0x3b<READ,WRITE,LIMITED,ENHANCED,GROUPING>
attribute groups: 0x1<STORAGE>
document types:
    1.0.8571.5.3     unstructured binary file (FTAM-3)
    1.0.8571.5.1     unstructured text file (FTAM-1)
```

```
1.3.14.5.5.9      file directory file (NBS-9)
estimated integral FADU size: 2034
```

Notice the application context, service class, FTAM quality of service, functional units, attribute groups, and document types available in this association. Notice again that most of this information was derived from the environment established when we invoked FTAM. All this detail is important for proper functioning of the protocols, but the user can usually accomplish the task of transferring a file without being aware of most of it.

SUMMARY

File systems range from the relatively simple needs of a single-user local filestore to a very complex environment where multiple users share files that may be partitioned or replicated on a number of locations. Many applications developed as distributed systems must deal with these complexities. File transfer requires a process in each of the two systems: the one where the user is initiating requests and the one where the remote file is stored. The processes must cooperate to mask differences in the file systems and to move the contents of a file accurately from one system to the other.

A number of protocols support transfer of a file from one system to another. FTAM goes well beyond simple file transfer to provide remote file access across heterogeneous file systems. FTAM depends on an abstraction of a file system called a virtual filestore to capture what is necessary for access to a file system. It builds on its predecessors to provide simple file transfer but also full-featured distributed file access.

In this chapter, we considered widespread access to files independent of the file's structure and the operating system under which it resides. In the next chapter, we move to widespread access to database entries, also independent of the database model and local operating system. These two chapters are bound by an important theme: access to information without requiring that the information be reformatted or reconfigured to be made available.

EXERCISES

1. Compare and contrast the Kermit and FTP approaches to file transfer. Under what circumstances would each be used?
2. What are the principal characteristics of the PC-based file transfer protocols described in the chapter?
3. How does file transfer over a dial-up connection differ from file transfer over a network connection?
4. Using Kermit, transfer a file between a PC-type system and a larger host.
5. Using anonymous FTP, retrieve a file of interest from somewhere in the Internet.
6. Notice the functional units listed in the ISODE file transfer example. What is the meaning of those functional units?
7. What is meant by the attribute group STORAGE in the ISODE file transfer example?
8. Explain why file transfer processes must be set for binary or text (ASCII) mode.

9. Why is the set of functional units {KERNEL, GROUPING, RECOVERY} not meaningful? What other groupings can you find that are not meaningful?

10. Consider an application that requires confirming that certain files have been created on various remote sites; it does not need to know anything about the files except that they exist. What is the minimum set of FTAM service classes required for this application?

11. Consider an application that must determine the time of the most recent file activity on a variety of remote sites. What is the minimum set of FTAM service classes required?

12. Consider three computer systems: A, B, and C. Running FTP on system A, transfer a file from system B to system C. (The details of how to do this are not in the chapter. How will you find the necessary information?)

13. Return to the inventory problem of Chapter 1. What file access is required to solve that problem? Would Kermit be useful? FTP? FTAM? If any of those could be used in the solution, describe how you would integrate it into the full inventory system.

CHAPTER 8

The Directory X.500 and LDAP

KEY CONCEPTS

- Characteristics
- The Distributed Directory
- Directory Protocols

The World Wide Web exploded onto the scene and became a widely available source of information in 1993 with the release of Mosaic. The need for organized access to a large body of information available through interconnected networks goes back much farther, however. In this chapter, we present a distributed database called the Directory in OSI terms and X.500 by ITU. Though the Directory, like many ISO applications, has developed more slowly than anticipated, it figures prominently in a number of efforts. See RFC 2312 S/MIME Version 2 Certificate Handling for a recent (March 1998) example. A "lightweight" version of the Directory, the Lightweight Data Access Protocol (LDAP), has been developed for use in the Internet, with commitments from many vendors to provide support. Existing Directory entries are now accessible with Weblike interfaces to simplify search and retrieval. Figures 8.1 and 8.2 show available entries as they appear to the user.

In addition to its practical applications, the X.500 work provides many lessons useful in the systematic and efficient search for information over a widely distributed database. Many of the models developed in this context will be of value in research and development efforts seeking to impose a semblance of order on the information space that is the World Wide Web.

A directory can be thought of as an electronic telephone book, providing both "white pages" (given the name, return the location and telephone number) and "yellow pages" (given some attribute, such as service offered, return the name and other information). The Directory Service, defined in ITU Recommendation X.500 and ISO 9594, provides services for creating, structuring, and accessing the data contained in a worldwide distributed database.

The information content of the Directory is limited only by what people choose to put into it and is constantly changing. Access to the information is limited by the access con-

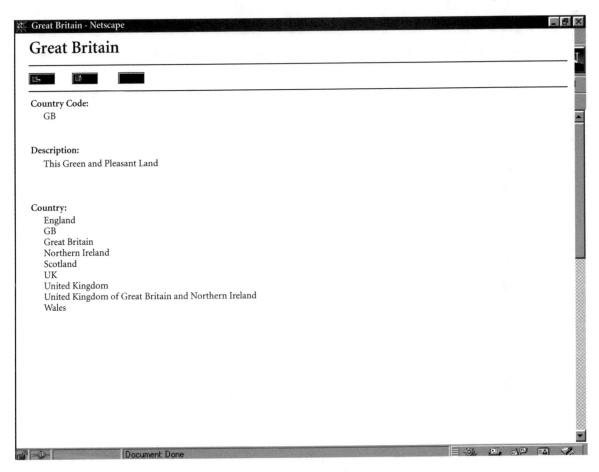

Figure 8.1. The top-level entry for Great Britain in the Directory

trols put in place by the organization responsible for each section of data. Items in the database are not restricted to information about people or organizations. You could use the Directory to find answers to questions such as these:

- Where is the nearest laser printer with PostScript capability?
- Who is chair of the Computing Sciences Department at Hathaway College?
- Are there researchers working in protocol analysis at any university in Western Australia?
- What Computer Science major has the highest grade point average in the graduating class of 2002?
- What conferences are scheduled in New England during June and July of 2001?
- What is a presentation address at which an instance of a particular application process can be reached?

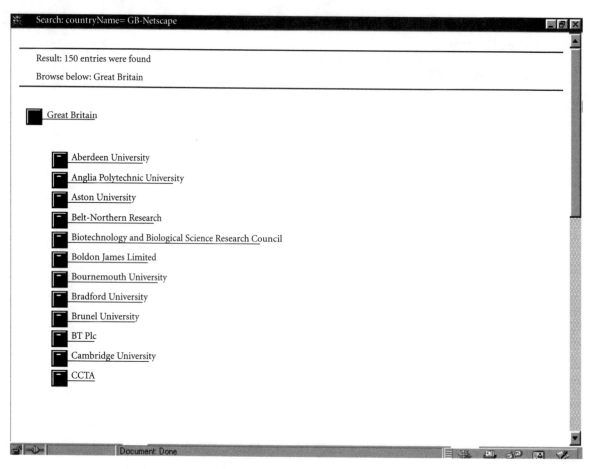

Figure 8.2. One level down in the Great Britain entry in the Directory (partial listing)

8.1 CHARACTERISTICS

An important characteristic of the Directory is its assumption that the most common use is to retrieve information; that is, there are many more queries to the Directory than there are updates. Thus, where tradeoffs must be made between efficiency for reading versus efficiency for writing, the preference will be for reading. Data in the Directory is distributed and duplicated to support fast access and availability despite failures at some system locations. Further, no requirement is made for instantaneous updates of all instances of any Directory entry. Thus, transient conditions will occur in which some part of the Directory information is inconsistent with other parts. From the perspective of a user accessing the data, this characteristic is similar to having a telephone book in which some numbers have changed; the book is still useful and correct for nearly all queries, despite some inaccuracies. The Directory inconsistencies are not permanent, like those in a printed telephone book. The advantages of having information easily available outweigh the potential of occasionally providing outdated information.

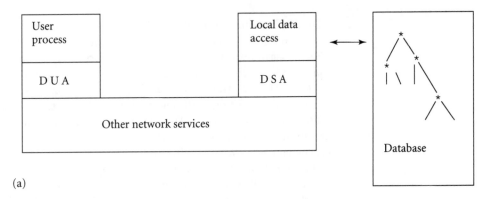

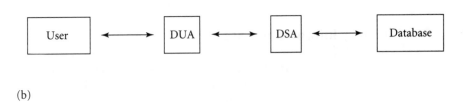

Figure 8.3. User access to the data in the Directory: (a) showing Network layering and (b) reduced to the basic components

Directory users gain access to the Directory through a **directory user agent (DUA)**, much as the user of an electronic mail system gains access to its services through a user agent.

The Directory is a distributed logical database of information about people and objects. Users of the Directory may be people or computer programs. Directory users gain access to the Directory through a **directory user agent (DUA)**, much as the user of an electronic mail system gains access to its services through a user agent. The DUA is an application process that interacts with the Directory through a **directory system agent (DSA)** to obtain the information requested by the user. The DUA is an application process and, subject to permission, can read or modify the information contained in the Directory, or some part of it. Figure 8.3 illustrates the relation between the user, the DUA, and the DSA.

8.2 THE DISTRIBUTED DIRECTORY

The Directory is defined in terms of four models, each of which describes some aspect of the Directory and its operation.

The **informational model** describes the directory information base (DIB): the relationship of the directory information tree (DIT), entries, attributes, types, and values. It includes the Directory schema, which determines how a component section of the DIB can be formed.

The **functional model** describes access to the Directory by a user and the response to the user by the Directory. The DSA is an application process that allows DUAs or other DSAs to access the DIB. The DSA may use information stored locally in its own database or may interact with other DSAs to carry out requests. Alternatively, it may direct the requestor to another DSA better able to process the request.

The **organizational model** describes the distribution of responsibility for maintenance of the component parts of the Directory. A set of one or more DSAs and zero or more DUAs managed by a single organization is a **directory management domain (DMD)**. An *administrative DMD (ADDMD)* is operated by a public telecommunications organization. *Private DMDs (PRDMD)* are operated by other organizations. For example, a corporation that maintains a portion of the Directory related to its employees, products, and resources would constitute a PRDMD. The corporation might have any type of local access procedures for use of its data within the DMD. It must make use of the Directory specifications in participating in the larger directory.

The **security model** describes the directory services in terms of authentication and authorization. A DUA must show the right of its user to access requested information or to make the modification included in the request. Similarly, DSAs interacting with each other on behalf of a DUA must present appropriate indication of rights to perform the requested actions.

8.2.1   The Directory Information Base

In the informational model, the Directory is described in terms of the information it contains and the organization of the information in the database. Information is stored in the Directory in a **directory information base (DIB)**, composed of entries that consist of information about one object. An object is anything that can be identified (named), such as

- A person
- A printer
- A company
- A state or province
- An application entity

Each entry in the DIB is made up of attributes. Each attribute consists of a type and one or more values. Figure 8.4 illustrates the structure of an entry in the DIB.

A single "thing" (for example, one person) may be two or more objects in the Directory through the use of an *alias* entry type. The DIB is the complete set of information to which the Directory provides access.

Objects are grouped into object classes. An **object class** is an identified family of objects sharing a set of common characteristics. For example, one object class is person. The person object class is a collection of objects, all of which contain the attributes commonName and surname. In addition, objects in the person object class may contain the attributes description, telephoneNumber, userPassword, and seeAlso.

An object can belong to a class that is the subclass of another class. For example, the class organizationalPerson is a subclass of person. As such, every entry in the class organizationalPerson must have all the attributes required in the class person. It may have the attributes that are optional in the class person. It also has attributes of its own. In this case, objects of the class organizationalPerson may also contain the following attributes: localeAttributeSet, postalAttributeSet, telecommunicationAttributeSet, organizational-

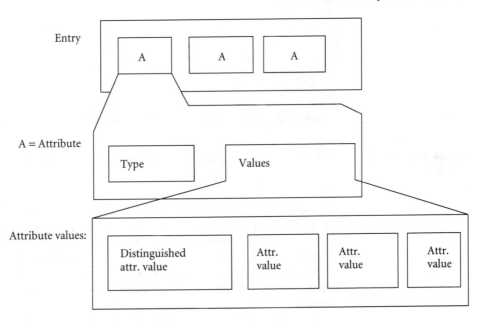

Figure 8.4. Structure
of a DIB entry

UnitName, and title. These attribute sets are defined in Figure 8.5. An example entry of the
class organizationalPerson appears in Figure 8.6.

The structure of the DIB is treelike, with entries forming the vertices of the tree. Arcs in
the tree define the relation between entries. For example, in the entries shown in Figure 8.7,
vertex A is the immediate superior of each of vertices B, C, and D, and vertices B, C, and D
are the immediate subordinates of A. The relation extends recursively to superiors of A and
subordinates of B, C, and D, and so on.

```
telecommunicationAttributeSet ATTRIBUTE := {

                                        facsimileTelephoneNumber,
                                        internationalISDNNumber,
                                        telephoneNumber,
                                        teletexTerminalIdentifier,
                                        telexNumber,
                                        preferredDeliveryMethod,
                                        destinationIndicator,
                                        registeredAddress,
                                        x121Address}

postalAttributeSet ATTRIBUTE ::= {

                                        physicalDeliveryOfficeName,
                                        postalAddress,
                                        postalCode,
                                        postOfficeBox,
                                        streetAddress}

localeAttributeSet ATTRIBUTE ::= {

                                        localityName,
                                        stateOrProvinceName,
                                        streetAddress}
```

Figure 8.5. Definitions
of useful attribute sets

Entry:

	Type	Values
Attribute:	surname	Cassel, Riley
Attribute:	commonName	L N Cassel, Lillian N. Cassel, Boots Cassel
Attribute:	telephoneNumber	001-610-555-1234, 001-610-555-3523

Figure 8.6. An entry in a DIB

Object entries can be either leaf or nonleaf entries. Alias entries point to object entries and are always leaf entries in the tree. These alias entries allow an object to have more than one name. Consider the following example: one individual, Robert Kenil, works as a member of two different departments within the organization. Aliasing his entry allows him to be found when a search is made for members of either department. At the same time, there is only one entry for him, so there is no chance of conflicting information in different entries.

Each entry in the tree is uniquely and unambiguously identified by a *distinguished name* (DN). The distinguished name of an entry is constructed from the identities of its ancestors in the tree along with a specially designated set of attribute values from the entry itself. For example, the distinguished name of the entry described in Figure 8.6 in the directory information tree of Figure 8.8 is (C=US,L=PA,O=VU,OU=Computing Sciences, organizationalPerson = Cassel). The particular attribute value *Cassel* has been selected as the *relative distinguished name* for the entry that also includes other attributes of the organizationalPerson. Some distinguished name must be selected for each entry in the DIT. The other entries shown in the tree as ancestors of the entry we have singled out may have additional attributes and values as well. Only the distinguished name is shown because that is the value used to refer to the entry.

CCITT Recommendation X.521, which defines selected object classes, including those used in this section, also includes the DIT structure diagram. The root, of course, is the common ancestor of all entries in the DIT. Immediate subordinates of the root can be *country, organization,* or *locality* entries. Immediate subordinates of locality entries may be *residential person* or *group of names* or *organizational unit* or *organization* or *location* itself. Further, *organization* has an immediate subordinate of *locality*, which has an immediate subordinate of *organization*. Figure 8.8 shows an example DIT.

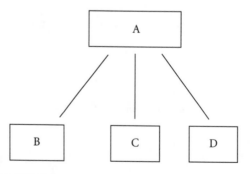

Figure 8.7. Tree arcs and vertices

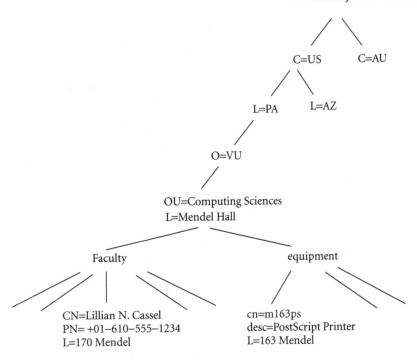

Figure 8.8. A Directory Information Tree

8.2.2 The Directory Schema

Since the Directory is distributed over a number of sites, with a number of organizations controlling the content of the various components, some common understanding of the nature of the entries in the DIB is required. This is provided in the form of a directory schema. The directory schema is a set of rules governing attribute types allowed for each class of object, form of values for each attribute type, and class of object that can be a child entry of a given class object.

Like the directory information base itself, the directory schema is distributed. In each autonomous administrative area, a subschema governs entries in a branch of the DIT. The directory schema is described in detail in ISO 9594.

8.2.3 The Directory Service

The Directory supports operations to interrogate and to modify the content of the Directory. There is also provision to control access to DIT entries. The Directory ensures that changes, whether made through a directory service request, or by some other (local) means, continues to obey the rules of the directory schema.

Parameters of the Directory Services

A number of interactions with the Directory make use of common information carried as arguments of an operation request or as results of an operation execution. These common information components include options describing the type of service required, security considerations, identification of the DIT entry sought, specification of the information to be returned from the DIT entry once it is located, and standard designation of the information returned by the DSA. Some of this commonly used description of the operation or its results constitute qualifications on the requests. We begin with a description of the qualifications, common arguments, and results; we then look at the operations supported on the Directory.

Qualifications   Qualifications can be *service controls, security parameters*, or *filters*. Service controls, described in Figure 8.9, allow a bound to be specified on the resources that might be expended in servicing a request. For example, a service might come with a limit on the time to be used in a search, the maximum result size, or the scope of the search. Security parameters, described in Figure 8.10, may include a user's request for various kinds of protection, including digital signature of the request and information to assist the correct party to verify the signature. Filters are conditions that an entry must satisfy to be returned as part of the outcome. For example, the entry must match a particular value *title* = *"Department Head,"* be greater than or equal to a particular value *gpa* $\geq$ 3.0, or be less than or equal to a particular value *speed* $\leq$ 1200. Other tests include *present*, which tests to see whether a particular attribute is present in the entry, and the selection of the initial substring, any substring, or the final substring in the entry. The boolean operators *and, or,* and *not* may be applied to form compound filters.

Common Arguments   Information called *common arguments* may be provided to constrain the action of the directory service in each of its operations. The common arguments consist of the following elements:

Service controls as seen in Figure 8.9.

Security parameters as seen in Figure 8.10.

Requestor distinguished name identifies the originator of a particular operation. It is the name of the user as determined during the binding to the Directory, and may be optional or required, depending upon the operations involved. If a signature is required, the requestor must be specified.

Operation progress describes the state of progress in carrying out an operation that involves more than one DSA. The default initial value of *notStarted* becomes *proceeding* and then *completed*.

Common results   Each retrieval operation causes a result. Information common to all results is described as follows:

Security parameters, described in Figure 8.10.

performer is a DistinguishedName that identifies the DSA that provided the result. Though optional, it may be required when a signature has been requested by the initiator in the Protection Request.

Options	preferChaining		
	chainingProhibited		
	localScope		
	dontUseCopy		
	dontDereferenceAliases		
	subentries		
	copyShallDo		
priority	low	medium	high
timeLimit			
sizeLimit			
scopeOfReferral			
attributeSizeLimit			

preferChaining indicates a preference for chaining rather than referrals in providing the requested service. The directory is not required to oblige in this request.

chainingProhibited specifies that the DSA is not to distribute the request through the Directory by chaining or in any other manner.

localScope specifies that the request is to be limited to the local attention. The meaning of local is defined locally and may mean a limit to the DSA or to any DSA in the local DMD.

dontUseCopy indicates that only the master copy of the information is to be used; no copies are allowed.

dontDeferenceAliases allows the operation to access an alias entry itself rather than the object entry to which the alias points.

subentries requests that subentries, not normal entries, be used in satisfying the request.

copyShallDo is meaningful only if *dontUseCopy* is not set. It indicates that if the information requested is only partly present in a copy, that portion of the result should be returned as a response to the request, and no further search for the remaining information should be undertaken.

sizeLimit is applicable only to list and search operations and limits the number of objects to be returned in response to the request.

scopeOfReferral, if used, limits the scope of a referral to the DMD or country.

attributeSizeLimit restricts the maximum length of any attribute (including the type and all values) returned in any entry information. If an entry exceeds this limit, all its values are dropped from the response and the parameter *incompleteEntry* is set in the returned entry information.

Figure 8.9.
Service controls

aliasDereferenced notifies the initiator of the operation that some target of the operation included an alias that was followed to an object entry.

EntryInformationSelection   Once a particular entry in the DIB has been located, there may be much more information available than the requestor wishes to have transferred. The EntryInformationSelection parameter specifies what to retrieve from the target entry:

certification-path is used to associate the sender's distinguished name and public encryption key.

name is the distinguished name of the first intended recipient of the argument or result that carries this set of security parameters.

time limits the validity of a signature to a specified length of time.

random number is used in conjunction with the time parameter to protect against replay of security information captured from network monitoring.

Figure 8.10. Security parameters

target Protection Request describes the degree of protection that the initiator of an operation wishes to have applied to its result and is either **none** or **signed**.

attributes allows the initiator of the operation to request that either all attributes of the entry be returned or that a selected subset of the attributes be returned. A subset is selected by listing the attribute types for which the type or values are requested. The default is all attributes returned.

infoTypes is one of attributeTypesOnly or attributeTypesAndValues, each with the meaning suggested by the name. The default is attributeTypesAndValues.

Entry information The EntryInformation parameter provides structure for the responding DSA to send information found at an entry to the requestor of the information. The EntryInformation consists of the following fields:

DistinguishedName of the entry or of an alias for an entry.

fromEntry a boolean value indicating whether the information comes from the entry (TRUE) or from a copy (FALSE).

a set of Attributes or AttributeTypes perhaps including values—this is the actual data returned as a result of the operation.

incompleteEntry a boolean that lets the requestor know if the result returned is incomplete (perhaps because of access control limitations, perhaps because of a size limit on the result).

Service Requests

Service requests are classified as *interrogation* or *modification* requests. All requests are operations and consist of an appropriate *argument, result,* and *errors* component. Interrogations consist of the following:

read applies to an entry and causes return of values of some or all attributes of that entry. The ReadArgument consists of the name of the entry to be read, EntryInformation-Selection, and CommonArguments (as described previously). The read operation may also request that the responding DSA notify the requestor of its rights regarding modification of the entry. The ReadResult consists of the EntryInformation of the requested entry, the ModifyRights information if requested, and the CommonResults described earlier. ModifyRights information indicates that the requestor can remove, rename, or move the entry to a new location in the DIT. It also indicates permission to add or to remove attributes or values of the entry.

DSAs may not retain information or provide it to a DUA other than the original requestor unless such use is consistent with any access controls that may be present. The Directory defines schema procedures to ensure internal consistency of an entry (that is, in a particular copy of an entry, all attribute values are updated or all are not at any given time).

The Directory defines procedures for manipulating the minimum knowledge needed by a DSA to ensure the accuracy of the DIT.

8.3 DIRECTORY PROTOCOLS

Three protocols are defined for the Directory. The directory access protocol (DAP) defines the exchange of requests and outcomes between a DUA and a DSA. The directory system protocol (DSP) defines exchange of requests and outcomes between two DSAs. Finally, the directory information shadowing protocol (DISP) defines exchange of replication information between two DSAs that have a shadowing agreement. Figure 8.16 shows the relationship between the DUA and a number of DSAs and their sections of the Directory from the perspective of the Directory protocols.

SUMMARY

We have seen the tools available at the Application layer for the development of distributed applications in the OSI environment. In Chapter 4, we saw the basic building blocks that are components of nearly all application entities. In Chapters 5, 6, 7, and 8, we saw three classes of applications built from these components and also candidates for inclusion in other application entities as well.

Specifically, in Chapter 8, we explored the distributed logical database called the Directory in OSI terms and X.500 by ITU. Four models define the Directory. The informational model describes the directory information base, DIB. The functional model describes access by a user and the response to a user. The organizational model describes maintenance responsibilities. The security model describes services in terms of authentication and authorization.

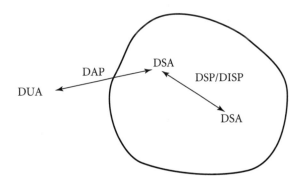

Figure 8.16. Directory protocols

The DIB is a treelike structure in which each entry contains information about one object. The entry is uniquely and unambiguously defined by a distinguished name (DN) constructed from identities of ancestors in the tree and by attributes consisting of types and values. Common understanding of the nature of entries across a number of sites is controlled by a directory schema. A number of services facilitate interactions with the Directory.

Now we begin looking "under the hood" to see and understand the underlying services that make these things work. The next section investigates the supporting structures.

EXERCISES

1. Using the example directory information tree of Figure 8.8, construct the distinguished name for each of the following:
   (a) The PostScript printer in Mendel Hall
   (b) Dr. Cassel's telephone number
   Fill in the DIT with additional, fictional entries representing people and devices in your own environment.

2. Using the DIT definition and rules, construct a tree showing each of the following:
   (a) Your entry as a residential person of your home community
   (b) Your entry as a student at your college, or as an employee in your company
   (c) A combination of the previous two parts of this question by making one entry an alias
   (d) A particular processor (for example, a file server in a lab)
   (e) A particular printer
   (f) An application entity (FTAM, for example) located on a specific host

3. (Programming Assignment) If you have access to a DSA, hence to the Directory, develop a DUA to provide a user-friendly interactive interface to the Directory. Support the operations *read, list, search, abandon*.

4. (Programming Assignment) If you do not currently have access to a DSA, use a database package available to you to develop a DSA to provide access to a locally held directory.
   (a) Use the directory schema to govern the permitted entries, their relationships and attributes.
   (b) Use a separate database, with different information, to provide another component of a distributed directory. Revise your DSA to include referencing capability.

5. Visit the Web site of the World Wide Web consortium (www.w3c.org) and investigate the current status of efforts to provide more organized access to information on the World Wide Web. Consider caching, for example. How are caching methods managed? What relationship do you find between issues under study by W3C and elements of X.500?

6. Look up the RFP that defines LDAP. Compare it to the full definition of X.500. In what ways are the two alike? How do they differ?

compare applies to an attribute of an entry and tests for a match between a value provided in the compare request and the value stored. An example use is verifying a password. The password is supplied by the user, and the Directory confirms that the password provided does match the value stored in the entry named.

list applies to an entry and returns the immediate subordinates (children) of the named entry. The ListArgument specifies the Name of the entry requested, CommonArguments as described earlier, and optionally requests that the response be returned a page at a time. The ListResult returns the DistinguishedName of the entry, and a set of subordinate entries each characterized by its RelativeDistinguishedName, whether it is an aliasEntry, whether it is from the main entry or a copy, and CommonResults as shown earlier.

search applies some filter and returns information from all entries within a certain portion of the DIT that satisfy the filter. The information returned is some or all attributes of the entries, as in `read`.

abandon notifies the Directory that the user wishes to abandon the operation currently in effect.

There are four directory modification requests:

add entry appends a new leaf to the DIT. The new leaf may be an object or an alias. It is not intended that this mechanism be applied repeatedly to build arbitrary new entries in the DIT, though that is possible. The intention is to provide a means to add a leaf entry only. Presently, arbitrary additions to the DIT are a matter for local implementation. An enhanced version of the service to address the more general case is anticipated. The AddEntryArgument includes the DistinguishedName of the new object; this name unambiguously defines the position the new entry will occupy in the DIT. The new entry is specified as a set of Attributes, including types and values. CommonAttributes complete the specification. The Result component of AddEntry is null.

remove entry is the complement of *add entry*. It deletes an entry at a leaf position of the DIT. It also is not intended for repeated use to make arbitrary modifications of the DIT. The entry to be removed is identified by its DistinguishedName. CommonArguments provide constraints on the operation. RemoveEntryResult is null.

modify entry allows attributes or attribute values to be added, removed, or replaced within an entry. The ModifyEntryArgument consists of the DistinguishedName of the entry and a sequence of modifications. Modifications consist of attributes and values to be added or removed. The Result component is null.

modify distinguished name changes the RelativeDistinguishedName of an entry or moves the entry to a new location in the DIT (though in the same DSA). The Argument of ModifyDN includes the DistinguishedName of the object, the new RelativeDistinguishedName for the object, instruction to delete the values in the old RelativeDistinguishedName or leave them present (though no longer part of the RDN), and the identification of the new location (the DN of the new superior node of this entry) if the entry is moved. The ModifyDNResult is null.

Failure to complete the service requested results if the request is improperly formed or if the DSA does not have access to the information requested. In the first case, an error message will be returned to the DUA with a best effort identification of the reason for failure. For example, if the name of an entry as provided by the user is not found, the error message will state that the entry name does not exist.

In the second case, the Directory may return a referral—an indication of a better DSA to contact in order to get the requested information. Whether the DSA returns a referral or makes an attempt to obtain the information from another DSA itself is a matter for negotiation between the DUA and the DSA at the time their association is established.

8.2.4   Operation of the Model

The functional model describes the Directory in terms of operations performed by a DUA and one or more DSAs serving the request of the DUA. A DUA gains access to the data stored in the Directory through a convenient DSA. The DUA binds to the Directory at an access point represented by a particular DSA. That DSA has direct access to a portion of the Directory. It also has knowledge about the rest of the Directory, allowing it to conduct inquiries about the location of information it does not have. When the DSA cannot provide the information requested, it exchanges information with other DSAs.

In Figure 8.3, a DUA interacts with a DSA that retrieves requested information from its local database; in Figure 8.11, the local DSA is seen as part of the distributed directory. If a DSA cannot satisfy a request, it proceeds in one of the ways shown in Figures 8.12 through 8.15.

In Figure 8.12, DSA-A passes the request to DSA-B. DSA-B does not have the information, but does have knowledge that DSA-C does have it. DSA-B provides this knowledge to DSA-A in the form of a referral. DSA-A passes the referral to the DUA, which repeats the request to DSA-C. DSA-C responds with the information.

In Figure 8.13, DSA-A again receives the referral from DSA-B. Instead of giving the referral to the DUA, however, DSA-A follows up on the lead, makes the request of DSA-C, and obtains the result for return to the DUA.

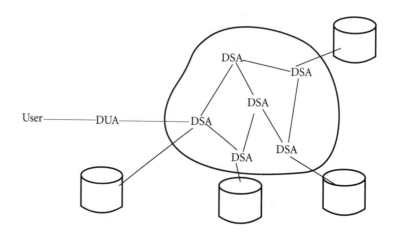

Figure 8.11. Several DSAs provide access to the whole distributed directory

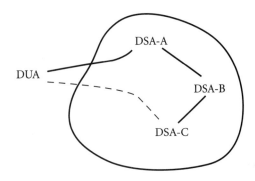

Figure 8.12. DSA
receives a referral
from another DSA
and passes it to the
requesting DUA

Referral ————————

Data connection – – – – – – –

Figure 8.14 illustrates *chaining*, in which DSA-A passes the request to DSA-B, which in turn passes it to DSA-C, which passes it to DSA-D. Finally, the information is provided and is passed back through the chain to DSA-A and eventually to the DUA.

Multicasting, illustrated in Figure 8.15, gets the request simultaneously to a number of DSAs. If at least one of them has the information requested, it will be returned to DSA-A to pass on to the DUA.

8.2.5   Replication

A large, globally distributed database presents a number of performance problems. If the data that is requested requires a large number of chaining steps, such as shown in Figure 8.14, response time could be poor. Further, some parts of the Directory might be inaccessible during intermittent failures by some components. Replication addresses both of

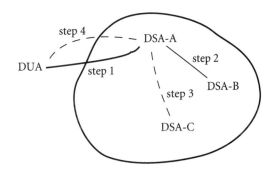

Figure 8.13. DSA
receives a referral
from another DSA and
follows it to obtain the
requested information
for the requesting DUA

Referral ————————

Data connection – – – – – – –

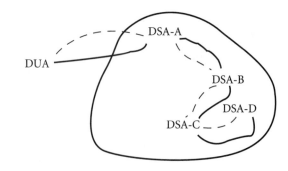

Figure 8.14. The DUA request is chained through several DSAs until the response is obtained and returned to the requesting DUA

Referral ——————————

Data connection – – – – – – –

these problems by allowing multiple copies of sections of the DIT. A DSA may store a copy of a section of the DIT for which it is not the master DSA. Updates will be directed to the master DSA, and there is no guarantee that the DSA holding a copy will not give outdated information in response to a request by a DUA before receiving the update information. A DUA will always know that it is receiving information from a copy of the data and will thus be aware of the potential for inaccurate data.

> A DUA will always know that it is receiving information from a copy of the data and will thus be aware of the potential for inaccurate data.

There are two types of data replication: *Cache* copies are obtained by a DSA and used in ways that are not covered by the Directory specification. Such copies might be termed unofficial copies. There is no guarantee that such a copy will eventually become updated. *Shadow* copies are obtained by a DSA in accordance with procedures in the Directory specification. Such a copy might be termed an official, controlled copy. Though the shadow copy may not be up to date at all times, there is a procedure for bringing it into conformance with the master copy, and its obsolescence has a time limit. The schedule for updating the copy is a matter of contractual agreement between the DSA holding the copy (the shadow consumer) and the DSA holding the master copy (the shadow supplier).

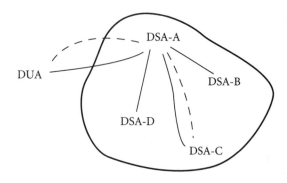

Figure 8.15. DSA uses multicast requests to obtain the information to return to the requesting DUA

Referral ——————————

Data connection – – – – – – –

DSAs may not retain information or provide it to a DUA other than the original requestor unless such use is consistent with any access controls that may be present. The Directory defines schema procedures to ensure internal consistency of an entry (that is, in a particular copy of an entry, all attribute values are updated or all are not at any given time).

The Directory defines procedures for manipulating the minimum knowledge needed by a DSA to ensure the accuracy of the DIT.

8.3 DIRECTORY PROTOCOLS

Three protocols are defined for the Directory. The directory access protocol (DAP) defines the exchange of requests and outcomes between a DUA and a DSA. The directory system protocol (DSP) defines exchange of requests and outcomes between two DSAs. Finally, the directory information shadowing protocol (DISP) defines exchange of replication information between two DSAs that have a shadowing agreement. Figure 8.16 shows the relationship between the DUA and a number of DSAs and their sections of the Directory from the perspective of the Directory protocols.

SUMMARY

We have seen the tools available at the Application layer for the development of distributed applications in the OSI environment. In Chapter 4, we saw the basic building blocks that are components of nearly all application entities. In Chapters 5, 6, 7, and 8, we saw three classes of applications built from these components and also candidates for inclusion in other application entities as well.

Specifically, in Chapter 8, we explored the distributed logical database called the Directory in OSI terms and X.500 by ITU. Four models define the Directory. The informational model describes the directory information base, DIB. The functional model describes access by a user and the response to a user. The organizational model describes maintenance responsibilities. The security model describes services in terms of authentication and authorization.

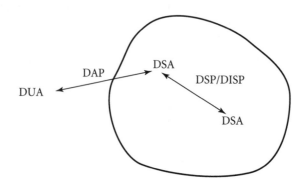

Figure 8.16. Directory protocols

The DIB is a treelike structure in which each entry contains information about one object. The entry is uniquely and unambiguously defined by a distinguished name (DN) constructed from identities of ancestors in the tree and by attributes consisting of types and values. Common understanding of the nature of entries across a number of sites is controlled by a directory schema. A number of services facilitate interactions with the Directory.

Now we begin looking "under the hood" to see and understand the underlying services that make these things work. The next section investigates the supporting structures.

EXERCISES

1. Using the example directory information tree of Figure 8.8, construct the distinguished name for each of the following:
   (a) The PostScript printer in Mendel Hall
   (b) Dr. Cassel's telephone number
   Fill in the DIT with additional, fictional entries representing people and devices in your own environment.

2. Using the DIT definition and rules, construct a tree showing each of the following:
   (a) Your entry as a residential person of your home community
   (b) Your entry as a student at your college, or as an employee in your company
   (c) A combination of the previous two parts of this question by making one entry an alias
   (d) A particular processor (for example, a file server in a lab)
   (e) A particular printer
   (f) An application entity (FTAM, for example) located on a specific host

3. (Programming Assignment) If you have access to a DSA, hence to the Directory, develop a DUA to provide a user-friendly interactive interface to the Directory. Support the operations *read, list, search, abandon.*

4. (Programming Assignment) If you do not currently have access to a DSA, use a database package available to you to develop a DSA to provide access to a locally held directory.
   (a) Use the directory schema to govern the permitted entries, their relationships and attributes.
   (b) Use a separate database, with different information, to provide another component of a distributed directory. Revise your DSA to include referencing capability.

5. Visit the Web site of the World Wide Web consortium (www.w3c.org) and investigate the current status of efforts to provide more organized access to information on the World Wide Web. Consider caching, for example. How are caching methods managed? What relationship do you find between issues under study by W3C and elements of X.500?

6. Look up the RFP that defines LDAP. Compare it to the full definition of X.500. In what ways are the two alike? How do they differ?

CHAPTER 9

Encryption and Compression

KEY CONCEPTS

- Secure Transmission of Messages
- Data Compression

The popularity and pervasiveness of the Internet raise serious concerns regarding secure message transmission. A company or other organization with an internal network must apply additional safeguards to protect proprietary material from unauthorized access when the network is connected to an external network such as the Internet. Electronic commerce requires a secure Internet banking system. Conflicts between the right to individual privacy and monitoring or surveillance for national security purposes are magnified. The issues are complex and wide-ranging; some, such as export control of security methods, have international implications. The political and societal nature of many of the issues places them outside the scope of this book, but provides a context and an impetus for discussion of relevant techniques and applications.

We will defer the discussion of ways to safeguard an internal network from unauthorized access until a later chapter. This chapter addresses two major issues pertaining to messages in a network: security and rate of transmission. Encryption is introduced as a means of enhancing the secure transmission of messages; data compression is considered as a process for increasing the rate of transmission.

After a brief introduction to the topic of encryption, methods such as private and public key encryption, digital signatures, and trusted server systems are illustrated. For each method, a common technique is described and then further specified with an algorithm and example. The selection of techniques includes PGP, a method that is especially useful for Internet e-mail users.

A similar structure is used for data compression. Terminology and categories are identified. Then a group of methods are described, some with algorithms and examples, for the compression and decompression of textual and graphical data.

9.1 SECURE TRANSMISSION OF MESSAGES

Three major concerns in sending private or secure messages over a network are the following:

- They come from the person who is identified as the sender.
- They are not altered.
- They are read only by the person for whom they are intended.

Numerous encoding and decoding methods have been developed with the goal of ensuring that messages arrive without being intercepted by unauthorized persons. A fourth concern is that a user can send a signed document securely. This concern is also addressed by encoding messages.

Very simple methods of disguising messages are not suitable for transmitting secure messages over networks. An example of a simple encoding method is the substitution of one letter for another. These are found on newspaper puzzle pages and are entertaining mental puzzles. However, they are easily solved by computer programs that try each possible option and then display the one that produces real words. Human puzzle-solvers do not try all the possible letter combinations. Instead, they use known characteristics of the language to crack the code. An effective encryption method must hide the number of characters in each word, the existence of double letters, the places where vowels must appear, and so on. Secure transmission over networks requires more complex techniques because so many people can eavesdrop on a network and possibly alter messages, without other users being aware that their messages are being read.

Several promising encoding and decoding approaches have evolved since the early 1970s: private key systems, public key systems, digital signatures, and combinations of these techniques. The techniques can be incorporated into an overall methodology for secure networks. Our focus is on the techniques. Graft et al. [GPP90] discuss the specification, design, and implementation phases of the methodology.

9.1.1 Terminology

The processes of encoding and decoding messages are called **encryption** and **decryption**. They have been practiced throughout history. **Cryptography** is the science and art of encryption, and **cryptanalysis**, the science and art of decryption. More commonly, cryptography is used to encompass both encryption and decryption. A sender's message in **plaintext** is encoded into **ciphertext** for transmission to a receiver, who decodes it into plaintext as illustrated in Figure 9.1. An **encryption method/key** maps the plaintext message into the ciphertext version of the message; a **decryption method/key** maps the ciphertext into the plaintext message.

Cryptography is used to prevent a message from being read or altered by an unauthorized third party, an **intruder**. The intruder may be passive, simply listening, or **eavesdropping**; or the intruder may be active, changing the message, or using part of it, without the receiver's (or sender's) knowledge. That is, the intruder may be **masquerading** as the original sender or as the intended receiver. Eavesdroppers listen in and receive all encoded or

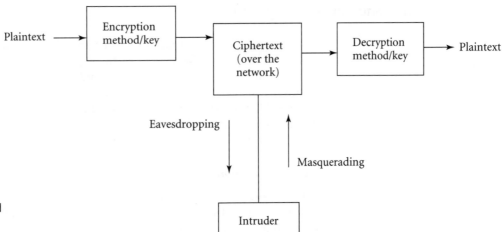

Figure 9.1. Encrypted message transmission in a network

The sender should assume the message can be intercepted or recorded and take whatever steps are appropriate, depending upon the amount of security required.

plaintext messages but do not interfere with the transmission. An active intruder interrupts the message flow from sender to receiver by becoming both a receiver to the original sender and a sender to the intended receiver. The original sender and receiver think they are communicating with each other, but the actual communication is between sender and intruder, and then intruder and receiver. Masqueraders (also referred to as **spoofers**) could change a military message and cause a misdirection of troops, or could use the sender's credit card number to charge expenses while on a trip. The sender should assume the message can be intercepted or recorded and take whatever steps are appropriate, depending upon the amount of security required. Friends can exchange e-mail messages over the Internet in plaintext, but a monetary transfer between banks needs the most secure encryption method possible.

9.1.2 Security Services

Four of the services characterizing a secure network system are *data integrity, authentication, confidentiality,* and *authorization.* **Data integrity** is the assurance that the data received is the same as the data generated. **Authentication** is the verification of the identity of a user who generated a message (data) and the integrity of the data. The user whose identity is verified is referred to as the **principal**, and the user who demands assurance of the principal's identity is the **verifier**. Authentication techniques differ in several ways: they may assure when the principal sent the message or that the principal was present when the message was sent; they may support one or multiple verifiers; or they may enable a verifier to prove to a third party that the message originated with the principal. **Confidentiality** is the protection of information from disclosure to those not intended to receive it. This service is often an option in authentication methods. **Authorization** is the process by which one determines whether a principal is allowed to perform an operation. The process typically follows authentication and may be based upon information available to the verifier or upon authenticated statements of others.

9.1.3 Private and Public Key Systems

Two types of cryptography, **symmetric** and **asymmetric**, pertain, respectively, to encryption and decryption keys being held privately by sender and receiver or being public. In symmetric cryptographic systems, encryption and decryption keys are inverse mappings and are privately shared by receiver and sender. Asymmetric cryptography uses public keys that are certified by a *trusted authority*, and the encryption key is computed from a public key, enabling the receiver to decode the ciphertext. The trusted authority is a mechanism for ensuring that the keys and associated user identities, all of which are public, are correct.

Private Key Encryption

Private key systems are characterized by both the encoding and decoding keys being known only by authorized senders and receivers. The most prominent of this type of method is the **data encryption standard (DES)**. Development of the DES began in 1973 by the National Bureau of Standards and IBM. The algorithm appeared in 1975. Its adoption as a federal standard did not occur until 1977 and subsequently was reaffirmed. The goals of the DES, which are common to any effective encryption technique, include the following:

- A high level of data protection against unauthorized disclosure or undetected modification of data
- Simple to understand
- Complex enough to cost more to break than the gain would warrant
- Protection based upon encryption key rather than on secrecy of the algorithm
- Economical to implement
- Efficient to operate
- Adaptable for different applications
- Available to all users and suppliers at reasonable cost

The following description illustrates the 19-step DES algorithm. The process is shown in Figure 9.2. Step 1 converts the input message into binary form, in blocks of 64 bits. Step 2 permutes each block of data and splits it into two 32-bit blocks, a left half (LH) and a right half (RH). Then step 3 transforms LH and RH into two new blocks, LH1 and RH1, where $LH1 = RH$ and $RH1 = LH < + > f(RH, K1)$. The operator $< + >$ is a bitwise EXCLUSIVE OR. The function f is a 32-bit block obtained through the following procedure: RH is expanded into 48 bits by appending half of its original 32 bits and scrambling the result. $K1$ is a 56-bit key. Its bits are rearranged, split in half, shifted, and then recombined into a 48-bit block. The two 48-bit blocks are combined and passed through eight distinct selection functions, each of which takes 6 bits as input and yields 4 bits as output. The resulting 32-bit block is $f(RH, K1)$.

The next 15 steps (steps 4–18) are repetitions of step 3, each accomplished with a new key and the two halves produced at the previous step. The last step (step 19) is the inverse of step 2. Each rearrangement of bits and combination of blocks follows a well-defined pattern.

The apparent complexity of the DES is deceiving; it is fast enough to be effective, especially for long messages. Hardware implementations exist that improve the speed of

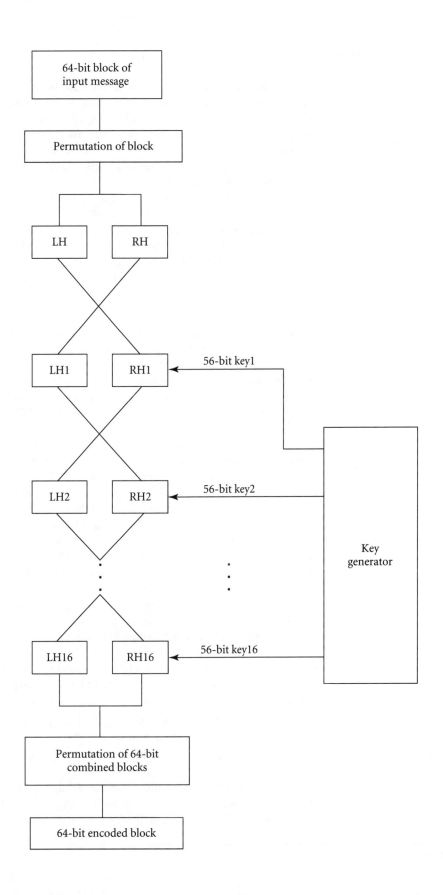

Figure 9.2. Data encryption standard process

software versions. DES, in its original implementation, cannot be considered a secure method [Way95]. One reason for this is that the same 64-bit plaintext block always produces the same 64-bit encrypted block. Several methods of **chaining** can be used to increase the security of the method, but they also increase its complexity. One method, **cipher block chaining**, performs an EXCLUSIVE OR on a plaintext block with the previous encrypted block before entering the DES process. DES is also used in combination with public key encryption described in the next section.

There are no known instances of breaking one of the modified DES techniques, although concern has been raised that larger blocks, for example, of 128 bits, should be used to prevent compromise. The availability of supercomputers and parallel computing increases the risk of current DES modifications being broken. Distribution of keys to remote sites remains a potential problem with DES. Both encryption and decryption use the same key, which requires its manual distribution to senders and receivers to maintain security.

Public Key Encryption

The traditional approach to encryption and decryption requires that both the encoding and decoding keys be secret, known only to authorized senders and receivers. This requirement can be compromised too readily when networks are the medium for transmitting encrypted messages, unless the keys are embedded in a complex algorithm such as the DES. Because of the large number of people transmitting over a network, either too many people know the same secret keys or each person must know too many different secret keys, one encoding–decoding pair for each other person.

In 1976, Diffie and Hellman [DH76] proposed a radically different approach to transmitting encrypted messages over networks. The concept, make the encrypting key public but keep the decrypting key secret, provides a viable alternative to the DES. It opened the door to expanding the role of cryptography in public and private sectors. The approach also enables users to apply a combination of the two methods, thus taking advantage of the best features of each method. A patent, issued for their method in 1980, expired in 1997.

A public key encryption system requires each user to have an encoding–decoding pair of keys. The encoding key, E, is made public; the decoding key, D, is known only to the user. When Alice wants to send an encrypted message to Bob, Alice uses Bob's public key E to encode the message. Bob then applies his secret decoding key D to decrypt the message. Any network user can send an encrypted message to Bob in this way. Other network users could see the message, but only Bob can decrypt it.

An effective public key encryption system must have the following components:

- The keys E and D must be inverse functions; that is, if M is the message, then $D(E(M)) = M$. This means that the message sent must be the message received.
- The amount of computation to apply E and D must be reasonable.
- E cannot be broken without knowing D; that is, an encrypted message cannot be decrypted by any other method than applying D.
- The amount of time and effort to discover (break) D must be computationally infeasible.

We give the outline of the most popular public key system (based upon an algorithm devised by Rivest, Shamir, and Adelman in 1978), referred to as the RSA method or the MIT algorithm [RSA78]. The method is widely used internationally and has became a de facto standard. It was part of the first commercial version of a public key encryption system that appeared in 1981. A patent, issued in 1983 for their method, expires in 2000.

1. Choose two large prime numbers, p and q, such that $p, q > 10^{100}$ (that is, p and q are primes consisting of 100 or more digits).
2. Compute $n = p \times q$ and $z = (p - 1) \times (q - 1)$.
3. Choose a number, e, relatively prime to z. n and e determine the receiver's public key.
4. Find d such that $(e \times d) \bmod z = 1$. n and d determine the receiver's private key.

Steps 1–4 are completed before encryption begins. The sender converts the message M into a bit string, then groups the bits into blocks P of size k, where k is the largest integer such that $2^k < n$. The bit string P, considered as a number in binary, must have a value $0 < P < n$. The sender then encrypts each block P by computing

$$C = P^e \bmod n$$

where e is the value in step 3. This process is the encoding key E. The receiver decrypts each P by computing

$$P = C^d \bmod n$$

where d is the value chosen in step 4. This process is the decoding key D. Encryption requires only e and n, both of which can be published. Decryption requires d and n, where d is maintained secretly by the receiver. The method is shown in Figure 9.3.

Consider the following example, where p and q are chosen as small primes to simplify computation. Let $p = 5, q = 13$. Then

$$n = 5 \times 13 = 65, \quad z = 4 \times 12 = 48$$

Choose $e = 11$. Then

$$11 \times d = 1 \times \bmod 48 \quad \text{and} \quad d = 35$$

To encrypt P, compute

$$C = 22^{11} \bmod 65 =$$

To decrypt the encoded message, compute

$$P = C^{35} \bmod 65 = 22$$

Figure 9.3 uses these keys to encrypt, send, receive, and decrypt a short message.
The following algorithm simplifies the computation of C:

```
C := 1,
begin for i = 1 to d do
  C := C x P mod n
```

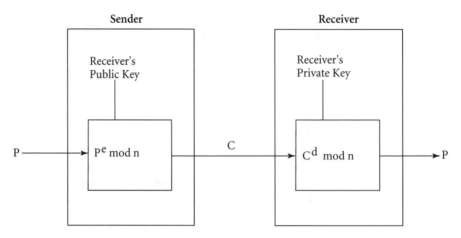

Figure 9.3. The RSA method on a single block P of plaintext

Why is this method considered secure? The answer lies in the difficulty of finding factors of large numbers. Factors of numbers with fewer than 100 digits can be discovered in approximately one day using supercomputers. Factoring a 200 digit number could take over a million years [RSA78].

Although public key encryption methods overcome the DES problem of secure key distribution, they have the disadvantage for a long message of being slower than DES because they are computationally intensive. A method that combines the best of DES and public key encryption, without the disadvantages of either system, involves using a public key system such as the RSA method to distribute electronically the master DES keys. The sender can then encrypt messages by means of the DES. The receiver decrypts the message containing the DES keys by applying the secret decoder key D. This combination method provides the desirable capability of extending key lengths to keep ahead of advances in factoring techniques.

The security of the DES and public key encryption combination stems from its ability to protect against intruders. Passive intruders, eavesdroppers who merely monitor the traffic over a network, with no secret decoding key D have no access to DES master keys encrypted with the public encoding key E. The active intruder must know all relevant keys in order to decrypt an encrypted message, change it, then encrypt the altered message. When the DES master keys are encrypted with an encoding key E, the active intruder must know the secret decoder key D to obtain the DES keys.

The scenario illustrated in Figure 9.4 makes apparent how active intrusion can easily be accomplished unless additional safeguards are imposed. Suppose the active intruder S intercepts a public key request from the sender A intended for a receiver B, and responds with S's public key. Because S has a secret decoder key D, any message sent by A using S's public key can be decrypted by S. Also suppose that S sends a public key request to the intended receiver B at the same time as obtaining the public key request from A. Then B sends its public key to S. Using B's public key, S can now encrypt any message and send it to B for decrypting with B's secret decoding key. In this scenario, S shares a DES key with the sender A and a second DES key with the receiver B. Neither A nor B would be aware that S exists.

There are safeguards to prevent active intrusion, particularly for connection-oriented networks. When the encrypted DES keys are transmitted initially, the sender A computes

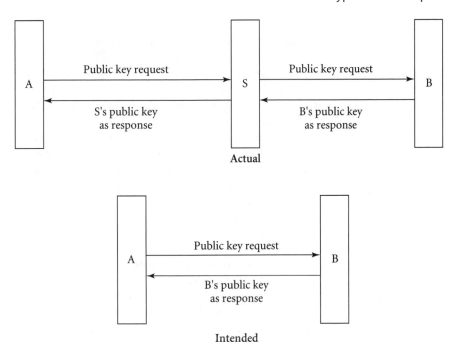

Figure 9.4. Interruption of a message by an active intruder

a checksum or message authentication code on the message, and appends the bit-block to the message. The intended receiver B also computes the checksum. A and B then compare checksums by telephone. Identical checksums indicate that the message, and therefore A's public key, was unaltered. If an active intruder S intervened and sent a different encrypted public key, the message's checksum computed by B would be different from A's. Similarly, a difference would be noted if S tried to alter the original message by substituting S's DES keys but encrypting them with A's public key. This security measure requires personnel on site during the initial transmission of the DES master keys.

Another security measure protects subsequent key transfers at those times when the sites are not attended. The sender A includes a verification key in the original message that transfers DES master keys. The checksum comparison as before guarantees that the message is unaltered. Any future message from B that transmits B's public key to A is then encrypted using the verification key. Further, when B uses A's public key to encrypt a message transmitting DES master keys to A, then B further encrypts the message, including the checksum, using the verification key. An active intruder must break a DES-encrypted message to break into the system at this point. The checksum as a verification key in message authentication is a form of digital signature in plaintext message transmission, as we will see in the next section.

9.1.4 Digital Signatures

In 1991, the U.S. National Institute of Standards and Technology (NIST) made public its support for a method called the *Digital Signature Standard (DSS)*, developed by the U.S.

National Security Agency. The algorithm is based upon ElGamal's 1985 public key encryption technique, which uses discrete logarithms [ElG85]. Prior to that time, NIST appeared to be considering the RSA method as the U.S. government standard. Early in 1991, a patent was issued for a digital signature method by Schnorr; it expires in 2008.

The Digital Signature Standard is not an encryption method; it is, however, an integral aspect of cryptography. Specifically, the DSS is proposed as an electronic means of verifying the integrity and source of unclassified information. It is intended to facilitate government-initiated, paperless transactions but is more widely applicable to any situation that requires verifying the integrity and source of a message. Whenever a receiver of an encrypted or a plaintext message needs to know that the sender is not an intruder, a digital signature sent along with a message authenticates the sender.

> Specifically, the DSS is proposed as an electronic means of verifying the integrity and source of unclassified information. It is intended to facilitate government-initiated, paperless transactions but is more widely applicable to any situation that requires verifying the integrity and source of a message.

Because of the potential impact of the DSS, we include its algorithm. First, however, we illustrate the idea of digital signature. The use of digital signatures is analogous to several familiar situations, such as entering a password to gain entrance to a computer account, cashing a check, or signing a contract. When you use a personal check for payment, you are usually asked for some form of identification. This protects you from a bogus check writer using your account. Moreover, when you sign a contract, someone verifies your signature. This protects the contractor in case you later say you never agreed to the terms of the contract. Digital signatures have a similar twofold goal: they protect the sender because no one else can send and impersonate, and they protect the receiver because the sender cannot later deny sending the message.

Authentication of a public–key–encrypted message imposes an additional requirement on the encoding and decoding keys E and D. We have already seen that $D(E(M)) = M$ for a message M. When authentication is involved, we must also have $E(D(M)) = M$. Assume the sender A has public encoding key EA, private decoding key DA, and knows receiver B's public encoding key EB. To send a signed message M to B, the sender A first encodes M with DA, then encodes DA(M) with EB. B then applies DB to the encrypted message EB(DA(M)) and stores the result DA(M). To obtain the plaintext message M, B applies A's public key EA to DA(M). Although anyone can read DA(M), only B can read the encrypted message sent by A. Note that once B decodes M, the sender A can no longer deny sending the message because B has both M and DA(M), and the latter could have been encoded only by A. Further, A's secret decoding key is still not known by B.

The Digital Signature Standard (DSS)

A high-level version of the DSS algorithm is given next. Notation in the algorithm is specified in the table. The algorithm consists of two parts: the sender preparing and sending the message followed by the receiver verifying the message and authenticating the sender.

p	prime number; 512 bits long with leading bit not 0
q	prime divisor of $p - 1$; 160 bits long
d	$(p - 1)/q$
h	any integer such that $0 < h < p$ and $h^d \bmod p > 1$
g	$h^d \bmod p$
x	integer such that $0 < x < q$; user's private key
y	$g^x \bmod p$; user's public key
M	the message

k random integer such that $0 < k < q$

H one-way hash function, not specified in the standard

p, q, and g are public. k is private and must be changed for each signature. H must be chosen so that it is computationally infeasible to create a message that results in a given hash value or to create a message whose hash value matches a given message. In other words, it must be computationally infeasible to fake a message.

The DSS Algorithm

The Sender

1. Determine p, q, and h.
2. Compute g. Publish p, q, and g.
3. Generate x.
4. Compute and publish y.
5. Apply H to M.
6. Generate k.
7. Compute $r = (g^k \bmod p) \bmod q$
8. Compute $s = k^{-1}(H(m) + xr)) \bmod q$, where $(k^{-1}k) \bmod q = 1$ and $0 < k^{-1} < q$.

r and s constitute the signature of the message; they are sent along with M.

The Receiver p, q, and g, the sender's public key and identity, must be available to the receiver in an authenticated manner.

1. Assume m', r', and s' are received.
2. Check to see that $0 < r' < q$ and $0 < s' < q$. If either condition is not satisfied, then the signature is rejected, and no further computation is necessary.
3. If the conditions are met, then compute

   - $w = (s')^{-1} \times \bmod q$, where $((s')^{-1}s) \bmod q = 1$ and $0 < (s')^{-1} < q$
   - $u1 = ((H(m'))w) \bmod q$
   - $u2 = ((r')w) \bmod q$
   - $v = ((q^{u1} y^{u2}) \bmod p) \bmod q$

4. If $v = r'$, then the signature is verified.

It can be shown that $v = r'$ when $m' = m$, $r' = r$, and $s' = s$; that is, the message and signature received are the same as the message and signature sent. If $v \neq r'$, then the message may have been modified, incorrectly signed by the sender, or signed by an imposter.

9.1.5   Trusted Server Systems

When a sender changes digital signatures, say from s1 to s2, the receiver can no longer prove that a specific message sent with s1 originated from the sender. Legal problems can result when the message is a contract between two persons or an agreement between two organizations. Trust between the two parties breaks down. The situation can be avoided by introducing an automated service as a third party (a mediator or central authority) into the network. This service, referred to as a **trusted server**, acts as an automated security administrator. It can have any of the following functions:

- Maintain public and private keys
- Maintain time and date of digital signatures
- Manage data access across multiple networks
- Perform protocol conversions
- Make security decisions based upon preprogrammed policies

The trusted server is an asset in any network, but it is critical to data access management in networks that consist of subnetworks, such as those operating in large organizations. Each organizational component having a subnetwork has its own security level for information access. A user in one component asks for a file from another component. The request is first processed by the trusted server to authenticate the user's identity and to determine that the user has the appropriate security level to gain access to the file. If the determination is positive, the file is provided to the user, possibly after the server reads the file to verify that it conforms to the user's request. If the determination is negative, access is denied to the user, and the system administrator is notified.

Kerberos

The **Kerberos** system is a trusted third-party authentication service, most widely used in application protocols such as telnet and FTP, and less frequently in lower-layer protocols. Modeled after a key distribution system of Needham and Schroeder [NS78], Kerberos was designed by Miller and Neuman [MNSS87] for open network computing environments. It is based upon a private key system and has the versatility to provide an applications programmer a choice of three levels of authentication, encryption methods (initially, Kerberos was based upon DES), and a database management system. Authentication can be established at the beginning of a network connection with the assumption that the sender of additional messages from the same address is the authenticated sender. Increasing levels of security provide for **safe messages**, authentication of each message with no concern for disclosure; and for **private messages**, authentication of each message with encryption included. Kerberos uses DES for encryption but can support DES extensions. Authorization and accounting are not provided by Kerberos, but secure versions can be added.

The software components of the Kerberos system include an applications library (including routines for handling authentication requests and creating both safe and private messages), encryption and database libraries as replaceable modules, database administration programs, administration and authentication servers for interacting with the database, and user programs (including logging in, changing Kerberos passwords, and displaying or destroying identification *tickets*). The database contains each principal's name, private key, expiration date, and other information for administrative purposes. The administration server has read/write access to the database; the authentication server has read-only access. The database, along with the authentication server, can be copied to, and exist on, other

It is based upon a private key system and has the versatility to provide an applications programmer a choice of three levels of authentication, encryption methods (initially, Kerberos was based upon DES), and a database management system.

(slave) machines as read-only copies. Master machine updates are then provided to all slave machines.

In Kerberos, network services requiring authentication, and users requiring the services, register by negotiating private keys that are then entered into the database. The private key of a user is an encrypted password. Most of the remaining Kerberos operations are transparent to the client. Kerberos generates **session keys**, temporary private keys for exclusive use of the user, the Kerberos system, and the applications server that enable them to encrypt messages. The appropriate level of authentication is then determined. The user agent at the workstation gets a request from a user, receives credentials from Kerberos for accessing services, requests authentication for a service, and presents the credentials to the applications server (for example, a file server or e-mail server that will perform the service), as illustrated in Figure 9.5.

Credentials consist of **tickets** and **authenticators**. A ticket contains the names of the server and client; the client's Internet (IP) address; the beginning and ending times for which the ticket can be used (this pair is referred to as a **nonce**, an identifier used only once); and a randomly generated session key. All are encrypted with the private key of the server to prevent the client from altering the ticket. Until the ticket expires, the client may use the ticket repeatedly for access to the server. The time span limits the opportunity for intruders to intercept the communications. An authenticator is single use and only for the specified service. Authenticators contain the client's name, workstation's IP address, and current time at the workstation. This information, encrypted with the session key on the ticket, is used to prove that the client who presents the ticket is identical to the one issued the ticket. Note that the client can construct the authenticator with information on the ticket and at the client's workstation.

An algorithm for Kerberos can be expressed in the five steps indicated in Figure 9.5. Each step, however, involves additional details:

1. Request initial ticket.

   User logs in at workstation (client), responding to prompt from user agent (UA) within the workstation.

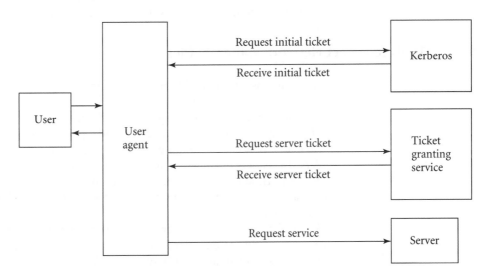

Figure 9.5. Kerberos authentication process

UA sends request containing client name and the name of a special service, the ticket granting service (TGS), to authentication server (AS).

AS validates that user is registered; randomly generates a session key; creates a ticket containing client's name, name of TGS, a nonce (current time and lifetime of ticket), client's IP address.

Session key encrypted with user's private key (based upon user's password).

Ticket information encrypted using private key of TGS (known only to AS and TGS).

2. Receive initial ticket.

AS sends both encrypted parts to UA.

UA requests user password; creates authenticator (including user name and timestamp encrypted with session key, the encrypted ticket, name of server being requested, and a second nonce) to verify that user has been authenticated.

3. Request server ticket.

UA sends authenticator to TGS.

TGS decrypts authenticator with session key; generates new session key for use by UA in communications with server; creates a response in two parts: new session key and second nonce encrypted with the original session key, and a new ticket encrypted with the server's private key; sends response to UA.

4. Receive server ticket.

UA decrypts the first part of response with original session key to obtain the second nonce (for confirmation that response relates to request to TGS) and the second session key (for creating an authenticator to verify user has permission to access the server); creates message (containing authenticator, ticket from TGS, and a third nonce).

5. Request server.

UA sends message to server.

Server decrypts ticket with its private key to obtain user name and second session key; decrypts authenticator with second session key to confirm user has been authenticated as a registered user and has permission to access the server; sends response to UA containing third nonce encrypted with second session key.

9.1.6 Tools to Detect Network Vulnerabilities

Methods such as DES and RSA are prevalent and viable, but additional ones have entered the scene to address security needs made more apparent by the Internet. We explore a sampling of the methods. Details for almost all of them are readily available on the Internet. We first look at types of mechanisms to detect and reduce vulnerabilities of networks.

No matter how effective and well administered, a network is vulnerable to attack by intruders. The variety of vulnerabilities includes password file access, sendmail, remote shell access, and writeable FTP home directory, among many others. A number of tools are available to assist the network administrator in detecting them and in implementing security fixes when necessary.

An excellent source for current information on security problems and tools to help solve them is CERT (Computer Emergency Response Team) advisories. CERT, formed by DARPA in 1988, maintains its Coordination Center in the Software Engineering Institute on the campus of Carnegie Mellon University. Advisories and bulletins are posted on the USENET newsgroup comp.security.announce and are available via anonymous FTP.

There are a number of tools for detecting and handling network vulnerabilities. SATAN (Security Administrator Tool for Analyzing Networks) is both a testing and reporting tool. Its capabilities include collection of information (topology, what equipment) about specified hosts and networks, production of summary reports, and investigation of potential security problems. For each problem it identifies, SATAN provides a brief description and suggested fix. SATAN's ease of use and extensibility make it an attractive tool for potential intruders to find out vulnerabilities of specific networks. Documentation of SATAN and the other tools is available on the Internet via anonymous FTP.

One type of intruder attack on a network involves creating and sending packets with spoofed IP addresses to gain root access on systems using IP address-based authentication. Once root access is gained, the intruder can dynamically modify system kernels to hijack any user's terminal and login connection. One preventive measure is a router (see Section 13.5) that filters packets entering a system's external interface (see Section 12.3 for a discussion of firewalls).

9.1.7 Secure Sockets Layer

Netscape provides Secure Socket Layer (SSL), an open, non-proprietary protocol that has become accepted as a de facto standard among software vendors.

Electronic commerce is an ever-expanding industry. It is viable only when the Internet banking system is secure enough that a person wanting to purchase a product via the Internet can be assured that his or her credit card information will not be intercepted by unauthorized individuals. To meet this need, Netscape provides Secure Socket Layer (SSL), an open, nonproprietary protocol that has become accepted as a de facto standard among software vendors. Microsoft's Internet Explorer supports both version 3.0 and the earlier 2.0. Version 3.0, published in March 1996, was submitted to the Internet Engineering Task Force (IETF) for validation as the official Internet standard for Transport Layer Security (TLS) and to the W3 Consortium (W3C) working group for review as a standard for World Wide Web browsers and servers.

SSL is layered between application protocols, such as FTP, HTTP, or telnet, and TCP/IP. You can enable SSL when building your own Web site, by configuring a security-enabled HTTP process and then specifying which pages you want to require SSL access. If that method fails, you can apply to download Netscape's reference implementation, SSLRef, an advanced application software toolkit. SSLRef requires application development experience. It is also useful for developing non-Web-based applications.

SSL employs a variety of techniques to ensure secure transmission. Authentication is achieved through RSA public key cryptography with digital signature. It allows Diffie–Hellman key exchanges and chains of certificates, and incorporates a symmetric cryptography algorithm (for example, DES). Handshakes can be initiated by a client or requested by a server during an open session, enabling parties to change algorithms and keys at any time.

The Internet banking system, for example, employs layers of security measures to prevent unauthorized users from accessing sensitive data. A customer logs on with a private account number and password. The browser then automatically secures the session using SSL. The customer's request reaches the bank's internal network system, where other

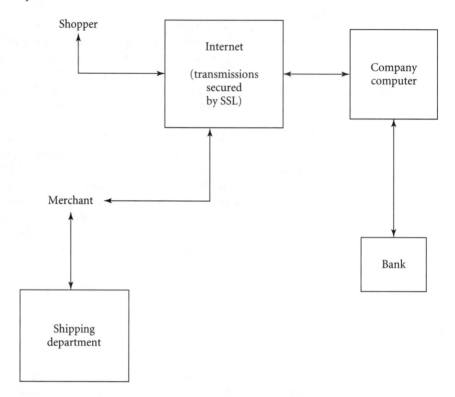

Figure 9.6. Internet shopping application of SSL

security devices called firewalls and routers make sure that only the customer, not an unauthorized user, is being served.

Shopping via the Internet provides another application of SSL. In the scenario illustrated in Figure 9.6, all Internet transmissions are secured by SSL. A shopper decides to purchase an item from a merchant. The order form and credit card information are transmitted to an intermediary company's server. A receipt appears on the shopper's screen, the order information is stored locally, and the merchant is notified by fax or e-mail. The merchant reviews the order, makes changes as appropriate, and sends payment information to the company's computer. The computer sends payment to the bank and a detailed status of the payment and the contents of the order to the customer by e-mail. After receiving word that the funds are approved, the merchant processes the order by notifying the shipping department and inserting the package tracking number on the order entry. The tracking number enables the customer to determine where the package is at any time prior to delivery.

9.1.8 Electronic Mail Security

Consistent with the increasing popularity of the Internet is the rise in cryptography as a means of improving authenticity, confidentiality, and integrity of messages. Versions or combinations of the DES and RSA methods are available to address security issues in message transmission on the Internet and connected networks. The status and acceptance of any method changes. We identify several methods—Privacy Enhanced Mail (PEM), Pretty Good Privacy (PGP), and Skipjack/Clipper—and briefly describe their impact.

Privacy Enhanced Mail

Privacy Enhanced Mail (PEM) is designed primarily for Internet e-mail users. Begun in 1985 by the Privacy and Security Research Group (PSRG) of the Internet Architecture Board (IAB) and developed with ARPA funding, PEM has evolved into a virtual Internet standard for secure mail. PEM also has become a commercial product. Steps in the PEM process involve transforming the message into a network standard representation, calculating a message integrity code (MIC), encrypting the message (an option), and transforming the resulting message into a suitable character set for transmission. PEM allows a choice of algorithms, including DES for encryption and RSA for sender authentication and key management [Lin93b].

Pretty Good Privacy

P. R. Zimmerman developed Pretty Good Privacy (PGP) for secure e-mail and file encryption on the Internet. The method appeared in 1991 as a free product available via anonymous FTP on the Internet. This caused immediate controversy, including a court case, because of the U.S. government's approach to the control of the export of cryptography. The method has proved to be effective and is used by a number of countries as a de facto standard.

From a user's point of view, PGP is a public key system; internally, it is a hybrid of IDEA, a version of the data encryption standard developed by X. Lai and J. Massey in Switzerland in the early 1990s. IDEA is considered to be faster and stronger than DES because it uses a 128-bit key and RSA. PGP is a combination of methods previously discussed, it is periodically updated, and software and ample descriptions of how to use PGP are readily available on the Internet. We will not detail the method but will summarize how it works and indicate some of its capabilities by illustrating the process of sending a message by e-mail.

Briefly, the basic encryption/decryption steps in PGP include:

- Sender: Use IDEA to encrypt a message with a randomly generated key.
- Sender: Use the recipient's public key to encrypt the randomly generated key.
- Receiver: Use the recipient's private RSA key to decrypt the IDEA key.
- Receiver: Use the IDEA key to decrypt the message.

PGP can also sign plaintext messages by applying a hash function MD5 (or NSA's algorithm SHA1) to the message, then encrypting the hash output of 128 bits with the sender's secret RSA key. Any recipient calculates the same hash function of the message, then uses the sender's public key to decrypt the signature. Agreement of the decryption output with the recipient's calculated hash output guarantees that the sender actually sent the message and that the message has not been altered during transmission.

As developed by Zimmerman, PGP uses a UNIX-style command line; it is not menu driven. However, more recent software provides menu interfaces. Each command begins with the letters *pgp* followed by a space, then one or more arguments preceded by a single hyphen. Arguments with a -k trigger key commands (-kg generates a key, -ka adds a key,

-kr removes a key, -kv views a key, and -kx extracts a key). Keys are maintained on public and secret key rings (files). The only other arguments trigger encryption commands (-a for armor specifies e-mail format, -c specifies conventional encryption, -e indicates public key encryption, -s indicates signature, and -t indicates text contains binary data). For example, a command beginning with `pgp -sac` sends a message with a signature, using ASCII `armor\radix-64` (to convert text that can't be transmitted over the net into an ASCII form that can be sent by e-mail), and conventional cryptography (one key is used to encrypt and decrypt the plaintext message).

The internal operation of PGP is transparent to a user. A file is encrypted and sent through a sequence of commands that reference downloaded PGP software. A sample process follows in which, for example, Bob sends to Alice a message copied into a file named netbook.doc.

1. Generate a unique public/secret key pair.

   - Bob enters pgp -kg. A PGP prompt then asks for the following:
   - a key size, usually 1024 bits or more
   - a user ID, which for e-mail transmission, must have the form firstname lastname <Internet mail address>, where the <> are included
   - a pass phrase

   The pass phrase permits entry into Bob's secret key file, so it should be chosen with care. It should be longer than the usual password, difficult for someone else to guess, and easy to remember. Then a prompt asks Bob to enter some text. PGP uses the timing of keystrokes and the characters entered to generate random numbers that will derive the public/secret keys. The public key is stored in a file with the default name pubring.pgp, and the secret key is in secring.pgp. The filenames can be changed; the default extension is .pgp.

2. Sign the public key.

   - Bob enters pgp -ks bobskey -u bobskey. This signs Bob's public key bobskey with Bob's secret key. This step is optional, but should be taken because it makes changing Bob's key by someone else virtually impossible.

3. Extract the public key from the key ring. Bob enters pgp -kxa bobskey. A prompt asks to which file. He enters a filename, say bob, which causes the file bob.asc to be created. He mails this file to Alice. She has followed the same process to generate alice.asc, which she sends to Bob.

4. Add a key to a public key ring. Bob enters pgp alice.asc. After PGP interprets the file as a public key, it prompts Bob by asking if he wants to add the key to his public key ring. Alice follows the same procedure. Messages can now be sent, but a key verification should be done first.

5. Verify public keys. An optional key verification can be performed before sending by Bob entering pgp -kvc alice to see the PGP fingerprint (a list of letters and numbers) of Alice's public key. Alice also enters pgp -kvc alice and gets a PGP fingerprint; Bob

contacts Alice and reads the fingerprint he obtained. If it matches the list Alice has, they both know Bob has Alice's correct public key. They repeat the process for Bob's public key.

6. Encrypt the plaintext message. Bob enters pgp -e netbook.doc alice. This produces a file netbook.pgp encrypted with Alice's public key, which only Alice can decrypt. The command is the simplest way to send a file but not the surest. Some characters could be corrupted during e-mail transmission, preventing Alice from reading the file. To prevent this, encase the PGP file in ASCII by using the -a command. A further enhancement adds the -t command, which enables the file to be read by different systems and adapts to differences such as end-of-line commands. Thus, Bob enters pgp -eat notebook.doc alice, producing the file netbook.asc.

7. Sign the ciphertext. Instead of the command in step 6, Bob could enter pgp -seat netbook.doc alice -u bob. This option ensures that the message could only come from Bob because it is signed with his secret key.

8. Mail the ciphertext. This part of the process varies according to the e-mail package Bob uses. Cut-and-paste and enclosing the file in a message are two possibilities.

9. Decrypt the ciphertext. Alice sees the .ASC extension and knows the file was encoded with PGP. She copies the file to her PGP directory (or PGP disk) and enters pgp netbook.asc. A prompt asks for Alice's pass phrase, then PGP produces a plaintext file called netbook. Alice reads the file with her word processor or text editor.

There are other options possible with PGP, but the preceding example provides a flavor of what is involved in using the method. Note that PGP does all the work; the user merely enters commands.

Skipjack/Clipper

Early in 1994, the National Institute for Standards and Technology (NIST) approved the Escrowed Encryption Standard (EES) [NIS94]. The standard consists of a classified algorithm, Skipjack; a chip for encyrption, Clipper; and secret encryption keys held in escrow by the U.S. government. EES is voluntary and is intended to cover encryption of voice, fax, and computer transmissions over circuit-switched telephone systems.

The encryption/decryption algorithm Skipjack relies on public key management techniques. Because it employs an 80-bit key, the method is considered millions of times stronger (more secure) than the 56-bit key DES. The Clipper chip contains an additional key. At the time equipment is manufactured, the chip is installed and the key is split into two parts, each half being placed in the custody of a trusted institution (the *escrow agent*). The escrowed keys can be made available to authorized agencies with prior approval, for example, to law enforcement agencies for monitoring messages of groups suspected of being terrorist organizations—an updated version of wiretapping.

Issues leading to the 1994 announcement of EES began surfacing in the 1980s. It became apparent that implementation of essentially unbreakable cryptographic methods would negate the possibility of monitoring electronic messages within groups considered a threat to national security. Laws regulating wiretapping would no longer be adequate, so the development of a more sophisticated method was considered necessary. Internet growth and the U.S. government's National Information Initiative (NII), the "Information Highway,"

The feasibility, therefore, of the Skipjack/Clipper is not a technological issue. However, EES raises substantial political and societal issues, especially regarding an individual's right to privacy versus the government's duty to protect its citizens.

were factors in the eventual announcement in 1993 by the government of the Escrowed Encryption Initiative followed by NIST's declaration of the EES.

It is technologically possible to embed a chip into a device so that messages through that device can be monitored. The feasibility, therefore, of the Skipjack/Clipper is not a technological issue. However, EES raises substantial political and societal issues, especially regarding an individual's right to privacy versus the government's duty to protect its citizens. Much debate has occurred and will continue to occur. See [Rot93], [Lev94], [Lan94], and [Hof94] for discussions of the issues at about the time the EES was announced. In particular, [Hof94] includes trends in encryption technology and policy in the environment of the debate over national security and privacy, and identifies four possible scenarios for the control and decontrol of cryptography.

9.2 DATA COMPRESSION

Numerous applications benefit from increasing the rate at which data is transmitted. Multimedia, television, text and graphics over the Internet, fax, and financial transfers between banks are but a few of the situations that rely upon fast transmission of data. The transmission rate depends upon the amount of data and upon the physical size of the representation of the data. If a given amount of data is represented with fewer bits, then the data can be transmitted in less time. For example, the time required to send the 6 bytes of character data CCCCCC can be reduced to one-third when the representation 6C (2 bytes) is sent. **Data compression** is the process of converting data from one format to a smaller-sized format. Data transmitted in compressed form must be decompressed and restored to its original form, or nearly so, to be read at the receiving end. Decompressing transmitted data requires knowing the compression algorithm.

Methods for compressing data have taken on new importance with Internet and multimedia demands. Graphical images and motion, so vital to both applications and to interactive multimedia in particular, require that vastly more bits be transmitted than text representations require. Moving the data rapidly so that the user does not have long wait times is a necessity. Variations on compression methods continue to appear to satisfy this need. Before examining specific methods, we introduce some terms, image types, and categories to facilitate understanding. The keywords appear in Figure 9.7.

Terms	Uncompressed Data	Compressed Data	Compression Ratio
Image Types	Bitmap	Vector	Metafile
Categories	Physical Symmetric Lossy Nonadaptive	Logical Asymmetric Lossless Semiadaptive	Adaptive

Figure 9.7. Relevant terms and categories for compression methods

9.2.1 Terminology

Data before compression is referred to as **unencoded data**, **uncompressed data**, or **raw data**. After compression, it is **encoded data** or **compressed data**. **Compression ratio** is the ratio of uncompressed to compressed data. For example, a compression ratio of 7:1 is achieved when 1 is sent as the representation of 0000001; the uncompressed data is seven times larger than the same data in a compressed format.

Compression of graphical data is a more serious concern than text data because of the larger number of bits required for representing graphical images. Types of graphics data are **bitmap**, **vector**, and **metafile**. Only the image is compressed in bitmap files, not the header, footer, and other portions of the file. The image composes most of the file. Vector files contain a mathematical representation of an image; they are rarely compressed because the representation is already compact and relatively slow to process. Data compression methods for metafiles can be similar to bitmap techniques.

9.2.2 Categories

The data compression methods in this section are physical rather than logical. This categorization refers to how the data is compressed. **Physical compression** transforms a given bit sequence into a more compact one. This compression is achieved by removing redundancy that exists in the uncompressed data. **Logical compression** substitutes an abbreviated form for the original data, for example UK for United Kingdom, or a caricature for a full drawing of a face.

Compression methods can be symmetric or asymmetric. This categorization refers to the comparison of work required to compress and decompress data. A **symmetric method** takes approximately the same amount of effort to compress raw data as it does to restore the original representation. If decompression requires appreciably more (less) time than compression, then the method is **asymmetric**. When data compression is used in backing up a number of files, an asymmetric method is acceptable, one that compresses the data in files much faster than when the backup file is decompressed for use. The reverse is desirable when putting a file on a network server for access by many users.

Sometimes data is lost when decompression is performed; more often the original representation is preserved exactly. The term **lossless** is applied to compression methods in which no data is lost during decompression. The term **lossy** refers to the category of methods in which data is lost. It may be acceptable to lose a slight amount of data when the compression/decompression method is substantially faster than a method that loses no data, especially when a considerable amount of data is available for transmission. For example, a user accessing a home page through the World Wide Web is unlikely to notice if selected colors of a compressed digitized image of a photograph are missing when the image is decompressed and shown on the user's screen.

Yet another way to categorize compression methods is by how static the dictionary is. For example, as a line of text is scanned, comparisons with phrases in a dictionary are made to determine the compressed representation to be transmitted. If the dictionary is static, already available when the algorithm is applied, then the compression method is called **nonadaptive**. If the dictionary is constructed dynamically, at the time of scanning, then the method is **adaptive**. Methods that combine the two approaches are called **semiadaptive**.

9.2.3 Methods

Several standard methods are discussed in this section and their variations, particularly to accommodate graphical image transmission, are indicated. Selected methods—run-length encoding (RLE), Huffman coding, dynamic Huffman encoding, CCITT Groups 3 and 4, and the Lempel–Ziv–Welch (LZW) technique—are addressed in some detail by means of description, example, algorithm, and variations of each method. Applications, effectiveness, and efficiency are considered. The combination of methods referred to as JPEG is also included, but in less detail. A few methods, such as relative encoding and discrete cosine transform (DCT), are treated in a more cursory fashion. Pixel packing, although not a compression method, is also cited.

Run-Length Encoding (RLE)

The run-length encoding (RLE) scheme can be used on any kind of data, but works best when the data contains repeating strings, or **runs**, such as the same character or consecutive pixels of the same color. In its simplest form, RLE involves scanning a line of text and converting strings of consecutive, like characters into 2-byte **packets**, the first byte containing the integer number of repetitions, or **run count**, and the second byte containing the character, or **run value**. For example, the 31-byte string

```
RRRRRSSSSSSSSSSSTTTTTTUUVVVWXXXX
```

would be represented as the 14-byte string

```
5R10S6T2U3V1W4X
```

The compression ratio is 2:1. Each time the character changes, a new packet is generated. Although this method implements easily and executes rapidly, it is not always efficient. Note that in the example, the 1-byte character W converts to the 2-byte representation 1W, a negative compression. It follows that a string containing no repeating characters (maximum run-length = 1) would be doubled in size by the RLE method. Also note that the representation in the example simplified the algorithm for ease of understanding. Actually, 1 byte can represent integers from 0 to 255 (11111111), and the run count, therefore, is one less than the number of repetitions up to a maximum of 255. That makes best use of the values available: 0 represents one occurrence, 255 represents 256 occurrences, and so on. In general, RLE is unlikely to achieve compression ratios as high as those achieved by a number of other techniques, but its ease and quickness are worth considering in lieu of no compression or a more complex method.

The following algorithm for the RLE method encodes a bitmap by scanning horizontally across one line at a time from left to right and beginning in the left-hand corner, as in Figure 9.8(a).

```
Repeat until no more data
  Begin
    Read RunValue
    Repeat until no more data in the line
      Begin
        Set RunCount = 0
```

```
      Read NewValue
        Repeat until (NewValue /= RunValue) or (RunCount > 255)
          Begin
            Increment RunCount
            Read NewValue
          End
        Write RunCount
        Write RunValue
        Set RunValue = NewValue
      End
    Write RunCount
    Write RunValue
    Mark end of line
  End
```

Processing of the one-dimensional stream is sequential and an end-of-line marker, a unique packet, guarantees that the scan does not merge consecutive lines. Decompression involves reading the contents of both bytes in each packet and writing the run value one more than the number of times indicated by the run count.

Two variations are shown in Figures 9.8(b) and (c): a vertical scan and a scan that encodes a bitmap into two-dimensional tiles. RLE and these two variations are lossless. A zigzag scan and a lossy version are also variants but are seldom implemented. There is also an application-dependent variant that uses vertical replication packets to encode data in cases where repetitions of a scan line occur. RLE can also be adapted to run at the bit, byte, or pixel level. The algorithm flow is the same, but in the bit-level version, only bits are read; byte and word boundaries are ignored. Another variant can improve the compression ratio when data contains relatively few repetitions. In this version, strings with one to three characters are simply copied into the compressed stream. Longer strings of the same character (bit or pixel) require 3 bytes. The first byte contains a flag that is unique, if possible, from any other likely character. The second and third bytes contain the run count and value, respectively, as in the RLE method described earlier. At decompression, when a flag is en-

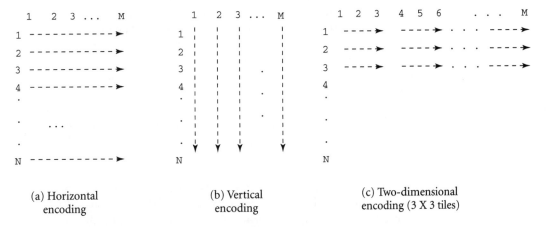

(a) Horizontal encoding

(b) Vertical encoding

(c) Two-dimensional encoding (3 X 3 tiles)

Figure 9.8. Three modes of scanning data

countered, the run value is written one more than the number of times indicated by the run count. When no flag is present, the characters themselves are written.

Huffman Encoding

In 1952, David Huffman published what has become a very well known and widely used compression method [Huf52]. Versions of Huffman encoding have been used in facsimile transmission and document imaging. As we will see, the baseline JPEG standard incorporates Huffman encoding as a final step in an image compression process.

This compression method replaces standard bit representations of symbols with shorter bit strings. It is a statistical method based on the frequency of occurrence of each symbol in a file. Predetermined probabilities of symbol occurrences are used to construct a binary tree from the bottom up. This guarantees that the symbols that occur the least will have the longest bit strings. In the tree, symbols are terminal nodes, branches are marked 0 or 1, and the bit representation of the path from the root to a symbol is that symbol's compressed bit-string representation.

As an example, consider the character string

ASIANANDAFRICAN

The number of occurrences of each character is 5 As, 3 Ns, 2 Is, 1 F, 1 R, 1 C, 1 D, and 1 S. For purposes of this example, we use the number of occurrences rather than the probability (number of occurrences divided by total number of characters) to construct the tree. We first list all characters in nondecreasing order; the order of characters with the same number of occurrences does not matter. Make two of the characters with the lowest number of occurrences the terminal nodes of a binary tree. Set the root value to the sum of the number of occurrences of the two nodes. Repeat this step until no more characters remain. The value at the root of the tree that is constructed by this process is the total number of characters in the string (or is 1 if probabilities are used). Label all left (right) branches 0 and all right (left) branches 1.

Figures 9.9 and 9.10 illustrate the method and include the compressed representation of the example string. Notice that at step 2 any two of the letters with number of occurrences = 1 could have been combined. The choice will usually be determined by the order in which the letters were written down in step 1. In step 3, another pair of letters that occur once in the original string are joined; S, D, C, and R have now entered the tree. (Actually, there appear to be two small trees at this point, but that will sort itself out.) In step 3, the one remaining node with value 1 (F) is joined to the node resulting from placing S and D into the tree. It would have been equally correct to join F with the node that joins C and R or the node that represents I. Each of those nodes has a value of 2 and produces a node with a value of 3 when joined with F. Similarly, at each step, two nodes are connected to form the smallest possible value at the newly created node. When all the nodes have been joined, the result is a tree structure whose root node value is the number of characters in the original string.

There are 120 bits (15 characters × 8 bits/character) in the uncompressed string and 41 bits in the compressed format, a compression ratio of approximately 3:1.

The average bits per character (symbol, in general) can be obtained by summing the products of the number of occurrences of each character and the length of the character's

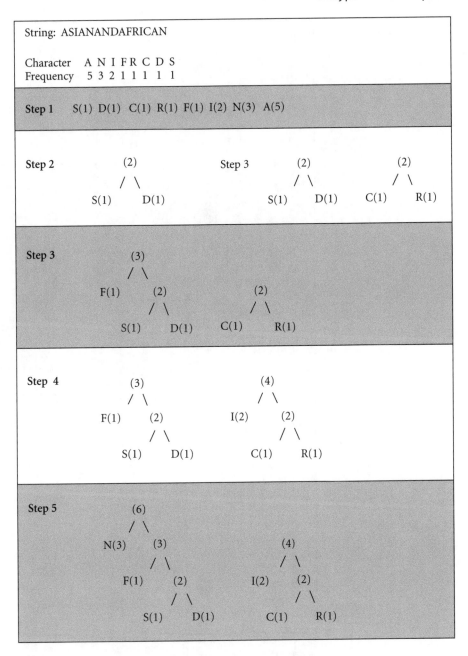

Figure 9.9. An illustration of Huffman encoding: part 1 of 2

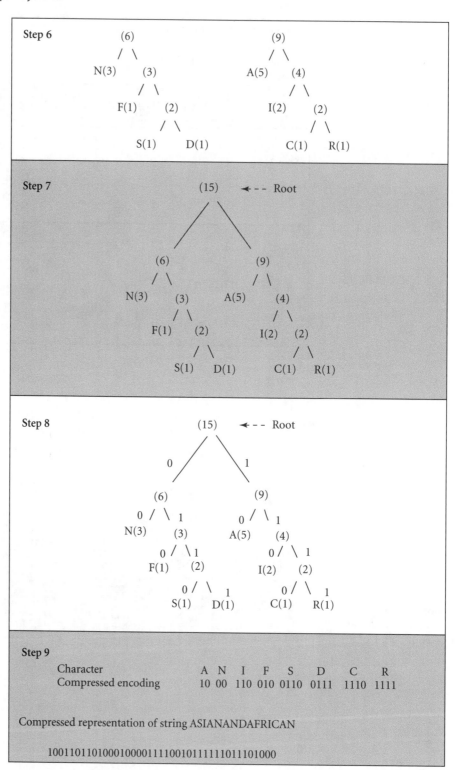

Figure 9.10. An illustration of Huffman encoding: part 2 of 2

bit string, then dividing the result by the total number of characters in the original string. For the example, the average bits per character is

$$(5 \times 2 + 3 \times 2 + 2 \times 3 + 1 \times 3 + 1 \times 4 + 1 \times 4 + 1 \times 4 + 1 \times 4)/15 = 41/15 = 2.73$$

This value can also be interpreted as the average amount of information in each character. Information theory tells us that the information content, or **entropy per symbol**, of a symbol is

$$-\sum_{i=1}^{n} p_i \log_2 p_i$$

where n is the number of symbols, and p_i is the probability of occurrence of the ith symbol. Applying this formula to the example string, we obtain the value 2.68. This result indicates that Huffman encoding is efficient for the example string; the result approximates the theoretical limit, which is also true for most strings. In general, Huffman encoding is a practical technique for compression of character data, especially in light of the relative ease of implementation of its algorithm.

An algorithm for Huffman encoding follows the description of the method. In the algorithm, probabilities and symbols are used instead of frequencies and characters. We assume that probabilities have been assigned to symbols based upon the kind of material being transmitted and that the probabilities sum to 1. Each node of the binary tree has an associated probability; each terminal node also has a symbol:

```
List all symbols and associated probabilities.
Repeat until the probability at a node is 1
   Begin
      Find the two smallest unmarked probabilities
      Mark them
      Create a parent node with the two probabilities as children
      Assign a probability to the parent equal to the sum of the
          probabilities of the children
   End
Beginning at the root, label all left branches 0 and all right
                   branches 1 (or vice versa)
Repeat until no more symbols
   Begin
      Read next symbol
      Represent the symbol by the bit string obtained by
          tracing the path from the root to the symbol
   End
```

The encoding scheme must be known to apply the decompression process, which is the reverse of the compression algorithm. This indicates that the method is symmetric. It is also lossless and adaptive. The method is effective and efficient for files in which the symbol set is known and the probability distribution is wide. (Try implementing the algorithm with an input stream of ten characters, all with the same probability.)

Dynamic Huffman Encoding

A variation of the Huffman encoding method, **dynamic Huffman encoding**, generates the binary tree dynamically as symbols are read, both at the transmitting and receiving ends. At the beginning of transmission, both sender and receiver have a tree consisting of a root and a left branch (labeled with a 0) to an empty leaf node, indicating an occurrence frequency of zero. The tree being constructed dynamically at both ends of the transmission will always have a subtree with this characteristic, a root with a left branch to an empty leaf node. The sender transmits the first character in uncompressed form. It becomes the leaf node of the right branch of the root, and the right branch is labeled 1. For each character after the first, the sender determines whether it is already on the tree. If so, the sender transmits the current path to the character (the compressed encoding form of the character), increments the weight of each branch node in the path, and increments the number of occurrences of the character. If not, then the sender transmits the path to the empty node followed by the character in uncompressed form and updates the tree by converting the empty node to a branch node with an empty left leaf (with branch labeled 0) and the character as a right leaf (with branch labeled 1); incrementing the weight of each branch node in the path; and restructuring the tree, if necessary, in weight order.

Restructuring according to weight order involves the following steps: (a) list the weights of all nodes from left to right beginning with the bottom level of the tree and working upward to the top level; and (b) if any two weights are out of numerical order, then restructure the tree by interchanging the position of the node of greater weight with the rightmost node of lesser weight in the list, along with its subtree. If no weight is out of order, then no interchange is done. The restructuring guarantees maximum compression.

The receiver follows the same process. The first character is added as a right leaf to the initial tree. The encoded form of each character that follows enables the receiver to locate the character on the tree or create a new node for the character just as the sender does. The receiver can also restructure the tree, if necessary, after each character is received. Both sender and receiver, then, always have the same tree (encoding table) after each character is transmitted successfully.

Figures 9.11 through 9.15 illustrate the method with the string ASIANAND. As before, we use the number of occurrences rather than the frequency of occurrences. For the example string, the first character, A, is transmitted in uncompressed form and assigned to the leaf node of the right branch (labeled with a 1) of the root. The next character, S, is checked against the character already in the tree. It is found to be different, so a 0S is sent, a new empty node is added to the tree, and the weight of the new branch node is incremented as shown in step 2 in Figure 9.11. Similarly, the character I is sent as 00I. An empty node is added, weights at branch nodes are incremented, and the tree is restructured (because the nodes are not in weight order) as in step 3. The next character, A, is already on the tree so its encoded form (the single bit 0) is sent and its occurrence number is incremented. The process continues as shown in the figures.

Assuming an 8-bit representation for characters, the compressed string transmitted is 56 bits. The uncompressed string is 64 bits. For this example, the compression ratio, 1.14, is not impressive. However, notice that after the second N is transmitted, the restructured tree provides a much shorter path for the character. In general with this method, as in the standard Huffman encoding method, characters with the highest frequency of occurrence have the shortest bit strings. Thus, the compression ratio for longer strings usually is con-

String :   ASIANAND

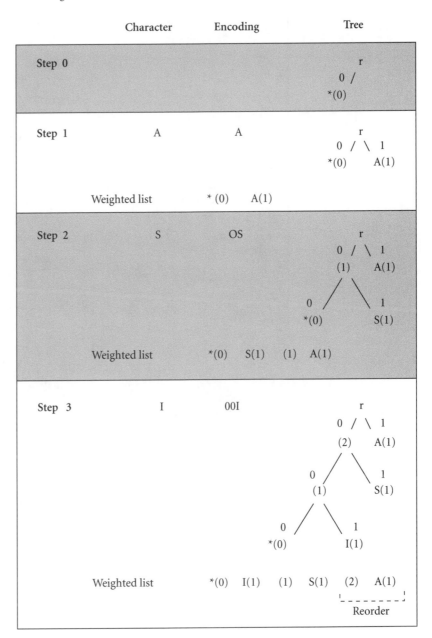

Figure 9.11. An illustration of dynamic Huffman encoding: part 1 of 5

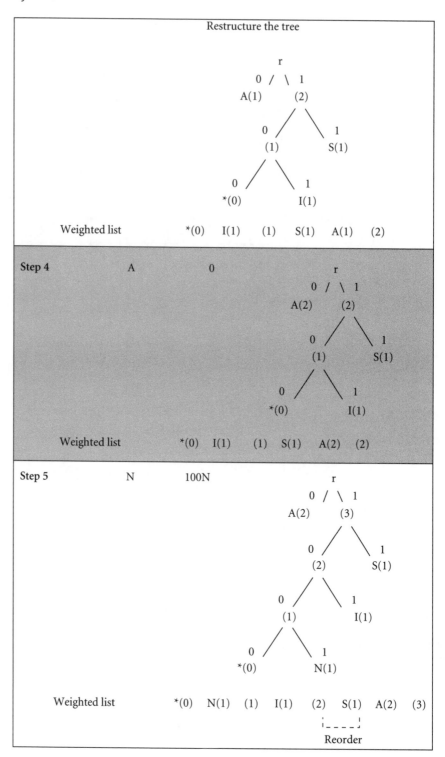

Figure 9.12. An illustration of dynamic Huffman encoding: part 2 of 5

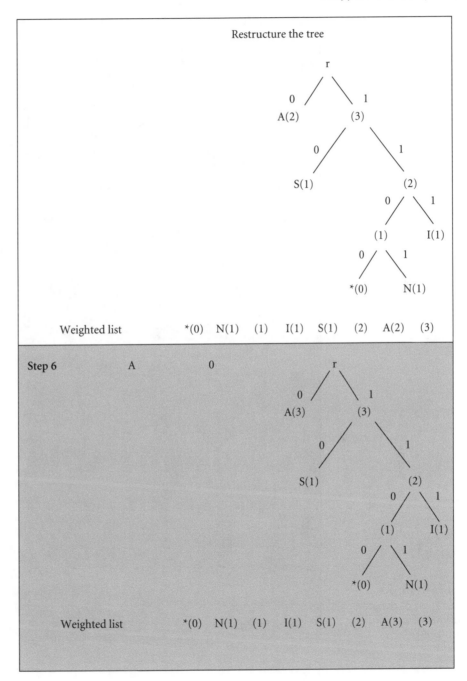

Figure 9.13. An illustration of dynamic Huffman encoding: part 3 of 5

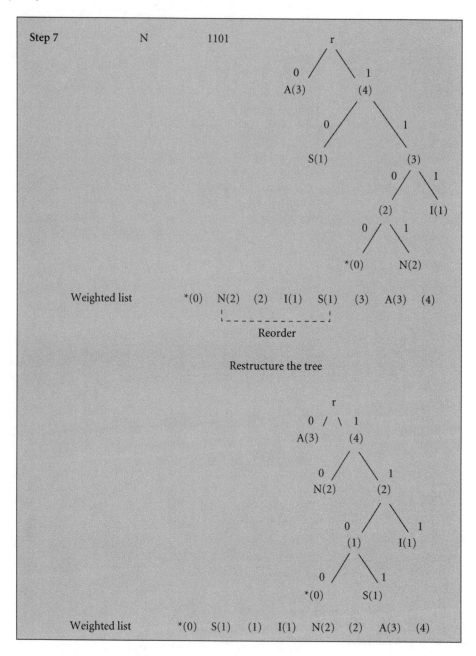

Figure 9.14. An illustration of dynamic Huffman encoding: part 4 of 5

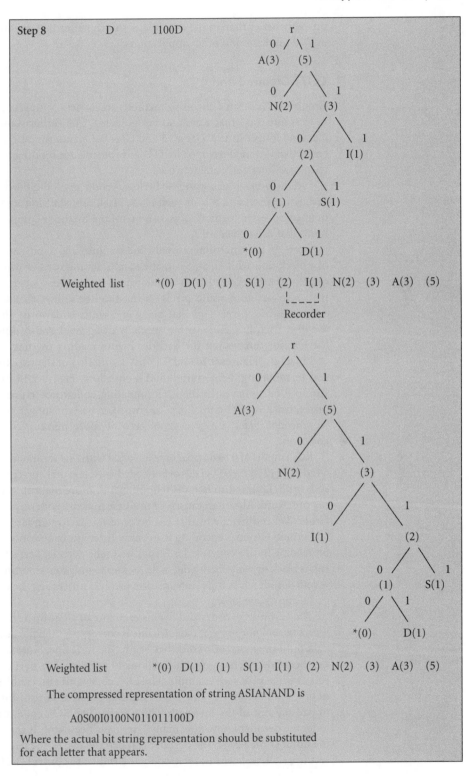

Figure 9.15. An illustration of dynamic Huffman encoding: part 5 of 5

siderably better than in the example, so much better that dynamic Huffman coding is used in V.32 modems and other applications.

CCITT Groups 3 and 4

Group 3 and Group 4 encoding methods are lossless compression algorithms implemented in facsimile (fax) machines and fax modems. The earlier standards, Group 1 and Group 2, are no longer in use. Group 3 and Group 4 standards, also called T4 and T6 standards, respectively, were developed by ITU as protocols for sending black-and-white images over telephone lines and data networks.

Facsimile machines scan line by line, producing a digitized image consisting of a 0 for each white pixel and a 1 for each black pixel. Transmitting a page involves millions of bits in uncompressed form. Group 3 and Group 4 methods compress the digitized image with ratios that can exceed 10:1.

Group 3 is a one-dimensional (line-by-line) and 1-bit encoding method. As each line of a black-and-white image is scanned, alternating runs of white and black pixels (picture elements) are encoded with standardized codewords (strings of bits). Each line begins with zero or more white pixels so the receiver knows that the first codeword refers to a run of white pixels and that black and white codewords alternate through the rest of the line. Each line ends with a specially designated end-of-line (EOL) codeword so that the receiver can realign the decoder before reading the next line should an error occur within a line. Figures 9.16 and 9.17 list a sampling of the two kinds of codewords, **makeup** and **terminating**, for Group 3 and 4 encoding. Figure 9.18 includes several examples of Group 3 encoding with them. Terminating codewords represent run lengths of 0 to 63 pixels, black or white. Makeup codewords represent longer runs of the same color pixel. An encoded pixel run consists of zero or more makeup codewords and a terminating codeword.

Run lengths of 0 to 63 pixels are encoded with one terminating codeword. Run lengths of 64 to 2623 (2560 + 63) pixels are encoded with one makeup codeword and one terminating codeword. Longer run lengths require two or more makeup codewords and one terminating codeword. Although the use of multiple makeup codewords is really an extension of the Group 3 encoding, the feature has become a de facto standard.

Because Group 3 encoding uses variable length codewords, decoding requires a bit-by-bit reading until a codeword is recognized. The decoder keeps track of whether the current run is black or white, reducing table lookup to only one column. A faster and more efficient way to decode a facsimile transmission involves processing the encoded data 1 byte at a time and using a state table.

The 12-bit EOL codeword begins each line of a Group 3 transmission. This use of EOL serves several purposes. If data in a line is corrupted, then the decoder can discard unknown data until the EOL codeword that begins the next line. Normal transmission then continues. Some decoders contain algorithms to replace all or part of the corrupted line; with a run of white pixels for example. The EOL codeword also enables the decoder to keep track of line width. A shorter line might indicate an error in transmission or cause the decoder to pad the rest of the line with white pixels. The EOL codeword also serves as a counter to let the decoder know how many lines have been sent. If the number of lines is less than the number on a page, the decoder can pad the rest of the page with white pixels. Six consecutive EOL codewords, referred to as a **return to control** (**RTC**) code, signal the end of a

White Run Length	Terminating Codeword	Black Run Length	Terminating Codeword
0	00110101	0	0000110111
1	000111	1	010
2	0111	2	11
3	1000	3	10
4	1011	4	011
5	1100	5	0011
6	1110	6	0010
7	1111	7	00011
8	10011	8	000101
9	10100	9	000100
10	00111	10	0000100
11	01000	11	0000101
12	001000	12	0000111
13	000011	13	00000100
14	110100	14	00000111
...	...	...	...
61	00110010	61	000001011010
62	00110011	62	000001100110
63	00110100	63	000001100111

Figure 9.16. Group 3 and 4 codewords: part 1 of 2

transmission. When an RTC code is decoded, the receiver changes from the high-speed to the low-speed carrier to await a post-page command.

Group 3 encoding is one-dimensional, lossless, and nonadaptive. It works best on documents that are typed, handwritten, or contain line drawings. For these documents, compression ratios can reach 8:1. Scanning a document of 200 line-per-inch resolution at the rate of approximately 8 pixels per millimeter produces about two million binary digits of uncompressed data. An 8:1 compression ratio saves considerable transmission time. Compression ratios are distinctly worse, and could be negative, on other types of documents. This may occur, for example, with a document containing continuous-tone, rather than black-and-white, images characterized by a large number of short runs. Group 3 encoding and decoding are efficient for black-and-white images and provide some error detection and correction—for example, the EOL features—without additional hardware.

Group 3 also has a two-dimensional encoding method, but it has generally been replaced by Group 4 two-dimensional encoding. Rather than scan each line independently from others, the two-dimensional method takes advantage of the fact that two successive lines differ very little from each other. Additional compression is achieved by encoding differences between lines rather than the total contents of each line.

White Run Length	Makeup Codeword	Black Run Length	Makeup Codeword
64	11011	64	0000001111
128	10010	128	000011001000
192	010111	192	000011001001
256	0110111	256	000001011011
320	00110110	320	000000110011
384	00110111	384	000000110100
...	...	...	...
1664	011000	1664	0000001100100
1728	010011011	1728	0000001100101
1792	00000001000	1792	00000001000
1856	00000001100	1856	00000001100
1920	00000001101	1920	00000001101
1984	000000010010	1984	000000010010
...	...	...	...
2496	000000011110	2496	000000011110
2560	000000011111	2560	000000011111
EOL	00000000001	EOL	00000000001

Figure 9.17. Group 3 and 4 codewords: part 2 of 2

```
EXAMPLES:

Run length of 33 white pixels
Encoding is    0010010

Run length of 180 black pixels
Encoding is  10010000000100100
             128  +  52

Run length of 9000 white pixels
Encoding is 000000011111000000011111000000011111011011001001001001
            2560  +  2560  +  2560  +  1280 +  40
```

Figure 9.18. Group 3 example encodings

284

Group 4 encoding identifies the first pixel of each run length as a changing element. This pixel's location is where the image changes color, for example, from black to white or white to black, in a line. Knowing that the next changing element is n pixels away is the same as knowing that there is a run length of n before the next change occurs. Group 4 (and Group 3) encoding uses short codewords to locate the next changing element relative to the current one when the next one is three or fewer pixels away, and long codewords otherwise. The codes that identify this positional information are called **relative element address designate (READ)** codes.

In Group 4 two-dimensional encoding, scanning is accomplished two consecutive lines at a time, the current line, or **coding line**, and the previous line, or **reference line**. The first reference line is imaginary and assumed to be only white. The beginning of each successive line begins with an imaginary white pixel. The scan begins at the left of a page (at the white pixel). Three modes of encoding are possible, depending upon the location of the beginning of the next run length in the reference line relative to that in the coding line. If r_1r_2 is the run length in the reference line and c_1c_2 is the next run length in the coding line, then the **pass mode** identifies the case when r_2 is to the left of c_1, the **vertical mode** when r_1 is to the left or right of c_1 by no more than three pixels, and the **horizontal mode** otherwise. Figure 9.19 illustrates different possibilities for the three modes. In the figure, c_0 is the first pixel of a new codeword; it could be black or white. At the beginning of each new line, c_o is assumed to be white. r_1 and c_1 are the first pixels on the reference line and the coding line, respectively, to the right of c_0 with a different color.

The following algorithm for the Group 4 two-dimensional method encodes a bitmap by scanning two adjacent lines at a time (the reference line and the coding line) from left to right and beginning in the left-hand corner of a page. The notation refers to the examples in Figure 9.19.

```
Set reference line to all white
Set coding line to first line
Repeat until end of page
  Begin
    Repeat until end of line
      Begin
        Set c0 to (imaginary) first pixel in coding line
        Determine c1, r1, and r2
        If r2 is to the left of c1
        Then (Compute pass mode code)
          Encode the run length r1r2
          Set c0 to pixel immediately below r2
        Else if r1 is to the left or right of c1
               by no more than three pixels
            Then (Compute vertical mode code)
              Encode the run length c1r1
              Set c0 to c1
            Else (Compute horizontal mode code)
              Determine c2
              Encode c0c1 and c1c2
              Set c0 to c2
```

a. Pass mode

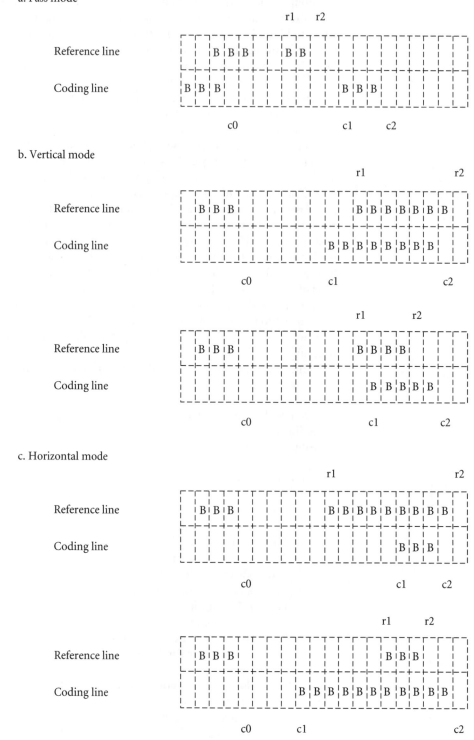

b. Vertical mode

c. Horizontal mode

Figure 9.19. Examples
of Group 4 modes

```
            Endif
        Endif
    End
    Set reference line to coding line
    Set coding line to next line
End
```

We note that the vertical mode is used most frequently because color changes from line to line usually vary by few pixels. The algorithm requires that c_0 is determined before the other locations where color change occurs. After the locations are determined, the encoding mode is identified. The relative locations and the encoding mode are both needed to create the code that is transmitted. Figure 9.20 contains the codes. An additional encoding mode, **extension mode**, is included in the figure. This codeword causes encoding to be aborted. Subsequent transmission is then in uncompressed form or in a different encoding method. Codes for run lengths are shown in Figures 9.16 and 9.17.

Graphical Image Compression

In this section, we introduce two popular methods for compressing graphical images. Because there are numerous variations of both methods and one involves several other methods, we will provide less detail than previous methods. References are cited that contain complete descriptions of the methods. The first method, **Lempel–Ziv–Welch (LZW)** compression, is found in GIF and TIFF file formats. LZW has gained additional recognition because GIF is the common format to all World Wide Web browsers. The second method, **JPEG** compression, is growing in importance as an increasing number of World Wide Web browsers support it. We also note that a method called MPEG is considered an international standard for compressing transmission of video.

LZW is a lossless method patented by both Unisys and IBM that can compress almost any kind of data. An early version was developed in 1977 by Lempel and Ziv [ZL77]. The method is dictionary based and writes compressed data as bytes. Its algorithm creates a data dictionary of uncompressed data substrings. Patterns in the data to be transmitted are identified in the dictionary, or if not, then a shorter code phrase is created and added to the dictionary listing. Hashing or tree-based methods are commonly used to search through the listings. The compressed stream consists of the dictionary entries.

Mode	Run Length	Codeword
Pass	r_1r_2	$0001 + r_1r_2$
Vertical	c_1 directly below r_1	1
	c_1 one to left of r_1	011
	c_1 two to left of r_1	000011
	c_1 three to left of r_1	0000011
	c_1 one to right of r_1	010
	c_1 two to right of r_1	000010
	c_1 three to right of r_1	0000010
Horizontal	c_0c_1 and c_1c_2	$001 + c_0c_1 + c_1c_2$
Extension		0000001000

Figure 9.20. Table of Group 4 codewords

Before compression begins, the first 256 entries in the data dictionary are initialized with the 8-bit ASCII character set. These entries are the only single-byte phrases that can occur. All other substrings in the uncompressed data are combinations of the initial phrases. Both the encoding and decoding dictionaries are initialized with these 1-byte phrases. The decoding process, which is the reverse of encoding, does not require the rest of the dictionary. During decoding, the dictionary is built dynamically, a characteristic that makes LZW different from, and more commonly used than, other dictionary-based compression methods.

The performance of LZW can be degraded by noisy images. Transforming the images to a different form to remove noise can improve compression. Differencing is another technique that can improve LZW and other compression techniques. Differencing reduces the amount of information in an image. Adjacent pixels may vary slightly in certain images, particularly continuous-tone images, so using the difference in values rather than the pixel value reduces the amount of information stored in a lossless way. The resulting data can be compressed more than the original data. An inverse operation can be performed during decoding to restore the actual representation.

Variations of LZW are common. Some variants are designed to improve efficiency and speed by systematically discarding or replacing dictionary entries. In GIF, each input symbol to LZW is a pixel value. The number of possible values for a pixel depends on the pixel depth. Pixel, or bit, depth is the number of bits or bytes comprising the individual data value, where the maximum value is 2 to the power bit depth. For example, each pixel of 8-bit image data can have from 1 to $2^8 = 256$ values. GIF allows 1- to 8-bit deep images, which correspond to 2 to 256 LZW input symbols for initializing the data dictionary. No matter how the pixels are originally stored, LZW processes them as a sequence of symbols. The pixel depth affects other aspects of LZW in addition to the dictionary, requiring a number of variants. Another characteristic of GIF that leads to variations is its storage of compressed codes with the least significant bit first, not necessarily the machine bit order.

JPEG is a combination of compression methods adaptable to individual users or applications. The Joint Photographic Experts Group (JPEG), a combined ISO and CCITT group established in 1987, evolved from a group with the acronym PEG originally formed within ISO in 1982. PEG's goal was producing an industry standard for graphics and image data transmission over digital communications networks.

JPEG works efficiently with continuous-tone images, such as photographs, having pixel depths of 6 to 24 bits. It is a lossy method designed to eliminate information that the human eye will not detect. The method can produce compressed images varying from very small and poor quality to somewhat smaller than original and very high quality. The quality of the image can be adjusted by the user on a 1-to-100 scale. Compression ratios of 20:1 without noticeable degradation can be obtained for images of photographic quality.

A baseline, or minimal, subset of the JPEG standard is defined and must be supported by all applications allowing JPEG. The standard specifies an 8-bit pixel depth. Baseline JPEG involves five steps:

- Transform the image, if necessary, to feature information most sensitive to the human eye.
- Downsample (reduce the sampling size) by averaging pixel groupings.
- Remove redundant image data by applying a discrete cosine transform (DCT) to pixel blocks.

- Divide the DCT output and discard the portions less sensitive to the human eye.
- Employ a Huffman variable word-length compression method to encode the resulting data.

An understanding of the first two steps, transforming the image and downsampling, requires an exploration of color concepts outside the scope of this book. We note, however, that gray-scale images contain information most sensitive to the human eye; they do not need to be transformed. Downsampling uses techniques similar to color TV transmission methods. The third step, DCT, involves a complex process of dividing pixels into 8×8 blocks and then converting a spatial image into a frequency map. This step costs more than the others in JPEG. It achieves a separation of high- and low-frequency image information so that the fourth step, quantizing, can more easily discard appropriate portions of the high-frequency information. By adjusting the setting on the 1-to-100 scale that determines quality, the user can control the quantizing that occurs in this step. The fifth step, Huffman variable-length encoding, losslessly removes redundant information resulting from the previous step. The compressed image data is then ready for transmission. Decoding is accomplished by reversing the five-step process.

There are some noticeable disadvantages to JPEG. Developing a software version can be difficult. The work is made easier with a JPEG library, but the software version tends to be slower than a hardware counterpart, especially for decompression. The number of file formats that support JPEG is growing, but each format is likely to be revised periodically. Some of the techniques in JPEG can introduce visible images within large areas of a single color, making it inappropriate for images containing large blocks of the same color.

Extensions to baseline JPEG are available, and more should be expected as JPEG's popularity increases. Details of the JPEG compression method and the complete text of the ISO standards can be found in [PM92]. A C programming language version of JPEG and a number of other compression methods are in [Nel91].

SUMMARY

Information transfer between two end-user systems not only must be accurate but also must be readable only by the receivers for whom the information is intended. Secure transmission is a major concern, and encryption/decryption methods to enhance it are implemented at the Presentation layer. Serious and much debated issues involve the selection of a standard encryption/decryption method that meets all the desirable criteria: high-level protection against unauthorized disclosure or modification that is based upon an encryption key rather than a secret algorithm; simple to understand but complex enough to discourage breaking; economical, efficient, and adaptable; and available at a reasonable cost. The data encryption standard (DES), various public key encryption algorithms, and digital signature methods each have merit for encrypting messages prior to invoking session-layer services. Inserting a central authority (trusted server) into a network provides additional security, especially when subnetworks are present.

Networks are vulnerable to attack from intruders. Tools are available to detect vulnerabilities, provide reports, and suggest implementations to reduce the possibility of attacks.

The rise in Internet popularity has encouraged the development of additional methods to ensure secure message transmission through e-mail or file transfer. In particular, electronic commerce requires secure communication.

Use of some security methods has increased to the point that the U.S. government is concerned about losing the ability to monitor messages within groups considered to be threats to national security. The government has advocated the Escrowed Encryption Standard as a means of maintaining the ability, especially over switched-circuit networks involving phones and fax transmission. The advocacy has prompted much debate over privacy and national security issues.

Data compression has grown in importance because of the extremely heavy use of networks and the numerous applications involving transmission of graphical images. The amount of data and the size of the representation of that data are critical factors in transmission rate. Data compression reduces the size of data by changing its representation, making the process an invaluable tool for transmission over networks, especially when graphical images are included.

Several data compression methods are implemented for textual data or black-and-white images transmission. In this category, run-length encoding (RLE), Huffman encoding and Huffman dynamic encoding, CCITT Groups 3 and 4, and the Lempel–Ziv–Welch (LZW) technique are discussed in detail. Algorithms and examples are included, as are ways to decompress the data at the receiving end of the transmission. Methods for compressing data representations of graphical images, such as JPEG, are dealt with in a more cursory fashion. The importance of these methods is growing, and the number of variations increasing. An application developer is advised to be aware of developments, for example, through the World Wide Web.

EXERCISES

1. Assume the lowercase alphabet is encoded as $a = 1, \ldots, z = 26$, and that the RSA method is used.
   (a) What values of d are possible if $p = 3$ and $q = 5$?
   (b) Encrypt "network" with $p = 11$, $q = 17$, and $d = 21$.

2. Send a short message to a receiver using the RSA method. Obtain verification that the correct message was received. Carefully choose relatively small prime numbers to control the computational complexity inherent in the algorithm.

3. Write a program that implements the DSS algorithm.

4. Determine the current status of the DSS as a standard. Summarize the pros and cons of the debate on its merits vis-à-vis the RSA method.

5. Identify at least two advantages and two disadvantages of allowing a third party, say, a government agency, to eavesdrop in a network. What constraints, if any, should be imposed upon the third party before allowing the activity?

6. Prepare a report on the current status of the U.S. policies on providing encryption algorithms for international use.

7. Write a program to implement the CCITT Group 4 two-dimensional algorithm. Run it with the following data and calculate the compression ratio (b and w represent black-and-white characters or pixels, respectively):

```
bbbbbbbbbbbwwwwwbbbbbbb
bbbbbbbbwwwwwwwwwwbbbb
bbbbbwwwwwwwwwwbbbbbbbb
bbbbbbbwwwwwwwwbbbbbbbb
bbbbbbbbbwwwwwwbbbbbbbb
bbbbbbbbbbbwwwwwbbbbbbbb
```

8. Write a program for the RLE method. Test your program with the string:

   BBBBBGGGRRRRRRRTTTTTZZZZ

9. Show a binary tree for each of the Huffman encoding methods (static and dynamic) for the string MISSISSIPPI.

10. Write a program to implement the Huffman encoding algorithm. Test your program with the following data: EUROPEASIAAUSTRALIA. Assuming the given data is the entire message, calculate the entropy per symbol and compare it to the compression ratio you obtained when encoding the message.

11. Produce the compressed representation of the string WINNING using dynamic Huffman encoding. Repeat using the strings BANANA, TENNESSEE.

12. List all categories for each of the following data compression methods: RLE, Huffman encoding, dynamic Huffman encoding, CCITT Groups 3 and 4, LZW, and JPEG. Refer to Figure 9.7.

13. Prepare a report summarizing the current status of support of JPEG in the World Wide Web.

PART THREE

The Supporting Structure

We use the layers of the OSI model to structure the discussion, but include significant attention to the TCP/IP environment.

The rest of the chapters of the book address services that are necessary for the Application layer to do its job. We use the layers of the OSI model to structure the discussion, but include significant attention to the TCP/IP environment.

We begin this part with a chapter on encryption and data compression, two key issues in network development because they are basic tools for transforming data in transit. We introduce each topic by specifying terminology, then we examine a selection of typical methods. Algorithms and examples are included to facilitate understanding and implementation.

Chapter 10 presents the services of the Presentation and Session layers. Though these topics are not treated as a separate layer in the TCP/IP model of network interactivity, examining the OSI work in this area gives a good understanding of the kind of interaction that must be built into distributed applications.

Chapter 11 addresses the Transport layer and investigates how the dependable network services to which we have often referred are actually provided. Research and development of effective, efficient transport services continues. The types of problems encountered at the Transport layer are central to interconnected networks and the development of distributed applications. We will see that providing dependable transport connections involves significant cost in processing requirements and time. An alternative is a more primitive connectionless service that is suitable for many types of applications.

A number of topics covered in this chapter are more usually found in discussions of the Data Link layer. This is a consequence of the top-down approach taken in this text. There is a similarity in the responsibilities of the Transport and Data Link layers. The difference is partly that the Transport layer deals with dependable communication over intervening networks, whereas the Data Link layer is concerned with communication over a direct connection. Since this is the first time we see the problems associated with reliable communication, the topic is treated in this chapter.

The layering of network operations allows Transport layer service to assume that it can find and interact directly with the intended partner in distributed operations. The Network layer assumes responsibility for address resolution and route determination to allow the Transport layer's end-to-end connection to occur. These responsibilities introduce a new set of problems and form the basis of Chapter 12. In this chapter, we include the topic of firewalls—those gateways that limit what Transport layer connections will be permitted with a particular organization's computing resources.

In the final three chapters, we consider topics appropriate to the Data Link and Physical layers of the OSI model. Medium access control in Chapter 13 presents common contention-based and controlled access techniques for accessing a shared medium. Chapter 14 addresses problems and common approaches to moving network traffic between distinct local area networks over bridges. Issues of privacy and vulnerability are included. Chapter 15 completes the discussion of the lowest layers by highlighting characteristics and issues related to logical link control and high-speed transmission.

By the end of the book, you should be well equipped to pursue application development in networked environments. However, the emergence of new techniques will keep the development area alive and will require you to update your knowledge and skills constantly. Thus, the end of this book is the beginning of your work as a network-based applications developer.

Presentation and Session Layers

KEY CONCEPTS

- Presentation Layer
- Basic Encoding Rules (BER)
- Session Layer
- Tokens
- Synchronization and Activity Concepts
- Connectionless Session Service

In an ideal environment, interoperating application processes share information required for their cooperation, without regard to how the information is represented or how it is passed between them. For example, applications might exchange personnel records, semester class schedules, a store's inventory, or advertising plans. Local storage methods on the two cooperating systems could be very different—different number of bits used to store integers, different conventions for addressing a group of bytes, different methods of storing and using negative values, even different codes for representing characters. Applications running on one system are developed with little or no consideration for the storage conventions of the local system; applications running on cooperating separate systems should be equally independent of storage details.

Of course, an indication of what a personnel record, semester class schedule, store inventory, or advertising plan is and what it contains must be understood. Further, the data of which the information is composed must be passed from one system to the other and converted from the representation of one to the other. The OSI model requires that an application entity determine what information it will share with its peer application entity, and that the information be described without reference to any particular storage characteristics. ASN.1 is a machine-independent description of the content of information exchanged between open systems application entities. Conversion of the abstract syntax to a specific representation suitable for transfer is the responsibility of the Presentation layer. The OSI Basic Encoding Rules (BER) accomplish this conversion.

In addition to a representation that all parties to a distributed application share in common, effective interactivity requires additional coordination. The OSI model defines a Session layer to account for the necessary communication coordination.

The Internet protocols do not include the Presentation and Session layers defined in the OSI model. That does not mean that applications built in the Internet do not need these aspects. The difference between the OSI model and the Internet approach is one of how and where these tasks are accomplished. In the OSI approach, a collection of services and protocols are defined and incorporated into applications as needed. In the Internet approach, each application builds the services of the Presentation and Session layers individually. Of course, libraries can be built, and objects and methods reused as needed, but no protocols or services for these activities are defined in the network protocol stack.

This chapter briefly describes the OSI Presentation and Session layers. Our purpose is to illustrate what must be accomplished by interoperable processes. Whether the OSI services and protocols are used, or the equivalent, or similar, interactions are built into individual applications, these types of activities are needed.

10.1 PRESENTATION LAYER

The responsibility of the Presentation layer is to transfer information between interoperating application entities in such a way that the semantics are preserved during transfer [Pre87b]. An application entity provides an abstract syntax to describe the information it will share with its peer. In turn, the presentation entities negotiate a particular representation to use for the information during transfer. The peer presentation entities must each be able to convert between the local storage conventions and the agreed-upon *transfer syntax*. The responsibility of the Presentation layer can thus be summarized:

- Negotiation of transfer syntax
- Transformation to and from the transfer syntax
- Preservation of semantics

In the Internet suite, no "Presentation layer" is defined; however, the function must be available.

Regardless of the network model used, the function defined for the OSI Presentation layer holds an important position in the interoperability of cooperating processes. In the Internet suite, no "Presentation layer" is defined; however, the function must be available.

In practice, a number of different transfer syntaxes will be available for use with a given abstract syntax. For example, a company's advertising plan could be transferred using an ordinary basic encoding scheme, or it could be sent in a compressed form. The peer presentation entities negotiate the choice.

10.1.1 Services Provided by the Presentation Layer

The presentation service provides capabilities for the following:

- Connection establishment
- Data transfer

- Context modification
- Dialog control
- Connection termination

In the OSI model, connection establishment and connection termination follow closely the similar services provided by ACSE (see Chapter 4, section 4.2). In the Internet suite, connection establishment is a concern of the transport service. Applications must establish a relationship in order to interact, but there are no standards and no established procedures for accomplishing that connection. Similarly, there is no defined role for a Presentation layer that concerns itself with the coordination of data representation. We examine the OSI services defined for this purpose because they provide a well-defined paradigm for accomplishing this coordination.

The services of the Presentation layer are concerned primarily with the representation of data for transfer to a peer presentation service user (PS user). The context established in connection establishment is an important part of the representation choice. The context in use during a communication between PS users can be modified with the context modification facility of the Presentation layer.

Dialog Control

Dialog control capabilities offered by the presentation service provider are actually conduits to the services offered at the Session layer and below. They are not directly related to the purpose of the Presentation layer, which is to relieve Application-layer entities of concerns related to representation of information at end systems and in transit between arbitrary end systems.

Data Transfer

Data transfer facilities are accessed by application entities through the services of the Presentation layer. The OSI model offers four types of data transfer service,

P-DATA is an unconfirmed service, and both the request and indication primitives have a single parameter: user data. The user data is delivered to the responding PS user, using the encoding rules agreed to in the connection establishment phase.

The service P-EXPEDITED-DATA provides the PS user with access to priority handling of the data at lower layers of the open system. It is possible for expedited data to overtake data sent earlier. The significance of expedited data to the presentation service provider is that it may overtake an earlier message that affects the presentation context. It is therefore not possible to determine the correct association of the abstract syntax used in expedited data with a transfer syntax. Because of this characteristic, the user data carried in P-EXPEDITED-DATA will always be transferred using the default context. The interpretation of the expedited data is a matter for the application entity using the service. An example use of this service would be to send a message such as "System going down in 5 minutes. Please log off." An application that chooses to use expedited data must request the appropriate support from underlying layers.

The service P-TYPED-DATA is used when restrictions exist concerning which side of a communication is permitted to send data at any particular time. P-TYPED-DATA gives the

PS user the capability of sending data to a peer process without regard to current ownership of the right to transmit. The presentation service attaches no significance to P-TYPED-DATA and hands it to the corresponding Session-layer entity without any special treatment.

The service P-CAPABILITY-DATA allows renegotiation of the conditions existing between the presentation entities. This is not a form of user data, but a communication between the presentation entities that allows the conditions of communication between the cooperating applications to be modified.

Context Modification

The **P-ALTER-CONTEXT** service is an option negotiated during connection establishment. P-ALTER-CONTEXT provides the following facilities:

- Creation of presentation contexts and their addition to the DCS
- Removal of presentation contexts from the DCS

Additions and deletions to the presentation context list are suggested in the P-ALTER-CONTEXT.request and conveyed to the responding PS user in P-ALTER-CONTEXT.indication. Each item suggested for addition consists of two parts: a presentation context identification and an abstract syntax name. Items proposed for deletion from the presentation context list are specified by their presentation context identifications.

The presentation context addition result list, if present, is a list of responses to the items in the presentation context addition list. If the parameter is not present, then all the proposed additions are acceptable both by the presentation service provider (PS provider) and the cooperating PS user. If the presentation context addition list parameter is present in the P-ALTER-CONTEXT.indication, its entries serve to notify the responding PS user that the PS provider cannot support one or more of the requested additions. The parameter consists of list entries corresponding to the entries in the presentation context addition list. If the PS provider rejects a proposed addition, it places the value "provider rejected" in the corresponding position in the result list. The responding PS user then places the value "accepted" or "user rejected" in each of the result list positions that do not already contain a "provider rejected" value. Communication options must be supported by three parties: the initiating PS user, the responding PS user, and the PS provider.

10.1.2 Basic Encoding Rules (BER)

Instances, or values, of the abstract notation ASN.1 are encoded for transfer between two application entities by the set of encoding rules, or transfer syntax, BER.

Basic encoding rules (BER) is the set of rules for encoding ASN.1-defined data into a particular representation for transmitting to another system. Chapter 3 compared the abstract syntax notation to the declaration section of a high-level language like C or Java. Continuing the analogy, we compare the transfer syntax BER to an assembly or machine language. Instances, or values, of the abstract notation ASN.1 are encoded for transfer between two application entities by the set of encoding rules, or transfer syntax, BER. Just as a high-level language is more frequently used than assembly language in applications programming, so too are network users and programmers more apt to be familiar with ASN.1 than BER in networking applications. For that reason, we dwelt on ASN.1 in some detail and discuss BER only briefly.

We give the structure of BER and examples, enough to acquire a flavor of the encoding and decoding rules that are used to transmit ASN.1-defined data types and values. ISO 8825 (or ISO 8825-Part 1: Basic Encoding Rules) and ITU's X.209 contain a detailed specification of BER. Later amendments in ISO 8825 PDAM 2 were combined with ISO 8825 to form ISO 8825 Part 1: Basic Encoding Rules.

Structure of Data Elements

Data elements are the fundamental units in BER. Encoding consists of expressing information as data elements; decoding is the reverse process. Each data element is an ordered list of three components: identifier, length, and content. A primitive data element is characterized by a content component containing no additional data elements. In a structured data element, the content component contains one or more data elements, as shown in Figure 10.1. Each component is encoded in octets; the encoded data element is the complete sequence of the octets.

Identifier The identifier, or tag, is encoded as one or more octets, as shown in Figure 10.2. It gives the type of the data specified in the content component. In a single-octet identifier, bits 8 and 7 represent a class (UNIVERSAL is 00, APPLICATION is 01, CONTEXT-SPECIFIC is 10, and PRIVATE is 11); bit 6 specifies the data element as primitive (0) or structured (1); and bits 5 through 1 give the tag number. For example, 00000011 indicates that the tag class is UNIVERSAL (00), the data element is primitive (0), and the tag number is 3 (00011), the BIT STRING tag number.

a) Primitive

b) Structured

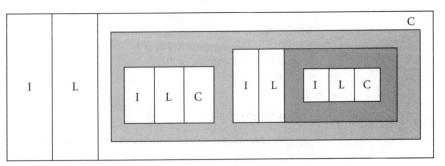

Figure 10.1. BER data element structures

a. Single byte

Class	Prim/Struct	5 bits (not all 1s)

b. Multiple bytes

Figure 10.2. Identifier (tag) encoding

Class	P/S	11111		1	7 bits	•••	1	7 bits		0	7 bits

More than 5 bits, hence additional octets, are required when the tag number is greater than 31. In that case, bits 5 through 1 of the first octet are 1, and each remaining octet has a 1 or 0 in bit 8, depending upon whether the tag number is continued in at least one or no octet, respectively. For example, the tag APPLICATION 293 is encoded as 01111111 10000010 00100101.

Length   The length component of the data element indicates the length (number of octets) of the content component with one of three forms:

- Short form—the length is given in one octet, representing a range of numbers from 0 to 127 since the first bit must be 0. For example, a length field of 01010110 indicates that the content field has $2^6 + 2^4 + 2^2 + 2^1 = 86$ octets.
- Long form—the length is given in 2 to 127 octets, allowing numbers from 128 through $2^{1016} - 1$. In practice, numbers are in the lower end of the range. A 1 or 0 in bit 8 of each octet has the same meaning as in the identifier field. For example, 10011001 00011010 indicates that the content field has 3226 octets.
- Indefinite form—the content of a structured data element (the only kind allowed with this form) has a specific end-of-content data element, given by two consecutive octets of all zeros. The length field contains one octet, 10000000, which signals that the end-of-content octets are present.

Content   In the content component, zero or more octets encode primitive data elements, and zero or more data items encode structured data elements. Encoding for ASN.1 data types is specified in Figure 10.3. For types BIT STRING and OCTET STRING, the content component may be encoded as primitive or structured. All character string types may also be encoded as primitive or structured, in which case each component data item represents a substring.

Encoding Examples

We give several examples to convey the flavor of BER. ISO 8825 contains a more complex example.

(a) Primitive

Primitive Type	Contents Encoding
BOOLEAN	A single octet: zero for FALSE; any non-zero value for TRUE
INTEGER	Value encoded in two's complement: first octet and bit 8 of second octet are neither all ones nor all zeros
BIT STRING	Value encoded in zero or more octets following an initial octet which contains a number from zero to seven indicating the number of unused bits in the final octet
OCTET STRING	Value encoded in zero or more octets
NULL	No octet (Length octet is zero)
OBJECT IDENTIFIER	An ordered list of encodings, the first two integers in the first octet, one integer in each of the subsequent octets
REAL	No octet for zero, "01000000" for PLUS-INFINITY, and "01000001" for MINUS-INFINITY. Other values expressed in exponential form: base (sender option), exponent, and sign encoded in first one to four bits; mantissa encoded in subsequent octets
ENUMERATED	Encoding of its associated integer value
CHARACTER STRING	Encoded as [UNIVERSAL x] IMPLICIT OCTET STRING, where x is the tag number of the string type

(b) Structured

Structured Type	Contents Encoding
SEQUENCE	Encode each element, then concatenate result
SEQUENCE OF	Same as SEQUENCE
SET	Same as SEQUENCE
SET OF	Same as SEQUENCE
CHOICE	Encoded as the chosen (primitive or structured) type
SELECTION	Encoded as the selected (primitive or structured) type
ANY	Encoded as the selected (primitive or structured) type
BIT STRING	Encoded as [UNIVERSAL 3] IMPLICIT SEQUENCE OF BIT STRING
OCTET STRING	Encoded as [UNIVERSAL 4] IMPLICIT SEQUENCE OF OCTET STRING
CHARACTER STRING	Encoded as [UNIVERSAL x] IMPLICIT OCTET STRING, where x is the tag number of the string type
Tagged (without IMPLICIT)	Encoded as the *base encoding*, the complete encoding of the corresponding data value of the type appearing in the Tagged Type notation
Tagged (with IMPLICIT)	Same as Tagged without IMPLICIT, except is structured or primitive depending on the base encoding

Figure 10.3. Content component encoding of ASN.1 data types

In section 3.3.2, the type SET was illustrated with the example

```
Person    ::=  SET
      {
       name        IA5String,
       age         INTEGER
       female      BOOLEAN
      }.
```

The BER encoding (in hexadecimal) of the instance "Maggie", 4, TRUE is

SET		IA5String		M	a	g	g	i	e	INTEGER		4	BOOLEAN		TRUE
31	14	16	06	77	65	71	71	73	69	02	01	04	01	01	FF

where 14, 06, 01, and 01 are lengths of content components. The identifier (I), length (L), and content (C) components are determined as follows. First, consider the encoding of name "Maggie". In this example, IA5String has class UNIVERSAL (00), type primitive (0), and tag 22 (binary 10110). Its 8-bit identifier component is 00010110, which is 16 in hexadecimal. The ASCII representation of the value "Maggie" consists of 6 octets. Thus, for name "Maggie", we get

```
I  L  C
16 06 77 65 71 71 73 69
```

Next, consider age 4. INTEGER has class UNIVERSAL, type primitive, and tag 2. Its value 4, is the single octet 04 in hexadecimal. Thus, for age 4, we get

```
I  L  C
02 01 04
```

Next, consider female TRUE. BOOLEAN has class UNIVERSAL, type primitive, and tag 1. The value TRUE is represented by the single octet 11111111, which is FF in hexadecimal. Thus, for female TRUE, we get

```
I  L  C
01 01 FF
```

Finally, SET has class UNIVERSAL, type structured (1), and tag 17. Its 8-bit identifier component is 00110001, which is 31 in hexadecimal. The content component consists of the 14 octets obtained by concatenating the three ILCs.

By examining the encoded version, it becomes apparent why the components in the SET type can be in any order, provided no two components are of the same type. For example, the encoded version of 4, TRUE, "Maggie" would be

```
31 14 02 01 04 01 01 FF 16 06 77 65 71 71 73 69
```

As an example of encoding the type SET with tagged components, consider the four cases in Figure 3.6 using the instance 180, 180, 0. The first case (a) is invalid. In case (b), each component has class APPLICATION (01) and type primitive. The integer value 180 has binary representation 10110100 (one octet), which is B4 in hexadecimal. The encoded version of INTEGER 180 is

```
I  L  C
02 01 B4
```

The identifier component of [APPLICATION 0] is 01000000, which is 40 in hexadecimal. The encoded version of [APPLICATION 0] 180 INTEGER, then, is

```
I   L   C
40  03  02  01  B4
```

Similarly, the encoded version of the occupied and vacant components of seats are 41 03 02 01 B4 and 42 03 02 02 00, respectively. The encoded version of the instance 180, 180, 0 of seats is

```
I   L   C
31  15  40  03  02  01  B4  41  03  02  01  B4  42  03  02  01  00
```

Note that the tags removed any ambiguity among the components of seats, which enables the components to be listed in any order.

The use of IMPLICIT in case (c) shortens the encoded string by making it unnecessary to encode the tag for INTEGER. In this case, 40 01 B4 encodes the value 180, and the encoded version of 180, 180, 0 is

```
I   L   C
31  09  40  01  B4  41  01  B4  42  01  00
```

Case (d) is encoded the same as case (b) except that the tags are CONTEXT SENSITIVE (10) rather than APPLICATION (01). In this case, the encoded version of 180, 180, 0 is

```
I   L   C
31  15  80  03  02  02  B4  81  03  02  01  B4  82  03  02  01  00
```

Comments About BER

A number of concerns and issues have been raised with regard to BER. We will cite some of them, but not address them in detail for the same reason we did not spend more time on the encoding rules themselves. In general, BER is widely implemented, but there is at least occasional concern about efficiency and speed. Two other issues, compactness and the number of options in BER, also are worth noting.

Lin reported on a set of experiments that addressed the efficiency and processing time of ASN.1 BER [Lin93a]. By applying to BER certain restrictions he considered realistic, he achieved experimental results that suggest BER is comparable to other known methods and that it can be viable when interoperability is sought.

Two enhancements of BER address the compactness and options issues. One enhancement, *packed encoding rules (PER)*, allows identifier or length components to be omitted under certain conditions. PER has other features that decrease the amount of encoding necessary for transmission. In circumstances where BER offers optional ways to encode a value, the other enhancement, *distinguished encoding rules (DER)*, select a single encoding. The standard ISO 8825 consists of three parts, one for each of BER, PER, and DER.

10.2   SESSION LAYER

The Session layer is the last of the three layers that provide services directly to the user process. The Application, Presentation, and Session layers all are concerned with the needs of the application process. Services of the lower layers are important, of course, but their relationship to the application invoking network services is indirect. We have seen hints of the services provided by the Session layer in several of the services of higher layers. In examining the OSI definition of the Session layer, we explore the ideas of dialog control, synchronization, and activity management.

The session service provides mechanisms for organized and synchronized exchange of data between cooperating session service users (SS users) [Ses87a, Ses87b]. The session service also supports the exchange of data between peer entities (and provides the mechanism for synchronization of that data exchange) and allows for the orderly release of the connection.

The session service provides support for the user of *tokens* in data exchange, synchronization, and connection release. Session services allow data transfer to be either half-duplex or full-duplex. Synchronization facilities of the session service allow establishment of checkpoints within the dialog so that the SS user can recover from errors by resuming operation at a checkpoint. This facility also allows interruption and resumption of a dialog at prearranged points.

10.2.1   Tokens

Tokens appeared in the context of virtual terminals in section 6.3. Tokens defined in the Session layer serve a similar purpose of enforcing access rights. A token is an attribute of a session connection that is assigned to one or the other of the SS users. Possession of the token implies the right to use a particular service to the exclusion of other potential users of the service. Four types of tokens are defined in the OSI session service: *data token, release token, synchronize-minor token*, and *synchronize major/activity token*. Each conveys rights to particular services. A token may be assigned to one of the SS users, or it may be unassigned. If the token is assigned to one user, that user has exclusive access to the services related to that token. If the token is unassigned, then no SS user has exclusive access to the service. This may result in both SS users having simultaneous access to the service (in the case of the data transfer and the release tokens) or neither SS user having access to the service (in the case of the synchronize-minor and the major/activity tokens).

10.2.2   Synchronization and Activity Concepts

A dialog between two SS users can be subdivided into *activities*. An activity, or a dialog that is not divided into activities, can be marked with synchronization points. It is important to note that the Session layer does not subdivide a dialog into activities, nor does it mark synchronization points. These actions are performed by the SS user (which is a presentation entity acting on behalf of an application entity). The session services do include the necessary functions to place these markers. The session service provider also maintains the correct serial number values for the counters used to distinguish among the markers.

Figure 10.4 illustrates the concepts of dialog subdivision. The section of dialog between two major synchronization points is called a *dialog unit*. All communication within a dialog unit is completely separate from all communication before or after it. Each major synchro-

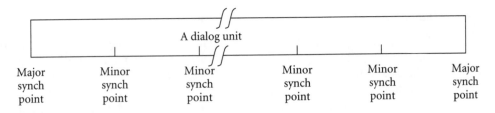

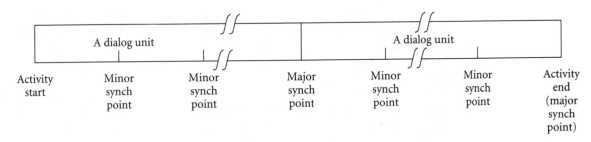

Figure 10.4. Synchronization points and activities

nization point is confirmed. Once a major synchronization point is passed, no return to any prior synchronization point is possible. Minor synchronization points subdivide a dialog unit. A minor synchronization point may or may not be confirmed.

Activities subdivide a dialog into logical components, perhaps separate pieces of work. Activities may have very different characteristics and may require different choices in the nature of the connection. For example, during a single dialog, the SS users may move from interactive communication, to large file transfer, and then back to interactive communication. Each of these phases can logically be designated a separate activity.

Resynchronization can be invoked by either SS user. Resynchronization returns the session to a defined state, including reassignment of tokens and changing the values of serial numbers attached to the synchronization points. All undelivered data is dropped on resynchronization. Resynchronization can occur in one direction or in both directions.

10.2.3 Services Provided by the Session Layer

The services of the Session layer are grouped by function into connection establishment, data transfer, dialog control, activity management, exception reporting, and connection termination. A selection of these is discussed further in the following sections.

Connection Establishment

Information specified during establishment of an association between application entities (use of A-ASSOCIATE in the OSI model) define the Session layer services needed by the application.

Dialog Control

There are two aspects to dialog control: regulating which side of the communication is sending data, and making arrangements to back up in a communication and repeat what has been done before. The Session layer provides both these facilities as options to its user. Controlling which side of the communication has the ability to send data simplifies the design of an application considerably. If either side can send, then the application must be designed to respond to data arrival at any time. If the permission to send is regulated, the application can exhibit more deterministic behavior: it is in sending mode, or it is in listening mode.

The ability to back up and repeat a part of a communication must not be confused with the notion of dependable data transfer, which is the responsibility of the lower layers. The Session layer service providing for checkpoints and retransmission is to recover from faults in the processing above the Transport layer. In other words, even if the data is delivered to the destination system, some problem may occur to prevent the application process from succeeding in final processing of the data. For example, suppose a disk write error occurs on a disk during a file transfer, and a portion of the data is lost. The Transport layer has succeeded in delivering the data to the end system; the application process is responsible for its use after that. The file transfer operation will require that the lost data be transferred again. The Session layer provides tools that the higher layers can use to mark places in the data so that a backup and restart can occur. The Session layer provides only the tools; it is the responsibility of the application process to use them.

S-SYNCH-MAJOR, S-SYNCH-MINOR   An SS user inserts synchronization points in a stream of data by using the services S-SYNCH-MINOR and S-SYNCH-MAJOR. Both of these are confirmed services, indicating the need for both sides of the communication to know where the synchronization points are located. A serial number is associated with the synchronization process and is incremented each time a synchronization point is inserted. If communication is controlled in the two-way alternate (TWA) mode, one serial number is used. Data is sent from one side or the other at any given time, and the serial number is incremented with each checkpoint placed in the data. If both sides are sending data at the same time (two-way simultaneous (TWS) mode) two separate serial numbers are used, one for each direction. In two-way simultaneous communication, minor synchronization points include only one serial number, the one associated with the sender of the data; major synchronization points have both serial numbers.

Separate tokens are used to control placement of minor and major synchronization points. It is possible to back up as far as the last major synchronization point or to any of the minor synchronization points placed since the last major synch point.

S-RESYNCHRONIZE   The SS user chooses where to resynchronize by using S-RESYNCH-RONIZE, another confirmed service. The SS user must keep track of the serial numbers associated with existing synchronization points and must resynchronize before the serial numbers become larger than their limit.

S-TOKEN-GIVE   The S-TOKEN-GIVE service allows one SS user to surrender one or more tokens to the other SS user, thus relinquishing exclusive access to the service restricted by the token. The service is unconfirmed and carries two parameters: identification of the token(s) surrendered and optional user data. The user data, if present, is passed to the peer SS user. The list of tokens surrendered can be any combination of the four token types: data token, synchronize-minor token, major/activity token, and release token.

S-TOKEN-PLEASE The S-TOKEN-PLEASE service allows one SS user to request one or more specific tokens from the other SS user. The service is unconfirmed, and the parameters are a list of requested tokens and optional user data. The user data, if present, is passed to the peer SS user. The list of tokens can be any combination of the four token types.

Activity Management

S-ACTIVITY-START S-ACTIVITY-START allows an SS user to initiate a new activity. Values for the next synchronization point serial number(s) are set to one. The service can be used only when no activity is in progress. The service is unconfirmed and carries two parameters: a mandatory activity identifier and optional user data. The activity identifier is provided by the SS user and allows the two SS users to identify the new activity. User data, if present, is passed to the peer SS user.

S-ACTIVITY-RESUME S-ACTIVITY-RESUME allows an SS user to indicate that a previously interrupted activity is resumed. The resumed activity is identified by providing its activity identifier and a new identifier is provided for the activity as it is resumed. The resumed activity may have been part of a previous session connection. In that case, the identity of the old session connection must also be provided. The invoking SS user must also provide the first serial number to be used in synchronization for the new activity. If synchronization was done separately for the two directions on the old activity, then a new synchronization serial number must be provided for each direction. The service is unconfirmed.

S-ACTIVITY-INTERRUPT S-ACTIVITY-INTERRUPT allows an SS user to terminate an activity abruptly. Work achieved before the interrupt is not canceled and can be resumed later. Restrictions on use of the service are governed by token holding. The parameters of the service include an optional reason and optional user data. The service is confirmed.

S-ACTIVITY-DISCARD S-ACTIVITY-DISCARD allows the SS user to terminate the activity abruptly. Though it is implied that the activity is canceled and cannot be resumed, this is not under control of the session service provider. The service can only be used subject to token possession restrictions. The service is confirmed and carries optional reason and user data parameters.

S-ACTIVITY-END S-ACTIVITY-END provides for "normal" termination of an activity and causes a major synchronization point to be set. The service can be used only if an activity is in progress and subject to token holding restrictions. The parameters of the service include a new synchronization point number (one for each direction if synchronization is done separately in the two directions) and optional user data.

S-CONTROL-GIVE S-CONTROL-GIVE allows an SS user to surrender all the tokens it currently holds. This service can be used only when the activity management functional unit is selected, and then only when no activity is in progress. There is no need for S-CONTROL-GIVE to carry a list of tokens since it transfers all tokens. The only parameter of the primitives is an optional user data field. If present, the user data is passed by the SS provider to the peer SS user.

Connection Termination

Like the connection establishment services, session connection termination closely resembles the related services at the Presentation layer and in ACSE. An orderly release of the connection is initiated with S-RELEASE. Abrupt termination, with the possibility of data loss, can be invoked by the session service user (SS user) through the unconfirmed S-U-ABORT service. S-P-ABORT is used by the session service provider (SS provider) to notify its user that the connection has been lost.

10.2.4   Connectionless Session Service

All the session services that we have seen in this chapter are connection oriented: they all assume that a connection will be established, then data will be transferred, and then the connection will be released. The OSI session service includes one connectionless service: S-UNIT-DATA. The S-UNIT-DATA request and indication carry calling session address and called session address parameters as well as the SS user data that is to be delivered. The request primitive also carries a quality-of-service parameter. S-UNIT-DATA is self-contained, not dependent on any previously established connection. No relationship is assumed between any S-UNIT-DATA data unit and any other. There is no provision for detection of transmission errors by the sending or receiving SS user. There is no guarantee of delivery of the data, much less any guarantee of order in data units delivered. There is no mechanism for negotiation between the SS users. On the positive side, no connection establishment or release phases are required, and data is delivered with minimal overhead.

SUMMARY

The Presentation and Session layers define an important intermediary between the Application layer and the lower-layer services. Primarily, Presentation-layer services involve connection establishment, modification, and termination. An abstract syntax (ASN.1) and its associated transfer syntax (BER) enable the Presentation layer to perform these services that facilitate communication between end-user systems. Several examples provide an introduction to the encoding rules and open the door to further study. The goal of these tools is to free application entities from concern with information representation details.

The Session layer defines services related to coordinating the activities of cooperating processes, running on separate systems. No corresponding service is defined in the TCP/IP network protocols. In the TCP/IP environment, these services are integrated into each application. The OSI model recognizes these as common requirements in network applications and defines standard services to meet the need.

Like other layers in the OSI stack, the Session layer offers both connection-oriented and connectionless services. The connection-oriented services are more complex and involve a large number of services and service primitives. These are divided into groups: connection establishment, data transfer, dialog control, exception reporting, activity management, and connection termination. In the connectionless model, only data transfer service exists.

The Session layer is the last of the three that directly serve the application. The Application, Presentation, and Session layers all take their purpose directly from the application and are independent of the network and communication requirements. We look next at the Transport layer, which must provide the service that protects the top layers from potential failures in communications.

EXERCISES

1. Encode the representation(s) in Exercise 13 of Chapter 3 in BER.

2. Write the BER encoding of the ASN.1 definition in Exercise 14 of Chapter 3.

3. Write the BER encoding of each of the following:
   (a) The integer -145
   (b) The value {5,7} of   example ::=   SEQUENCE

   ```
                                        {
                                        m   INTEGER,
                                        n   INTEGER
                                        };
   ```
   (c) The value {5,7} of   example ::=   SET

   ```
                                        {
                                        m   [0]   INTEGER,
                                        n   [1]   INTEGER
                                        };
   ```

4. Write the BER encoding for each example in section 3.3.5 (see Chapter 3).

5. Research the DER (distinguished encoding rules) for ASN.1 defined in ITU X.509. See what you can learn about the reasons for defining another set of encoding rules and how BER differs from DER.

6. The responsibility of the Session layer is heavily oriented toward synchronizing the actions of the two sides of a communication. For each of the following applications, determine whether such synchronization is necessary and, if so, how it should be applied.
   (a) A remote operation facility in which a command is sent to a specified system where it must be executed. The result of the command execution is returned to the originating system.
   (b) A distributed inventory system in which a sales clerk checks the availability of an item in the stock at other stores.

7. Explain the differences among activity, major synchronization, and minor synchronization. Give an example of the use of each.

8. Capability data is used only between activities. Why is capability data not available within an activity?

9. There are four kinds of data-carrying services in the Session-layer: S-DATA, S-EXPEDITED-DATA, S-TYPED-DATA, S-CAPABILITY-DATA. Give an example of the use of each. Could any one of these be deleted without loss of function? (In other words, could any one of these be replaced by use of other services, perhaps with additional constraints?)

CHAPTER 11

Transport Layer

KEY CONCEPTS

- The Services Provided by the Transport Layer
- The OSI Transport Service
- The Internet TCP Transport Service
- The Transport Protocol
- Connection-Oriented vs. Connectionless Services
- Application Program Interfaces (API)
- Services Required by the Transport Layer

In the top three layers of network software, the focus is on meeting the needs of the application process. We have discussed establishing an association, representing information in a form suitable for communication with a cooperating system (without being conscious of the architectural details of that system), arranging for access to remotely stored files, sending operation codes for remote execution, dealing with concurrency issues, and establishing checkpoints for possible restarts of communication. All these are related to solving particular application problems; none are directly related to using the network connections, overcoming network failures, making the best choices among network options, interacting with a particular local area network, and so on.

In this chapter, as we examine the Transport layer, we begin to consider the problem of network-based applications from the perspective of network services. These are the services whose existence we have assumed in previous chapters. Now we develop an understanding of what work is required to provide the services and what options are available regarding service levels and costs (both financial and computational).

We identify the services provided by the Transport layer and the "behind the scenes" activity needed to provide the services. We consider the often similar approaches to Transport-layer responsibilities taken by the OSI and Internet suites of protocols. In environments where the upper layer services are not developed, user applications must interface directly with the Transport layer; we therefore conclude the chapter with a description of application program interfaces to transport services for two common environments.

The idea of moving from the domain of the application process and the user to the domain of the network and its services and limitations is especially significant in understanding the Transport layer. In many cases, the Transport layer is the last layer directly under the user's control. Through parameters specified in calls to the transport service, the user describes the type of service required from the network. Services of the network and lower layers will often be provided by a service utility, such as the telephone company.

11.1 THE SERVICES PROVIDED BY THE TRANSPORT LAYER

The amount of effort that the Transport layer expends in this effort is under control, ultimately, of the user application process. The more thoroughly the Transport layer isolates the user from network defects, the more processing it must do—even when everything is functioning smoothly.

The Transport layer attempts to mask failures or deficiencies of the subnet from the application. Thus, it is the responsibility of the Transport layer to present to the Session layer (or directly to the application if no Session and Presentation layers exist) the illusion of a totally dependable, trouble-free network. The amount of effort that the Transport layer expends in this effort is under control, ultimately, of the user application process. The more thoroughly the Transport layer isolates the user from network defects, the more processing it must do—even when everything is functioning smoothly. Figure 11.1 shows the transport entity in place in the hierarchy of network entities. The service access points are the connections identifying specific locations. The network service access point identifies the particular machine in the interconnected set of networks and is unique among all machines in the world. The transport service access point identifies a particular application or session process connection to the transport service.

If an application process is willing to endure possible failures, or if the underlying network services are so reliable that failures are extremely rare, a less exhaustive effort by the Transport layer is appropriate. Another reason for the application process to request minimal processing by the Transport layer is that sometimes perfect performance is critical and the application will not trust even the most complete Transport-layer implementation to protect it from every possible failure. In that case, the application process reserves to itself the requirement to do the processing required for near perfect performance. Thus there are two reasons why an application process might select minimal transport processing over a network that is subject to some level of error occurrence:

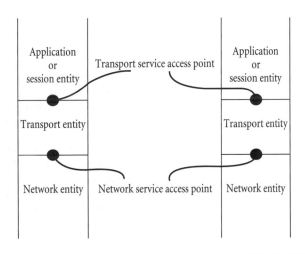

Figure 11.1. The transport service in relation to other layers of the network

1. The application process is not particularly concerned about an occasional error, such as a lost packet, and would prefer that packet delivery be as fast as possible.

2. The application process is so concerned with the possibility of an occasional error that it will do full checking of the completeness, correctness, and order of every packet itself, thus making the Transport-layer checking redundant.

An example of the first case is data consisting of spoken communication: the loss of a sound in the middle of a conversation might not be noticed, but a significant delay while that sound is retransmitted would interfere with the communication. An example of the second is a medical image for analysis and diagnosis by a remote physician.

Different types of transport service exist in both the TCP/IP and OSI protocols. The TCP/IP suite provides two levels of transport service: Transmission Control Protocol (TCP) is a connection-oriented protocol that provides the illusion of dependable delivery service to the applications above it; User Datagram Protocol (UDP) is a connectionless protocol that provides fast, best-effort transport service. In the OSI protocol suite, there are five connection-oriented transport protocols, TP4, TP3, TP2, TP1, and TP0, and one connectionless transport protocol. The OSI transport protocol development benefited from the experience of the TCP/IP networks, and TP4 is similar to TCP. Figure 11.2 distinguishes among the OSI transport connection-oriented protocols.

11.2 THE OSI TRANSPORT SERVICE

The OSI transport service provides capabilities for connection establishment, data transfer, and connection release.

These services are closely related to the Network layer but the transport services have the added responsibility of making the performance of the Network layer appear error-free.

OSI recognizes three different classes of Network-layer service and defines a number of different transport protocols. The transport protocol selected for a particular application

TP0	Simple, basic service on an underlying network that is assumed to be flawless and error-free
TP1	Basic service on an underlying network that provides perfect packet delivery, but may reset
TP2	Multiplexing transport service on an underlying network that is assumed to be flawless and error-free
TP3	Error recovery and multiplexing on an underlying network that provides perfect packet delivery, but may reset
TP4	Error detection and recovery over an underlying network that is unreliable, characterized by loss and duplication of packets, as well as resets

Figure 11.2. Five connection-oriented transport protocols

will depend upon the quality of service demanded by the user and upon the types of network service available to it. To further describe the options in the OSI Transport layer, we need to consider the types of service available from the network.

11.2.1 Network Service Relevant to Transport Services

In the OSI view, networks can be graded in terms of the types of errors that are likely to occur. In particular, OSI transport services recognize two classes of errors: those errors that the network service provider detects but does not attempt to correct and errors that the network service provider does not detect. The former are called **signaled errors**, because the network provider signals the user (Transport layer) when these errors occur. An example is the reset of the network service to some previous state, or complete loss of a network connection. The latter are called **residual errors**, those that the network provider does not know about and thus cannot report to the Transport layer. Examples include the loss or reordering of data units. Network service providers can then be classified in terms of these error types:

Class A. The service provided includes a nearly error-free environment, with both types of error occurring only at acceptable levels.

Class B. Residual errors are rare (occur at an acceptable rate), but signaled errors are frequent enough to require corrective action.

Class C. Both types of error occur at a rate that is not acceptable and requires Transport-layer enhancement.

The five classes of connection-oriented Transport layer services defined in OSI are designed to provide a specific level of service given that the underlying network service is in one of these classes:

TP0: TP0 is the simple class transport service. It provides no enhancement of network service and is intended to operate over a Class A network provider.

TP1: TP1 is the basic error recovery class transport service, intended to operate over a Class B network provider.

TP2: TP2 is the simple class with the addition of multiplexing service. It is also intended to operate over very high-quality (Class A) network providers because it provides no error detection or recovery service.

TP3: TP3 is the basic error recovery class with multiplexing added.

TP4: TP4 is the full-service Transport-layer provider; it offers error detection and recovery, and is suitable for use over Class C networks.

TP0 through TP4 are connection oriented. Not every OSI system needs to provide all the available transport protocols. Selection of appropriate transport provider is an item of negotiation in establishing a connection.

11.2.2   Connection Establishment in OSI

In the descriptions that follow, notice the roles of three participants in providing transport services: the initiating and the responding TS users and the TS provider. The two TS users are the processes that invoke the transport service. In the OSI model, the TS users are processes of the Session layer. The TS provider is the pair of Transport-layer processes that jointly implement the chosen transport service. To the transport user, the TS provider looks like a single entity that accepts data and delivers it to the peer transport user. The TS provider acts like a pipe through which data flow in the data transfer phase, but is an active participant in transport connection and transport release phases.

> To the transport user, the TS provider looks like a single entity that accepts data and delivers it to the peer transport user.

Connection-oriented transport service begins by establishing a connection between transport entities with agreed conditions for the communication. T-CONNECT provides this service.

T-CONNECT is a confirmed service initiated by a TS user (a session entity) to establish a connection between two systems. The **calling** and **called transport SAPs** (service access points) identify the initiating TS user and its intended responder. A transport address consists of a **transport selector** and one or more **network addresses**. The network address portion of the transport address identifies the machine at one end of the communication. The transport selector portion of the transport address identifies the program on that machine that will provide Transport-layer service. Within the OSI protocol suite, the transport selector identifies a process providing TP0, TP1, TP2, TP3, TP4, or the connectionless transport service. The chosen transport service could also be the Internet TCP or UDP or some other program. The Transport- and Network-layer protocols and services usually come from the same suite, but other combinations are theoretically possible.

The **expedited data** parameter takes the value **enabled** or **disabled** to show if the use of expedited data is requested on this connection. The TS provider can change this value before delivering the T-CONNECT.indication if expedited data is requested but not provided by the TS provider. The responding TS user may also change the value from enabled to disabled if it does not wish to establish a connection with expedited data allowed.

Quality of service (QOS) describes the level of service the TS user wishes on the connection. The QOS parameter is actually a list of options that reflect the specific needs of the application. For example, real-time applications will give precedence to speed in the Transport-layer, whereas applications requiring transfer of large blocks of data will emphasize continuity of connection and protection from data loss. The requested quality of service can be altered by the TS provider if it is unable to meet the requested levels. The responding TS user can also reduce the values in the quality of service parameter list, depending upon its capability to meet the requested level of service.

User data carries up to 32 octets of data provided by the TS user. Unlike higher layers where the user data of the connect service carries the protocol data unit of the service user, the Transport layer's CONNECT service user-data parameter does not carry information for the session protocol. As we saw in Chapter 10, the session connect protocol data unit is carried in T-DATA after the transport connection is established.

The **responding address** is provided in the T-CONNECT.response and T-CONNECT.confirm primitives and usually matches the called address in the request and indication. Alternatively, it could specify another address to be used if the connection is broken and must be reestablished.

11.2.3   Data Transfer in OSI

The Transport layer provides two services for transferring data: T-DATA, for normal data transfer, and T-EXPEDITED-DATA. Each is an unconfirmed service that carries data in a user-data parameter.

The T-DATA service provides for ordinary data transfer over an established transport connection. The service is unconfirmed, but a connection-oriented transport service provider gives reliable delivery. If reliable delivery is not possible because of service failure, the Transport layer will notify the TS user. There is no limit to the quantity of data in the user-data parameter. Data ordering is preserved in delivery of T-DATA.

T-EXPEDITED-DATA is available if it was selected and accepted upon connection establishment. The data carried in user data is limited to 16 octets; data ordering is not preserved in the transfer of expedited data, which may pass data sent previously. Expedited data is exempt from flow control restrictions that block normal data transfer.

11.2.4   Connection Release in OSI

Connection release is provided by the T-DISCONNECT service. The service is used by either the initiating TS user or the responding TS user to terminate a connection.

T-DISCONNECT is an unconfirmed service. It carries a single parameter, user data, of up to 64 octets. The T-DISCONNECT can be issued by either of the TS users in the form of T-DISCONNECT.request; the transport service responds by issuing a T-DISCONNECT.indication to the other user. T-DISCONNECT.indication can also be issued by the TS provider to reject a connection. If the TS provider issues T-DISCONNECT.indication, an additional parameter identifies the connection release as provider initiated.

11.3   THE INTERNET TCP TRANSPORT SERVICE

TCP provides reliable stream transport service. This means the application process sends bits across the network connection, by means of the TCP services, with assurance that the bits will arrive in order, without duplication or loss. The application sends any number of bits, grouped as octets. For the sake of efficiency, TCP collects the octets until a reasonably sized packet forms before sending it across the network by invoking Network-layer services. See Figure 11.3. At the receiving side, TCP delivers the octets to the application in exactly the same order as they were sent. If an application requires that the octets go out before a full packet is formed, it must tell TCP to *push* the packet out, regardless of the number of octets it contains. There is no notion of data types in the stream of octets carried by TCP. An application using TCP is completely responsible for knowing the meaning of the data exchanged and treating it correctly.

The services of TCP can be described in terms similar to those used for the OSI transport services. Figure 11.4 lists the services available to the user of TCP; the following sections describe their use.

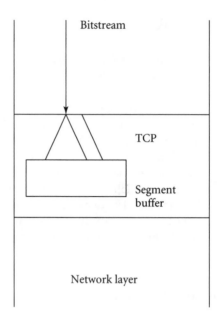

Figure 11.3. TCP collects a stream of bits into a segment before sending

Bitstream
TCP
Segment buffer
Network layer

Function	Service Primitive	Type	Initiator/Responder
Connection establishment	ACTIVE_OPEN	Request	Initiator
	ACTIVE_OPEN_WITH_DATA	Request	Initiator
	FULL_PASSIVE_OPEN	Request	Responder
	UNSPECIFIED_PASSIVE_OPEN	Request	Responder
	OPEN_ID	Local response	Initiator
	OPEN_SUCCESS	Confirm	Initiator
	OPEN_FAILURE	Confirm	Initiator
	OPEN_RECEIVED	Indication	Responder
Data transfer	SEND	Request	Either
	DELIVER	Indication	Either
Status/error reporting	STATUS	Request	Either
	STATUS_REPORT	Local response	Either
	ERROR	Indication	Either
Connection termination	CLOSE	Request	Either
	CLOSING	Indication	Either
	TERMINATE	Confirm	Either
	ABORT	Request	Either

Figure 11.4. TCP services

11.3.1 Connection Establishment in TCP

TCP provides specific service primitives for each side of a communication to use in establishing a connection. The responder, often called the **server**, must first issue the primitive that allows it to listen for an incoming connection request. A server process issues a **passive open**, which allows it to accept a request for a connection. The passive open may be either **unspecified**, which means any other process can connect to it, or **fully specified**, which means that only a specific partner may connect to it. The responder provides a **port** number as identification of itself to potential partners.

The initiator of a connection, often called the **client**, requests a connection to a particular responder by issuing either an ACTIVE_OPEN or ACTIVE_OPEN_WITH_DATA TCP primitive. Either type of ACTIVE OPEN must specify to what responder it wishes to connect.

The identification of a desired responder consists of two elements: the IP (network) address of the machine on which the responder resides and the port number of the particular TCP service it wishes to contact. The port number corresponds to the transport selector of the OSI transport address. Port numbers may be permanently and globally assigned, assigned for a particular application but not globally known, or reserved. Figure 11.5 lists some of the currently assigned TCP ports. A current listing of Internet assigned numbers can be found in RFC 1010 [RP87]. Globally known port numbers, called **well-known ports**, allow an application process on one system to connect to a particular server on another system. The initiator must know the network address of the destination system and the port number of the desired process. Well-known ports simplify the task of obtaining the

Port Number	Service Available
0	Reserved
1–4	Unassigned
7	Echo
11	Show active users (USERS)
13	Daytime
15	Netstat
17	Quote of the day (QUOTE)
20	FTP-DATA
21	FTP
23	Telnet
25	SMTP
37	Time
42	Name server
70	Gopher
79	Finger
80	HTTP
102	ISO-TSAP
103	X.400
133–159	Unassigned
160–223	Reserved
247–255	Unassigned

Figure 11.5. TCP well-known ports

necessary information. For example, the ECHO server is an application process that listens for connection requests from any source. The process accepts data and sends it back to the sender. The ECHO server listens at port 7 and can be reached by an ACTIVE_OPEN that specifies its machine address and destination port = 7. Notice that the list of well-known ports includes port 102 assigned to ISO-TSAP.

An open connection must have an identifier to allow communication to flow between the correct sender and receiver even if a number of connections are open between the same pair of machines. The connection identifier is provided by TCP and communicated to the initiator process in an OPEN_ID primitive. The connection identifier must be provided in many of the TCP primitives' parameter lists. The parameters required by each TCP connection establishment primitive are shown in Figure 11.6.

11.3.2 Data Transfer in TCP

TCP provides one primitive for data transfer: SEND/DELIVER. SEND allows the TCP user to provide data for TCP to transport. DELIVER permits TCP to notify the recipient of the arrival of data on the connection. The OSI notion of expedited data corresponds to the use of the urgent flag in the TCP SEND/DELIVER primitives. The push flag allows a user process to force TCP to move the data without waiting to fill a packet. Parameters associated with TCP data transfer primitives appear in Figure 11.7.

11.3.3 Status and Error Reporting in TCP

A TCP user can obtain information on the status of the connection by using the STATUS primitive. The resulting STATUS_REPORT returns information relevant to the health of the connection. The ERROR primitive allows the TCP service provided to report the existence of an error condition on a specific connection. Parameters associated with TCP status and error reporting appear in Figure 11.8.

11.3.4 Connection Termination in TCP

TCP connection termination attempts to protect against lost data by continuing to accept incoming data, even after a CLOSE is initiated, until the CLOSE has been acknowledged by the other side of the connection. TCP service primitives for connection termination are CLOSE, which is issued by both sides of the connection and indicates that the TCP user has no further data to send; CLOSING, which is notice from the TCP service provider that the remote user has requested closing the connection; and TERMINATE, which is delivered to each user by TCP to indicate that the connection is closed.

An abrupt termination of the connection consists of ABORT issued by one user and a resulting TERMINATE delivered by TCP to the other user. Parameters associated with TCP connection termination primitives appear in Figure 11.9.

TCP Primitive	Parameter
ACTIVE_OPEN	Source port Destination port Destination address [timeout] [timeout-action] [precedence] [security range]
ACTIVE_OPEN_WITH_DATA	Source port Destination port Destination address Data Data length Push flag Urgent flag [timeout] [timeout-action] [precedence] [security range]
FULL_PASSIVE_OPEN	Source port Destination port Destination address [timeout] [timeout-action] [precedence] [security range]
UNSPECIFIED_PASSIVE_OPEN	Source port [timeout] [timeout-action] [precedence] [security range]
OPEN_ID	Connection identifier Source port Destination port Destination address
OPEN_SUCCESS	Connection identifier
OPEN_FAILURE	Connection identifier

Figure 11.6. TCP connection establishment services

Computer Networks and Open Systems

TCP Primitive	Parameter
SEND	Connection identifier
	Data
	Data length
	Push flag
	Urgent flag
	Timeout
	Timeout action
DELIVER	Connection identifier
	Data
	Data length
	Push flag
	Urgent flag

Figure 11.7. TCP services

TCP Primitive	Parameter
STATUS	Connection identifier
STATUS_REPORT	Connection identifier
	Source port
	Source address
	Destination port
	Destination address
	Connection state
	Receive window
	Send window
	Waiting ack
	Waiting receipt
	Urgent
	Precedence
	Security
	Timeout
ERROR	Connection identifier
	Reason code

Figure 11.8. TCP status and error reporting services

TCP Primitive	Parameter
CLOSE	Connection identifier
CLOSING	Connection identifier
TERMINATE	Connection identifier
	Reason code
ABORT	Connection identifier

Figure 11.9. TCP connection termination services

11.4 THE TRANSPORT PROTOCOL

We noted earlier that the transport service provider appears to the transport service users as a single entity, when it is actually a pair of cooperating processes residing on separate computers. The rules that govern how the two processes interact to provide this service are defined in the transport protocol.

The transport service provider executes a protocol in cooperation with a peer transport service provider to meet the needs of the TS user and provide the services described in section 11.2. The work required to provide the transport service varies with the dependability of the underlying network services and the requirements of the user. In this section, we examine the work done to provide the transport service and some approaches to solving the problems encountered.

11.4.1 Connection Establishment

If the underlying network services could be depended upon to deliver the PDUs reliably, there would be little need for the Transport layer to exist.

Connection establishment results from the exchange of protocol data units, as seen in Figure 11.10. The initiating transport service provider sends a **connection request** PDU (CR) to its peer. The other transport service provider responds with a **connection confirm** PDU (CC). The initiator and responder each provide appropriate information in the parameters of the PDUs. Nothing could be simpler.

Unfortunately, there is a complication. If the underlying network services could be depended upon to deliver the PDUs reliably, there would be little need for the Transport layer

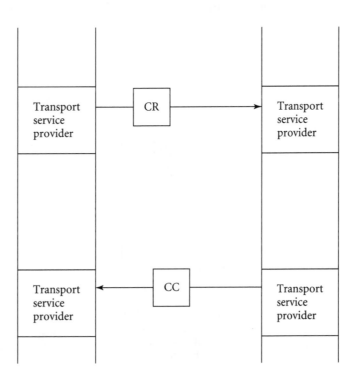

Figure 11.10. Connection establishment PDUs

to exist. Since the network services cannot be depended upon to deliver the user's traffic, they cannot be depended upon for delivery of the Transport-layer PDUs either.

Failure to deliver either the CR or the CC PDU causes the initiating transport service provider to time out and try again. Figure 11.11 illustrates some problems that could arise. In the first case, the initiating Transport-layer entity issues a connect request, which fails to arrive at the responding entity. However, an old connect request pops out of the network at a time that allows it to replace the lost CR. The responding entity creates a connection record corresponding to the CR it sees, and sends a connect confirm (CC). Unless there is a way to associate a particular CC with a CR, the two sides of the connection may have different characteristics. In the second example of Figure 11.11, the responding entity has refused the connection, but an old CC arrives at the initiating Transport-layer entity, causing it to believe that a connection has been established safely. If these examples of potential error conditions seem far-fetched, they are. The likelihood of exactly these sequences of events occurring *is* very small. However, they could happen. Correct protocol design and implementation requires that even very unlikely events must be anticipated and planned for. Consider this: when millions of connections are established every day, a condition with a probability of 0.0001 is expected daily. Millions of connections is a very conservative estimate of daily connection. To illustrate: every time a user of the World Wide Web invokes HTTP to transfer a document or image or sound clip or video, HTTP establishes a TCP connection, requests the transfer, and terminates the connection. HTTP is only one of many protocols generating TCP connections. Protocol designers have good reason to be paranoid.

To protect against these failures in the connection establishment phase of a transport connection (TC), the transport entities assign identification numbers to the TC. The initiating Transport-layer entity assigns a value chosen locally by any procedure so long as it is not possible for there to be a still surviving CR in the Internet containing that same iden-

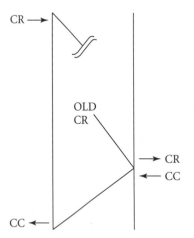

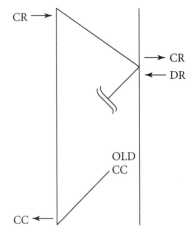

Figure 11.11. Some things that could go wrong in connection establishment

A connection request is lost, but an old connection request surfaces and causes a connection confirm to be sent.

The connection is refused, but an old connection confirm occurs and causes the initiator to complete a connection.

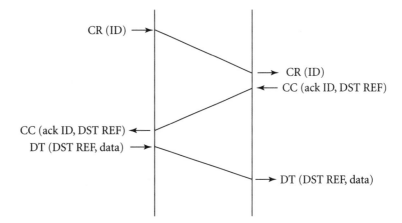

CR (ID) ⟶

⟶ CR (ID)
⟵ CC (ack ID, DST REF)

CC (ack ID, DST REF) ⟵
DT (DST REF, data) ⟶

⟶ DT (DST REF, data)

Figure 11.12. ISO Transport connection protocol steps

tification value. On receiving the CR, the responding Transport-layer entity issues a CC that carries another identification, again chosen locally, but such that there is no duplicate CC still in existence that could carry the same identification value. The CC also carries an acknowledgment of the identification found in the CR. When the CC arrives, the initiating Transport-layer entity can see that the CC is in response to the CR it has sent, and it establishes a connection. All subsequent PDUs carried on this transport connection will carry the responder's identifier, called the **destination reference:DST REF**. The first PDU carried on the connection, a DT PDU that carries the Session layer's connection request PDU, will serve to confirm to the responding Transport-layer entity that its CC and accompanying connection identification arrived safely at the initiator. The interaction between the initiating and responding transport entities is shown in Figure 11.12.

In the Internet's TCP, a third protocol step is required in the exchange of connection establishment information. When a TCP user issues an ACTIVE_OPEN service request, TCP sends a SYN PDU carrying its assigned identification number. The responding TCP entity issues a SYN PDU carrying its ID value and an acknowledgment of the ID sent by the initiator. The acknowledgment is carried in the ACK field of the PDU and consists of a value one greater than the ID value received (that is, the value it expects to see in the next data it receives). The initiator then sends an ACK PDU carrying the acknowledgment of the responder's connection ID value (again by sending the next higher value, the sequence number expected in the next data received). These steps, which constitute a **three-way handshake**, are illustrated in Figure 11.13.

The two protocol diagrams are similar, of course. Both require a three-step process to establish a connection with confidence. The difference is that the TCP protocol specifies three PDUs to accomplish the connection establishment. The OSI approach piggybacks the acknowledgment of the connection onto the first data transmission.

11.4.2   Data Transfer

Error Detection

Error detection occurs at several layers in network communication. The general model of error detection resembles parity checking: extra bits, computed from the contents of

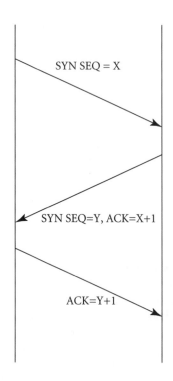

SYN SEQ = X

SYN SEQ=Y, ACK=X+1

ACK=Y+1

Figure 11.13. TCP transport connection protocol steps

the packet, are appended by the sender. At the receiver, the extra bits are recomputed and checked against those found in the packet. If the two computations are identical, the transmission is considered correct; otherwise, the receiver rejects the packet and the sender retransmits. TCP and TP4 use different computations to produce and verify the checksum. The differences reflect the tradeoffs often required in protocol design. Piscitello and Chapin summarize the differences: "the checksum used in TCP is faster, but the one used in TP4 is stronger" [PC93].

Both TCP and TP4 compute a checksum on the contents of the entire data unit, the header and the user data. TCP also includes a prepended pseudoheader that contains the source and destination IP addresses, the TCP segment length, and the protocol id field of the IP packet that will carry the data unit. The TP4 checksum computation may be disabled by the user process; TCP checksum computation is mandatory.

The checksum provides a reasonable amount of error checking to help ensure that data in the packet is not corrupted during transmission.

The TCP header of each packet includes the 16-bit field **checksum**. The checksum provides a reasonable amount of error checking to help ensure that data in the packet is not corrupted during transmission. When the packet is sent, the checksum is computed by finding the one's complement of the sum of all 16-bit blocks in the packet and then inverting the result. The example in Figure 11.14 illustrates the process.

In the figure, four 5-bit blocks are sent with their checksum. One's complement arithmetic is used to compute the sum of the four blocks. End-around carry is used in the addition. The result is inverted and sent with the four blocks. At the receiving end, the four blocks and the checksum are added using one's complement arithmetic. If the packet arrives without error, then the sum is zero (all 1 bits in one's complement arithmetic). This happens because inverting the sum results in a value that is the negative of the sum; adding a value and its negative at the receiving end produces a zero. In the event that the com-

```
           Sending                              Receiving

           10011                                10011
           00111                                00111
           11100                                11100
           10011                                10011
           -----                                10101    Checksum
    (1)    01001                                -----
               1   End-around carry      (1)    11110
           -----                                     1   End-around carry
           01010   One's complement sum           -----
    Invert                                       11111   One's complement sum
           10101   Checksum                               equals zero
```

Figure 11.14. Computation of checksum for a packet of four 5-bit blocks

putaton at the receiving end is not a zero, an error in transmission has occurred, and the receiver requests that the packet be resent.

Although all computation of a checksum is done in binary, the process is time consuming. Each block in a packet must be included in the computation. Hardware implementations exist that can significantly lessen computation time, but they must first be able to recognize that a TCP packet is being sent.

Error Correction

When a data unit does not arrive, it must be retransmitted. When a received data unit has errors, it must be corrected or retransmitted. Data correction requires adding redundant bits to the data unit so that the receiver can detect both the fact of an error and which bits are incorrect. For most networks, the probability of errors in transmission is sufficiently small that the cost of producing, transmitting, and checking the extra bits exceeds the cost of retransmitting a damaged data unit. Since a data unit with errors is essentially a data unit that did not arrive, we consider simply the requirement to replace a missing data unit. Clearly, it is the intended receiver of the data unit that must detect the failure and request corrective action. We consider here the methods by which this can be done, including the method chosen for use in both TCP and TP4.

Stop-and-Wait   The simplest approach to coordination between sender and receiver so that any delivery failure will be noticed and corrected is the stop-and-wait protocol. This requires that the sender transmit a data unit, then wait for an acknowledgment from the intended receiver before sending the next. If no acknowledgment arrives within a specified length of time, a copy of the data unit is transmitted. Even such a simple strategy has some potential problems. Figure 11.15 illustrates normal operation of the protocol in parts (a) and (b). In part (c), the acknowledgment is lost and the sender times out and sends a second copy of a data unit that has already arrived at the receiver. Thus, even when each data unit is acknowledged before the next is sent, a sequence number must be included in the header provided by the transport protocol so that duplicate data units can be detected and extra copies discarded. The sequence number of the data unit is included in the acknowledgment so that no combination of lost transmissions will lead to confusion about what data unit has arrived safely.

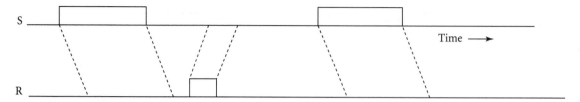

(a) Normal events: data unit sent, received correctly, acknowledgment sent, received correctly, next data unit sent.

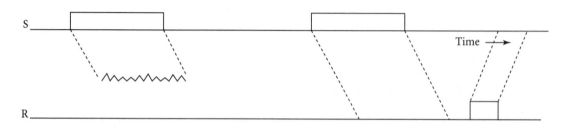

(b) A data unit is sent but does not arrive at the destination. After a time out period, the sender retransmits the data unit, and it arrives successfully and is acknowledged.

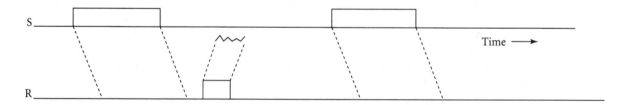

(c) A data unit is sent and arrives successfully; however, the acknowledgment does not get back to the sender. Thus, the sender times out and retransmits the same data unit. The receiver now has two copies of the same data unit.

Figure 11.15. Stop-and-wait retransmission strategy

Go-Back-N The problem with stop-and-wait is that too much delay is injected into the process of transmitting the data. The sender could transmit other data units while the first is traversing the network, the receiver is generating the acknowledgment, and the acknowledgment is getting through the network.

The go-back-N protocol allows a sender to transmit up to N data units before an acknowledgment arrives. As the name suggests, this protocol requires the sender be prepared to back up and retransmit up to N previously sent data units. Figure 11.16 illustrates the go-back-N protocol for $N = 5$. The can-send permissions noted in the figure represent the sequence numbers of data units that the sender can transmit without receiving an ac-

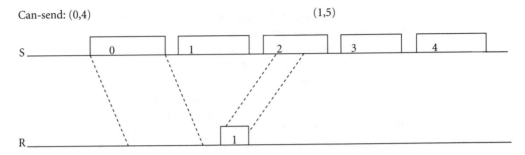

Can-send: (0,4)   (1,5)

(a) The sender begins with a can-send permission for data units numbered 0 through 4. When data unit 0 arrives, the receiver acknowledges it by requesting that the sender transmit data unit 1. When this acknowledgment arrives at the sender, the can-send permission is changed to allow transmission of data units 1 through 5.

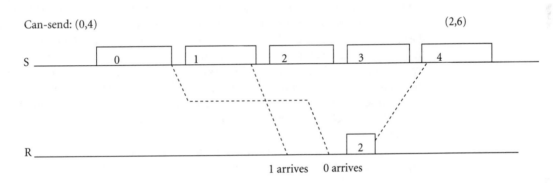

Can-send: (0,4)   (2,6)

1 arrives   0 arrives

(Note: Only the trailing end of the data unit is shown here to simplify the figure a bit.)

(b) For some reason, data unit 0 arrives later than data unit 1 (perhaps because they followed different routes through the network). The receiver does not acknowledge data unit 1, but continues to receive data units. When data unit 0 arrives, the receiver sends an acknowledgment that says it is looking for data unit 2, thereby acknowledging all data units with lower sequence numbers. On receipt of this acknowledgment, the sender changes its can-send permission to (2,6) and continues to send.

Figure 11.16. Go-back-N retransmission strategy

knowledgment. This is actually a window on the whole set of data units. All data units currently in the window are eligible for transmission. Each must stay in this window until successful delivery has been acknowledged. In Figure 11.16(a), a single data unit arrives and is acknowledged, the acknowledgment arrives, and the sender slides its can-send window one position to reflect the new state. In Figure 11.16(b), the window slides two positions because an acknowledgment arrives that confirms delivery of data units 0 and 1.

In the figure, the reason for acknowledging two data units is that the data units arrived out of order and the receiver waited long enough to allow the earlier data unit to arrive. In some protocols, an acknowledgment might refer to more than one data unit because it is incorporated into a data unit going in the reverse direction. In other words, if data units are flowing in both directions, the receiver may tack an acknowledgment onto a data unit it is sending anyway. If there is a data unit going where an acknowledgment is needed, the receiver will wait until its data unit is ready to send and will include acknowledgment of the last data unit it received. If data is flowing more frequently in one direction than the other, or if the receiver's data units are longer and take more time to transmit, some number of data units will be acknowledged in each piggybacked acknowledgment. If the receiver has nothing ready to send, it must send an acknowledgment alone in order to provide the feedback the sender needs to keep operating. Any protocol policy that might delay the sending of an acknowledgment requires care that the sender does not give up too soon and timeout, or be kept waiting when it could be sending additional PDUs.

Figure 11.17 illustrates two more cases: loss of a data unit and loss of an acknowledgment. In the case of a lost data unit, the go-back-N strategy allows the sender to continue sending until a timer expires. The sender then retransmits all the data units in the window because it does not know how many of them did not arrive successfully. Retransmission of data that has arrived successfully without the sender knowing it generates unnecessary traffic. The alternative is for the sender to retransmit the first unacknowledged data unit and wait for the next acknowledgment to arrive before retransmitting additional data. Though that strategy reduces the traffic generated, it leaves the sender idle until an acknowledgment arrives. If some number of data units failed to arrive, the necessary retransmission will have been delayed. Each approach has a negative side; both result in successful delivery of all the data units.

The loss of an acknowledgment in Figure 11.17(b) causes no problem because the subsequent acknowledgment of data unit 1 implies acknowledgment of data unit 0 as well.

Data Unit Ordering

To provide the illusion of error-free communication over the network to the TS user, the transport protocol must present the data units to its user in the correct order. The same window mechanism that allows the transport service provider to hold data units that arrive out of order while waiting for others that may have been delayed also allows handing the data units to the TS user in order. At the same time that an acknowledgment is sent for some set of data units that are now complete, those data units can be passed up to the user.

Flow Control

If a transport service provider is serving only one user and has allocated buffer space equal to the window size in a go-back-N protocol, flow control should not be a problem. The receiver has enough space available to hold all the TPDUs that could arrive before it has acknowledged receipt and handed off responsibility to the higher layers. However, if a transport server has multiple users and has allocated buffer space that is less than the combined needs of all the TS users based on estimation of the traffic rate, there is a potential for the receiver transport provider to be overwhelmed by the sender. It would be inefficient to require that every transport provider allocate the maximum amount of buffer space that could possibly be needed. The alternative is to provide a mechanism to slow down or tem-

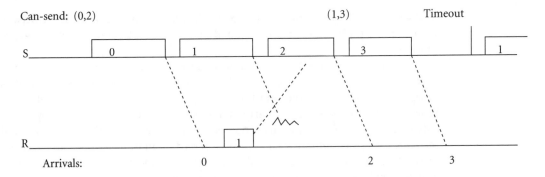

(a) Data unit 1 never arrives. The sender continues to transmit frames while awaiting acknowledgment of data unit 1. When all the data units in the can-send window have been sent, the sender waits for a time, then gives up and resends all the data units in the current window (i.e., all the data units that have not yet been acknowledged). As soon as the receiver gets data unit 1, it can send an acknowledgment requesting data unit 4.

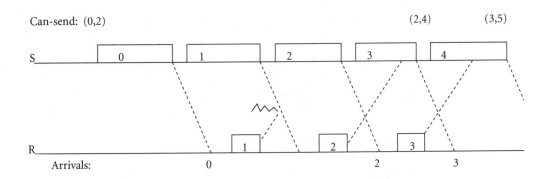

(b) Here the data units all arrive safely, but the acknowledgment of data unit 0, which requests that the sender transmit data unit 1, is lost. Since the sender does not know that the acknowledgment is lost until it sees a request for data unit 2, which implies arrival of data units up to and including data unit 1, the loss of acknowledgment 1 has no effect.

Figure 11.17. Go-back-N retransmission strategy with losses ($N = 3$)

porarily halt the flow of TPDUs over a transport connection. Since the sender's can-send window size effectively limits how far ahead of the receiver's acknowledgments the sender can get, reducing the sender's window accomplishes the desired result. When an acknowledgment arrives, it might be accompanied by a new upper limit for the sender's window. If the new upper bound is 0, the sender is required to cease transmission. The receiver can tell the sender to begin again by sending a new, nonzero, upper window value.

Slow Start and Congestion Avoidance A fairly simple system provides a degree of flow control in the network. Slow start requires the sender to begin with a very small can-send window and increment it only if the sender receives indications that the network can support more traffic. Slow start is required in TCP networks and is starting to appear in TP4 as well.

Slow start requires that the initial can-send window size of the sender be 1, regardless of the window size agreed upon with the recipient. The sender transmits one data unit (a segment for TCP) and waits until the acknowledgment returns before sending another. When the first acknowledgment arrives, the window size is incremented by 1, and two data units are sent. Each time an acknowledgment arrives safely, the size of the window is incremented by one until it reaches the size agreed upon in the connection establishment phase. Assuming that the acknowledgments continue to come for each transmitted data unit, the sender can maintain the size of the window.

When an acknowledgment does not come for a data unit, the sender must resend that data unit and any others that follow it in the send window. Clearly the sender would prefer to avoid having to retransmit more data units in the future. The philosophy behind congestion avoidance is that the most likely cause of lost packets is that the packets were dropped at a congestion point in the network. The sender responds by cutting back on the window size, slowing the transmission of new data units until there is an indication that the congestion has cleared.

When the sender detects congestion (that is, when a data unit acknowledgment fails to appear), the sender calculates a **slow start threshold value** equal to one-half of the current window size. Depending on the particular congestion indicator received (timeout with no acknowledgment or a double acknowledgment for the same packet), the sender sets the window size to the new threshold value or back to 1. When the window size is 1, the slow start algorithm is used to increase the window by one segment with each acknowledgment received. Once the window reaches the size of the threshold value, the window size increases more slowly until it reaches the window size agreed upon by the sender and the receiver.

Use of slow start and congestion avoidance allow the sender to control the rate of sending. The window size negotiated when the connection was established is the receiver's flow control mechanism. The receiver reacts to its own ability to receive and process incoming data. The sender reacts to indications of congestion in the network.

TCP and TP4

Both TCP and TP4 use go-back-N retransmission to confirm safe delivery of data units. The transport headers for TCP and for TP4 DT (data) PDU are shown in Figures 11.18 and 11.19, respectively. The acknowledgment field in the TCP header is the location in which a piggybacked sequence number is carried back to its sender. The TCP sequence numbers and ACK numbers refer to the octet number of the first octet of the data unit relative to the entire message stream. TP4 uses a separate PDU to acknowledge data: the AK PDU includes the sequence number of the next expected data unit in the field N(R).

In general, the data units received can be passed up to the higher layer as consecutive data units arrive. However, in specific cases, there may be reasons to retain the data units until some condition is met. In particular, in OSI TP4 data is given to the Transport layer by the Session layer in TSDUs. These service data units are not limited in size. (Remember, data does not have to be moved to be handed from the Session layer to the Transport layer. The TSDU most likely consists of a pointer to the beginning of the data to be transferred and a length indicator.) The sender side of the transport service provider will break the

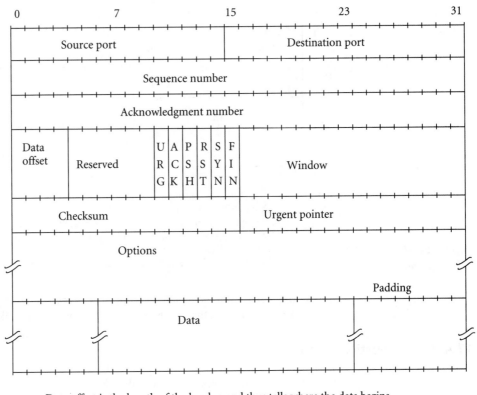

```
0              7              15              23              31
+-+-+-+-+-+-+-+-+-+-+-+-+-+-+-+-+-+-+-+-+-+-+-+-+-+-+-+-+-+-+-+-+
```

Source port	Destination port

Sequence number

Acknowledgment number

Data offset	Reserved	U R G	A C K	P S H	R S T	S Y N	F I N	Window

Checksum	Urgent pointer

Options		Padding

Data

Data offset is the length of the header, and thus tells where the data begins.
Reserved = for future use
Code bits = URG = Urgent pointer is valid and points to the location
                  of urgent (expedited data) in the PDU.
           ACK = The number in the Acknowledgment field is valid and
                  identifies the octet number expected next, relative
                  to the start of the message of which this PDU is part.
           PSH = Deliver this data immediately.
           RST = Reset sequence and acknowledgment numbers.
           SYN = Synchronize the sequence numbers to the value
                  carried in this PDU.
           FIN = End of byte stream from the sender.

Figure 11.18. TCP
header format

TSDU into pieces to be transmitted as TPDUs. (TPDU length depends upon the quality of network service available to the Transport layer.) As the TPDUs arrive, the receiver side of the transport service provider will reassemble the entire TSDU before handing it up to the Session layer.

TCP operates in a similar fashion. TCP offers a "reliable stream transport service." Data arriving from the Application layer (recall that there is no Presentation or Session layer in the TCP/IP suite of protocols) is organized into segments by TCP before transfer. Short data transfer requests will wait until the segment buffer is full before being sent. Long transfers, such as in file transfers, will be broken into segments. An optional field in the TCP header allows the application to specify that the transport service should "push" the data out with-

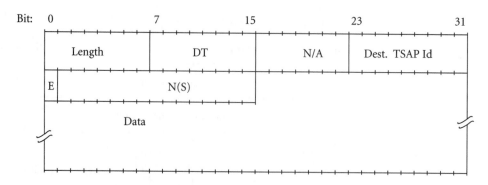

Bit: 0	7	15	23	31
Length	DT	N/A	Dest. TSAP Id	
E N(S)				
Data				

DT = Code bits designating this a DT PDU.
E = End of SPDU indicator.
N/A = Not applied here. In other PDUs (specifically, CR, CC, ACK, and RJ), this field contains the number of outstanding TPDUs the receiver can accept.
N(S) = Send sequence number.
Length = Length of the header, excluding the 4 octets of the Length itself.

Figure 11.19. TP4 DT TPDU Format

out waiting for the buffer to fill. The optional *urgent* designation allows data to bypass flow-control restrictions that might be in effect, thus behaving like the OSI expedited data.

11.4.3 Connection Release

Orderly connection release requires that both sides of the connection recognize the end of the connection, and that no data is sent by one side after the other has "hung up." This would result in loss of data, as illustrated in Figure 11.20. In the OSI Transport layer, T-DISCONNECT is an unconfirmed service. Once a TS user has issued T-DISCONNECT.request, it will not receive any further data over its transport connection. In the protocol, receipt of T-DISCONNECT.request causes the Transport-layer entity to issue a DR PDU. The Transport-layer entity that receives DR, responds by sending a DC PDU, confirming the termination of the connection. The initiating Transport-layer entity will not accept any PDUs except DC on a connection, once it has sent DR. Synchronization of the two sides of the transport connection, so that data will not be lost during the connection closing phase, is managed at the Session layer, where we saw options to require that both the data and the release token are held by the same side of the connection.

In TCP, there is no Session layer to provide synchronization between the two sides of the transport connection. TCP includes an opportunity for more data to be delivered to a TS user after the user has requested a termination of the connection. This case is illustrated in Figures 11.21 and 11.22. In Figure 11.21, the responding side has no data left to send when it is notified that the initiator has requested termination of the connection. TCP sends the CLOSING message to the user, sends an ACK PDU to acknowledge the FIN PDU indicating the connection closing, and waits for further instruction from the user. The user has no further data to send, so issues the CLOSE service request. The TCP provider sends the FIN PDU and gives the TERMINATE message to its user. In Figure 11.22, the responder TCP user still has data to send. When the TCP provider gives the user the CLOSING message, the user continues to issue requests to send data. The TCP provider sends the data and the side that initiated a CLOSE continues to accept the data that arrives. When the

TCP includes an opportunity for more data to be delivered to a TS user after the user has requested a termination of the connection.

DT
DR
DT
DR
DC
DC
DR
DT
DT
DTs
ignored
DR
DC
DC
PDUs arriving after DR is issued
are ignored, except the expected.

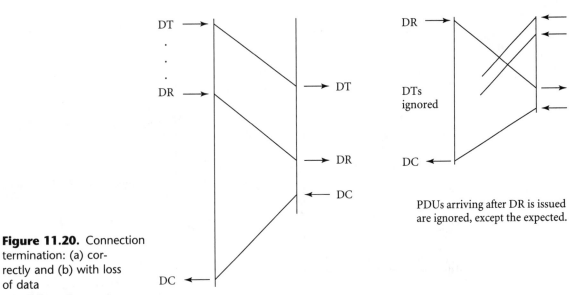

Figure 11.20. Connection termination: (a) correctly and (b) with loss of data

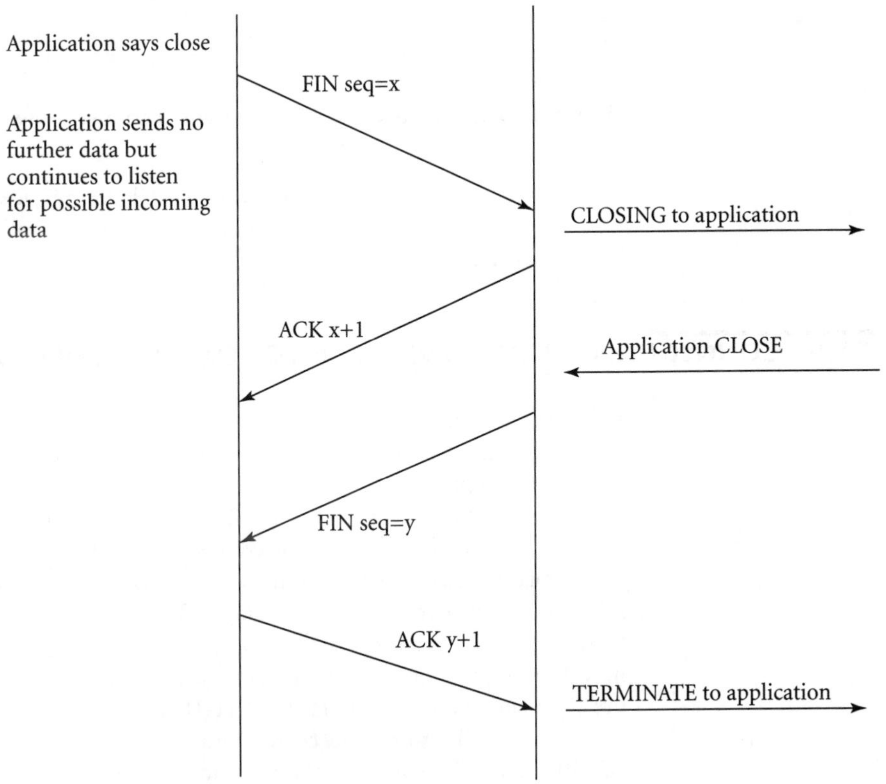

Application says close
FIN seq=x
Application sends no
further data but
continues to listen
for possible incoming
data
CLOSING to application
ACK x+1
Application CLOSE
FIN seq=y
ACK y+1
TERMINATE to application

Figure 11.21. Operation of TCP in closing a connection when no more data remains

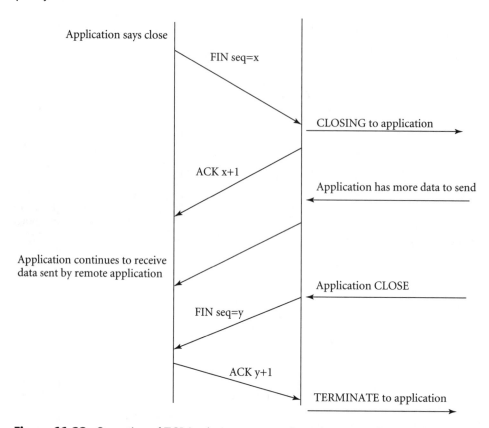

Application says close

FIN seq=x

CLOSING to application

ACK x+1

Application has more data to send

Application continues to receive
data sent by remote application

Application CLOSE

FIN seq=y

ACK y+1

TERMINATE to application

Figure 11.22. Operation of TCP in closing a connection when more data remains

responder has issued its last data, it calls the CLOSE service. The TCP provider sends the
FIN PDU, awaits an ACK PDU to confirm receipt of the data and the FIN PDU, and sends
TERMINATE to its user.

11.5 CONNECTION-ORIENTED VS. CONNECTIONLESS SERVICES

All the services described in sections 11.2 and 11.3 are connection oriented. They require a
connection establishment and a connection termination for every transfer of data between
interoperating processes.

In the OSI suite of protocols, the T-UNIT-DATA service allows data transfer between
systems without the overhead of connection establishment and termination. T-UNIT-
DATA carries the user-data obtained from S-UNIT-DATA at the Session layer and from
P-UNIT-DATA at the Presentation layer. T-UNIT-DATA, like the similar services at the
higher layers, carries user data, and also all information required to establish the type of
network service required for its delivery, and the sending and receiving addresses. Figure 11.23 shows the format of a T-UNIT-DATA data unit.

In the TCP/IP suite, the corresponding protocol is called **user datagram protocol
(UDP)**. UDP relies entirely upon the underlying services to deliver the data it carries. The

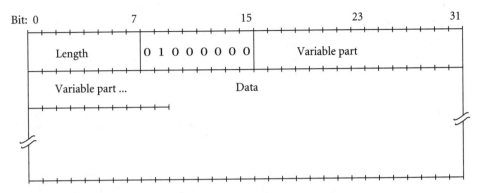

Figure 11.23. TP0 TPDU format

Length = Length of the header, excluding the Length field itself.

Variable part = Source and destination TSAP addresses and optional checksum.

01000000 identifies this as T-UNIT-DATA data unit.

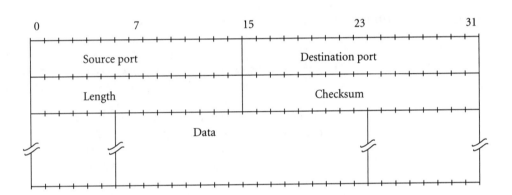

Figure 11.24. UDP header

UDP header identifies the destination process within the host identified in the network protocol. UDP provides no additional services; UDP allows the user to invoke the services of the Internet protocol (IP) without adding overhead associated with additional services. IP is a connectionless, best-effort network protocol. The UDP header appears in Figure 11.24.

11.6 APPLICATION PROGRAM INTERFACES (API)

In this section, we consider in some detail the specific tools available to invoke Transport-layer services.

The goals and operation of the Transport layer have been described in abstract terms that emphasize the approaches to addressing needs and the compromises that result when conflicting requirements appear. In this section, we consider in some detail the specific tools available to invoke Transport-layer services. We consider the X-Open interface to the OSI transport services and the UNIX interface to tcp.

Transport interfaces give access to synchronous (blocking) and asynchronous (nonblocking) modes of transport service. In the synchronous mode, a calling TS user attempts to connect to another TS user and waits (blocks) for an acceptance of its call. At the re-

T-LISTEN	the arrival of a connection request from a peer TS user
T-CONNECT	the arrival of a connection confirmation
T-DATA	arrival of normal data
T-EXDATA	arrival of expedited data
T-DISCONNECT	arrival of disconnect indication
T-ORDREL	arrival of orderly release indication
T-UDERR	(connectionless mode only) error found in previously sent datagram
T-GODATA	flow control on normal data transfer lifted; normal data transfer available
T-GOEXDATA	flow control on expedited data transfer lifted

Figure 11.25. Events that affect a transport endpoint

mote side of the connection, the called TS user attempts to connect and listens passively for a connection request to arrive. In asynchronous mode, the calling TS user attempts to connect and continues with other tasks while waiting for the connection acceptance. The called TS user requests a connection as a background process while it continues with other work.

11.6.1   X-Open Interface to OSI Transport Services

The X-Open transport interface (XTI) describes a TSAP as a transport endpoint (TEP). The TEP is established when a TS user issues a call to t-open(). The TS provider maintains state information on each TEP. Figure 11.25 lists a number of events that may affect the state of the TEP independent of any actions by the TS user.

A TS user examines the state of the TEP by using t_look(), which retrieves the events. In addition, each event has a corresponding event-clearing function. The events remain visible in the TEP state information until explicitly cleared.

Creation of a TEP requires two steps, open and bind:

t_open   obtains information about the specific transport provider the TS user intends to use. Parameters include the location of a file that describes the transport provider wanted, a set of flags describing options in the use of the transport service, and information about the TEP returned by the t_open call. The returned information has the structure shown in Figure 11.26. A call to t_open returns an integer "file descriptor" that will serve as the identification of the TEP. The call to t_open to produce the file descriptor `fd` also appears in Figure 11.26. The term `ISO_TP` identifies the transport service provider desired, `O_RDWR` selects read/write accessibility to the TEP, and a 0 supplied in the `t_info` parameter indicates that the

```
struct t_info{
    long addr;        /* max size of transport address              */
    long options;     /* max #bytes in protocol options field       */
    long tsdu;        /* max size of transport service data unit, TSDU */
    long etsdu;       /* max size of expedited sdu, ETSDU           */
    long connect;     /* max amount of user-data in T-CONNECT       */
    long discon;      /* max amount of user-data in T-DISCONNECT    */
    long servtype;    /* service type supported                     */
};
```

Figure 11.26. T_open

```
fd = t_open(ISO_TP, O_RDWR, (struct t_info *) 0)
```

t_connect request a connection to a remote TS user. If the TEP is asynchronous, return control without waiting for a response

t_rcvconnect in asynchronous mode, check status of a t_connect call sent previously

t_listen receive connection indications

Figure 11.27. TLI connection establishment

t_accept the listening TS user accepts a connection request after it receives an indication

t_snddis the listening TS user rejects a connection request

Figure 11.28. TLI data transfer

t_snd send data over a transport connection. A parameter identifies the data as normal or expedited

t_rcv receive (read) data over a transport connection

Figure 11.29. TLI disconnect

t_snddis initiate destructive disconnect
t_rcvdis obtain the reason for a destructive disconnect

Figure 11.30. TLI connectionless data transfer

t_sndudata send a datagram (unit data)

t_rcvudata receive a datagram (unit data)

t_rcvuderr retrieve error information associated with a previously sent datagram

---

user does not want to receive the `t_info` information. (These values are useful if the space for structures will be allocated and released dynamically.)

t_bind binds a transport address to the TEP and activates the TEP. The invocation of t_bind also directs the TS provider to begin accepting connection indications.

Use of t_open and t_bind establishes a TEP and makes it ready for use. Additional commands give access to the tools required in connection establishment (Figure 11.27), data transfer (Figure 11.28), and disconnect (Figure 11.29) phases of a communication.

In connectionless mode, the communication functions are limited to the instructions shown in Figure 11.30.

Figure 11.31 maps the functions provided in XTI to the familiar OSI primitives. In the figure, a connection is established, one data unit is sent, and the connection is broken.

11.6.2 UNIX Interface to TCP

We describe access to TCP through use of the Berkeley UNIX socket interface. This section will present and describe the necessary system calls and provide an example of a functioning server and client. For much more detailed treatment of the UNIX interface to network programming, see the books dedicated completely to that topic, for example, *UNIX Network Programming* by Stevens [Ste90].

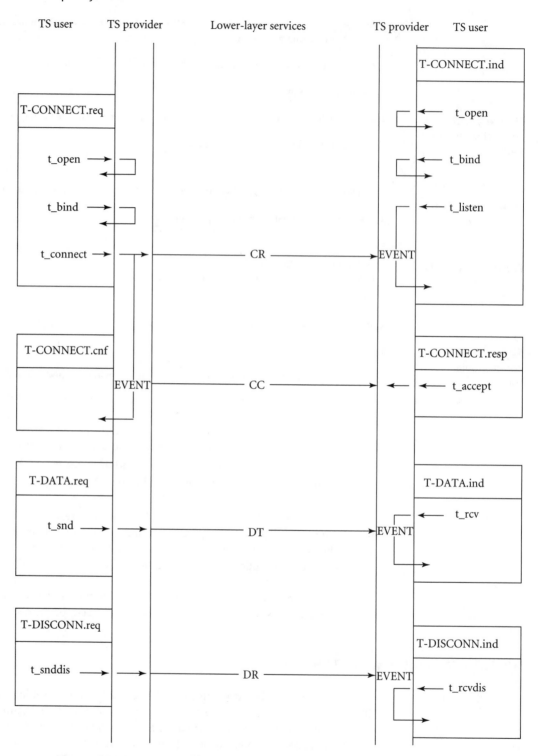

Figure 11.31. Mapping between XTI functions and OSI transport service primitives

int socket (int family, int type, int protocol)

int bind (int sfd, struct sockaddr *myaddr, int addrlen)

int connect (int sfd, struct sockaddr *servaddr, int addrlen)

int listen (int sfd, int queuelength)

int accept (int sfd, struct sockaddr *client, int *addrlen)

int send (int sfd, char *buff, int nbytes, int flags)

int recv (int sfd, char *buff, int nbytes, int flags)

int sendto (int sfd, char *buff, int nbytes, int flags,
            struct sockaddr *dst, int addrlen)

int recvfrom (int sfd, char *buff, int nbytes, int flags,
              struct sockaddr *dst, int *addrlen)

Figure 11.32.
Elementary UNIX system calls for network communication

Figure 11.32 shows the principal system calls for communicating with another process over a network using TCP. The socket through which an application reads from or writes to a network connection is similar to a file access device. Defining a socket resembles opening a file. Reading and writing involve the same parameters as reading from and writing to a file, and a few new ones related to the fact that the target is on another computer system. There are a few additional system calls as well, which we will see shortly.

The UNIX system calls provide access to a number of network services. Here we illustrate only access to TCP. The parameter AF_INET in the call to socket specifies the Address Family = Internet (TCP/IP) protocols. The parameter SOCK_STREAM in the call to socket requests TCP. Other choices for that parameter include SOCK_DGRAM, which selects UDP, and SOCK_RAW, which selects access directly to IP.

socket returns a small integer value that serves the purpose of a file descriptor. After the return from socket, the protocol has been identified and a name is assigned to the connection between the process and the network data flow. The call to bind connects the process to the socket and makes input and output on the network connection possible.

A client process uses connect to establish a connection with a particular server. In issuing the connect call, the client is doing the equivalent of CONNECT.request. As a result, the TCP protocol operation will perform its three-way handshake to establish the connection. A return from connect (equivalent to CONNECT.confirm) will occur only when the protocol operation is finished and the connection is established. A client process does not have to bind before calling connect.

The listen call allows a server to indicate that it is willing to receive connections. The parameter queuelength says how many connection requests can be queued by the system while the server processes the accept for an incoming request.

accept takes the first connection request on the input queues and creates another socket with the same properties as sfd. If no connection requests are pending, accept blocks. In client, the call returns the address of the connected client process. addrlen will contain the length of the address of the client.

The calls `send`, `sendto`, `recv`, and `recvfrom` are similar to calls to `read` and `write`. The parameter `sfd`, `*buff`, `nbytes` serve the same purpose as in those calls. `flags` may be set for special options or be set to zero. `*dst` is a pointer to the address to which the data is to be sent. `*from` is a pointer to the address from which data is coming. `addrlen` and `*addrlen` provide information on the length of the address. All four of these system calls return the length of the data as the function value.

The example in Figure 11.33 is an **iterative server**. An iterative server receives a request from a client, processes the request, and prepares to accept and service another request. A server that has many clients and provides a time-consuming service would not perform well in iterative mode. A **concurrent server** accepts a request, forks a child process to handle the request, and goes back to accepting requests.

11.7 SERVICES REQUIRED BY THE TRANSPORT LAYER

The Transport layer operates above the Network layer, shielding user processes from the operations required within the network. It provides a logical end-to-end communication independent of the complexities of underlying network activity. The amount of service provided by the Transport layer is dependent upon the type of service provided to it by the Network layer.

In the Internet, the IP protocol provides a connectionless, best-effort class of service. The approach taken in the Internet is to leave the correction and compensation effort to be done once, at the Transport layer. There is no facility to correct transmission errors, keep data units in order, detect lost data units. IP deals with addressing, routing, and revising routing information as paths become congested or fail. The two classes of transport service, UDP and TCP, allow the user to build directly on the IP service (UDP) or enhance that service to provide a virtual circuit (TCP).

SUMMARY

The Transport layer provides its users with a virtual path independent of lower-layer network services. The tasks associated with the Transport layer can be summarized as connection establishment, data transfer, and connection release. The amount of effort required at the Transport layer to provide these services is dependent upon the quality of service required by the users and the level of service provided by the Network layer.

The Internet suite of protocols provides two choices: UDP, which allows the user to access Network-layer services without the overhead of enhancement, and TCP, which provides a reliable byte stream data transfer over a network that is assumed to be not dependable. The OSI Transport layer provides a connectionless service, equivalent to the service offered by UDP, and five classes of connection-oriented service: TP0 through TP4. An appropriate match between the service requirements of the user and the quality of service provided in the network can be selected.

In the chapters that follow, we consider the services provided by the network and the choices available to the transport provider in selecting an appropriate vehicle for its users.

```
/*
 * Example of client using TCP protocol.
 */

#include <stdio.h>
#include <sys/types.h)
#include <sys/socket.h>
#include <netdb.h>
#include <netinet/in.h>
#include <sys/time.h>
#include "inet.h"




main(argc, argv)
int argc;
char *argv[];
{

 int              sockfd;
 srtuct sockaddr_in    serv_addr;
 pname = argv[0];

 /*

  * Fill in the structure "serv_addr" with the address of the
  * server that we want to connect with
  */

 bzero(char *) &serv _addr, sizeof(serv_addr));
 serv_addr.sin_family     = AF_INET;
 serv_addr.sin_addr.s_addr = inet_addr(SERV_HOST_ADDR);
 serv_addr.sin_port        =htons(SERV_TCP_PORT);

 /*
  *Open a TCP socket (an Internet stream socket).
  */

 if ((sockfd = socket (AF_INET, SOCK_STREAM, 0)) <0)
             err_sys("client: cannot open stream socket");

 /*
  * Connect to the server.
  */

 if (connect(sockfd, (Struct sockaddr *) &serv_addr, sizeof(serv_addr))<0)
     err_sys(Client: cannot connect to server");
 str_cli(stdin, sockfd);
 close(sockfd);
 exit(0);

 }
```

Figure 11.33. UNIX access to TCP example

EXERCISES

1. Consider the go-back-N protocol of section 11.4.2. What is the relationship between the range of sequence numbers possible in the transport header and the size of the can-send window? (Can the window be larger than the range of sequence numbers allowed? Can it be smaller? Must both be the same?)

2. The initial sequence number used in a TCP SYN PDU or a TP4 SRC-REF must be absolutely unique among any possibly still existing sequence numbers from that system in order to guard against the emergence of an old duplicate connection request that could lead to a badly formed connection. What is the significance, if any, of the standards process in determining how the sequence number is formed?

3. Using the material of Exercise 2 as an example, discuss the difference between local implementation decisions and standards conformance.

4. Explain how the sender and the receiver sides of a transport connection control the rate at which packets move between them.

5. (Programming Exercise) Write a program to establish a connection with the ECHO server on a remote Internet host, send a stream of characters, receive the echo in response, and display the echo. Modify your program to display the time elapsed from when the stream of characters is sent until the response is received. Allow the user of your program to specify what host to connect to. Run the program repeatedly, and note the difference in time of response by hosts in locations near you and in very remote locations.

6. (Programming Exercise) In Figure 11.5, well-known port number 13 is associated with the DAYTIME server. When a connection is made to that port number, the server responds with date and time information intended for use by humans (that is, not requiring further processing before being presented to human readers). The information comes as an ASCII string. No specific format is required. Well-known port 37 is used for the TIME protocol. When a connection is made to that port, the server returns a 32-bit binary number, in network byte order (most significant bit first), giving the number of seconds since January 1, 1900 GMT.
    (a) Using one of these servers, establish a connection and get the date and time at the server. (Which service provides the needed information?)
    (b) Use the results of (a) to query servers in many locations around the world regarding the current local date and time. Develop an application that accepts a remote host id and calculates the time difference between the client site (your machine) and the server site.

7. Implement a service that listens for a transport request, identifies the service desired from a list of services available, wakes up the process that provides the service, binds the client to the requested server, and returns to listening for requests.

8. What advantages would the service described in Exercise 7 have over having each possible service listening for incoming connection requests?

CHAPTER 12

Network Layer

KEY CONCEPTS
- Addressing
- Routing
- Firewalls
- Services Provided by the Network Layer

The Network layer is responsible for delivering a packet from the source machine to its final destination, through whatever intervening machines and networks are necessary. To accomplish this, the Network layer must know about the topology of the communications subnet in order to choose a path, must distribute traffic to avoid congestion, and must deal with differences of network types.

Until now, when we referred to an address, such as the *called presentation address* or the *called session address*, we were designating one process among possibly many processes running in a particular open system (machine). These addresses are often called *selectors* because they are used to select one process from among a small number that could receive an incoming data unit.

At the Network layer, the significance of the address is different. Now we mean a particular machine on which the process is running (in addition to the selection of process). This change matters considerably. For one thing, there are many more machines to choose from than there are processes within a single system. For another, the machines belong to many different people and many different organizations. The machines are connected to different types of networks, with different addressing conventions. The task of uniquely identifying and designating each of these machines is a tremendous challenge. In section 12.1, we consider this task and the approaches taken in OSI and in the Internet to solve these inherent problems.

Providing a unique identifier for each machine accessible through networks is only the first step in connectivity. Somehow, each machine must have a way to reach each other machine reliably and efficiently. This part of Network-layer responsibility, known as **routing**, is treated in section 12.2. Because **firewalls** use either a gateway, an Application-layer service, or a routing filter, a Network-layer service, we discuss them in this chapter, in section 12.3.

Users access the services of the Network layer at the boundary between the Transport and Network layers. In section 12.4, we describe the connection-oriented network services of OSI and the connectionless network services of TCP/IP and OSI.

12.1 ADDRESSING

There are three aspects to the identity of a particular machine: a name that should be easily readable by humans, an address that uniquely identifies it and its location, and a detailed route to the machine from any other machine. That is, we can specify a particular machine by *what it is, where it is*, and *how to get to it* [Sch78].

12.1.1 Internet Addresses

Typical machine names in the Internet are *tiger.villanova.edu* and *cs.umd.edu*. These names are registered with the Network Information Center (NIC) and have assigned Internet-style addresses. The NIC is the central authority charged with allocating a unique address to each host interface to the Internet. Internet addresses comprise a network address and a host address. The NIC accepts requests for addresses and assigns a network address. Individual host addresses are assigned by the network administrator from the block of host addresses associated with a particular network address.

The need for an address is inherent in the fact that what is good for human readability and processing is not what is good for machine readability and processing. Specifically, names can vary in length (the parts of the names, set off by dots, vary in both length and number), are sometimes written with uppercase letters and sometimes with lowercase letters, and may even have local aliases. For example, tiger.villanova.edu is known as just tiger on its local network. Machine processing is faster and more accurate if the name it receives is always in the same format, has the same parts in the same places, and is always the same size.

In the Internet, 32-bit addresses have distinguished individual network interfaces from the beginning. This scheme has finally become insufficient, due to the unforseen (and unforseeable) growth of the Internet. The designers of these addresses cannot be blamed for not anticipating the emergence not only of personal computers but of many types of devices requiring Internet addresses.

We begin with a description of the long-standing 32-bit addresses still dominating the Internet. We follow with a description of the new addressing scheme expected to replace this one over a period of transition.

For flexibility in accommodating the many different types of networks that make up the Internet, the initial 32-bit addresses are divided into classes. Each class is distinguished by the location of the first 0 bit in the addresses of that class.

Figure 12.1 shows the form of the address classes. Each address consists of two parts: a network part and a host part. The network part defines the network to which a device is connected. The host part identifies the particular network connection of a device, which may be a computer, a printer, a personal digital assistant (PDA), or any device that can communicate over a network. Some addresses have special significance: an address of all 1s

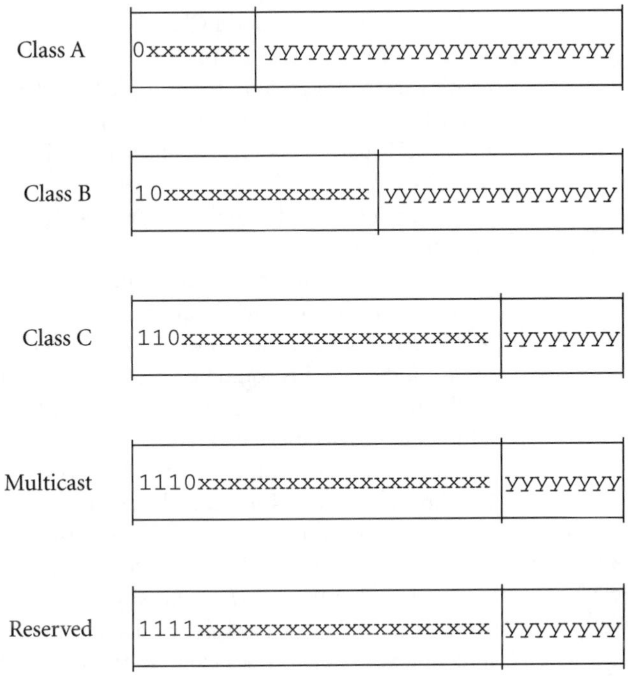

Figure 12.1. Internet address formats

means broadcast to all entities in this domain; an address of all 0s means this device itself. The special meaning of all 1s and all 0s removes two potential addresses from the set of addresses possible in each of the configurations.

Class A consists of addresses that have a zero in bit position 0. The next 7 bits constitute the net ID, and the remaining 24 bits form the host ID. Thus, Class A networks allow up to $2^{24} - 2$ hosts on each of $2^7 - 2$ networks. Class B network addresses have their first 0 in bit position 1. Bits 2 through 15 are the net ID, and bits 16 through 31 are the host ID. Class B networks, therefore, permit up to $2^{16} - 2$ hosts on each of $2^{14} - 2$ networks. Class C addresses have their first 0 in position 2. Bits 3 through 23 contain the net ID, and bits 24 through 31 contain the host ID. Thus, class C networks allow up to $2^8 - 2$ hosts on each of $2^{21} - 2$ networks. Addresses that begin with 1110 are multicast addresses; they indicate a destination that is a group of end systems (hosts). Addresses beginning with 1111 are reserved.

The 32-bit addresses used in the Internet are commonly represented in the **dotted decimal notation**. Each octet of the address is represented in decimal digits, a value in the range 000 to 255. Class A networks have addresses with first octet value between 000 and 127. A complete Class A address is of the form 000.x.y.z to 127.x.y.z, where the x, y, and z together form the host address within a network. Class B networks have net IDs written as 128.000.y.z to 191.255.y.z. Class C networks are in the range 192.000.000.z to 223.255.255.z.

Further subdivision of the host ID part of an address into a subnet ID and a host ID allows multiple networks within an organization to appear as a single network to the Internet as a whole. Thus, a network of workstations in an office or laboratory does not have to consume an Internet-wide net ID. Instead, it will share the net ID of all the networks within an organization and will have a subnet ID unique within the organization.

For example, consider a Class B network, belonging to a large city government. There are $2^{16} - 2$ host IDs available for assignment by the network administrator. The network administrator assigns bits 16 through 24 to designate subnets. The address structure is now in the form NNN.NNN.SSS.HHH in dotted decimal representation, with N designating the network ID part, S designating the subnet ID part, and H the host ID part. The department of parks and recreation, given subnet ID 001, can support up to $2^8 - 2 = 254$ hosts attached to the city network. The police department, given subnet ID 010 through 110, can support 1270 individual hosts.

Other subnets are assigned to other departments according to their need. Control of subnet host ID assignment can be delegated in any departments that have staff assigned to computer support activities. Where such departmental support is not available, assignments of the host ids could be done by the organization's network administrator.

Because the network ID is combined with a host ID to provide an address, the Internet address actually describes a connection between a host and a network, rather than just the host. That means that when a host is connected to more than one network, it must have more than one Internet address. It also means that when an address is specified for a machine, the address also determines the particular network connection to be used in reaching the machine. Thus, the address affects the route by which the machine is reached.

The fact that the net ID can easily be extracted from an Internet address is very useful. To reach a particular machine from a remote network, it is necessary to reach a network interconnection machine attached to the same network as the destination machine. Internet routing algorithms must deal with the network part of an address only, continuing to pass a packet toward a network interconnection device that is attached to the same network as the destination machine.

> To reach a particular machine from a remote network, it is necessary to reach a network interconnection machine attached to the same network as the destination machine.

12.1.2 IPv6 Addressing

The Internet has grown to a size that could not have been foreseen by its creators. There are two aspects to this problem. First, the number of Class A and Class B addresses is limited, and the demand is growing. Though there are many more Class C network addresses, these too are limited and will eventually be depleted. Projections of when the end will come vary, but it is near enough to cause serious concern. The second aspect of the problem has to do with the number of network addresses that must be recognized in each router. There are too many potential addresses to permit fast, efficient operation of the routers.

IP version 6 (IPv6) began life as IPng (IP next generation). It was approved by the Internet Engineering Steering Group in November 1994 and became a proposed standard. IPv6 is the successor to the current IP version 4 (IPv4). One of the challenges involved in revising IP and its address scheme is the sheer magnitude of the task of replacing IP in all the machines of the Internet. A transition plan must accommodate a lengthy changeover. A clear lesson from the current situation is to plan for growth that cannot be imagined. Hence, there must be a transition plan that allows a lengthy changeover, and there must be the ability to grow with the addition of new types of devices to appear on the Internet. Internet nodes that move about are already common, and their presence will increase as the devices become cheaper and smaller and more integrated into daily life. Other sources of new nodes for the Internet come from the entertainment industry, where video on demand and digital high-definition television will increase demand for network connectivity. Device controllers that will allow consumers to turn on their lights and start the music playing or to adjust the heat or air-conditioning level from the office will further fuel the need for network addresses. IPv6 intends to meet these needs and others we cannot yet imagine.

Figure 12.2 displays the header format for IPv6 packets [Hin95].

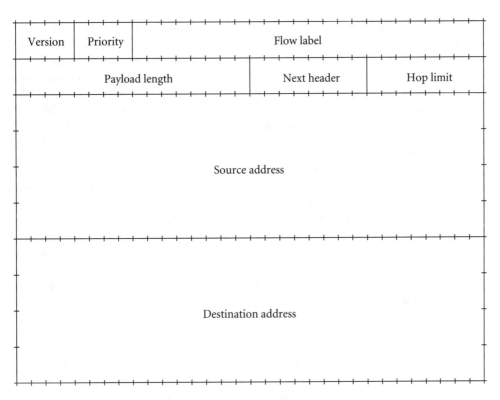

Version	4-bit Internet Protocol version number = 6.
Priority	4-bit Priority value.
Flow label	24-bit field.
Payload length	16-bit unsigned integer. Length of payload, i.e., the rest of the packet following the IPng header, in octets.
Next header	8-bit selector. Identifies the type of header immediately following the IPng header. Uses the same values as the IPv4 Protocol field.
Hop limit	8-bit unsigned integer. Decremented by 1 by each node that forwards the packet. The packet is discarded if Hop Limit is decremented to zero.
Source address	128 bits. The address of the initial sender of the packet.
Destination address	128 bits. The address of the intended recipient of the packet (possibly not the ultimate recipient, if an optional Routing Header is present).

Figure 12.2. IPv6 header format

The 2^{128} potential addresses of IPv6 comes to approximately 665,570,793,348,866,943, 898,599 addresses per square meter of the Earth's surface [Hin95]. Though the number of addresses probably meets the need for expansion, it presents an intimidating task for devices that must distinguish among network interfaces represented by the addresses. Some type of hierarchy is clearly called for.

The leading bits of an IPv6 address, a variable-length field called the format prefix (FP), determine its place in the hierarchy. Addresses fall into one of three basic types: unicast, anycast, or multicast. A **unicast address** identifies a single host interface and is used for point-to-point communication. An **anycast address** identifies a group of host interfaces, one of which is to receive the communication. The interface selected will be the closest one by some measure used in routing. A **multicast address** refers to a group of interfaces, all of which are to receive the communication. There is no broadcast address type in IPv6. In the initial allocation of addresses, approximately 85 percent of the potential addresses are unassigned, leaving significant room for future use. Figure 12.3 shows the initial allocation of prefixes and the fraction of address space allocated to each type of IPv6 address [Hin95].

Address space reserved for NSAP (ISO addresses) and IPX allow IPv6 to accommodate other types of network addressing schemes and facilitates interoperation. Provider-based unicast addresses provide a hierarchical scheme based on registration authorities, providers, subscribers, subnets, and interface identification. The scheme builds on the experience in IPv4 of classless interdomain routing (CIDR), which was developed to reduce the burden on routers as the number of Internet network IDs became burdensome.

Local use addresses have meaning within a very restricted domain. The format of the local use address includes the format prefix shown in Figure 12.3 and an identifier of a specific network interface. In many cases, that address is the IEEE 802 48-bit address. Link local use addresses have no other fields and are valid only on a particular link (local area network, for example, an Ethernet LAN). Site local use addresses also have a subnet field and have validity through a collection of LANs at a site. An organization can therefore have a rather extensive network environment addressed with interface identifiers and subnet identifiers. This allows an organization to have locally assigned Internet addresses without involving the Internet registration overhead. Since the addresses have only local significance and there is no connection to the global Internet, the assignment of the field values is under local control. If the organization later connects to the Internet, the addresses are made globally unique through the assignment of registration authority, provider, and subscriber information.

Multicast addresses identify a group of interfaces to which a message will be delivered. The group may be permanent or transient. A given interface may belong to more than one group. Transient multicast addresses are useful for such things as online conferences. Each conference participant sends transmissions to the group, and the message is received by each other participant. When the conference ends, the group is dissolved. Permanent multicast groups might identify the members of a team with long-term shared responsibility for a specific activity.

The flexibility attempted in designing the address space for IPv6 intends to make this addressing scheme last for the foreseeable future. Of particular importance is the attempt to allow for transition from IPv4 to IPv6 and future transition from what has been defined for IPv6 to what may be needed as new applications of the Internet appear.

Allocation	Prefix (binary)	Fraction of Address Space
Reserved	0000 0000	1/256
Unassigned	0000 0001	1/256
Reserved for NSAP allocation	0000 001	1/128
Reserved for IPX allocation	0000 010	1/128
Unassigned	0000 011	1/128
Unassigned	0000 1	1/32
Unassigned	0001	1/16
Unassigned	001	1/8
Provider-based unicast address	010	1/8
Unassigned	011	1/8
Reserved for neutral-interconnect-based unicast addresses	100	1/8
Unassigned	101	1/8
Unassigned	110	1/8
Unassigned	1110	1/16
Unassigned	1111 0	1/32
Unassigned	1111 10	1/64
Unassigned	1111 110	1/128
Unassigned	1111 1110 0	1/512
Link local use addresses	1111 1110 10	1/1024
Site local use addresses	1111 1110 11	1/1024
Multicast addresses	1111 1111	1/256

Figure 12.3. Initial allocation of IPv6 address types and the format prefix of each type

12.1.3 OSI Addresses

The Network-layer addressing scheme used in OSI is a compromise that reflects the existence of a number of existing schemes and corresponding administrative authorities, all of which could make a strong case for their use in the OSI network. The scheme has the flexibility to support a large number of address formats and the ability to define extremely large networks.

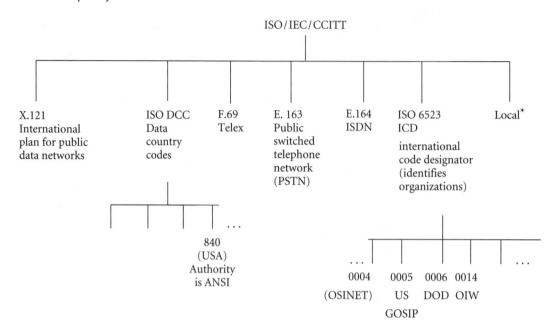

*Global registration not required, but local registration is needed to assure unique addresses within the local environment.

Figure 12.4. ISO address domains

The specification of network address formats and values is delegated in a hierarchical scheme illustrated in Figure 12.4. The structure of an NSAP address is shown in Figure 12.5. The address consists of two parts: an **initial domain part (IDP)**, which describes the kind of address it is, and a **domain specific part (DSP)**, which may provide further address information. The IDP is further divided into two parts: an **authority and format identifier (AFI)** and an **initial domain identifier (IDI)**. The AFI is a two-digit, binary-coded decimal value assigned by ISO and CCITT. The particular value used indicates which authority assigned the address (that is, which of the branches from the root of the global addressing hierarchy) and what format (decimal, binary, character, or national character set) is used in the address. The AFI values and their meanings are shown in Figure 12.6.

Let's look at some examples of the IDP. The AFI is determined by assignment. An ordinary telephone number, for example, will have AFI = 42 or 43. If the AFI is 42, the telephone number is written in decimal numbers (each decimal digit coded as a 4-bit binary number). If the AFI is 43, the telephone number is written as a binary value. The second part of the IDP is assigned by the agency given authority over that set of numbers. In the

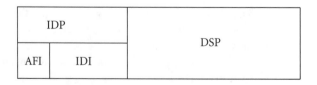

Figure 12.5. OSI address format

AFI	Format	Authority
36	Decimal	X.121
37	Binary	(Public data networks)
38	Decimal	ISO DCC
39	Binary	(Data country codes)
40	Decimal	F.69
41	Binary	(Telex)
42	Decimal	E.163
43	Binary	(PSTN)
44	Decimal	E.164
45	Binary	(ISDN)
46	Decimal	ISO 6523
47	Binary	(ICD — organizations)
48	Decimal	
49	Binary	Local
50	Character	
51	National character set	

Figure 12.6. Authority and format identifiers

case of telephone numbers, the controlling agreement is the public switched telephone network (PSTN). In the PSTN address design, the phone number appears in the IDI part of the IDP. There is no use of the DSP at all. Figure 12.7 contains an example. The phone number shown is in the familiar format: country code (1 = US), U.S. area code (410), local exchange (555), individual phone (1234). Phone numbers in other countries have slightly different formats but the same basic structure. Incorporating this well-established addressing scheme into its addressing format is a practical step in OSI address design.

Other examples of address formats are shown in Figure 12.8. In each case, the format of the OSI address allows an address to be used even if the address was not designed for computer networking. The scheme is flexible, gives many separate organizations control over the kinds of addresses they use, and scales to allow virtually unlimited growth in the number of devices that must be addressable.

The content of the IDI and DSP depends upon the authority that assigns its values. Some authorities subdivide their domains into subdomains, which may further subdivide the domain. The limit of 20 octets in the entire address and the use of the first octet to designate the AFI are the only restrictions imposed by the OSI standard. Thus, "OSI addresses" can look very different from each other, as the examples in Figure 12.8 indicate.

The format :

IDP		DSP
AFI	IDI	
42	1 410 555 1234	

Sample value :

Figure 12.7. OSI PSTN address example

a) AFI = 36 :   X.121   address, decimal format

AFI	IDI	DSP
36	496584511200	1

b) AFI = 39 :   ISO DCC address, binary format
IDI = 840 :   Country = US, whose address authority is ANSI.
DSP is defined by ANSI

AFI	IDI	DSP						
		DFI	org	res	rd	area	system	selector
39	840	DFI	org	res	rd	area	system	selector
	(US)	1	3	2	2	2	6	1

(number of octets used for each subfield)

DFI = DSP format identifier (version of the ANSI
            standard in use.   1000 0000 = 1992   version)
org = organization that assigned this address value
res = reserved for future use
rd = routing domain
area = area within a routing domain
system = specific end station
selector = selected network layer entity

c) AFI = 47 :   ISO 6523   International Code Designator for organizations
            binary format
IDI = 0005 :   US GOSIP   DSP defined by USGOSIP

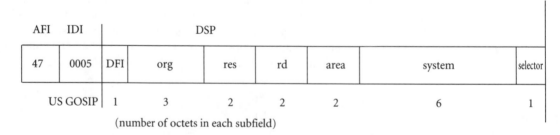

AFI	IDI	DSP						
47	0005	DFI	org	res	rd	area	system	selector
	US GOSIP	1	3	2	2	2	6	1

(number of octets in each subfield)

AAI = Administrative authority identity; equivalent to org in ISO DCC US example. Other fields have the same meaning as in the ISO DCC US example.

Figure 12.8. OSI address examples

The flexibility in forming OSI addresses allows the needs of each environment to be addressed directly. It is not surprising that an address based on X.121 and intended to support connection-oriented communication looks a lot like a phone number used in the PSTN. It is also not surprising that these look different from addresses intended to support connectionless data communication and the necessary routing functions these involve. Both the IDI 39-840 and the 47-0005 examples include a routing domain, an area, and an end system designation in the address. We will see the significance of these fields as we look at the routing function of the Network layer.

12.2   ROUTING

The Network layer, upon receiving a network service data unit (NSDU), delivers it to the intended destination anywhere in the world. Since it is not reasonable to expect every network service provider to know the location of every possible destination site, some technique is needed to move the NSDU toward its destination, with only limited information available. The process is called **routing**.

12.2.1   Routing Techniques

Routing is a procedure for moving packets from a source to a destination in an efficient and reliable way. Routing can be accomplished in several ways. One technique is **centralized routing**. Centralized routing requires some entity to have complete knowledge of the destinations available in a network. It could be constructed to be an active participant in all routing activities—every host sends every message to the central router, which in turn sends the message to its destination. This approach is feasible in a small network, where routing is one function of an active hub. It quickly becomes infeasible, however, when the network is very large.

Another way to use a central routing facility is to have it send copies of routing information to every other participant in the network. This allows every routing decision to be based on the same information. There are some problems associated with this approach in very large networks. One problem is that the need to send information to every site in the network is a heavy burden to place on the one station on which every other depends. Congestion in the vicinity of the central routing node could become a serious problem in the network operation. Further, if the central node fails, all routing information exchange is lost.

Two types of routing are needed: each node must have a way to reach other nodes in the same "area," nodes that might be considered local or part of a common environment; each node must also be able to start a NPDU on a path toward a node outside its own network.

A more practical approach to the routing problem is to have the routing process distributed among the nodes in the network. To see how this is accomplished, we need to consider the architecture of the environment in which the routing process occurs. An internet is a collection of interconnected networks. Two types of routing are needed: each node must have a way to reach other nodes in the same "area," nodes that might be considered local or part of a common environment; each node must also be able to start a NPDU on a path toward a node outside its own network. Nodes that are connected to more than one network and are thus able to participate in routing are called **routers**.

Different types of routing are required to meet the needs of different parts of the internet architecture. In both OSI and TCP/IP networks, there are three levels of routing: routing from an end system (ES) to another ES or to an intermediate system (IS), routing between ISs in the same administrative domain, and routing between ISs in different administrative domains.

12.2.2 Discovery

An end system does not participate in routing, except to provide data units for delivery to another end system. To do this effectively, the end system must know what other system receives its data unit. If the destination end system is directly connected (part of the same local area network or metropolitan area network), the source end system should send the data unit directly to the destination. If more than one IS is available to the source, a choice must be made. Similarly, the ES must be known to other ESs in the local environment and to connected ISs that receive data units from outside the local environment destined for the given ES. To "know and be known," the ES participates in a process of discovery.

There are two basic approaches to the discovery process. One is practiced in OSI networks, the other in TCP/IP networks. In the OSI approach, each end system periodically sends a message called ESH (end system hello). Each connected intermediate system learns of the existence of the end system and its physical address on the network. (Other end systems may also listen for ESH messages and record the location of attached end systems.) The TCP/IP approach to the discovery process is based upon request/reply communication. When an IP process receives a data unit from TCP for delivery, it first searches a table to find the physical address associated with the given IP address. If the IP address is not in the table, the address resolution protocol (ARP) is used. An ARP packet is constructed with the IP address for which a physical address is needed. The ARP packet is broadcast to all systems in the local environment, and every station receives the ARP packet. If one of the stations recognizes its own IP address, it sends a response with its physical address.

The two techniques are different, but the result is basically the same. Nodes on a network learn what other nodes are reachable on the network and announce their own presence. In the OSI approach, ESH messages are broadcast periodically. The periodic repetition of the message allows the other nodes to learn that a node has failed or moved by detecting the absence of the expected hello. A new IS or one that has failed and recovered learns about reachable hosts within a preset amount of time, without having to send queries. In the TCP/IP approach, an ES that is well behaved and has not moved does not have to send messages repeatedly to allow others to know it is still there.

12.2.3 IS to IS Routing

End systems must learn about the ISs that are available to carry data units out of the local environment. ISs announce their presence by sending an ISH (intermediate system hello). The message is received by all connected end systems and by other ISs. The ISs will use the information in establishing IS to IS routing.

There are two forms of IS to IS routing. ISs within a single administrative domain have the advantage of shared administration, and generally a level of trust and cooperation that can be assumed. ISs of separate administrative domains must deal with the same technical concerns as ISs of one administrative domain but also face complications of border problems: authorization to pass the boundary, security concerns, and cost allocation.

IS to IS routing within an administrative domain is **intradomain routing**. An administrative domain consists of one or more routing domains. Within a routing domain, the same routing protocol, algorithm, and cost metrics are used. The primary concern of intradomain routing is finding the best route to use. Issues include the cost of exchanging information for making routing decisions and the cost of sending data along a chosen route. IS to IS routing across the boundaries of administrative domains is **interdomain routing**.

Two families of routing protocols exist: **distance vector** and **link state**. Here we consider the principles of operation of each.

Distance Vector Routing

In the **distance vector routing** approach to distributed routing, each node maintains the distance from itself to each possible destination and the best link to use as the first step toward the destination. The node builds a routing table by regularly exchanging information with its immediate neighbors:

1. Each node enters its own identity into the routing table, with the distance to itself set to 0.
2. Each node knows all the connections it has and can learn the identity of the node at the other end of each connection. The node enters into the routing table the identity of and distance to each neighbor, along with the identity of the connection to use. The "distance" could be measured in terms of delay involved in reaching the neighbor or in some other measure of cost, perhaps a tariff for using that connection. Clearly, all costs must be measured in the same units for any comparisons to be meaningful; however, a number of different measurements are meaningful.
3. Each node exchanges information with its immediate neighbors, and thereby learns of the nodes adjacent to each neighbor. The node adds the cost of reaching the neighbor to the cost of getting from the neighbor to each of its neighbors. If the result is a lower cost than some destination that the node had known about previously, that information replaces what was in the routing table about reaching that destination.

The process of learning about neighbors and exchanging information about neighbors is repeated regularly. It is all that is needed to have each node in the network learn the least cost path to each other node. For example, consider the network shown in Figure 12.9. Ini-

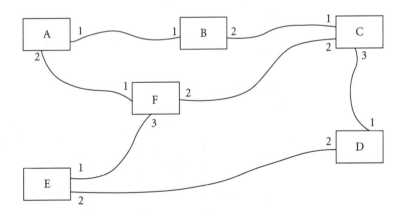

Figure 12.9. A network routing example

tially, each node knows itself and its immediate neighbors. In the tables held by each node and shown next, D = destination, L = link to use to reach the destination, and C = cost of reaching the destination. In this example, we have equated the cost of reaching a node to the number of hops needed to reach it. In actuality, a different cost could be associated with each link. An implication of using cost = hops is that the paths discovered early in the routing process will never be replaced with other paths discovered later. Exercise 5 illustrates the effects of different cost allocations on routing.

In the example, each node initially stores a cost of 0 for reaching itself, and a cost of 1 for reaching any immediate neighbors.

Node A			Node B			Node C			Node D			Node E			Node F		
D	L	C	D	L	C	D	L	C	D	L	C	D	L	C	D	L	C
A		0	A	1	1	B	1	1	C	1	1	E		0	A	1	1
B	1	1	B		0	C		0	D		0	D	2	1	C	2	1
F	2	1	C	2	1	D	3	1	E	2	1	F	1	1	E	3	1
						F	2	1							F		0

After one exchange of information between neighbors, each node has the table listed next. (We assume that information is processed in alphabetical order by the name of the node, and when a newly found cost is equal to the one already known, no change is made in the node's table (routing table).) For example, A receives the tables of B and F, and learns of node E (reachable through F) and node C (reachable through either B or F). Since the paths from A to C are the same length, our assumption about alphabetical processing means that A will learn of the path through B first and will not change the path when it learns of the path through F. The new routing tables after this iteration appear next.

Node A			Node B			Node C			Node D			Node E			Node F		
D	L	C	D	L	C	D	L	C	D	L	C	D	L	C	D	L	C
A		0	A	1	1	A	1	2	B	1	2	A	1	2	A	1	1
B	1	1	B		0	B	1	1	C	1	1	C	2	2	B	1	2
C	1	2	C	2	1	C		0	D		0	D	2	1	C	2	1
E	2	2	D	2	2	D	3	1	E	2	1	E		0	D	2	2
F	2	1	F	1	2	E	2	2	F	2	2	F	1	1	E	3	1
						F	2	1							F		0

Nodes C and F now have complete tables. After one more iteration, all the tables are complete.

Node A			Node B			Node C			Node D			Node E			Node F		
D	L	C	D	L	C	D	L	C	D	L	C	D	L	C	D	L	C
A		0	A	1	1	A	1	2	A	1	3	A	1	2	A	1	1
B	1	1	B		0	B	1	1	B	1	2	B	2	3	B	1	2
C	1	2	C	2	1	C		0	C	1	1	C	2	2	C	2	1
D	1	3	D	2	2	D	3	1	D		0	D	2	1	D	2	2
E	2	2	E	1	3	E	2	2	E	2	1	E		0	E	3	1
F	2	1	F	1	2	F	2	1	F	2	2	F	1	1	F		0

If a node fails, its neighbors note the absence of the hello messages usually exchanged and assign a high value to the cost of reaching that node. The new information propagates through the network, and the routing tables are updated.

Distance vector routing works and is simple to implement. In a large network, however, it converges slowly, and there are particular configurations where the algorithm behaves very poorly in the face of node failures, as illustrated in Exercise 3.

Link State Routing

Link state routing is a technique whereby each node obtains and retains the information as to the distance from every node to each of its neighbors. Note the difference from distance vector routing, where each node obtained each of its neighbors' knowledge of other reachable nodes and the cost of reaching each one. In the distance vector example, node A learns that node F is reachable in three hops using connection number 1. However, node A does not learn what other nodes the path from itself to F includes, nor what nodes are adjacent to F.

In link state routing, each node obtains the connections and costs of connections between every pair of nodes in the graph. In an interconnected network, this means that every router knows the identity of every other router and the complete set of connections between routers, as well as the costs of those connections. This information is obtained by having each router send a message containing its connections and their costs to each other router. This information is updated and resent on a regular basis so that changes in network topology are soon known to all the routers. Complete details of the propagation of this information are beyond the scope of this book. A thorough discussion can be found in Radia Perlman's book on the subject of network connections [Per92].

Once it knows all the connections in the internet, a router can discover the best route from itself to any other router (and thus to the end nodes on the network where the destination router is connected) by an algorithm such as the Dijkstra shortest-path-first graph traversal. The algorithm is illustrated here for the network of Figure 12.9.

We produce the routing table for node D. A similar process occurs independently at each of the other nodes also. First, D places into its routing data its own identity and the special information that it is accessed by no connection and at a cost of zero.

Destination	Connection	Cost	Status
D	0	0	

Next, D examines its own link state data, which shows what other nodes are directly attached and the connection to use to reach each. These are placed into the routing data table with status = tentative (T). The resulting routing data is as follows:

Destination	Connection	Cost	Status
D	0	0	
C	1	1	T
E	2	1	T

Next, the algorithm examines the entries marked with status T and finds the one with lowest cost. Since we are using hop count for cost, both the neighbors of D have a cost of 1, and either could be used. We select the first to appear in the table, the entry for neighbor C. The algorithm now looks at the link state data for node C, which shows that the neighbors of C are B, F, and D with costs all equal to 1 since hop count is used for cost and all are neighbors of C. For each of C's neighbors, the algorithm computes the cost of reaching that node by adding the cost of getting to C to the cost of getting to C's neighbors. The cost of getting from D to C is 1, and the cost of getting from C to each neighbor is 1. Thus D can reach B, F, and D at a cost of 2. B and F do not exist in D's routing data, so the cost of 2 is the best-known cost of reaching these nodes. They will be entered into D's routing data table. The cost of getting to D through C is 2, which is clearly greater than the cost of getting to D found in the table, so the new path will not be used. The new routing data table for D is as follows:

Destination	Connection	Cost	Status
D	0	0	
C	1	1	
E	2	1	T
B	1	2	T
F	1	2	T

The entry for C is no longer tentative since its information has been fully incorporated into the routing data.

The process is repeated, taking the next tentative entry with smallest cost and using the link state data associated with that node. When the link state data of a node is used, the node entry is no longer tentative. When there are no more tentative entries in the routing data, the table is complete and the process stops. The following tables show the successive iterations of the algorithm.

The entry for E is tentative and has a cost of 1. Thus the link state data for E is used next. E's neighbors are F and D. Each of these can be reached by the cost of getting to E (1) plus the cost of getting from E to its neighbor (1) for a total cost of 2. This is no improvement on the cost of reaching either D or F, so no new entry is added to the routing data. However, the entry for E is no longer tentative.

Destination	Connection	Cost	Status
D	0	0	
C	1	1	
E	2	1	
B	1	2	T
F	1	2	T

The neighbors of B are A and C. Each is reached by the cost of reaching B (2) plus the cost of getting from B to its neighbors (1), for a total cost of 3. We have a less costly path to C, but the path to A is the first we have discovered. It is added to the routing data, and the entry for B is no longer tentative:

Destination	Connection	Cost	Status
D	0	0	
C	1	1	
E	2	1	
B	1	2	
F	1	2	T
A	1	3	T

Next, the entry for F causes us to consider the link state data of F. The neighbors of F are A, C, and E. Each is reachable at the cost of reaching F (2) plus the cost of getting from F to its neighbors (1) for a total cost of 3 for reaching A, C, or E. All those destinations are known and at cost that is no higher than 3. Thus, the information from the link state data of F will not be incorporated into the table, and the entry for F will no longer be tentative:

Destination	Connection	Cost	Status
D	0	0	
C	1	1	
E	2	1	
B	1	2	
F	1	2	
A	1	3	T

Finally, the link state data for node A is considered. We obtain no new nodes and no improved cost paths, so no changes are made to the routing data. The entry for A is no longer tentative. The new table follows:

Destination	Connection	Cost	Status
D	0	0	
C	1	1	
E	2	1	
B	1	2	
F	1	2	
A	1	3	

There are no more tentative entries, thus the algorithm is complete. D now has the identity of all reachable nodes, the number of hops in the shortest path to each, and the connection that should be used in reaching each node.

Uses of the Routing Protocols

Link state routing is used in OSI networks for intradomain IS to IS routing. Distance vector routing is the basis of the **routing information protocol (RIP)**, the most common intradomain routing protocol in the Internet. More recently, the Internet has begun to use the **open shortest path first (OSPF)** protocol, which is a link state routing protocol using Dijkstra's algorithm.

Interdomain routing in both OSI networks and the Internet relies on distance vector routing techniques. The information exchanged among neighbors in separate administrative domains includes attributes of the path available to reach a next node on the path to a particular destination, in addition to the usual cost information. The use of distance vector routing results from practical and political considerations involved in the free exchange of information about connectivity across administrative boundaries.

12.3 FIREWALLS

Personnel using their organization's internal network for interchanging messages, sometimes of a confidential nature (new product information, for example), want to be free from concern that unauthorized persons can intercept the messages. The same personnel want access to the Internet for its many benefits, however. Unfortunately, an internal network's workstation with connection to the Internet also provides a path for other Internet users to gain access to the internal network unless some protective mechanism prevents access. An organization faced with protecting its internal network from unauthorized access, while also allowing personnel access to the Internet, implements a mechanism called a **firewall**.

A firewall is one or more systems that enforce an access policy between two networks. It is a static traffic routing service that may be placed between an organization's internal network and its connection to an external network, usually the Internet, or between two internal networks in a large organization. A firewall has the dual purpose of blocking and permitting traffic, both into and out of the protected network. Like a medieval castle's drawbridge, a firewall creates a single point for entry and exit, thus simplifying the task of securing an internal network. A firewall is used to stop intruders and to implement company policy on protecting data. Further, a company can use a firewall to store information about products and services that the public can access on the Internet.

Basic implementations of firewalls involve a gateway, which is an Application-layer service, or a routing filter, which is a Network-layer service. Application gateways are more costly but allow greater control and monitoring. The most effective firewalls implement both gateways and routing filters. For that reason, we discuss firewalls in this chapter rather than in the Application-layer chapters.

In this section, we illustrate a selection of architectures for common types of firewalls, include relevant terminology, and give several examples of filtering rules in routers. We then identify some of the major advantages and disadvantages of the selected firewalls, as well as tradeoffs involved when implementing them.

> A firewall has the dual purpose of blocking and permitting traffic, both into and out of the protected network.

12.3.1 Architectures

An application gateway is a firewall that prohibits any service between two networks that is not expressly permitted. One firewall of this type is shown in Figure 12.10. Called a **dual-homed gateway**, this firewall consists of a secure host running proxy software that has two network interfaces, one with the Internet and the other with the internal network. The function of this secure host, commonly referred to as a **bastion host**, is to block di-

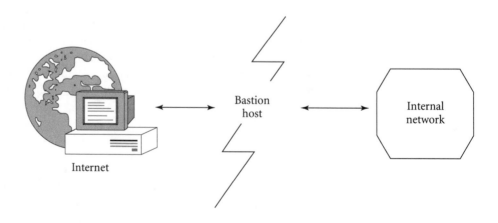

Internet

Bastion host

Internal network

Figure 12.10. A dual-homed gateway

rect traffic between the two networks. The proxy server on the host logs and audits traffic and also translates addresses. When one network connects to the proxy server on the bastion host, the proxy server determines whether the service is expressly permitted. If so, the proxy server relays the requested service to the second network; otherwise, any other services are prevented from reaching the second network. Users have access only to the services supported by the proxy server running on the bastion host. The dual-homed gateway disables IP routing/forwarding, preventing an IP source address attack on the internal network.

Operating at the network level, a routing filter, or **screening router**, acts as a firewall that permits any service between two networks that is not expressly prohibited. This type of firewall uses a packet filtering capability to screen transmissions. Direct connections between two networks are allowed, but unwanted services are blocked. IP network packets are scrutinized for all traffic between the two networks. Predefined rules determine which packets are passed through. Only those packets that match one of the rules allowing traffic are transmitted. Any information in the TCP/IP packet header could be analyzed by a screening router. Usually, however, only the set of information referred to as the **full association**– the protocol, source address, source port, destination address, and destination port—undergoes analysis.

Screening router firewalls are more flexible than application gateways, but generally provide less security against intrusion. Companies developing firewalls to protect networks are more likely to create screening routers; commercial firms offering firewalls usually implement application gateways or hybrids consisting of both types.

A common type of network level firewall, called a **screened host gateway**, is shown in Figure 12.11. Implementation of these firewalls involves both a screening router and a bastion host. A usual configuration places the screening router between the Internet and the bastion host, blocking traffic on specific ports. The bastion host is most commonly part of the internal network. Host systems on the internal network connect directly to the bastion host, which is the only system on the internal network that connects directly to the Internet.

Another type of network level firewall, called a **screened subnet**, is shown in Figure 12.12. In this architecture, a subnet is placed between the Internet and the internal network. A screening router lies between the subnet and each of the two networks. Packets from either network that are permitted to pass through the screening router will enter the subnet at a bastion host, which provides an additional security layer. Should the bastion host be compromised, the attacker has access only to the subnet and can gain access to either network only through a screening router.

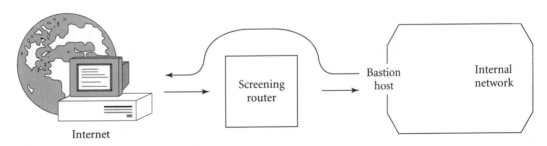

Internet

Figure 12.11. A screened host gateway

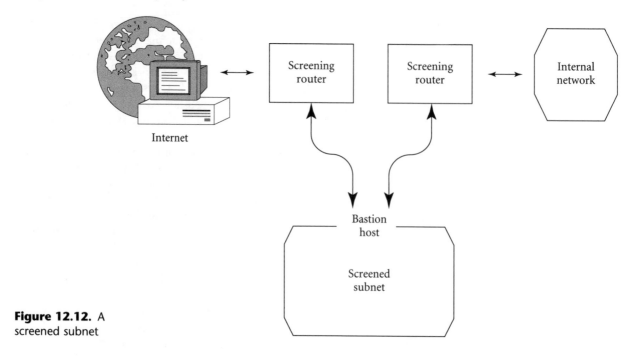

Figure 12.12. A screened subnet

12.3.2 Examples

Proxy servers in firewall implementations are application specific. Proxies for telnet, rlogin, FTP, X-Window, http/Web, and NNTP/Usenet news are included in the TIS Internet Firewall Toolkit (FWTK). A generic proxy system called SOCKS, based on the Winsock application protocol interface, can be compiled into a client-side application. This system facilitates developing proxies in support of new protocols [NEC98].

Toolkits are also available for implementing screening routers. Examples include the PC-based kit Karlbridge [Ohi95], versions of the Digital Equipment Corporation kernel screening software, and the free iplifter. Both of the latter two kits are for BSD-based systems.

Industry-standard routers such as Cisco support screening and can be configured to operate as filtering routers. Figure 12.13 and the accompanying explanation are from an example in *Internet Firewalls Frequently Asked Questions* by Marcus J. Ranum [Ran95]. The IP access list assumes Cisco IOS v. 10.3 or later. It shows the implementation of the following specific policy for securing a network: allow all outgoing TCP-connections, incoming SMTP and DNS to mailhost (mail and DNS are only incoming services and all incoming connections go through mailhost), and incoming FTP data connections to high TCP port (>1024). Further, try to protect services that live on high port numbers. The company has Class C network address 195.55.55.0, and its network is connected to Internet via IP service provider.

In the example, only incoming packets from the Internet are checked. Rules are tested in order, and testing stops when the first match is found. An implicit deny rule at the end of the access list denies all UDP traffic to protect RPC services.

```
 1. no ip source-route
 2. !
 3. interface ethernet 0
 4. ip address 195.55.55.1
 5. !
 6. interface serial 0
 7. ip access-group 101 in
 8. !
 9. access-list 101 deny ip 195.55.55.0 0.0.0.255
10. access-list 101 permit tcp any any established
11. !
12. access-list 101 permit tcp any host 195.55.55.10 eq smtp
13. access-list 101 permit tcp any host 195.55.55.10 eq dns
14. access-list 101 permit udp any host 192.55.55.10 eq dns
15. !
16. access-list deny tcp any any range 6000 6003
17. access-list deny tcp any any rangee 2000 2003
18. access-list deny tcp any any eq 2047
19. access-list deny udp any any eq 204
20. !
21. access-list 101 permit tcp any 20 any gt 1024
22. !
23. access-list 101 permit icmp any any
24. !
25. snmp-server community FOOBAR RO 2
26. line vty 0 4
27. access-class 2 in
28. access-list 2 permit 195.55.55.0 255.255.255.0
```

Figure 12.13. An example of using Cisco as a filtering router

The set of rules in Figure 12.13 indicates the complexity and amount of control in a routing filter implementation. The line numbers and formatting are for reference and readability. Comments on some of the rules follow. Line 1 prevents address-spoofing attacks through source routing by dropping all source-routed packets. Router-based firewalls are vulnerable to this kind of attack. Line 9 drops any packet that claims to be from the local network. Line 10 allows all packets that are part of already established TCP connections to pass through without further checking. Lines 12–14 block all connections to low port numbers except SMTP and DNS. Lines 16–19 block all services listing TCP connections in high port numbers. This includes X-Windows (port 6000+), OpenWindows (port 2000+), and NFS (port 2049). NSF usually runs over UDP, but not always. Line 21 requires incoming connections from port 20 into high port numbers to be FTP data connections. In Line 28, access-list 2 limits access to the router itself (telnet and SNMP).

12.3.3 Tradeoffs

Implementing firewalls involves tradeoffs. An organization has much to consider before implementing an effective firewall. What amount of message blocking and permitting is feasible in order to prevent intrusion and still allow workers to get their jobs done? What level of monitoring, redundancy, and control should be imposed to meet the organization's objectives and requirements? What is the cost in money and staff time to develop a firewall within the organization? Is it better to purchase a product? What maintenance will likely be involved? What part does organizational politics play in the final decision? What firewall architecture (application or network level, or hybrid) will achieve the desired goals? In simplest terms, the tradeoff is between ease of use and security.

In considering the implementation of a firewall, it is important to realize that firewalls cannot protect against every kind of attack. In particular, they are not effective against an attack that does not go through the firewall, such as a virus, a traitor within the company, or a careless employee who leaves a password where someone else can read it. A virus is an example of a data-driven attack; it is read into a host and executed there. Firewalls do not protect against data-driven attacks. A traitor could bypass a firewall by exporting sensitive information by telephone, fax, or disk. A firewall, then, should be part of an overall security plan of an organization if it is to be effective.

12.4 SERVICES PROVIDED BY THE NETWORK LAYER

Two classes of service are available in the OSI Network layer: connection-oriented network services (CONS) and connectionless network services (CLNS). CONS provides a service closely related to the connection-oriented transport services described in Chapter 11. CLNS provides a best-effort delivery service, without the steps involved in connection establishment and release. Each data unit carried in CLNS is routed independently of others, and may arrive out of order—or not arrive at all. Most network service providers are connectionless, thus the need for end-to-end connection management by the Transport layer. The OSI CLNS is closely related to the Internet network protocol (IP). There is no CONS; the CCITT network protocol X.25 provides some of the features of a CONS, and procedures have been defined to map between X.25 and OSI CONS service.

12.4.1 Connection-Oriented Network Services

The services provided by the CONS Network layer are shown in Figure 12.14. N-CONNECT and N-DISCONNECT, respectively, relate to the connection establishment and connection termination operations of the Transport layer. Data transfer of the Transport layer maps to N-DATA, N-DATA-ACKNOWLEDGE, and N-EXPEDITED-DATA. N-RESET serves to reestablish a lost connection.

Service	Type
N-CONNECT	Confirmed
N-DISCONNECT	Unconfirmed
N-DATA	Unconfirmed
N-DATA-ACKNOWLEDGE	Unconfirmed
N-EXPEDITED-DATA	Unconfirmed
N-RESET by NS user	Confirmed
N-RESET by NS provider	Indication only

Figure 12.14. Services of the Network layer

Fixed part	Address part--					Options	User data
	Destination address length	Destination address	Source address length	Source address	Segmentation part		

Fixed part:

Network layer protocol ID	Header length	Version	Life time	Flags	Segment length	Header checksum

Segmentation part:

Data unit identifier	Segment offset	Total length

Options part:

Code	Length	Value

Figure 12.15. CLNP data PDU format

The use of N-DATA-ACKNOWLEDGE and N-EXPEDITED is optional and negotiated during connection establishment by use of the receipt requested and expedited data flags, respectively. Normal data transfer, provided by the N-DATA service, may include a request for acknowledgment if this service was negotiated during connection establishment. If acknowledgment is requested, it is returned on the basis of an individual network service data unit (NSDU). The acknowledgment, provided by the N-DATA-ACK unconfirmed service, carries no parameters. N-RESET request and indication carry the reason for the reset. Since either a NS user or NS provider could initiate the N-RESET, N-RESET.indication includes the identity of the reset initiator.

The QOS parameter of N-CONNECT specifies the quality of service expected. It is derived from the QOS parameter of the T-CONNECT primitives. An example of QOS negotiation at the Network layer would be a request for a transit delay of 250 msec with maximum acceptable delay of 1 sec. These values are presented to the NS provider in the N-CONNECT.request primitive as the desired and acceptable values for transit delay. The NS provider presents to the responding NS user original acceptable delay and the best transit delay it can provide, perhaps 1 sec and 500 msec, respectively. The responding NS user (transport entity, recall) will include the value it can provide in the N-CONNECT.response—perhaps 650 msec. That value will be delivered to the initiating NS user in N-CONNECT.confirm.

12.4.2 Connectionless Network Service

The Network-layer connectionless service, like that of the higher layers, consists of a single, unconfirmed service: N-UNIT-DATA. Because there is no connection over which the data flow, all the information needed to deliver the data must accompany each data unit. The

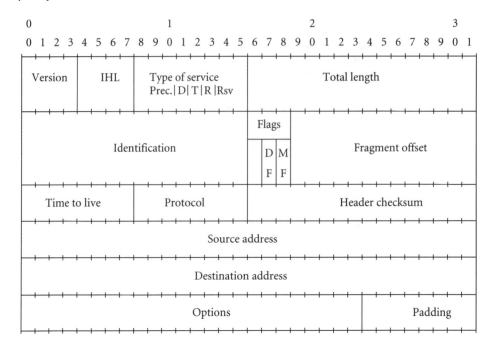

Version: 4 bits

IHL: 4 bits Internet header length. Length of the IP header in 32-bit words, and thus points to the beginning of the data

Type of service: 8 bits

Total length: 16 bits Measured in octets, includes header and data

Identification: 16 bits Used to reassemble fragments

Flags: 3 bits

        Bit 0: Reserved, must be zero
        Bit 1: (DF) 0 = May fragment, 1 = Don't fragment
        Bit 2: (MF) 0 = Last fragment, 1 = More fragments

Fragment offset: 13 bits Position of this fragment in the original data unit, measured in units of 8 octets

Time to live: 8 bits Measured in seconds

Protocol: 8 bits Identifies the next higher layer process, which is to receive this data unit

Figure 12.16. The Internet IP data unit format

Options: Variable length

Padding: Variable length as needed to ensure that the IP header ends on a 32-bit boundary. Contains zero bits

QOS parameter carried in N-UNIT-DATA.indication reflects the service received by that data unit, which may differ from the requested service.

Figure 12.15 shows the format of a data unit in the connectionless network protocol (CLNP). Figure 12.16 shows the format of an Internet IP data unit. Figure 12.17 compares the fields in the CNLP and IP headers [PC93].

The IP type of service is used in networks that provide various levels of service. Higher costs may be associated with higher service levels. There is generally a tradeoff among delay, throughput, and reliability; a particular data unit should request high service in not more than two of these. Figure 12.18 provides the choices defined for IP type of service.

The total length field in the IP header refers to the current data unit, which may be a fragment of an original data unit. IP does not carry the length of the original data unit.

The identification field is set by the source and replicated in any fragments resulting from the original data unit. It is used to identify fragments of one data unit so they can be restored.

The **don't fragment** flag states that this data unit may not be subdivided. If it cannot be forwarded without fragmentation, it is discarded. The **more fragments** flag is used to distinguish between intermediate fragments and the last fragment. The offset field determines where a given fragment belongs in the original data unit; however, without a total length of the data unit, there must be an indication of the last fragment.

Comparison of the Fields in CLNP and IP Headers		
Function	ISO CLNP	Internet IP
Version number	8 bits	4 bits
Header length	8 bits, counts in octets	4 bits, counts in 32-bit words
Quality of service	QOS option	Type of service
Segment / fragment length	16 bits, counts in octets	16 bits, counts in octets
Total length	16 bits, counts in octets	Not present
Data unit identification	16 bits	16 bits
Flags	Don't segment, more segments, suppress error reports, don't fragment, more fragments	
Segment / fragment offset	16 bits, counts in octets	13 bits, counts in octets
Time to live	8 bits, counts in half-second units	16 bits, counts in 1 second units
Higher-layer protocol	Not in header	Protocol field
Addressing	Variable length	32-bit fixed
Options	Security Priority Complete source routing Partial source routing Record route Padding No timestamp option	Security Precedence bits in type of service Stricter source route Loose source route Record route Padding Timestamp

Figure 12.17. Comparison of ISO CLNP and Internet IP protocol headers

Type of service:
Bits 0-2: Prec. = Precedence

    111 - Network control
    110 - Internetwork control
    101 - CRITIC/ECP
    100 - Flash override
    011 - Flash
    010 - Immediate
    001 - Priority
    000 - Routine

Bit 3: D = Delay; 0 = Normal, 1 = Low
Bits 4: T = Throughput; 0 = Normal, 1 = High
Bits 5: R = Reliability; 0 = Normal, 1 = High
Bits 6-7: Rsv. = Reserved for future use

Figure 12.18. IP type of service choices

Time to live (TTL) is measured in seconds. However, every module that processes the data unit must decrement the TTL field by at least one. Thus, the TTL value is an upper limit on the length of time the data unit may continue to exist in the Internet. It is important for the source IP user to know that there is a time after which no data unit survives with a particular identification or sequence numbers, so that those numbers can be safely reused.

The protocol field serves as a service access point in the OSI model. It identifies the next higher layer protocol, which will receive and process the data part of the IP data unit. Examples include representations of TCP or UDP. The complete list of codes recognized is included in RFC 1010: Assigned Numbers [RP87]. Figure 12.19 contains some examples.

The IP header checksum algorithm is:

The checksum field is the 16-bit one's complement of the one's complement sum of all 16-bit words in the header. For purposes of computing the checksum, the value of the checksum field is zero [Pos81].

That is, the header checksum is computed by adding together the contents of each 16-bit piece of the header using one's complement (end around carry) arithmetic. The resulting 16-bit number is complemented and used as the checksum. Since the checksum itself is part of the header, it must be included in the computation before it is computed. This difficulty is solved by using a value of zero for the checksum while doing the computation. Parts of the header change at each module that processes the data unit (the TTL field at least), so the header checksum must be recomputed by each process that accesses the data unit.

A number of options are available in IP. The options must be available at each site that processes the data unit. They are optional in that the user may choose to use them or not. There are two formats for options: a single octet of option-type, or a type-length-value format in which the type and length are each one octet and the option data follows. Some available options include source routing, record route, security, and internet timestamp. Source routing allows the sender to specify the full route to be used in reaching the destination. Two forms of source routing exist: strict source routing requires that the data unit follow exactly the path indicated; loose source routing requires that the nodes listed be used, but allows the routers to use additional nodes to reach the ones listed. Record route specifies that the path taken by the data unit be recorded as it progresses. Internet timestamp

There are two formats for options: a single octet of option-type, or a type-length-value format in which the type and length are each one octet and the option data follows.

Assigned Internet Protocol Numbers

Decimal	Keyword	Protocol
0		Reserved
1	ICMP	Internet control message
2	IGMP	Internet group management
3	GGP	Gateway-to-gateway
4		Unassigned
5	ST	Stream
6	TCP	Transmission control
8	EGP	Exterior gateway protocol
9	IGP	Any private interior gateway
11	NVP-II	Network voice protocol
12	PUP	PUP
13	ARGUS	ARGUS
14	EMCON	EMCON
15	XNET	Cross net debugger
16	CHAOS	Chaos
17	UDP	User datagram
18	MUX	Multiplexing
20	HMP	Host monitoring
21	PRM	Packet radio measurement
27	RDP	Reliable data protocol
28	IRTP	Internet reliable transaction
29	ISO-TP4	ISO Transport protocol class 4
30	NETBLT	Bulk data transfer protocol
33	SEP	Sequential exchange protocol
34-60		Unassigned
62	CFTP	CFTP
63		Any local network
80-254		Unassigned
255		Reserved

Figure 12.19. IP protocol id values

requires the nodes that process the data unit to write the time into the data unit. Security specifies 1 of 16 levels of security.

12.4.3   Segmentation and Reassembly

As a data unit travels from its source to its destination, it may cross the borders between different networks. The data unit must meet any conditions required of data passing through each network. One such condition is maximum data unit length. There are valid reasons both for short and for long maximum data unit length. Short data units reduce the chance of damage in networks where errors occur frequently. If a short data unit is corrupted, the cost of retransmission remains low. On the other hand, a long data unit is more efficient in terms of the ratio of data bits to total data unit length. The header size is not reduced for short data units; long data units make better use of the overhead incurred for sending header information. A network with very low error rates will usually permit longer data units. Another consideration in determining data unit length is fairness. Some limitation on data unit length is needed, even when errors occur very infrequently, to protect network resources from being clogged by very long transmissions from one user.

As a data unit passes through various networks, it must be fragmented when its length exceeds the network maximum data unit size. Fragmenting a data unit requires replicating the header, providing header information regarding the fragments, and breaking up the data part of the data unit so that the resulting fragments meet the length requirements of the network.

The principal issue involved in fragmentation regards reassembly. Should the data unit be reassembled as it leaves the network that required the fragmentation, or should it remain fragmented until it reaches its destination? The first approach is called **intranet fragmentation**, and the second is **internet fragmentation**. Each has advantages and disadvantages:

- Intranet fragmentation may result in wasted effort if the reconstructed data unit must again be fragmented at a later step in its path. On the other hand, because the complete data unit is available on entry to each network, the data unit can be divided into optimal size subunits for the next part of its journey.

- Internet fragmentation saves the effort of reassembling data units as each intervening network is left, but means that smaller than optimal data units may be used.

SUMMARY

This chapter examined the principal functions of the Network layer. One of the responsibilities of the Network layer is to provide a unique identifier for each individual device attached to any network, anywhere in the world. We looked at the scheme for addressing that has been used successfully in the Internet community for nearly 30 years, and noted the need to increase that address space. We looked at the inherently scaleable, but somewhat cumbersome, address scheme used by the OSI community. That approach allocates a share of the address space to each of many organizations and allows each to define addresses as they will. The result is variable length addresses of no one pattern, but with essentially unlimited capacity to grow with the need.

The Network layer is also responsible for finding a path by which data units can travel from sending station to destination station. Data units travel through intermediate networks during the trip, and the intermediate networks often belong to unrelated organizations. Routing involves cooperative efforts by systems in different administrative domains. Routing requires a knowledge of network architecture. Techniques for discovering paths and for distributed routing, including distance vector and link state, are provided at the Network layer. Algorithms, such as Dijkstra's shortest-path-first graph traversal, are available. We summarized the use of these tools in both TCP/IP and OSI networks.

Firewalls offer several approaches to protecting a network against attacks. Protection comes at a cost, making use of the network somewhat less convenient for its legitimate users. The degree of protection required determines the most appropriate approach to a particular organization. Ultimately, however, the only sure protection against network dangers is complete disconnection from outside access.

The networks through which data units travel have different characteristics. One important characteristic is the maximum size of a data unit. Data units that are too large must be fragmented before entering the network. This is another responsibility of the Network layer. The decision to reassemble the data unit on exit from the network or to retain the smaller fragments until the data unit reaches the destination impacts efficiency and affects performance.

We looked at the services of the Network layer as seen by the user, the Transport layer. The Internet IP and OSI CLNS are similar, offering connectionless network service. OSI also defines a connection-oriented network service, CONS.

All upper layers through the Network layer have at least some orientation to the user. We now turn to the lower layers where the orientation is machine to machine. We regard these lower layers much as an application developer on a single system regards the details of the machine. Though the programmer will rarely think of how floating-point numbers are stored or what machine-level instructions are found in the machine, a general (and sometimes detailed) understanding of how the machine works is often important in developing well-constructed applications. In this same spirit, we now look at the structure and operation of the lowest levels of the network.

EXERCISES

1. In the example of section 12.1, a Class B network is divided into subnets with a particular allocation of bits associated with a subnet ID and the remainder of the host ID field actually identifying a host. How many subnets are possible in this allocation, and how many hosts can be on each subnet? Critique this particular subdivision. Should there be more (and smaller) subnets or fewer (larger) subnets? What are the advantages and disadvantages associated with each choice?

2. Assume that node B fails in Figure 12.9. Find the new routing tables produced by the distance vector routing method.

3. Apply the distance vector algorithm to the following small network (assume the link cost is 1 for each connection):

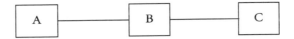

   Now assume that node A fails, and node B assigns a value of 9 (a very big value in this network) to the cost of the link between A and B. What happens in the next two iterations of the algorithm?

4. In the description of distance vector routing, we noted that "with cost equated to hops, paths discovered on later iterations will not replace paths found earlier." Explain why that is so.

5. In Figure 12.9, assign the following costs to the links:

A - B	5
A - F	1
B - C	2
C - D	3
C - F	1
D - E	2
E - F	2

   (a) Determine the routing tables for each node, using the distance vector scheme.

   (b) Determine the routing tables for node D, using link state routing.

6. (Programming Exercise) Implement distance vector routing. Remember that new networks appear frequently and that speed is important. What major issues can you identify in relation to scaling and efficiency?

7. (Programming Exercise) Implement link state routing. Assume that the link state information for all other routing nodes is available locally. Remember that new nodes appear frequently and that speed is important. What major issues can you identify in relation to scaling and efficiency?

8. Consider the journey of a packet of length 2048 octets. The packet passes through networks with maximum packet sizes as shown. Show what happens to the packet using intranet fragmentation and internet fragmentation. Discuss the performance of each scheme. (Assume that the packet header is 40 octets.)

Network	Maximum Packet Length
A	2048 octets
B	512 octets
C	1024 octets
D	256 octets
E	1024 octets

9. In the scenario of Exercise 8, consider two cases:

   (a) The packet is a data unit submitted to the Network layer by a connection-oriented transport service.

   (b) The packet is a data unit submitted by a connectionless transport service.

   Further, consider that network D is very unreliable. What is the difference in the two cases in regard to network performance with the two fragmentation schemes?

10. (Programming Exercise) Develop a simulator that allows you to experiment with questions such as those in Exercises 8 and 9. Include a user interface that allows the user to specify a number of different scenarios—including the number of intermediate networks the data unit must traverse, the maximum size data unit handled by each network, and the choice of connectionless or connection-oriented transport service user.

11. (Programming Exercise) Write a program to read a string of 20 octets and produce the IP checksum. Write another program to receive a string of 20 octets of IP header and confirm that the delivery was uncorrupted. (These are two separate programs and could run on two separate systems. Send the output of the first to be the input of the second.) Next, make some random changes in the output of the first program before sending it to the second.

Medium Access Control

Beginning at the Data Link layer, we see an important change in the role of network standardization. The Data Link layer concerns communication between *adjacent machines*. There is a wide range of possibilities for what constitutes "adjacent," but the important point is that each side of the communication knows a lot about the way the other sends and receives data. Communication between adjacent machines concerns sharing a common link—whether it be a cable, a broadcast channel involving a satellite or microwave or radio transmission, or something else entirely.

The functions of the Data Link layer are usually described in two groups: the medium access control, which focuses on the logical connection between two separate systems and the way they cooperate to share a common communication medium; and the logical link control, which deals with error detection and correction and with connection management. In this chapter, we look at the medium access control—the characteristics that differentiate among the major types of local area networks. In Chapter 14, we look at how these differences affect the requirements for joining similar LANs together with bridges. We complete our treatment of the lowest layers of network protocols in Chapter 15 with a brief description of logical link control functions and the physical-layer protocols that allow connected machines to transmit bits over a shared link.

13.1 VARIATIONS ON MEDIUM ACCESS CONTROL

Contention-based
access is similar to the
use of a shared phone
line... Controlled
access is like the use of
a traffic signal to show
whose turn it is to travel
through an intersection.

When a number of stations share one communications medium, they must coordinate their transmissions so that they do not interfere with each other. There are two approaches to this coordination: contention-based access and controlled access. Contention-based access is similar to the use of a shared phone line. If you want to make a call, you pick up the receiver and listen. If no one is speaking, you make your call. If someone else is using the line, you replace the receiver and try again later. Controlled access is like the use of a traffic signal to show whose turn it is to travel through an intersection. Contention-based systems allow access to the channel with minimum delay. At any time that the channel is free, the station with something to send can proceed. However, contention-based systems do expose traffic to interference from other stations, if more than one tries to use a clear channel at nearly the same time. Controlled access prevents the multiple user interference problem, but at the cost of delay that is sometimes unnecessary. (Have you ever sat patiently at a red light with no other cars in sight?)

Our discussion of transmission medium access control (MAC) techniques begins with a very simple contention-based system, Aloha, and continues with later systems, including the protocol for the standard Ethernet local area network. We will then look at controlled access schemes, beginning with the token ring and token bus, and then higher-speed medium access protocols. One conclusion from the discussion will be that techniques that worked well at lower speeds do not work well at higher transmission rates.

In all protocols for sharing the use of a communication channel, several criteria will be considered: access must be available fairly to all the stations, with no station receiving preferred treatment; the channel should be used efficiently with minimum capacity lost to overhead associated with the channel access method; and frames should be transmitted as soon as a station is ready and the channel is clear. Protocols are also evaluated on the delay they impose on a station that has a frame ready to send. Ideally, every station should have an equal chance at obtaining the channel, the full data carrying capacity of the channel should be used, and each station should be able to transmit as soon as it has a frame ready, unless another station is using the channel.

13.2 CONTENTION-BASED ACCESS

13.2.1 Alohanet

In 1968, planning began for an experimental radio-linked computer network to link facilities at seven locations, all parts of the University of Hawaii [Abr85]. A number of experimental efforts had begun to show that something other than the existing telephone system would be better suited to the requirements of data communications. The use of broadcast radio channels instead of the traditional point-to-point telephone communication began with the Aloha project and is an important aspect of many types of networks today.

In the Aloha system, the remote sites communicate with a central facility by sharing a common broadcast channel. If two or more stations transmit at the same time, their signals interfere with each other, and no meaningful communication occurs. The central site transmits to the remote sites using a different channel, so there is no interference possible with its transmissions. The remote sites do not hear each other's transmissions, so they have no way of knowing if another site is broadcasting. A site knows that its message got through successfully when it receives a response or acknowledgment from the central site. Since a site has no way to know if any other site is transmitting, it simply transmits whenever it has anything to send. If the message fails to get through, the station must resend.

The natural question is, of course, what degree of success in communicating can be obtained in such an undisciplined system? Is there any hope of getting real work accomplished? To answer these questions, we must consider the probability that a given message will be delivered successfully, without interference from another station's transmission. Let's consider the vulnerability of a fixed-size frame sent over the Alohanet. From the time the first bit of the frame leaves the sending station until the last bit of the frame is received by the central site, the frame is occupying the channel. If any other data is sent on the channel during any part of that period, the overlapping frames will be destroyed. It may seem strange that a small overlap of transmissions will totally destroy both frames. What if 99 percent of the frame has arrived safely before the overlap occurs? Why is that frame destroyed? The answer lies in the requirement to verify the transmission received by calculating a checksum and comparing the calculated checksum with that carried in the frame. Even a single bit corruption will lead to an invalid checksum computation and no way to determine where or how much the data was corrupted.

Consider the frame shown shaded in Figure 13.1. If t is the time the frame occupies the channel, then it is clear that no other frame can be sent during that time if the frame is to arrive safely. However, since the sending station knows nothing of the state of the channel when it sends its frame, it is also necessary that no other frame has been sent in the previous time of length t. If such a transmission had occurred, that frame would still be on the channel and the new frame would overlap it, and both would be destroyed. Thus, we see a period of vulnerability for a time of length $2t$ during which no station may begin transmitting if this frame is to be delivered safely.

To evaluate the *throughput* (that is, the percentage of the channel's capacity that can actually be used with this protocol), we must make some assumptions about the rate at which frames are generated by the remote stations. Clearly, if frames are generated rarely, so that there is almost never an overlap of frames on the channel, then every frame will be delivered successfully, and the throughput will be determined entirely by the amount of data generated. Thus, if the channel capacity is 9600 bps (the original Aloha rate) and the combined data generated by the stations amounts to 960 bps and no frames ever overlap, then throughput $= 960/9600 = 10$ percent of the channel capacity. If overlap (a *collision*) occurs, then both frames must be retransmitted. The lost transmission constitutes a waste of channel capacity and is not an effective data transmission. For example, suppose that, on average, the combined traffic generated by the remote sites amounts to 960 bps, as before.

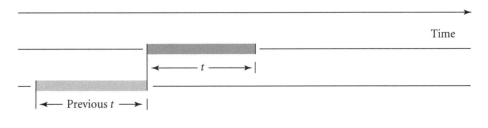

Figure 13.1. Vulnerability for a frame sent in pure Aloha

However, suppose that 192 bits of the 960 is retransmitted data due to prior collision. Then the throughput is $(960 - 192)/9600$ or 8 percent.

Standard assumptions about the generation of data are represented by the Poisson model. Assuming Poisson behavior, the probability that n frames will arrive during a time of length t, when the rate of arrival is λ is

$$P_n(t) = \frac{(\lambda t)^n e^{-\lambda t}}{n!}$$

Define the **offered load** $G = \lambda t$ = the number of frames generated in the time t. Then the probability that exactly k frames will begin transmission during the time t that it takes to send one frame is given by

$$P_k(t) = \frac{G^k e^{-G}}{k!}$$

For a given transmission to succeed, there must be no other transmissions begun during the time required to complete the first one. In other words, we need $k = 0$.

$$P_0(t) = \frac{G^0 e^{-G}}{0!} = e^{-G}$$

Further, there must have been no transmission begun during a preceding time long enough to allow a frame to be still on the channel. Thus, we want

$$P_0(2t) = \frac{(2G)^0 e^{-2G}}{0!} = e^{-2G}$$

The throughput, S, is the offered load, G, times the probability that no collisions will occur. Thus,

$$S = Ge^{-2G}$$

Evaluating for various values of G, we see how the Aloha access method responds to various levels of offered load. As we would expect, when the offered load is very low, all transmissions succeed, and throughput matches offered load (the curve goes up from the origin at a 45 degree angle). We also expect that the upward curve cannot continue for all possible values of G. S, after all, is limited to 100 percent of the channel capacity, where G can grow without bound if great numbers of frames are generated. In fact, we see that the slope of the curve remains positive as long as $2G < 1$ and then falls off. The derivative of S with respect to G gives us a function for the slope of the curve:

$$\frac{d(Ge^{-2G})}{dG} = (1 - 2G)e^{-2G}$$

Setting the slope equal to 0 and solving for G, we find that the slope of the curve is 0 at $G = 0.5$. At that point the amount of wasted capacity due to retransmission is such that the throughput decreases as more traffic is generated. The value of S when $G = 0.5$ is 18.4 percent, the maximum throughput achievable for pure Aloha channels.

Another characteristic of traffic in channel access schemes must be considered as well. That is the delay implied by the channel access protocol. How long must a station wait to transmit, once it has a frame ready to send. As we consider the various access schemes discussed in this chapter, we will look both at throughput and at delay. Pure Aloha is not strong in throughput, but its delay characteristic is ideal: a station with a frame ready to send has no wait at all. In examining other channel access protocols, we will look for ways to improve throughput while maintaining the advantage of minimal delay.

Slotted Aloha

One reason for the low throughput on pure Aloha is the fact that the frame is vulnerable to collision for twice as long as the time required to send it. That is, the frame must be sent when no other frame is on the channel, and no other frame must be sent during the time this frame is using the channel. Slotted Aloha reduces the vulnerable period to one frame transmission time. The method requires synchronizing all the stations and restricting frame sending to the beginning of fixed-length time slots. Any frame that becomes ready to transmit during a slot must wait until the beginning of the next slot. Figure 13.2 illustrates the idea, showing a successful transmission and also a case with three frames competing for one slot.

This method eliminates vulnerability to collision by frames that might begin transmission during the time the frame is occupying the channel. The only competition is from other frames that became ready to send during the previous time slot. All such frames will begin transmission at the beginning of the new slot and will thus interfere with each other. The analysis of throughput is the same as for pure Aloha, except that we are interested in the probability that exactly 0 frames will be generated during the slot (of time length t) before the one in which our frame is sent [Kei89]. The probability of 0 frames generated by other stations during one slot of time length t is

$$P_0(t) = \frac{G^0 e^{-G}}{0!} = e^{-G}$$
$$S = Ge^{-G}$$

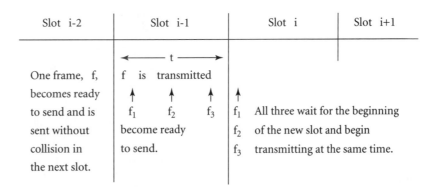

Figure 13.2. Slotted Aloha

Once again, we use the derivative to see that the throughput curve increases as long as $G < 1$ and reaches a maximum value of 0.368. Slotted Aloha increases throughput at the cost of a delay in transmitting a frame that is ready until the beginning of the next slot. It also requires synchronization among the stations, which is a significant requirement.

13.2.2 Carrier Sense Multiple Access

Slotted Aloha eliminates the problem of other frames beginning to transmit after one is on the channel. Another way to reduce the time of vulnerability is to eliminate the possibility of a station beginning to transmit while another station is transmitting. If that could be done, we would eliminate all collisions except those occurring between frames whose transmissions begin simultaneously. For a station to know that a channel is in use, and thus to defer sending its frame, the station must listen to the broadcast channel before attempting to send. This technique is called **carrier sense multiple access (CSMA)**. It is also known as **listen before talk (LBT)**. Central to the operation of this technique is the fact that the propagation delay (the time it takes a bit to travel from its source station to the destination station) is very small compared to the transmission time (the time it takes to put all the bits of the frame onto the channel).

There are three variations on this approach:

Non-persistent If a station with a frame to send detects an idle channel, it sends the frame. If the station detects a busy channel, it waits for a random amount of time and checks again. (Essentially: call; if the phone is answered, talk; if there is a busy signal, do something else and try again later.)

p-persistent If a station with a frame to send detects an idle channel, it will send the frame with probability p or delay a time approximately one propagation delay with probability $1 - p$. If the channel is busy, it will listen continuously until the channel is free, then transmit with probability p.

1-persistent This is a special case of p-persistent, with $p = 1$.

***p*-persistent CSMA** The p-persistent approach, in which a station might decline to send a waiting frame, even if the channel is free, appears strange at first glance. In fact, p-persistent CSMA achieves the highest throughput of all. The reason is indicated in Figure 13.3. When

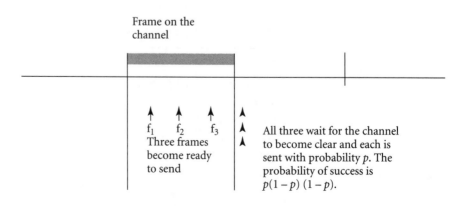

Frame on the channel

f_1 f_2 f_3
Three frames become ready to send

All three wait for the channel to become clear and each is sent with probability p. The probability of success is $p(1 - p)(1 - p)$.

Figure 13.3. p-persistent CSMA

the number of frames generated is large, the probability that more than one frame will become ready to send during the time the channel is busy with another frame increases. If that happens, all the stations that have frames to send will wait until the channel becomes idle. As soon as the channel becomes idle, all the waiting stations will transmit at the same time, guaranteeing a collision. Both non-persistent and *p*-persistent CSMA address this problem by spreading out the times at which the waiting stations attempt to transmit. Both non-persistent and *p*-persistent CSMA reduce the chance of a collision occurring at the cost of wasted opportunities for successful transmission, and both delay the transmission of a frame.

Though these methods improve throughput, they do not completely eliminate collisions. First, there is still a possibility that two or more stations will transmit at the same time. Second, there is a time after a station begins transmitting before other stations become aware that the channel is busy. If another station listens to the channel in that brief interval, hears a clear channel, and transmits, then a collision occurs. Figure 13.4 shows the complete picture of what occurs as two stations transmit over a shared channel using a CSMA channel access protocol. The numbers in the figure correspond to the following notes:

1. A vulnerable period—a station has begun to transmit, but at least some other stations on the channel have not yet learned of the transmission.
2. For some time after the transmission ends, at least some other stations do not know that the channel is now free.
3. An idle period—the channel is free, but no station has a frame ready to send.
4. At some time into the vulnerable period for a new frame, another station begins to transmit.
5. If there is no collision detection mechanism, the collided frames will be sent completely, and the channel will not be available again until the end of the period after the last transmission is completed and all the other stations know of the free channel.
6. For some time after the collision, the first frame is still vulnerable to collision from frames from other stations that have not heard the frame on the channel.

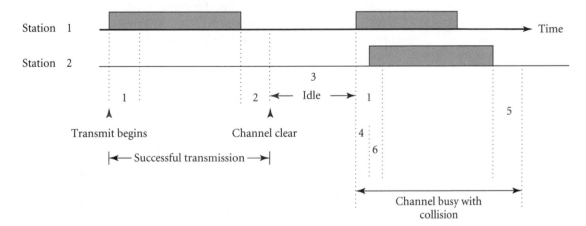

Figure 13.4. Successful transmission and a collision on a CSMA channel

Analysis is simplified if we normalize time by defining one time unit to be the time required to transmit one frame. Then the time the channel is occupied with a successful transmission is $1 + a$, where a is the time required for a bit to travel from a sending station to the last station to hear it—the time shown in Figure 13.4 as 2. If a collision occurs, the channel is busy for a time $1 + a$ for the second (or last if there are more than two frames involved in the collision) plus the time that passed after the first frame transmission began and before the last colliding frame began (shown in the figure as 4)—call it Y. That is, the channel is occupied a total of $1 + a + Y$ time units for a collision.

Using the Poisson model of behavior, we find that the probability of no other station transmitting during the vulnerable period is

$$P_0(a) = \frac{(aG)^0 e^{-aG}}{0!} = e^{-aG}$$

and the average length of time that the channel is used successfully, U (the time required to transmit a frame, 1, times the probability of success, $P_0(a)$), is

$$E[U] = e^{-aG}$$

Computing the expected value (average length) of the idle time and of the time within the vulnerable period before a colliding frame is sent, we can compute the throughput (the average amount of time spent doing useful work) as

$$S = \frac{E[U]}{E[B] + E[I]}$$

where B is the time the channel is busy, whether with a successful or unsuccessful transmission, and I is the time the channel is idle. We have a representation for $E[U]$; we now require $E[I]$ and $E[B]$. $E[I]$ is obtained from the properties of the Poisson behavior as

$$E[I] = \frac{1}{G}$$

Intuitively, since G represents the number of frames generated in a period of time, we expect idle time to reflect the inverse—the time per frame generation.

We have seen that the busy time for the channel is

$$B = 1 + a + Y$$

where $Y = 0$ for successful transmissions. Since 1 and a are constants, Y provides the variation in B, thus,

$$E[B] = 1 + a + E[Y]$$

Y is a random variable, and reflects the probability of a given colliding frame being the *last* one to collide. In other words, the value of Y is related to the probability that no other frame will begin transmitting in the vulnerable period for the first frame sent. The period of interest then is of duration $a - Y$ and is labeled 6 in Figure 13.4. The probability of no other transmission in a time of length $a - Y$ is $Ge^{-G(a-Y)}$. Since Y can take on any value between 0 and a, its expected value is obtained by considering every possible value for Y and its corresponding probability represented by its probability density function, $f(y)$.

$$f(y) = Ge^{-G(a-y)} \quad 0 \le y \le a$$

$$E[Y] = \int_0^a y f(y) \, dy$$

$$= a - \frac{1}{G}(1 - e^{-aG})$$

Substituting all the pieces in the equation for S yields

$$S = \frac{Ge^{-aG}}{G(1 + 2a) + e^{-aG}}$$

$$\lim_{a \to 0} S = \frac{G}{G + 1}$$

Thus, in theory, for non-persistent CSMA, as the offered load grows, the throughput approaches 1, the maximum possible value.

1-persistent CSMA   Figure 13.5 shows the operation of stations using a channel in 1-persistent CSMA mode. Since the frames that become ready to send while the channel is busy are lying in wait and try to transmit as soon as the channel is free, the probability of collision increases as the offered load on the channel increases [Kei89].

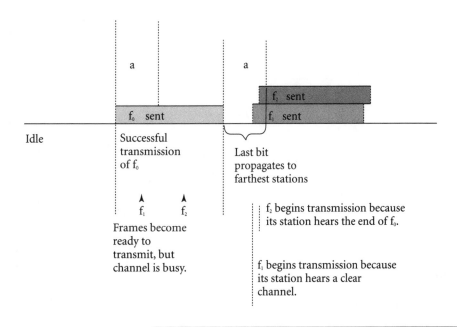

Figure 13.5. 1-persistent CSMA

The throughput calculation yields

$$S = \frac{Ge^{-G}(1+G)}{G + e^{-G}}$$

As the offered load, G, gets very large,

$$S \rightarrow Ge^{-G}$$

which approaches 0.

CSMA/CD

We can see from the descriptions of CSMA channel sharing protocols, that channel capacity is wasted by continuing to transmit a frame after a collision occurs. This waste suggests an opportunity for throughput improvement that is addressed by **carrier sense multiple access with collision detection (CSMA/CD)**. This access control method requires a transmitting station to listen to the channel while sending a frame so that a collision will be identified if it occurs. The transmission then ceases and a backoff procedure is invoked. CSMA/CD is also known as **listen while talk (LWT)**. The behavior of two stations whose frames have collided is shown in Figure 13.6 [Kei89].

When a collision occurs in CSMA/CD, each station involved in the collision learns of it by continuing to listen to the channel while sending its frame. This implies that each sending station must continue to transmit and listen long enough for any possible interference to be detected. Consider the situation illustrated in Figure 13.7. The line in the figure is now the transmission channel, not time as in the other figures.

Let τ be the time required for a bit to propagate from one station to another when the stations are as far apart as possible. In Figure 13.7, assume that the first bit of a frame from

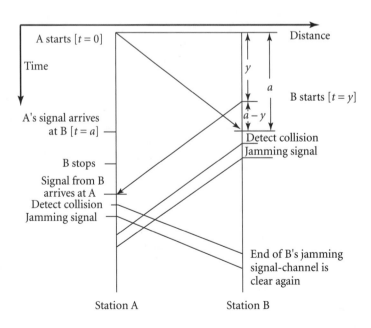

Figure 13.6.
CSMA/CD behavior
with collision

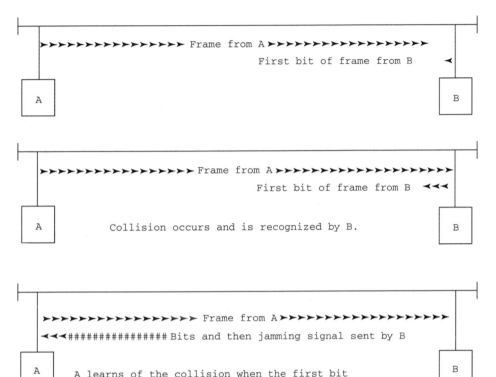

Figure 13.7.
CSMA/CD collision
detection requires
listening long enough
to hear any possible
interference

B is sent just before the first bit of the frame from A arrives at station B. To be sure that any possible collision will be detected, each transmitting station must continue to listen to the channel for a time equal to 2τ. This requirement is encoded in the standards for CSMA/CD protocols as a minimum frame length. Two implementations of CSMA/CD, Ethernet and the nearly identical IEEE 802.3, specify maximum distance between stations, a particular transmission speed (the rate at which bits are put onto the channel), and a minimum frame length. These parameters are defined in such a way that any collision will be detected by all stations involved.

Binary Exponential Backoff   When a collision occurs, all stations involved must respond by ceasing to transmit. In fact, a station detecting a collision stops sending its frame and transmits a special signal to alert any other station that is preparing to transmit that a collision has occurred and at least two stations will be attempting to regain the channel. Of course, if the stations involved in the collision begin to transmit as soon as the channel is cleared of the collision, there will be another collision. To prevent continuous collisions, each station independently calculates a value—either 0 or 1. Each station, if it calculated a 0, again attempts to transmit. If it calculates a 1, it waits a period of time and listens to the channel to see if it is clear. If exactly two stations are involved in the collision, the probability of another collision is 0.5. If a second collision occurs, the stations involved again calculate a random value, this time in the range (0, 3). Again, if a station computes 0, it attempts to transmit. If it calculates a value greater than 0, it waits the indicated amount of time and listens for the channel availability. If another collision occurs, the stations again double the range of values from which to draw a random number. This technique is called **binary exponential backoff**. The Ethernet standard calls for stations participating in the backoff procedure to double the range of values until the selection is made from the values (0, 1023) and then to continue for five more tries of values selected from that range. If after 15 tries, the station still gets a collision, it gives up and reports an error to the higher layers.

The Ethernet and IEEE 802.3 standards employ the CSMA/CD protocol with the 1-persistent version of the CSMA. Though 1-persistent access increases the chance for collisions and therefore decreases throughput, it does provide minimal access delay. The Ethernet/802.3 approach is to allow collisions to occur more often than is necessary and to use the binary exponential backoff procedure to deal with collisions when they do occur. Another important characteristic of the Ethernet/802.3 standards is that they assume a transmission rate of 10 Mbps. At this rate, the propagation delay is much lower than the transmission time, an important factor in the performance of this type of network.

We can calculate the average time required to launch a message successfully on the bus [Sch87]. The reciprocal of this time is the maximum throughput of the protocol.

In the worst case, time $= 2\tau$ is required to detect the occurrence of a collision. If the average number of retransmissions required to succeed in transmitting after a collision is J, then $2\tau J$ time units are required to resolve the collision. The average time to launch a message between the most widely separated stations is then

$$m + \tau + 2\tau J$$

where m is the time required to transmit the message, and τ is the time it takes for the message to leave the channel (reach the farthest end of the bus).

With $a = \frac{\tau}{m}$, the message launching time t is

$$m(1 + a(1 + 2J))$$

We can determine J, the only unknown in the expression, by introducing v = probability of success after one retransmission attempt. Then the probability of success after two attempts is $(1 - v)v$, after three attempts is $(1 - v)^2 v$, and so on. The average number of retransmissions required, what we called J, is the sum over all possible numbers k of the number k times the probability of success after k of retries:

$$J = \sum_{k=1}^{\infty} kv(1 - v)^{k-1} = \frac{1}{v}$$

To determine v, let p be the probability that any one station wants to transmit in a 2τ interval. The probability that exactly one station transmits and is successful is

$$v = np(1 - p)^{n-1}$$

Because the maximum value of v occurs when $p = \frac{1}{n}$, we get

$$v_{max} = n\left(\frac{1}{n}\right)\left(1 - \frac{1}{n}\right)^{n-1} \rightarrow e^{-1}, n \rightarrow \infty$$

$$J = \frac{1}{v} \rightarrow e$$

From before,

$$t = m[1 + a(1 + 2J)]$$
$$= m[1 + a(1 + 2e)]$$

So, the time to launch a message successfully, including time for retransmission after collisions, is

$$t = m[1 + 6.44a]$$

Suppose, for example, that we have a 10M bps channel and a message length of 1000 bits. That is,

$$\frac{1 \text{ message}}{1000 \text{ bits}} * \frac{10,000,000 \text{ bits}}{\text{second}}$$

Then the time to transmit this message

$$m = \frac{1}{10,000} \frac{\text{seconds}}{\text{message}} = 0.0001$$

and

$$t = 0.0001[1 + 6.44a]$$

For $a = 0.1$,

$$t = 0.0001644 \frac{\text{seconds}}{\text{message}}$$

Scalability of CSMA/CD   We began with an interest in throughput. The throughput is obtained from the transmission time.

$$S = \frac{1}{t_v}m \leq \frac{1}{1 + 6.44a}; a = \frac{\tau}{m}$$

Now consider that we want to increase the throughput. What are the options? To increase S, we must decrease a. That means that we must either decrease τ or increase m. In other words, we can shorten the length of the bus (decrease the maximum time to move the first bit from the sender to the farthest station on the bus) or increase the length of the time it takes to put a message on the channel (increase the length of the message). We cannot change the rate at which bits move on the channel—essentially the speed of light. The only way to decrease τ is to shorten the bus. The other variable, m, is the time required to put the message onto the bus. If we were able to dramatically increase the rate at which we write the bits to the channel, what would be the effect on throughput? As m becomes much smaller, a becomes larger, and S decreases!

As we increase the transmission rate on a CSMA/CD network, we decrease the throughput, thus getting less and less use of the channel capacity. This is why the use of CSMA/CD channel access is not considered the best plan for high-speed networks, operating at 100 Mbps or more.

Ethernet and IEEE 802.3

The CSMA/CD protocol offers a number of advantages over other options for implementing local area networks. The behavior required of each participating station is simple and easy to implement. Failure by any subset of the stations leaves the others unaffected (unless the failure involves continuous transmission). Stations are easily added to or removed from the network without effect on the other stations. In addition, the CSMA/CD scheme was an early solution to the question of how to allow communication among attached network stations. Early on, details of the method were agreed to by Digital Equipment Corporation, Intel, and Xerox (DIX). The resulting DIX standard for Ethernet communications gained the distinct advantage of a large market share. This historical event is partly responsible for the dominance of Ethernet in the local area network arena. When the IEEE committee on local area network protocols began to produce standards, they essentially adopted the, by then, defacto standard Ethernet.

Frame Format and Addressing   The format of a frame on a CSMA/CD LAN is shown in Figure 13.8. The frame is transmitted most significant bit first (MSB), that is, in left-to-right order as shown in the figure. The **preamble** is a sequence of 8 bytes, each consisting of the bit pattern 10101010, used for synchronizing the electronic interfaces between stations on the network. The preamble is immediately followed by the single-byte **start frame delimiter (SFD)**, which consists of the bit pattern 10101011 and signals the start of the actual transmission. The **destination address (DA)** identifies the station that is expected to receive the transmission. All stations on the network must be listening for all transmissions. When a station's interface recognizes its own address, it copies the rest of the transmission and passes it up to the logical link control sublayer for further processing. If the DA seen in the frame does not match the local address, the frame is ignored. The **source address (SA)** field identifies the sender of the frame. This is needed for acknowledgment of frames and other network control operations. The **length** field specifies the number of bytes in the logical link control (LLC) field that follows. The **LLC** field is the data that this frame carries. It was handed to the MAC layer for framing and transmission. Because of the requirement for a minimum frame length, which we saw in section 13.2.2, a **pad** is added if necessary to make the frame long enough to guarantee proper operation of the channel access protocol. The **frame check sequence (FCS)** is the 32-bit CRC code described in section 15.1.2. The FCS is computed as the frame is generated and is appended to it. When the frame is received, the FCS is recomputed. If the remainder calculated is not 0, the frame is rejected as containing a transmission error.

Bytes:	7	1	2/6	2/6	<= 1518	Varies	4
	Preamble	SFD	DA	SA	LLC	PAD	FCS

Figure 13.8.

The IEEE 802.x standards all use the same addressing scheme. Addresses are either 16 bits or 48 bits. Addresses of 16 bits are set locally and may be repeated in other LANs. The longer 48-bit address form may be assigned a value locally or may be universally unique, assigned by a central authority. LAN segments connected by repeaters constitute one LAN for the purposes of address resolution, and must consist of unique physical addresses, all of the same length. An address of all 1s is a broadcast to all stations. In both address forms, one bit is used to indicate that the address refers to a single station or to a group of stations. The 48-bit addresses lose another bit in specifying whether the address is locally assigned or universally unique. Of the 48 bits in the address field, 46 are used for individual station addresses. A destination address that is all 1s, whether in the short or long address format, indicates a broadcast transmission that is to be received by all stations.

Initialization, Station Addition and Deletion, Fault Management A distinct advantage of the CSMA/CD protocol for medium access control is its simplicity. The complete independence of the stations means that no special procedures are needed for initializing the network, or for adding or deleting stations. The failure of one station will not affect others. As we will see in the sections that follow, these are significant issues in controlled-access (token-based) schemes. In fact, there are very few problems that can develop in CSMA/CD. If an interface fails, its station will not be able to send or receive, but the other stations will continue to have access to the network. If an interface fails while locked in a transmitting mode, so that the channel becomes inaccessible to other stations, the situation will be detected when a station with a frame ready to send finally gives up gaining access to the channel and reports an error to the higher layers.

13.3 CONTROLLED ACCESS

The CSMA/CD approach to sharing the channel does not require any communication or direct interaction among the stations sharing the channel. This independence means that some collisions will occur. Recovery from the collisions allows the transmission to be completed, but does waste time and channel capacity. Another approach to sharing the channel is by direct communication among the stations such that each is explicitly assigned permission to transmit in turn. Such schemes constitute controlled access to the channel and are implemented by passing a special message, called a token. Token passing requires an ordering among the stations to determine which station receives the token next. The ordering can be either physical ordering, in which each station is connected to its predecessor and successor in a point-to-point link, or logical ordering, in which each station addresses the token to a logical next station on the ring. Each of these approaches has been standardized, as IEEE 802.5 and IEEE 802.4, respectively.

13.3.1 IEEE 802.5: The Token Ring

Stations on a token ring are connected in a closed loop. Each interface to the ring is a repeater, a device that receives an arriving bit and retransmits it. Since each interface resends the bit, the distance that the ring can cover is larger than the bus-based CSMA/CD protocols.

No collisions occur in the token ring because a station sends only on the segment of cable that connects it to the next station in the ring. At the tap, where a station is connected to the network, the only conflict concerning access to the network is between incoming bits and the station that has a frame ready to send. The tap sends from its attached station when the station holds the token. Otherwise, the tap receives a bit from the network, its input line, and then resends it on its output line.

The token consists of 3 bytes that must circulate continuously on the network until captured by a station that has data ready to send. The requirement to keep a token circulating imposes a constraint on the network performance similar to the requirement for a minimum frame length in CSMA/CD that keeps a transmitting station listening long enough to guarantee that it will hear any possible collision. In this case, the problem is that it takes a very long cable to "hold" 24 bits. At the original token ring standard transmission rate of 4 Mbps, it takes 6 μsec to put 24 bits on the channel. For the whole token to fit on the channel at the same time, the first bit must stay on the channel at least 6 μsec. Since the bits move along the channel at a speed approaching the speed of light, this requirement calls for approximately a mile of cable to hold the 24 bits of the token!

To address this problem, the token ring must have an active monitor that includes a 24-bit delay buffer. The buffer effectively slows the bit propagation speed so that 24 bits can be contained on the ring.

The frame formats for the token ring are shown in Figure 13.9. Two types of frames travel around the ring, in addition to the token: MAC-level frames that convey information

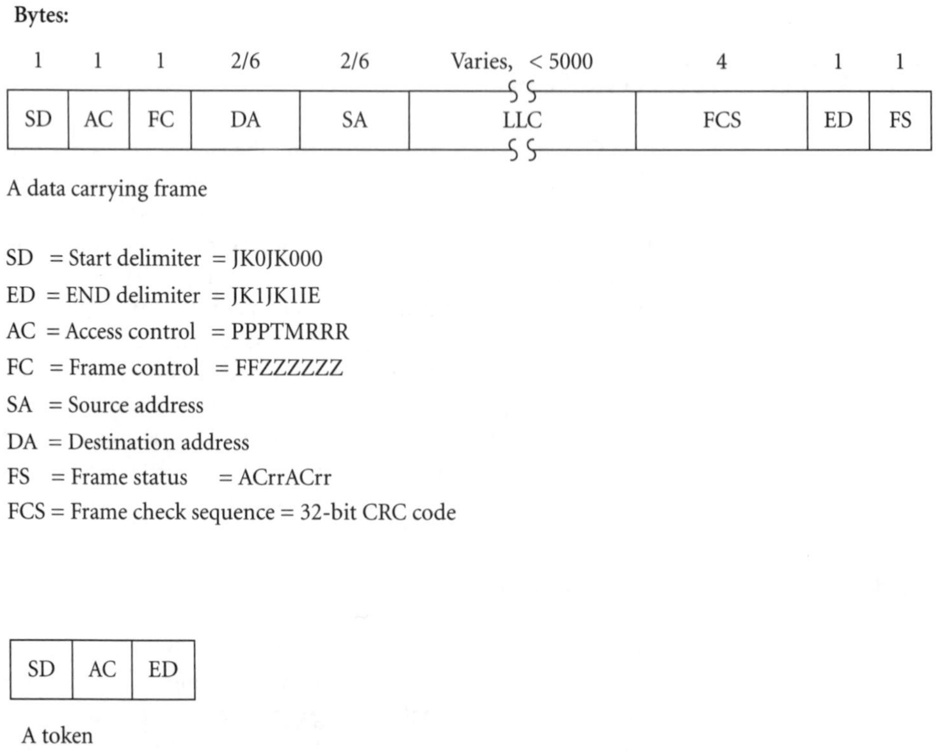

The requirement to keep a token circulating imposes a constraint on the network performance similar to the requirement for a minimum frame length in CSMA/CD that keeps a transmitting station listening long enough to guarantee that it will hear any possible collision.

Bytes:

1	1	1	2/6	2/6	Varies, < 5000	4	1	1
SD	AC	FC	DA	SA	LLC	FCS	ED	FS

A data carrying frame

SD = Start delimiter = JK0JK000
ED = END delimiter = JK1JK1IE
AC = Access control = PPPTMRRR
FC = Frame control = FFZZZZZZ
SA = Source address
DA = Destination address
FS = Frame status   = ACrrACrr
FCS = Frame check sequence = 32-bit CRC code

SD	AC	ED

A token

Figure 13.9. Token ring frame format

among the MAC layers to control and coordinate channel access, and data link frames that carry Data Link layer control information and user data.

The 3 bytes of the token frame are a start delimiter (SD), access control (AC), and end delimiter (ED). The SD alerts the interface that a new frame is beginning. It consists of the 8 bits JK0JK000, where J and K each represent a specific signal voltage that cannot be mistaken for a 0 or a 1 bit.

The SD is followed by an AC byte whose 8 bits are represented as PPPTMRRR. The P bits specify a priority associated with this token and determine which station will gain the token. The T bit is set to 1 to indicate that this is a token. The R bits provide a reservation facility. A station that has a frame ready to send can grab a token if the frame has a priority at least as high as the priority set in the token. If the frame has lower priority, the station can attempt to reserve a future token by setting the reservation bits RRR to match the priority of the frame it has to send. A station can change the reservation bits only if it can raise their value.

In each part of the frame and token formats, the leftmost (high order or most significant bit) is received first. As a station interface receives an incoming bitstream, it first sees the 8 bits of SD, which it regenerates and sends to the output line. Next the 3 priority bits arrive. At this point, the interface does not know if it is receiving a token or a frame.

If the station has a frame ready to send and the frame has higher priority than shown in the incoming priority bits, then if the T bit is set (that is, this is a token), the station changes the T bit to 0, making this a frame, and sends its data. Notice that this is done while seeing only 1 bit at a time. Once a bit has passed, it cannot be changed. To compare priority and reservation bit values with the priority of waiting data and to change the values appropriately without seeing all the bits, the station *must* receive the high-order bits first.

If the incoming bits are part of a frame (T = 0), the data must be sent on, regardless of its priority. If the priority of the waiting data is greater than the reservation bits of the frame, the reservation is changed. When the station that sent the data regenerates the token, it will set the token's priority bits to the value currently in the reservation bits.

The new token will be grabbed by the first station with data priority greater than the token priority—not necessarily the one whose reservation bits were put into the new token's priority bits. If a token is not grabbed by the station receiving it, the AC byte is followed by the end delimiter (ED), which consists of the bits JK1JK1IE. The J and K bits are the same special voltage signals used in the SD. The I bit indemnifies this frame as an intermediate frame of a multiframe sequence. I = 0 if this is the last frame; if I = 1, there are more frames. E is the error-detected bit. As each station's network interface unit (NIU) passes on incoming bits, it checks for the occurrence of transmission errors. If an error is detected, the station issues a warning to other stations by setting E = 1. By noting how frequently it generates an E = 1 bit, the station interface helps identify cable segments that produce a lot of errors. This makes it easy to isolate faulty segments.

If a station has data to send and priority considerations allow it to grab the token, the station generates a **frame control (FC)** byte to follow the AC byte. The FC byte indicates the type of frame this is: MAC or LLC.

The frame control byte is followed by the destination address (DA) and then the source address (SA). A receiving interface compares the destination address with its own station address, bit by bit. If a match occurs, the interface begins copying the incoming bits to its own buffer. If no errors are found in the arriving bitstream (that is, the receiver detects no errors and E = 0 in the ED), the arriving frame is handed up to the LLC. If any errors are detected, the frame is not delivered to the LLC, and the interface and the **frame status (FS)** byte is constructed to inform the sender of the frame of its fate. The FS byte has format ACrrACrr, where the bits labeled r are reserved for future use and are set to 0. The A and C bits describe what occurred when the frame reached its destination. A = 1 means the destination address was recognized. This means that the address was valid and that the station addressed was functioning and able to receive data. C = 1 confirms that the data frame was copied to the destination's buffer for hand off to higher layer processing.

Addressees in all the 802.x MAC protocols are of the same format. Addresses are either 16 or 48 bits in length. Short addresses are assigned locally, and the same address may occur on many individual networks. The first bit of the address is 1 if the address refers to a group of destinations, and 0 if the destination is a single station. This bit is called the **I/G bit** for individual or group address.

13.3.2   IEEE 802.4: The Token Bus

The protocol controlling token passing is more complex on the token bus than on the token ring because all the stations are attached to the common bus, and the token must be addressed to its intended receiver.

The token bus combines the flexible layout of a bus with the controlled access of the token ring. A logical ring is formed from the stations connected to a bus network. The protocol controlling token passing is more complex on the token bus than on the token ring because all the stations are attached to the common bus, and the token must be addressed to its intended receiver. Thus each station must know about its successor on the logical ring. Each station must also know about its predecessor. If a station goes down, and thus cannot receive the token, the sender must be able to locate the next logical station after the one that is not responding.

Though the stations in the logical ring of the token bus all access the same physical channel, collisions are avoided by having each station refrain from transmitting until it possesses the token. The station holding the token has control of the channel for a fixed amount of time. The time a station has access to the channel must be shared among four priority classes: 0, 2, 4, and 6 (highest). A station assigns a share of its time to each class with definite preference for the higher priorities.

The combination of token passing access control and the use of a common bus to carry transmissions implies a number of maintenance requirements. First, the ring must be initialized. Each station must be given its logical position in the ring, and must learn the identity of its predecessor and its successor on the ring. One station must be given first use of the token. Second, provision must be made for stations to join the ring and to leave it. Addition of an extra station will change the token rotation time (the time it takes for the token to get back to a station that hands it off). The new station must also be assigned a position in the ring, and the information stored by its predecessor and successor must be adjusted. Removing a station from the ring also changes the token rotation time, this time reducing it. The deleted station's predecessor and successor must have their tables adjusted also. Finally, there must be a provision for error recovery. If a station goes down and cannot receive the token, a procedure is needed to allow the token holder to discover which is the next logical station to receive the token. If a station goes down while holding the token, a procedure is needed to note the loss of the token and to generate exactly one replacement. Each of these issues must be addressed whenever a network design requires a token and explicit knowledge of other stations by individual stations. In the following sections, we will look at how the issues are addressed in the IEEE 802.4 token bus standard.

Ring Initialization The ring must be initialized whenever there is no activity occurring. This could be at the time of the initial setup or because an error condition has resulted in the loss of the token. A station detecting lack of activity on the ring will issue a *claim token* MAC control frame. It will wait for a period of time equal to some number of maximum round-trip delay times (response windows). The number of windows it will wait is determined from the first 2 bits of the station's address. If the station hears activity on the channel before the number of windows it is waiting, it will assume that some other station is also soliciting the token, and it will defer to the other station. After waiting the indicated number of response windows, the station cannot just generate a token. It is possible that some other station has also sent a claim token frame and has heard no activity on the bus. (Remember that there is no collision detection mechanism in the token bus. A station does not listen while it is transmitting.) Thus, on hearing silence in the number of windows specified, the station will issue another claim token frame and wait again, this time using the second 2 bits of its address to determine the number of response times to wait. This process is repeated until the station has used the last 2 bits of its address and has still heard silence after its claim token frame. At that point, it will generate a frame that is the token and proceed to send data or pass on the token to its successor.

In the case of ring initialization before any transmissions have occurred, the station will not have a successor identified. It then uses the solicit successor frame as described in the next section.

Adding a Station A new station is given an address, which will determine its logical position in the ring, and listens to the channel, waiting for an invitation to join. Periodically, a station holding the token must send the MAC control frame **solicit successor**. The data unit of a solicit successor frame contains the address of the station that is currently the next station. A new station waiting to join the network sees the address of the station that is looking for a new network participant in the source address of the solicit successor frame. If its address lies between the source address and the next station address in the frame, it responds by sending a **set successor** MAC control frame. The new station now has a position in the ring and participates in the network.

If more than one new station is waiting to join the network and they have addresses between the source address and next station address, a collision will occur when both try to respond. In that case, the station that invited a response from a new station will send another MAC control frame, this time **resolve contention**. The station will wait for a period of time equal to four times the maximum round-trip propagation delay on the network. These four round-trip times constitute four windows of opportunity for a new station to send a response. Stations wanting to join the ring respond in the time window indicated by the first 2 bits of their own address. Thus, if a new station has an address that begins with 00, it will respond immediately. If it has an address that begins with 01, it will wait for the next window to respond. The first new station to respond "wins" and the token will be passed to it. Other stations will wait for the next invitation to join the cycle initiated by the new station. If more than one new station has the same first 2 bits, their responses will collide, and the process is repeated using the second pair of bits. This process is repeated as many times as necessary to get a single response from a new station. Since no two stations have exactly the same address, the process must eventually lead to a resolution and a new station joins the ring. If more than two stations are involved in one collision, but one or more is not involved in the next collision, the stations will realize the collision occurred before they responded because they will hear a transmission on the channel in the period before they would reply to the solicit successor frame.

Once the new next station is identified, the current token holder passes the token to the new station. The station that was previously the next station will learn of the new addition from the source address in the token that it will receive later. If a station sending *solicit successor* receives no response, no new station is waiting to join the network in the position between that station and its successor, so the station sends the token to its successor.

Deleting a Station   A station wishing to leave the ring must first update the successor information of its predecessor. It waits until it has the token. Then the departing station (A) sends a *set successor* MAC control frame to its predecessor (B), giving it the address of its own successor (C). A then passes the token to C and departs. The next time B receives the token, it will pass it to C, at which point C will learn the identity of its new predecessor from the source address field in the token.

Fault Management   Several problems can occur during the operation of a token bus. The problem of a lost token is corrected by the initialization procedure described previously. Other error cases and their corrections are described next.

If more than one token exists at any time, all transmissions will collide and no communication can occur. Multiple token detection occurs when the holder of the token hears a transmission that suggests some other station also holds a token. When a station detects this condition, it immediately defers to the other station, thus reducing the number of tokens. Since all stations behave in this way, the number of tokens will drop to one or zero. If the number of tokens drops to one, then normal operations proceed; otherwise, the ring initialization process will regenerate a token and operation is restored.

When a station passes the token to its successor, it must verify that the successor is active and participating in the network. The station that passes the token thus listens to the channel for a transmission originating at its successor. If the successor is active, a valid frame will be sent—either a data frame or the token being passed. In that case, the station can return to a state of listening for frames addressed to itself. If no valid frame is heard, the station again tries to send the token to its successor. If a second retransmission of the token also fails, the station assumes the successor is not responding, and it then sends a MAC control frame *who follows* with the address of its successor, looking for the next logical station in the network. If two tries of *who follows* also fail, the station sends *solicit successor*, inviting a response from any station on the network. If that succeeds, a ring is reestablished, with the responder becoming the new successor of the station passing the token. If there is no response to the *solicit successor* frame, a major fault has occurred that involves complete loss of network communication. The reason could be a break in the transmission medium, a failure of the receiver of the station holding the token, or failure of all other stations on the network.

Frame Format and Addressing   The frame format of the token bus is shown in Figure 13.10. The preamble is used for timing and coordination between sender and receiver stations. The standard requires that the preamble lasts a minimum of 2 microseconds. The beginning of the actual frame is a start delimiter (SD) whose form is JK0JK000, where J, K are nondata signals that are clearly distinguishable from a 0 or a 1. The frame control (FC) byte tells what type of frame this is—a MAC frame or a data link frame. If the frame is a

A data carrying frame

Bytes: >=1	1	1	2/6	2/6	Varies, > 0	4	1
Preamble	SD	FC	DA	SA	LLC	FCS	ED

SD = Start delimiter = JK0JK000

ED = End delimiter = JK1JK1IE

FC = Frame control = FFZZZZZZ

SA = Source address

DA = Destination address

FCS = Frame check sequence = 32-bit CRC code

Figure 13.10. Token bus frame format

MAC-level control frame, bits of the FC byte also identify its function (token, solicit successor, claim token, set successor, who follows, or resolve contention), as described under the preceding ring operation sections. If it is an LLC frame, the data unit carries a Data Link-layer protocol data unit. The frame check sequence (FCS) is the CRC-32 code calculated on the contents of the frame to detect any transmission errors. The receiving station recomputes the FCS and compares its calculation to the value found in the frame. The **end delimiter (ED)** marks the end of the frame and allows the receiving station to know where the FCS is. The format of the ED is JK1JK1IE, where the JK bits again indicate nondata voltage signals. $I = 1$ indicates that this is an intermediate frame; $I = 0$ indicates that this is the last frame of this data. The E bit is set to 1 if an error is detected. The E bit is set by a repeater that sends this frame on to another cable segment. A repeater that detects errors retains a count of them to help in identifying error-prone cable segments.

The addressing scheme used by the IEEE 802.4 token bus is the same as that used by the other IEEE LAN standards.

Priorities and Token Rotation Time   Both the token ring and the token bus standards include provision for assigning priorities to data as an option. The token ring supports four priority classes:

Class	Description
6	Synchronous
4	Asynchronous urgent
2	Asynchronous normal
0	Asynchronous time available

Each station must be aware of a total token rotation time associated with each priority class. In addition, it has a **token holding time (THT)**. On receiving the token, a station transmits its class 6 data for as long as class 6 data is still available and the THT has not expired. Class 6 data has hard time constraints, such as real-time voice that must not be delayed. Classes 4, 2, and 0 provide for transmission of data with varying degrees of time constraints. A separate timer is associated with each class of data, assigning it some portion of the station's access to the channel. A token rotation time is maintained to guarantee the maximum time a station must wait to receive the token again.

13.4 JOINING LANS

There are advantages to each of the medium access control methods described in the previous sections. It is often necessary to pass data from one LAN to another; sometimes between LANs of the same type, sometimes between LANs of different types. The complexity of this inter-LAN communication depends on the types of LANs to be joined.

A single station connected to both LANs performs the task of taking a transmission from one LAN and retransmitting it to the other. In this section, we introduce in general terms the requirements for inter-LAN communication. In Chapter 14, we look in greater detail at common connections between LANs.

13.4.1 Bridges

A bridge performs filtering on addresses in addition to retransmitting. Filtering requires that the bridge recognize the address field in a data unit and make a decision whether data units with that address should or should not be forwarded. In Figure 13.11, Br2 is a bridge that forwards from LAN B to LAN C all data units that appear on LAN B and have destination address on LAN C.

When the networks connected by bridges are Ethernets, each segment is separate as far as common channel sharing is concerned. The maximum propagation delay on LAN A is the time required for a bit to travel from Host A1 to Host A5, for example.

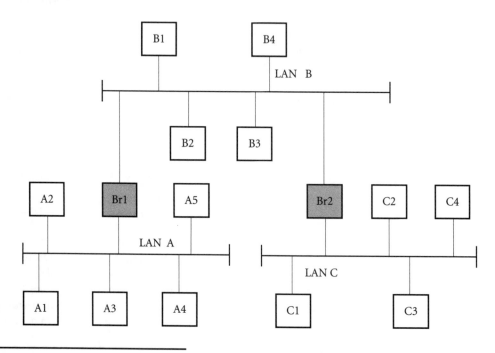

Figure 13.11. Bridges joining networks

A bridge that joins Ethernets listens for a clear channel, then transmits and continues to listen to the channel to determine that no collision has occurred.

A bridge is itself a host on each network to which it is attached. A bridge that joins Ethernets listens for a clear channel, then transmits and continues to listen to the channel to determine that no collision has occurred. If a collision does occur, the bridge participates in the binary exponential backoff (see section 13.2.2) like any other Ethernet host. This implies that the bridge must be able to receive frames from one network, and buffer them until it can retransmit them onto the other network.

Consider the example network of Figure 13.11. If Host B4 is sending a large file to Host A2, B4 will produce a number of frames that must pass through bridge Br1. If the traffic on LAN B is light, B4 will send the frames in rapid succession. If traffic is heavy on LAN A at that time, Br1 will not be able to forward the frames as fast as they arrive from B4. Data Link-layer flow control procedures will be invoked to slow down sending from B4.

A bridge operates only at the Data Link and Physical layers; thus it is not able to perform functions associated with higher layers. For example, a bridge cannot split frames into smaller frames or reassemble frames as specified in Network layer operation (see section 12.4.3). This is not an issue when a bridge connects two identical networks because the sizes of the frames will be the same on both networks. However, if a bridge were to join LANs with different maximum frame sizes, the bridge might receive a frame that is too large to pass on to the other LAN. The bridge would drop the frame.

Because bridges must make forwarding decisions based on addresses, the addresses on all the LANs interconnected by bridges form a single domain. The addresses of all the hosts shown in Figure 13.11, for example, form a single address space. The addresses must all be of the same type, and there must be no duplicate addresses. The addresses defined in IEEE 802.3, 4, and 5 are all of the same type and could appear on both sides of a bridge. The choice of 16-bit or 48-bit addresses, allowed by those standards, must be the same on both sides of the bridge. If globally unique addresses are used, there is no problem assuring the uniqueness of addresses in the set of hosts connected by bridges. If addresses are locally assigned, they must be carefully chosen to make unique addresses throughout the domain connected by bridges.

13.4.2   Routers

Routers connect networks at the Network layer and can translate from one data link protocol to another. In addition to acting like a host on each network, the router looks at the internetwork address to choose the path on which to forward the frame. A router can fragment an incoming frame before forwarding it if necessary. Because routers use the Network-layer address, they can forward frames toward any host in the world that uses the same type of Internet addresses. A particular router recognizes Internet IP addresses or OSI IP addresses, for example. Because it can fragment and reassemble frames, a router is the usual choice for interconnecting different IEEE 802.x networks.

The distinction between bridges and routers has become blurred with the introduction of hybrid machines that act as bridges and perform some of the functions of routers, such as fragmentation and reassembly of frames. **Brouters** may act as bridges and be able to route only some specific protocols.

13.4.3   Higher-Layer Gateways

Use of different Transport-layer protocols can prevent systems from communicating. It sometimes happens that a particular network will have some hosts that use one Transport-layer protocol (Internet TCP, for example) and some that use another (perhaps Digital's LAT). Since the hosts are on the same network, their communications can be delivered since they will use the same data link protocol. However, they will not be able to perform Transport-layer functions. This problem is addressed by placing a transport protocol converter on the network. This special-purpose host receives each frame. If it determines that the source and destination addresses for the frame correspond to hosts that use different transport protocols, it converts the frame from the transport format of the sender to the transport format of the destination host and passes the converted frame to the destination.

If the hosts employing different Transport-layer protocols are on different networks, several possibilities exist for allowing them to interact. If the different networks are connected by bridges, then the frames can be exchanged without regard to differences in the Transport layer. Once the frame arrives on the destination LAN, it can be translated with a Transport-layer protocol converter, as described previously.

If the hosts employing different transport protocols cannot exchange messages through bridges, then they must communicate through a device that joins networks at a higher layer. An ordinary router is not sufficient because network and transport protocols are selected from the same suite. Thus a network that uses TCP will also use Internet IP; a network that uses Digital's LAT will also use a corresponding network protocol from Digital. Communication between such systems requires a protocol converter and router that can translate both Transport and Network layers. Since this device may be attached to dissimilar LANs, it may also have to translate between two different LAN protocols.

Communication between such systems involves processes above the Transport layer that need to communicate and that have different network services at the Transport layer and lower. Such situations are unusual, though not impossible. An example is an implementation of the mail system MH (see section 5.2) developed for an IBM SNA host exchanging mail with MH running on a UNIX system on a TCP/IP network. Here the application processes (MH on both systems) are compatible, but the network services over which they run are not compatible. A Transport-layer gateway would allow them to interact.

13.4.4   Application Gateways

An application gateway is required when two different approaches to a particular application need to interact. An example is electronic mail. Independently implemented approaches to electronic mail might include different entries in the message headers, and different formats of similar entries. Sender and receiver addresses might be in different forms in the two mail systems. Differences in the user interface are not significant because they do not affect the way mail is handled within the network. Thus if one person uses Pegasus and another uses MH, they can still communicate. What is important are those aspects of mail handling that allow the message to be transmitted and delivered. The interaction between the user agent and the message transfer agent and between message transfer agents is important to communication between mail system users. A **mail gateway** accepts deliv-

A mail gateway accepts delivery of a mail message sent with one system and resends the message with a different system.

ery of a mail message sent with one system and resends the message with a different system. Mail gateways exist to convert between SMTP and X.400, and between many other pairs. To avoid the proliferation of such mail system gateways, X.400 is used as a common denominator by many systems. A mail gateway converts from one mail system to X.400, and then another converts from X.400 to another system. Thus each individual mail system does not need a gateway to each other mail system, but only a gateway to and from X.400.

SUMMARY

Transmission in networks consisting of a number of stations sharing one communication medium requires coordination. Two approaches are contention-based access and controlled access. The protocols for both of these medium access control (MAC) techniques are based on fair access to all stations, efficient channel use, and frame transmission as soon as a station is ready and the channel is clear.

In contention-based networks, concerns include vulnerability of a frame, throughput, delay, and collisions. Important measures are the probability of a frame getting through and the maximum throughput. Increasing capabilities are found in the Aloha network, the slotted Aloha network and the Ethernet, but each has shortcomings. The slotted Aloha network reduces vulnerability to collision compared to Aloha and increases throughput, but at the cost of delay in frame transmission. Further, its stations must be synchronized.

A carrier sense multiple access (CSMA), or listen before talk (LBT), network reduces the time of vulnerability and improves throughput, but still allows collisions and does not recognize them when they occur. Three variations of CSMA are discussed: non-persistent, p-persistent, and 1-persistent. A CSMA/CD network adds collision detection to CSMA. Ethernet is CSMA/CD with 1-persistent CSMA. Simplicity characterizes the CSMA/CD approach, but as transmission rate increases, throughput decreases resulting in lower usage of channel capacity.

Controlled access MAC techniques involve direct communication among stations, with each station explicitly assigned permission to transmit in turn. These techniques are implemented by token passing. Ordering among stations is required to determine which gets the token next. The ordering is physical, as in the token ring network, or logical, as in the token bus network. IEEE 802.5 and IEEE 802.4 are standards documents for the token ring and token bus, respectively. In a token ring, there are no collisions. Each station interface is a repeater; it receives and retransmits each frame. In a token bus, the protocol is more complex because each station must know its successor and predecessor. If a station goes down, the next logical station must be identified.

EXERCISES

1. Distinguish between contention-based and controlled access.
2. Determine the current status of Aloha (or slotted Aloha).
3. Which of Aloha's principles are found in Ethernet? What do networks that contain mobile hosts (for example, systems carried by individuals) have in common with Aloha?
4. Verify that the maximum throughput achievable for pure Aloha channels is 18.4 percent using Poisson behavior.

5. Why is throughput not the only criteria for an effective and efficient network architecture?

6. What is a realistic tradeoff between throughput and delay? Which access method comes closest to this tradeoff? Explain your answer.

7. Under what conditions will collisions occur in a p-persistent CSMA?

8. Graph the throughput in a p-persistent CSMA for values of offered load from 0 to 10 in increments of 1.

9. List several advantages and disadvantages of physical and logical ordering in token ring networks.

10. Specify at least two industry applications in which a token bus is used. Could a token ring, CSMA, or CSMA/CD be used more effectively in the applications? Explain.

11. Token ring priorities range from 000 to 111, with 111 highest. Suppose a station has data with priority 011. Show all possible incoming priority bit patterns and the changes that result. Show the decision as each bit arrives. Repeat for priority 101.

12. Distinguish between MAC and LLC frame types.

13. What is the only possible value for the I/G bit in a source address field?

14. How many different stations can be accommodated with the 16-bit address format?

15. What are all possible combinations of values of the EAC bits and their meanings in the token ring?

16. Review the process of adding a new station to a token bus. What is the ordering of addresses with respect to token passing? (That is, do the stations pass the token to the next higher or the next lower address?) Assume stations with addresses as shown here (in hex) are currently part of a token ring. Show the steps by which a station with the address 3AD2 would join the ring. Current ring station addresses: 21A4 2D35 3592 3D2B 3FC3.

17. Assume one station on a LAN is a file server and the other stations are user/clients. On this LAN, why should passwords be encrypted? What other privacy or security issues pertain to this type of LAN? Which of these issues are common to all other types of LANs?

CHAPTER 14

Bridges Between LANs

KEY CONCEPTS
- Transparent or Spanning Tree Bridges
- Source Routing Bridges
- SRT Bridges
- SLIP and PPP
- Vulnerability and Privacy Issues

The tasks that fall to bridges were described in general terms in section 13.4.1. In this chapter, we will describe techniques used to accomplish these requirements.

Two very different approaches to bridging networks have appeared. The key difference between them is where the burden of required processing is placed—in the bridge or in the host that sends the frame. There are advantages to each approach. If the processing burden is in the host (or the host's **network interface unit, NIU**, specifically), then the bridge can be very simple and operate at greatest speed in forwarding frames. If the processing is done by the bridge, NIUs can be kept simple and inexpensive. As we will see, placing the burden in the NIU also allows optimal routing among connected LANs, at a cost.

We look first at the approach that puts the burden on the bridge (transparent or spanning tree bridges) and then at the less common approach of putting the burden on the NIU of each host (source routing bridges).

14.1 TRANSPARENT OR SPANNING TREE BRIDGES

The **spanning tree bridge** is also called a **transparent bridge** because its existence and functioning is transparent to hosts attached to the network. In Figure 14.1, Host A2 would send a frame to Host C3 without knowing where C3 is located or that the frame must pass through two bridges to reach its destination. The transparent bridge is also easy on the network administrator: it requires no configuration and no initialization. It is connected to each of the networks it will link and left to learn which addresses are on each network.

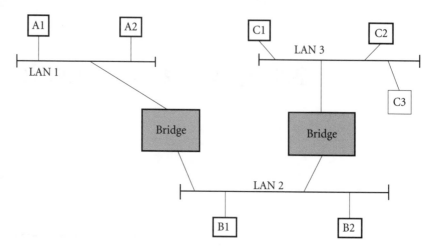

Figure 14.1. The spanning tree bridge

When first installed, the bridge has no information about the hosts on the attached networks. Each time the bridge sees a frame, it records in a **forwarding database** where the sender of the frame is located. When it sees a frame with a destination that is in the forwarding database, it knows whether or not to forward the frame. The bridge quickly learns the location of each host and efficiently forwards only those frames that belong on the other network. Each entry in the bridge's forwarding database contains the address of a host, the bridge port corresponding to the LAN on which the host was detected, and a timer value. Each time the host address is seen as a frame source, the timer is updated. When an entry becomes "old," usually in a few minutes, it is deleted from the database. This allows the bridge to adjust quickly if a station is moved.

The bridge quickly learns the location of each host and efficiently forwards only those frames that belong on the other network.

Figure 14.2 illustrates a potential problem for a bridge behaving as we have just described. The figure shows two bridges between the same two networks. If station A sends a frame to any station that is not known to either bridge, each bridge will forward the frame to the other network. Each bridge on the second LAN will see the frame forwarded by the other bridge. Still not knowing where the destination host is, each bridge will forward the other's frame back to the network from which it was sent. There it will be seen by each bridge and forwarded again. The looping will continue and bring down both networks. To

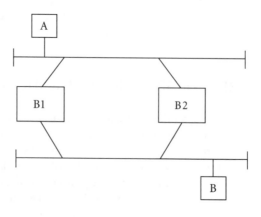

Figure 14.2. Loop in the topology

prevent this looping, the topology of the interconnected networks must form a **spanning tree**. A spanning tree is the set of all nodes in a graph plus a subset of the links such that all the nodes are connected, but there is only one path between any pair of nodes. In the case of bridged networks, the spanning tree is constructed from the bridges, assuring that there is only one path from any bridge to any other bridge. The networks are the links between pairs of bridges.

Any number of bridges can be used to connect networks into any topology. The transparent bridges construct a spanning tree, without the intervention of a network administrator, by executing a spanning tree algorithm. The spanning tree algorithm involves **bridge protocol data units (BPDUs)**, by which the bridges communicate with each other. Each bridge must have a unique bridge identifier; there must also be an address that is received by all the bridges that see it in any transmission, and each port of a bridge must have an identifier that is unique within that bridge. All these come with the bridges; no human setup is required.

The spanning tree is constructed as follows. The bridge with the lowest bridge identifier becomes the root of the spanning tree. Each other bridge then determines which of its ports provides the best access to the root bridge. That port becomes the *root port* for that bridge. Next, exactly one bridge on each network is selected as the bridge that will forward traffic toward the root bridge, the **designated bridge**. This is always the bridge that offers the least cost path toward the root bridge.

In each designated bridge, the root port and all ports for LANs for which it is designated are placed in a *forwarding* state. All other ports are placed in a *blocking* state. Some of the bridge-forwarding capacity is lost if there are redundant connections. This is necessary to prevent the looping problem described earlier. Though it is not possible to split traffic over parallel bridges due to the spanning tree requirement, parallel bridges do provide backup.

Bridge ports in the forwarding state are part of the spanning tree. They move frames toward the root bridge and toward the destination LAN. Bridge ports in the blocking state are idle, except that they do receive BPDUs addressed to all bridges. This is necessary to allow detection of bridge failures.

14.1.1 Sample Connections

Figure 14.3 shows a topology involving six LANs and five bridges. The designation Bx means a bridge with unique id $= x$. B1, having the lowest identifier, becomes the root bridge. On each network, one bridge is found to have the shortest distance to the root. For LAN A, this is bridge B4; LAN B has two bridges that are each one intervening LAN removed from the bridge. The tie is broken by selecting the bridge with the lower id; thus, B3 becomes the designated bridge on LAN B. LAN C also has two bridges. Two paths exist from LAN C to the root bridge: through B3, over LAN F to B1; or through B2, over LAN D, through B5, over LAN E to B1. The path through B3 is shorter, so B3 becomes the designated bridge on LAN C. The shortest path from LAN D to the root is through B5. LAN E is connected to B1.

In Figure 14.4, the designated bridge for each LAN is shown by a double line connecting the bridge to the LAN. Port numbers shown with an *, such as port 3 of bridge B3, are the ones used by that bridge to reach the root. Ports that do not connect a LAN to its

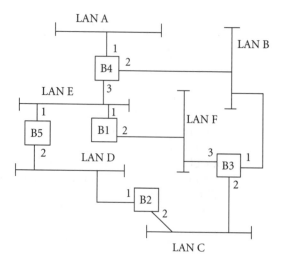

Figure 14.3. Networks connected by bridges

designated bridge and are not used by a bridge to reach the root are in a blocking state and do not forward frames.

Bridge B2 is not the designated bridge for either of its attached LANs and can be used only in case of failure of bridge B3 or B5. At this stage, we can see that any frames on LAN B will be considered by B3 as candidates for forwarding. If B3 recognizes that the destination address of a frame is on LAN B, it will not forward the frame. If B3 does not know where the destination is, or if it knows that the destination is not LAN B, B3 will forward the frame. Similarly, each of the other designated bridges will examine frames and choose whether or not to forward each one.

Consider how frames move in this interconnected network. A frame that begins on LAN B and has a destination on LAN F is detected by bridge B3. Checking its forward-

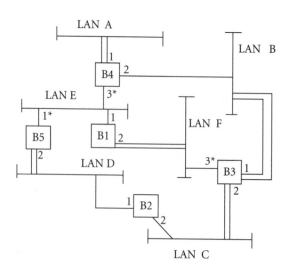

Figure 14.4. Networks connected by bridges showing designated bridges and root ports

ing database, B3 determines that the frame must be forwarded. B3 transmits the frame on port 3. B1 detects the frame on LAN F but finds that it does not require forwarding.

Consider a frame that originates on LAN C with destination on LAN D. Bridge B2 cannot be used to move the frame because the spanning tree algorithm has placed B2's ports in the blocking state. The frame is forwarded by B3 through its root port onto LAN F. Root bridge B1 receives the frame from LAN F and forwards it to LAN E. On LAN E, the frame is seen by bridges B4 and B5. If B4 recognizes the destination address (finds it in its routing table), it will ignore the frame. If B4 does not recognize the address, it will forward it on its port 1 to LAN A. B5 will forward the frame from LAN E to LAN D, and the frame will reach its destination.

This example clearly illustrates a weakness of the spanning tree or transparent bridge. Some frames will take nonoptimal routes to reach their destinations because of the requirement that no loops be present in the topology.

Remember that all the LANs connected by bridges constitute one expanded virtual LAN. All the addresses in the expanded LAN must be unique. The address tables built in the bridges will include all the stations in the expanded LAN, not just the stations on the LANs directly attached to particular bridges. Each bridge, on receiving a frame, examines its forwarding table and does one of three tasks:

- If the destination address of the frame is found to be in the direction of the port on which it arrived, the bridge does nothing with the frame.

  Example: Frame with source and destination both on LAN A would not be forwarded by B4.

  Example: Frame with source on LAN E and destination on LAN A would not be forwarded by B1 because both source and destination of the frame are reached by port 1 of B1.

- If the destination address is found to be on other than the port through which the frame arrived, the frame is forwarded on the port that moves the frame toward its destination. Note that the forwarding is not always toward the root. When a bridge corresponds to the root of a subtree in the spanning tree, it may forward a frame from one of its children to another.

  Example: Frame with source LAN A and destination LAN D is forwarded by B4 on port 3 to move toward the root.

  Example: Frame with source LAN B and destination LAN C is forwarded by B3 on port 2.

- If the destination address does not have a current entry in the forwarding database, it is forwarded on all nonblocking ports except the one on which it arrived.

  Example: Frame with source on LAN B and destination not recognized by B3 is forwarded by B3 on ports 2 and 3.

  Example: Frame with source on LAN A and destination not recognized by B4 is forwarded by B4 on port 1, but not on port 2, which is in a blocking state.

14.1.2 Spanning Tree Diagram

Marking designated bridge connections and root ports in a network diagram help mark the paths available to frames. As the number of LANs and bridges increases, however, the

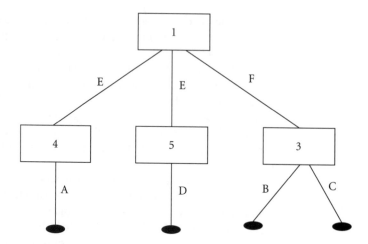

Figure 14.5. First representation of the spanning tree topology

picture becomes more difficult to read. A simple abstraction that captures the relevant information clearly is needed. A first approach at such a view is shown in Figure 14.5. In the diagram, each node corresponds to a bridge, and each branch or arc represents one of the LANs. Bridge B2, whose ports are in the blocking state, does not appear in the tree. Using this representation, we see that a frame with source on LAN D and destination on LAN C must travel through B5 to root bridge B1, then through B3.

Since bridges B4 and B5 both reach the root through LAN E, two different branches are labeled E. This is unsatisfactory and somewhat misleading. In this tree, it appears that traffic going between LANs A and D must be forwarded by the root. In fact, such traffic reaches LAN E and is then forwarded appropriately by B4 or B5.

The tree in Figure 14.6 is a more accurate reflection of the LAN connections. Traffic between bridges B4 and B5 travels over LAN E, the common arc shown above the combined node. Though this example shows only two bridges (B4 and B5) sharing a common LAN (E) for access to the root bridge, there could be any number of such bridges sharing a LAN

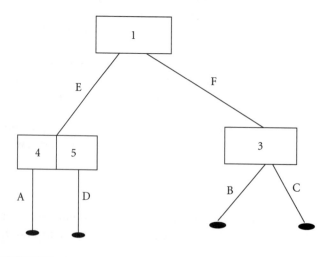

Figure 14.6. Revised representation of the spanning tree topology

Bridges Between LANs

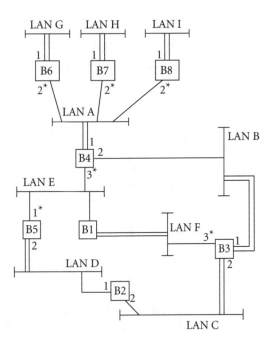

Figure 14.7. Additional LANs in the interconnection

for access to another bridge on the path toward the root. Figure 14.7 shows the LANs of Figure 14.4 with four additional LANs each attached by a bridge to LAN A. The corresponding spanning tree is shown in Figure 14.8.

Using the spanning tree diagram, we can calculate the length of the journey for a frame traveling between any two LANs in terms of the number of LANs traversed and the number of bridges that must forward the frame. In any such computation, each transfer between children of a multibridge node counts as two bridges and one LAN traversal, regardless of

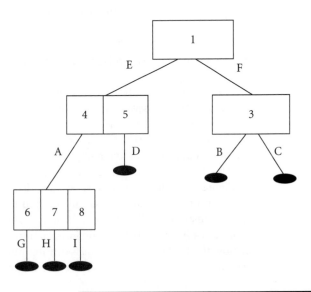

Figure 14.8. Spanning tree topology for the expanded example

the number of bridges represented by the node. Consider the following examples, using the interconnections of Figure 14.7 and the spanning tree representation of Figure 14.8:

Source	Destination	Number of LANs (LAN ids)	Number of Bridges (Bridge ids)
G	I	1 (A)	2 (B6,B8)
H	E	1 (A)	2 (B7,B4)
I	D	2 (A,E)	3 (B7,B4,B5)

The spanning tree diagram makes it easy to determine the maximum path length between nodes. This is the distance from the lowest leaf to the root plus the distance from the root to the lowest node that is not a descendent of the same multinode as the first leaf. In Figure 14.8, the maximum path length is the distance from any one of {G, H, I} to the root plus the distance from the root to either of {B, C}. The leaf corresponding to LAN D cannot be used in this calculation because it is a child of the multinode 4/5 and the LANs G, H, and I are descended from that multinode also.

The spanning tree diagram is easily represented as a modification of the abstract data type *tree*, giving access to standard tree analysis algorithms and their programming language implementations.

Spanning tree bridges construct the spanning tree by exchanging messages called bridge protocol data units (BPDUs). The operation is transparent to users and requires no intervention by a network administrator. The disadvantage of the spanning tree bridge is that the requirement that there be no loops in the topology means that nonoptimal paths may be required of some traffic.

14.2 SOURCE ROUTING BRIDGES

Source routing originated in the IBM token ring community. The approach differs fundamentally from that of the transparent bridge paradigm. In source routing, the responsibility for determining the path a data unit will follow rests with the originating host (more accurately, with the originating host's network interface unit). By placing this responsibility at each host, the source routing scheme achieves two advantages:

- Bridge operation is kept simple.
- The sending host controls the path the data unit follows.

The cost of these advantages is increased complexity at the NIU of each host. There is also extra traffic generated as the hosts send discovery transmissions to determine a route to the destination. The sending host must place into every data frame header, in addition to the source and destination address, a specification of which bridges are to forward the frame and over which intervening networks the frame will pass.

The IEEE 802.5 token ring frame format was presented in Figure 13.9 and is reproduced in Figure 14.9. This format must be expanded to carry the routing information required by source routing. The additional information is inserted following the source address field, and is illustrated in Figure 14.10. A source-routing bridge attached to the token ring network must interpret the routing information in the frame header. An immediate problem is how the bridge will distinguish routing information from ordinary LLC field content. The bridge should look for routing instructions only in those frames that are to leave the

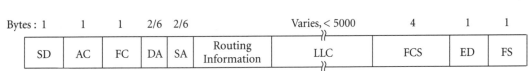

Bytes: 1	1	1	2/6	2/6	Varies, < 5000	4	1	1
SD	AC	FC	DA	SA	LLC	FCS	ED	FS

A data carrying frame

SD = Start delimiter   = JK0JK000
ED = End delimiter   = JK1JK1IE
AC = Access control   = PPPTMRRR
FC = Frame control   = FFZZZZZZ
SA = Source address
DA = Destination address
FS = Frame status   = ACrrACrr
FCS = Frame check sequence = 32-bit CRC code

Figure 14.9. Token ring frame format

local network. This problem was solved by making use of a bit in the source address that is otherwise useless: the one bit that designates an address that refers to a group of stations (section 13.2.2). Since the source address must refer to a single station, the bit that designates a multicast address is superfluous. Source routing uses that bit to indicate that there is routing information in the frame.

Figure 14.11 illustrates the behavior of a source-routing bridge connecting token ring networks. In Figure 14.11(a), Host A transmits a frame with destination Host B. Both hosts are on the same ring, and no routing information is included in the frame header. The bridge acts like every other station on the ring: it reads the header, determines that the frame is not addressed to itself, and repeats the bits onto the ring. Host B receives the frame and also repeats the bits. Host A receives the frame and removes it from the ring. The first bit of A's source address contains 0, indicating a single host address.

In Figure 14.11(b), Host A transmits a frame with destination Host Y. Since Host Y is on a different ring, the frame header includes routing information telling the bridge to forward the frame. The bridge must participate in the token ring protocol just like every other node on the network. In addition, the bridge must examine the source address for an indication that the data unit contains source routing information. The 1 in the first bit of

> The bridge acts like every other station on the ring: it reads the header, determines that the frame is not addressed to itself, and repeats the bits onto the ring. Host B receives the frame and also repeats the bits. Host A receives the frame and removes it from the ring.

Bytes: 1	1	1	2/6	2/6	Varies, < 5000	4	1	1
SD	AC	FC	DA	SA	Routing Information	LLC	FCS	ED	FS

A data carrying frame

SD = Start delimiter   = JK0JK000
ED = End delimiter   = JK1JK1IE
AC = Access control   = PPPTMRRR
FC = Frame control   = FFZZZZZZ
SA = Source address
DA = Destination address
FS = Frame status   = ACrrACrr
FCS = Frame check sequence = 32-bit CRC code

Figure 14.10. Token ring frame format with routing information added

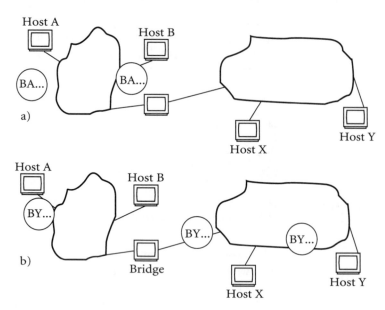

Figure 14.11. Source routing bridge operation

A's address tells the bridge to look for routing information. The routing requires that this bridge forward the frame. The bridge will also repeat the bits onto the ring where they will eventually arrive at A to be removed from the ring. Notice that the confirmation of delivery that A receives in the frame status byte only confirms the delivery to the bridge, not to the final destination station.

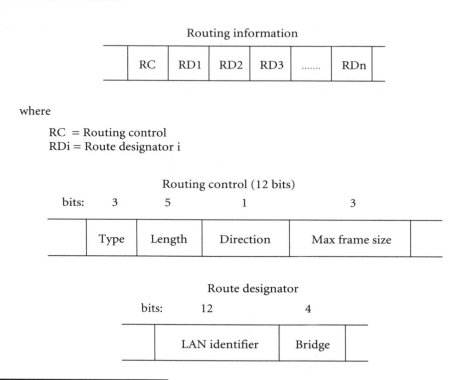

Figure 14.12. Source routing information fields

type One of the following:

  specifically routed The exact route the frame will follow is coded in the routing information

  all paths explorer A discovery frame that is to explore all possible paths between the source and destination

  spanning tree explorer A discovery frame that will only follow paths that are part of a spanning tree

length Number of octets in the routing information field

direction Read the route right to left or left to right

max frame size Selects one of eight possible values: 516, 1500, 2052, 4472, 8144, 11407, 17800, 65565

Figure 14.13. Routing information

route Sequence of two-octet route designators. Each consists of a 12-bit LAN number and a 4-bit bridge number

Routing information consists of a routing control field followed by as many route designators as needed. The format appears in Figure 14.12. The fields contain information shown in Figure 14.13.

The bridge number is useful in path descriptions, but also helps keep the number of message copies down. If a bridge sees a discovery frame, it looks for its own identifier in the accumulated routing information. If the bridge has forwarded this frame before, it does not do so again.

A route consists of LAN Bridge LAN Bridge LAN Bridge . . . LAN. Each route designator consists of a LAN identifier/Bridge pair, so the last route designator contains a LAN identifier and an unused Bridge identifier. The unused 4 bits of the last Bridge identifier is coded as all zeros in implementation, but are ignored by the bridge protocol.

14.3 SRT BRIDGES

Interconnection of LANs using a combination of source routing bridges and transparent bridges clearly won't work. In a world in which both types of bridges could exist, the combination defeats the goal of connectivity.

The solution was removal of source routing bridges from the LAN standards. In its place, SRT (source routing transparent) bridges provide transparent bridge behavior and source routing. Bridges that provide only transparent bridge operation remain in the standards. The compromise allows a source station to attempt to discover the best route to a destination and then use source routing to force traffic onto that route. Because source routing can only use the SRT bridges (not the strictly transparent bridges) between the source and destination, source routing can no longer guarantee the best route.

Operation of an SRT bridge is straightforward. If the bridge observes an RI (route indicator) field in the frame header, it uses source routing procedures; otherwise, it uses transparent bridge procedures.

14.4 SLIP AND PPP

Serial Line IP (SLIP) [SLI88] provides access to serial lines for applications running over Internet IP. SLIP encapsulates an IP datagram, sends it over a serial connection, receives suitably encapsulated datagrams, and hands their contents up to IP for further handling. SLIP, therefore, acts as a form of Data Link layer.

Because serial connections are slow (compare a 56Kbps modem to a 10 Mbps or 100 Mbps Ethernet connection), interactive connections over serial lines are generally unsatisfactory. To improve performance, **compressed SLIP (CSLIP)** [CSL90] simplifies the TCP and IP headers usually carried in an IP datagram. CSLIP reduces the usual 40-byte headers to 3 or 5 bytes. CSLIP maintains state for up to 16 TCP connections on each link. Header compression results from understanding that most fields in the headers do not change from one frame to another or change in predictable ways. The smaller headers greatly improve interactive response time.

The point to point protocol (PPP) [PPP94] builds on the SLIP experience and corrects the shortcomings of SLIP [PC93]. PPP, like SLIP, encapsulates IP datagrams on a serial link. PPP also includes a link control protocol (LCP) to establish, configure, and test the data link connection. Finally, PPP includes a set of network control protocols (NCPs) specific to different Network-layer protocols. Definitions of PPP exist for IP [PPP92b], the OSI Network layer [PPP92c], and AppleTalk [PPP92a], for example. Figure 14.14 shows the format of a PPP frame. The format was chosen to resemble the ISO HDLC definition.

PPP provides header compression like CSLIP; it also provides some other services not available in either SLIP or CSLIP. The presence of the CRC fields provides a check on the transmission of each datagram. Services in NCP allow dynamic negotiation of the IP address on each end of the connection. By contrast, SLIP requires that the IP addresses on both ends be known in advance in order to establish a connection. PPP provides option

Bytes:	1	1	1	2	<= 1500	2	1
	Flag 7E	Addr FF	Control 03	Protocol		CRC	Flag 7E

7E = The flag designating the beginning and ending of the frame: 01111110.
FF = The address field always contains all 1s.
03 = The control field is always 03.

The protocol field serves the same purpose as the Ethernet type field. It identifies the protocol using this service. The following codes are among those defined:

0021 = IP datagram
C021 = Link control data
8021 = Network control data

Figure 14.14. Format of the PPP datagram

negotiation through its link control services. Finally, PPP allows multiple protocols on a single serial line at the same time. SLIP and CSLIP support only IP.

14.5 VULNERABILITY AND PRIVACY ISSUES

In the IEEE 802.3, 4, 5, and 6 standards, all stations have access to all transmissions. The destination address specifies which station is to copy the transmission from the medium and pass it to higher layers for processing. The interface will receive any transmission in which the destination address matches what it is expecting. It is not difficult to make an interface expect all addresses, or just some address that matches the one of another station. Notice that in all these protocols, the intended receiver has no way of knowing if some other station also received the message.

In most cases, a station that receives all transmissions (promiscuous mode) is serving a legitimate and often necessary network management function. It is watching network traffic for the purpose of detecting unusual activity that might indicate a faulty station, or a sudden change in traffic patterns that might signal the need to reconfigure the network. It is also observing the level of traffic to recognize when a split of one LAN into two or more connected by bridges might be called for. In some cases, however, the station in promiscuous mode belongs to an intruder whose sole purpose is to eavesdrop. Remote logins are a favorite source of material for such intruders. The easily read account identifier and password give access to otherwise unavailable resources.

Regardless of whether the promiscuous mode operation is legitimate or the work of an intruder, all transmissions over these local area networks are subject to reception by stations other than the intended receiver. For both security and privacy considerations, every LAN user should be conscious of the openness of transmissions. Passwords sent over LANs need frequent changing. Confidential or private communications require encryption.

SUMMARY

Connection of LANs and MANs at the Data Link layer is possible if the networks use compatible headers and a single physical address space. (No addresses of the network interface units can repeat in the interconnected networks.) The devices that connect such networks are called bridges. The bridge behaves like any other node of each network to which it is attached. It obeys the token-passing protocol of a token ring or token bus network and the contention resolution protocol of an Ethernet. In addition, the bridge notices data units that need to leave the network on which they originated. The bridge decides whether it has responsibility for accepting the data units on their original network and writing them onto another network to which the bridge is connected.

Two approaches for making that decision were presented in this chapter: transparent bridges observe the source of data units they see and thus learn over time where each host is located. The transparent bridges in a set of networks communicate with each other to form a spanning tree that connects all nodes to all others with no loops in the topology. Transparent nodes are designed to take on the work involved in moving data units from one network to another. As the name implies, the operation of these bridges, and the path taken by the data units, are transparent to the sending and receiving network stations. The disadvantage of the transparent bridge approach is that cycles in the topology cannot be allowed. As a result, some paths are not available for data units to follow, and nonoptimal paths result.

An alternative to the transparent bridge approach places responsibility for discovering and specifying the data unit's path in the sending host. Source routing bridges provide this type of service. The bridges are simple; they only need to look at the route that is given in the data unit's header and follow the instructions. The disadvantage associated with source routing is the added complexity needed in every host's network interface unit. In addition, the need for discovery frames adds traffic to the networks.

To provide compatibility among bridges and allow extensive network interconnection, the SRT bridge provides a compromise. Transparent bridge operation is required in all bridges. Source routing is optional. Source stations that wish to specify the route may do so, but are limited to paths that go through bridges that implement the source routing option. All stations can communicate with the transparent bridge operation.

EXERCISES

1. For the following interconnected LAN configuration, determine
   (a) which bridge is root,
   (b) which port is used by each bridge for traffic toward the root,
   (c) which is the designated bridge for each LAN.

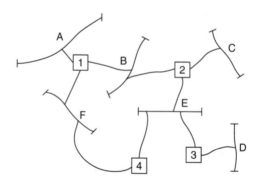

2. For the interconnected LAN configuration of Exercise 1, construct the spanning tree topology graph, similar to the one of Figure 14.8.

3. For the interconnected LAN configuration of Exercise 1, make a table showing the number of LANs traversed and their ids; and the number of bridges passed and their ids for the frames going from LAN A to LAN D, LAN B to LAN A, LAN D to LAN B, LAN C to LAN B.

4. Define a network configuration that illustrates a case where SRT bridges cannot find an optimal route because some of the bridges on the optimal path are transparent bridges only.

CHAPTER 15

Logical Link Control and the Physical Layer

KEY CONCEPTS

- The Data Link Layer: Logical Link Control
- Synchronous and Asynchronous Transfer
- The Physical Layer

We began this book with the intention of emphasizing the computer networking subjects most closely related to application development in a distributed environment. Greatest attention was given to the highest layers of the OSI reference model. We then spent some time in the middle of the stack, learning about the functions of the Transport and Network layers, which provide a dependable communications link over which to build our applications. Still, at those layers, the network is somewhat intangible; it is made up of rules and recovery strategies and is not something we can really get our hands on. We came closer to the real equipment when we discussed the medium access control strategies in Chapter 13; there we got down to actual machines, or at least their network interface cards, attempting to send real bits over a physical medium. We saw how conflicts over use of the resource are resolved and how various strategies provide reliable, more or less simple communication. In Chapter 14, we looked at the methods available to extend a LAN by joining multiple LANs and allowing stations to communicate over the inter-LAN boundaries.

In this final chapter, we attempt to tie up the ends of the story. Though it is seldom of interest to one whose task it is to develop a new application that runs on a network instead of on a single host machine, there are still some necessary elements involved in making a network operable. We will not study these elements in depth, but simply give an introduction to these lowest-layer issues. Whole books and courses in data communications deal with these matters for those who will work closely with them. That is not our purpose. We wish only to give a final word to the story of computer networks.

We begin this final piece with the Logical Link Control component of the Data Link layer and finish it with a very brief overview of the Physical layer. Some topics related to high-speed networks are also introduced.

15.1 THE DATA LINK LAYER: LOGICAL LINK CONTROL

The Data Link layer accepts a packet from the Network layer and, invoking the services of the Physical layer, sends the packet to the next machine on the path to its destination. The function of the logical link control sublayer is to provide services that are common, independent of the particular type of network connection over which the packet will travel.

The responsibilities of the Data Link layer include:

- Delimiting frames so that frame boundaries are clearly discernible
- Detecting errors, including corrupted bits and lost and damaged frames
- Using flow control to limit the rate at which data is sent to the rate at which the receiver can accept it
- Employing link management, including connection establishment and release, and control of sequence numbers used

Communication between machines that share a common resource also involves gaining access to that resource. Because that function involves details of the particular communication link connecting the machines, and varies considerably among the types, it is generally considered separately from the common requirements of the Data Link layer. We discussed medium access control in Chapter 13.

15.1.1 Framing

The Data Link layer verifies the correctness of the bits before handing them up to the higher-layer functions.

The Data Link layer uses the services of the Physical layer to transmit a stream of bits. The Data Link layer verifies the correctness of the bits before handing them up to the higher-layer functions. In order to check the accuracy of transmitted bits, the Data Link layer groups the bits into frames and appends extra bits to serve as check bits. Determining the boundaries of frames, given the possibility of errors in transmission at the Physical layer, requires some thought. Two common techniques are described here: starting and ending flags with bit stuffing and Physical-layer coding violations.

Starting and Ending Flags with Bit Stuffing

A common technique for marking the beginning and end of a frame is to use a reserved bit pattern. The pattern 01111110 begins and ends each frame, for example; all bits between the delimiters constitute the actual transmission. The Data Link layer includes additional bits to verify the accuracy of the others. We look at the generation and interpretation of the check bits in section 15.1.2.

Naturally, if the pattern 01111110 indicates the end of a frame, it is critical that that pattern not occur in the data carried by the frame. Bit stuffing eliminates any possibility of the pattern appearing in the data. The process works as follows. As the data bits of a transmission are handed to the Physical layer, the Data Link layer monitors the number of consecutive ones in the transmission. If a pattern of five ones ever appears, the Data Link layer inserts a zero after the fifth one. Only in sending the end-of-frame pattern will six ones appear consecutively. To compensate for this modification of the data sent, the receiving Data Link layer removes any zero that follows five ones. The result is the restoration of the original transmission. The following example demonstrates the process:

```
Original transmission:  10010011100111111111100111111001111101110
Note that the end-of-frame sequence 01111110 appears in the
data, and further the sequence 0111110 also appears.

Frame delimited sequence sent:
    01111110100100111001111101111100011111010011111001110011001111110
    --------            -       -       -       -      --------
```

All the bits added by the framing and bit stuffing procedure are underlined.

Notice that the example includes the string 0111110, which would not be confused with the delimiter but would be incorrectly handled by the receiver if it were transmitted without change. (The receiving Data Link layer, on seeing five ones followed by a zero, would assume that the sending Data Link layer had inserted the zero after seeing five ones and would remove it.) To make the final string correct, the sending Data Link layer must insert a zero after the five ones in the data string. When the receiver removes the zero after every string of five ones in the example, the original string is restored.

The flag 01111110 delineates the beginning and end of frames in SDLC (synchronous data link control protocol, the data link portion of IBM's SNA), ADCCP (advanced data communications protocol, a modification of SDLC adapted by ANSI), HDLP (High-level data link protocol, the ISO modification of SDLC), LAP and LAPB (link access procedure, the CCITT version of HDLP and part of the X.25 network interface standard), and the IEEE 802 LLC (logical link control, based on HDLC and resembling LAPB). Bit stuffing prevents the flag pattern from appearing in the data stream. Describing these protocols, Andrew Tanenbaum made his often quoted observation, "The nice thing about standards is that you have so many to choose from"[Tan88].

Physical Layer Coding Violations

The use of an invalid Physical layer coding takes advantage of the fact that there are more options available in representing bits on the line than are actually needed. The sender and receiver have an agreement on what means zero and what means one. Anything else is an invalid code. The advantage of using an invalid signal to delimit frames is clear—the invalid code cannot possibly appear in a legitimate data stream, so no bit stuffing is required. Chapter 13 includes the use of physical layer coding violations by several medium access layer control schemes.

15.1.2 Error Control

Error control includes detection and correction of transmission errors. There are two approaches for accomplishing this:

- Put the minimum information into the transmission to find that an error exists and then request retransmission of the frame to obtain the correct result.
- Put enough information into the transmission so that the receiver not only finds errors but also determines where the errors are.

Retransmission is an appropriate strategy for correcting the occasional error in a network where transmissions are usually error-free because the extra information required to locate the error bits is a heavy burden. In situations where retransmission is not practical, the extra burden of bits that locate the errors as well as detect them is the only choice. Such situations include transmissions to very remote space probes, and transmissions in locations where the sender or receiver might be destroyed and unable to participate in a retransmission.

Parity and Block Parity

The simplest form of error detection is the familiar parity check; a single bit added to a character code forces the total number of 1 bits in the code to be even (even parity) or odd (odd parity). Clearly, the parity check will detect any single bit error. In fact, it will detect any odd number of bit errors. Parity checking can determine that there is an odd number of errors, but cannot tell how many bits are bad or which ones are in error. Errors detected by parity checking require retransmission for correction since the parity check does not determine the location of the error.

A simple way to augment parity checking is to extend the scheme to two dimensions. Figure 15.1 illustrates this method. A block of characters appears as an array. Each row of the array is a single character. Each column corresponds to one bit position. The column labeled P consists of the parity bits for the characters. The row labeled C consists of the parity bits computed on each bit position. If an even number of bit errors occur in a character, the column parity bits will detect them. If a particular set of errors occurs such that an even number of bit inversions occur in both rows and columns, the errors will go undetected. Thus, the probability of undetected errors is greatly reduced compared to performing parity checks on the characters alone.

Parity checking by character or in blocks is effective when errors occur in a single bit here and there. In many types of transmission, errors tend to occur in bursts, and the block parity checking scheme is too vulnerable to missed errors. Polynomial error detecting schemes, such as the **cyclic redundancy check (CRC),** are preferred.

```
                       P
          0100  0001  1
          0100  1110  1
          0100  1110  1
          0100  0001  1
          0100  1101  1
          0100  0001  1
          0101  0010  0
          0100  1001  0
          0100  0101  0
        C 1010  1101  1
```

Figure 15.1. Block parity checking

Cyclic Redundancy Check

Polynomial error detection consists of interpreting a stream of bits as the coefficients of a polynomial and then performing computations on the polynomial. For example, `0100 0001` becomes

$$0x^7 + x^6 + 0x^5 + 0x^4 + 0x^3 + 0x^2 + 0x + 1$$

or just $x^6 + 1$.

The sender and receiver of the data must agree on a **generator polynomial** to be used to produce check bits for the data. Check bits will be added to the data such that the polynomial represented by the data augmented by the check bits is evenly divisible by the generator polynomial. The sender appends the check bits, and the receiver divides the incoming data by the generator polynomial. If there is any remainder, an error has occurred.

We can illustrate the basic idea, using decimal numbers. Suppose the data consists of the value 37 and we use a generator of 7. The data, 37, is not evenly divisible by 7; $37/7 = 5$ and with a remainder of 2. If we subtract 2 from the data, we make it evenly divisible by 7. To send the data and check data, we send 37 and 2 (the original data and the remainder). The receiver could subtract 2 from 37, then divide by 7. The resulting remainder of 0 verifies the transmission.

The encoding done to produce the polynomial frame check sequence (FCS), also known as the CRC, uses modulo 2 arithmetic in which both addition and subtraction are the same as EXCLUSIVE OR (XOR). Long division becomes a fast and simple operation consisting of many XOR operations. The method used to produce the CRC is as follows:

1. Append as many 0s as the degree of the generator polynomial to the end of the data.
2. Divide the new polynomial by the generator polynomial.
3. Subtract the remainder from the augmented polynomial and transmit the result.

Though we describe the operation as long division, the steps consist of simple bit shifts and comparisons. When we finish the computation, the remainder is contained in the trailing bits of the transmission; the original data appears in the lead bits. An example of the computation appears in Figure 15.2. On the receiver's side, the data that arrives is evenly divisible by the generating polynomial if no error has occurred. The receiving side recomputes the CRC on the entire data unit. If the remainder is zero, the data unit contains no error. If the remainder is not zero, the data unit is rejected.

The choice of generator polynomial is critical to the effectiveness of the CRC. Remember that the data transmitted is viewed as the coefficients of a binary polynomial and that the generator is another polynomial. If we refer to the data polynomial as $D(x)$ and the generator as $G(x)$, the earlier procedure modifies $D(x)$ to produce a message for transmission, $M(x)$ such that $M(x)/G(x)$ produces a quotient, $Q(x)$, and a remainder, $R(x)$, such that $R(x)$ is zero. The message received after transmission is $M'(x) = M(x) + E(x)$. That is, the message that arrives is the message that was sent plus any errors that occurred in transmission. The receiver recomputes the CRC on $M'(x)$. The computation done by the receiver is

$$\frac{M'(x)}{G(x)} = \frac{M(x) + E(x)}{G(x)} = \frac{M(x)}{G(x)} + \frac{E(x)}{G(x)}$$

417

```
        Data = 10010100010001
   Generator = 10010
```

Append 4 0s to the end of the data because the generating polynomial is of fourth degree.

```
                 10000100110111
         10010 )100101000100010000
                 10010
                 ‾‾‾‾‾
                   10001
                   10010
                   ‾‾‾‾‾
                    11000
                    10010
                    ‾‾‾‾‾
                     10101
                     10010
                     ‾‾‾‾‾
                      11100
                      10010
                      ‾‾‾‾‾
                       11100
                       10010
                       ‾‾‾‾‾
                        11100
                        10010
                        ‾‾‾‾‾
                         1110
```

The remainder, 1110, replaces the four 0s appended to the data. The sender transmits 100101000100011110.

Figure 15.2. Computing the cyclic redundancy check

Since the remainder of $M(x)/G(x)$ is 0, any remainder observed by the receiver comes from $E(x)/G(x)$. Any $E(x)$ that is evenly divisible by $G(x)$ will go undetected. Since we cannot control the errors, we need to choose $G(x)$ to reduce the probability of an error slipping by.

Clearly, any $E(x)$ that is smaller than $G(x)$ will be detected. Thus, if $G(x)$ is a polynomial of degree 5, any error occurring only in bits 0 through 3 will cause a remainder. For example, if $E(x) = x^3 + x + 1$ and $G(x) = x^4 + x^2 + 1$, $E(x)/G(x)$ gives a remainder equal to $E(x)$. Suppose there are some error bits, fewer than the degree of G, but not at the end of the transmission. The part of the transmission that contains the errors is called a **burst**. A burst error begins with an error bit and ends with an error bit and has some mix of correct and error bits in between. The burst error $B(x)$ also represents a polynomial. $B(x) = x^i + \ldots + x^j$ for some $i \geq j$. If $E(x)$ contains a burst error, $E(x)$ consists of $B(x)$ followed by zeros in all the bit positions that do not contain errors. Here is an example:

```
   Correct message:  100010101001001010010101010100000111010101
   Received message:  100010100011011010010101010100000111010101
Coefficients of E(x):        1010010000000000000000000000000000000
Coefficients of B(x):        101001
```

Write $E(x)$ as $E(x) = x^j B(x)$. $B(x)$ is not divisible by $G(x)$ if the degree of $B(x)$ is less than or equal to the degree of $G(x)$. If $G(x)$ contains an x^0 term as well as other terms, it will never divide evenly into x^j. Thus, any generator polynomial of degree r with coefficient of $x^0 = 1$ will detect any burst error of length less than r. Clearly, that includes all single bit errors. A burst error with value exactly equal to $G(x)$ will go undetected. Since both $G(x)$ and $B(x)$ begin and end with 1, the probability of an exact match is the probability that all the $r - 1$ bits between the first and last are exactly the same. That is, $(\frac{1}{2})^{r-1}$.

Some burst errors of length greater than the degree of $G(x)$ can also be detected. In particular, the properties of modulo 2 arithmetic imply that no polynomial with an odd number of terms (odd number of coefficients = 1) is divisible by $x + 1$. To illustrate, assume that $E(x)$ has an odd number of terms. Then evaluate $E(1)$. Using modulo 2 arithmetic, any even number of 1s sums to 0 (mod 2), and any odd number of 1s sums to 1 (mod 2). So, $E(1) = 1$ if $E(x)$ has an odd number of terms. If $E(x)$ has $x+1$ as a factor, $E(x) = (x+1)F(x)$ for some $F(x)$. But then $E(1) = (1 + 1)F(1) = 0 * F(1) = 0$. Thus, $E(x)$ cannot have both an odd number of terms and $x + 1$ as a factor. A generator function that contains $x + 1$ as a factor will thus catch all errors with an odd number of terms.

Two versions of the 16-bit checksum are international standards:

$$CRC - 16 = x^{16} + x^{15} + x^2 + 1$$
$$CRC - CCITT = x^{16} + x^{12} + x^5 + 1$$

Tanenbaum summarizes the effectiveness of a 16-bit CRC check as follows:

A 16-bit checksum, such as CRC-16 or CRC-CCITT, catches all single and double errors, all errors with an odd number of bits, all burst errors of length 16 or less, 99.997% of 17-bit error bursts, and 99.998% of 18-bit and longer bursts. [Tan88]

The CRC computation and verification done at the Data Link layer provides very good, but not perfect, checking of data transmitted from one machine to another. As we have seen, accuracy is further checked at the Transport layer if TCP is used and is optionally checked if TP4 is used. Applications that require more reliable data transfer may add additional checking.

15.1.3 Flow Control

Flow control refers to the need to coordinate the workings of a sending device with the capacity of a receiving device. A principal method for controlling the rate at which frames arrive at a destination is the sliding window protocol, described in section 11.3.2. The difference is that the Transport layer works end to end, whereas the Data Link layer works between adjacent machines. An alternative approach, XON/XOFF, was described in section 7.2. XON/XOFF involves an explicit squelch message sent from the receiving device to the sender to stop the transmission of bits; a complementary message is required to restore transmission.

15.1.4 Link Management

Link management involves establishment and termination of a connection and initialization of sequence numbers for the flow control window in a connection-oriented data link communication. In the event of an interruption of communication, sequence numbers must be reinitialized as well.

15.2 SYNCHRONOUS AND ASYNCHRONOUS TRANSFER

An important component of the communication needs of many applications is the time delay or the acceptable variation in time delay. In a phone conversation, long delays (about 1 second) in delivery make smooth conversation difficult. If a movie is played at a service site and delivered to a television set over a communication line, a modest delay is acceptable, but it must be consistent. (If the movie starts at 8 p.m. and the first bits arrive 10 seconds later, no one will notice. However, if delay varies greatly, reception will suffer.) Finally, an electronic mail message can tolerate reasonable delay and variation without degrading service.

These different types of needs require different types of service: synchronous communication provides service for time-dependent users; asynchronous communication provides flexibility to deliver service as needed.

In pure synchronous transfer mode, each user is given access to the communication channel in regularly occurring chunks of time. For example, in a DS1 communication channel, there is capacity for 1.5 Mbps; good voice communication requires 64 Kbps. Each of 24 voice links could have a share of each second of transmission, or the capacity could be shared in units of various sizes—several 64 Kbps chunks for voice, and the remainder in chunks of different sizes for data communication.

The problem with synchronous transmission is that once the capacity is allocated, it cannot be used for another purpose. Data applications are bursty, with quiet periods interspersed among very high-traffic bursts. If capacity to carry the largest burst is allocated, the channel will be idle during quiet times and the capacity wasted.

Asynchronous Transfer Mode (ATM) provides access to channel capacity as needed. The network provides a steady stream of cells, each composed of 5 header and 48 payload octets. A station can acquire cells at fixed intervals to support voice or video or other synchronous traffic; other cells can be used to send nontime-dependent traffic, such as file transfers. Complete information about the development of ATM can be obtained at the ATM Forum Web site (http://www.atmforum.com).

15.3 THE PHYSICAL LAYER

The Physical layer consists of the protocols that govern communication at the very lowest level. (Notice that the Physical layer is still a protocol layer, not physical materials.) These protocols specify how bits are represented, and how a sending device and a receiving device coordinate to recognize the start and end points of an information-carrying signal.

Designs at the Physical layer are influenced by important classical results in communication theory. In 1924, H. Nyquist derived an expression for the maximum data rate achievable over a noiseless channel of finite bandwidth. In 1948, Claude Shannon extended this work to express the maximum achievable data rate on a channel with random noise.

These expressions take into account the bandwidth of the transmission medium, the number of different levels (different symbols) coded, and in Shannon's work, the ratio of signal to noise.

The Nyquist formula states

$$\text{max data rate} = 2H \log_2 V \; bits/sec$$

where H is the bandwidth in Hertz, and V is the number of different symbols carried. For example, a 1 MHz channel, carrying just two symbols, 0 and 1, has maximum data rate of

$$2(1M)log_2(2) = 2M \; bits/sec$$

Shannon's work takes noise into account thus factoring in the inability of the medium to carry a completely clear, uncorrupted signal. The resulting expression is

$$\text{max data rate} = H \log_2 \left(1 + \frac{S}{N}\right) \; bits/sec$$

where H still represents channel bandwidth in Hertz, and $\frac{S}{N}$ is the ratio of signal to noise.

Protocols at the Physical layer are directly concerned with the characteristics of the medium that will carry the bits. Important characteristics include the vulnerability to noise and the distance over which a signal can travel without losing strength to the point that a receiver can no longer extract information reliably.

Media vary in cost and in ease of installation. Today, the emergence of mobile computing based on cellular radio transmissions adds a new dimension to the requirements of protocol options at the Physical layer.

Traditional telephone communication systems represent information as analog signals during transmission. Computers require modems to translate between their digital representations and the analog representations required for transmission over phone lines. Telephone systems have changed gradually to digital transmission, and there is a lot of excitement (and hype) about the potential of services that will be offered once an all-digital system is in place. It will mean sufficient bandwidth to each subscriber residence to bring emerging services on the World Wide Web and many other applications—video links to sites around the world, for example.

15.3.1 High-Speed Transmission

Fiber optics makes very high-speed transmission a feasible option for widely separated network nodes. High-speed transmission does not refer to how fast the bits move—that is a fraction of the speed of light and is not going to change. High speed comes from putting the bits onto the medium faster, which means sending shorter (smaller) bits. At 100 Mbps, the bits are 0.1 times the length of bits at 10 Mbps. Gigabit speeds mean even smaller bits. These smaller bits are feasible now because fiber optics provides much more dependable representation of the bits from one end of the transmission to the other. Since the bits are not corrupted, the receiving circuitry does not need as large a sample to recognize the data accurately. Encoding schemes in which the voltage level detected represents more than one bit also becomes more practical (for a similar reason).

In Figure 15.3, you can see the decreasing size of bits at increasing speeds. The figure uses a simple bit encoding where high voltage is 1 and low voltage is 0. Other bit-encoding schemes are also used.

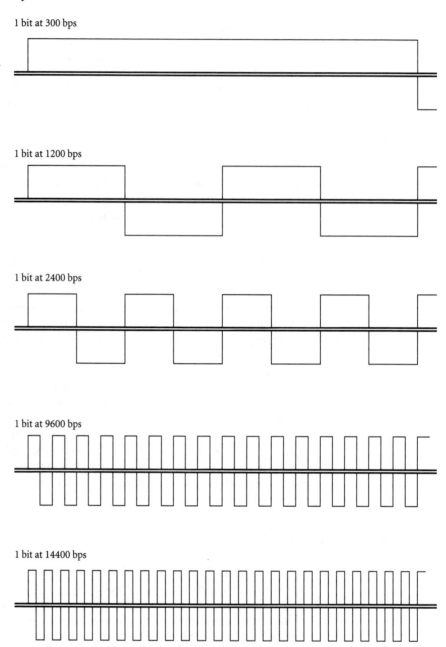

Figure 15.3. Relative bit sizes at increasing speeds

To convey more than one bit at a time, there must be more than two recognizable voltages. To have a single signal carry 2 bits, for example, there must be four different voltages recognized—one to represent each of 00, 01, 10, and 11; Figure 15.4 illustrates the idea. The need to recognize a signal with these smaller changes in voltage imposes still more stringent requirements on the circuitry that generates and reads the bits.

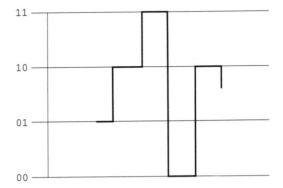

Figure 15.4. Encoding more than one bit in a signal change

SUMMARY

This chapter concludes our trip down the seven layers of the OSI reference model. The logical link control sublayer of the Data Link layer and the Physical layer deal with the realities of transmitting bits over communication lines. These topics are treated in summary form here because they are worthy of whole books in their own right. They are the central topics in courses and books in data communications.

An important concept in this final chapter is that the very bottom of the OSI reference model is still about protocols and not about wires and physical items. At the Physical layer, the protocols deal with how electrical signals will be used to convey data bits between communicating systems. Without this basic function, none of the higher layers would have any meaning. Without the work in physics and engineering that allow signals representing bits to move from one place to another, there would be no need for routing, no need for addressing, no sense in worrying about missing packets, no synchronization, no coordination of compression and encryption techniques, no file transfer, no e-mail, no World Wide Web.

EXERCISES

1. For each of the following bit strings, show the sequence of bits transmitted after bit stuffing:
   (a) 0011111011111101111111011111111101111111111011111111111101111111111111110
   (b) 000111011101111110111111110111

2. Look up at least one method used in error correction. Analyze the cost of error correction using this method compared to error detection and retransmission. Be realistic in characterizing the environment. For example, consider the cost of both methods in communicating with a space probe with a very long transmission propagation time and in a high-speed local network with very low error rates.

3. (Programming Exercise) Write a program to take as input a string of bits for transmission and to send them out with the properly calculated CRC at the end. Write a corresponding program to receive a transmission and verify that the CRC is correct.

4. What is the maximum data rate on a 100 MHz channel carrying two different signals? What is the maximum data rate if the signal-to-noise ratio is 0.99995?

5. Look up typical characteristics of network environments. What should you expect as a signal-to-noise ratio? Has that ratio changed significantly in recent years?

Internet Archive Server

One of the advantages of the interconnection of many networks around the world is the accumulation of valuable resources that are accessible to users of the networks. A significant problem that presents itself in this context is knowing what is available and where it resides. We saw the OSI solution to this question in Chapter 8. In the Internet, several sites maintain lists of available resources and the locations from which they are available. All the sites listed can be accessed without previously establishing an account. Figure A.1 shows a telnet session to an archiver (Archie) site. We log in as `archie`; a welcoming message appears along with a line stating that our terminal type has been determined to be a vt100 with 24 lines of 80 characters. If we type `help` at this point, we will get information about the commands that can be used.

The command `pager` causes output to be stopped after a screen is full until we request that it continue. `Whatis <keyword>` gives a list of items with that word in the description. In the figure, we asked `whatis osi` and got a long list of items, including a number of RFCs that address issues involving OSI. In Figure A.2, the command `prog rfc1074` asks where the particular file called rfc1074 can be found. The resulting list shows a number of sites where the file is available to an anonymous login. In Figure A.3, we will retrieve the file containing RFC 1074, based on the description here. The Internet archives contain a wealth of items to explore.

Anonymous FTP

We have seen an example telnet session in which we queried the archive service to find a particular document we wanted to retrieve. Now let us get the document. All the sites listed in the archiver accept anonymous FTP connections. Access is restricted to directories open for public display. When someone wants to retrieve a document or program from an archive, he or she uses FTP with the login name `anonymous`. The password requested is usually an identifier, such as an e-mail address of the person logging in. Once logged in, the user can display directory listings, move through the directory structure, and retrieve files. The anonymous user does not have write privileges to the directory, so there is no opportunity to put files there for use by others.

Figure A.3 shows a session in which a user logs into a site discovered by the telnet session in this appendix.

```
AIX telnet (nis. ans. net)


IBM AIX Version 3 for RISC System/6000
(C) Copyrights by IBM and by others 1982, 1990.
login: archie
```

```
*** As of 02/19/92, the default search method is set to "exact".
*** Type "help set search" for more details.


Australian users:        archie.au (139.130.4.6)
Canadian users:          archie.mcgill.ca     (132.206.2.3)
European users:          archie.funet.fi      (128.214.6.100)
                         archie.doc.ic.ac.uk  (146.169.11.3)
Other U.S. servers:
 archie.sura.net (128.167.254.179)            archie.unl.edu (129.93.1.14)
 archie.rutgers.edu (128.6.18.15)


 o Type 'help' for help
 o Send questions/comments to archie-admin@ans.net, site add/
 delete/change requests to archie-updates@cc.mcgill.ca



 Client software is available on ftp.ans.net:/pub/archie/clients;
 documentation can be found in /pub/archie/doc.
```

```
# term set to vt100 24 80
archie> pager
archie> whatis osi
```

```
PROSITE                  Dictionary of Protein Sites and Patterns (A.
                         Bairoch, Geneva)

RFE 1070                 Hages, R.A.; Hall, N.E.; Rose, M.T. Use of the
                         Internet as a subnetwork for experimentation with the
                         OSI network layer. 1989 February; 17 p.

RFE 1161                 Rose, M.T. SNMP over OSI. 1990 June; 8 p.

RFE 1165                 Crowcroft, J.; Onions, J.P. Network Time Protocol
                         (NTP) over the OSI Remote Operations Service.
                         1990 June; 10 p.

 .....
<<<<Additional listings cut>>>>
```

Figure A.1. A session with the archive server

```
archie> prog rfc1074
# matches / % database searched:      6 /100%



Host ucdavis.ucdavis.edu     (128.120.2.1)
Last updated 10:50  1 Oct 1992


    Location : /rfc
       FILE        r--r--r--        10590  Dec 21  1988   rfc1074


Host utkuxi.utk.edu    (128.169.200.67)
Last updated 23:51 30 Sep 1992


    Location: /pub/internet/rfcs
       FILE        rw-r--r--        10590   Nov  2  1991   rfc1074


Host tamu.edu    (128.194.15.32)
Last updated 18:58 30 Sep 1992


    Location: /rfc
       FILE        r--r--r--        10590   Nov 10  1990   rfc1074

<<<< Three additional, similar responses cut >>>>


archie>
```

Figure A.2. Finding places to obtain a copy of a particular document

In Figure A.2, we used the archive server to find a site that stores copies of the RFCs. Now we use anonymous FTP to contact one of those sites (UCDAVIS here) and download a copy of RFC 1074:

```
111 /mnt/a/cassel> ftp    128.120.2.1
Connected to 128.120.2.1.
220 ucdavis.ucdavis.edu FTP server (Version 4.114
        Tue Jun 9 17:42:20 PDT 1992) ready.
Name (128.120.2.1:cassel) :    anonymous
331 Guest login ok, send ident as password.
Password :
230 Guest login ok, all files are read-only.
ftp> cd rfc
250 CWD command successful.
ftp> get rfc1074
200 PORT command successful.
150 Opening data connection for rfc1074 (153.104.7.161,1260) (10590 bytes).
226 Transfer complete.
local : rfc1074 remote: rfc1074
10872 bytes received in 2.5 seconds (4.2 Kbytes/s)
ftp> bye
221 Goodbye.
```

Figure A.3. Anonymous FTP and file transfer

A Review of HTML

The HyperText Markup Language (HTML) is a tool for producing hypertext documents. HTML is an application of the Standard Generalized Markup Language (SGML) [Gol90]. HTML contains facilities for producing documents with many kinds of elements. HTML originated to allow scientists to have research papers with links to related work and references. Once the commercial world discovered the benefits of a Web presence, HTML was stretched far beyond its original design. Although we cannot present all of HTML or these newer tools in this book, we will introduce the basic features, enough to allow production of meaningful documents.

Figure B.1 shows the basic format of an HTML document. An HTML document consists of a **head part** and a **body part.** Words and symbols enclosed in < > are **tags,** meaningful to an HTML reader.

<HTML> signifies the beginning of an HTML document and alerts an HTML reader to expect HTML codes.

<HEAD> marks the beginning of the head section of the document.

<TITLE> introduces the title of the document. The title applies to the document and will appear in a box or border around the document. It does not provide a title to the contents of the document.

</TITLE> marks the end of the title.

</HEAD> marks the end of the head part of the document description.

```
<HTML>
<HEAD>
<TITLE>  A Sample Document  </TITLE>
</HEAD>
<BODY>
```

Figure B.1. The basic HTML document structure

```
</BODY>

</HTML>
```

<BODY> introduces the body of the document. The body may contain a title for the document as well as any material wanted, and should end with the name and e-mail address of the author and the date of last revision.

</BODY> marks the end of the body of the document.

</HTML> marks the end of the HTML document description.

A document containing HTML tags requires a program to read it and to present it to the human reader, formatted and ready to use. A browser interprets the codes embedded in the HTML document and uses them to determine how to present the document to the user. The browser strips away the codes (anything embedded in < >) and displays the remaining text according to the rules it implements. There are a number of browsers (see section 2.2.1), and each has its own way of displaying the elements of a document defined in HTML.

B.1 WHY A MARKUP LANGUAGE

As we look at HTML, you will notice that documents are *described* and that the description must be interpreted by another process. The descriptive elements in HTML are limited and not nearly as powerful or as convenient as those used by standard WYSIWYG (what you see is what you get) word processing packages. You might wonder about this apparent backward step to less convenient tools. Two factors support this approach to document creation and dissemination: the effect of file size on the transfer time, and the need to have the file viewed on a variety of equipment types.

An important constraint in convenient access to resources on a network is the time it takes to move the resource from its storage location to the system making a request. Try a simple experiment. Use a simple text editor to type in a modestly sized document. Format it as well as you can within the constraints of the editor. Now read the same file into a modern word processing package. Make some font changes and do ordinary formatting that you would have included in the document if you had entered it into the word processing package in the first place. Save the file in the word processor format. Compare the sizes of the two files.

The large size of files created with WYSIWYG word processors is not the only issue; the display depends upon the characteristics of the display device, both monitor and printer. To display a WYSIWYG file, it must be formatted for the display device, or the word processor software that created the file must be invoked to display it correctly. Neither alternative is attractive.

Using a markup language such as HTML allows the file to be stored in plaintext form and interpreted and displayed by whatever browser the user selects. Use of a markup language greatly facilitates document sharing.

B.2 SIMPLE FORMATTING

HTML can describe a simple document, without hypermedia content. Figure B.2 shows the principal codes available for use in an HTML document for formatting purposes. Most

`<H1>   </H1>`	Heading, level 1 (usually used for the title of the document)
`<H2>   </H2>`	Heading, level 2 (levels 2 through 6 available)
`<P>   </P>`	Paragraph
`<!-- Comment -->`	Comment
`<OL>   ...   </OL>`	Numbered (ordered) list
`<UL>   </UL>`	Unnumbered list
`<LI>`	A list item
`<DL>   ...   </DL>`	A definition list, with list items defined by DT and DD codes
`<DT>`	A definition term (to be followed by its definition)
`<DD>`	Definition for the corresponding DT term
`<B>   ...   </B>`	Boldface
`<I>   ...   </I>`	Italic
`<TT>   ...   </TT>`	Typewriter font (all characters the same width)
`<PRE>   ...   </PRE>`	Preformatted (verbatim)
`<HR>`	Horizontal rule (line)
` `	Break (line break)
`<ADDRESS>   ...   </ADDRESS>`	Signature for the page

Figure B.2. HTML document formatting codes

of the HTML formatting codes have a begin and an end indicator. The first-level header is introduced by `<H1>` and terminated by `</H1>`, for example. The first-level header may be displayed in any of a number of ways, depending on the browser. However, this is the most dominant format available. It is often used to title the document.

Other headers, `<H2>... </H2>` through `<H6> ... </H6>`, designate text to be displayed in successively less conspicuous form. If the H1 header gives the name of a book, for example, H2 might name chapters, H3 might name major sections within chapters, H4 might name subsections, and so on. The important thing is that the headers are levels and can be reused as needed. Higher numbers designate less significant items, which should be arranged hierarchically. Figure B.3 shows an arrangement of items designated with appropriate headers. Figure B.4 shows the way the browser Netscape displays the document of Figure B.3.

Browsers ignore spacing in HTML documents, except in special cases discussed later. To indicate that a group of lines belongs together, mark the beginning and end of the paragraph with `<P>... </P>`. Some browsers will leave extra space between paragraphs; some will indent the first line of the paragraph. The spacing in the source file is completely irrelevant. Since `<P>` begins a new paragraph, the use of `</P>` seems redundant. In fact, browsers currently do not use `</P>`. Future extensions to HTML may make the `</P>` significant.

It is often convenient to leave a note in the file, perhaps a reminder to insert something later. Browsers will ignore any line set off with a code meaning "This is a comment." The HTML code for a comment is `<!-- Comment -->`.

Lists allow an orderly presentation of information. Several types of lists serve this purpose in HTML. An ordered list includes a number for each item; an unnumbered list sets

```
<HTML>
<HEAD>
<TITLE> An Illustration of Headers </TITLE>
</HEAD>
<BODY>
<H1> An Example of the Use of Headers </H1>
<H2> A Major Section of this example </H2>
<H3> A lesser section, supporting the Major Section </H3>
<H3> Another section at the same significance as the previous one </H3>
<H2> Back to the higher level of significance </H2>
<H3> A final subsection </H3>

</BODY>
</HTML>
```

Figure B.3. The hierarchy of headers

off each item with a bullet; items in a definition list consist of two parts: a term and its definition or description. Figure B.5 shows the use of the three types of lists; Figure B.6 shows how the lists are displayed with Netscape. Lists can be nested as needed.

HTML includes some basic options in text display. The code <B> ... </B> causes text to be set in boldface type if possible. Similarly <I> ... </I> selects italics. Not all systems can display bold and italic text. The browser will substitute something else to set off

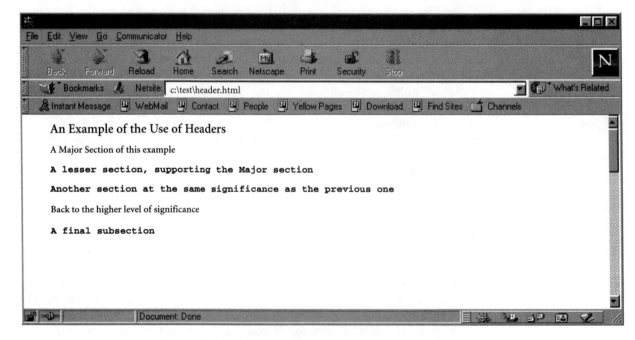

Figure B.4. Netscape display of the hierarchy of headers

```
<ul>                                            Begin an unnumbered list
<li>shoes                                       A list item
<li> ships
<li> sealing wax


</ul>                                           End the unnumbered list


<br>
<br>


<ol>                                            Begin an ordered (numbered) list
<li>Pick up plane tickets                       A list item
<li>Make transparencies
<li>Leave instructions for replacement
</ol>


<br>
<br>


<dl>
<dt>protocol
<dd>a set of rules that describe how two systems communicate
<dt>client server computing
<dd>a paradigm in which one system provides a service that can be used
by other systems that are called clients
</dl>
```

Figure B.5. Three list formatting tools of HTML

this text if the chosen format is not available. The code `<TT>` ... `</TT>` designates text to be set in typewriter font. Typewriter font makes all characters the same width and is useful for lining up characters. Similarly, `<PRE>` ... `</PRE>` specifies that the spacing of the text is to be maintained in the displayed document. This is useful in incorporating documents from a text file and maintaining the arrangement of paragraphs and the alignment of tables without having to add formatting codes throughout the text.

A horizontal line can be useful to separate sections of the document displayed. Line breaking allows the author to control line content, perhaps in displaying verse or lines of an address. The HTML codes for a horizontal line and for an end-of-line break are `<HR>` and `<BR>`, respectively. These are unusual because they do not have beginning and ending markers. A horizontal line is the full width of the screen. A line break is a break; it does not need a beginning and ending marker.

`<ADDRESS>` ... `</ADDRESS>` sets off the information of a signature for the page. Each document should contain the name and contact information of the author and the date of last revision. The ADDRESS tag delimits this information and allows the browser to choose a suitable font for this information.

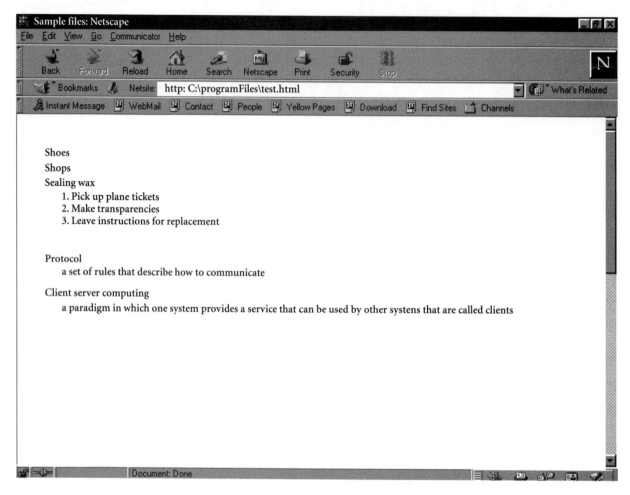

Figure B.6. Netscape display of list formatting tools

B.3 LINKS AND ANCHORS

The HTML codes of section B.2 allow us to create a document with basic formatting. Now we add the features that make HTML documents *hyper*text. The key concept here involves establishing a connection between a place in a document and some resource—another document or document section, or an image or other object to be accessible from that place. To establish a link, we must designate the jumping off point in one place, plus the name and location of the other end of the link. The browser will distinguish the jumping off point in some way—usually by making the text a different color.

The link may point to another section of the same file, to a different file in the same file system, or to a file on a remote system. If the end of the link is located on a different file system from the document that refers to it, we must also provide information about how

Filename	Location of the file
picture.gif	Same directory as the document that includes the reference
../picture.gif	In the parent directory of the document that includes the reference
c\/html/pictures/picture.gif	Absolute reference starting at the root of the file system
accessprotocol://machine/file location	General form to access a resource on a separate machine, for example, http://renoir.villanova.edu/html/oreo.gif

Figure B.7. Location specification in links

to retrieve the object. Most frequently, the way to retrieve the object will be through the use of the **hypertext transfer protocol (HTTP)**, introduced in section 2.3.

HTML was designed specifically to interact with HTTP to support moving resources in hypertext documents. Figure B.7 summarizes specification of location of the desired object, using an image file called picture.gif as an example. (The significance of .gif is explained in section 2.2.3.) An important point is the difference between opening a local file to process and display its contents versus transferring a resource from a remote system to the user's site and then displaying the resource. When the file is local, the location specification needs only to show exactly where the file is found. When the file is on a remote system, the two systems must cooperate to identify the desired resource and transfer it to the location where it is needed. The access protocol is identification of the set of rules for communicating between the two systems to accomplish the transfer.

The HTML tag that designates a link is **A**. The tags we have seen so far designate the beginning and end of some item in the text—a header, for example. The A (or anchor) tag may mark the beginning and end of text that will be highlighted to mark a connection (the jumping off point) to another object, and also includes one or more attributes of the connection. The most commonly used attribute in the A tag is the HREF attribute, which describes the location of the item on the other end of the link. An example is the most effective way to show the use of the A tag. The following sentence is part of an HTML document:

```
The <A HREF="http://www.acm.org/events/"> ACM Conference
Calendar </A> includes several hundred conferences at any given time.
```

The <A> tag includes the reference to the other end of the link. The part of the sentence between the <A ... > and the </A> will appear highlighted, as shown in Figure B.8. If

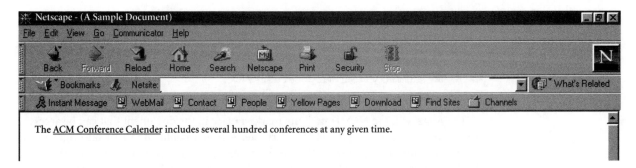

Figure B.8. The appearance of a hypertext link

the reader clicks on the highlighted text, the document will be retrieved from the machine acm.org and displayed on the reader's monitor. (Note that no filename is specified. The browser will access a default file, usually called index.html, in the directory events.)

While the events document is loaded, the reader can follow any links in that document. The browser will provide some mechanism to return to the previous location (a button labeled with a left-pointing arrow or the word back, usually).

The HREF entry in the example A tag (<A HREF="http://www.acm.org/events/">) includes three distinct parts:

http:// http is an access protocol. It specifies the rules of communication to be used between the computer that displays the document and the computer that holds the object needed for insertion into the document.

www.acm.org This is the machine, or a particular location in the directory tree of a system, where the desired object is stored. Public access to information may be restricted to a portion of the file system for security reasons. Often the section accessible through the World Wide Web is designated as www.

events The final part of the reference designates the path to the file in which the object is stored. If a file named index.html exists in the directory, it will be retrieved. If no such file exists, the path must end with a specific filename. The file extension is significant on the Web. The extension html indicates that this file contains html tags and informs the browser to interpret those tags as the file is displayed.

The format for identifying objects for insertion into the document is standard and is called a **uniform resource locator (URL)**. (URLs are sometimes described as *universal resource locators* or *unified resource locators*.) We will see a number of examples, but they will all be in the general format:

access protocol://machine/path/filename.extension.

The second A tag attribute of interest is the NAME attribute. An HREF specifies a file to access. NAME allows specification of a place within a file. Again, an example illustrates the use of the feature:

```
At the end of this report you will find a <A HREF="#summary">summary
a</A> of the budget figures given below.

< detailed budget numbers >



<A NAME="summary">Summary Screen</A>
Totals:          ....
```

The A tag with the NAME attribute marks a place in the document that can be accessed from another A tag using the HREF attribute. A reader could choose to skip right to the summary figures by clicking on the word summary in the first sentence. The new screen display will begin with the location of the NAME tag and will have "Summary Screen" in the title box of the screen.

Once it has a name, a section of a document can be reached from anywhere in the same document by giving HREF= and the name assigned. A section of a document can be reached from other documents also. If the previous example document resides in file `year95.sales.html`, the summary section can be reached from other documents as

`year95.sales.html#summary`

The URL can be expanded with path name, machine name, and access protocol for use from another computer system.

B.4 IMAGES

An attractive feature of hypertext documents accessible on the World Wide Web is the use of images interspersed with text. Images must be used with care; they are often large files and can slow display on a system that has a low bandwidth connection. Some browsers are not able to display images at all.

There are two ways to include images in an HTML document: **inline** and **external.**

Inline images are part of the document. When the document is opened, the image will display unless the browser does not display images or the user has turned off the option to display them.

External images must be requested by clicking on a highlighted portion of text or another image. External images do not consume time in displaying the primary document and also provide flexibility in the format used in storing the image. File formats and external media are described in section 2.2.3.

An IMG (image) tag provides access to an image for inclusion in a document, an inline image. Like the A tag, the IMG tag has attributes. In particular, the SRC (source) attribute provides the location of the image file. A URL specifies the location, just as for the HREF. An example illustrates its use:

```
The phrase ''Meet me at the Oreo'' is a common reference to a
campus landmark. <IMG SRC="http://renoir.villanova.edu/html/oreo.gif">.
```

Inline images are used extensively to provide special fonts and formatting not available through the standard HTML text-formatting tags. Often, the content of the image is completely text; the image is used for creative presentation. A simple example appears in Figure B.9.

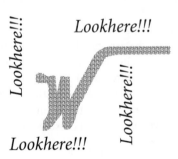

Figure B.9. An image used to display text

Other optional parameters of the IMG tag specify the alignment of the image and the amount of space around it. The `align = left` or `align = right` tag positions the image at the left or right margin, with the text flowing around the image. `align = center` puts the image in the center of the line and prevents text wraparound. Other options control space between the image and surrounding text, limit the length and width to a specific size, and provide a border of given width around the image.

There is no end tag to IMG. Use of IMG produces a graphic image in the document where the tag occurs. There is no label or highlighted text associated with the IMG. An ALT (alternative) attribute provides an alternative for cases where the image cannot be displayed. The following sentence from an HTML document includes instructions on what to display if the image cannot be used inline:

```
The phrase ''Meet me at the Oreo'' is a common reference to a
campus landmark. <IMG SRC="http://renoir.villanova.edu/html/oreo.gif"
ALT="[PICTURE OF CAMPUS LANDMARK]">.
```

Use of the `<IMG>` tag places the image in the page or displays the contents of the ALT phrase if the image cannot be displayed. To link an image to a page requires use of the same `<A>` tag used to link other elements. This example

```
The phrase ''Meet me at the
<A HREF= "http://renoir.villanova.edu/html/oreo.gif"> Oreo</A>''
is a common reference to a campus
landmark.
```

makes the word `Oreo` a link to a picture of the artwork.

Finally, an inline image can also be a link to another image or other material. In this example

```
The phrase ''Meet me at the Oreo'' is a common reference to a campus
landmark.<A HREF="HTTP://www.csc.villanova.edu/html/oreo.history.html>
<IMG SRC="http://renoir.villanova.edu/html/oreo.gif" ALT="[PICTURE
OF CAMPUS LANDMARK]"> </A>.
```

the image is displayed as part of the page and has a border around it to indicate that it is a link. Clicking on the image brings up another page for display. In this case, the other page contains information about the artwork shown in the image. Often a small image is embedded in the page and is linked to a larger image that the reader can download.

We conclude this section with one final use of graphics in an HTML document: to make a background for the page. The `<BODY>` tag may include a pointer to an image that will be used to fill the background of the page. The image will be tiled—repeated as needed to fill the page. This option allows interesting textures and colors that capture attention and make a page noticeable on first sight. In choosing a background, be very careful about how it looks with text and images appearing in the foreground. Remember, too, that the image will look different when displayed on different monitors. Choose something that will not be cluttered or interfere with the display of the primary material on the page. Popular choices include paneling, stucco, and textured paper. Sometimes a logo is used. The background shown in Figure B.11 results from the following `<BODY>` tag:

```
<BODY background="gif/panel.gif">
```

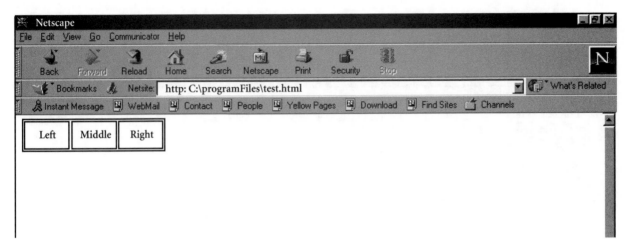

Figure B.10. A simple table

B.5 TABLES

Tables extend control over the format of a Web page to two dimensions. Figures B.10 and B.11 show samples of tables in HTML documents. A table consists of rows and columns. The intersection of a row and a column is a cell. Cells can be enlarged to encompass multiple rows or columns, as shown in Figure B.12. Tables thus divide a Web page into discrete areas, each of which can be formatted with any HTML feature.

Table definitions include the familiar open and close tags:

```
<TABLE>
```

```
</TABLE>
```

The default definition makes a table with no lines—no border around the table and no lines separating the rows and columns. Options in the TABLE tag provide borders and lines and extra spacing in the cells:

```
<TABLE CELLPADDING=2  BORDER=3>
```

Table contents are divided into rows (`<TR>` ... `</TR>`), which are further divided into columns (`<TD>` ... `</TD>`). Figure B.13 defines a table of one row and three columns.

The Netscape display of the result appears in Figure B.10. Remember that spacing in HTML is irrelevant. The table definition could have been written as

```
<TABLE CELLPADDING=3  BORDER=2>
<TR> <TD> Left </TD>   <TD> Middle </TD>   <TD> Right </TD></TR>
</TABLE>
```

The lengths of cell entries usually require multiple lines for each row definition. Indenting helps keep the structure clear to readers and makes it easier to revise the table.

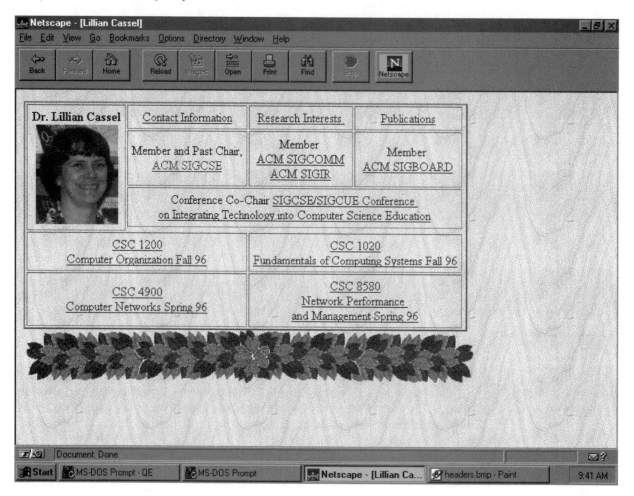

Figure B.11. Web page with background and table. (See current version at www.csc.villanova.edu/~cassel.) This page corresponds to the HTML code of Figure B.12.

To make a cell span multiple columns requires COLSPAN=n, where n is any number of columns. Similarly, ROWSPAN=n causes a cell to span multiple rows. The total number of rows and columns in a table is determined by the browser by counting <TR> and ROW-SPAN entries and using the largest number of <TC>and COLSPAN entries in any one row. Uneven rows result in poor table displays. A break (<BR>) in any empty cell position makes a complete table definition that will display properly. Figures B.13 and B.12 define the tables of Figures B.10 and B.11, respectively.

```
<HTML>
<HEAD>
<TITLE>Lillian Cassel<TITLE>
</HEAD>
<BODY background="gif.files/panel.gif">

<table border =2 cellpadding=5>
<tr align=center>
<td ROWSPAN=4>
<b>Dr. Lillian Cassel</b><IMG align=left SRC="gif/cassel.gif"></td>
<td align=center><a href="mydesc.html">Contact Information</a></td>
<td align=center><a href="#speciality">Research Interests </a></td>
<td align=center><a href="/mnt/a/cassel/html/vita/resume/pubs.html">Publications</a></td>
</tr>
<td align=center>Member and Past Chair,<br>
<a href="http://www.acm.org/sigcse/">ACM SIGCSE</a></td>
<td align=center>Member <br>
<a href="http://www.acm.org/sigcom/">ACM SIGCOMM</a><br>
<a href="http://www.acm.org/sigir/"ACM SIGIR</a></td>
<td align=center>Member <br>
<a href="http://www.acm.org/sigs/">ACM SIGBOARD</a></td>
<tr align=center>
<td align=center colspan=3>Conference Co-Chair
        <a href="http://www.csc.villanova.edu/html/sigcse/html">
        SIGCSE/SIGCUE Conference <br>
        on Integrating Technology into
        Computer Science Eduction</a></td>
<tr align=center>
</tr>
<tr align=center>
<td align=center colspan=2><a href="/mnt/a/cassel/html/1200/index.html">
CSC 1200<br>Computer Organisation Fall 96</a></td>
<td align=center colspan=2><a href="/mnt/a/cassel/html/1020/index.html">
CSC 1020<br>Fundamentals of Computing Systems Fall 96</td>
</tr>
<tr align=center>
<td align=center colspan=2><a href="/mnt/a/cassel/html/4900/index.html">
CSC 4900<br>Computer Networks Spring 96</a></td>
<td align=center colspan=2><a href="/mnt/a/cassel/html/8580/index.html">
CSC 8580<br>Network
Performance <br>and Management Spring 96</td>
</tr>
</table>
<img src="gif/1fban02.gif">
```

Figure B.12. Table with a variety of cell shapes

```
<TABLE CELLPADDING=3    BORDER=2>
<TR>
        <TD>  Left  </TD>
        <TD>  Middle  </TD>
        <TD>  Right  </TD>
</TR>
</TABLE>
```

Figure B.13. A simple table definition

Bibliography

[Abr85]   Norman Abramson. Development of the ALOHANET. *IEEE Transactions on Information Theory*, IT–31(2):119–123, March 1985.

[AC88]   Richard H. Austing and Lillian N. Cassel. *File Organization and Access: From Data to Information*. D.C. Heath Co, 1988.

[BF96]   N. Borenstein and N. Freed. *MIME (Multipurpose Internet Extensions)*. The Internet RFCs, http://info.internet.isi.edu:80/in-notes/rfc/files/rfc2045.txt, November 1996.

[BHWW83]   J. H. Benjamin, M. L. Hess, R. A. Weingarten, and W. R. Wheeler. Interconnecting SNA networks. *IBM Systems Journal*, 22(4):344–365, 1983.

[CG89]   Editor Christing Gianone. *Kermit User Guide*. Columbia University Center for Computing Activities, Kermit Distribution, 612 West 115th Street, New York, NY 10025, March 1989.

[Col99]   Columbia University Center for Computing Activities, http://www.columbia.edu/kermit/index.html. *The Kermit Project*, May 1999.

[Com95]   Douglas E. Comer. *The Internet Book*. Prentice Hall, 1995.

[Cou]   International Organization for Standardization, Secretariat of ISO/IEC JTC1/SC21, American National Standards Institute, 1430 Broadway, New York, New York 10018. *ISO Standard 3166 COUNTRY CODES*.

[Cro82]   David H. Crocker. *RFC822: Standard for the Format of ARPA Internet Text Messages*. The Internet RFCs, nic.ddn.mil in directory /rfc via anonymous ftp, August 1982.

[CSL90]   *Compressing TCP/IP Headers for Low-Speed Serial Links*, The Internet RFCs, nic.ddn.mil in directory /rfc via anonymous ftp, February. 1990.

[DH76]   W. Diffie and M. E. Hellman. New directions in cryptography. *IEEE Transactions on Information Theory*, 22:644–654, November 1976.

[Dou91]   Joe Doupnik. Kermit,tcp/ip, packet drivers, and the future. *Info-Kermit Digest (Info-Kermit-Request@WATSUN.CC.COLUMBIA.EDU)*, 14(5), September 1991.

[ElG85]   T. ElGamal. A public key cryptosystem and a signature scheme based on discrete logarithms. *IEEE Transactions on Information Theory*, 31(4):473–481, July 1985.

[FA89]   Donnalyn Frey and Rick Adamss. *!%@:: A Directory of Electron Mail Addressing and Networks*. O'Reilly & Associates, Inc., 632 Petaluna Avenue, Sebastopol, CA 95472, 1989.

[For95]   Andrew Ford. *Spinning the Web*. VNR Communications Library. International Thomson Publishing, Van Nostrand Publishing, International Thomson Publishing, Berkshire House, 168–173 High Holborn, London WC1V 7AA. Van Nostrand Publishing, 115 Fifth Avenue, 4th Floor, New York, NY 10003, 1995.

[Gol90] Charles F. Goldfarb. *The SGML Handbook*. Clarendon Press, Oxford, 1990.

[GPP90] D. Graft, M. Pabrai, and U. Pabrai. Methodology for network security design. *IEEE Communications Magazine*, pages 52–57, November 1990.

[Hal92] Fred Halsall. *Data Communications, Computer Networks and Open Systems*. Addison-Wesley, third edition, 1992.

[Hin95] Robert M. Hinden. *IP Next Generation Overview*. http://playground.sun.com/pub/ipng/html/INET-IPng-Paper.html#CH5, May 1995.

[Hof94] Lance J. Hoffman. Cryptographic policy. *Communications of the ACM*, 37(9), September 1994.

[Huf52] David Huffman. A method for the construction of minimum redundancy codes. *Proceedings of the IRE*, 40(9):1098–1101, September 1952.

[Hut88] David Hutchison. *Local Area Network Architectures*. Addison-Wesley, 1988.

[ISO9545] International Organization for Standardization, Secretariat of ISO/IEC JTC1/SC21, American National Standards Institute, 1430 Broadway, New York, New York 10018. *Editor's Text of ISO/IEC 9545 with DAM 1 Applied*, August 1991.

[JA90] Bijendra N. Jain and Ashok K. Agrawala. *Open Systems Interconnection: Its Architecture and Protocols*. Elsevier, 1990.

[Kei89] Gerd E. Keiser. *Local Area Networks*. McGraw Hill, 1989.

[Kes88a] Gary Kessler. Ring on a bus. *LAN Magazine*, pages 75–79, February 1988.

[Kes88b] Gary Kessler. Tokenism. *LAN Magazine*, pages 56–59, September 1988.

[Keu90] Steven F. Keukes. Cooperative processing: A long-term investment. *Computer Technology Review*, pages 28–29, Spring 1990.

[KKL88] Keith G. Knightson, Terry Knowles, and John Larmouth. *Standards for Open Systems Interconnection*. McGraw Hill, 1988.

[KS94] G. Kessler and S. Shepard. *RFC 1739 A Primer on Internet and TCP/IP Tools*. The Internet RFCs, nic.ddn.mil in directory /rfc via anonymous ftp, December 1994.

[Lan94] Susan Landau. Crypto policy perspectives. *Communications of the ACM*, 37(8), August 1994.

[Lev94] Steven Levy. Battle of the clipper chip. *The New York Times Magazine*, pages 44–51, 60, 70, June 12 1994.

[Lin93a] Huai-An (Paul) Lin. Estimation of the optimal performance of asn.1/ber transfer syntax. *Computer Communication Review*, pages 45–58, July 1993.

[Lin93b] J. Linn. *RFC 1421 Privacy Enhancement for Internet Electronic Mail: Part I: Message Encryption and Authentication Procedures*. The Internet RFCs, nic.ddn.mil in directory /rfc via anonymous ftp, February 1993.

[MB76] R. M. Metcalfe and D. R. Boggs. Ethernet: distributed packet switching for local computer networks. *Communications of the ACM*, 19(7):395–405, July 1976.

[MNSS87] S. P. Miller, B. C. Neuman, J. I. Schiller, and J. H. Salzer. *Section E.2.1: Kerberos Authentication and Authorization System*. MIT Project Athena, Cambridge, MA, December 1987.

[Mor95] Mary E. S. Morris. *HTML for Fun and Profit*. SunSoft Press. Prentice Hall, 1995.

[NEC98] NEC Systems Laboratory, 110 Rio Robles Drive, San Jose CA 95134. http://www.socks5.nec.com. *SOCKS The Border System Enabler: A Technology Backgrounder*, September 1998.

[Nel91] Mark Nelson. *The Data Compression Book*. M&T Books, Redwood City, CA, 1991.

[Net91]   NetLine, Incorporated, Provo, UT. *NetLine*, February 1991.

[NIS94]   *Escrowed Encryption Standared (EES) FIPS PUB 185*, February 1994.

[NS78]   R. M. Needham and M. D. Schroeder. Using encryption for authentication in large networks of computers. *Communications of the ACM*, 21(12):993–999, December 1978.

[Ohi95]   Ohio State University Public Access Site, ftp://ftp.net.ohio-state.edu/pub/kbridge. *Karlbridge Kit*, February 1995.

[OSI]   International Organization for Standardization, Secretariat of ISO/IEC JTC1/SC21, American National Standards Institute, 1430 Broadway, New York, New York 10018. *ISO Standard 7498 Information Processing Systems—Open Systems Interconnection—Basic Reference Model.*

[OSI91]   International Organization for Standardization, Secretariat of ISO/IEC JTC1/SC21, American National Standards Institute, 11 West 42nd Street, New York, New York 10036. *Revised Text of CD 10731, Information Technology—Open Systems Interconnection—Conventions for the Definition of OSI Services*, August 1991.

[PC93]   David M. Piscitello and A. Lyman Chapin. *Open Systems Networking*. Addison-Wesley, 1993.

[Per92]   Radia Perlman. *Interconnections Bridges and Routers*. Addison-Wesley, 1992.

[Pic89]   John Pickens. The convergence of appn and subarea networking: The new sna of the 1990s. *SNA Perspective*, pages 1–8, February 1989. Monthly newsletter published by CSI, 2125 Hamilton Avenue, San Jose CA 95125.

[Pic90]   John Pickens. Breaking the chains of hierarchical networking: Integrating node type 2.1. *SNA Perspective*, pages 1–16, January 1990. Monthly newsletter published by CSI, 2125 Hamilton Avenue, San Jose CA 95125.

[PM92]   W. B. Pennebaker and J. L Mitchell. *JPEG Still Image Data Compression Standard*. Van Nostrand Reinhold, New York, 1992.

[Pos80]   Jon Postel. *RFC765: File Transfer Protocol*. The Internet RFCs, nic.ddn.mil in directory /rfc via anonymous ftp, June 1980.

[Pos81]   J. Postel. *RFC 793 Transmission Control Protocol*. The Internet RFCs, nic.ddn.mil in directory /rfc via anonymous ftp, September 1981.

[PPP92a]   *The PPP AppleTalk Control Protocol (ATCP)*. The Internet RFCs, nic.ddn.mil in directory /rfc via anonymous ftp, November 1992.

[PPP92b]   *The PPP Internet Protocol Control Protocol (IPCP)*. The Internet RFCs, nic.ddn.mil in directory /rfc via anonymous ftp, May 1992.

[PPP92c]   *The PPP OSI Network Layer Control Protocol (OSINLCP)*. The Internet RFCs, nic.ddn.mil in directory /rfc via anonymous ftp, November 1992.

[PPP94]   *The Point-to-Point Protocol (PPP)*. The Internet RFCs, nic.ddn.mil in directory /rfc via anonymous ftp, July 1994.

[PR83]   Jon Postel and J. Reynolds. *RFC854: Internet Telnet Protocol and Options*. The Internet RFCs, nic.ddn.mil in directory /rfc via anonymous ftp, May 1983.

[Pre87a]   International Organization for Standardization, Secretariat of ISO/IEC JTC1/SC21, American National Standards Institute, 1430 Broadway, New York, New York 10018. *Information Processing Systems—Open Systems Interconnection—Connection Oriented Presentation Protocol Specification*, 1987.

[Pre87b]   International Organization for Standardization, Secretariat of ISO/IEC JTC1/SC21, American National Standards Institute, 1430 Broadway, New York, New York 10018. *Information Processing Systems—Open Systems Interconnection—Connection Oriented Presentation Service Definition*, 1987.

Bibliography

[Pro91]	*Procomm Plus User Manual*. Data Storm Technologies, Inc., PO Box 1471, Columbia, MO 65205, 1991.
[Ran95]	Marcus J. Ranum. *Internet Firewalls Frequently Asked Questions*. V-ONE, http://www.v-one.com/documents/fw-faq.htm, 1995.
[Ros96]	M. Rose. *Post Office Protocol—Version 3*. The Internet RFCs, http://info.internet.isi.edu:80/in-notes/rfc/files/rfc1939.txt, May 1996.
[Rot93]	Marc Rotenberg. Communications privacy: Implications for network design. *Communications of the ACM*, 36(8):61–68, August 1993.
[RP87]	J. Reynolds and J. Postel. *RFC1010: Assigned Numbers*. The Internet RFCs, nic.ddn.mil in directory /rfc via anonymous ftp, May 1987.
[RSA78]	R. L. Rivest, A. Shamir, and L. Adleman. On a method for obtaining digital signatures and public key cryptosystems. *Communications of the ACM*, 21, February 1978.
[Sac90]	George C. Sackett. Sna and osi integration. *Enterprise Systems Journal*, pages 27–30, December 1990.
[Sch78]	John Schoch. Internet naming, addressing, and routing. *Proceedings of COMPCON*, 1978.
[Sch87]	Mischa Schwartz. *Telcommunication Networks*. Addison-Wesley, 1987.
[Sch88]	Patricia Schnaidt. Nfs now. *LAN Magazine*, pages 62–69, October 1988.
[Sch92]	Patricia Schnaidt. X.400 messaging. *LAN Magazine*, June 1992.
[Ses87a]	International Organization for Standardization, Secretariat of ISO/IEC JTC1/SC21, American National Standards Institute, 1430 Broadway, New York, New York 10018. *Information Processing Systems—Open Systems Interconnection—Basic Connection Oriented Session Service Definition*, August 1987.
[Ses87b]	International Organization for Standardization, Secretariat of ISO/IEC JTC1/SC21, American National Standards Institute, 1430 Broadway, New York, New York 10018. *Information Processing Systems—Open Systems Interconnection—Basic Connection Oriented Session Protocol Specification*, 1987.
[SLI88]	*A Nonstandard for Transmission of IP Datagrams over Serial Lines: SLIP*. The Internet RFCs, nic.ddn.mil in directory /rfc via anonymous ftp, June 1988.
[SM89]	Editor Sape Mullender. *Distributed Systems*. ACM Press, 1989.
[Sou89]	Alan Southerton. The basics of servers. *Unix World*, pages 54–70, April 1989.
[Ste90]	W. Richard Stevens. *UNIX Network Programming*. Prentice Hall, 1990.
[Ste91]	Peter Stephenson. The peer connection. *LAN Magazine*, pages 121–128, June 1991.
[Str91]	John Strang. *Programming with Curses*. O'Reilly & Associates, Inc., 103 Morris Street, Suite A, Sebastopol, CA 95472, 1991.
[Tan88]	Andrew S. Tanenbaum. *Computer Networks*. Prentice Hall, second edition, 1988.
[TOMW98]	K. Toyoda, H. Ohno, J. Murai, and D. Wing. *A Simple Mode of Facsimile Using Internet Mail*. The Internet RFCs, http://info.internet.isi.edu:80/in-notes/rfc/files/rfc2305.txt, March 1998.
[Way95]	P. Wayner. Picking the crypto lock. *Byte*, pages 77–80, October 1995.
[Wor96]	World Wide Web Consortium, http://www.w3.org/TR/REC-CSS1. *Cascading Style Sheets, level 1*, December 1996.
[X4088]	CCITT, ITU Geneva, Switzerland. *Message Handling System and Service Overview*, 1988.
[ZL77]	J. Ziv and A. Lempel. A universal algorithm for sequential data processing. *IEEE Transactions on Information Theory*, 23(3):337–343, March 1977.

Index

Privacy issues, 411
PRIVATE class, 93
Private key encryption, 252–254
Private messages, 260
Programming interface, 210
Proprietary systems, compared to open systems, 5
Protocol data units, 28–29
Protocol definition, 30
Protocol machines, 34–36
Protocol specification, 33
Protocol stack, 16
Protocols
  ADCCP, 415
  ASCE, 112–114
  brouters and, 395
  CCR, 129–130
  CLNP, 367
  communication between cooperating entities,
    143–144
  Directory X.500, 247
  FTP, 17, 200, 207–208
  go-back-N, 326–328
  HTTP, 57–58, 435–436
  IP protocol, 369
  Kermit, 181, 183, 205, 206–207
  layering and, 15–16
  MAC, 390
  message transfer, 149–150
  OSI, 312
  Physical layer, 420–421
  PPP, 410–411
  ROSE, 119
  routing, 359
  RTSE, 123
  SDLC, 415
  for sharing communication channels, 374
  SLIP, 410–411
  standards and, 13–14
  stop-and-wait, 325–326
  TCP/IP, 312
  UDP, 17, 312, 334, 362
  upper-level ISO, 224
  virtual terminal protocol, 184
  YMODEM, 206
  ZMODEM, 206
PSAP (Presentation Service Access Point), 110
PSTN (public switched telephone network), 350,
  351
Public key encryption, 254–257

Q

Qualifications, Directory Services, 240
Quality of service (QOS)
  connection establishment and, 314

expected by applications, 30, 109
  parameter, 367
Quarantine delivery control, 191
Querying the domain name server, 151

R

Raw data, 269
RDF (Resource Description Framework), 77
READ (relative element address disignate) codes,
  285
REAL values, 88
Reassembly, 369–370
Recursion, 97–98
Remote files, for sequential access, 226–230
Remote operation of instructions, 114–121
Remote sites, file copy to, 224–226
Remote systems
  receiving mail, 165–166
  RTSE and, 123
Repeaters, 43
Replication, X.500, 245–247
Request primitives, 31
Residual errors, 313
Resolve contention, MAC control frame, 391
Responding address, 314
Response primitives, 31
Resynchronization, Session layer, 305
Retransmission, 416
Retrieval operations, X.500, 240–241
RFC 2305, *A Simple Mode of Facsimile Using
  Internet Mail*, 143
RFC 2312 S/MIME Version 2 Certificate Handling,
  232
Ring initialization, 391
Ring topology, 41, 42
RIP (routing information protocol), 359
RLE (run-length encoding), 270–272
Robots, 75
ROSE (Remote Operations Service Element)
  distributed applications and, 108
  ERROR macro in, 99–100
  example, 119–121
  protocol, 119
  remote operation of instructions, 117
Routers, 43, 353, 393
Routing protocols, 359
RSA method, 254–255, 256
RTC (return to control) code, 282–283
RTSE (Reliable Transfer Service Element)
  ASE and, 172
  definition, 108
  delivery of bulk data, 119
  processes, 121–122
  protocol, 123

NOTES

NOTES

NOTES

NOTES

NOTES

NOTES

NOTES

NOTES

NOTES

NOTES